Third Edition

NOLO PRESS BERKELEY

Your Responsibility When Using a Self-Help Law Book

We've done our best to give you useful and accurate information in this book. But laws and procedures change frequently and are subject to differing interpretations. If you want legal advice backed by a guarantee, see a lawyer. If you use this book, it's your responsibility to make sure that the facts and general advice contained in it are applicable to your situation.

Keeping Up-to-Date

To keep its books up-to-date, Nolo Press issues new printings and new editions periodically. New printings reflect minor legal changes and technical corrections. New editions contain major legal changes, major text additions or major reorganizations. To find out if a later printing or edition of any Nolo book is available, call Nolo Press at (510) 549-1976 or check the catalog in the Nolo News, our quarterly newspaper.

To stay current, follow the "Update" service in the Nolo News. You can get the paper free by sending us the registration card in the back of the book. In another effort to help you use Nolo's latest materials, we offer a 25% discount off the purchase of any new Nolo book if you turn in any earlier printing or edition. (See the "Recycle Offer" in the back of the book.)

This book was last revised in: **April 1995.**

THIRD EDITION

Second Printing	APRIL 1995
Printer	CONSOLIDATED PRINTERS, INC.
Book Design	JACKIE MANCUSO
Cover Design	TONI IHARA
Illustrator	MARI STEIN
Production	MICHELLE DUVALL
Proofreader	ELY NEWMAN
Indexer	SAYRE VAN YOUNG
Manuscript Preparation	STEPHANIE HAROLDE

PRINTED IN THE U.S.A.

Printed on paper with recycled content

Clifford, Denis
Plan your estate / by Denis Clifford & Cora Jordan.
p. cm.
Rev. ed. of: Plan your estate with a living trust. 2nd national ed. 1992.
Includes index.
ISBN 0-87337-239-5
1. Estate planning--United States--Popular works. 2. Living trusts--United States--Popular works. I. Jordan, Cora, 1941- II. Clifford, Denis. Plan your estate with a living trust. III. Title.
KF750.Z9C59 1994
346.7305'2--dc20
[347.30652]

94-973
CIP

Acknowledgements

Even more than most Nolo books, this one would never have seen the light of day without the generous efforts and contributions of many fine people. So our thanks to all those friends who helped us with this book, both putting it together and with previous editions over the years:

Four friends at Nolo Press, without whose efforts this book wouldn't have existed: Jake Warner, as ever, a great editor, writer and critic; Mary Randolph, another great editor, writer and organizer extraordinaire; Barbara Kate Repa, another superb editor and writer; and Stephanie Harolde, who read all our editing scrawls and turned them into coherent pages, and also did much fine editing as she was preparing yet another draft of the manuscript.

Mark Peery of Greenbrae, California, a superb estate planning lawyer (and great friend); Marilyn Putnam, San Francisco, another estate planning wizard.

All our other friends and colleagues at Nolo Press. In the past, we've listed everyone, but now we have 50 or more employees, plus more outside writers and an employee manual. Still, Nolo retains the relaxed, friendly atmosphere that makes it such a pleasant (as well as productive) place to work.

Dorcas Moulton, Amanda Cherrin and Naomi Puro, for their contributions to the original cover painting;

Ken Fischer, Orinda, California, a fine insurance agent; Bill Hudspeth, Austin Trust Co., Austin, Texas; Magdelen Gaynor, another fine estate planning attorney, White Plains, New York;

And our continued appreciation to other friends who also helped with other editions of this book: David Marcus; Paul Remack, R.G. Financial Service, San Francisco; Dave Brown, Peter Jan Honigsberg, Robert Wood of Athearn, Chandler & Hoffman, San Francisco, members of the Bay Area Funeral Society, Walter Warner; people who helped prepare the manuscript—Sandy Wieker, Christy Rigg, Cathy Cummings and Bethany Korwin-Pawloski; and Keija Kimura, Carol Pladsen and Linda Allison.

And finally, Denis's heartfelt thanks to the many readers who have written to him with suggestions, comments, corrections and other thoughts for improving earlier editions of this book.

Table of Contents

Introduction: How to Use This Book

1

Personal Concerns and Estate Planning

2

An Overview of Estate Planning

3

State Property Ownership Laws

4

Inventorying Your Property

5

Beneficiaries—Deciding Who Gets Your Property

6

Children

7

Probate and Why You Want to Avoid It

8

Chart: Probate Avoidance Methods

9

Revocable Living Trusts

10

Joint Tenancy and Tenancy by the Entirety

18

Estate Tax-Saving Bypass Trusts

19

Other Estate Tax-Saving Marital Trusts

20

Charitable Trusts

21

Other Estate Tax-Saving Trusts

22

Disclaimers: After-Death Estate Tax Planning

23

Trusts for Second or Subsequent Marriages

24

Trusts and Other Devices for Imposing Controls Over Property

25

Combining Ongoing Trusts

26

Incapacity: Health Care and Financial Management Directives

27

Body Organ Donation, Funerals and Burials

28

Business Ownership and Estate Planning

29

Social Security and Pensions

30

Using Lawyers

31

After Your Estate Plan Is Completed

32

After a Death Occurs

33

Some Estate Plans

Glossary

Appendix : State Death Tax Rules

Introduction: How to Use This Book

This book is designed to enable you to understand how to sensibly plan for the transfer of your property and otherwise provide for your loved ones after you die. Depending on your situation, this can be straightforward and simple, involving little more than the preparation of a will. But if your estate is large or your family needs are complicated, it can also necessitate sophisticated estate tax planning and the use of complicated legal devices to control what happens to your property after your death.

Whether simple or complex, lawyers call all these concerns "estate planning." Your "estate" is simply all the property you own, whatever it's worth. The "planning" required can be understood by normal, intelligent people—you don't have to be a nuclear physicist or even an attorney. Indeed, with the aid of this book, some people will learn that they can safely do much, or even all, of their planning themselves. Others will conclude that they need at least a measure of professional help.

WARNING TO LOUISIANA RESIDENTS:

This book is designed for residents of all states except Louisiana, which has a legal system based on Napoleonic Code, different from the other states. If you live in Louisiana, please return this book to Nolo Press for a full refund.

While this book focuses on legal and practical issues of estate planning, it's important to recognize that, viewed from a larger perspective, these are often of minor concern in the face of the overwhelming emotional force and mystery of death. Chapter 1 discusses some of the human realities that can be involved in estate planning. Nevertheless, this book doesn't attempt to deal with the larger meanings of a death; they are appropriately left for philosophers, clergy, poets and—ultimately—to you. But it's important to recognize that when we think about planning our estate, we necessarily think about our own mortality, and death is a difficult subject to think about, to talk about, and to plan for. The ancient Greeks believed the inevitability of death could best be faced by performing great deeds. Christian religions offer the promise of eternal life; preparing for death means preparing to "meet your maker." Other cultures have prepared for death in a wide variety of ways.

However anyone chooses to emotionally prepare for death—his own or someone he cares for—there are also practical consequences that someone must deal with. In the U.S., if there has been no planning, the normal result is that the survivors, upset and confused, turn everything over to "professionals." A body must suddenly be disposed of, so a funeral parlor is called. A myriad of financial problems can arise: how are bills to be paid and tax returns prepared? How is title to the family house transferred to the inheritors? Who pays death taxes? Enter a host of highly paid professionals, often including lawyers, CPAs, real estate advisors and insurance brokers.

While trying to deal with the emotional trauma and the physical reality of death, it's easy for thousands of dollars to be consumed by the excessive or unnecessary fees of professionals. The money wasted comes from the estate of the person who died—money that would otherwise be available for the family, friends or others to inherit. In addition to curtailing this kind of waste, planning can save substantial amounts on death taxes for larger estates. So, in the final analysis, preparing an estate plan is an act of love for your inheritors. Although you don't directly face the consequences of procrastination and avoidance, they will, unless you decide to act.

Plan Your Estate is designed for people with estates of any amount, from relatively modest to many millions. This is possible because many of the methods this book covers are equally useful for large estates as well as small ones. For instance, the probate avoidance methods, such as living trusts or joint tenancy and explained (Chapters 9 and 10), work well for estates worth thousands, as well as those worth millions. Similarly, planning for what happens if you become incapacitated involves substantially the same concerns, no matter what the size of an estate. But it's also true that larger estates tend to require more complicated and more in-depth estate planning. So to help people whose estates are larger than $600,000, we provide a thorough discussion of the principal trusts that can be used to save on estate taxes. (An estate less than $600,000 is not subject to federal estate tax. See Chapter 15, Estate Taxes.)

In addition, many people with estates larger than $600,000 will need the assistance of an expert lawyer to actually prepare one of the trusts discussed in this book. But even if you eventually decide you need a lawyer to help you prepare your final estate plan, you'll benefit greatly by gaining an overview of the basic issues involved, and the types of legal devices you may want to use. In sum, the information you gain by reading this book should enable you to work more effectively with a professional.

A. What This Book Helps You Do

This book will enable you to understand what estate planning is: what choices you have, how they work, and the advantages and drawbacks of each.

In contrast with many Nolo books, this is not a do-it-yourself law book, with legal forms you can tear out and complete. Rather, *Plan Your Estate* presents a comprehensive discussion and overview of all major aspects of estate planning, from simple wills to complex estate tax-saving trusts. Because estate planning can involve so many different factors—from concerns about saving on taxes, to how to avoid probate, to worries about the care of small children or providing for all family members when there has been a second or subsequent marriage, to mention just a few—we believe that it will be well worth your time to understand the choices possible in your situation before you can sensibly decide which ones are best.

This book also provides thorough charts, designed for you to itemize your property and list all your beneficiaries. Since you won't be preparing any legal documents using this book, it's not mandatory that you do this. However, doing so accomplishes two valuable goals. First, it allows you to figure out your net worth (assets minus liabilities), a figure that is extremely important for tax planning purposes. Second, it gives you a head start on actually preparing your estate, the next step after you read this book. An alternative is to simply make a rough estimate of your present net worth (assets minus liabilities).

The first thing that comes to many people's minds when they think of estate planning is property. Who gets what? Not surprisingly, most of us desire to conserve as much of our property as possible for the people and charities we care about, minimizing the amount siphoned off by lawyers and taxes. And, of course, a major concern of people with minor children or dependent adult relatives is providing for their care and support. All of these issues are important aspects of estate planning, but there are many other significant concerns explained in this book. To give you a comprehensive overview of key estate planning issues, the book is organized into a number of major units:

- **Part I, Introduction to Estate Planning.** Here's where you get your feet wet and begin to learn the language and basic goals of estate planning. (Introduction, Chapters 1 and 2)
- **Part II, Groundwork.** In this section, you focus on your personal situation, your finances and who you

want to leave your property to (your beneficiaries), including special concerns if you want to leave property to children.

- **Part III, Avoiding Probate.** Probate is the court legal process generally required when property is left by a will. Eventually—usually after a long time and excessive lawyer's fees—the property is distributed as the will directs. Because so many people understand that probate is often little more than a lawyers' racket, probate avoidance is a high priority in this book. (Chapters 3 through 6)

The major probate avoidance methods, including living trusts, joint tenancy, pay on death designations and life insurance, are explained in detail. But don't assume that planning to avoid probate is the main brick in the wall of your estate plan. Especially if yours is a larger estate, planning to limit federal—and sometimes state—death taxes is equally, if not more, important. (Chapters 7 through 13)

- **Part IV, Preparing Your Will.** Everyone should have a will, even though avoiding probate for your property is usually desirable. This section explains why, and presents the range of different styles of wills possible for different situations. (Chapter 14)
- **Part V, Estate and Gift Taxes.** Many people will be pleased to learn that no death taxes will be assessed against their estates. However, people with larger estates (over $600,000) do face federal estate taxes. Also, if you make a gift of over $10,000 a year to any person, you'll be liable for federal gift taxes, which are the same rates as estate taxes. This part offers a thorough explanation of how these estate and gift taxes work. (Chapters 15 and 16)
- **Part VI, Use of Ongoing Trusts.** An ongoing trust is irrevocable and an independent legal entity. Typically, an ongoing trust lasts for a long period of time—years or decades. There are varied uses of ongoing trusts in estate planning, including:
  - Using ongoing trusts to save on estate taxes. There are a number of sophisticated trusts that may be useful to those with larger estates to reduce estate taxes.
  - Trusts imposing controls over your property after you die. This is often done in second or subsequent marriages, to ensure that a spouse's property will ultimately go to children from a prior marriage.

  (Chapters 17 through 25)
- **Part VII, Special Practical Concerns.** Here we cover a potpourri of subjects that people may consider in their planning, including:
  - Handling special estate problems facing owners of small businesses;
  - Deciding who will handle your medical and financial affairs and make legal decisions for you if you become incapacitated;
  - Organ donations, funerals and burial;
  - Understanding how Social Security and pension programs should influence your estate planning.

  (Chapters 26 through 29)
- **Part VIII, Going Further.** This part first discusses how to find and use a good estate planning lawyer. It also discusses the option of doing your own research. Then it covers what happens after your planning is done, and the legal documents you want completed. Subjects covered include:
  - Starting your estate planning documents and making copies;
  - Keeping your estate plan up-to-date;
  - What happens with your estate after you die.

  (Chapters 30 through 33)

LOOK FOR THESE ABBREVIATIONS AND ICONS

To aid you in comprehending the information presented, we use several icons to advise you of some special alert. These icons are:

A caution that there may be some serious risk, or danger, that can arise in this facet of your estate planning.

Indicates where we are definitely offering our own (best) advice, not merely "objective" information.

Lets you know when we believe you need the advice of an attorney, often an estate planning expert.

Flags situations which apply to couples in particular.

B. Tailoring Your Estate Plan to Your Needs

Let's take a minute to put the term "estate planning" into plain English. The word "plan," especially, can be misleading. It doesn't mean you'll have a document that looks like a map, or one that has lots of charts and graphs. It doesn't even mean you'll end up with a thick file of papers filled with obscure legalese. Your estate plan will simply consist of the methods and documents you've decided on, and prepared, to handle what happens after your death to the matters that concern you. For example, you might decide to use a simple will to name a guardian for your minor children and make some minor gifts, a living trust to pass your real estate and other major items to your beneficiaries, and an insurance policy to pay debts, taxes and provide for your family's immediate needs.

Some lawyers have attempted to present pre-packaged estate plans that apply to certain "standard" situations. For example, if a husband and wife have minor children and an estate of approximately \$200,000, Plan A is proposed. But a husband and wife with no minor children and an estate over \$200,000 should use Plan B. Then there's plans C, D and E, and who knows how many more.

The problem with these off-the-shelf estate plans is that, as we all know, real life isn't that standardized. There are too many variables in most people's situations to make a one-size-fits-many approach work well. A far better approach is for each individual to take stock of her own needs and desires, and determine what her goals are. Then, with the broad-based information we present here, you should be able to come up with a general idea, at least, of the estate plan you want—one that is geared to your personal situation.

We suggest that you read through the entire book once before you actually begin to formulate your own estate plan. Different aspects of estate planning are often intertwined. Thus, it simply doesn't make sense to decide what should go in your will until you understand whether some of your property might be better passed to your beneficiaries using probate avoidance methods. Similarly, if you have a good-sized estate, you'll need to understand how estate taxes work before you can determine the wisest ways to transfer property to your loved ones. Again, the point is, you need to get a good overview of the whole field before you begin to make your plan. Of course you can safely skip those parts of the book which obviously don't apply to you.

We encourage you to use *Plan Your Estate* as a workbook. That is, you should feel free to underline and highlight text or make notes in the margins whenever you come across material that seems pertinent to you particular situation, or raises questions you will want to further consider.

C. Will You Need Professional Help?

For most people with moderate estates, the actual process of estate planning isn't nearly as forbidding as many professionals make it seem. For example, one pillar of estate planning is respect for conventional lawyer language and accepted forms. What can be surprising is how simple it often is for non-lawyers to learn how to use these legal tools. It's our experience in working with this material for over 20 years that most people who have estates worth no more than $600,000, and who have clear desires about their property, can safely prepare their own estate planning forms from other Nolo resources, listed in Section D, below.

As we've already said, many individuals or couples with estates exceeding $600,000 will want to consult a legal expert, or possible tax expert, as part of making estate planning decisions; depending on what's needed, they may want to hire a lawyer to prepare some or all of their estate planning documents, particularly if these include complex trusts.

After finishing this book, you should be able to determine whether you want or need help from an expert. Make this judgment carefully, of course, but do remember that lawyers, accountants and other experts aren't magicians. The cost of hiring an expensive estate planner, if you have a moderate estate, is often greater than any savings or certainty you can achieve beyond what you accomplish yourself by the methods presented here. If you do decide you need expert help, the knowledge you gain here should help keep your costs to a minimum. Since you already know the basics, you won't need to purchase this information at upwards of $200 per hour. Also, if you educate yourself and do much of your initial planning, you're more likely to end up with something that fully expresses your own desires.

Finally, two disclaimers are in order. This book doesn't claim to present definitive advice on every aspect of estate planning. Many subjects covered, such as estate taxes, life insurance, probate avoidance, ongoing trusts or even will-drafting, can get very complicated and esoteric for people with very large estates or complicated family situations. This partially explains why there are volumes of books on each topic in any good-sized law library. *Plan Your Estate* does cover the basics of all major aspects of estate planning, including those for people with estates of at least several million dollars. Wherever possible, we recommend self-help methods to accomplish your plan. Where appropriate, we recommend seeing an expert.

Second, we do not cover retirement issues, from financial investing for old age, to pension/retirement plans such as IRAs or Keoghs, to choosing nursing home care. This is a separate field, and this book is big enough. Where appropriate, we do refer you to other resources on these topics. And to the extent these matters can directly impinge upon your estate planning, we discuss those interactions.

D. Other Resources

Nolo Press publishes other materials that may be useful to you in your estate planning. If it seems self-serving for us to recommend other materials, let us tell you why we do so. About a dozen of us who know each other well and share information on an almost daily basis have developed and updated these materials carefully over many years. Our materials are specifically written to help people safely do it themselves and, quite frankly, we believe they are by far the best for self-help purposes.

Estate planning resources include:

- *WillMaker,* Nolo's computer will program, which enables you to prepare a comprehensive will, including a basic trust for your minor children, allowing you to choose the age at which your children inherit property you leave them.
- *Nolo's Living Trust,* Nolo's computer living trust program, which enables you to prepare a probate-avoidance living trust.
- *Make Your Own Living Trust,* a complete explanation, including forms, of how to prepare a living trust. Included are forms and information enabling a married couple with a combined estate between $600,000 to $1,200,000 to prepare an estate tax-saving "marital life estate" trust, or "AB" trust.
- *Nolo's Simple Will Book,* an in-depth explanation of how to prepare a will that covers all normal needs, including simple trusts for your minor children.
- *Nolo's Law Form Kit: Wills,* contains information and forms enabling you to prepare a basic will.
- *How to Probate an Estate* (California Edition), enables Californians to do normal probate without an attorney.
- *The Deeds Book* (California Edition), explains how to use deeds to transfer real estate for estate planning.
- *Beat the Nursing Home Trap: A Consumer's Guide to Choosing and Financing Long-Term Care,* a practical guide which provides all the information you need to help make the best arrangements for long-term care. It shows how to protect assets, arrange home health care, find nursing and non-nursing home residences, evaluate nursing home insurance and understand Medicare, Medicaid and other benefit programs.
- *Social Security, Medicare and Pensions,* offers invaluable guidance through the current maze of rights and benefits for those 55 and over, including Medicare, Medicaid and Social Security retirement and disability benefits, and age discrimination protections.

Throughout *Plan Your Estate,* we alert you when one of these materials is particularly pertinent and provides more coverage of an aspect of estate planning than this book does. You can order any of these books direct from Nolo Press. A catalogue of books and software is at the back of this book. ■

1

Personal Concerns and Estate Planning

Underlying the creation of any estate plan are profound human concerns: a primary urge for order and the desire to pass on property to loved ones. So a good estate plan is an accurate reflection of your deepest personal wishes. While much of this book is about mechanics, methods and documents, it's important to remember that no matter how well you deal with the legal technicalities, your estate plan won't succeed unless you take human concerns into account, too.

We make no claim to being experts on the psyche. Indeed, we are wary of "experts" who claim they have precise understanding of something as complex and mysterious as human beings. Happily, you don't need an expert to cope with the human realities that can come up in your estate planning. You do need common sense, candor about the strengths, weaknesses and genuine needs of close family members and an ability to consider legal technicalities, but not let them interfere with what you know in your heart needs to be done.

For many people, no serious personal problems arise in their estate planning. They know who they want to give their property to. They do not foresee any possibility of conflict between their beneficiaries, nor threat of lawsuit by someone claiming they should have been a beneficiary. On the human level, these people can, happily, focus on the satisfactions they expect their gifts to bring.

Other people's situations are not so clear and straightforward. They must deal with more difficult human dynamics, such as possibilities of family conflicts, or dividing property unequally between children, or providing care for minor children, or handling complexities arising from second or subsequent marriages.

Before beginning your legal planning, it's vital that you assess your personal circumstances and consider how you want to resolve them, often by doing the best you can to compromise conflicting needs. If you're planning to leave all your property to your spouse or two compatible children, or are otherwise sure you don't face any human problems, wonderful. You can safely go on to Chapter 3, State Property Ownership Laws. If, however, you think you might face complications—or if you're not sure what kinds of problems can come up—read the balance of this chapter, which discusses a number of human concerns based on examples drawn from Denis' estate planning practice.

A. Avoiding Conflict

Estate planning involves money—whether cash or other assets that can be sold for cash. Money, as most of us learn as we get older, is strange stuff—or, more accurately, people can often do strange things because of the desire for money. (If the love of money isn't *the* root of all evil, it's certainly up there as a big one.) So Step 1 in creating an estate plan is to recognize that if you plan unwisely, your plan may lead to bitterness, strife and lawsuits rather than conferring the benefits you surely intend. Against this background, avoiding conflict after your death to the extent reasonably possible should be a central goal of estate planning.

Start by asking yourself if there is the potential for conflict in your family situation. If this potential does exist, think of what can be done to eliminate or at least reduce it. One important thing to remember here is that disputes are not always over property that is worth a great deal of money. If different family members have deep emotional attachments to family heirlooms, or what they stand for, fighting can become fierce, even if the heirlooms themselves won't make anyone rich.

John Gregory Dunne, in his autobiography *Harp* (Simon-Schuster), has an excellent description of one family's fight over heirlooms. His Aunt Harriet failed to specifically state who got what of her many items of personal property. Dunne aptly describes how much meaning that property seemed to have to the beneficiaries, and the wisdom of one lawyer in resolving their conflicts over the property.

> *In legal terms, Aunt Harriet became..."Estate of Harriet H. Burn," appraised and organized, room by room, into "8 carved Hepplewhite mahogany chairs" and "Coalport 'Kings Plate' china service for twelve" and "Repro Victorian loveseat, blue brocade" and "Light blue upholstered settee, soiled." The house was sold, the belongings apportioned [left to] to the surviving children and grandchildren. There is something so metaphorical and final in the act of dividing up the possessions a family has accumulated over several lifetimes and more generations; for the first time I thought there might be a good argument for primogeniture. It was not that the furniture and china and crystal and silver and linens had great worth; it was just that each piece, each object had a private history, a special meaning for one or the other of us. For a family, the process of apportionment is like psychoanalysis or the confessional box; long-buried resentments surface, old hurts and forgotten slights. In the end, a lawyer drew up the order of selection; his ground rules were worthy of Solomon:*
>
> *The order of selection will be determined as follows: each of you is requested to pick a number from one to ninety-nine and advise me of it by return mail: the person whose number is closest to the first two numbers of the Connecticut Daily Lottery on Tuesday, October 7, will have first pick, and so forth....If the first person who selects property picks an item in an amount worth $1,400, the second person will be entitled to pick as many items as he or she wishes up to $1,400 in value. The third person would then have the right to choose property in the amount equal to the value selected by the person who preceded him or her and so forth until all items have been selected. In this way, each family unit will have an opportunity to select property, in turn and essentially of equal value.*
>
> The Connecticut State Lottery: God, if there is one, must have a sense of humor.

With some planning, the conflicts between the beneficiaries could have been forestalled. After all, a lawyer could have drawn up his distribution method, complete with the Connecticut State Lottery, well before Aunt Harriet died. So even if you can't, or don't want to, decide before your death exactly who gets what, you can still create a binding method for resolving distribution of your property after you die.

Let's explore general ways to avoid conflict by looking at three different family situations. Then, in the sections that follow, we will discuss conflict avoidance in the context of several typical family situations where it's most likely to arise. Our concern here is to indicate how to cope with potential human problems—not to provide comprehensive estate planning information, which will come later. Finally, we do want to note that, in some cases, conflict simply can't be avoided.

Example 1: Patrick and Clara have five children. One, Sean, is a lawyer. Patrick and Clara admit to themselves, though they never reveal it to others, that Sean is their one grasping child, who has always wanted the most, materially, from his parents and the world. Indeed, by sheer persistence, Sean has already managed to acquire a substantial number of family heirlooms. Sean tells his parents he wants to supervise distribution of their property (after both die) as executor of their wills and successor trustee of their living trust, stating that he's obviously the most professionally qualified.

At first, Patrick and Clara aren't sure what to do. Their concern isn't that Sean will violate their wills and distribute their major items of property unequally. Rather, they worry that the personal possessions they have left to all their children won't be divided fairly. After considerable discussion, they decide they don't want Sean to have sole authority to supervise the distribution of their estate. Basically, they conclude that while they love him as they do their other children, they simply can't rely on him to be able to put his own desires aside and distribute their heirlooms impartially. They'd prefer to have their daughter Maude, the kindest and most level-headed of their kids, be both executor and successor trustee, which will allow her to preside over the division of the personal items. However, they're afraid that doing this will offend Sean, something they're determined not to do.

After much thought, they decide to have three executors and successor trustees—Sean, Maude and another daughter, Maeve. (Patrick, Jr. lives in Europe and isn't interested, and Polly is still a minor). While this may be a little awkward, and sets up the possibility that Maude and Maeve may have to combine forces to cope with Sean (as they've had to do for 30 years), Patrick and Clara feel they have arrived at a solution that has a good chance of success. They plan to talk to Maude, Maeve and Sean to try to work things out, including the rules for authority—such as whether two of three can determine what's done, even if one is opposed. While this may involve some conflict with Sean, there's far less risk of serious family strife than if Sean were named sole trustee and executor.

Example 2: Sol and Bernice have two children in their late 20s, Abel and Alexis, and a combined estate worth about $530,000. Sol also has a 34-year-old daughter, Lilith, from his first marriage, who he's seen very rarely since his marriage to Bernice. Sol wants to give Lilith a gift of $100,000 in his living trust. Bernice says "That's absolutely ridiculous. You're just trying to absolve yourself of the guilt you feel for ignoring Lilith all these years." Sol replies "Isn't it my money?" Bernice points out that half of it is her money, as their property lists both their names as owners (see Chapter 3, State Property Ownership Laws). Sol says, "Yes, but half of $530,000 is $265,000, so I can give $100,000 to Lilith if I want to." But he soon admits that this "divide my estate" approach would mean he would only be leaving Bernice $165,000, with nothing for his other two children, who, in truth, he is closer to. In short, Sol realizes that Bernice is right—his children from his present marriage would almost surely feel hurt.

Sol and Bernice decide to work through this problem together. After some lengthy talks, they decide that Sol will give $50,000 to Lilith, and the rest to Bernice in his living trust (assuming Bernice survives Sol). When Bernice dies, she will pass on everything that's left to Abel and Alexis. They then check with the two children to see if this seems fair to them as well. Happily, it does. Abel says, "Hey, it's your money, Pa." Their daughter adds, "So enjoy." Both convince Sol and Bernice that they think the gift to Lilith is fair.

Example 3: Al is a widower with three children. Although there's no problem dividing up his big ticket items among his children equally—they all

agree on that—all three children have expressed deep attachment to a number of relatively inexpensive family treasures. Al decides they have to talk it out. He gets all three children together and says "You're going to have to work it out among you. Come up with something you all agree on and I'll do it. But don't make me guess, and don't leave me worrying that you'll be fighting amongst yourselves when I'm gone." A family retreat is planned and carried out. It takes longer than any of them anticipate, but the kids stick with it, and eventually, a few flashes of temper and some weary hours later, they've worked out an agreement to divide some items of property and share others. Everyone is in good spirits. Al studies the agreement and, while he secretly thinks it's more complex than necessary, he agrees that it's fair. That evening, everyone drinks and toasts to Al's good health and long life.

B. Leaving Unequal Amounts of Property to Children

Sometimes parents want to leave unequal amounts of property to their children, but don't want to give the impression that they favor the child who is given more. Here are some examples of how people have handled this matter.

Example 1: Dolly, a widow with no children, asks her three nieces and two nephews which of her heirlooms they want. Most requests are reasonable, and Dolly sees how she can use her will to reflect everyone's wishes. But there is one big problem. Four of the five ask for her valuable Daumier etchings, and none of them seems willing to give way. Dolly discusses this with them. Two are adamant that they do not want the etchings sold and the profits divided between all five, so Dolly decides that option is out. All eventually agree to all own the etchings and rotate possession every year. Dolly secretly thinks the solution is awkward but is proud of herself for coming up with a plan that will keep peace in her family.

Example 2: Ira's parents, Mort and Leah, have paid for his college and dental school education and helped him purchase his first house. Melinda, their other child, has always been an independent sort who, while a loving daughter, has prided herself on making it on her own. Now Mort and Leah want to equalize their gifts by giving more to Melinda in their estate plan. Some hints of their thinking are enough to disturb Ira, and he argues that he still should get half. Mort and Leah retreat, talk it over and decide they'll stick to their original plan, giving Melinda more, and won't discuss the subject with Ira again. But in their estate planning documents (a will and a living trust), they'll take the time to explain why and how they determined the distribution. They'll emphasize that they love both children equally and are determined to treat them equally. Mort and Leah hope that being fair and firm with Ira will gain his respect in the end.

Example 3: Ayyad, a widower with a modest estate, has four grown children. Three are very well-established in conventional business careers with excellent future prospects. One is a serious, but impoverished, jazz musician. Because of his greater need, Ayyad considers giving the jazz musician most of his estate, but decides to confer with his children before finalizing that plan.

To Ayyad's surprise, he learns that two of his children don't agree with his plan. One has never much cared for the jazz musician, finding him irresponsible and indulgent. (Besides, this child has never liked his music, anyway.) Another child points out that she has two children and that, in today's market, neither her nor her husband's jobs are really secure. The jazz musician, she reminds Ayyad, has provided him with no loving grandchildren. The daughter asks whether her children shouldn't receive some "rainy-day" funds from their grandfather.

Ayyad says he'll think this over. He decides he doesn't want to talk it over further with his kids. This is, after all, his decision. He's gotten their input but it's up to him to decide.

Finally, he decides to divide his total estate by percentages: 50% will go to the jazz musician (Ayyad admires his son and thinks him sincere, not lazy), 12 ½% will go to each of his other two children with no children of their own, and 25% to the daughter with children. If any of his other children has a child, or if the musician gains a measure of financial success, Ayyad plans to revise these percentages.

In an effort to soothe feelings, Ayyad writes a detailed letter explaining his decision and expressing his love and good wishes for each child. He attaches the letter to his living trust, and does not plan to have the letter revealed to his children until after his death.

Example 4: Barbara and Barry have two children and a substantial estate. One of the children is a doctor, and the other a graduate student currently working as a waitress. Barbara and Barry consider leaving the bulk of their wealth to the student, figuring that their son is much more secure. But then, on reflection, they decide they don't want to be locked into such an imbalance. Medicine, they reason, is surely changing, and may not be as lucrative in the future. And the doctor already has one child, with more hoped for. Who knows what his needs may become in the future. And anyway, his sister is doing well and will likely be established in her own career in a few more years. So Barbara and Barry decide, for the time being, to divide their estate equally between the two children. But they also agree: 1) They will continue to give $20,000 a year to the student, while she still needs their help; and 2) they will periodically review their plan, to see if it now might make more sense to leave more of their property to one child.

C. Providing Care for Minor Children

A prime concern of parents of minor children is who will take care of their children if the parents die. If both parents are involved in raising the child (together, or in the case of divorce or separation, with the participation of both), the principal worry is what happens if both parents die. Obviously, if there is only one parent, because the other is dead or has effectively abandoned the child, the sole parent is likely to be even more concerned that his children will be well cared for if he dies.

In either case, the primary issues are who will raise the child *and* who will be responsible for supervising property the parent(s) leave to the child. These issues are discussed in depth in Chapter 6, Children. Here we want only to indicate some of the emotional concerns that may be raised when trying to resolve them.

Example 1: A married couple, Taylor and Sondra, have two grade school age children. Taylor and Sondra discuss who will raise their children if they both die before the kids are adults. Taylor strongly promotes his sister, Beth, as the suitable guardian. Sondra thinks Beth is a snob and declares she doesn't want her children raised in that household. She suggests her older brother, Louis. Taylor retorts that Louis may be good with money, but he has a terrible temper and doesn't have the most stable marriage.

Fortunately, Taylor and Sondra are sensitive enough to realize they have to talk seriously to reach an agreement on who would make the best guardian. After considerable discussion, and a fairly successful effort to feel out the kids, they settle on Sondra's best friend, Hilda, who they both trust and respect, and who has children about the same age and is willing to accept the responsibility for raising the children.

But both Sondra and Taylor agree that Hilda is not very sensible with money. They worry that she couldn't sensibly manage the money they would leave for the children. Hilda isn't overjoyed to hear this, but she is good-hearted. She accepts Sondra and Taylor's solution—she will be the children's personal guardian, and Louis supervises the money left them until they're old enough to get it outright. Louis also agrees to this arrangement.

Example 2: Marcie, a single parent, wants her best friend, Shoshana, to be the guardian of Katherine, Marcie's nine-year-old daughter, should Marcie die before Katherine is 18. To Marcie's surprise, Shoshana says she can't accept the responsibility. She has two kids of her own, and that's all she can handle. Marcie is hurt, and worries there's no one she trusts who will do the job. After some reflection and discussion with other friends, Marcie realizes that her brother Alex is willing to be guardian. Marcie is not overjoyed: Alex and she weren't really close as kids and still aren't. But she realizes that Alex is a trustworthy person and that Katherine would be well cared for with him. She concludes that her best estate plan is to stay alive until her daughter is an adult, but if she doesn't, she will rely on Alex.

D. Subsequent Marriages

People who marry more than once may face problems reconciling their desires for their present spouse and family with their wishes for children from their prior marriages. Individual situations can vary greatly, often depending on whether marriages occurred relatively early or late in life and on how well family members get along. But one thing is obvious—if yours is a non-traditional family, you must carefully consider, and do your best to reconcile, needs that may be competing and conflicting. These issues are covered in more depth in Chapter 23, Trusts for Second or Subsequent Marriages.

Example 1: Katerina and Pavel get married when they are in their 50s. Katerina has a son from her prior marriage. Pavel has three children, two daughters and a son. Katerina and Pavel both work. Pavel has a slightly higher income, and savings of $400,000 to Katerina's $130,000. They buy a house, with each spouse contributing half the down payment, and equally sharing the monthly payments. Both spouses want to insure that, when the other dies, the survivor gets to live in the house for the rest of his or her life. When both spouses die, they want the house to be divided equally, with one share going to Katerina's son and the other share divided between Pavel's three children. Similarly, by use of an estate planning tool called a "marital life estate trust to control property" (see Chapter 18, Estate Tax-Saving Bypass Trusts, Section C), each spouse's assets will be left for the "use" of the surviving spouse, with "use" defined to mean the right to receive income the property generates or literal use of some property (for example, a car). Neither spouse can invade the other's principal.

Katerina and Pavel consider the wisdom of discussing their plan with all their children. Since they have chosen Eve, one of Pavel's daughters, to wind up their affairs after their death in the role of the successor trustee of their living trust, they have already discussed it with her. But because Katerina's son, Tad, has never accepted Pavel, and remains hostile to him, Katerina and Pavel sadly decide that talking their plan over with Tad will only provide an occasion for more rancor. So they simply don't tell him what they've agreed upon.

Example 2: Angelina Bellows, in her 70s, is a wealthy widow with three grown children. She remarries Arthur Rice, also in his 70s. They live in Angelina's house. Arthur, who has very little property, has two children from a prior marriage who Angelina does not particularly care for. As she plans her estate, Angelina realizes she wants to allow Arthur to remain in the house if she dies before he does, but doesn't want him to be able to rent out the house, nor be able to sell it and buy another one. She discusses her concerns with him. He is bothered that she doesn't trust him fully. She explains frankly that her children, who are delighted she has remarried Arthur, are nevertheless concerned that his children might end up with what they see as their inheritance.

Angelina decides to leave much of her property outright to her children. She will create a trust for the house, and leave enough money in the trust to pay for mortgage and upkeep on the house, plus a little extra to supplement Arthur's Social Security and small pension. The trust will be managed by the most responsible of her children. Arthur will have the right to live in the house for the duration of his life and receive the income produced by the trust.

Arthur agrees with this arrangement, but asks what happens if he gets ill and must be hospitalized? Will he be thrown out of the house? His concern prompts Ms. Bellows to realize that there are aspects of the trust to pin down. She doesn't want to allow the possibility that Arthur can be thrown out of the house if he's in the hospital for a week. But also, if he moves permanently to a nursing home, she prefers that the house then be turned over to her children rather than remain in trust until Arthur dies. She discusses her concerns with Arthur. He's understanding but concerned, himself, about becoming ill and having to leave the house for a while and then not being able to return to it.

After considerable discussion, Angelina and Arthur agree that he will retain the right to live in, or return to, the house if he's lived away from it for up to eight consecutive months. If he's been away from it for a longer period than that, the house will come under management by the trustee, who can rent it out. But the trustee cannot sell it or live in it or allow other children to live in it while Arthur lives. Any income from the rental is added to the trust income available for Arthur.

Since Angelica is leaving much of her property outright to her children, outside this trust, she feels it is fair for them to wait to inherit the house until Arthur's death. He's in this 70s after all. Anyway, she may well outlive him, and she'll certainly keep the house herself until her death. Angelica then sees a good estate planning lawyer to prepare the trust she wants. With the lawyer's aid, Angelica pins down precisely how the trust will work.

E. Long-Term Care for a Child With Special Needs

Parents of mentally and sometimes physically disabled children may need to provide care and support for those children whether they are minors or adults. Providing this care often requires the help of experts, particularly to coordinate the parents' contributions with rules on government benefits. This is particularly true when creating an estate plan to provide for a disabled child for possibly many years. Also, it may well be that, in their estate planning, parents, like it or not, may need to concentrate most of their resources for their disabled child, leaving less for any other children.

Example: The Balfour family has a disabled child Bob, age 15, who will need care all his life. They have two other children, both of whom are healthy. The Balfours' primary estate planning concern is doing all they can to arrange for Bob's care after they die. They realize this means leaving Bob most of their modest estate. They discuss this with their 19-year-old daughter, Rebecca, who says "that's fine." Their other son, Jeb, resents Bob a little and isn't so acquiescent. But the Balfours decide that protecting Bob remains their top priority. They hope that, as Jeb matures, he will understand the difficulties Bob faces and that his resentment that Bob got more than his share (as Jeb defines it) of parental attention will fade.

There are many questions the parents must resolve about Bob. Who will be responsible for Bob's personal care after they die? How can they best leave money for his use? How will any money they leave be treated when determining eligibility for government benefits? After all, it makes no sense to leave money to Bob if it means he will be ineligible for government help until it's all used up.

The Balfours must chose a personal guardian to be responsible for Bob until he becomes a legal adult, at age 18, and a financial guardian or manager to supervise any money they leave for Bob, as long as Bob lives.

The Balfours discuss these concerns themselves and then broaden their discussion to include Rebecca and other family members and close friends they are considering for these two tasks. Eventually, they choose Mrs. Balfour's younger sister to be Bob's personal guardian if needed. They name their closest friend, William, to be Bob's financial manager, until Rebecca turns 30. After that, she will become Bob's financial manager.

To understand how to dovetail money they leave Bob in trust with government benefits, the Balfours do some preliminary research. They decide to establish a "special needs" trust for Bob. They have this trust drafted by an expert who designs it to maintain Bob's eligibility for government assistance programs and to provide control for the trustee (the property manager) over trust property used for Bob's benefit.

F. Concerns of Unmarried Couples

Unmarried couples have no legal right to each other's property, unless each member of the couple makes a will or other estate plan specifically leaving property to the other. A central concern of most unmarried couples is to do just this. Happily, unmarried people—whether lesbian, gay or heterosexual—have the right to leave their property to whomever they want, as long as they're competent. (Even if one or both has been legally married in the past, they have no obligation to their ex-spouse, unless specific support is still required by the divorce decree.) In case of serious threat by hostile family members, a couple may take action to establish by clear proof that they were competent when they prepared their estate plan.

Example: Ernest and Linda have lived together for many years. Aside from a few small gifts to friends or family, each wants to leave all their property to the other after death. They're concerned with efficiency and economy, but above all they want to be sure that their estate plan can't be successfully attacked by several close relatives who have long been hostile to their lifestyle. Ernest and Linda each prepare a living trust leaving their property as they desire. They videotape their signing and the notarization of this document to provide additional proof they were both mentally competent and not under duress or undue influence when they signed.

G. Worries About the Effect of Inheriting Money

Sometimes people worry that someone they want to leave money or property to cannot handle it. In other words, they fear their gifts will have destructive results: the beneficiaries may be too young or too immature, for example. Resolving these concerns always requires a careful examination both of the strengths and weaknesses of the potential beneficiaries. Sometimes it also involves putting one's own worries and prejudices under as objective a personal microscope as possible.

Example 1: Ely is quite wealthy, and worried about the effects of his wealth on his children and grandchildren. He grew up poor, worked hard all his life and made a small fortune. Shouldn't his kids, now in their 20s and 30s and just making their way in the world, be encouraged to continue to work hard, at least until they're old enough to keep a large inheritance in perspective? If Ely dies soon, and each child inherits over $1 million will they lose their incentive to strive for goals they might strive for otherwise? Ely is not the type to question whether losing the incentive to strive might be a good thing. He had it, he wants his kids to have it. Ely wonders if his best estate plan wouldn't be to say "Being of sound mind, I spent all I could and I give the rest to charity"? And what about his grandchildren? Should he give money only to those who join his business? (The fact that none of his children did still rankles.)

No matter how much Ely learns about the intricacies of tax planning and probate avoidance, he needs to do some serious thinking and reflecting on the subject of his money and his family before he can hope to make a decent estate plan. Or put another way, Ely needs to better understand the complicated nature of his own emotions and expectations pertaining to his money. Once over this hurdle, he should be better able to make up a plan to benefit his children and grandchildren.

For example, perhaps Ely will realize that his dedication to making it the hard way is perhaps a tad extreme, but does contain some truth. If so, he may leave (or even give) moderate amounts of property to his children outright to help them cope better with parenting their young children. Ely will leave the rest of his estate in trust for his children. Each child will receive a moderate amount of income for a number of years, only getting the bulk of the property at the age Ely has chosen. (For example, Joseph Kennedy, Sr. established trusts for each of his children that didn't release the trust property until that child became 50 years old.)

Ely decides he doesn't want to pressure, or hire, a grandchild into his business by promises of additional inheritance. Instead, he creates an education trust for each grandchild, leaving each $50,000 for college or other educational costs.

Example 2: Sylvia, a wealthy widow, has two children in their 30s: Yvonne, the sensible one, and Colleen, who's always been improvident and often more than a little self-destructive. Sylvia wants to leave her estate equally to her two daughters. She'll give Yvonne's half to her outright, but she's troubled by the thought of Colleen receiving several hundred thousand dollars. After reading Chapter 16, Sylvia decides it's sensible to give Colleen her money in what's called a "spendthrift" trust, where a trustee, someone other than Colleen, controls the money (principal), and Colleen receives only the trust income. She can only draw on any of the trust principal if the trustee agrees she needs it for educational, medical or other essential needs.

Sylvia still faces three important problems: First, who is to be trustee of the trust? Second, should she tell Colleen what she's decided upon? Third, when should the trust end? Sylvia discusses both questions with Yvonne, who convinces her mother that, for reasons having to do with sibling rivalry, she—Yvonne—shouldn't be the trustee. Sylvia reluctantly agrees that, given the personalities involved, and the fact that Colleen will hate not to get the money outright, it's sure to be personally destructive if one sister controls the other's inheritance. So, Sylvia decides to appoint her younger brother as trustee. She also decides the trust will end when Colleen becomes 45, at which point she will get all the money outright. She hopes Colleen will be fully responsible by then.

Finally, she decides to tell Colleen her plan, although she's not joyously anticipating that discussion. She softens the blow by also telling Colleen that if, over the coming years, she decides Colleen has matured and can handle money, she will change her estate plan and leave Colleen her money outright.

H. Disinheriting People, Including Children

Some parents want to disinherit a child, or children. Other people want to ensure that certain relations or ex-friends get none of their property. Legally, there is no need to disinherit friends or relatives other than your spouse or children—they inherit nothing unless you say so. When it comes to your spouse, he or she normally has rights to a certain percentage of your property. (See Chapter 3, State Property Ownership Laws.) It is legal to disinherit a child, however, if you take affirmative steps to do so. (See Chapter 6, Children, Section F.) But deciding to disinherit a child is often not easy to do, emotionally.

Example 1: Zorba and Kyria have three children—two daughters and a son— and a substantial estate. They are very close to the two daughters, but bitterly on the outs with their son, Nikos. Zorba and Kyria had originally intended to leave most of their property to each other, with some to the two daughters they're close to. Then, when the surviving spouse dies, the remaining property would be divided between the two daughters. But they have second thoughts. Do they really want to cut their son out entirely? This feels too harsh, too rejecting. And if they do cut Nikos out entirely, are they creating any real risk that he will be able to invalidate their estate plan? Although their lawyer tells them that since they are clearly competent, and can legally disinherit Nikos with little danger of him overturning their estate plan, they decide that both parental charity and prudence dictate the same decision. Each will leave Nikos $25,000 and include a "no-contest" clause in their wills. This clause states that if any beneficiary challenges a will, he gets nothing if his challenge is unsuccessful. The parents expect that Nikos will take the certain $50,000 he'll receive from both parents rather than the risk and the cost of a lawsuit he's almost sure to lose. Also, despite the bitterness they feel towards Nikos, both Zorba and Kyria are relieved that they haven't allowed it to cause them to completely disinherit one of their own children.

Example 2: Peter has two grown children, both very prosperous. Peter decides he wants to leave most of his estate to his favorite charity—a cause he deeply believes in—and the rest to his children. He hints at this to them. One child is supportive; the other is very upset, arguing that property should stay in the family. Peter decides to stick to his plan, accepting whatever disapproval or conflicts it will cause. In his living trust, he states expressly why he has decided his property is best given to the charity, and that even though he has done this, he loves his children deeply.

I. Communicating Your Decisions to Family and Friends

Many of the examples we've just discussed demonstrate our belief that communication can usually, but not always, resolve many potential estate planning difficulties with family and friends. Happily, in many families, talking about the older generation's estate planning isn't difficult. Both the parents and the children want the planning to be out in the open, so there will be no surprises down the road. Of course, there are certainly families where raising the subject of the parents' (or grandparents') estate plan may bring up tension, or touch on old conflicts—and others where the response will not be easy to predict. Only you can decide whether, when and how to talk about your plans, but here are some suggestions that may help with your thinking process:

- Whom do you want to talk to? Obviously, you need to talk to anyone you are naming to have responsibility for your minor children, or for supervising the distribution of your property after you die. But what about some, or all, of your beneficiaries?
- What should you talk about?
- Do you want to tell people what you've already decided and why, or ask for advice, or state that, within reason, you're open to suggestions? Or do you want to discuss the mechanics of how your estate plan will work with your inheritors? (You should, of course, with your executor and successor trustee.)
- Do you want to give your inheritors copies of your estate plan?

Talking is not invariably a panacea. Certainly, there are times when someone doesn't want to hear or talk, or other times when communication only reveals a deep and unbridgeable gulf. And from the older generation's point of view, there can be risks involved with communication: if they promise money to beneficiaries, they may feel guilty if a future medical necessity eats up some—or all—of that money. They may also worry that their revealing their plans will expose undesirable qualities like greed and hard-heartedness in those promised to inherit.

From the younger generation's viewpoint, it can be very difficult to open up estate planning discussions with parents. You certainly don't want to try to force a parent to talk about his or her property or plan. At the same time, you may need or want the reassurance that sensible planning has been done. We can suggest no magic formula to make this easier. All you can do is be tactful and genuinely concerned and see if that opens any doors.

But we do think it makes sense for all parents to at least indicate that planning has been carried out. If not, it's a good idea for communication to be initiated by a child, especially if that child knows or suspects her parent, or parents, have not taken care of even the basics. Saying this is easy, but of course, there can be many barriers to candor, such as:

- a general societal code that death is an unmentionable, especially with one's own parents
- fear that motives can be misunderstood. A parent may fear being seen as trying to manipulate a child by offering inherited money for demonstrations of love. A child, in turn, may fear that raising the subject will be seen as pushy or greedy
- the sense that honor lies in not caring about a parent's property, or that of any other loved one.

Still, the results of talking openly are usually positive. For example, we know of a situation in which a child who had done very well financially asked her parents to leave a disproportionate share of their estate to the other children. The children's discussion provided the impetus for their parents to do estate planning they'd intended to do for years. They were quite relieved to finally have it accomplished. Even where there are less dramatic results, we feel that communication, particularly among family members, about one's estate plan is a healthy process that can aid in preventing later conflicts. ■

2

An Overview of Estate Planning

There are a number of ways to leave property to those you want to have it after your death. The peculiarities of our system of inheritance mean that substantial amounts of money and time can often be saved if property is labeled and transferred by certain legal means rather than others. For example, if you leave your affairs to be handled by lawyers, a considerable sum of your money may end up in their pockets as fees for that time-consuming and unnecessary legal exercise called probate. Also, those with larger estates, over $600,000, can sometimes save substantially on estate (death) taxes by use of certain types of trusts, making gifts while alive or a combination of both.

Fortunately, the essentials of estate planning, even for those with larger estates, can be understood by most people, if they're willing to focus on, and carefully read, the information in this book. After understanding this information, you'll be able to tell whether you can do your estate planning yourself (using other Nolo resources) or whether you'll need an attorney. Many people with estates over $600,000 will sensibly conclude that they need an attorney for their estate planning. Still, understanding the basics of what they want their attorney to do for them should make matters go smoother, and the attorney's bill smaller.

Although we believe this book to be the most thorough estate planning manual written for the non-lawyer, it nevertheless does not cover some of the more esoteric, and extremely complex, areas of estate planning, such as planning for someone who owns property in several countries, or detailed planning for owners of valuable copyrights or patents. For special concerns like these, you need a lawyer, straight off.

A. The Language of Estate Planning

Estate planning is one of the more jargon-ridden areas of law. We've tried to keep use of this lawyer dialect to a minimum, but because some legal terms have become part of the law itself, it isn't possible to eliminate it entirely. To make this material as comprehensible as possible, each important term is defined when it's first used in the text and then redefined periodically. There's also a glossary near the back of the book. Please use it early and often to be sure you really understand what you are reading.

There are a few legal terms that anyone who wants to learn about estate planning must know. Some are euphemisms. For example, a dead person is referred to as a "decedent." Others are technical terms, including:

- "Testate" means to die leaving a will or other valid property-transfer device, such as a living trust.
- "Intestate" means to die without one, in which case, your property passes to your beneficiaries following the dictates of state law.
- "Real property" is real estate—land and the buildings on it.
- "Personal property" is every other kind of property, from stocks to cash to furniture to wedding rings to your pet canary and your old magazines. Of course, land isn't any more "real" than a car or wallet. Nevertheless, it apparently seemed more real to our ancestors. So we're stuck with the definition.
- "Gift" means property you transfer freely (not by sale or trade) to a person or institution. Throughout this book, "gift" is used both to describe property you give away during your lifetime, and property you leave at your death. This saves us from having to use the legalese "bequest," "devise" or "legacy."

B. What Is An Estate?

In common sense terms, your "estate" includes all the property you own, minus anything you owe (assets minus liabilities). To actually plan your estate sensibly, you first have to estimate its value. Another way to say this is that you must determine your "net worth." For purposes of this book, you may wish to make a rough general estimate, since you aren't doing any final planning now. Or you can choose to make a more complete and accurate listing of your assets and liabilities, as is discussed in Chapter 4, Inventorying Your Property. However, as you'll learn in subsequent chapters, there are two other ways to value your estate that can also be important for your planning:

- **The taxable estate.** This is the property that's subject to federal estate taxes (and state death taxes, too, if there are any in your state) when you die. Very generally, this is the same as the value of your estate, or net worth (assets minus liabilities), except that certain property included in your estate is excluded from your taxable estate. For example, for federal tax purposes, property left to a surviving spouse or to charity is not subject to tax, and therefore excluded from the taxable estate.
- **The probate estate.** This is the portion of your estate that is required by law to go through probate before it can be distributed. Most property left by will must go through probate. Everything that is transferred by probate-avoiding methods such as living trusts, joint tenancy or insurance, is not part of the probate estate, simply because the law allows it to be transferred directly to its inheritors with no need for probate. For those who plan wisely, the "probate estate" will be considerably less than the taxable estate; some people will eliminate it entirely.

Example: Maureen's taxable estate amounts to $500,000. She decides to transfer the major items in her estate—her house and stock account worth $460,000—by a living trust, not her will. Thus, her probate estate totals only $40,000.

C. Deciding Whom You Want to Receive Your Property

Deciding whom you want to receive your property is the heart of estate planning for most people. Most people approach their estate planning with a strong personal conviction as to what they want to do with their property. However, as you proceed through the book and move deeper into estate planning, we'll introduce a number of options that might affect the way you choose to distribute property to your beneficiaries, such as:

- giving money away before you die
- estate tax considerations that can affect how you leave property to your beneficiaries
- naming alternate beneficiaries
- leaving property to an adult for use for a minor, instead of leaving that property to the minor
- leaving property in trust for a spouse, child or other beneficiary.

D. What Is Probate and How Do You Avoid It?

Probate is the name given to the legal process by which a court oversees the distribution of property left by a will.[1] Probate proceedings are generally mere formalities, since there's rarely any dispute about a will, but they are nevertheless cumbersome and lengthy. (We explain why in Chapter 7, Probate and Why You Want to Avoid It.) During probate, the assets of the decedent are identified, all debts and death taxes are paid, fees for lawyers, appraisers, accountants and for filing the case in court are paid, and the remaining property is finally distributed to the inheritors. The average probate proceeding drags on for at least a year before the estate is actually distributed.

The very word "probate" has acquired a notorious aura. Although probate doesn't involve evil officials or outright corruption, it is commonly an institutionalized rip-off of a dead person's estate by lawyers, and sometimes executors, who get large fees for what in most cases is routine, albeit tedious, paperwork. For example, if a parent dies and leaves a will dividing his estate equally among his three children, and no one contests the division, why should a lawyer be paid a hefty sum to shuffle some routine papers through a bureaucratic maze?

Since probate lawyers are so expensive, we are often asked by beneficiaries if it's possible to safely handle probate without them? Unfortunately, except in California, Maryland and Wisconsin, the answer is normally "no," at least not without considerable difficulty.[2] Legally, it's permissible in most states (but not, for example, in Florida) for the executor named in a will to act for the estate, appear in probate court and handle the proceedings without an attorney ("in pro per"). But probate is a technical and tedious area of the law. Without good instructions, which are unfortunately non-existent outside of lawyer texts in most states, the necessary forms can seem complicated to the uninitiated. In some situations, there are court proceedings to attend. In short, learning how to do probate from scratch normally takes considerable time—and risks continuing frustration. Worse, the courts and clerks can be unhelpful, or even hostile, to laypeople. (This isn't to defend such bureaucratic hostility—there's obviously no defense—but it's important to note it exists.)

The far wiser approach is to plan to avoid probate altogether. Fortunately, this can be done without great difficulty for most estates. Several probate avoidance methods avoid court proceedings, transfer property quickly after a death, and can often be prepared without a lawyer. These methods are:

- Living trusts (Chapter 9)
- Joint tenancy (Chapter 10)
- Informal bank account trusts (pay-on-death accounts) and, in a few states, transfer-on-death registration for stocks or vehicles (Chapter 11)
- Life insurance (Chapter 12), and
- Probate exemption or simplification procedures, which are available in many states for small estates in the $5,000-$60,000 range (Chapter 13).

E. Why You Should Have a Will

Everyone should make out a will. Even those who plan to transfer all their property by probate avoidance methods, such as living trusts or joint tenancy, should prepare a will to back up these other transfer devices. You need a will to:

[1] If there was no will or other valid transfer device, such as a living trust or joint tenancy, probate occurs under the "intestacy" provisions of state law.

[2] Simple estates can be probated without a lawyer in California by using the excellent book, *How to Probate an Estate,* by Julia Nissley (Nolo Press). Maryland and Wisconsin provide simplified probate systems, with court clerk assistance for completing forms. (See Chapter 13, State Law Exemptions From Normal Probate, Sections B and C.)

- transfer property somehow overlooked when establishing probate-avoidance devices, since a living trust only transfers identified property transferred to the trust
- transfer property unexpectedly acquired after probate-avoidance devices are set up (a sudden inheritance, lottery winnings, etc.)
- appoint an executor, the person responsible for supervising the property left by will. Even if you leave most, or all, of your property by other methods, it's prudent to have a formal executor too, and sometimes essential, such as when you use a QTIP trust (see Chapter 19, Other Estate Tax-Saving Marital Trusts, Section A)
- nominate personal guardians for your minor children (discussed in Chapter 6, Children). You can't do this using any other estate planning device.

Some people eventually decide all the estate planning they want is a will. They prefer the ease of using a will to the more complicated methods needed to avoid probate or reduce death taxes. In other words, they decide to keep things simple for themselves, in spite of the additional complexity and cost probate and death taxes impose on their inheritors.

Although you may find it surprising, limiting estate planning to making a will can, in the right circumstances, make good sense. For example, younger people in good health often sensibly decide to postpone detailed estate planning for later. A will naming a personal and property guardian for minor children and leaving their usually modest amount of property to a spouse, living together partner or a few close relatives is all they need now. Since probate doesn't happen until death, most people will have plenty of time to plan to avoid it later in life. But for older people with a reasonable amount of property, it makes little sense to depend on a will alone. The amount of time and effort it takes to plan to avoid probate is just not that much—certainly far less than inheritors will expend going through it, not to mention the significant costs saved.

Some experts argue that in cases where estate taxes must be paid, or estate tax returns filed, avoiding probate is not wise, and that it makes sense to have a probate lawyer, experienced in these tax matters, do the paperwork as part of a formal probate. Bunk—don't fall for it. It's not difficult to hire a tax expert to prepare any needed estate tax returns for an estate that avoids probate—and generally, for far less than the cost of probate

In unusual situations, probate can be useful. If your estate will have many debts or claims by creditors, probate provides a forum for resolving those claims with relative speed and certainty. And, if creditors' claims are not filed within a set period of days, they can be barred forever. (This is covered in Chapter 7, Probate and Why You Want to Avoid It, Section D.)

F. Death Taxes and How to Minimize Them

Death taxes are taxes imposed on the property of a person who dies. Some people confuse probate avoidance devices, such as living trusts and joint tenancy, with death-tax-saving schemes. Unfortunately, avoiding probate doesn't have any effect on, or reduce, death taxes.

Death taxes are called by various names. The federal government, which imposes the stiffest taxes, calls them "estate taxes." Some of the states that impose death taxes (many states don't) call them "inheritance taxes." In theory, these states tax the recipients of a deceased person's property rather than the property itself, but the reality is the same—the taxes are paid out of the deceased's estate.

Whether or not your estate will be likely to be required to pay death taxes depends on two factors:

- the value of your taxable estate (your taxable estate is your net estate minus any gifts or expenses that are tax-exempt), and
- the laws of the state where you live.

If the net worth of your estate will be less than $600,000, you'll have no liability for federal taxes—assuming you haven't made large gifts during your lifetime. (See Chapter 15, Estate Taxes, Section A.) Each person has a $600,000 personal exemption from federal estate taxes. If you are single and you are pretty sure your estate will not be larger than this amount soon, you don't need to worry about federal taxes, or the material in this book discussing them—at least for now. If your estate exceeds $600,000 or soon will, it will usually owe federal estate tax on your death, unless you make substantial tax-exempt gifts, such as gifts to spouses, gifts for someone's education or medical costs, and gifts to charity.

If you're married (or in a couple) and the total combined estate belonging to you and your spouse amounts to over $600,000, you will almost certainly want to consider tax planning if each spouse plans to leave most of his or her property to the other. This is particularly important if both spouses are elderly. This type of marital estate tax planning, which usually involves establishing what we call a "marital life estate trust," is designed to preserve each spouse's $600,000 estate tax exemption. (See Chapter 18, Estate Tax-Saving Bypass Trusts, Section C.) In this situation, if spouses don't do any tax planning, the estate of the survivor will end up with more than $600,000 and therefore end up paying a hefty federal estate tax on the excess.

FAMILY LIMITED PARTNERSHIPS

Some people in the estate planning field, particularly certain insurance agents, have urged many families to use "family living partnerships" to save on estate taxes. The notion is that the parents can (somehow) transfer their property into the partnership business entity, with their children, and possibly grandchildren, sharing ownership as limited partners. By doing this, they hope the partnership will then be transferred to younger generations tax-free.

Guess what? This usually won't work. The IRS will disallow any family limited partnership it regards as a tax-avoidance scam. For such a plan to succeed, the IRS must be convinced that the limited partnership has a real business purpose. This means more than having alleged "business" records. The IRS looks to reality to make sure there really was a valid business, and that all the limited partners were actually involved in managing it.

There are a number of strict IRS requirements that must be met for a family limited partnership to be valid. If you are considering one, you must see a lawyer who is an expert in this specific area.

The state where you have your home is, generally, the one that determines if you're liable for state death taxes. Many states have no death taxes. (State death tax rules are discussed in Chapter 15, Estate Taxes, Section C.) Some states do impose stiff death taxes, particularly on property left to non-family members. This can be a particular problem for unmarried couples. People who divide their time between a high estate tax state (usually in the northeast and midwest) and a no estate tax state (usually in southern and western states) often can achieve significant tax savings by establishing permanent resident in the no tax state.

There are a number of different types of trusts called, in general, "ongoing" trusts, as well as other legal devices such as "disclaimers" or tax-free gifts made during one's lifetime, that can be used to reduce, postpone or, occasionally, even eliminate estate taxes for large estates. These trusts and devices are discussed in:

- Chapter 16: Gifts and Gift Taxes
- Chapter 17: Ongoing Trusts: An Overview
- Chapter 18: Estate Tax-Saving Bypass Trusts
- Chapter 19: Other Estate Tax-Saving Marital Trusts
- Chapter 20: Charitable Trusts
- Chapter 21: Other Estate Tax-Saving Trusts
- Chapter 22: Disclaimers: After Death Estate Tax Planning

G. Planning for Possible Incapacity

Thorough estate planning includes considering what happens if you become incapacitated and are unable to make medical or financial decisions for yourself. For many people, the most important concern here is to insure that their life is not artificially prolonged using life support systems, if they are in the last stages of a terminal illness or are in a permanent coma and cannot make their own medical decisions. No one can be compelled to subsist on life support systems against their will. But, of course, the problem is, if you are unconscious or mentally incompetent, how can you enforce your decision? Fortunately, there are legal documents, such as "Durable Powers of Attorney for Health Care" or living wills that you can use, depending on your state, to:

1. Specify your decision regarding use of life support systems, and

2. Appoint someone to have authority to act for you and enforce your written decision if you are incapacitated.

These devices are discussed in Chapter 26, Incapacity: Health Care and Financial Management Directives, Section A.

Catastrophic Illness Clause

Many people are concerned that if they contract a serious illness, all their savings—indeed, all their assets—will be consumed to pay medical/health care costs. This is far from an irrational concern—it has happened to many people. To address this worry, some people ask for a will clause, or a trust, or anything that will prevent their assets from being used for expensive medical costs. Unfortunately, there's no simple clause or trust that can legally accomplish this. About the best you can do is:

- Seek advice from an expert attorney in your state on its laws and regulations regarding protecting your assets in case of immense medical bills. State laws vary considerably here. The attorney must also know applicable federal laws and regulations.
- If you're a member of a couple, research how you can best protect the assets of the member who doesn't become ill. Many states do allow one spouse to shield his or her property from liability for medical bills of the other spouse. (This is covered in depth in *Beat the Nursing Home Trap*, by Joseph L. Matthews (Nolo Press).)
- Consider transferring some of your property to trusted family members before you become seriously ill.

All this can be tricky, and both federal and state legal rules can, and sometimes do, change rapidly. Nevertheless, a lawyer in your state experienced in elder law issues should be able to provide you with some measure of asset protection. Unfortunately, this is likely to be less than you want, but the best you can do.

To arrange for handling of your financial matters should you become incapacitated and unable to manage them yourself, you need to prepare another document, called a "Durable Power of Attorney for Finances." (See Chapter 26, Section B.) In this document, you appoint a person with authority to manage your financial affairs if you can't. Also, you can impose whatever limits or restrictions on this person's authority that you want to.

H. Choosing Someone to Supervise Your Estate

However you plan to transfer property at your death, you need to name someone who will actually be responsible for supervising your estate after you die and seeing to it that your expressed desires are carried out. This person is your "executor" (called a "personal representative," in some states) if named in a will, or your "successor trustee," if named in a living trust. Since many people use both a living trust and a will, they name the same person in each capacity.

Most people know who they want to be their executor or successor trustee—their spouse or mate or most trustworthy child. Others select a best friend or close family relation. If there's no obvious person who comes to mind, work through your possible selections, using common sense to decide who would be the wisest choice. Do remember that human concerns are usually more important than technical "expertise." Of course, the person you name must agree to do the job, but the most vital criterion here is good honest character. Competence and expertise can be purchased, but at the most personal level, trust, honesty and an ability to treat all family members fairly cannot.

Some conservative estate planners recommend that you select a "corporate fiduciary" such as a bank, or even a "team of professional experts," to handle your affairs after you die. We strongly recommend against this in most instances. Your personal representative is your link to the future, the one who's in charge of distributing your property after your death. You want someone human, with genuine concern, not an impersonal institution that charges fees for every small act. In short, if your most trusted friend is your banker, name him as executor, but not the bank itself.

I. Providing for Care and Support of Minor Children

If you have minor children, you'll want to plan ahead for what will happen if you and the other parent (if there is one) die before your children become legal adults—18 years old in most states. These issues are discussed in detail in Chapter 6, Children. Here we only alert you to the most basic ones.

First, whom do you want to name as the "personal guardian" for your children—the adult who will be responsible for raising them if both parents die, or if the other parent can't or won't accept responsibility for them? While your nomination isn't automatically legally binding, courts normally confirm the person you name if the other parent isn't available.

Next, how much property do you want to leave for your minor children, and who will supervise it? There are two good legal methods you can use to leave property to your minor children: 1) establishing a child's trust, or 2) using the Uniform Transfers to Minors Act (UTMA), available in most states, which allows you to name a trusted person to manage property for a child, doling it out slowly for needed purposes, such as living costs and education. Only when the child reaches an age you establish does she get the remainder of her inheritance outright. This is important because many parents worry that age 18 (the age children are normally entitled to obtain outright property left to them) is far too young for the responsibility of handling money and property.

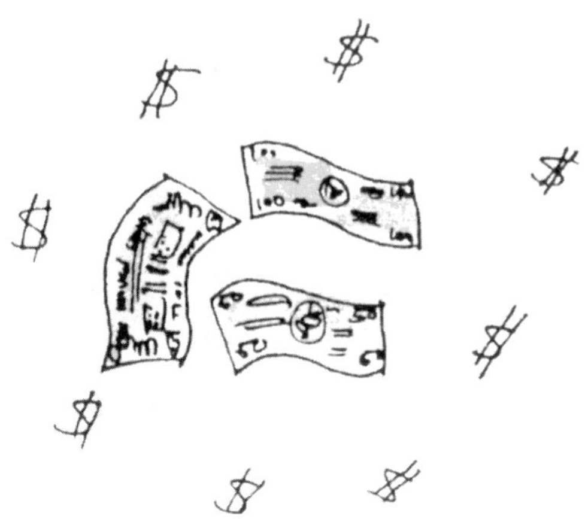

J. Providing Ready Cash

Another important goal of estate planning is to provide ready cash (also called "liquidity") for immediate family needs or, later on, to pay any death taxes or other debts of the deceased. Particularly if you are your family's main provider, your survivors will immediately need cash for living expenses. Cash will also be needed for the "costs of dying"—hospitalization and funeral and burial expenses, and to pay other debts and taxes that are due promptly.

If most of your property is to be transferred by will, your family won't get it while probate drags on. Limited amounts for family necessities can normally be obtained by petitioning the probate court, but it's wiser to plan to have sources of money available that don't require going to court and paying attorneys' fees.

If most of your property will be transferred outside of probate, there is much less reason to worry about arranging for ready cash, since property in a living trust or owned in joint tenancy can often be transferred to inheritors in a few days. However, if most of your assets aren't "liquid"—cannot easily be converted to money—you may still need to provide a source of ready cash. For example, if your worth is in real estate and shares of a private corporation that can't readily be sold, your family might have trouble obtaining cash for daily expenses.

A life insurance policy payable to a survivor or survivors is one traditional method of providing ready cash, but it's by no means the only available one. For example, money held in a joint bank account can often be released immediately, or in a few days, if you plan it properly[3]. Also, most banks offer informal trust accounts (often called "pay-on-death" accounts) that can be used to promptly provide the cash in the account to named beneficiaries free of probate. An advantage of this type of account as compared to some types of joint tenancy accounts is that the person named as an account beneficiary cannot take any money from the account before the depositor dies. (See Chapter 11, Pay-on-Death Designations, Section A.)

K. Funeral and Burial Plans

As part of your estate plan, you may want to decide on, and arrange for, a funeral and burial plan. Doing this in advance can be a great gift to your loved ones, freeing them from burdensome tasks immediately after your death and almost always saving significant amounts of money. (You will almost surely spend less than they will.)

There are a number of possible choices, including:

- services offered by commercial funeral homes
- services offered through no-profit funeral societies
- cremation, and
- donation of body parts to organ banks for medical transplants.

[3]If your state has an inheritance or estate tax (see Chapter 15, Estate Taxes, Section E), it is wise to check with your bank to learn if joint accounts are "frozen" upon the death of one of the account holders, and if so, how to get the account released. In most states, even if accounts are frozen by state tax authorities, it's only for a short period.

These issues are discussed in Chapter 27, Body Organ Donation, Funerals and Burials.

L. Do You Need Professional Help?

By the time you're finished with this book you'll be able to make a sensible evaluation of whether or not you need to hire a lawyer or other expert to help you. Many readers don't need professional help to adequately plan their own estate. This is especially true if the estate is worth less than $600,000, because no federal estate taxes will be assessed (with the exception, already noted, of couples whose combined estate exceeds $600,000). Others, especially those with larger estates or special needs, such as the responsibility to provide long-term care for a serious mentally or physically disabled child, will need a lawyer to prepare their final estate plan. If you own assets in more than one country, you should see a lawyer knowledgeable in "multinational" estate planning. In a number of situations, we believe getting legal help is essential. These are clearly indicated throughout this book. (Use of lawyers, accountants and other estate planning experts is discussed in Chapter 30, Using Lawyers.)

Even if you do conclude that you need the assistance of a lawyer or decide that you simply feel more comfortable consulting one, you'll be sufficiently informed so you should have a clear general idea of what you want. In addition, you'll be able to evaluate whether the lawyer you talk to is dealing honestly and appropriately with you.[4]

As we noted in the Introduction, this is the symbol you'll see throughout *Plan Your Estate* when we suggest that you consult a lawyer, accountant or other estate planning expert. If you face a complicated situation, please take seriously our advice that you get expert help.

Finally, anyone who takes a do-it-yourself route—in whole or part—must develop a skin thick enough to ward off derisive comments by lawyers. Some members of the legal establishment have tried to frighten the public with horror stories of disasters that befell some benighted person who prepared her own estate plan. For example, a renowned lawyer once remarked sarcastically that anyone who can take out his own appendix can write his own will. This analogy is just plain false. A more accurate one is that if you can understand a standard tax form, doing your own estate planning should present you with no insurmountable problems, especially if your estate is under $600,000. ■

[4]For instance, lawyers have been known to charge hundreds or even thousands of dollars to set up elaborate tax-saving devices for people whose estates are quite likely to be exempt from federal taxation.

3

State Property Ownership Laws

To sensibly plan your estate, you obviously need to know what property is yours, and roughly what your net worth is. Many people choose to go further and inventory and assign a value to each significant item of property they own before proceeding with their planning. You'll have the opportunity to do this in the next chapter.

But however precise you choose to be about listing and valuing your property, you also need to know the basic rules governing property ownership. This will allow you to be sure you don't include any property in your planning that you don't actually own, or overlook property you do own.

What you own is determined by the laws of the state where you live, with one important exception: if you own real estate in another state (or country), the laws of that other state (or country) govern its ownership. Within the U.S., property ownership rules are very similar from one state to the next, with this major exception: eight states (mostly in the west) follow a community property ownership system which is substantially different from that of the other 41 states and Washington, D.C. (Remember, this book does not cover estate planning for residents of Louisiana.)

Fortunately, many readers, married or single, will find state property ownership laws raise no worries. If, as you read Section A of this chapter, you conclude that your property ownership situation is simple, you can skip the rest of the chapter and move on. But if your situation isn't so clear, as can often be true for married couples, be sure you understand how state property laws affect you before you go ahead.

A. How Marital Status Affects Property Ownership

The rules for property ownership vary depending on whether you are single or married.

1. Unmarried People

If you're single and own all your property outright, your property ownership situation is definitely simple. You should have no estate planning problem with any state ownership law. By "outright," we mean that you don't share ownership, of property with anyone else as would be the case, for example, if you owned property with a friend in "joint tenancy" or in a partnership. For these purposes, the fact that an institution has a mortgage on your home or a claim to title to your car for a loan isn't shared ownership, because you're entirely free to give that home or car (subject to the debt, of course) to whomever you choose.

If you do own any property with someone else—such as property in joint tenancy,[1] tenancy in common,[2] partnership or a small, closely-held corporation in which there are other owners—you'll need to understand how this shared ownership affects ownership rights to the property and your power to give away your share. Joint tenancy and marital tenancy by the entirety are discussed in greater detail in Chapter 10, Joint Tenancy and Tenancy by the Entirety; partnership and small business corporate ownership are discussed in Chapter 28, Business Ownership and Estate Planning.

2. Married People

Property ownership situations are often more complex for married people than for singles. This is primarily because spouses often own property together. In the eight community property states,

[1]Joint tenancy is a form of property ownership by two or more persons where surviving owners automatically inherit the share of a dead owner.

[2]Tenancy in common is another form of shared ownership; the surviving owners of tenancy-in-common property don't automatically inherit the share of the deceased owner. Each owner is free to give her share—but only her share—by will or living trust to whomever she chooses.

UNMARRIED COUPLES: WHO OWNS WHAT?

Unless an unmarried couple—gay, lesbian or heterosexual, it makes no difference—agrees to share ownership of specified property, each member of the couple owns only his or her own property. An agreement to own property jointly must often be in writing to be enforceable. In most states, an oral agreement is effective if it can be proved, but that can often be difficult. In short, it is best for unmarried couples to put any property-sharing agreement in writing.

If you're part of an unmarried couple where each person has kept all property separate (a written agreement to do this, listing the property of each person, is a good idea here as well), each of you is free to give your property to whomever you wish. However, if property ownership is shared, either under the terms of a written contract or in a tenancy in common or partnership, you're only free to dispose of your share, unless the contract or partnership agreement provides otherwise.

Property held by unmarried couples in joint tenancy goes to the survivor automatically.

For more information on property ownership problems of unmarried couples and sample property-sharing agreements, see either *The Living Together Kit*, by Ihara and Warner (Nolo Press), a detailed guide designed to help unmarried couples minimize their entanglements with the law, or *The Legal Guide for Lesbian and Gay Couples*, by Curry, Clifford and Leonard (Nolo Press).

spouses typically share ownership of most property, even if only one spouse's name is on the title slip or deed. (See Sections A3 and B of this chapter for a list of these states and an explanation of community property.) In these states, each spouse can leave his or her share of property as desired, but has no control over the other spouse's share.

In the other 41 "common law" states and the District of Columbia, the spouse whose name appears in the ownership document is the owner of that property. However, unlike the legal situation in the community property states, state laws provide that each spouse has a legal right to inherit at least a minimum portion of the other's property at death, even if the deceased spouse has left it all to someone else. (See Section C for a list of states and an explanation of common law property rules.)

If you and your spouse plan to leave all, or the lion's share, of your property to each other, it's not of much practical importance to understand who legally owns each item of property. After all, as long as the survivor will get all, or even most, of the property, it's not important how it's labeled. However, if you plan to make substantial gifts of property to someone other than your spouse (especially if your spouse might prefer that you didn't), it's essential that you understand both who owns the property and whether there are any rules in your state which give your spouse the right to at least a minimum portion of it at your death. Otherwise, your decision to give property to someone other than your spouse may occasion a nasty conflict after your death.

To understand how marital property laws affect your situation, you need to know:

1. The property ownership laws of the state where you have your home. The legalese term for where you permanently live is "domicile." You can only have one domicile. The state of your domicile governs your marital property—except real estate in another state or country. If you have homes in two or more states, it can be important which you choose as your legal domicile, both for property ownership and state inheritance tax purposes. Given a choice, it's usually best to opt for a state that imposes no, or low, property taxes. (See Chapter 15, Estate Taxes, Section C, for information on state tax rates.)

If You're Unsure of Your Marital Status

Most people are quite certain of their marital status. If you're not, here's what you need to know.

The divorce decree. You're not divorced until you have a final decree of divorce (or dissolution, as it's called in some states) issued by a state court in the United States, or under limited circumstances by the legally empowered authorities of a foreign country. (See below.)

If you think you're divorced but never saw the final decree, contact the court clerk in the county where you think the divorce was granted. Give the clerk your name, your ex-spouse's name and the date, as close as you know it, of the divorce.

Legal separation. Even if a court has declared you and your spouse legally separated, and you plan to divorce, you are still married until you get the divorce decree.

Foreign divorces. Divorces issued to U.S. citizens by courts in Mexico, the Dominican Republic or another country may not be valid if challenged, especially if all the paperwork was handled by mail. In other words, if you or your your spouse got a quickie foreign divorce, you may well well be still married under the laws of your state. On the other hand, foreign divorces, where both spouses were present in person or through a representative, may be recognized as valid in the U.S. If you think that someone might make a claim to some of your property after your death based on the invalidity of a foreign divorce, see a lawyer.

Common law marriages. In some states, a couple can become legally married by living together, intending to be married and clearly presenting themselves to the world as a married couple. Even in states that allow such common law marriages, most couples who live together don't have common law marriages. Folk law notwithstanding, no magic number of years of living together automatically establishes a common law marriage. If you really do have a valid common law marriage, you must go to court and get a divorce to end it—there's no such thing as a common law divorce.

If you are confused about where you legally live (are domiciled). If you own two or more homes in the U.S. or live both in the U.S. and abroad, see a lawyer to discuss how this affects your estate planning, to determine which state's or country's laws govern your marital property and what, if anything, you can do to change this if you so desire.

2. The property ownership laws of any state or country where you own real estate. The marital ownership laws applicable to real estate are the laws of the state or country where the real estate is located, no matter where you live.

Divorce means a new estate plan. If you get divorced, you should always re-examine your estate plan and bring it up to date. One obvious reason for this is that, in some states, divorce doesn't automatically revoke your will as to gifts made to your former spouse. Even in the majority of states, where a divorce invalidates an earlier will as far as property left to the divorced spouse is concerned, you still need to designate whom you now want to get that property. Also, in almost all states, divorce does not revoke a living trust, even if an ex-spouse benefits from it. The moral is simple: If you get divorced, be sure you revise your estate plan to keep it current.

3. Community Property and Common Law States

As we've mentioned, states can be broadly divided into two types for the purpose of deciding what marital property is in your estate when you die:

- community property states, and
- common law property states.

Community Property	Common Law
Arizona California Idaho Louisiana Nevada New Mexico TexasWashington Wisconsin[3]	All other states and the District of Columbia (except Louisiana which has a different basis for its laws).

- If you live or own real estate in a community property state, you should read Section B of this chapter.
- If you live or own real estate in a common law state, you should read Section C.
- If you have moved, while married, from a community property state to a common law state, or vice versa, also read Section D.

[3]Although the terminology is different, Wisconsin's marital property law works much like those found in community property states.

Varying State Property Ownership Laws By Contract

If you and your spouse don't like the way your state's law defines how the two of you share ownership of jointly-owned property, you can normally agree to change it. To accomplish this, you need a valid contract between you and your spouse. For example, in most states you can agree to change the ownership status of property acquired prior to marriage, which would normally be owned as separate property by the acquiring spouse, to joint ownership. A written agreement to do this made before a marriage, where the couple set out the terms by which their property, before and after marriage, shall be owned, is called a "prenuptial contract" or "marital contract."

Prenuptial contracts must comply with your state's laws governing them. Generally, this means they must be in writing, voluntarily agreed to by both spouses, and have been agreed to after fair disclosure by both spouses of their partnership ownership and financial obligations. These agreements often explicitly inheritance, and partnership ownership for estate planning. Of course, valid agreements can also be made after a couple is married.

Marital contracts and inheritance rights are often a confusing combination. If you have a marital property contract and are in doubt as to how its provisions affect your rights to give that property away at death, or if you want to explore preparing this kind of contract after marriage, see an attorney.

Property ownership can be confusing. The discussions in these three sections present the basic rules that apply to marital property in your state. It's impossible, short of a ten-volume treatise, to cover every complexity and nuance of marital property law for every state. If you have a question that isn't answered in these pages, you'll need to see a lawyer or research it yourself. (See Chapter 30, Using Lawyers.)

B. Marital Property in Community Property States

The basic rule of community property law is simple: During a marriage, all property earned or acquired by either spouse is owned in equal half shares by each spouse—except for property received as "separate property" by one of them through gift or inheritance. This community property concept derives from the ancient marriage laws of some European peoples, including the Visagoths, which passed to Spain and then to many Western states through Spanish explorers and settlers. For estate planning purposes, there are no restrictions on how each spouse can give away his or her half of their community property. Neither is required to give it to the surviving spouse, although, of course, many spouses do.

In community property states, "separate property" is property owned entirely by one spouse. Property owned by one spouse before a marriage remains separate property even after the marriage, as long as it's kept separate. Also, property given to one spouse or left by will or living trust to one spouse at someone's death is his or her separate property.

Using common sense. For many couples in long-term marriages, characterizing their property is relatively easy: it's all community property. Any property owned by either spouse before marriage is either long gone or so totally mixed with community property that it has long since lost its separate property status; and neither spouse has inherited or been given any substantial amount of separate property during the marriage, or if they have, it, too, has been merged into the community pot. Still, even if you believe this to be your situation, read the next few pages to be sure.

1. What Is Community Property?

Unless the husband and wife agree to something different (usually in writing), the following is community property:

- all income received by either spouse from employment or by other means (except by gift or inheritance to one spouse) during the marriage[4]
- all property acquired with community property income during the marriage, and
- all separate property that is transformed into community property under state law. This transformation can occur in several ways, including when one spouse makes a gift of separate property to both of them. Generally, this must be done with a written document.

Example: Ned Terrlin owned a home for five years before he married Sally. He then signed a new deed for the house, listing the new owners as "Ned

[4]This generally only refers to the period when the couple is living together as husband and wife. From the time spouses permanently separate, most community property states consider newly-acquired income and property as the separate property of the spouse receiving it.

and Sally Terrlin, as community property." Thus, Ned has given one-half ownership of the house to Sally.

Community property can also be transformed into separate property by gifts between spouses. The rules for how to do this differ somewhat from state to state. Normally, if real property is given, the gift must be in writing. And even for personal property, the strong trend is to require that, to be binding, a gift must be made in writing.

Another common example of transformation of separate property is when it gets so mixed together with community property that it's no longer possible to tell the difference between the two. Lawyers call this "commingling."

Example: When she was married, Felicity had a bank account with $10,000 in it, her separate property. During her marriage, now in its 27th year, she maintained this account, depositing money she or her husband earned and making frequent withdrawals. She no longer has a separate property interest in any money in the account. The original $10,000 has long since been "commingled" with community property funds.

Each spouse can keep his or her own income as separate property. All community property states except Washington allow spouses to treat income earned after marriage as separate property if they sign a written agreement to do so and then actually keep their income separate (as in separate bank accounts).

2. What Is Separate Property?

The following property qualifies as separate property:

- all property owned by either spouse prior to marriage
- all property received by one spouse after marriage by gift or inheritance, and
- all property earned or accumulated by one spouse after permanent separation.

As mentioned, separate property keeps its separate property legal status only so long as it is not:

- hopelessly mixed (commingled) with community property, or
- transferred to joint ownership by its separate property owner, in writing.

Income from separate property. Community property states have different rules for classifying certain types of income derived from separate property:[5]

California, Arizona, Nevada, New Mexico and Washington: Any income from separate property during a marriage is also separate property.

Texas and Idaho: Income from separate property during a marriage is community property.

3. Pensions

Generally, private pensions (and pensions from the military) are considered community property—at least the proportion of them attributable to earnings during the marriage. However, certain major federal pension programs, including Social Security and Railroad Retirement, aren't community property because federal law classifies them as the separate property of the employee.

[5]Wisconsin's statutes on this point are confusing; if this point matters to you, see a Wisconsin lawyer.

4. Distinguishing Community and Separate Property

Most married couples have little difficulty determining what's community property and what is each one's separate property. However, these issues can get complicated. Divorce courts churn out a continual stream of decisions on the fine points of community versus separate property. Here are a few potential problem areas in estate planning.

Appreciated property. In most community property states, when the separate property of one spouse goes up in value, this appreciation is also separate property. However, sometimes one spouse owns separate property before a marriage, but both spouses contribute to the cost of maintaining or improving that property during the marriage. The result can be that the property is part community, part separate. If the property substantially appreciates in value over the years, it can be difficult to determine what percentage of the current value of the property is separate property and what is community property.

A common example of this would be a house that was originally owned by one spouse. Then for a length of time, say ten or 30 years, both spouses pay, from community funds, the costs of maintaining the house (mortgage, insurance, upkeep). Assuming the value of the house grows during the marriage, the couple can determine what portion of the present value is community property by agreeing in writing on any division they decide is fair.

Businesses. A family-owned business can pose difficult ownership questions, especially if it was owned by one spouse in whole or part before marriage and grew later. As with home ownership, the basic problem is to figure out whether the increased value is community or separate property. Again, a married couple can agree on any division they want to. One sensible approach is if both spouses work in the business, then the increase in value which the business undergoes during that period is community property. However, if only the spouse who originally owned the business as separate property works in it, resolving ownership can be more difficult. If it's likely the business would have grown in value anyway, the increase could more reasonably be regarded as separate property.

Monetary recovery for personal injuries. As a general matter, personal injury awards or settlements are the separate property of the spouse receiving them, but not always. In some community property states, this money is treated one way (community property) while the injured spouse is living and another way (separate property) upon his death. Also, the determination as to whether it's separate or community property can vary when the injury is caused by the other spouse. In short, there's no easy way to characterize this type of property.

5. Resolving Conflicts Over Property Ownership

Remember, it's not crucial to define which spouse owns what property if the spouses plan to leave all or most of their property to each other, or in a way the other approves of. However, if you and your spouse discover any conflict over your property ownership that will significantly affect your estate planning (for example, you want to leave a certain item of property to your brother and your spouse doesn't), we highly recommend that you talk it out. It's best, of course, if you are able to resolve any disagreements among yourselves. But failing this, it's far better to get professional help—from a mediator, lawyer, or even a therapist—than to allow confusion to remain unresolved. If a mutually-agreeable compromise isn't reached prior to death, and one spouse tries to leave property the other believes he or she doesn't own, there is real danger of a nasty court fight. After resolving any problems, both spouses should sign a written "Marital Property Agreement" setting forth the determinations.

> **ADDITIONAL RESOURCES**
>
> Good sources of information if you're interested in pursuing this subject further are:
>
> - *Community Property Law in the United States*, by W. S. McClanahan (Bancroft-Whitney)
> - *Nolo's Pocket Guide to Family Law*, by Leonard & Elias (Nolo Press).

C. Marital Property in Common Law States

In common law states, there's no rule that property acquired during a marriage is owned by both spouses. Common law principles are derived from English law, where in feudal times the husband owned all marital property and a wife had few legal property ownership rights and couldn't even leave any property at all by will. And still today, in the common law states, the spouse who earns money or acquires property owns it separately and solely, unless, of course, he or she transfers it into shared ownership.

In common law states, the property you own for estate planning purposes, whether you are married or not, consists of:

Community Property	**Common Law**
Arizona California Idaho Louisana Nevada New Mexico Texas Washington Wisconsin[6]	All other states and the District of Columbia (except Louisiana which has a different basis for it's laws).

- everything held separately in your name if it has a title slip, deed or other legal ownership document (this always includes real estate, vehicles, securities and bank accounts), and
- all other property you have purchased from your assets or income.

For example, if you earn or inherit money to buy a house, and title is taken in both your name and your spouse's, you both own it. But if your spouse earns the money to buy it, but somehow title is placed in your name alone, you own it.[7] Similarly, no matter who puts up funds to buy a house, if title is in your spouse's name, he or she owns it.

---

[6]Although the terminology is different, Wisconsin's marital property law works much like those found in community property states.

[7]Despite the general rule stated here, courts in most common law states have legal rules designed to prevent blatant injustice from occurring. Specifically, all common law states employ some type of "Equitable Distribution Law" for divorces. Under these laws, the court has the power to distribute marital property fairly (often equally) no matter what the ownership documents say. While those equitable distribution laws haven't been applied to the characterization of property upon death, in extremely unjust inheritance cases a court could use its "equity powers" (its inherent authority to do justice). Still, this isn't certain, and would always involve a lawsuit, so it's far wiser to resolve all marital property ownership questions amicably while both spouses are alive.

1. Family Protection in Common Law States

Because property ownership rules can result in one spouse legally owning all or most of a couple's property, all common law states have laws designed to protect the other spouse from being disinherited and winding up with nothing. To accomplish this, common law states normally give a surviving spouse legal rights to a certain portion—usually one-third to one-half—of the other's estate. (See Section 2, below.)

Suppose, for example, one spouse owns the family house, the car and bank accounts in his name alone and attempts to leave it all to a stranger (or, worse, a lover). Can the stranger kick the surviving spouse out of the house, empty the bank accounts, and so on? Of course, this rarely happens, but just in case, the common law property states prevent the surviving spouse from being completely, or even substantially, disinherited.[8] While many of these protective laws are similar, they do differ in detail.

The chart below provides a summary outline of the basic rights that states give to the surviving spouse. It doesn't contain the specifics of every state's law. Also, please realize that many states' laws are quite complex in this area. If this issue is significant to you, see a lawyer.

[8]Some common law states and some community property ones provide additional, relatively minor protection devices such as "family allowances" and "probate homesteads." These vary from state to state in too much detail to discuss here. Generally, however, these devices attempt to assure that your spouse and children are not totally left out in the cold immediately after your death, by allowing them temporary protections, such as the right to remain in the family home for a short period, or funds (most typically while an estate is being probated). Accordingly, they shouldn't prove unwelcome to any of you.

2. The Spouse's Minimum Share

Methods of protecting families currently in use in common law states were developed hundreds of years ago by English courts, which were confronted with the same problem of a few people disinheriting their spouses. In response, they developed the legal concepts called "dower" and "curtesy." "Dower" refers to the rights of a surviving wife; "curtesy" is the share received by a surviving husband. When the United States was settled, most states adopted these concepts. To this day, all common law states still retain some version of dower and curtesy (although many have dropped the old terminology and simply provide for "spousal inheritance rights" or some similar phrase). Note that no such legal protections are needed in community property states, because each spouse owns one-half of all property acquired from the earnings of either (or both) during the marriage.

In most common law property states, a spouse is entitled to one-third of the property left by the other. In a few, it's one-half. The exact amount of the spouse's minimum share often depends on whether the couple has minor children. In some states, the surviving spouse must be left only a certain percentage of the estate transferred by will. In other states, property transferred by means other than a will, such as a living trust, is included when calculating whether a spouse has received his or her minimum legal share of property. (This is called the "augmented estate" and is discussed in Subsection 3, below.)

What happens if a person leaves nothing to a spouse or leaves less than the spouse is entitled to under state law? In most states, the surviving spouse has a choice of either taking what the will or other transfer document provides or rejecting the gift and instead taking the minimum share allowed by state law. Taking the share permitted by law is called "taking against the will."

Example: Leonard's will gives $50,000 to his second wife, June, and leaves the rest of his property, totaling $400,000, to his two children from his first marriage. June can take the $50,000 or elect to take against the will and receive her statutory share of Leonard's estate. Depending on the state, this will normally be from one-third to one-half of Leonard's total estate.

When a spouse decides to take against the will, the property which is taken must come out of one or more of the gifts given to others by the will (or in many states, other transfer documents, such as a living trust, as well; see Section 3, below). In other words, somebody else is going to get less. In the above example, the children will receive much less than Leonard intended. So, if you don't provide your spouse with at least the statutory share under your state's laws, your gifts to others may be seriously reduced.

If you want to leave your spouse little or nothing, see a lawyer. Put bluntly, if you don't wish to leave your spouse at least one-half of your property, and you haven't gotten your spouse's unforced and written consent to your plan, your estate may be heading for a legal mess and you should see a lawyer.

3. The Augmented Estate

As mentioned above, in many common law states, all property of a deceased spouse, not just the property left by will, is considered in determining whether a spouse has been left the statutory share. This is called the "augmented estate." It means that in determining whether a surviving spouse has been adequately provided for, courts in most common law property states look to see the value of the property the spouse has received outside of probate, though devices such as living trusts, as well as counting the value of the property that passes through probate. This makes sense because many people devise ways to pass their property to others outside of wills—with living trusts or joint tenancy, for example—to avoid probate fees.

Example: Alice leaves her husband, Mike, $10,000 and her three daughters $90,000 each in her will. However, Alice also leaves real estate worth $500,000 to Mike by a living trust. The total Mike receives from this augmented estate, $510,000, is more than one-half of Alice's total property, so he has nothing to gain by insisting on his right to make a claim against her estate.

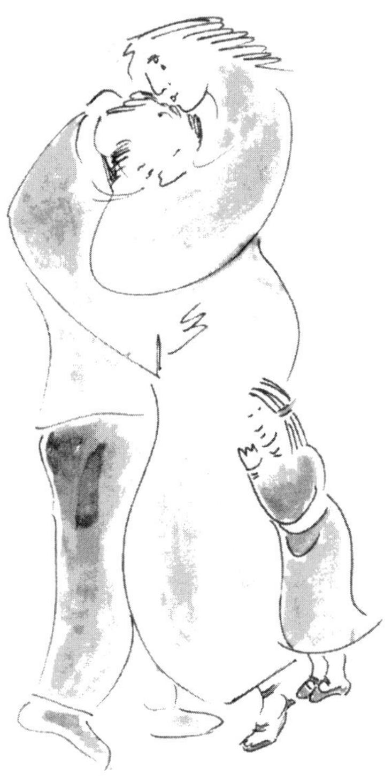

FAMILY PROTECTION IN COMMON LAW STATES

I. Surviving spouse receives right to enjoy one-third of deceased spouse's real property for life

Connecticut*
Kentucky*
Rhode Island
Vermont
West Virginia

II. Surviving spouse receives percentage of estate

a. Fixed percentage

State	Share
Alabama *	1/3 of augmented estate
Alaska*	1/3 of augmented estate
Colorado	1/2 of augmented estate
Delaware	1/3 of estate
District of Columbia	1/2 of estate
Florida	3/10 of estate
Hawaii*	1/3 of estate
Iowa	1/3 of estate
Maine*	1/3 of augmented estate
Minnesota*	1/3 of estate
Montana*	1/3 of augmented estate
Nebraska*	1/3 of augmentedestate
New Jersey*	1/3 of augmented estate
New York*	1/3 of augmented estate
North Dakota*	1/3 of augmented estate
Oregon*	1/4 of estate
Pennsylvania*	1/3 of estate
South Carolina	1/3 of estate
South Dakota*	1/3 of augmented estate
Tennessee	1/3 of estate
Utah*	1/3 of estate

b. Percentage varies if there are children (usually one-half if no children, one-third if children)

Arkansas*
Illinois*
Indiana*
Kansas
Maryland*
Michigan
Missouri
Mississippi
New Hampshire
North Carolina*
Ohio
Virginia
Wyoming*

III. One year's support

Georgia

D. Moving From State to State

A will or living trust validly made in one state is, broadly speaking, valid in all. However, problems can develop when married people move from a community property state to a common law property state or vice versa. This is because the property each spouse owns (and is therefore free to give away) may change. If spouses move from one state to another which follows the same property ownership system (for example, New York to Florida, or California to Texas), there is normally no need to worry about property ownership.

Remember, technical property ownership rules are not a worry if spouses plan to leave all (or the lion's share) of their property to each other, or in a way the other spouse approves of.

1. Moving From a Common Law State to a Community Property State

What happens when a husband and wife acquire property in a non-community property state but then move to a community property state? California and Idaho (community property states) treat the earlier acquired property as if it had been acquired in a community property state. The legal jargon for this type of property is "quasi-community property." The other community property states don't recognize the quasi-community property concept and instead go by the rules of the state where the property was acquired.[8] Thus, if you and your spouse moved from any non-community property state into California or Idaho, all of your property is treated according to community property rules. (See Section C, above.) However, if you moved into any of the other community property states from a common law state, you'll need to assess your property according to the rules of the state where the property was acquired.

2. Moving From a Community Property State to a Common Law Property State

When spouses move from a community property state to a common law property state, each generally retains one-half interest in the property accumulated during marriage while the couple lived in the community property state. However, the courts have not been entirely consistent in dealing with the problem in situations where the property is in one spouse's name.

If you have moved from a community property state to a common law state, and you and your spouse have any disagreement or confusion as to who owns what, check with a lawyer.■

[8]Arizona and Texas recognize quasi-community property for divorce purposes, but not for will or living trust purposes.

4

Inventorying Your Property

Preparing a thorough written inventory of your property is often necessary for thorough estate planning, so you can:

- remind yourself of what you own
- determine what you owe
- carefully estimate the net value of your estate (now) as an aid to estate tax planning
- pin down any shared ownership of property
- make a handy list to refer to when making gifts to beneficiaries, and
- have your assets organized in case you later consult an estate planning lawyer.

This being said, it's still up to you to decide whether you want to itemize your property in detail or simply estimate its overall worth. For some people, arriving at an exact number is part of the process—we wouldn't dare say fun—of planning their estate. For others, giving the subject enough thought so as to arrive at a decent ballpark estimate suffices. For example:

- If someone knows she want to leave all her property to one other person (usually a spouse), or first to her spouse for his lifetime use and then equally to her children, there is far less need to itemize all major items of property than if a person wants to leave a number of separate gifts to a good-sized list of people.
- For federal estate tax purposes, the key figure, as we've previously mentioned, is $600,000. (See Chapter 15, Estate Taxes.) If you are confident that your net estate is worth less than this sum, you won't owe any federal estate tax. However, if you're a member of a couple, and plan to leave most or all of your property to the other member, and your combined estates exceed $600,000, there will be eventual estate taxes assessed.

  If your estate won't be liable for federal estate taxes in the first place, then one major reason to come up with a fairly precise number of the worth of your assets disappears.

Example: Jane wants to leave all of her woodworking tools and equipment to her friend Alice, her car to her friend Amy, and everything else she owns (which includes stocks, jewelry, money market funds and personal household possessions) to her longtime companion Mary. She knows her estate is worth no more than $400,000, that the state she lives in has no death taxes, and that she has no significant debts. Jane decides there's no need for her to list separately each item of property, since with two easy-to-remember exceptions, she's giving it all to Mary.

A. Instructions for the Property Inventory Worksheet

Section B of this chapter contains a worksheet to help you inventory your property. As you'll see, the worksheet is designed to permit recording a wide range of property. Take a minute to get acquainted with its structure.

The following detailed description of the chart and the suggestions for completing it are for those who want or need to be thorough. It's up to you to decide how extensive and detailed your own listings need to be.

In Section I of the chart, you list your assets—all the property you own. There are four kinds of information to give for each item of property:

- Column 1—a description of the item of property
- Column 2—if ownership of that item is shared, enter the type of shared ownership
- Column 3—the percentage of any shared ownership property you own
- Column 4—the net value of each item of property (or share of shared property) you own.

Now let's take a minute to review the information that should be entered in each column.

YOU MAY BE WORTH MORE THAN YOU THINK

We've been surprised to learn that quite a few people who have worked hard for years, and live a frugal life, find it difficult to admit that their assets could be worth more—sometimes substantially more—than $600,000.

This can occur with owners of appreciated real estate or a successful small business. When asked how much a residence or business is worth, the owner may think in terms of what was paid for it, plus a small mark-up. We've seen a number of situations where this estimate was hundreds of thousands of dollars off the mark. Or a person may have become so accustomed to the family furniture and paintings he doesn't consider the possibility that the heirlooms are now much sought-after antiques or valuable art.

What all this lack of realism often adds up to is that some people just don't want to admit that they have money—it doesn't suit them. But indulging in denial at the cost of not planning one's estate carefully is clearly no favor to one's beneficiaries, who most likely hope you'll take sensible steps to pass money to them, rather than giving a large amount to the government in taxes. So, c'mon—be sure your estimates as to how much your property is worth are up-to-date.

COLUMN 1

Identify and Describe Your Property

Here you identify your property with sufficient detail so there can be no question what it includes. This worksheet divides your property into four groups:

A. Liquid assets, which include cash, savings, checking and money market accounts, CDs and precious metals.

Examples:

- Certificate of Deposit No. 10235, Lighthouse Savings and Loan Association, Ventura, CA
- My savings account at Bay Bank (if you have only one savings account)
- My savings account number 18-17411 at Bay Bank (if you have more than one savings account).

B. Other personal property, which includes all your property except liquid assets, business interests, and real estate. This catch-all category includes stocks, mutual fund shares, other securities, bonds, automobiles, jewelry, furs, art works, antiques, tools, life insurance, collectibles, etc.

Examples:

- 50 shares Transpacific Corporation common stock
- $10,000 El Dorado Drainage and Water System, District of Alameda, 1980 bond series C, 10.5% due June 1, 2000
- 1986 Ford automobile, License # 123456
- All my fishing equipment
- Gold earrings with the small rubies in them purchased from Charles Shreve and Co. in 1971
- Daumier print captioned "Les beaux jours de la vie"
- Life insurance policy #A106004, You-Bet-Your-Life Insurance Co.
- All my carpenter's tools, including my power saws.

Note on miscellaneous personal property. If you are like most people, you have all sorts of minor personal possessions you don't want to bother itemizing. To deal with these, you can group a number of items in one category ("all my tools," "all my dolls," or baseball cards, or records, or machines and equipment or household furniture). Of course, some items without large monetary value have great emotional worth to you and your family: a photo album, an old music box, a treasured chair. These can be separately listed as you desire.

As another alternative, you can conclude your list with one catch-all item such as "all my other personal possessions and furnishings."

C. Business personal property, including all business interests, except any real estate used in that business.[1]

Examples:

- My shares of stock in the Mo-To Corporation
- My business d/b/a Ace Stationery Store, Boca Raton, Florida
- My partnership interest in JTL Partnership Enterprises, Main Office, Detroit, Michigan
- All my copyrights and rights to royalties in the book with the following titles, currently published by Acme Press, Berkeley, California [titles listed].

D. Real estate, including all business real estate, and all home, coop/condominiums, mobile homes attached to land,[2] undeveloped or agricultural land, etc.

To describe real estate, simply list its address or location. This is normally the street address, or condominium number. If there's no post office address, as is the case if you own undeveloped land, simply describe the real property in normal language "my 120 acres in Lincoln County near the town of Douglas". You don't need to use the legal description from the deed.

Examples:

- 126 Oceanview Terrace, Mendocino, California
- My lot on Keeler Street, Middletown, Ohio
- 1001 Main Street (the Fullerton Hardware Building), Moose, New York.

Real property often contains items which are properly classified as personal property. For instance, farms are often sold with tools and animals. If you intend to keep both together (as a gift) generally indicate what this "together" consists of. It's best to specify the large ticket items (tractor, cattle) and refer generally to the rest of the items as "personal property."

Examples:

- My 240-acre truck farm in Whitman County with all tools, animals, machines and other personal property located there
- My fishing cabin on the Wild River in Maine with all the fishing gear, furniture, tools and other personal property which are found there
- My ownership of the mobile home located at E-Z motor camp, and all possessions and furnishings contained in it.

[1]In Chapter 28, we discuss major estate planning concerns of small business owners, whether sole proprietors or shared owners, like partners or shareholders in small closely-held corporations.

[2]The rules on when an attached mobile home becomes "real estate" vary. If this matters to you, see a lawyer.

USE YOUR COMPUTER TO KEEP PROPERTY LISTS

Nolo's Personal RecordKeeper (computer program) allows you to enter all of your property and estimate how much it's worth easily and quickly.

Nolo's Personal RecordKeeper also has helpful fields to enter valuable information about each item, such as its location, whether it's owned jointly or separately, where title documents are kept and much more. Best of all, it's easy to use your computer to keep your property list up-to-date.

See the Nolo Catalog at the end of this book for more information.

COLUMN 2

Type of Shared Ownership

You only need to be concerned with Columns 2 and 3 if you own one or more items of property listed in Column 1 with someone else. If you are single and own all your property outright, you can simply skip to the instructions for Column 4. However, if you are married or have entered into personal or business shared ownership transactions, please read what follows carefully. Obviously, before you can sensibly plan your estate, you must clearly understand what you own and therefore have the power to give away.

Most people know whether they own property with others. However, occasionally, you may have to do some investigating to be sure about the ownership status of a particular piece of property, For example, you may have to locate the deed to your house or stock certificates to clarify whether you own property in joint tenancy. You can check real property records at the county real property recorder's office. Never guess. If you're not sure how you own an item of property, take the time to find out.

If you live in a community property state, are married, and you and your spouse own both separate and community property, you may have some difficulty determining exactly what you and your spouse own. (We discuss this in Chapter 3, State Property Ownership Laws, Section B.) For example, if you are unsure whether a $10,000 bank account is community property or your separate property, bear in mind that you and your spouse can resolve the confusion by jointly characterizing this account in either ownership category. To do this legally, however, it's important to put your conclusion in writing, signed by both of you.

Below we give you a summary of the different legal forms possible for shared ownership. Some of these concepts may be new to you. If after reading what follows you don't understand exactly what a particular form of shared ownership means, you needn't worry. They are explained in more depth in the chapters identified. Simply note on your chart that the property is held in some form of shared ownership. Once you understand precisely what "joint tenancy," "tenancy in common" or another type of shared ownership means, complete the "Shared Ownership" category for that property.

Here are the symbols you can use to record the major types of shared ownership on the chart:

- **Joint Tenancy (J.T.):** Property held with a written ownership document identifying the owners either as Joint Tenants or Joint Tenants With Right of Survivorship.[3] Under these forms of ownership, each joint tenant owns an equal share of the property with all other joint tenants. The share of the first tenant to die must go to any survivors, even if there's a will or living trust to the contrary. (Joint tenancy is discussed in detail in Chapter 10.)

  Joint tenancy must be created by a written document. If you own property using the phrase "Joint Tenancy With Right of Survivorship," there is no question what type of shared ownership you have. But what about writings that are less clear? For example, suppose your real estate deed says "Tenancy in Common With Right of Survivorship" In Oregon, this has the same practical effect as joint tenancy; in some other states, it surely doesn't. The point is—don't guess. If you're not clear what kind of legal animal you've got, check it out by doing your own research or checking with a lawyer knowledgeable about real property law.

Similarly, suppose owners are listed simply with an "and" or an "or"? For example, two people own real estate with the title listed as held by "Smith and Jones." Two others own real estate with title listed as "Smith or Jones." Are either of these joint tenancy? The answer is that it depends on the state in which the property is located. Under most states' laws, neither by themselves constitutes joint tenancy, but if you hold ownership with another person with "and" or "or" in the title document, you need to know the specific rules of your state.

- **Tenancy by the Entirety (T.E.):** This form of ownership is recognized in a minority of states. It consists of joint tenancy with right of survivorship between spouses. Its use is limited to a married couple and must be created in writing. (Discussed in Chapter 10.)
- **Community Property (C.P.):** In the eight community property states (listed in Chapter 3, State Property Ownership Laws, Section A), property spouses earn or acquire during a marriage is jointly-owned community property, with a few exceptions. The biggest ones are for property that is given to or inherited by one spouse which is the separate property of that spouse. Separate property also includes property owned by each spouse prior to marriage, if it's kept separate. You can leave your one-half share of community property to whomever you want to have it. The other one-half of the community property already belongs to your spouse and you have no power to give it away in your will.
- **Separate Property:** In the eight community property states, all property that isn't community property is held separately. (See above.)

  In the other 41 common law property states (listed in Chapter 3, Section A), separate property means all property that each spouse owns individually, including all property where one spouse's name appears on the title document, unless there is a written contract to the contrary.
- **Partnership (P.):** Property owned by business partners, regulated by a partnership agreement (including shares in a limited partnership). Partnership agreements often contain detailed rules as to what happens to a partner's share at death. (Partnership property is discussed in Chapter 28).
- **Corporate Shares (C.S.):** Shares of a small or closely-held corporation may be freely transferable at death. However, your freedom to transfer them may also be regulated by corporate bylaws or a separate shareholders' agreement. (Corporate shares are discussed in Chapter 28).
- **Tenancy in Common (T.C.):** Any property held in shared ownership which isn't in another type of ownership—in other words, all shared property not owned in joint tenancy, tenancy by the entirety or community property, partnership or corporation. This includes a great deal of the property spouses own together in the 41 common law property states. You can own any percentage of tenancy in common property (.005%, 95%, etc.)—owners' shares don't have to be equal, as they must be for joint tenancy property. If the

[3]In a few states, the words "with right of survivorship" added to "joint tenancy" or "joint tenants" are necessary to create a joint tenancy. In most, the words "joint tenants" or "joint tenancy" do the job. In Oregon, the term "tenancy in common with right of survivorship" means the same thing.

ownership deed doesn't specify the type of shared ownership, it's probably tenancy in common, although, as mentioned above, in some states the words "or" or "and" may indicate joint tenancy ownership. Unlike joint tenancy, where there is an automatic right of survivorship for joint tenants, you can leave your portion of property held as tenants in common as you choose, unless restricted by a contract.

Example: Natalie and Jeremy Engels live in North Carolina, a common law property state. They hold several securities, their house and a piece of land with both their names on the title documents, but no joint tenancy designation. They are presumed to own the property as tenants in common, with each owning a 50% share.

COLUMN 3

Percentage of Shared Property You Own

In this column, list the percentage of each item of shared property you own. People who own property as tenants in common, or in partnership, should be particularly careful —you can own any percentage of property in this ownership form, from 1% to 99%. Especially with a partnership, you must check your partnership agreement to be sure. With a tenancy in common, co-owners normally own equal shares (33.3% if you are one of three), unless there is a written agreement to the contrary.

Also, if you own an interest in a partnership or a small corporation, make sure you check your agreement to see if there are any restrictions on your rights to transfer your interest at death. Often other business owners have a right to purchase your shares if they wish.

Don't overlook the fact that you and your spouse may own partnership interests, corporate shares, or own interest in a tenancy in common as community property if you live in one of the eight community property states. Working all this out can be tricky, but it's necessary—not only to determine what is in your estate, but also for purposes of establishing the net value of your property for tax purposes.

If the property (or a share of property) is owned as community property or a tenancy by the entirety, ownership is shared equally. So, if there are two joint tenants, the ownership is 50-50; if there are three, each owns one-third, and so on.

Example: Johnny Ryan is a one-third partner in Electric City, an electric product distributor in Washington state. Johnny has been married to Maeve for 40 years, and used money he earned while married to her to help start the business. Since Washington is a community property state, Johnny and Maeve each own one-half of his one-third partnership interest, and both can leave their share as they choose.

Assume Johnny and Maeve live in Maine, a common law property state. Johnny owns his one-third partnership share outright. However, as discussed in Chapter 3, State Property Ownership Laws, Section C, under Maine law, Maeve is entitled to inherit a significant part of it (or other valuable property) if Johnny doesn't adequately provide for her.

While deciding what property you own is a fairly easy task for many people, this is obviously not always the case. If you have trouble or questions, see a lawyer. You don't want to die leaving a property ownership mess.

COLUMN 4

Net Value of Your Ownership

In this column, you estimate the "net value" of each item listed. Net value means your equity in your share of the property—the market value of your share, less your share of any debts on that share, such as a mortgage on a house or the loan amount due on a car. Doing this not only helps you determine the value of the property you have to dispose of, but also tells you whether you're likely to be subject to death taxes, especially federal estate taxes. (See Chapter 15, Estate Taxes, Section A.)

Obviously, listing net values for your property means making estimates. That's fine; there's no need to burden yourself with seeking absolutely precise figures. After all, your death taxes, if any, will be based on the net value of your property when you die, not its current worth. For example, if you think the net worth of your house, after you subtract the mortgage, is about $200,000, your car $5,000, and your stamp collection would fetch $2,000 if you put an ad in a philatelist's journal, use those numbers. (If these items are owned as community property with your spouse or in joint tenancy with someone, divide each of these amounts in half to determine the value of your share.) Only with more complex types of property, in particular business interests, are you likely to need expert help.

Example 1: Clay owns a house with a market value of $250,000 as a tenant in common with his sister Ava; each owns half. Clay computes the net value of his share by first subtracting the amount of mortgages, deeds of trust, liens and past due taxes from the market value to arrive at the total equity in the property. There's a $100,000 mortgage and a $10,000 lien against the property. The total equity, then, is $250,000 minus $110,000, or $140,000. The net worth of Clay's half of the property is $70,000.

Example 2: Stacey is sole owner of the Maltese Falcon Restaurant, a successful business she has run for 20 years. She has only a vague notion of its market value since she has never been interested in selling it. To competently plan her estate, she needs a reasonable estimate of the worth of the business. This can be difficult to make, since the market value of her restaurant includes the intangible of "good will." Stacey talks to an accountant or tax lawyer to help her arrive at a sensible estimate of the worth of the restaurant.

The last step in Section I of the Property Worksheet is to add up the net value of all your assets, and list that sum in Part E.

In Section II, Liabilities, list any liabilities—debts—you haven't already taken into account in Section I. For example, in Section II, list any significant personal debts—the $10,000 loan from a friend or $5,000 unsecured advance on a line of credit. Also list all other liabilities, such as tax liens or court judgments. Remember, you have taken account of mortgages on your real estate and payments owed on your motor vehicle in Section I, so don't list them here.

Add up your estimate of all your liabilities and list that sum in Part D of Section II.

Finally, in Section III of the chart, estimate your current net worth. To get this figure, simply subtract your total liabilities listed in Section II from your total assets listed in Section I.

B. YOUR PROPERTY WORKSHEET

Remember, this chart is purely for your convenience. It can be as messy or as neat as you care to make it. Also, pencil is recommended (unless you're the type who does *The New York Times* crossword puzzle in ink).

PROPERTY WORKSHEET

I. ASSETS

Column 1 Description of Your Property	*Column 2* Type of Shared Ownership	*Column 3* Percentage You Own	*Column 4* Net Value of Your Ownership
A. Liquid Assets			
1. cash (dividends, etc.)			
2. savings accounts			
3. checking accounts			

Column 1 Description of Your Property	*Column 2* Type of Shared Ownership	*Column 3* Percentage You Own	*Column 4* Net Value of Your Ownership
4. money market accounts			
5. certificates of deposit			
6. mutual funds			

Column 1 Description of Your Property	*Column 2* Type of Shared Ownership	*Column 3* Percentage You Own	*Column 4* Net Value of Your Ownership

B. Other Personal Property

(all your property except liquid assets, business interests and real estate houses, buildings, apartments, etc.)

1. listed (private corporation) stocks and bonds

2. unlisted stocks and bonds

3. government bonds

Column 1 Description of Your Property	*Column 2* Type of Shared Ownership	*Column 3* Percentage You Own	*Column 4* Net Value of Your Ownership
4. automobiles and other vehicles, including planes, boats and recreational vehicles			
5. precious metals			
6. household goods			
7. clothing			

Column 1 Description of Your Property	*Column 2* Type of Shared Ownership	*Column 3* Percentage You Own	*Column 4* Net Value of Your Ownership
8. jewelry and furs			
____	____	____	____
____	____	____	____
____	____	____	____
____	____	____	____
9. art works, collectibles and antiques			
____	____	____	____
____	____	____	____
____	____	____	____
____	____	____	____
10. tools and equipment			
____	____	____	____
____	____	____	____
____	____	____	____
____	____	____	____
11. valuable livestock/animals			
____	____	____	____
____	____	____	____
____	____	____	____
____	____	____	____

Column 1 Description of Your Property	*Column 2* Type of Shared Ownership	*Column 3* Percentage You Own	*Column 4* Net Value of Your Ownership
12. money owed you (personal loans, etc.)			
13. vested interest in profit sharing plan, stock options, etc.			
14. limited partnerships			
15. vested interest in retirement plans, IRAs, death benefits, annuities			

Column 1 Description of Your Property	*Column 2* Type of Shared Ownership	*Column 3* Percentage You Own	*Column 4* Net Value of Your Ownership
16. life insurance			
17. miscellaneous (any personal property not listed above)			

C. Business Personal Property

Column 1 Description of Your Property	*Column 2* Type of Shared Ownership	*Column 3* Percentage You Own	*Column 4* Net Value of Your Ownership
1. patents, copyrights, trademarks and royalties			

Column 1 Description of Your Property	*Column 2* Type of Shared Ownership	*Column 3* Percentage You Own	*Column 4* Net Value of Your Ownership

2. business ownerships *(partnerships, sole proprietorships, corporations, etc.; list separately and use a separate sheet of paper if you need to elaborate)*

name and type of business

3. miscellaneous receivables *(mortgages, deeds of trust, or promissory notes held by you; any rents due from income property owned by you; and payments due for professional or personal services or property sold by you that are not fully paid by the purchaser)*

Column 1 Description of Your Property	*Column 2* Type of Shared Ownership	*Column 3* Percentage You Own	*Column 4* Net Value of Your Ownership
D. Real Estate			
address			
address			
address			

Column 1 Description of Your Property	*Column 2* Type of Shared Ownership	*Column 3* Percentage You Own	*Column 4* Net Value of Your Ownership
address			
address			

E. TOTAL NET VALUE OF ALL YOUR ASSETS $______________

II. LIABILITIES *(what you owe)*

Many of your liabilities will already have been accounted for because you listed the net value of your property in Part I of this chart. For example, to determine the net value of your interest in real estate, you deducted the amount of all mortgages and encumbrances on that real estate. Similarly the value of a small business is the value after business debts and other obligations are subtracted. For this reason, the only liabilities you need list here are those not previously covered. Don't bother with the small stuff (such as the phone bill, or what you owe on your credit card this month), which changes frequently. Just list all major liabilities not previously accounted for, so you can get a clearer picture of your net worth.

Column 1 To Whom Debt Is Owed	*Column 2* Net Amount of Debt You Owe

A. Personal Property Debts

1. personal loans (banks, major credit cards, etc.)

______________________	__________
______________________	__________
______________________	__________
______________________	__________
______________________	__________
______________________	__________

2. other personal debts

______________________	__________
______________________	__________
______________________	__________
______________________	__________
______________________	__________
______________________	__________

Column 1 To Whom Debt Is Owed	*Column 2* Net Amount of Debt You Owe

B. Taxes

(include only taxes past and currently due. Do not include taxes due in the future or estimated estate taxes)

C. Any Other Liabilities

(legal judgments, accrued child support, etc.)

D. Total Liabilities

[excluding those liabilities already deducted in Section I]

III. NET WORTH

Total Net Value of All Your Assets (Section I. E.)
minus Total Liabilities (Section II. D.) $______________

5

Beneficiaries—Deciding Who Gets Your Property

Deciding what persons or organizations you want to receive your property—who will be your beneficiaries—is obviously a main focus of your estate plan. This chapter raises some important concerns about choosing them and provides a chart where you can list each beneficiary and what property you give him or her.

Even if you are positive as to whom you want to receive your property and are tempted to skip directly to the chart, please read at least Sections A through H first. These sections cover important beneficiary information everyone should take into account.

After these "mandatory" sections come some optional ones, I through O. Read these only if the subjects concern you.

Finally, in Section P of this chapter, you can make a tentative list of your beneficiaries. It's prudent to regard this list as preliminary. You may wish to revise it as you gain more knowledge by reading this book.

A. Some Thoughts About Gift Giving

Before plunging into technical concerns about how to name beneficiaries, let's pull back for a moment and consider what gifts are. In our predominantly commercial culture, whether they are made during life or at death, gifts are special. They are free, voluntary transfers of property, made without any requirement of receiving anything in return. The essence of gift giving is generosity, an open spirit. To say one makes gifts "with strings attached" is not a compliment.

Much of the real pleasure of estate planning comes from contemplating the positive effects your gifts will have on those you love. Sometimes, these pleasures are quite focused—you know how much Judith has always liked your mahogany table, and now she'll get to enjoy it. Others are more general—your son can buy a house with the money you leave him, which will hopefully relieve some of the financial and emotional pressures that have been weighing on him.

We mention the spirit of giving here because we've learned that it's easy to get entrapped by the details of estate planning and lose sight of your real purpose. So, if technicalities and legalities start to get to you, take a break and remember whom you're giving your property to, and why. And if you wish to explore in profound depth what gift giving is, or can mean, read Lewis Hyde's *The Gift* (Vintage/Random House), a brilliant exploration of how gifts work in many cultures.

Simple Beneficiary Situations

If you know you want to leave all your property to your spouse or children, you don't have much need to list "all" your beneficiaries. But even when desires are this clear and simple, you still face some additional complexities. Do you want to name an alternate beneficiary, in case the person you've originally named dies before you do? Suppose you want to name two or more alternate beneficiaries. What happens if these alternate beneficiaries wind up receiving your property? Does each one receive an equal share? If they inherit real estate, must it be sold unless all agree to keep it? In sum, even with a seemingly very simple beneficiary situation, you'll almost always need to go further than just naming one person to receive all you've got.

B. How to Name Beneficiaries

There are no laws requiring gifts you leave to be written in legalese, none that penalize you for stating your intentions in simple, plain English. You will enter the names of your beneficiaries and the property they will receive in your estate planning documents—your living trust, will, or both. We call these people your "primary" beneficiaries. You can safely use the names by which your beneficiaries are normally known.

Even if a beneficiary later changes his or her last name, that's no reason for you to revise your estate plan. For example, if a daughter later marries and decides to change her last name, legally taking her husband's name, you don't need to revise her name as listed as a beneficiary in your living trust or will. She, and others concerned, will be clear whom you meant.

Fred Rubellem shall be given all stock in International Merger Corporation.

Elizabeth Danford shall be given the grantor's[1] *interest in the house and real estate at 44 White Deer Road, Ardmore, Pennsylvania.*

Note on gifts to a married person. When you make a gift to a person who's married, the property belongs only to that person, not to his or her spouse. For example, suppose your will says: "I give my antique clock to Mary Kestor," or "I give $10,000 to Mary Kestor." This means Mary owns the entire property and her husband has no interest in it. It follows that if Mary later divorces, she is entitled to keep the entire gift if she divorces (assuming the property has been kept separate, not commingled with other shared marital property so that the gift could no longer be separately identified. (See Chapter 3, State Property Ownership Laws.) If you want to emphasize this intent, you can say: "I give my antique clock [or $10,000] to Mary Kestor, as her separate property."

By contrast, if you wish to make a gift to a married couple, simply make it in both their names. For example: "I give my silver bowl to Edna and Fred Whitman." Again, you can provide clarity by expressly stating your intent: "I give my silver bowl to Edna and Fred Whitman, as husband and wife."

Pets as beneficiaries. As a part of their estate planning, many pet owners arrange informally for a friend or relative to care for a pet. But what if the person you asked to provide care can't afford to keep an animal, or isn't available when needed? Usually, more formal arrangements are better. These issues are discussed in detail in *Dog Law*, by Mary Randolph (Nolo Press). Here are a few things to keep in mind:

- In all but two states, you can't leave money or property to a pet, either through a will or a trust. In California or Tennessee, you can name a pet as the beneficiary of a trust. All other states' laws provide that animals are property, and one piece of property simply can't own another piece. So, if you do name a pet as a beneficiary in your will, or set up a trust naming a pet as the beneficiary, in most all states, whatever property you tried to leave it will go, instead, to the residuary beneficiary (the person who gets everything not left to the beneficiaries named in the will). If there's no residuary beneficiary, the property will be distributed according to state law.
- You can use your will or living trust to leave your pets, and perhaps some money for expenses, to someone you trust to look out for them. Don't make the gift of an animal a surprise—make sure the people you've chosen are really willing and able to care for pets.
- Consider making arrangements for veterinary care for your animals. You can leave money to a vet (working out an amount with the vet in advance) or write out a life care contract with a vet. A vet may agree to provide lifetime care in exchange for a lump sum, or to use the money as a credit toward services.

[1] The word "grantor" is used if the gift is made from a living trust. See Chapter 9, "Revocable Living Trusts," Section B.

C. Naming Alternate Beneficiaries

It normally makes sense to name alternate beneficiaries to receive property if your first choices (again, your primary beneficiaries) die before you do. This is especially appropriate if you've made some gifts to older people, or people in poor health. But it's a good idea in all cases. You simply might not have the time, or inclination, before your own death, to revise your estate plan after a beneficiary dies.

On the other hand, this is one of the many estate planning issues where there is no one way you must do it. Some people decide they don't want the morbid bother of worrying about their beneficiaries dying before they do. They make their gifts—as many people do—to those considerably younger than they are. If a beneficiary dies before them, they'll normally be able to modify their will, trust or other document to name a new beneficiary. If they don't, the property will go to their residuary beneficiary (see below), which may, anyway, be the same person or persons they would name as their alternate.

The beneficiary chart in this chapter provides space for listing alternate beneficiaries for each gift you make.

Mike McGowan shall be given the Mercury Outboard Motor, or, if he fails to survive me, that property shall be given to his son, Pat McGowan.

It's up to you to decide whether you want to complete these spaces.

D. Naming a Residuary Beneficiary

Whatever you decide about alternate beneficiaries, you should definitely name a "residuary" beneficiary in your will and/or living trust who will receive all property you don't specifically give to other beneficiaries. The residuary beneficiary you name in your living trust (assuming you use one) receives only the remaining property in the trust that is not given to other named beneficiaries. The residuary beneficiary you name in your will receives all property covered by the will not given to other named beneficiaries in the will.

Example: Edward places his house in a living trust and leaves it to his wife, Lila. He leaves his car to his son, Alan, through his will. He does not name any beneficiary for his clothes and personal checking account. Edward does not name alternate beneficiaries and names his daughter-in-law Monica as the residuary beneficiary of his living trust and Ned, his grandson, as the residuary beneficiary of his will. Both Lila and Alan die before Edward does. When Edward dies, Monica inherits the house and Ned inherits the car, the clothes and the bank account.

As this example shows, if you don't name an alternate beneficiary for a specific gift in your will or living trust, and that beneficiary dies before you, your residuary beneficiary receives that gift. Thus, you always have one back-up plan for all your gifts. It's a good idea to name an alternate residuary beneficiary as well in both your living trust and will, so you have another back-up in case your choice for residuary beneficiary in either document dies before you.

E. Making Shared Gifts

Sometimes people want to make shared gifts, particularly to their children.

Example: Virginia wants to leave her house to her three children—Alan, Patsy and Philip. Seems simple, but even in this very straightforward situation, important questions should be asked and resolved. First, do the three children share ownership equally? Second, who controls what happens to the house? Third, what happens if one child dies before Virginia does?

One obvious way to avoid these problems is to not make shared gifts. Often there are other ways to accomplish the same purpose. For example, Virginia, in the above example, might have directed that the house and its contents be sold and the profits divided equally among the three beneficiaries.

But in some situations, particularly gifts from parents to children, shared gifts are desired. If you decide on a shared gift, read the rest of this section on the three major concerns that must be resolved when making a shared gift.

1. Percentage of Ownership

The key here is to say in the estate planning document how ownership is to be divided between the beneficiaries. If you don't specify shares of ownership, it's generally presumed that you intended equal shares, but this rule isn't ironclad, and there's no good reason to be silent on this matter. If you want a gift shared equally, say so.

I give my house at 1123 Elm St., Centerville to my three children, Anne, Rob and Tony, in equal shares.

I give my stock accounts equally to my daughters Maxine and Simone.

In a number of situations, there may be a good reason to leave a larger share of a piece of property to one beneficiary of a shared gift and smaller shares to another, or others. You can divide ownership any way you want. For example:

I give my house and real estate known as 111 11th St., Muncy, Iowa, as follows:

40% to my spouse Mary,
25% to my son Jon,
25% to my daughter Mildred, and
10% to my brother Tim.

2. Control

Control is the most basic problem with shared ownership. Suppose the people to whom you've given a gift disagree about how to use it. In most states, any co-owner can go to court and force a sale, with the net proceeds divided by percentage of ownership. To return to the example of the house given to the three children, suppose one wants to sell it, and two want to remain living there. The house would be sold. Do you want to allow this?

You can put provisions governing the issue of what the shared owners can do in the estate planning document (will or living trust) where the gift is made. For instance, "The house cannot be sold unless all three of my children agree on it." But often other problems follow. If two want to sell the house, but one doesn't, who manages the house? Does it have to be rented at market value? Can the child who wants to keep the house live in it? If so, must that child pay the others rent? And what happens if one child dies? The difficulties of dealing with these types of complications is why it seems more sensible not to specify details of long-term control of property you leave your beneficiaries. Let them work it out. If you don't think they can, a shared gift probably isn't appropriate.

If you are apprehensive about a particular shared gift, discuss it with the proposed beneficiaries. If there's genuine agreement between them, potential problems are less likely to become real ones. If you conclude there's genuinely no risk of conflict, you can simply make the shared gift without any conditions or directions, leaving it up to the beneficiaries to resolve any problems. Or you can direct that if there are any problems or conflicts over the property, any of the beneficiaries can compel the property to be sold and the proceeds distributed between the beneficiaries as you've directed. Otherwise, you might want to see what other solutions an attorney can come up with.

3. Naming Alternate Beneficiaries for a Shared Gift

Things can become quite complicated if you decide to move on to the next level of contingencies—naming alternate beneficiaries for a shared gift. To return once more to the house Virginia wants to give to her children, Alan, Patsy and Philip, what are Virginia's options if she wants to name alternate beneficiaries?

- She can specify that a deceased beneficiary's share is to be divided between her remaining children.
- She can provide that a deceased child's share is to be divided equally between that beneficiary's own children, or, if there are none between the surviving children.
- She can name another alternate beneficiary (a friend or other relative) to receive the interest of any child who dies before she does.
- She can name three separate alternate beneficiaries, one for each child (for example, each of their spouses).

As you can see, juggling these types of remote contingencies is tricky. Often the wisest solution is to provide that the other beneficiaries of a shared gift divide the interest of a deceased beneficiary.

Example:

Mollie Rainey, Allen Rainey and Barbara Rainey Smithson shall be given my house at [address]. If any of them fail to survive me, his or her interest in my house shall be divided equally between the survivors.

Alternate beneficiary provisions for a shared gift can quickly become very complicated. For example, suppose Bernice is an alternate beneficiary for a shared gift. What happens if: 1) Bernice dies? 2) Bernice is married and dies? 3) Bernice has children and dies? Before you worry about such contingencies, consider carefully whether you really want to bother about this kind of complexity in naming alternate beneficiaries. After all, once you get started worrying about remote possibilities, where do you stop? For example, you could also worry about what happens if all your alternate beneficiaries, as well as the beneficiaries themselves, die before you, and so on. In other words, there's no total security, no matter how many alternate beneficiaries you name.

Also, as we've said, you should always name a residuary beneficiary in your will and living trust to take any property left by that document but not validly given to a specific beneficiary. That way, you always have a back-up if one—or all—beneficiaries of a shared gift dies before you and you didn't name alternate beneficiaries.

F. How Naming Your Residuary Beneficiary Works

As we've stressed, in your estate planning documents where you make your gifts—your living trust and will—you should always name a residuary beneficiary to receive all property covered by the document not specifically given to named beneficiaries. You should also name an alternate residuary beneficiary who will inherit if the residuary beneficiary dies before you.

It's possible, and fairly common, to make the residuary beneficiary your main beneficiary. This is appropriate where you plan to leave all, or almost all, of your property to one person. Thus, some people's estate plan consists of a few relatively small gifts to specifically-named beneficiaries, with the bulk of their estate given to the residuary beneficiary.

Example: Jennifer wants to give her two Tiffany lamps to her friend Linda, $5,000 to her niece Martha, and her car to her sister Joan. She wants to leave all the rest of her extensive estate—houses, stocks, limited partnerships—to her long-time living together partner, Paul. She can simply name Paul as her residuary beneficiary of her living trust, after listing her three specific gifts. She names Joan as her alternate residuary beneficiary.

It's also common to split the bulk of your estate among children by making a few specific gifts and then naming the children as residuary beneficiaries. For example, after leaving some cash gifts and heirlooms to other friends and charities, you could name as residuary beneficiaries "my children, Henry and Aaron, in equal shares."

G. Explanations and Commentary Accompanying Gifts

If you wish, you can provide a brief commentary when making a gift. You can do this whether you use a will or a living trust as your primary estate planning document.

The grantor's business associate, Mildred Parker, who worked honestly and competently with her over the years, and cheerfully put up with her occasional depressions, shall be given $40,000.

I give my best friend, Hank Salmon, whom I enjoyed fishing with for so many years, all property listed on Schedule A, including my cabin on Lake Serene and boat and outboard motor.

There are times, particularly in family situations, when an explanation of the reasons for your gifts can help avoid hurt feelings or family fights. For example:

I give my house at 465 Merchant St., Miami, Florida, and all stocks and bonds I own as follows:

40% to my son Theodore Stein
40% to my daughter Sandra Stein Smith
20% to my son Howard Stein

I love all my children deeply and equally. I give 20% to Howard because he received substantial family funds to go through medical school, so it's fair that my other two children receive more of my property now.

I give Matt Jackson my bank account #41-6621-9403 at First Maple Bank. I love all my children deeply and equally. I give more of my property to Matt than my other children because Matt is physically disadvantaged, and is likely to need special care and attendants throughout his life.

Another approach is to write a letter stating your views and feelings, and attach the letter to your will or living trust. If you have a lot to say, a letter can be a better way to do it than trying to include it all in your will or living trust. Your letter isn't officially a part of a legal document, and has no legal effect. It is prudent for you to state in your letter that you understand this, to eliminate any possibility someone could claim you intended the letter to somehow modify the terms of your legal documents.

Short of libel,[2] the scope of your remarks is limited only by your imagination. Some writers have expressed, at length and in their own chosen words, their love for a mate, children and friend. By contrast, Benjamin Franklin's will left his son William, who was sympathetic to England during our Revolution, only some land in Nova Scotia, and stated, "The fact he acted against me in the late war, which is of public notoriety, will account for my leaving him no more of an estate that he endeavored to deprive me of." And the German poet Heinrich Heine wrote a will leaving his property to his wife on the condition that she remarry, so that "there will be at least one man to regret my death." William Shakespeare cryptically left his wife his "second best bed," a bequest that has intrigued scholars for centuries.

H. Disinheritance

You can disinherit most people simply by not making them beneficiaries of your estate. If you don't give someone any of your property, he has no rights to it, period. However, as discussed in the next section, special rules control disinheriting your own children, or the children of a deceased child. And when it comes to your spouse, no disinheritance is possible except in the eight community property states. (See Section 2, below.)

[2]If you write something so malicious (and false) that you libel someone in a will or living trust, your estate can be liable for damages.

1. Disinheriting a Child

The rules for disinheriting a minor child are discussed in detail in Chapter 6, Children, Section F. Here we briefly summarize them. In all states, you have the power to disinherit any or all of your children. However, unlike the situation with other people, merely leaving a child (or child of a deceased child) out of your estate plan doesn't "disinherit" that child. Those children who aren't mentioned in your estate planning documents (or in some states, who aren't provided for in your will) have a legal right to claim part of your estate. This doesn't mean you must directly leave some of your property to your children. After all, many spouses leave all their property to the other spouse, naming their children as alternate beneficiaries. This is sufficient to show you have not legally omitted your children from your estate planning documents.

If you want to disinherit a child (or children of a deceased child), you have two options:

- **You can explicitly disinherit a child in your will.** If you want to explicitly state that a child is totally disinherited, you must do so by a specific clause in your will. There is no legal requirement that you state a reason, but if you wish, you can include a statement of why you disinherited that child. If you decide you want this approach, you need an express disinheritance clause.
- **You can leave them a minimal amount in your will, which, functionally, serves as a disinheritance.** Obviously, mentioning a child and leaving him or her only this one dollar, and no more, effectively disinherits that child.

2. Disinheriting a Spouse

If you live in one of the 41 common law states or the District of Columbia, you cannot disinherit your spouse. As discussed in Chapter 3, State Property

Ownership Laws, Section C, these states allow a spouse to claim a significant portion (often one-third) of your estate despite your wishes (although many states do allow a spouse to waive these rights in a written marital property agreement).

By contrast, in community property states, a spouse has no legal rights to receive any of the other spouse's property. Or, put another way, each spouse has the right to leave their one-half of the community property and all his or her separate property as he or she sees fit.

Unmarried couples. Unmarried couples living together have no rights to inherit any of each other's property. In short, each person can leave his or her property to anyone he or she wants to. However, if the couple has created a valid contract which gives the other the specific right to inherit specific property, that contract will normally be enforced.

3. General Disinheritance Clauses

You may have heard that some lawyers recommend leaving $1 to certain close relations or even to each of your relatives. This is not legally necessary. There's generally no need to mention a relative or anyone else but your children and your spouse in your will. No one else has a legal right to any of your property.

4. No Contest Clauses

A "no contest clause" in a will or living trust is a device used to discourage beneficiaries of your estate plan from suing to void the plan and claiming they are entitled to more than you left them. Under a no contest clause, a beneficiary who unsuccessfully challenges a will or living trust forfeits all her inheritance under that document.

Example: Pip leaves his daughter Estelle $10,000 in his will, and includes a no contest clause in that document. If Estelle challenges the will and loses, she does not receive the $10,000.

No contest clauses can be sensible if there's a risk a beneficiary might challenge your estate plan, claiming that you were incompetent or unduly influenced. Normally, a no contest clause isn't necessary, since your estate plan (we presume) treats family members fairly. Also, you don't have to be "fair" anyway. It's your property, and you can leave it however you want to (with the exceptions for spouse or child noted above). But if for some reason you leave the minimum legal amount to your spouse, or prefer one child to another by leaving one a great deal and the other very little, you might want to include one, just in case the person who gets less tries to claim that somehow you weren't competent to make your will.

See a lawyer if you fear a will contest. If you think you want a no contest clause because you sense the possibility of a court fight, see a lawyer to discuss how you can best arrange to handle that risk. There are a number of things that can be done to establish that you are competent to make your will and free of undue influence.

I. Forgiving Debts

When you're thinking about whom you want to leave gifts to, consider the people who owe you money. One type of gift you can make is to forgive a debt—release the person who owes you the debt from responsibility to pay it. Any debt, written or oral, can be forgiven.

Example: Bud loaned his daughter Kathlyn and son-in-law Tyrone $30,000 for a down payment on a house, but doesn't want them to be obligated to his estate for this loan after he dies. So, in his will, Bud includes a provision stating "I forgive the loan of $30,000 I made to Kathlyn and Tyrone Benson in 1988."

If you're married and forgiving a debt, be sure you have full power to do so. If the debt was incurred while you were married, you may only have the right to forgive half the debt (especially in community property states) unless your spouse agrees in writing to allow you to forgive his or her share of the debt as well.

J. Minors as Beneficiaries

Estate planning issues concerning children are discussed in Chapter 6. Here we briefly summarize the options available if you're considering naming a minor child as a beneficiary, including an alternate beneficiary.

Minor children can only own a small amount of property outright in their own names. This amount, which is set by state law, varies from $2,500 to $5,000. Any property belonging to a minor above this amount must be legally controlled and supervised by an adult. Anyone contemplating making a substantial gift to a minor must therefore choose an adult to be responsible for the gift. This decision can be made in different ways:

- If the gift is intended for your own children, it can be made outright to the other parent, who will use the gift for the children's benefit. If spouses—or even ex-spouses—get along and trust one another to manage money well, this is usually the simplest way to handle the matter.
- The gift can be expressly given to the child, and you name an adult to be responsible for supervising that gift. That adult can be one of the child's parents, but doesn't always have to be. When you have decided who the adult supervisor will be, your next step is to decide what legal form you want to use to make the gift. Options include establishing a simple children's trust, making a gift under the terms of the Uniform Transfers to Minors Act (if it has been enacted in your state) or naming a property guardian in your will.

K. Restrictions and Controls on Gifts

There are two possible types of restrictions on gifts:

- restrictions you, the giver, want to impose, and
- restrictions imposed by law.

1. Personal Restrictions on Gifts

Most people simply leave their property outright to family, friends or charities. However, sometimes a person wants to make a gift with restrictions on it. Sometimes called "dead-hand control," the obvious risk is that circumstances are almost sure to change, so you must try to anticipate what is likely—or even possible—to occur in the future, and provide for it. This, at best, is complex work, and all too often ends up enriching lawyers, who must later help sort out how to get around unworkable restrictions.

Example: Cindy wants to give her house to her sister, Karen, to use during her lifetime, then leave it in trust equally to Karen's two young children, until each becomes 40. Then each will receive half the property, unless only one is married and has children, in which case she shall receive 75% ownership of the house. Some of the issues that must be resolved are: Can Cindy's sister sell the house? Who is the trustee of the trust? Can he sell the house if he thinks that's a good business decision?

If you want to make a gift where you impose personal restrictions or conditions, you'll need to consult a lawyer. If conditions or restrictions are imposed on a gift, someone must be responsible for being sure they are complied with. Many conditional gifts, such as "John, if he quits smoking," create far more problems than they solve. Who could ever tell if John fully quit smoking? He can't be watched around the clock each day. And how long is "quit"? But if you're determined to go ahead, the best way to do it is to leave the property in a trust to be managed by a trustee, who has authority to see if the conditions are met. You'll need a lawyer to help you establish the trust.

Example: Don wants to leave money to a nephew, Ed, if he goes to veterinary school, but, if he doesn't, to his niece Polly. This sounds simple, but here are just a few problems inherent in this approach: How soon must Ed go to veterinary school? What happens if he applies in good faith but fails to get in? Who decides if he's really studying? What happens to the money before Ed goes to veterinary school? What happens if Ed goes to veterinary school but drops out after a year and says he'll go back eventually? What happens if he graduates but doesn't become a vet?

2. Legal Restrictions on Gifts

With very few limits, you can give your property however you choose. While the few existing legal restrictions rarely apply, let's be cautious and review them briefly.

First, there are a few legal restrictions all states impose on gift-giving:

- Some felons and anyone who unlawfully caused the death of the person who wrote the will (or living trust) cannot inherit under it.
- You cannot attempt to encourage or restrain some types of conduct of your beneficiaries. For example, you cannot make a gift contingent on the recipient's marriage, divorce or change of religion.
- You cannot validly leave money for an illegal purpose—for example, to establish the Institute for the Encouragement of Using Psychedelics.

Second, a few states (the District of Columbia, Florida, Georgia, Idaho, Mississippi, Montana and Ohio) have laws restricting your ability to make gifts to charities. These laws, holdovers from centuries past, were enacted primarily to discourage churches and other charitable organizations from using unfair means, such as promising elderly people a place in heaven, to fill their own coffers at the expense of a surviving family.

If you're in one of these states, you should check with an attorney if you desire to leave a large part of your estate (certainly more than half) to a charitable institution, especially if you believe your spouse or children will object or that you may not have too long to live. However if you're leaving a relatively small percentage of your estate to a charity, you needn't worry about these restrictions no matter where you live.

L. Establishing a Survivorship Period

A survivorship period requires that a beneficiary must survive you by a specified time period to inherit. The purpose of a survivorship period is to insure that if the beneficiary dies soon after you do, the property will go to the alternate you've selected, rather than to the people the beneficiary chose to inherit his property.

> *I give my 1955 T-Bird to my best friend, Francois de Croissy, or, if he fails to survive me by 45 days, to my cousin Jacques Marquette.*

Survivorship periods can make sense if most of your property is transferred by will and will be subject to probate. Since probate takes months anyway, you're not tying up your property by imposing a short survivorship period on it.

Using the same reasoning, establishing a survivorship period isn't usually desirable for property transferred by living trust, since, as explained in Chapter 9, Revocable Living Trusts, a principal advantage of a living trust is precisely that property can be transferred quickly to the new owners. No sense in setting up a living trust to allow quick transfer of property and then frustrating it by saying beneficiaries must survive for many months to inherit.

M. Simultaneous Death

Many couples, married or not, who leave their property to each other wonder what would happen to the property if they were to die at the same time. (Another common concern of couples—what happens to their children if the parents die simultaneously—is discussed in Chapter 6, Children.) If property is left to a spouse by will or trust without a specific clause to cover simultaneous death, and you and your spouse die simultaneously, your property could pass to your spouse or mate, and then immediately to your spouse's inheritors. That might not be the result either of you want.

Most living trusts and wills contain a "simultaneous death" clause to prevent one spouse's property from going to another spouse's estate when both died at or near the same moment. Functionally, these clauses provide that when it's difficult to tell who died first, the property of each spouse or mate is disposed of as if he or she survived the other.

Example: Under their shared living trust, Edith and Charles leave much of their property to each other. However, Charles wants his property to go to his daughter from his first marriage if Edith dies before he does. Edith wants her property to go to her sister if Charles dies before she does. Edith and Charles are killed in a car crash. Under the simultaneous death clause in each one's trust, Charles's property would go to his daughter, and Edith's to her sister.

You may ask, "How, logically, can simultaneous death clauses work? How can I be presumed to have outlived my spouse for my purposes, but then she's presumed to have outlived me for her purposes?" Yes, it is a paradox, but it does work. Under the law, each estate is handled independently of the other. After all, this does allow both spouses to achieve the results each wants in the event of simultaneous death. As Oliver Wendell Holmes put it, "The life of the law has not been logic, it's been experience."

N. Property You Give Away by Will or Trust That You No Longer Own at Your Death

Before your estate can pay your cash gifts, it must pay all your last debts and taxes, including death taxes. After that, if your estate doesn't have enough money available to pay your cash gifts, there's trouble. For example, suppose in your living trust you give your house to your daughter Anne and $30,000 to your cousin Joan. But when you die, the only property in your living trust is the house. Can Joan force Anne to mortgage or sell the house to pay Joan the $30,000? The answer is that Joan might be able to prevail in this type of lawsuit, depending upon how a court interpreted your "intent" in creating the trust. Even if Anne prevailed, she's had the burden of a lawsuit.

If your will or living trust makes more in money gifts than you have ready cash, this necessitates what's called an "abatement" in legalese. An abatement means a reduction of gifts when there isn't enough to go around.

Fortunately, it's easy to plan to avoid this sort of nasty post-death mess. Don't give away more cash than you have. If you make cash gifts by a living trust, be sure the trust itself owns liquid assets sufficient to pay those gifts. So, aside from calculating the amount of your cash gifts, you need to estimate what you owe and what your estate will need to pay for death taxes. Revise your estate plan if you ever don't have enough liquid assets to pay cash gifts.

O. Naming Your Living Trust as a Beneficiary of Your IRA or Profit Sharing Plan

Many people have an individual retirement plan like an IRA or Profit Sharing Plan, and also create a living trust. So a common question is, "Should I name my living trust as the beneficiary of my retirement plan, and then name specific beneficiaries for any money in that plan in my trust?" The answer is that this is a bad idea, except possibly when your beneficiary is a minor. You should make the primary beneficiary of your IRA your spouse or another individual of your choice.

If you designate your living trust as the primary beneficiary of your individual retirement account, certain limitations will apply at the time distributions from that account are made. First, mandatory distributions must begin at age 70-1/2, if a trust is the beneficiary. Distributions will be based on your life expectancy alone and not the joint life expectancy of you and another beneficiary (as is possible if you'd named a living person as beneficiary of your IRA). Second, at your death, any account balance must be fully distributed within five years instead of longer periods that might be available if the trust weren't the beneficiary.

There is one possible exception here. If your beneficiary is a minor (or a young adult not capable of handling money) and you are elderly, you might want to make your living trust the beneficiary. This way, any funds remaining in your account at your death can go to the beneficiary through a child's trust, or as a gift under the Uniform Transfers to Minors Act (UTMA), as part of your living trust. (See Chapter 6, Children, Sections A, B and C.) Otherwise, if a minor receives the money, there must be a legal property guardian appointed to supervise it, since minors cannot own significant amounts of money outright. And an immature young adult will receive the money freely unless you create some kind of trust or UTMA device to impose mature adult control over that money.

P. The Beneficiary Chart

In the following chart, you can list your gifts by describing the items of property and who it's given to.

Note. If you think you'll need more space than this chart provides, simply photocopy the blank chart before you begin filling it

BENEFICIARY CHART

1. Specific Cash Gifts

_____________ to _____________
Amount *Beneficiary*

____
Alternate Beneficiary

_____________ to _____________
Amount *Beneficiary*

____
Alternate Beneficiary

_____________ to _____________
Amount *Beneficiary*

____
Alternate Beneficiary

_____________ to _____________
Amount *Beneficiary*

____
Alternate Beneficiary

_____________ to _____________
Amount *Beneficiary*

____
Alternate Beneficiary

_____________ to _____________
Amount *Beneficiary*

____
Alternate Beneficiary

2. Gifts of Specific Personal Property

______________________ to ______________________
Item *Beneficiary*

____
Alternate Beneficiary

______________________ to ______________________
Item *Beneficiary*

____
Alternate Beneficiary

______________________ to ______________________
Item *Beneficiary*

____
Alternate Beneficiary

______________________ to ______________________
Item *Beneficiary*

____
Alternate Beneficiary

______________________ to ______________________
Item *Beneficiary*

____
Alternate Beneficiary

______________________ to ______________________
Item *Beneficiary*

____
Alternate Beneficiary

3. Debts Forgiven

_________________________ to _________________________
Amount Forgiven *Debtor*

____
Date of Loan

_________________________ to _________________________
Amount Forgiven *Debtor*

____
Date of Loan

4. Gifts of Real Estate

_________________________ to _________________________
Property Address *Beneficiary*

____
Alternate Beneficiary

5. Residuary Beneficiary or Beneficiaries

(to receive the rest of your estate after all specific gifts are made)

____
Residuary Beneficiary

____
Alternate Residuary Beneficiary

6

CHILDREN

For estate planners, "children" can have two meanings. The first is "minors"—those not legal adults. The second meaning is offspring of any age; parents who live long enough can have "children" who are in their 40s, 50s or even older. The primary focus of this chapter is on minor children because of the special problems inherent in planning for people who are not adults. But we also present information of interest to parents with adult children.

Most parents of minor children are extremely concerned about what will happen to their children if disaster strikes and the parents die unexpectedly. If both parents are raising the children, the major concern is usually simultaneous death of the parents. If only one parent is involved—because the other parent is deceased, has abandoned the child or is unavailable for some other reason—the single parent wants to arrange for someone else to care for, and quite possibly, help and support the child if that parent dies.

Providing for your minor children if you die involves two distinct concerns:

1. Who will raise the children if you can't (that is, who will be each child's legal (personal) guardian)?

2. How can you best provide financial support for your children? (What money or property will be available? Who will handle and supervise it for the child's benefit? And what legal method is best for managing it?)

These concerns are addressed in depth in this chapter.

This chapter does not deal with adult "children" in as much detail as minor children, largely because no supervision is legally required either for the children themselves or for gifts made to any competent child over 18. However, because some parents understandably don't want to risk allowing their children to be able to receive substantial amounts of property outright while they're still in their 20s or even early 30s, this chapter explains how you can impose supervision over gifts you make to your younger adult children.

Disinheriting a child or children is not common, but there certainly have been, and are, parents who desire to do this. There are special rules for disinheriting any child, no matter what age, which are covered in Section F(1) of this chapter.

A. Custody of Your Minor Child

If two biological or adoptive parents are willing and able to care for the child, and one dies, the other normally has the legal right to assume sole custody. If the parents are married, or even if they are divorced, as long as both parents are cooperating to raise their children, this rule normally presents no problem. But what happens if both parents die? Or suppose there's only one parent in the picture, and he dies?

If there's no parent available who is competent and willing to do the job, some other adult must become the child's legal manager, unless she's legally emancipated.[1] This adult is called the child's "personal guardian."

A child's personal guardian must be named in a will. You cannot use other estate planning devices, such as a living trust, for this purpose, which is one reason why a will is essential even if you rely primarily on a probate-avoiding living trust to transfer the bulk of your property. Nevertheless, it's important to understand that a person named as a minor's personal

[1]An "emancipated minor" is a minor who has achieved legal adult status. The rules for emancipation are governed by your state's laws; normal grounds are marriage, military service or factual independence validated by court order for children who are within a year or two of becoming a legal adult. Emancipation is uncommon. Most importantly, for this book's purposes, you cannot emancipate your child through estate planning.

guardian in a will doesn't actually become the legal guardian until approved by a court. The judge has the authority to name someone other than the parent's choice if she is convinced it is in the best interests of the child. In short, children are not property, and naming a personal guardian in a will doesn't have the same automatically-binding effect as a provision giving a lamp to a beneficiary. However, if, as usual, no one contests your choice for your child's personal guardian, a court will almost certainly confirm this person. In practice, a court will only reject an unopposed nominee if there are obvious grave and provable reasons, such as alcoholism, a serious criminal background, or record of marital instability. A responsible parent should not, of course, select a guardian with such problems.

Most people with minor children probably know whom they want to name as their child's personal guardian. You should always name an alternate personal guardian as well, just in case your first choice is unable or unwilling to serve. When choosing a guardian and alternate guardian, remember the obvious: You can't draft someone to parent your kids. Be sure any person you plan to name is ready, willing and able to do the job.

Where two parents are involved in raising their kids, they should obviously agree on whom they want to appoint—naming different people almost guarantees a nasty conflict. With an intact family this normally isn't a problem, but divorced parents, particularly, should make sure to coordinate their planning. And it's best not to name a couple as joint managers, even if they will likely function that way. Doing this raises many potential problems, including what happens if the couple splits up. Better to simply name the member of the couple you rely on the most.

1. Complications in Naming a Personal Guardian

For some parents, appointing a personal guardian for their minor child is, unfortunately, not cut-and-dried. Here are some fairly common problems:

> *I don't want my ex-husband, who I believe is mentally unstable [or violent, or a substance abuser—or otherwise a lousy choice], to get custody of my children if I die. Can I choose another guardian?*
>
> *I have legal custody of the kids and I've remarried. My present wife is a much better mother to my daughter than my ex-wife, who never cared for her properly. What can I do to make sure my present wife gets custody if I die?*

There is no definitive answer to this type of question. Assuming a contested case was presented to a court, a judge's decision would very likely turn on both the facts of each situation and the judge's own belief system (prejudices). Here are a few general rules that usually are followed:

One parent (whether he has custody or not) cannot usually succeed in appointing someone other than the other natural parent to be guardian, unless the second parent:

- has abandoned the child,[2] or
- is unfit as a parent.

It's usually quite difficult to prove that a parent is unfit, absent serious problems such as alcohol abuse, a history of child molestation or violence or mental illness. The fact that you don't like or respect the other parent is never enough, by itself, to deny custody. If you want to name someone other than the

[2]This normally means not providing for or visiting the child for an extended period. "Abandonment" must be declared in a court proceeding, where a judge finds that a parent has substantially failed to contact or support a child for an extended period of time, usually (depending on state law) at least a year or two. Abandonment can be declared at a guardianship hearing if, after your death, the other parent, who has not visited or supported for an extended period, contests your choice in your will of someone else as guardian.

other parent as personal guardian for your children, and that person is fully apprised that this may lead to a custody fight, you should write a letter to accompany your will.

If my husband and I die simultaneously, his mother is sure to try to get custody. Neither my husband nor I want this to happen. How can we be sure that our good friends Betty and Carl, who know the kids well and would make great substitute parents, get custody instead?

It's not a serious problem to cope with this one. Name either Betty or Carl as personal guardian (not both, for reasons already discussed) in both wills. A judge will normally follow your recommendation. However, it can be wise to attach a letter to your will explaining why you prefer Carl or Betty to a grandparent.

If I die, I want my sister to raise my kids, but she isn't sensible with money. Can I have my sister take care of the kids and someone else manage the money I leave?

You can, but there are obvious risks of conflict in having one person have legal authority to raise a child and another to manage money used to support and educate the child. However, in some situations, a parent or parents will decide that splitting this authority between two persons is by far the best idea. Then the key is being sure that both people you want to name—one as personal guardian, one as property guardian—are willing to accept this split in authority. If the two potential guardians do really accept this, your major problem is solved.

2. Explaining Your Choice of Personal Guardian

If you honestly believe the other natural parent is incapable of properly caring for your children or simply won't assume the responsibility, or if you think that a particular relative or friend will try to be appointed personal guardian against the wishes you have expressed in your will, here is how to proceed:

1. Name the person you want to be your child's personal guardian in your will.

2. Explain why you're making your choice in your will or in a separate letter, and attach it to your will. Here's an example of such a letter:

> I have nominated my companion, Peter N., to be the guardian of my daughter, Melissa, because I know he would be the best guardian for her. For the past six years, Peter has functioned as Melissa's parent, living with me and her, helping to provide and care for her, and loving her. She loves him and regards him as her father. She hardly knows her actual father, Tom D. She has not seen him for four years. He has rarely contributed to her support or taken any interest in her.
>
> Date: January 15, 1994
>
> [Signed by:] Juanita R.

It is also possible to explain your choice of guardian in your will. Nolo's will-writing resources are provided in the Introduction, Section D.

If you don't want the other biological parent to gain custody, it's wise to discuss the details of your situation with a lawyer who specializes in family law. If there's a disputed custody proceeding after your death, a judge has wide discretion in deciding how much weight, if any, to give to written statements about your child's custody you made before you died. A good lawyer should help guide you to prepare the most persuasive case you can. This might include preparing your detailed statement of why the other parents shouldn't get custody, and identifying two people who will back up your statements by their court testimony, if necessary.

I want to appoint different guardians for different children.

This used to be unusual, but today, in many families children don't share the same two biological parents and the need occurs to name different guardians for different children. Naming different personal guardians for different children is certainly legal, but it might take some persuasion to convince a court that this was in the best interests of the children. But, under the right circumstances, this could be achieved.

Example: Irene is a single parent with two sons, aged 14 and 15, from her first marriage, and a daughter, age 2, from her second. Her first husband has never taken any interest in the children. Her second husband is deceased. Irene's brother, Biff, is close to her sons, and she and they feel he would be the best personal guardian for them. But Biff does not want to raise a young child, and there is such an age difference between her daughter and sons that Irene feels it's best to have her daughter raised (if need be) by the person who would care for her best, Irene's closest friend, Terry, even though that would mean separating her from her brothers. So, in her will, Irene names Biff as personal guardian for her sons and Terry as guardian for her daughter, and includes a thorough explanation in her will of why she made these choices.

B. Naming an Adult to Manage Your Child's Property

Minor children cannot own property outright, free of adult control, beyond a minimal amount—usually in the $1,000 to $5,000 range, depending on the state. This means there must be an adult legally responsible for supervising and administering all property owned by a child. Therefore, a vital part of your estate plan is arranging for responsible supervision of property of your minor children. This includes both property you leave for your child's benefit and any other substantial amounts of property they may acquire by gift or inheritance, which does not come with an adult supervisor already written in. It also includes any substantial amount of income they earn (for example, your 12-year-old is a genius computer programmer and is about to earn more than you do).

In addition to providing supervision for property left to children under 18, you may wish to provide that an adult you choose will manage any property you leave your younger adult children. It's common that parents don't want property to be turned over to children when they become legal adults, at age 18. Rather, the parents want that property supervised by a more mature person, until the children become 25, or even 30 or older, and are (presumably) more responsible.

1. Choosing Your Child's Property Manager

Assuming you have property you want to leave for your minor or young adult child's benefit, the next question is who will manage it for them? Although lawyers use confusing and often overlapping terminology, such as "custodian," "trustee" and "guardian," let's simply call this adult your child's "property manager." After you have chosen this person, you must select the legal form you want to use for that property manager to handle the child's property. These choices are discussed in the Section C, which follows.

When deciding whom to name as your minor child's property manager, here's a sensible rule: Name the same person you choose to have custody of the children (their personal guardian) unless there are compelling reasons to name someone else—for example, you're concerned that the personal guardian doesn't have sufficient economic or practical experience to manage property prudently. You should also name an alternate property manager in case your first choice can't serve. Again, name the same person you designated as the child's alternate personal guardian unless there are strong reasons to choose someone else.

The duties of the property manager are to act honestly with the property you leave for your children and in their best interests. This means using the money you leave to provide for normal living expenses and health and education needs. If you pick someone with integrity and common sense, your child's property will probably be in good hands. If substantial funds are involved, the property manager can pay for help to handle the more technical aspects of financial management. For instance, where large amounts of property are involved, it's routine for a property manager to turn tax and accounting functions over to an accountant.

Obviously, it's important to name a property manager who is sincerely willing to do a job which may, depending on the ages of your children, last for many years. It's also wise to choose someone the other members of your family respect and accept. You want your children to inherit money, not family arguments.

Except as a last resort, don't name a bank or other financial institution to be property manager. Most banks won't manage accounts they consider too small to be worth the bother; as a rough rule, this means accounts worth less than $250,000. And even for larger estates, they charge hefty fees for every little act. In addition, it's our experience that banks are simply too impersonal to properly meet your own child's needs. Far better, we think, to name a human being you trust than a bureaucracy. But if you can't find any adult who's willing and competent to be your child's property manager, it's normally better to name a financial institution than to make no choice at all, which amounts to leaving the matter up to a court. You'll need to check around with different banks and private trust companies to see which ones will accept the job, and seem most likely to do it for reasonable fees.

2. Selecting Different Property Managers for Different Minor Children

In some rare situations, you may want to name different property managers for different minor children. Doing this is legal. And unlike naming a personal guardian, it doesn't require court approval. The right to leave your property as you choose includes the right to name one adult as the property manager for one child's property and another adult as property manager for other children.

3. Leaving Property to Your Spouse for the Benefit of Your Children

One alternative for parents of minor or young adult children is for each to give property outright to the other spouse to be used for their child's benefit. If you do this, you don't need to worry about appointing someone to manage that property—you've already done it by leaving it to your spouse. This approach makes sense if the parents trust each other, but obviously isn't a good choice if the other parent is not available or financially imprudent.

But even if you leave all property to your spouse, it's always wise to name a child's property manager. This takes care of the possibility that you and your spouse might die simultaneously. Also, having a property manager in place means someone will be available to handle any property the children acquire directly from some other source, such as a grandparent.

C. Choosing the Legal Method to Leave Property to Your Children

Your next task is to choose which legal method you want to use to leave property to your minor children, or younger adult children. This assumes you want to impose mature adult supervision over any of your property inherited by your younger adult children. If it's acceptable to you that your children receive property outright when they become legally adult at age 18, you don't have to create any adult supervision method for this situation.

There are three basic options for leaving property to children or young adults:

- the Uniform Transfers to Minors Act
- a children's trust or family pot trust, and
- a property guardianship.

> **Taxation of a Child's Income**
>
> Income received by a minor child age 14 or over is taxed at the normal income tax rate applied to that income. But income to a child 13 or under is taxed differently. Under the "kiddie tax," all income to a child 13 or under is taxed at the higher of the two parents' tax rate. This kiddie tax has eliminated any income tax incentive for parents, or others, to transfer income-producing property from themselves, and their own high tax brackets,. to a minor under age 14.

1. The Uniform Transfers to Minor's Act

You can leave gifts to your child in your will or living trust under what is called "the Uniform Transfers to Minors Act" (UTMA),[3] if it's applicable in your state. Here your child's property manager is called a "custodian." The custodian's management ends when the minor reaches age 18 to 25, depending on state law. If the gift is made from your living trust, the property doesn't go through probate. If the gift is made from your will, it does go through probate.

---

[3] Uniform laws, as the name indicates, are standardized laws created by a legal commission. However, when it adopts a uniform law, a state legislature can make changes to the "uniform" version.

All states have adopted the UTMA, except: Connecticut, Delaware, Michigan, New York, Pennsylvania, South Carolina, Texas and Vermont. If you are a resident of one of these states, you cannot use the UTMA in your will or living trust and must use another method to leave property to minors or young adults.

Assuming the UTMA has been adopted in your state, you may use it to name a custodian to manage property you leave a minor until the age at which the laws of your state require that it be turned over to the minor. Depending on your state, this varies from 18 to 21, except that Alaska, California and Nevada allow you to extend management until 25.

Here's how the Uniform Transfers to Minors Act works for leaving property to your minor children. Under the Act, in either your will or living trust, you make a gift by identifying the property given and the minor it is given to. You then appoint a "custodian" to be responsible for supervising the property until the age you select (18-25, depending on your state law). You state that the custodian is to act "under the [your state] Uniform Transfers to Minors Act." You can also name a "successor custodian" in case your first choice can't do the job. The "custodian" is the person you've selected as your child's property manager. The "successor custodian" is your child's alternate property manager.

Basically, the custodian has great discretion to control and use the property as she determines is in the child's interest. Among the specific powers the UTMA gives the custodian are the right, without court approval, "to collect, hold, manage, invest and reinvest" the property, and to spend "as much of the custodial property as the custodian considers advisable for the use and benefit of the minor." The custodian must also keep records so that tax returns can be filed on behalf of the minor and must otherwise act as a prudent person would when in control of another's property. The custodian is entitled to be paid reasonable compensation from the gift property. No bond is required. And normally, no court supervision of the custodian is required.

Each gift under the Uniform Transfers to Minors Act can be made to only one minor, with only one person named as custodian. Once the child reaches the age the Act specifies for termination, the custodian gives her the remaining balance of the gift, with an accounting of all funds distributed.

The downside to the UTMA for some people is that property management in most states ends at age 21, or even 18. If your children are already teenagers and your estate is substantial, you may want to provide for property management until one or more of your children is older. If so, you may wish to use a children's trust which allows you to designate an older age for property management to end. (See Section 2, below). But the trade-off between using the UTMA or a children's trust is further complicated by the fact that trust income tax rates are now higher than individual rates. (See Chapter 17, An Overview of Ongoing Trusts, Section F.) So income retained in a children's trust (above $1,500) is taxed at higher rates than is property subject to the UTMA, which is fixed at the individual child's tax rate. Whatever the income tax rate applied to a child's income, it will be a lower rate than if any income from property left in a child's trust is retained by that trust.

As we've said, state law defines the age at which property left to a custodian under the UTMA must be turned over outright to the child. The age limits are:

- **Property management must end at age 18 in:** District of Columbia, Kentucky, Oklahoma, Rhode Island and South Dakota.
- **Property management must end at an age you choose between age 18 and 21 in:** Arkansas, Maine, New Jersey, North Carolina and Virginia.

- **Property management must end at age 21 in:** Alabama, Arizona, Colorado, Florida, Georgia, Hawaii, Idaho, Illinois, Indiana, Iowa, Kansas, Maryland, Massachusetts, Minnesota, Mississippi, Missouri, Montana, Nebraska, New Hampshire, New Mexico, North Dakota, Ohio, Oregon, Tennessee, Utah, Washington, West Virginia, Wisconsin and Wyoming.
- **Property management must end at an age you choose between age 18 and 25 in:** Alaska, California and Nevada.

2. A Child's Trust

To provide property management you can leave property to your children through a child's trust. A trust is a legal entity under which a person, called a "trustee," has the responsibility of handling money or property for someone else (in this case, your child), called a "beneficiary." A written document creates the trust and sets out the trustee's responsibilities and the beneficiary's rights. With a trust, the child's property manager is called a "trustee" or "successor trustee."

A child's trust can be established either by will, or as part of a living trust. If it is established as part of a living trust, the property placed in the child's trust avoids probate. If a will is used, the property in the child's trust must go through probate before it's turned over to the trust.

There are two principal types of children's trusts: a "pot" trust—a collective trust for a group (at least two) children—and an individual trust for each child.

- **Family pot trusts.** With this type of trust, all the property you leave for your child's benefit is held together, in one common fund or "pot." Most family pot trusts are drafted so that they convert to individual trusts when the youngest child reaches 18 (or some other age). These trusts are often advisable for families with younger children. If one child has a serious illness or other extraordinary needs, the money is there for him or her. The trustee decides how much money shall be spent on each child. Although family pot trusts clearly have the advantage of flexibility, they can make the trustee's (property manager's) job tougher as compared with a child's trust, where each child's property is legally separate from the trust property of other children. With a pot trust, the trustee may literally be called on to choose between one child's need for expensive orthodonture and another's desire to go to a pricey college.
- **Individual Trusts.** With this type of child's trust, you designate specific property to be used for a named child's benefit. You appoint a trustee who manages the property for the benefit of your child after you die. If you have more than one child, you can create an individual trust for each child. For older children, this is probably desirable, because each knows precisely how much she or he has, for college costs or other needs.

Some parents whose children are young and fairly close in age decide a pot trust is best for the children now. Then, when the kids are older—say the eldest reaches 16—the parents may decide to pull that child out of the pot, leaving his share under the terms of an individual trust or the UTMA. Or the parents could wait until the children are all over the age when the pot trust automatically converts to individual children's trusts.

The major difference between a child's trust and creating a custodianship under the UTMA is that, with a child's trust, you can specify any age at which the beneficiary receives her property outright. There are no cut-off limits imposed by state laws. Because there is time, these trusts can be, and often are, established for young adults already over age 18 or 21 who a parent (or other older adult) believes are not good bets now for responsibly handling any significant amounts of property they might inherit.

A child's trust is legal in all states. If you create a trust, any property inherited by a minor beneficiary will be managed by a person or institution you choose to serve as trustee until the beneficiary turns an age you choose. The trustee's powers are specified in the trust document. The trustee may use trust assets for the education, medical needs and living expenses of the minor or young adult beneficiary. All property you leave to a beneficiary for whom a trust is established will be managed under the terms of the trust.

A child's trust shouldn't last a lifetime. If you want a child's trust to last beyond age 30 or 35, you need to face the likelihood that their problem goes deeper than their youth, and they may never be able to manage their own finances. Whether their problem has to do with substance abuse, gambling or simply the inability to cope with finances, chances are you'll need a more complicated trust, perhaps a "spendthrift trust." (See Chapter 24, Trusts and Other Devices for Imposing Controls Over Property, Section D.)

3. Should You Use the UTMA or a Child's Trust?

For each minor child or young adult to whom you leave property, you need to decide which management approach to use—the UTMA or a trust. If you decide on a trust, you need to further choose between a family pot trust and individual trusts. Because both the UTMA and the two types of children's trusts are efficient and easy to put in place, any one of them can be used for many situations. Above, we have already discussed some key factors in deciding which is most appropriate for your family. But because this issue is so important, it's appropriate to examine it in more detail. This section can help you decide which is best for you and yours.

a. When to Use the UTMA

As we've said, you cannot use the UTMA in Connecticut, Delaware, Michigan, New York, Pennsylvania, South Carolina, Texas or Vermont.

As a general rule, the less valuable the property involved and the more mature the child, the more appropriate the UTMA is because it is simpler and often cheaper, from a tax point of view, to use than the children's trust. There are a couple of reasons for this.

Because the UTMA is built into state law, financial institutions know about it and should make it easy for the custodian to carry out property management duties. To set up a children's trust, the financial institution would have to be given a copy of the trust document and may tie up the proceeding in red tape to be sure the trustee is acting under its terms.

Also, a custodian acting under the UTMA need not file a separate income tax return for the property being managed; it can be included in the young beneficiary's return. However, with a children's trust, both the beneficiary and the trust must file returns.

In states where the UTMA allows for property management until 21 or 25, gifts to your children under the Uniform Transfers Act can be particularly sensible if you leave property worth less than $50,000-$100,000 to your child. Normally, amounts of this size will be fairly rapidly expended for the child's education and living needs, and are simply not large enough to tie up beyond age 21.

Another factor can be the age of the child at the time you create your will or living trust. If your daughter is now two-years-old it will obviously take (use up) far more money to support her until adulthood than if she is currently 17. For instance, $100,000 left to a two-year-old will likely be used up before she gets to college, while $100,000 left to a 17-year-old should at least last through college or whatever else she plans in the next four years.

b. When to Use a Pot Trust or a Child's Trust

As a general rule, the more property is worth, and the less mature the young beneficiary, the better it is to use a family pot trust or a child's trust, even though doing so is a bit more work for the adult property manager than using the UTMA. For example, if a minor or young adult stands to inherit a fairly large amount of property—such as $200,000 or more—you might not want it all distributed by your state's UTMA cut-off age, which is usually 18 or 21. In such circumstances, you will be better off using a child's trust. Remember, under the child's trust, management can last until an age you choose. Also, if you have two or more younger children, a family pot trust allows the trustee to spend any trust principal for the child she determines needs it. If you use your state's UTMA, you must create a different custodianship for each child's property, so you cannot lump all that property together as you can in a pot trust.

But if you live in Alaska, California or Nevada, where the UTMA can provide property management until age 25, your choice might be different. Except for truly big estates or very immature children, age 25 is often as sensible a time to end property management as any.

Example: Marilyn, a single parent, creates a living trust leaving her estate, worth $720,000, equally to her two children, Todd, age 25, and Carolyn, age 27. Carolyn has always been frugal, if not parsimonious, with money. She has been saving money from the time of her first allowance. Todd is the flip side of the coin. He runs through whatever cash he has at the blink of an eye and, from Marilyn's perspective, often goes beyond generosity to recklessness with money. So in her living trust, Marilyn leaves Carolyn her half of Marilyn's estate outright. However, Todd's half is left in a "child's trust," with Marilyn's brother—a stable type if ever there was one—as trustee. Todd will not receive any trust property outright until he becomes 35. By that age, Marilyn hopes he will have become sensible enough to manage a large amount of money.

4. Leaving Property to Your Minor Children to Be Supervised by the Property Guardian Named in Your Will

You probably have noticed that we've discussed using the UTMA or a children's trust, without (yet) mentioning your third option—leaving property to be supervised by the children's property guardian.

We list this method last because it is rarely, if ever, wise to leave property to your children to be supervised by the property guardian. The reason is that to have a property guardian manage property left to a minor, it must go through your will, which means it will go through probate. Even worse, property guardians are often subject to court review, reporting requirements and strict rules as to how they can expend funds. All this usually requires hiring a lawyer and paying significant fees, but in our view does little to guarantee that the property manager will do a good job. And those lawyer fees, of course, come out of the property left to benefit the minor. Another downside is that a property guardianship must end at age 18.

By now you are probably convinced that using either the UTMA or a children's trust is a better way to provide property management for minors. While this is true, your will should still name a property guardian to serve as a back-up to handle any property which for some reason isn't covered by a more efficient management device.

Specifically, naming a property guardian in your will provides a supervision mechanism in case:

- Your minor children earn substantial money after you die, or receive a large gift or inheritance which doesn't, itself, name a property manager.
- Spouses leave property to each other to use for their children, naming the children as alternative or residuary beneficiaries without bothering to add an UTMA designation or establish a children's trust. If both spouses die simultaneously, the parents' property will be managed for their children by the property guardian.
- You failed to include in an UTMA custodianship or a child's trust some property you want your children to inherit. This can occur because of oversight or, more likely, because you didn't yet have ownership of the property when you established your will or living trust and didn't amend that document later.

Creating a child's trust or a custodianship under your state's UTMA is really quite simple to do, so normally the children's property guardian should be used only for the back-up purposes listed above. However, for those who want to postpone estate planning or keep it to the bare minimum, it is far wiser to leave property to minor children to be managed by a property guardian rather than ignore the issue altogether. Having your minor child's property supervised by a property guardian you name in your will is certainly preferable to having a judge appoint someone to supervise that property. So, for example, a young couple, both healthy and unlikely to die for decades, may not want to deal with establishing a child's trust, or even an UTMA custodianship, now. But if they do both die, they don't want a court deciding who'll manage the property they leave for their children. So, they create wills, where each names a property guardian to manage property for their children's benefit if both die simultaneously.

5. Comparison of the Three Major Ways to Leave a Child or Young Adult Property

Below is a chart that summarizes the rules and reasons for each of the three major methods you can use to leave gifts to your minor or young adult children:

MAKING GIFTS TO YOUR MINOR OR YOUNG ADULT CHILDREN

	Gift Under UTMA	Child's Trust or Family Pot Trust[4]	Property Guardian
Legally Permitted	Must be authorized by your state's law	Yes, in all states	Yes, in all states
Amount of Property	If maximum age for release of gift is 18 in your state, then use is often best for mature children or for smaller gifts under $50,000 (depending on current age of child). If age for release is 21 or 25, sensible for gifts for $50,000 to $100,000 or more, especially to make sure money will be managed to last through college	Often good for gifts of any amount if UTMA age for release of gift in your state is 18, or if UTMA isn't applicable in your state. Often good for gifts in excess of $100,000 if UTMA applies in your state and age for release of gift is 21 or perhaps even 25	Last resort no matter what the amount
Paperwork	No trust tax returns required, but minor must file a yearly return based on money actually received. Custodian must give accounting when property turned over to child	Trustee must file yearly income tax returns for trust. Trust income over $1,500 taxed at higher rate than child's individual rate	Usually substantial because reports must be presented to court
Court Supervision	None	None	Guardian must make regular reports to court
Termination	In most states, custodian must turn over property to child at age specified by statute, usually 18-21 (25 in CA, AK, NV)	You specify the age at which the minor gets control of the trust property	Guardian must turn property over to child at age 18
Uses of Property	Custodian has broad statutory power to use property for child's living expenses, health needs and education	Trustee normally has power to use any of child's trust property for minor's needs for living expenses, health needs and education	Heavily limited and regulated by state law

[4]In Section C(2) we discussed the differences between a family pot trust and an individual child's trust. These differences primarily affect how trust principal can be used when children are younger. Because this chart is designed to illustrate the differences in how property is managed after age 18—and both types of trusts for children allow for continuing management—we don't make a distinction between these trusts here.

D. Naming Children as Beneficiaries of Life Insurance

Some may think we've put the legal cart before the financial horse here—all this discussion about how to leave property to your minor children before any talk of how to acquire some valuable property to begin with. One good reason for this order is this is a book on how to dispose of an estate, not about how to acquire an estate. Indeed, if we were masters of that, maybe we wouldn't have bothered writing this book. So all we can offer here is some general advice.

For more affluent families, creating a financial reserve to leave to their children isn't really necessary—their nest egg is already big enough for all the nestlings. However, many families need every nickel for living in the here and now, and don't have the luxury of putting significant amounts aside. For families in this category, the best way to be sure cash will be available for the children if the parents die is to purchase some low-cost term life insurance. Term is the cheapest form of life insurance. Younger parents can obtain a significant amount of benefit coverage for relatively low cost (for the obvious reason that statistically they are unlikely to die soon, or during the set term of the policy, so the risk to the insurance company is low).

Life insurance is discussed in depth in Chapter 12. The main point we want to make here is that it doesn't make good sense to name your minor children as beneficiaries of a life insurance policy, or as alternate beneficiaries, should the primary beneficiary (probably your spouse or co-parent) fail to survive you. If you die while the children are minors, the insurance company cannot legally give the proceeds directly to the children. Instead, court proceedings will be needed—to confirm a child's property guardian if you named one, or to name one in the first place if you neglected to do this. Either way, as we've discussed already in this chapter, means this property guardian can become enmeshed in the time-consuming court reporting requirements state laws typically impose. It also means the property guardian can only spend money under the terms of state law, which in some instances can be quite restrictive.

As we noted earlier, one simple way to avoid this problem is to name your spouse, co-parent or other adult as the beneficiary of your life insurance policies and trust him or her to use the proceeds to benefit the children. But if, for some reason, you don't want to do this, or you and this other adult die simultaneously, then your best approach is to establish a child's trust and name it as the beneficiary (or alternate beneficiary) of the policy. You can do this in a will or living trust. For example, in a living trust document, you can make a gift to your children of any insurance proceeds received by the trust and create a child's trust for this gift. If you die while your children are minors (or young adults), the proceeds paid to the living trust will be held in the child's trust. The result is that the insurance proceeds would be paid directly to the trust, free of probate or other court proceedings, to be managed for the benefit of your children by the trusted person you have named as trustee.

Of course, you do have to complete whatever paperwork the insurance company requires to have your living trust named as beneficiary of the policy. This may require sending your insurance company a copy of your living trust.

E. Leaving Property to Minor Children Who Are Not Your Own

If you want to leave property to minor or young adult children who aren't your own, you have the following legal choices:

- Make the gift outright to the child's parent or legal guardian, and rely on the parent to use the gift for the benefit of the child.

- Make the gift in your will or living trust through the Uniform Transfers to Minors Act. (The Act, and the states where it can be used, are discussed in Section C, above.) This is usually desirable for gifts under $100,000.
- Make the gift through your living trust or will, by creating a child's trust for that gift. You can create a child's trust for any young adult beneficiary who you believe is not presently capable of managing property wisely. You name the trustee of this child's trust, to manage all property in it. Doing this makes sense for large gifts—roughly, more than $100,000. This plan can make good sense for gifts to grandchildren, particularly if the trustee is the child's parent and will supervise that child's trust.

Example: John, an elderly widower, wants to make a cash gift to his 12-year old grandniece Sally from his living trust. He decides to make the gift using his state's Uniform Transfers to Minors Act. He names Sally's mother, Mary, to be the custodian. Her husband Fred is the alternate custodian. In his living trust, John makes the following gift: "Sally Earners shall be given $20,000; Mary Earners is to be custodian under the Minnesota Uniform Transfers to Minors Act. If Mary Earners is unable to serve, or continue serving, as custodian, the successor custodian shall be Fred Earners."

- Simply leave the gift in your will. If the child is a minor, when you die this will probably require court proceedings to appoint a property guardian to supervise the gift, and is therefore the least desirable method. And since you are not a parent of the child, you can't even appoint or suggest a property guardian for him or her in your will.

[5]Except that the Florida Constitution (Art. 10, § 4) prohibits the head of a family from leaving his residence in his will (except to his spouse) if he is survived by a spouse or minor child.

WHAT HAPPENS IF THE MINOR DOES NOT INHERIT PROPERTY OR RECEIVES IT OVER THE AGE YOU'VE SPECIFIED

If you arrange for property management for a minor, but the minor never inherits the property, no damage is done. The management provisions for that minor are simply ignored. For instance, suppose you identify a favorite niece to take property as an alternate beneficiary, and create a child's trust for that property until the niece turns 30. If the niece never gets to take the property because your primary beneficiary survives you, no child's trust will ever be established for her.

F. Children of Any Age

You can leave property outright to your adult children, just as you can to any adult beneficiary. Or, as discussed, you can leave property to your adult children in a children's trust. But in two areas, special rules apply to one's children no matter what their age: disinheritance of one's own children and concerns about adopted children or children born outside marriage.

1. Disinheriting Children

To an outsider, it may seem sad that a parent would want to disinherit a child, but nevertheless, it's surely been known to happen. Whatever the reasons, it's legal for a parent who intends to disinherit a child to do so. At the same time, legal rules protect children, and children of a deceased child, from being accidentally disinherited. The legalese for accidentally overlooked children is "pretermitted heirs." In most states, your children (and the children of deceased children) have a statutory right to inherit from you if you leave them out of your will or fail to make one. Grandchildren do not have any statutory right to inherit if their parent (your child) is still alive, so there is no need to disinherit them if you don't want them to inherit.

It's not that you can't exclude or disinherit a child if you wish. You can.[5] It's simply that laws on the books in most states require that you mention the child in your will. You can name the child and then expressly disinherit him, or functionally disinherit him by leaving him a very small gift. Even if you transfer all your property by a living trust, you must use a will to disinherit a child, or the children of a deceased child. The reason is simple: some state laws require disinheritance to be accomplished by will, and only by a will.

If you don't mention a child (or the children of a deceased child) in your will, the general rule is that the omitted child, or the children of a child who has died before you, are entitled to some of your property anyway. How much they get depends on whether you leave a spouse and how many other children you have. In addition, the laws of most states protect your children who are born after the will is made ("afterborn children") by entitling them to a similar share of your estate.

You may wonder how it can be that if you provide for your children outside your will—by giving them property from your living trust, for example—but didn't mention them in your will, these children may be able to, at least in theory, successfully claim to be accidentally overlooked heirs and demand additional shares of your estate. The answer is that, in defining whether a child is pretermitted (overlooked), and therefore entitled to receive a share of your estate, some state's laws specifically refer to omitting a child from a "will." Read literally, these statutes don't allow property left to a child by a living trust (or in joint tenancy, or by life insurance proceeds) to be considered to determine if a child has been overlooked. Of course, given the purpose of the pretermitted heir statutes—to protect children from being accidentally disinherited—it's senseless to read the statute so literally. But who says the law can't be senseless?

So, to be absolutely safe, even if you generously provide for your children outside of your will, you should list the names of all your children (and children of a deceased child) in your will and make some provision for them.

Note of sanity. Remember, for the "pretermitted heir" issue to become a real problem, a child must file a lawsuit contesting your will and estate plan. If you trust that your children aren't going to sue, you don't have to worry.

Revise Your Estate Plan When a Child Is Born or Dies

If, after preparing your estate plan, you have an additional child or children, you must revise that plan by providing for (or disinheriting) the new child.

If a child dies, leaving children (your grandchildren), you should revise your estate plan to provide for or disinherit these grandchildren because, legally, these grandchildren now stand in the shoes of the deceased child (their parent) and have a legal right to inherit if not specifically mentioned in your will. You should also, of course, make sure that all property left to the deceased child is redirected to other beneficiaries.

2. Adopted and Out-of-Wedlock Children

For centuries, courts have been confronted with the issue of whether a gift to "my children" includes adopted children and children born out-of-wedlock. To avoid any confusion in this area, when you prepare your will, simply name all your children, including any born while you were not married and any you have adopted.

If there is some question about who is included in a gift to "my children," judges attempt to determine what the person making the will intended. Most states automatically consider adopted persons, whether they were minors or adults when adopted, as "children" for the purpose of a gift to "children." This means that if you've legally adopted a child and leave a gift to "my children," the adopted child will take a share.

The rule for children out-of-wedlock cannot be so clearly stated. Basically, for inheritance purposes, states recognize an out-of-wedlock child as a child of the mother unless the child was formally released by the mother for adoption. However, an out-of-wedlock child isn't a child of the father for inheritance purposes unless the father has legally acknowledged the child as his. Just what constitutes legal acknowledgment differs from state to state. Generally speaking, if a father signs a paternity statement or later marries the mother, the child is acknowledged for purposes of inheritance in all states and has the same legal standing as a child born to parents who are married. Also, in some states, a father who welcomes a child into his home, and publicly states that the child is his, also establishes a parent-child relationship for inheritance purposes. ■

7

Probate and Why You Want to Avoid It

Many people aren't sure what probate actually is, except that it involves lawyers in transferring property after one's death. One thing they do know is they want to avoid it. That's a sound instinct. In most instances, probate is a costly and time-consuming business, providing no benefits except to attorneys.

A. What Is Probate?

Probate is the legal process that includes:

- Filing the deceased person's will with a local court (depending on the state, the court can have various names, such as the "probate," "surrogate" or "chancery" court).
- Identifying and inventorying the deceased person's property.
- Having that property appraised.
- Paying off legal debts, including death tax.
- Having the will "proved" valid to the court. (This is almost always a routine matter; Indeed, it's so routine that it's done without a formal hearing in many states, unless there is a contest, which is extremely rare).
- Eventually distributing what's left as the will directs.

If the deceased person didn't leave a will, or the will isn't valid and the deceased didn't use any other valid transfer device, such as a living trust or joint tenancy, the estate will undergo probate through what is called "intestacy" proceedings—with the property distributed to immediate family members as state law dictates.

People who defend the probate system (mostly lawyers, which is surely no surprise) assert that probate prevents fraud in transferring a deceased person's property. In addition, they claim it protects inheritors by promptly resolving claims creditors have against a deceased person's property. In truth, however, most property is transferred within a close circle of family and friends, and few, if any, estates face creditors' claims. Whatever bills the deceased had—often not many—are readily paid out of the property he left. (According to a study by the American Association of Retired People (AARP), the great majority of creditors' claims are filed by the funeral industry, who have learned to use it as a collection device.) In short, most people have no need of these so-called probate "benefits," so the system usually amounts to a lot of time-wasting, expensive mumbo-jumbo of use to no one but the lawyers involved.

The actual probate functions are essentially clerical and administrative. In the vast majority of probate cases, there's no conflict, no contesting parties, none of the normal reasons for court proceedings. Likewise, probate doesn't usually call for legal research, drafting or lawyers' adversarial skills. Instead, in the normal, uneventful probate proceeding, the family or other inheritors of the dead person provide a copy of the deceased person's will and other needed financial information. The attorney's secretary[1] then fills in a small mound of forms and keeps track of filing deadlines and other procedural technicalities. In some states, the attorney makes a couple of routine court appearances; in others, the whole procedure is normally handled by mail.

Because of the complicated paperwork, a typical probate takes up to a year or more, often much more. Denis once worked in a law office that was profitably entering its seventh year of handling a probate estate—and a very wealthy estate it was. By contrast, property transfers by other legal means, such as a

[1] There is so much money in the probate business that some lawyers hire probate form preparation services to do all the real work. In most instances, the existence of these freelance paralegal services is not disclosed to clients, who assume that lawyers' offices at least do the routine paperwork they are paid so well for.

living trust, can usually be completed in a matter of weeks.

Probate usually requires both an "executor" (called a "personal representative" in some states) and someone familiar with probate procedures, normally a probate attorney. The executor is a person appointed in the will[2] who is responsible for supervising the estate, which means making sure that the will is followed. The executor, who is usually a spouse or friend of the deceased, hires a probate lawyer to do the paperwork.[3] Then the executor does little more than sign where the lawyer directs, while wondering why the whole business is taking so long. For these services, the lawyer and the executor are each entitled to a hefty fee from the probate estate. It's common for the executor to waive her fee, especially if she is a substantial inheritor.

Probate sometimes evokes exaggerated images of greedy lawyers consuming most of an estate in fees, while churning out reams of gobbledygook-filled paper as slowly as possible. While there is more truth in these images than lawyers care to admit, the lawyer's fees won't actually devour the whole estate. But still, a report by the American Association of Retired People estimated that probate attorneys annually receive fees of $1.5 billion dollars. In many states, the fees are what a court approves as "reasonable." In other states, the fees are based on a percentage of the estate subject to probate. Either way, probate attorney fees for a "routine" estate with a gross[4] value of $400,000 (these days, this may be little more than a home, some savings and a car) can normally amount to $10,000 or more. And, in addition, there are court costs, appraiser's fees and other possible expenses. Moreover, if there are any "extraordinary" services performed for the estate, the attorney or executor can often petition the court for additional fees. Some lawyers even persuade (or dupe) clients into naming them as executors, enabling the lawyers to hire themselves as probate attorneys and collect two fees—one as executor, one as probate attorney.

Marilyn Monroe's estate offers an extreme example of how outrageous probate fees can be. She died in debt in 1962, but over the next 18 years, her estate received income, mostly from movie royalties, in excess of $1,600,000. When her estate was settled in 1980, her executor announced that debts of $372,136 had been paid, and $101,229 was left as the final assets of the estate, for distribution to inheritors. Well over a million dollars of Monroe's estate was consumed by probate fees.

[2]If the person died without a will, the court appoints an "administrator" (whose main qualification may be that he's a crony of the judge) to serve the same function.

[3]The executor often hires the decedent's lawyer (who may even have possession of the will), but this is not required.

[4]"Gross" probate estate means that debts on property are not deducted to determine value. Thus, if a house has a market value of $200,000 with a mortgage balance of $160,000 (net equity of $40,000), the gross "value" of the house is $200,000.

B. Avoiding Probate

In response to the manifest waste perpetrated by the probate system, a number of legal methods have been developed to avoid probate entirely. Because leaving property in a will usually results in probate, probate avoidance methods involve arranging, prior to death, to transfer property by other legal means. The major probate avoidance methods are:

- revocable living trusts (discussed in Chapter 9)
- joint tenancy (discussed in Chapter 10)
- "pay-on-death accounts," most often used for bank accounts, but also available for use for securities (stocks and bonds) and vehicles in a small but growing number of states (discussed in Chapter 11)
- life insurance (discussed in Chapter 12)

- state laws that exempt certain (small) amounts of property left by will from probate (discussed in Chapter 13), and
- gifts (discussed in Chapter 16).

Deciding which method, or combination of methods, is best for you is a major part of estate planning. So please read all the chapters on probate avoidance methods before you decide how to proceed. To assist you in reaching your decision, Chapter 8 provides a summary chart of the pluses and minuses of each method.

1. Informal Probate Avoidance

Some people ask, "Why not just divide up a deceased relative's or friend's property as the will directs, and ignore the laws requiring probate?" Indeed, some small estates are undoubtedly disposed of this way, directly and informally by family members. The people involved may not think of such an arrangement as avoiding probate, but that's what occurs.

For example, an older man lives his last few years in a nursing home. After his death, his children meet and divide the personal items their father had kept over the years. What little savings he has have long since been put into a joint account with the children anyway, so there's no need for court proceedings there. If the father owned no other property, the children have, in effect, "probated" his estate.

For this type of informal procedure to work, the family must be able to gain possession of all of the deceased's property, agree on how to distribute it, and pay all the creditors. Gaining possession of property isn't difficult when the estate consists entirely of personal effects and household items. However, if real estate, securities, individually-owned bank accounts or other property bearing legal title papers, such as cars and boats, are involved, informal family property distribution can't work. Title to a house, for example, can't be changed on the say-so of the next of kin; someone with legal authority must prepare, sign and record a deed transferring title to the house to the inheritors.

One good rule is that whenever outsiders are involved with a deceased's property, do-it-yourself division by inheritors is not feasible. For instance, creditors can be an obstacle to a family disposing of an estate informally. A creditor concerned about being paid can usually file a court action to compel a probate proceeding.

Another stumbling block for an informal family property disposition can be getting family members to agree on how to divide the deceased's possessions. If there's a will, doing this may not be a problem, since the will acts as a legal blueprint for distribution. If there is no will, things can be trickier. One alternative is for the family to look up and agree to abide by the intestate succession rules established to specifically cover situations in which there is no will by the law of the state where the deceased person lived. Or, in either case, the family may simply adopt their own, mutually agreed on settlement. For example, if, despite a will provision to the contrary, one sibling wants the furniture and the other wants the tools, they can simply trade. All inheritors must agree to the estate distribution if probate procedures are bypassed. Any inheritor who is unhappy with the estate distribution can, like creditors, file for a formal probate.

In sum, informal probate avoidance, even for a small estate, isn't something one can count on. Realistically, probate avoidance must be planned in advance.

2. Planning to Avoid Probate

Because probate has justifiably come to be viewed as an unnecessary device designed to fill lawyers' coffers, some have concluded that probate must be avoided for every last bit of one's property. In our view, this is too rigid. True, most people who take the time to plan their own estate decide they want to avoid probate, at least for the major items of property they own (house, business interests, stocks, money market funds). However, many younger people sensibly elect to put off planning to avoid probate until later. For example, a younger couple may decide that making wills sufficiently accomplishes their principal needs, which are to leave most or all property to the survivor, and to provide money and a guardian for their children if they should die at the same time. They understand that using probate avoidance methods will require some paperwork now, and perhaps some legal fees. Since it's highly unlikely they will die soon and suddenly (should they become ill, they'll normally have time to plan), and because they haven't yet accumulated a great deal of property, they decide to wait a few decades before engaging in probate avoidance planning.

There are even a couple of circumstances in which probate can be desirable.

- **If your estate owes a lot of debts.** Most estates don't involve complex creditor problems. Most deceased persons leave little more than conventional household debts (mortgages, utilities, magazine subscriptions, auto loans, credit cards). Probate is not necessary to handle these debts. But if there's a significant risk that many creditors, especially those owed large sums, will make claims against your estate, probate can be advisable, especially if your executor will contest one or more of these claims. For example, if you own a failing business, or are involved in complex financial transactions, probate can provide benefits because it provides a ready-made court procedure for resolving creditors' claims faster than by normal lawsuit. Creditors who are notified of the probate proceeding must file their claims promptly with the probate court, often within four or six months of the filing of petition for probate, or they needn't be paid. This is a much shorter "statute of limitations" than would otherwise apply and can allow beneficiaries to take their property (or their remaining property) free of anxiety about future creditors' claims.

  One type of potential claim that may make probate desirable is if a person owns land where there's a possibility of toxic chemical contamination, even if this occurred many decades ago. Under federal law, claims against land and landowners for damages from previous toxic waste contamination—and cost for its clean-ups can run forever. But there is one big exception—such potential claims can be cut off if the land is subject to a probate court proceeding. By contrast, transferring the same property by a living trust does not cut off such claims.

Get legal help if you fear toxic contamination. The law involving who is liable to clean up toxic waste is as fast-changing as it is brutal. Do not attempt to transfer contaminated property during life or at death without expert advice.

- **If you believe someone may challenge your estate plan in court.** Any estate planning device, whether it be a will, living trust, or any combination of legal methods, can be attacked by a lawsuit after your death. Fortunately, however, the legal grounds for attack are quite limited. The challenger must prove the estate plan is a result of someone's illegal act, such as fraud, duress or undue influence over the person who signed the documents, or the challenger must establish that the deceased person was mentally incompetent when the estate plan was authorized. Both of these legal theories are as hard to prove as they are easy to allege. If you believe there's a risk that your estate may be subject to legal attack, even by someone who has little chance of success, probate may be advisable as part of your plan to defeat that attack. Under probate law, only a brief time is allowed for attacking a will, and the people who witnessed the signing of the will should be able to testify to the will maker's competence.

If you're worried about a lawsuit, you should discuss your estate planning with an attorney, and decide together what your best course of action is.

C. How to Reduce or Eliminate Probate Fees

One way to reduce probate fees is for the executor to appear in court without an attorney ("in pro per") as the representative of the estate. Unfortunately, a few states don't permit the executor to act without a lawyer. And some judges in states which do officially permit executors to act in pro per make doing so difficult. The only states in which pro per representation is truly accessible for probate proceedings are California (see *How to Probate an Estate,* by Nissley, (Nolo Press), an excellent self-help book designed for, and used by, thousands of non-lawyers), Wisconsin, which has an established pro per procedure (see Chapter 13, State Law Exemptions from Normal Probate, Section B), and Maryland. In other states where in pro per action is theoretically possible, there are no comprehensive published materials, nor is other help available which makes probate easily accessible to non-lawyers. Without help, learning to complete the forms, understanding the intricacies of court petitions, estate inventories, proof of service declarations, and so on, is likely to be difficult. And to make matters worse, court clerks and judges are likely to be unsympathetic (to put it mildly), so any mistake is likely to cause delay, as well as, possibly, embarrassment. But handling a probate without a lawyer is far from impossible. Legal secretaries and paralegals typically copy necessary forms and follow procedures set out in lawyer practice manuals. These are usually available at public law libraries, and many people have successfully used them.

In all states (including California and Wisconsin), rather than trying to save money by considering having your estate probated without an attorney, it generally makes more sense to see if you can avoid probate altogether. As mentioned earlier in this chapter, this means transferring your property by probate avoidance methods. Obviously, if there is no probate, there are no probate fees. At the very least, we recommend that you consider reducing the size of the estate that will be subject to probate in order to reduce probate fees.[5] This approach involves transferring the big ticket items of your property—for example, your house and stock portfolio—outside of

[5]In some states, probate fees are based on the value of the estate. In the majority of states, where the fee is based on the hours the attorney works, or on some "reasonable" fee fixed by a judge, the fee should be substantially less for a smaller, less complicated estate than for a larger one.

probate, leaving only less valuable items to be passed by your will.

Finally, if some of your estate will be subject to probate, you can try to reach an agreement with your future executor and attorney that they'll do your probate for less than the conventional fees. However, you cannot bind your executor, or an attorney, to handle the probate of your estate for a reduced fee. In fact, legally you don't have the power to select the attorney at all. The law gives this authority to the executor. Indeed, the executor can legally revoke any waiver of fees made while you were alive, and claim full statutory fees. Fortunately though, most executors are close family members, who wouldn't revoke a prior fee agreement. Indeed, many executors don't charge any fee for their services, because they inherit a substantial portion (at least) of the deceased's estate.

There's no reason for you to pick an executor you don't completely trust. Usually, for moderate estates, an executor is a spouse or a close friend who will see to it that an attorney who agreed to handle the estate at a reduced fee will actually do so. If the probate of your estate is routine, it will be sufficiently profitable even at a fee lower than the conventional rate. There's nothing illegal or unethical about bargaining with an attorney to reduce fees. If you do arrange with an attorney to handle your estate at a reduced fee, be definite about the terms of the fee, and put something in writing, even if it's only a letter confirming this arrangement.

D. Debts, Taxes and Probate Avoidance

What about debts? If an estate is probated, debts and taxes are paid before property is distributed to inheritors. If duly notified creditors don't make their claims within the allotted time, they're simply cut off. This raises the question of how the deceased's debts, including death tax, get paid if there's no probate. Obviously, a probate court can't ensure that debts get paid if property is transferred outside of probate. However, there's no indication any judicial policing is needed. Many people leave no significant debts, and even if some do, they normally leave sufficient assets to pay them. It's important to realize here that the primary financial obligations most people do have—mortgages on real estate, or loans on cars—aren't debts which must be paid off promptly after the owner dies. Normally, these kinds of assets are transferred to an inheritor who becomes liable for the mortgage or loan. In other words, mortgages or car loans pass with the property and don't need to be paid off separately.

If no probate occurs to cut off creditors' claims, all the deceased's property remains liable for his debts, including any death tax. This is true even after the property is transferred to inheritors. If only one person will inherit from you, that person will be responsible for paying your debts and any death tax from the inherited property. If there are several inheritors, the responsibility for paying debts and taxes can theoretically become more confusing, but this confusion can be eliminated in advance by earmarking money in your estate plan to pay debts. One way to do this is to allocate, in a living trust, specific assets (a bank account, or a particular stock) to pay debts and taxes. If you don't have a suitable asset available to do this, consider purchasing insurance to accomplish it.

Tax note. In Chapter 15, Estate Taxes, we show you how to estimate whether any federal or state death tax will be due at your death. If the answer is "no," this is one less thing to worry about. If the answer is "yes," plan to leave adequate cash or property that can easily be sold, to cover your estate's likely tax obligation.

E. Probate Reform

Why is probate so time-consuming and expensive? Why is probate court approval required for so many routine actions when there's normally no conflict whatsoever? Aside from the mystique of professionalism and good old greed, the history of probate supplies most of the answer. Probate became legal business through a quirk of English history. In medieval England, wealth and power resided almost exclusively in the ownership of land. It passed, by feudal law, to the eldest son. Inheritance of land was a political matter of direct concern to the king, so land transfers after a death were done through the king's courts.

The proceedings were technical, formal and costly. Personal property (everything except real estate) was transferred by much simpler ways. When the United States became independent, it accepted and followed the traditional British legal system for land inheritance. But instead of distinguishing between land and personal property, our new nation tossed everything into the new "probate" court. Over 200 years later, all types of property can still be transferred through these formal judicial proceedings. Over the years, there have been countless efforts to reform probate by making it easier, cheaper or, in some instances, simply doing away with it. But because a complicated, formal probate system means substantial fees for lawyers, the legal profession continues to fiercely defend it.

Lawyers' assurances that probate is necessary sound increasingly hollow. Even the British eliminated tedious, expensive probate proceedings over half a century ago. In 1926, England reformed its probate system to provide that the person named in the will as the executor (normally a non-lawyer) simply files an accounting of the estate's assets and liabilities with the tax authorities, who appraise the inventory and assess any death tax due. If the papers are in order (as they should be in all routine probates), a "grant of probate" is issued in as little as seven days. Without any further court proceedings, the executor then handles all the estate's problems—paying the bills, collecting assets and distributing gifts to inheritors. Only if there's a problem, such as a will contest or a contested debt claim, is the matter referred to the Principal Registry, the functional equivalent of our probate courts.

In most civil law countries (including those in Western Europe and Central America), probate is even simpler. Wills are presented to a notary when signed. A notary, under civil law, is a quasi-judicial official who's responsible for ensuring the validity of documents. Upon death, the deceased person's successor named in the will performs the probate functions without any judicial supervision. If there are disputes such as contests of the will or disputed creditors' claims, they are handled like any other legal conflict.

Will our probate system be reformed soon? While some improvement may occur, it is likely to be slow and grudging. True, most people favor probate reform, in a vague way. And there's some real pressure on a number of state legislatures to adopt genuine probate reform, on the order of the simplified estate distribution system used in England or civil law countries. HALT (Help Abolish Legal Tyranny), a Washington, DC-based law reform organization, is one leader in this movement, having been instrumental in the probate reform legislation adopted in Maryland, which allows for self-help probate and requires probate court clerks to assist the public with the forms. Unfortunately, though, probate reform isn't a hot, glamorous issue that deeply moves lots of voters; without lots more public pressure, politicians (many of whom are lawyers, or sensitive to the lobbying of lawyer groups) are unlikely to become seriously interested in it. Unfortunately, much of what passes currently for probate reform merely simplifies probate procedures for the lawyers, but keeps the overall system, particularly the fees, intact. For example, under names like "Independent Administration of Estate Act," or "Unsupervised Administration Law," a number of states have passed laws simplifying probate procedures. Sadly, because these laws make no reasonable provision for non-lawyer access, the result is that lawyers have continued to do the vast majority of probates, charging their same high fees while doing less work.

There's more at work to prevent probate reform than lawyer greed, however. Ours is a society professing devotion to equality, but also to freedom, and that leaves us a little confused about money, especially inherited wealth. We don't have any blood aristocracy, but the grandchildren of wealthy people like Rockefeller, Vanderbilt or Kennedy and tens of thousands of others inherit money taxed at a much lower rate than any English lord or French duke can.

Surely it's not much of an exaggeration to say that a principal role for American lawyers is to legitimate wealth. So corporate lawyers are the clergy of money, and present themselves accordingly—dressed in dull garb, displaying grave demeanors and occupying somber offices. Wherever the millions originally came from—whether hard, honest toil or robber baron's thievery—a lawyer, or more likely, several of them, will be standing by. Even when money is filthy to start with, after a couple of generations of lawyers get through with it, it becomes more respectable and—when a few suitable charities are involved—almost holy. And the inheritors receive the money in clear conscience. After all, they didn't have anything to do with any earlier shenanigans.

Probate has been an essential part of this sanctification process. The idea seems to be that if you make the legal process surrounding the transfer of money on death complex and formal, it keeps attention off who decided what the rules are for inherited money anyway and gives the inheritors a fresh start.

But despite inertia and greed, there is one real incentive to probate reform, and that's the fact that many middle-class people are learning to avoid the system. An endearing trait of Americans is that they are as good at avoiding rules as they are at inventing them. As we'll discuss in more detail in later chapters, the living trust is currently the most popular of a small flock of safe, easy probate-avoidance schemes—so popular, indeed, that unless lawyers make probate simpler, cheaper and fairer, Americans may succeed in killing it through almost universal avoidance. ■

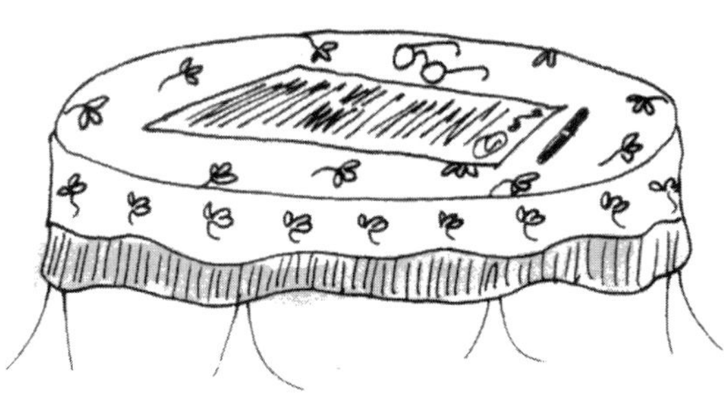

8

Chart: Probate Avoidance Methods

This chart summarizes the advantages and disadvantages of each of the major methods for transferring property after one's death. Each probate avoidance method is explained in depth in the following six chapters. You can use the chart now to gain a rough understanding of the basics of probate avoidance methods. And, if you wish, you can refer to it later to remind yourself of the pluses and minuses of one, or several, methods.

TRANSFER DEVICE	AVOIDS PROBATE?	MAJOR ADVANTAGES	DRAWBACKS
Will	No, except in limited circumstances for small estates. (See Chapter 13.)	Simple and easy to prepare; can serve other purposes, such as naming guardian for minor children. Often a good interim device to use until later in life.	Normally puts property in probate where inheritors face attorney's fees and other costs and time delays.
Living Trust		Complete control over property while alive; flexibility in providing for beneficiaries. Allows for property management in case of incapacity.	More trouble to establish than a will. Initial attorney's fees can be higher. More trouble to maintain than a will.
Joint Tenancy	Yes.	Can be simplest probate avoidance device to create.	Fine for long-term couples owning property together, but usually not a good substitute for a living trust later in life, because each joint tenant can normally sell their interest. There may be gift taxes involved in creating joint tenancy and putting property in joint tenancy. May mean partial loss of stepped up tax basis.
Tenancy by the Entirety	Yes.	Easy to create.	Available only in some states; limited to married couples. Can be a problem if one spouse becomes incapacitated.
Pay-on-Death Bank Accounts (Totten Trust)	Yes.	Very easy to create; no additional costs.	Limited to bank accounts and some government securities. Not a good idea when small children may inherit, since a property guardian will have to be appointed. (See Chapter 6.)

TRANSFER DEVICE	AVOIDS PROBATE?	MAJOR ADVANTAGES	DRAWBACKS
Transfer on Death Car Registration	Yes.	(If available) can be easy to create, and simplest way to transfer car.	Available only in California and Missouri, but proposed in several other states.
Transfer on Death Registration for Securities	Yes.	Easy to do. Name inheritor on securities' registration form.	Currently available only in Arkansas, Colorado, Kansas, Minnesota, Missouri, Montana, Nebraska New Mexico, North Dakota, Ohio Oregon, Virginia, Washington, West Virginia, Wisconsin and Wyoming.
Naming beneficiary to Pension Plan or Retirement Account	Yes.	Generally easy to do.	Can be limits imposed by specific policy, program, plan.
Life Insurance	Yes.	Good way to provide quick cash for beneficiaries or to pay estate taxes. Proceeds don't go through probate.	An expensive way to transfer property. If family members will not need immediate cash (or if they don't rely on you for support), the expense of policy may not be justified.
State law exemptions to normal probate	Yes.	Can work well if state allows this method to be combined with other probate avoidance methods.	Only relatively small amounts of property qualify. Rules vary for each state. (See Chapter 13). You have to understand your state's laws; research or hiring an attorney may be required.
Dying intestate, without creating any property transfer method	No.	No effort required.	Usually a terrible choice. Property will be distributed according to state law, which is likely not to be exactly as you wish. Your executor (administrator) will be appointed by judge. Guardian for your minor children selected by a judge.

9

Revocable Living Trusts

The purpose of a basic living trust is to avoid probate. Fortunately, a living trust is also an efficient and effective way to transfer property at your death. Essentially, a living trust is a legal document (a few pieces of paper) that controls the transfer of any property you have placed in the trust; when you die, whomever you have designated to receive that trust property obtains it free from probate. If this sounds a lot like a will to you, you're right. A living trust allows you to do the same basic job as a will, with the advantage of avoiding probate.

One big advantage of living trusts is that they are extremely flexible: You can transfer all your property by living trust, or, if appropriate, use a living trust to transfer only some assets, transferring the rest by other efficient methods. Also, living trusts normally are not made public at your death. Wills, on the other hand, are routinely made public as part of the probate process.

Living trusts are called "living" or sometimes "inter vivos" (Latin for "among the living") because they're created while you're alive. They're called "revocable" because you can revoke or change them at any time, for any reason, before you die. While you live, and as long as you are mentally competent, you still effectively own all property you've transferred to your living trust and can do what you want with it, including selling it, spending it or giving it away. In short, a revocable living trust is merely a document that becomes operational at your death to transfer your property privately and outside of probate to the people or organizations you've named as beneficiaries in the trust.

Aside from some paperwork necessary to establish a probate avoidance living trust and transfer property to it, there are no serious drawbacks or risks involved in creating or maintaining the trust. You don't even need to maintain separate trust tax records; all transactions which are technically made by the trust are reported on your personal income tax return.

It's important to realize that a basic probate avoidance living trust can also be combined with other types of trusts. For example, you can create a living trust which first avoids probate and then continues as an ongoing trust for years after your death for such purposes as saving on estate tax or imposing controls on property, as is commonly done for gifts to people with special needs, or for spouses in second marriages. Ongoing trusts to save on estate tax or control property are discussed in detail in Chapters 17 through 25.

For many people of moderate means, whose estates won't be subject to federal estate tax liability, the job is simply to avoid probate. Here's a summary of how a living trust works to accomplish that. You create a document called a living trust. No law specifies the form a living trust must take. As a result, there is no such thing as a "standard" living trust. Indeed, there are a bewildering variety of living trust forms, including some attorney-created forms that contain vast piles of verbiage that serve little real-world purpose, except to generate attorney fees.

But there are some essentials that must be covered. In your living trust document, you must name a trustee (normally yourself) to manage the trust property, and a successor trustee (often a family member or close friend), to distribute the property when you die. You also must name the trust beneficiaries, who receive the property when you die. You then formally transfer property into the trust's name. When you die, the successor trustee simply obtains the property from whoever holds it, and transfers it to the named beneficiaries. No probate or other court proceeding is required.

A. Does Everyone Need a Living Trust?

Given the advantages of avoiding probate that a living trust confers, shouldn't every prudent person use one for all their property? Despite our enthusiasm for living trusts, our answer is "not necessarily." The reason for saying this is two-fold. First, some people don't really need to plan to avoid probate now and, second, there are other probate avoidance methods which may fit a particular estate planning situation better.

Good estate planning can't be reduced to one universal formula. To make sensible decisions about using a living trust, you need to understand what it can and cannot accomplish, given your personal, family and property situation, and how it can be used with other estate planning methods in devising your overall plan. Norman Dacey, in his pioneering work *How to Avoid Probate* (Crown), essentially asserts that living trusts should be used by all people in all situations. A number of lawyers now make the same claim in advertisements and seminars. These claims are much too broad. Generally, there are a number of categories of people who may conclude that creating a living trust is not their best estate planning strategy, at least not right now, including:

- **People who are young, healthy and unlikely to die for a long time.** People in their 30s, 40s, and sometimes older, usually have the primary goal of seeing that their property will be distributed as they want in the highly unlikely event they die suddenly, and to provide financial resources and a person to care for any minor children. A will (perhaps coupled with the purchase of life insurance) often achieves these goals easier than a living trust. Here's why: A will is simpler to prepare and far easier to revise than a living trust. While using a will normally means property goes through probate, this only occurs after death. As long as a person is alive, the fact that probate will be avoided is of no benefit. Because very few younger, healthy people die without any warning (and because they often don't yet own enough property that probate fees would amount to that much anyway), it can make good sense now to make and revise (or replace) a will for a number of years. Later in life, when the prospect of death is more imminent, and the person has accumulated more property, a revocable living trust can be established to avoid probate.
- **People who can more sensibly transfer their assets by other probate avoidance devices, including joint tenancy, informal bank trusts ("pay-on-death" accounts), life insurance and gifts.** In addition, the laws in some states allow certain amounts or types of property (and occasionally property left to certain classes of beneficiaries, such as a surviving spouse) to be transferred without probate even if a will is used. None of these devices has the overall breadth of a living trust, which can be used to transfer virtually all types of assets. However, each can be easier to use, and equally efficient, in particular circumstances. In short, it's best to understand all probate avoidance methods and then to decide which ones will work best for you.
- **People who have, or may have, complex debt problems or business property subject to claims for toxic cleanup.** If you have a business that has many creditors, probate provides an absolute cut-off time for notified creditors to file claims. If they don't do so in the time permitted, your inheritors can take your property free of concern that these creditors will surface later and claim a share. A similar cut-off period applies in probate to claims for toxic clean-up. A living trust doesn't create any such cut-off period, which means your property could be subject to creditors' clean-up claims for a much longer time.
- **People who don't currently have title to property but expect to receive it.** A living trust only works to transfer property you currently own. If you've been left property by someone's will that is still in probate, or you expect to get money from a lawsuit settlement, only a will can be securely used to transfer that property. Of course, no one knows what property they might receive shortly

before death, which is one reason it is always wise to back up a living trust with a will.

- **Younger people without lots of property whose primary goal in making an estate plan is to name a personal guardian to care for their minor children.** A living trust can't be used for this; a will can. Of course, if you have a great deal of valuable property, you may want to create a living trust (or other probate avoidance device) to transfer that property and name a personal guardian for your minor children in a "back-up" will.
- **People who own little property, so there isn't much point in bothering with a living trust and probate avoidance.** Often younger parents with minor children who find themselves in this situation will provide financial resources for their children by purchasing term life insurance. But since the proceeds of insurance do not go through probate, there is no need to use a living trust to plan to avoid it. However, if the policy is fairly large, you will want to establish a way to manage any property your children will receive if you die before they reach the age of 18. Establishing a children's trust (as part of a will or living trust) and naming it as beneficiary of the policy—not the children—can be a good way to do this. (See Chapter 12, Life Insurance.)

Despite these exceptions, the fact remains that for all those who want to arrange to avoid probate now, including the elderly, the seriously ill and anyone with lots of valuable property who doesn't want any risk of subjecting it to probate, living trusts are usually the best probate avoidance device. Or put another way, most people who plan their estates eventually turn to a living trust as the best method to transfer some, and often the bulk, of their property.

B. Living Trusts Explained

Don't let the word "trust" scare you. True, the word can have an impressive, slightly ominous sound. Historically, monopolists used trusts to dominate entire industries (for example, the Standard Oil Trust in the era of Teddy Roosevelt's "trust-busting"). And while many people don't know exactly how a trust works, they do know, vaguely, that trusts have traditionally been used by the very wealthy to preserve their riches from generation to generation. (Indeed, isn't one version of the American dream to be the beneficiary of your very own trust fund?) Trusts may even appear to some as a particularly obnoxious form of lawyers' black magic, somehow enabling people to escape tax or other financial obligations. The reality—as it tends to be—is more mundane.

1. What Is a Living Trust?

Living trusts are, in basic concept, simple. Here's a valid bare-bones living trust:

> *I, Cynthia Sims, hereby place my diamond necklace in trust for my niece, Sara Sims. The necklace shall be given to her outright when she is 35. I retain all rights in the necklace until I die. I appoint myself as trustee of this trust, and Sara's mother, Nancy Sims, to be successor trustee after I die.*

Here is how this trust operates: The person who establishes the trust (Cynthia Sims) can be called, in legalese, the "grantor" or "creator" or "settlor." We use the term "grantor" to define the person who creates a trust, because that term is widely accepted in the financial and legal worlds. She puts something of value (in this case, the diamond necklace) in a legal entity ("legal fiction" might be a better term) called a "living trust." This trust entity is simply a written document that states that it's a living trust and specifies:

1. The "trustee," who manages the trust property. This is normally the person who establishes the trust. In legalese, the trustee holds "legal title' to the trust property.

2. The "successor trustee," who takes over after the grantor dies and turns the trust property over to the beneficiary.

3. The "beneficiary" or beneficiaries of the trust, who are named to receive the trust property at the grantor's death.

The beneficiaries hold "equitable title" to the trust property. "Legal title" and "equitable title" simply mean that one person, the trustee, has the authority to manage property for the benefit of another, the beneficiary.

4. The property that is subject to the trust.

5. The terms of the trust, including the fact that it can be amended or revoked by the grantor at any time.

A Mini-Glossary of Living Trust Terms

Although we've already used and defined some of these terms, we want to provide a summary of basic trust terms that are essential when preparing or understanding a living trust.

The person or persons (a couple) who sets up the living trust (that's you, or you and your spouse) is called the **grantor(s), trustor(s)** or **settlor(s)**. These terms mean the same thing and can be used interchangeably. As we've said, we use the term **grantor** in this book.

The grantor creates a written trust **document** or **instrument,** containing all the terms and provisions of the trust.

All the property you own at death, whether in your living trust or owned in some other form, is your **estate**.

The market value of your property at your death, less all debts and liabilities on that property, is your net or **taxable estate**. (Technically, the IRS allows your successor trustee to determine the market value of your estate at your death or six months later.)

The property you transfer to the trustee, acting for the trust, is called, collectively, the **trust property, trust principal** or **trust estate**. (And, of course, there's a Latin version: the trust corpus.)

The person who has power over the trust property is called the **trustee**.

The person the grantor names to take over as trustee after the grantor's death (or, with a trust made jointly by a couple, after the death of both spouses) is called the **successor trustee**.

The people or organizations who get the trust property when a grantor dies are called the **beneficiaries** of the trust. (While a grantor is alive, technically he or she is the beneficiary of the trust.)

2. How a Living Trust Works

The key to a living trust established to avoid probate is that the grantor (remember, the person who sets up the trust) isn't locked into anything. She can revise, amend or revoke the trust for any (or no) reason, any time before her death, as long as she's legally competent. The grantor appoints herself as the initial trustee, to control and use the trust property as she sees fit. If the grantor becomes mentally incapacitated, the successor trustee steps in and manages the trust property for the grantor's benefit, as long as she lives. If she regains her mental capacity, she regains the authority to manage her living trust property herself.

And now for the legal magic of the living trust device. Although a living trust is really only a legal fiction during the grantor's life, it assumes a very real presence for a brief period after death. When the grantor dies (or if he becomes mentally incapacitated), the living trust can no longer be revoked, or altered by a will. Once the grantor dies, the trust really does own the property. And since property held in living trust does not need to be probated, the successor trustee can immediately transfer all property owned by the trust to the trust beneficiaries.

It's evident that one crucial element to have a living trust work effectively is that you have someone you fully trust to be your successor trustee. There is no court or any governmental supervision to be sure your successor trustee complies with the terms of your living trust. So, if you don't have a spouse, child, other relative, trusted friend or someone else you believe is truly trustworthy to name as successor trustee, a living trust isn't for you.

Practically speaking, after the trust grantor dies, there is some paperwork necessary to complete transfer of the trust property to the beneficiaries, such as preparing new ownership documents, and paying any death tax assessed against the estate. Still, these matters can normally be handled without a lawyer in no more than a few weeks. Once the trust property is legally received by the beneficiaries, the trust ceases to exist.

Example: Travis intends to leave his painting collection and his house to his daughter, Bianca, but he wants to have complete control over the house and the collection until he dies, including the right to sell any painting in the collection if he chooses. At the same time, he doesn't want the $300,000 value of this house and the $250,000 value of the collection to be subject to probate. (Travis reasons that it's pretty silly to pay thousands of dollars in probate fees just to have his own house and paintings turned over to his daughter.)

So Travis establishes a revocable living trust, with the house and paintings as the trust's assets. He names himself as trustee, with full power to control the trust property. Bianca is named as the successor trustee, to take over after he dies. He also names Bianca as the trust beneficiary.

When Travis dies, Bianca, acting as successor trustee, turns the paintings over to the beneficiary, herself, as directed by the terms of the trust. And, as trustee, she prepares and records a deed transferring the house from the trust to herself. The trust then ceases to exist. All probate proceedings, delays and costs are avoided. Because the estate is worth less than $600,000, no federal estate tax is assessed. (See Chapter 15, Estate Taxes, Section A.)

3. Living Trusts and Your Income Taxes

Fortunately, once a living trust has been created, and property is placed in it, maintaining the trust is easy. During the grantor's life, the trust doesn't exist for income tax purposes. The IRS treats the trust property as it does any other property owned by the grantor; all transactions that are technically made by the trust are included as part of the grantor's regular income tax return. So, you don't have to maintain separate books, records or bank accounts for your living trust. While you live, the trust isn't functionally distinct from you, which means it can't be used to lower your income tax. But, when you die, the trust is, as we've stated, treated as a separate legal entity for probate avoidance purposes. So, for once, you can have your cake and eat it too.

4. Living Trusts and Death Tax

Let us say it loud, clear and in big type: REVOCABLE LIVING TRUSTS DESIGNED TO AVOID PROBATE DON'T SAVE ON DEATH TAX. We emphasize this because when some people hear the word "trust," they feel it must mean "tax savings." But now, to complicate matters, a revocable living trust designed to avoid probate can be combined with a second trust designed to save on death tax. A common example of this is when a spouse uses a living trust to first avoid probate and then to establish a "marital life estate" trust to pay income to the surviving spouse for his or her life, with the property in the trust going to the children or grandchildren when that spouse dies. (See Chapter 18, Estate Tax-Saving Bypass Trusts, Section C.)

5. Living Trusts and Your Debts

Property in a revocable living trust is not immune from attack by the grantor's creditors while he's alive. Some "authorities" have inaccurately stated that property in a revocable living trust can't be grabbed by the grantor's creditors to pay his debts during his life. These authorities argue that, for collection purposes, a revocable living trust is legally distinct from its creator. We know of no law or case that supports this position. It's most likely that a judge would rule that living trust property is not protected from the grantor's creditors. After all, during his life, the grantor has complete and exclusive power over the trust property, so why would a judge let him use the paper legality of a living trust he can revoke at any time to evade his creditors?

On the other hand, if property is put in a trust that can't be revoked or changed by the grantor (called an "irrevocable trust"), it's a different legal matter. (See Chapter 17, Ongoing Trusts: An Overview.) Property transferred to a bona fide irrevocable trust is immune from the grantor's creditors. The key words here are "bona fide." If an irrevocable trust is set up to defraud creditors, it's not bona fide. The irrevocable trust must have a valid purpose, and the grantor must be able to convince a judge, if need be, that this independent purpose makes the trust bona fide.

If you're concerned about protecting your assets from creditors, see a lawyer. The materials in this book aren't designed for you.

6. Living Trusts for Couples

A living trust can work as effectively for a couple as for a single person. And any couple, married or not, needs only one living trust for their shared property. Because most couples who use living trusts are married, the discussion that follows is cast in terms of "spouses" and "marital property." However, the concepts discussed apply equally to unmarried couples. We will remind you of this point occasionally, but in the meantime, if you are a member of an unmarried couple, we will count on you to make the necessary semantic substitutions.

The fact that a couple can create a shared living trust to cover the property of both doesn't mean they must. In some circumstances, it may make sense for each spouse to make their own living trust. For example, if each spouse owns mostly separate property, a combined living trust makes little sense. But if spouses share ownership of much or all of their property, as is usually the case, it's generally preferable that they use one revocable living trust for their shared property.

Shared ownership is almost always the situation of married couples in the eight states that follow the community property ownership system, under which spouses equally own most property acquired after marriage. Even in the other (common law) states, where one spouse may legally be the sole owner of much property, spouses who have been married for many years typically regard most or all property as owned by both. (See Chapter 3, State Property Ownership Laws, for a list of common law and community property states and an explanation of both systems of property ownership.) Unmarried couples can also share ownership of property, if that's how they choose to do it, and register any ownership/title document in both their names as co-owners.

Why is setting up two separate living trusts for shared property owned by a couple generally undesirable? Because each owner can transfer only his or her share of the property to his or her separate trust. To accomplish this, ownership of the shared property must be divided. Why go to the trouble of doing this? Worse, dividing shared marital property in half could lead to unfair and undesired imbalances—for example, one spouse's stocks might go up in value while the other's declines.

Fortunately, there is no need for spouses to divide property ownership as long as one trust is created to handle both spouses' shared property. In this type of shared trust, each spouse has full power to name the beneficiaries of his or her portion of the property put in trust. When the first spouse dies, the shared marital property is then divided into two trusts. One trust contains all property of the deceased spouse. The other trust contains all property of the surviving spouse. The deceased spouse's property is transferred to the beneficiaries he or she named in the trust document. One beneficiary is commonly the surviving spouse, but children, friends and charities may also receive property.

The diagram below shows how this type of marital living trust works. In this example, the husband and wife transfer their shared ownership property into one living trust. The husband is the first spouse to die, the "deceased spouse." The wife is the "surviving spouse."

How a Marital Living Trust Works

1. Husband and wife transfer shared property to trust.
2. Husband dies. Trust property is divided in half.
3. Husband's property goes to his beneficiaries. Property left to wife remains in her trust.
4. Wife's property stays in living trust.

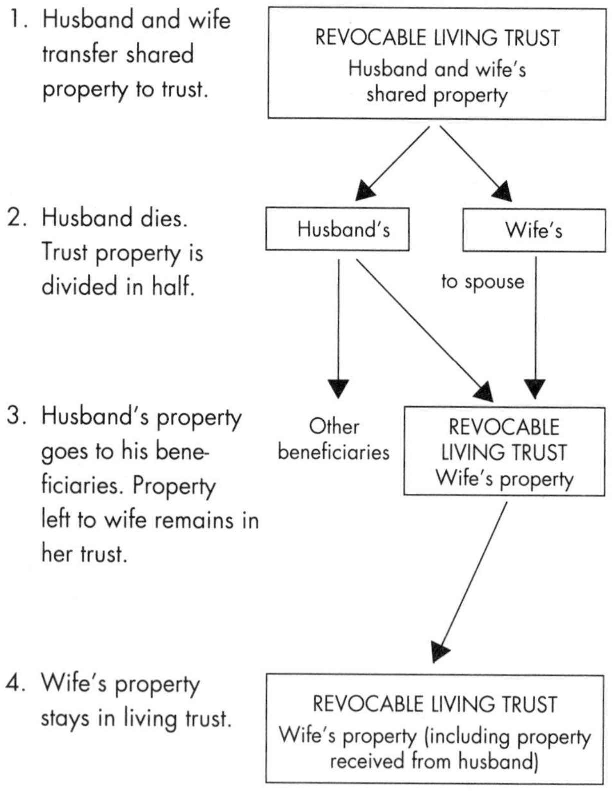

> **SEPARATELY OWNED PROPERTY**
>
> A spouse who owns some property separately has a choice as to whether to place this property in a separate living trust or in a shared living trust. If spouses choose this latter option, they clearly identify any separate property as the sole property of the spouse who owned it.

7. Naming Your Living Trust as a Beneficiary of Your IRA

It is a bad idea to designate your living trust as the primary beneficiary of your individual retirement account (IRA), because if you do, money in the account will have to be distributed earlier than might otherwise be the case. Specifically, mandatory distributions must begin at age70½, if a trust is the beneficiary. In addition, distributions will be based on your life expectancy alone and not the joint life expectancy of you and another beneficiary (as is possible if you'd named a living person as beneficiary of your IRA). If you use a second life, the distributions can be made slower if you wish. Also, at your death, any account balance must be fully distributed within five years instead of longer periods that might be available if the trust weren't the beneficiary. To avoid these limitations, you should make the primary beneficiary of your IRA your spouse or another individual of your choice.

8. Preparing Your Own Living Trust

Many individuals and couples can safely prepare their own living trust, without the assistance of an attorney. *Make Your Own Living Trust,* by Denis Clifford (Nolo Press), and Nolo's *Living Trust Maker* computer program, both enable you to prepare the following types of living trusts:

- A living trust for a single person with an estate worth less than $600,000 (the federal estate tax threshold, see Chapter 15, Estate Taxes, Section A).
- A basic living trust for a couple with a total estate (shared and separate property) with under $600,000.

In addition, *Make Your Own Living Trust* enables you to prepare a basic living trust for a married couple with a total estate (shared and separate property) worth between $600,000 and $1,200,000 (called a "marital life estate trust"; discussed in detail in Chapter 18, Estate Tax-Saving Bypass Trusts, Section C). The marital life estate trust contained in *Make Your Own Living Trust* is designed for married couples in first marriages. Couples where either spouse is in a second marriage, or has other special desires or needs, should not use this trust form.

BE WARY OF "FREE" LIVING TRUST SEMINARS OR HIGH PRESSURE TRUST SALESMEN

Newspapers, radio and TV are full of ads for free seminars on living trusts. Usually, these events are nothing more than elaborate pitches for paying a lawyer (or some non-lawyer entity or service) $1,000 or more to write a living trust. Sometimes living trust salesmen contact prospective customers directly, by phone, and pressure them to make an appointment to buy a living trust. Is it worth it? Usually not.

Seminar sponsors try and sell the idea that much of a person's estate is likely to be gobbled up by estate tax and probate unless they set up trusts now to avoid some of the tax and buy life insurance to pay the rest. The problem is, most people don't have estates large enough to generate estate tax liability. Further, some people hold the bulk of their property in joint tenancy, so they don't even need to worry about avoiding probate. (See Chapter 10, Joint Tenancy and Tenancy by the Entirety.)

Even though the sponsors know this, they try to sell:

- a lot of life insurance, to pay for supposed estate tax, and
- a fill-in-the-blanks trust that they claim will avoid probate while reducing estate tax—a version of what we call a "living trust with marital life estate."

Be sure you need these alleged benefits before paying what will be a substantial amount to acquire them. Do you really need to avoid probate now? Is your estate likely to be liable for estate tax? If so, and you are married, what type—if any—marital life estate trust makes sense? Is your situation more complex than what can be handled via a standard form? In conclusion, buying a trust from a seminar is a bit like buying aluminum siding from a door-to-door salesperson. If you really need exactly what the person is selling, you can satisfy yourself by checking references and making certain that the company the salesman represents provides a quality product, and that the price is fair. But this takes a lot of work, and we think there are normally better ways to find legal help. (See Chapter 30, Using Lawyers.)

9. Trusts for Minor or Young Adult Children

Minors cannot own any substantial amount of property outright. If any of your living trust property is given to a beneficiary who's a minor when you die, an adult must manage that property for the minor.

In Chapter 6, Children, Section C, we discussed the various legal devices that can be used to leave property to minors. In some circumstances, where an estate is relatively modest and there is a trusted person to care for the child (usually the other parent), it's easiest simply to leave property directly to the adult who will care for them. If the gift is larger, or there is no financially reliable spouse to leave it to, it can be desirable to use the Uniform Transfers to Minors Act, if it is applicable in your state. This allows you to appoint a financial manager for the money should something happen to you before the minor reaches an age from 18 to 25, depending on the version of the UTMA adopted by your state. But for much larger estates, where the money is unlikely to run out while the child is young, the best way to leave property to minor children is in a children's trust, which allows you to designate a more advanced age at which the child will receive what's left of the property (say 25, 30 or even 35), and name a trusted person to manage the trust for the children's benefit.

A children's trust may be created as a part of a revocable living trust. If you die before a child beneficiary has reached the age you designated, the children's trust becomes irrevocable, and continues until the child does reach that age. (If the child has reached that age when you die, she receives her property outright, and no children's trust is created for her.)

Example: One of Edward's beneficiaries of his living trust is Abigail, age 17. Edward establishes a child's trust for her, in his living trust, naming his brother Myron as trustee. Abigail is to receive her trust property when she becomes 35. Edward dies when Abigail is 26. Her property is maintained in her child's trust until she becomes 35. In the meantime, the trustee manages the trust property for her benefit, spending income or principal on her needs as he decides is appropriate.

C. Common Questions About Living Trusts

Now, let us change gears and answer some common questions about living trusts we've been asked over the years.

1. Real Estate

Will real estate be reappraised for property tax purposes if I transfer it to a living trust?

Generally, no. In some states, some real estate sales or transfers to new owners who aren't family members can result in property being immediately reappraised for property tax purposes. By contrast, if the property is not transferred to new owners, it usually won't be reappraised for a set period of years, or (in a few states) at all. Because you and your living trust are considered the same basic entity while you're alive, no taxable transfer is seen to have occurred when you transfer your property to it. But to be absolutely sure that this is true in your state if you're transferring real estate into a living trust, check with your local property tax collector to make sure you know exactly what reappraisal rules apply. A few localities do impose hefty transfer and recordation tax. Also there may be special local forms that must be completed for the transfer to be recorded. For example, in California, even though transfers to a living trust don't trigger a new appraisal, the transfer must be reported on a "Preliminary Change of Ownership" form, available at County Recorders offices.

If I'm over 55, do I keep my one-time federal tax benefits if I sell the home I live in after I've placed it in a living trust?

Yes. If you're over 55, you have the right, under Internal Revenue Code § 121, to sell your principal home once and exclude $125,000 of capital gains from income taxation, even if you have transferred that home to a living trust. And you also retain your rights to defer or "roll over" all profits from the sale of one home by using that gain to purchase another within 24 months of the sale.

Will I lose the homestead on my home if I transfer it to a living trust?[1]

Generally, no. State homestead protections, which typically protect a homeowner's equity interest in a home from creditors up to a designated amount, should not be lost because real estate is transferred to a living trust. However, if you're in debt and concerned that a creditor may try to force a sale of your house, check your state's homestead rules carefully. If you are not seriously in debt, there is no need to worry about this one.

2. Moving

Does my living trust remain legal and valid if I move to a different state after establishing it?

Yes. Revocable living trusts are valid and used in every state. However, as discussed in Chapter 3, Section D, if you're married, and you move from a

[1] A "homestead" is a legal device, available under the laws of most states, to protect your equity in your home, up to a statutorily specified amount, from creditors. In some states that allow homesteads, you record a Declaration of Homestead with the County Recorder; in others, the protection is automatic. In either case, if you qualify for a homestead, your home is protected against forced sale by creditors (other than mortgage holders) if your equity is below the statutory limit. If your equity is larger than the amount protected by the homestead laws, the house can be sold, but in many states you get that protected amount to invest in another house.

community property state to a common law state, or vice versa, you may want to check the marital property ownership laws of your new state to make sure that the property you believe is yours really is.

3. Gift Tax

Do I make a legal gift, possibly subject to a gift tax, when I transfer my property to my living trust?

No. Since your living trust can be revoked at any time before you die, you don't make a gift simply by transferring property to the trust. Therefore, no federal or state gift tax can be assessed. (See Chapter 16 for a discussion of gift taxes.)

4. Selling or Refinancing Property That Is in a Living Trust

Will it be difficult for me to sell or refinance property that I have transferred to my living trust?

No. If you decide to sell or refinance property owned by your trust, you can either:

- sell or refinance the property directly out of the trust. Title to all trust real estate should be held in the name of the trustee "as trustee for the [name] living trust." Acting in your capacity as trustee, you sign the title document or otherwise authorize the sale by completing a bill of sale, sales contract or other document. The trustee powers clause in most living trust forms specifically provides that the trustee has the power to sell or refinance trust property, including real estate and stocks or bonds; or
- in your capacity as trustee of the living trust, first transfer title of the particular item listed as trust property back to yourself as an individual, from yourself as trustee, and then sell or refinance the property in your own name.

Whichever way is most convenient is the one to use. When selling or refinancing real estate owned by a trust, what is most convenient is generally what the title company involved requests.

You should amend your revocable living trust if real estate given in that document to a particular trust beneficiary is no longer owned by the trustee for the trust. Obviously no document can validly give away what you don't own. (Amending living trusts is discussed in Section E4 of this chapter.)

D. Major Decisions in Creating a Living Trust

Okay, enough general information. Now let's focus on the key decisions you will need to make to create your trust, whether you prepare a revocable living trust designed to avoid probate yourself, or with the help of a lawyer.

Initially, you (the grantor or grantors) must make four major decisions:

1. What property will be in the trust?
2. Who will be the successor trustee(s), with the authority to manage the property if you are no longer competent to do so, and transfer the property in the trust to your beneficiaries after your death? (You'll be the initial trustee(s), to serve while you are alive and competent.)
3. Who will be your beneficiaries?
4. How will any debts and taxes outstanding at your death be paid?

1. Choosing Property to Put in the Living Trust

You can place all your property in your living trust, or transfer some, or even most, of your property by other means, such as a will or joint tenancy. But in general, if you decide to use a living trust to avoid probate, it's sensible to transfer all your "big-ticket" items to it, unless they are subject to another probate avoidance technique. For example, if you and your spouse already own your house in joint tenancy, you've already arranged to avoid probate of the house.

Example 1: Mr. and Mrs. Tramsey share ownership of a house with an equity of $150,000, held in joint tenancy, personal possessions worth $20,000, U.S. Government bonds worth $40,000, stock worth $100,000, two cars worth $20,000 each, and a joint savings account with $20,000 in it. Each wants to leave his or her half of the house, personal possessions, cars and stocks and bonds to the other. As the house is already in joint tenancy, the survivor will become the sole owner free of probate. To take care of the personal possessions, stock, bonds and cars, the Tramseys decide to create a revocable living trust.

However, when it comes to their savings account, they both decide that, at death, each will leave his or her half directly to their son, not to the surviving spouse. They learn that the simplest way to transfer bank accounts outside of probate is by using what's called an informal bank trust account, or "pay-on-death account." (We discuss this device in Chapter 11, Pay-on-Death Designations, Section A.) So, the Tramseys divide the money in their joint savings account in half, and each spouse then creates a separate pay-on-death account for their half, naming their son as beneficiary, to receive the money in that account when he or she dies.

Example 2: Violet McKensie, who lives in California, owns a house worth $200,000, a stock account, a car worth $12,000 and personal possessions worth $15,000. After reading Chapter 13, Section D, she learns that, under California law, she can transfer personal property worth up to $60,000 (with no need to count amounts transferred by probate avoidance devices) by her will free of probate.[2]

Violet decides to transfer her house and stock account by a living trust, thus avoiding probate on these items. Violet also understands that it is wise to have a back-up will (she plays the lottery occasionally, and who knows?). Since she plans to prepare a will anyway, she decides to use it for her car and personal possessions. One reason why Violet decides it makes sense to transfer her car by her will rather than by her living trust is that transferring title of the car to the living trust would require a trip to the Department of Motor Vehicles, something that experience in seemingly endless lines has taught is best avoided if possible. Also, she'd have to check with her insurance company to be sure it would continue her insurance if her car were technically owned by her trust—another hassle she'd prefer to avoid. And insurance companies are wary, at least, of insuring a car owned by a trust, or the trustee of a trust.

2. Choosing the Trustees of Your Living Trust

You must make two choices when it comes to naming a trustee to manage the trust property: who will be the initial trustee, and who will take over as the successor trustee when the first trustee dies or becomes incapacitated.

a. Your Initial Trustee

As discussed, the initial trustee of your living trust is usually you, the person (or, in a marital trust, the people) who set it up. Grasping this point is, of course, essential to understanding what a living trust

[2] Exemptions to probate are substantially lower in most other states. See Chapter 13, State Law Exemptions.

is—a device by which you continue to absolutely control your own property while you are alive, and at the same time you arrange to avoid probate of the property after you die.

With a marital living trust, both spouses (or members of the couple) are normally co-trustees. When one spouse dies, the other spouse continues as sole trustee.

One spouse as trustee. It's possible, but very unusual, to have only one spouse be the original trustee of a marital living trust. This option is not covered by the Nolo self-help materials mentioned previously, and you should see a lawyer.

Naming someone else as initial trustee. If you want to name someone besides yourself to be your initial trustee because you don't want to, or cannot, continue to manage your own assets, you again go beyond the scope of Nolo's self-help materials, and you should see a lawyer. When you make somebody else your initial trustee, you usually create a more complicated trust, often necessitating much more detailed controls on the trustee's powers to act. In addition, under IRS rules, if you aren't the trustee of your own living trust, separate trust records must be maintained, and a fiduciary trust tax return filed. However, completing this return need not be onerous, since all the IRS requires is filing the face page of this fiduciary return (Form #1041) and a summary listing of items of trust income and expense. These items are actually reported on the trust creator's regular 1040 income tax return.

b. Your Successor Trustee

In addition to naming yourself, or yourselves, as initial trustee(s), it's essential that you name at least one successor trustee. Your successor is the person who makes your trust work after you die, by distributing its assets to your beneficiaries. Also, the successor trustee is often authorized to take over management of the trust if you (or you and your spouse, with a shared marital trust) become incapacitated. This is a standard provision to avoid the need for court proceedings to manage property placed in the trust. (Chapter 26, Incapacity: Health Care and Financial Management Directives, discusses how you can create a durable power of attorney to choose someone to be responsible to handle property not held in your living trust should you become incapacitated.)

With a shared marital trust, the successor trustee takes over after both spouses die.

When you decide on your successor trustee, your job isn't done. You should also name an alternate successor trustee, in case the successor trustee dies before you do or for any other reason can't serve.

c. The Job of the Successor Trustee

To sensibly choose your successor trustee, you should understand what he or she will need to do under a living trust. The primary job of the successor trustee is to turn trust property over to the beneficiaries you have named. This is normally not difficult if the property and beneficiaries are clearly identified. Still, some effort is required.

Normally, the successor trustee obtains several certified copies of the death certificate of the grantor. Then she presents a copy of the death certificate and a copy of the living trust document, along with proof of her own identity, to financial institutions, brokers and other organizations having possession of the trust assets. If any documents of title must be prepared to transfer trust property to the beneficiaries, the successor trustee prepares them. For example, real estate owned by the trustee of a living trust is transferred to the beneficiaries, after the death of the grantor, by the successor trustee preparing, signing and recording (in the County Recorder's office) the following documents:

1. a deed from herself, as trustee of the living trust, to the specified beneficiaries, and

2. a declaration of death of the original trustee (the grantor) and assumption of trustee duties by the successor trustee.

No court or other administrative action is required.

What happens if an institution won't cooperate with the successor trustee? Happily, this is unlikely to happen. Institutions that deal with financial assets—from title companies to recorder's offices to stock brokers—are familiar with living trusts and how they work.

In addition to dealing with property subject to formal ownership (title) documents, the trustee supervises the distribution of all trust assets without documents of title—household furnishings, jewelry, heirlooms, collectibles—to the appropriate beneficiaries. The distribution process ends when all beneficiaries have actually received the trust property given to them in the trust document.

In some situations, additional tasks may be required of the successor trustee:

Preparing and filing death tax returns. If a death tax return (state, federal or both) must be filed, and death tax paid, the successor trustee is responsible for these tasks. (See Chapter 15 for a discussion of federal and state death tax.) If, as we strongly recommend, you also prepare a back-up will (see Chapter 14, Wills, Section A), the executor you name in the will shares legal responsibility for filing these tax returns. Since, usually, you will appoint the same person as the successor trustee and executor, the same person, in two different capacities, has the responsibility to file any death tax returns required by law.

Managing money left to minors. As mentioned, you can use the Uniform Transfers to Minors Act or create children's trusts as a component of your living trust. If you die before any child reaches the age you've specified in either legal device to receive property outright, the person you have named as a custodian (if you use the UTMA) or a named trustee (if you use a child's trust) will manage trust property left for the benefit of that child until she reaches that age. But if you go the child's trust route, income tax returns are required for each operational children's trust, and are the responsibility of the successor trustee.

The duties and burdens of a successor trustee who manages a children's trust can be substantial. The trust can last for decades and entail extensive financial responsibilities. If you have more than one minor beneficiary, the job can become even more demanding, as each minor's property can be managed in a separate trust.

d. Whom Should You Choose to Be the Successor Trustee for Your Living Trust?

Your successor trustee should be whomever you feel is most trustworthy to do the job, who's willing to do it, and can actually do it. Often a principal beneficiary, such as a spouse or adult child, is named as successor trustee. However, you aren't compelled to name a beneficiary as trustee. If you believe the beneficiary (much as you love him or her) will be troubled by having to handle the practical details and paperwork, it is preferable to name someone else, often another family member, to be successor trustee.

When you prepare a back-up will, the person you name as executor should be the same as your successor trustee. This eliminates any possible conflict that might arise if a different person fulfills each function.

If for some reason you want to name a person to be the successor trustee of your living trust and another to be the executor of your will, you should consult a lawyer.

Naming someone other than your spouse as successor trustee of a marital living trust. With a shared marital living trust, you both choose a successor trustee to take over after both spouses die. If you want someone other than a surviving spouse to be trustee for a deceased spouse's portion of a marital living trust, see a lawyer, because this raises many complexities and possible coordination problems between the surviving spouse and the other trustee.

e. Naming Co-Trustees

What about the idea of naming two successor trustees to serve together to wind up your living trust if you die or if you become mentally incapacitated, and thus unable to manage trust property? Legally, you can name as many successor co-trustees as you want, with power divided between them as you specify. However, as a rule, because of coordination and possible conflict problems between multiple trustees, it's generally best to name a single successor trustee. This isn't invariably true, however. For example, a parent may not want to be seen as favoring one child over others, and to avoid this could name two or more children as successor co-trustees. This can be especially appropriate if the children are equal beneficiaries of the trust. And if the children all get along, doing this rarely causes a problem. However, if the children are prone to conflict, you risk creating a serious problem (and doing none of them a favor) by having them share power as trustees. It's better just to name the most qualified and let the chips fall as they will.

Methods for handling potential conflicts between co-successors. If you're naming successor co-trustees, and have any fear of potential conflicts between them, see a lawyer. Such situations are too touchy to resolve without careful individual analysis. Methods a lawyer may recommend can include a provision that if there is a dispute, it be resolved by compulsory arbitration or perhaps simply that one identified trustee shall prevail.

f. Naming a Bank or Financial Institution as Successor Trustee

In our experience, it is usually a bad idea to name a bank or financial institution as successor trustee. There are plenty of horror stories involving the indifference or downright rapaciousness of banks acting as trustees of family living trusts. Think of it this way: Your successor trustee is your link with the ongoing life of your loved ones. You want that link to be a human being you trust, not a corporation dedicated to the enhancement of its bottom line. However, if there is no human being you believe will act honestly and competently as your successor trustee, and after reviewing the other probate avoidance devices discussed in this book, you are still determined to establish a living trust, you'll need to select some financial institution to do the job. Probably the best choice here is a private trust company. These companies generally offer more humane and personal attention to a trust than a bank or other large financial institution. Also, they can be more reasonable about fees charged to wind up a living trust than a bank is.

g. Should the Successor Trustee Be Paid?

Usually the successor trustee of a living trust isn't paid when the only purpose of the trust is probate avoidance, especially if the successor trustee is also a primary beneficiary. After all, the task of transferring assets to beneficiaries is not arduous and, in many instances, the successor trustee is one of the major beneficiaries.

However, trustees of ongoing, operational trusts (see Chapter 17, Ongoing Trusts: An Overview, Section E), which are often combined with a living trust, are often paid for their work as trustee. For example, since the trustee of the trust for a disabled person might have to manage property for some time, it seems fair to provide "reasonable compensation" for the trustee for doing this job, because it entails ongoing management responsibilities.

Of course, if the trustee is both a close family member or friend and financially comfortable, this may not be appropriate. If the possibility of compensation is provided, the living trust normally allows the trustee to decide what is a reasonable fee for these services. Since you wouldn't appoint this person in the first place unless she was highly trustworthy, this approach normally works fine. But if you're uneasy at this open-ended provision for compensation, a lawyer can prepare more limiting terms for payment of a trustee. But make sure that your trustee agrees on the method, or rate of compensation, you've chosen.

h. The Powers of the Trustee

A trustee of a trust must have a written authority defining what he can do. The legalese for this is "trust powers." Most living trust forms contain a broad general grant of powers to the trustees to transfer property to adult beneficiaries or institutions. A simple probate avoidance trust usually has no need for more than this, although some lawyers will include pages more of specific trustee powers.

3. Naming the Beneficiaries of Your Living Trust

Beneficiaries, of course, are simply the people or organizations you've chosen to receive your property after you die. You can select anyone you want to be beneficiaries for your living trust. And you can leave each beneficiary whatever trust property you want to. We've discussed choosing your beneficiaries in Chapter 5. Here we focus on the different classes of beneficiaries you can name in your living trust.

It's okay to explain why you are making—or not making—a gift. If you want to explain your gift intentions or feelings to your beneficiaries in your living trust, you can do this directly in your living trust document. Or you can also prepare a letter to accompany your living trust. This letter is not a valid legal document, and cannot be used to transfer any property. But to convey your thoughts and feelings, a letter works fine.

a. Direct Beneficiaries

Direct beneficiaries are those people you name to receive some trust property when you die. These include:

- The adult beneficiaries you name to receive their trust property promptly after your death.
- Minor beneficiaries who have their property retained in a children's trust until they reach the age you've specified for them to receive it.
- The young adult beneficiaries you choose to leave property through a children's trust.
- Beneficiaries you leave property to using your state's Uniform Transfers to Minors Act (if it's applicable in your state—see list in Chapter 6, Children, Section C).

Some people ask whether it's permissible to name only one beneficiary who also is the successor trustee. The answer is yes.

Example: Nikki, a widow, establishes a living trust. She transfers her house and personal possessions to the trust and name her adult daughter, Christine, as beneficiary. Christine is also named as successor trustee. After her mother dies, Christine puts on her successor trustee hat and executes a deed transferring the house out of the trust to herself, wearing her beneficiary hat.

b. Alternate Beneficiaries

For each item of property your living trust gives to a direct beneficiary, you can name an alternate beneficiary to receive that gift if the direct beneficiary dies before you do.

c. Residuary Beneficiary

You can name a person (or people) or organization(s) to receive all trust property not specifically given to a direct beneficiary or alternate beneficiary alive at your death. You can also name an alternate residuary beneficiary. The residuary beneficiary or alternate receives only property in the trust not given to another beneficiary. A trust residuary beneficiary cannot receive any property outside of the trust.

d. Beneficiaries of a Marital Living Trust

In a shared marital living trust, each spouse can name her or his own beneficiaries, alternate beneficiaries, residuary beneficiary and minor beneficiaries. Often, each spouse names the other as the sole beneficiary, with their children as alternate beneficiaries. In other situations, people may wish to divide their property between their spouse and children. Particularly if a spouse or spouses have a child or children from prior relationships, each spouse may want to name his or her own children as beneficiaries for some or all of their property. (See Chapter 23, Trusts for Second or Subsequent Marriages.) And of course, no matter how many times married, a spouse may want to make at least some gifts to people other than the other spouse and children—for example, him to his cousins, her to her sisters. No problem—spouses can name as many beneficiaries as they want.

Example 1: Malcolm and Ursula create a shared living trust. They have been married for 30 years; neither was previously married. They have one child, a daughter, Suzanne.

Each spouse leaves the bulk of his and her property to the other. Each also makes some smaller gifts to family relations, friends and charities. Both name Suzanne as their alternate beneficiary, and residuary beneficiary. They both name Suzanne's husband, Tom, as each of their alternate residuary beneficiary.

Example 2: Valerie and Eric create a shared living trust. They have been married for 18 years. They have two children, Meg and Marion. Valerie also has a child, Jarvis, from a prior marriage.

Valerie leaves most of her property to Eric, and the rest in a child's trust for Jarvis, age 21. She names Meg and Marion as co-alternate beneficiaries for all gifts, and also as co-residuary beneficiaries.

Eric leaves all his property to Valerie and names Meg and Marion as co-alterate beneficiaries, and also co-residuary beneficiaries.

4. Arranging for Your Debts and Taxes to Be Paid

Many people won't leave any significant debts or have any substantial income or death tax obligations when they die. If you fit into this category, you can go on to other concerns. However, if you will likely leave debts, including death tax obligations, and don't make provision to pay them, any of your property may be taken to pay for them.

As a general rule, if your debts are likely to be small, little planning is required. When you die, your successor trustee will pay whatever bills you have, and your estate accumulates, either from property you specified in your trust for this purpose, or from trust property generally. In either case, as debts are small, no beneficiary will suffer a substantial loss. If you have larger debts, including estate tax obligations, more planning is required.

Here's what can be involved.

a. Assessing Your Debts

When estimating your debts, don't include the kinds of obligations that are directly tied to specific items of property, such as the mortgage on a house or money owed on a car.[3] When you make a gift of these items, the debt on them goes right along. So, if you leave your house, which is subject to a mortgage, to your son, he gets both the house and the mortgage. These kinds of debts do not have to be paid off by your estate at death, unless you create a specific provision to do so in your living trust or will, and identify assets to be used for paying them.

Your estate will also be liable for any federal estate tax or state death tax assessed against your property. Your estate is liable for all other (unsecured) debts, which include such things as personal bank loans, court judgments and unpaid credit card balances. In adding up your debts, also consider funeral expenses and the possibility that you will incur expenses of a last illness. Many people prepay the former, and have insurance which covers the latter, but if any of these expenses aren't taken care of in other ways, your living trust property can be liable for these debts.

b. Do Death Taxes Have to Be Paid?

Before you worry about how your death tax will be paid, you need to learn whether you're likely to owe any. If the net worth of your estate is less than $600,000 when you die, there will be no federal

[3] These are usually called "secured debts" in legal parlance, and typically exist in situations when a creditor would have the right to repossess (foreclose on) the property if the debt isn't paid.

estate tax (unless you've made large gifts (taxable) during your life. (See Chapter 15, Estate Taxes, and Chapter 16, Gifts and Gift Taxes.) Also, all property, no matter how much it is worth, transferred to a surviving spouse is free of federal estate tax.

A majority of states, including California and Florida, impose no death tax. Other states do impose death tax; the minimum amount taxed and the tax rates vary substantially from state to state. In some states, whether a tax is imposed depends not only on the value of the estate, but who it is given to. (We provide state tax information in Chapter 15, Estate Taxes, Section C.)

c. Choosing Assets to Pay Debts and Taxes

Unless you plan to leave all, or the great bulk of, your estate to one person (say your spouse), in which case that person will be responsible to pay any debts or taxes as they see fit, you may want to designate specific assets to be used to pay them, especially if your estate is large. This can be done in a living trust simply by specifying which trust assets are to be used to pay debts—just make sure the assets are worth enough to cover all debts.

If you have substantial debts and/or tax liabilities, it's often a good idea to list several assets that are clearly large enough to cover their payment. Another approach is to list the order in which you want these assets used to pay debts and taxes. But no matter how you approach it, make sure you have provided enough cash—or property that can be turned into cash—to do the job. If you don't, all—or a portion of—your specific gifts to loved ones can be taken to pay these obligations.

Example: When she prepares her estate plan, Ms. de Soirée has several large debts totaling, roughly, $50,000. She also has substantial assets. Her living trust provides that her debts are to be paid from an identified trust stock account (presently worth $70,000). If that account proves to be insufficient, the remaining debts are to be paid from an identified trust savings account, with a current balance of $20,000.

When Ms. de Soirée dies, her debts total $96,000. The stock account is liquidated for $54,000. The savings account holds $29,000. The total amount in the specified property is $83,000, which is $13,000 less than her debts. Because Ms. de Soirée has not specified which additional property is to be used to pay her debts, her successor trustee can use any trust property she wants to pay this additional $13,000. This means the successor trustee can take the entire $13,000 from a gift to one beneficiary. There is no general legal requirement that this debt be pro-rated between the value of gifts to different beneficiaries. If you want that, you have to specify it in your living trust document.

Assuming you wish to designate specific assets to pay your debts, the best general rule is to select liquid assets over non-liquid ones. Liquid assets are those that are easily converted into cash. For instance, bank and deposit accounts, money market accounts and stocks and bonds can normally be converted to cash easily and at full value. By comparison, it's less desirable to designate tangible assets, such as cars, planes, jewelry, stamp and coin collections, electronic items and musical instruments, to be sold to raise the necessary cash to pay debts and taxes. Forced sales (often called "fire sales" or "distress sales") seldom bring in anywhere near the full value of the items sold; it's common to only receive 30%-50% of the item's full value. In short, if your successor trustee will have to sell tangible assets to pay your debts and expenses, the overall value of your estate will be reduced both by the costs of sale and the fact that full value will not likely be received.

When designating property to use to pay debts and taxes, review your specific gifts. Obviously, if property you select to pay debts and taxes is also earmarked for a specific beneficiary, that beneficiary is likely to feel slighted. For this reason, it is usually advisable to designate property that hasn't been left as a specific gift to pay debts and expenses. Or, if you do designate property that has been left to a specific person, make sure you have left them enough other property so that their entire inheritance isn't wiped out.

E. Preparing Your Living Trust

Some people have a lawyer prepare their living trust. If your estate plan calls for combining a living trust with one or more ongoing trusts designed to minimize taxes, it's likely you'll need a lawyer to prepare these trusts for you. But other people can safely prepare living trusts themselves, using Denis's book *Make Your Own Living Trust*, or Nolo's *Living Trust Maker* (computer program). Using either of these Nolo resources, many single people, or couples, with a (combined) estate of under $600,000 (to remind you, the federal estate tax threshold) can safely prepare a basic probate-avoidance living trust themselves, without an attorney. Further, many couples with a combined estate worth between $600,000 and $1,200,000, who decide they are good candidates for the tax savings made possible by creating a marital life estate trust (often called an "AB" trust), will find they can safely do this using *Make Your Own Living Trust*. Finally, these people can use these Nolo resources to educate themselves about living trusts or to prepare a draft trust, but also hire a lawyer to prepare the final version of their trust.

However, you decide to proceed, there are some basic steps you must follow:

1. Prepare your living trust document.

2. Have it notarized.

3. Transfer title to property into the name of your trustee (that is, you) as trustee for your living trust.

1. Preparing Your Living Trust

A living trust document is simply some sheets of paper that contain the terms and provisions of your living trust. In this document, you name the trustee(s) and successor trustee(s), your beneficiaries, and define what trust property is given to which beneficiaries. To help do this, you make a list (called a "schedule") of all property you have transferred to the trust.

To sensibly list your property on a schedule, you obviously need to identify each item of property in a way that your successor trustee and beneficiaries unambiguously know what's referred to. There are no legal rules which require property to be listed in any particular form. The whole point is to be clear as to exactly what property you transfer to the trust. General descriptions of property transferred to the trust are sufficient for listing it on a schedule. Thus, you can list:

- *The house, furnishings, and personal possessions at 1000 Eccles St., Burnfield, Michigan*
- *Bank account #88-124406 at First Savings, Burnfield.*
- *Securities Account #1344-0082, Flywheel & Flywheel, Stockbrokers, Ann Arbor, Michigan.*

When you name the beneficiaries for particular items of trust property, your gifts must, of course, be consistent with the property listed on the schedule. But your schedule listing does not automatically have to be as detailed as your gifts. For example, as just stated, you list, "The house, furnishings and personal possessions at [street address]" on the schedule. You can give all this property to one beneficiary, or you could divide it, naming one beneficiary for the house and another for the furnishings and possessions.

Normally, a living trust for a single person contains only one schedule.

Example: Mrs. Johnson wants to transfer her house, three different stock accounts, her valuable antiques and her jewelry to her living trust. She can list all this property on one trust schedule, "A."

Shared marital life estate trusts typically contain up to three schedules, one for shared property, one for the wife's separate property (if any), and one for the husband's separate property (likewise).

Example: Mrs. and Mr. Andrezly, in their 60s, have been married for 15 years. Each has children from a former marriage. When they got married, each owned property which they agreed would remain each's separate property. Since they have been married, they have acquired shared property, including a home. Each wants his or her separate property to go to their children from the first marriage and their shared property to go to the survivor. One simple way to list their property in the marital living trust is by using three schedules: Schedule A for the shared property, Schedule B for Mrs. Andrezly's separate property, and Schedule C for Mr. Andrezly's separate property. Another approach is to create three separate trusts—a marital living trust for the shared marital property and two living trusts for each spouse's separate property. If the Andrezlys did this, they would use only a Schedule A in the marital trust for their shared marital property.

Once your final living trust document is prepared, you (individually or both members of a couple) must sign and date the document in front of a notary, who then notarizes it. The document does not have to be witnessed.

2. Transferring Title of Trust Property Into the Trustee's Name

Your successor trustee can't transfer property to your beneficiaries that is not properly registered as being owned by the trust. To achieve this, you register title to trust property, if the item has a title document, in the trustee's name, as "trustee for the [named] trust." So, an essential step in making your trust effective is to transfer ownership (title) of property to the trustee.

If you decide to prepare your own living trust, the Nolo living trust resources provide thorough instructions on how to transfer different types of property into your trust. This will require some effort on your part—preparing new title documents, recording them if need be (as with real estate), and making sure the transfer actually occurs (which can sometime require several phone calls, for instance, to a slow-moving financial institution). Yet, this work is certainly manageable. It is not technical, nor does it require any special training or skills, beyond what you can acquire from Nolo resources.

Here we discuss what is involved in transferring title to major types of property into the trust. Many estate planning lawyers insist that they do this work. They don't necessarily do this to raise their fees—though that is one result. Many believe that a client can't be entirely relied upon to do the job right, and don't want to accept any risk that property won't be correctly transferred to the trust. But some attorneys do permit knowledgeable clients to do their own transfers, thus reducing the bill. Certainly this is an issue you should be able to discuss with your attorney. And even if your attorney insists on doing this work, it's sensible for you to understand what's involved, so you'll have a sense of whether he's charging a fair price for this work or not.

For the purposes of transferring title into the trustee's name, there are two types of property—those with ownership (title) documents and those without. Each type of property is treated differently when it comes to transferring it to your living trust.

a. Property Without Ownership (Title) Documents

Many types of property don't have title documents, including all kinds of household possessions and furnishings, clothing, jewelry, furs, tools, most farm equipment, antiques, electronic and computer equipment, art works, bearer bonds, cash, precious metals, and collectibles. You transfer these items to the trust simply by listing them on a trust schedule. Or you can use a "Notice of Assignment" form, a simple document that states that the property listed on it has been transferred to the trustee's name. "Notice of Assignment" forms can be obtained at some stationery stores or legal supply stores. These forms are also available in *Make Your Own Living Trust*, by Clifford (Nolo Press).

Example: Ms. Rotzinski lists on Schedule A: "All household goods and furnishings previously owned by the grantor." On the same schedule, she also lists her jewelry: "The gold bracelet, two star-sapphire pendants, and gold Huntingcase watch in possession of the grantor." She doesn't need to do anything else to legally transfer her household possessions, furnishings, and jewelry to the trust. But she can also use a Notice of Assignment form, listing each major item, and transferring the property to herself, as trustee of her trust. Of course, she will need to use one or more beneficiary clauses to actually give these items to a beneficiary.

b. Property With Ownership (Title) Documents

After the trust document has been signed and notarized, it is vital that all items of trust property that have ownership documents (title papers) be registered in the trustee's name.

The types of property owned by the trust which must have title documents re-registered in the trustee's name include:

- real estate, including condominiums and cooperatives
- bank accounts
- stocks and stock accounts
- most bonds, including U.S. Government Securities
- corporations/limited partnerships/partnerships
- money market accounts
- mutual funds
- safety deposit boxes
- vehicles, including cars, most boats, motor homes, and planes.

INSURANCE, IRAs, PROFIT SHARING PLANS AND OTHER PROPERTY NAMING A LIVING TRUST AS BENEFICIARY DON'T HAVE TO BE RE-REGISTERED

You do not have to re-register title for the types of property where you simply name the trust itself as beneficiary to receive specified property after you die. For example, if you want your living trust to receive your life insurance policy, IRA and Profit Sharing Plan, you do, of course, have to be sure the trust, or successor trustee, has been properly designated as the beneficiary. But you do not transfer ownership of the policy, IRA or Profit Sharing Plan accounts into the trustee's name. While you live, the trust, through the trustee, is not the legal owner of these types of property; you, personally, remain the legal owner. The trust is simply who you've named to receive benefits payable on your death—life insurance proceeds, or the balance in your IRA or profit sharing plan accounts. Since the trust never owned the insurance policy, IRA and Profit Sharing Plan, these assets were, of course, not listed on a trust schedule.

Don't delay transferring property to your living trust. Property subject to a title document (houses. land, securities, cars) must be transferred to the living trust promptly after the trust is prepared. The new ownership document of title must show that the trustee of the trust—not you, individually—is the legal owner of the property. Your living trust won't be effective for any property with an ownership document (title slip) which is not re-registered in the trustee's name.

If title to property listed on the trust schedules remains in your name (someone has failed to re-register it), that property will pass under the terms of your back-up will.[4] Since trust property isn't usually listed in this type of will, it will go to the residuary beneficiary, who, of course, may not be the person whom you intended to receive it. If you have no will, property not transferred to the trust will be left under the terms of your state's intestate succession law. In either case, it will be subject to all the expense and delay of probate—the very things you are trying to avoid.

Example: Ms. Dee Kaloia creates a living trust and lists her stock brokerage account on Schedule A, as trust property. In the trust document, she gives this stock account to her daughter. However, she never notifies her stock broker to re-register ownership of the account in the name of "Ms. Dee Kaloia, as trustee for The Kaloia Trust." When she dies, her successor trustee will be unable to successfully transfer the account to the daughter. The brokerage company will say to the successor trustee "We don't show that account owned by any living trust. It's owned by a Ms. Kaloia, and you have no legal authority to collect her assets." Thus, the account must pass by her will (assuming she has one) and go through probate, or pass to an inheritor designated by state law, which also requires probate.

[4] There is a California case, *Estate of Heggstad,* 16 Cal. App. 3rd 943 (1993), holding that simply stating in the trust document itself that real estate is transferred to the trustee is sufficient to legally get that property into the trust. However, this is not at all accepted practice, and many well not be legal in other states. Anyway, who wants to risk a court proceeding to have their living trust become effective? So don't make waves here. Transfer the property into the trust as it's traditionally done.

c. Real Estate (Real Property)

The term "real estate" includes land, houses, condominiums, cooperatives and any other interest in what lawyers call "real property." To transfer title of a piece of real estate to a living trust, you sign a new deed listing the trustee of the trust as the new owner of the property. Then that deed must be notarized and recorded at your local land records office. This isn't difficult, although it does involve some leg work. (This process is set out in far more depth in *The Deeds Book,* Mary Randolph (Nolo Press). This book specifically applies to California deeds, but much of the information it contains applies in any state.)

Here are the basics. You must:

- Locate your existing deed.
- Complete a quitclaim or grant deed form[5] deeding the property from yourself to yourself, or yourselves, as trustee(s) of your living trust.

Examples:

Janice Kingsley locates her old deed, which lists her as "Janice P. Kingsley." She would deed her property from "Janice P. Kingsley" to "Janice P. Kingsley, as trustee of The Janice P. Kingsley Trust."

Mary and Paul Jones' old deed identifies them as "Mary Meg Jones and Paul Mellon Jones, Tenants in Common." They list themselves in exactly these words on the new deed, transferring the real estate to "Mary Meg Jones and Paul Mellon Jones, as trustees of The Mary and Paul Jones Trust."

[5] A quitclaim deed is a simple deed form, where you transfer whatever ownership you have in real estate, without making any promises or guarantees of ownership. Since you are transferring your property from yourself to your trust, you're not worried about guarantees. Other types of deeds where guarantees are made are called "warranty" or "grant" deeds. These can safely be used as well.

d. Transferring Partial Ownership

If you share ownership of real estate with anyone except a spouse, it's wise to check with a title company to learn how it recommends you transfer title of your interest into a living trust. While you could simply deed "all [your] interest..." to the trust, some title companies prefer a transfer approved by all owners.

e. Stock Market or Mutual Fund Accounts

To register stocks, bonds, or mutual fund accounts in your trust's, or the trustee's, name, you can ask your broker or money fund officer what is required. Usually, they require a copy of the trust with your notarized signature for their files, and a letter instructing them to register the account in the trust name. They should then confirm in writing to you that this has been done.

If you have personal possession of the stock certificates or bonds (most people don't), you will need to get new certificates issued, listing the trustee of your living trust as owner. Your broker may be willing to do it for you. If your broker won't help, get another who will, or deal directly with the "transfer agent" of the corporation. Your broker (or the corporation) can tell you who this is. Ask the transfer agent for instructions, which will likely involve sending in your share certificates or bonds, a stock power, and a copy of the trust, and asking that new certificates or bonds be issued in the trustee's name.

Mutual Funds: Mutual funds should be re-registered in the name of the trustee of your living trust (that is, yourself, or yourselves) by communicating with the company and meeting its requirements. These normally consist of sending a letter of instructions (or form which they provide) and a copy of the trust.

Government Securities: To re-register T-Bills and other government and U.S. bonds, notes, bills and securities in the trustee's name, you must contact the appropriate government office directly (or, have your broker do it).

f. Bank Accounts

Title to bank accounts can be readily transferred to the trustee's name simply by completing the appropriate bank form. Before you decide to transfer bank accounts into your trust's name, be sure you've checked out whether you'd rather use an informal "pay-on-death" bank trust account, as described in Chapter 4, Pay-on-Death Designation, Section A. With this type of account, you name a beneficiary (who can be anyone you choose, including your living trust) on the account form, to receive the funds in the account after you die; the account itself remains in your name. This can be particularly desirable for your personal checking account used to pay normal bills, because most people don't want to hold that account—and its checks—in the name of a living trust.

g. Limited Partnerships

Limited partnerships are a form of investment, governed by securities laws. To re-register a limited partnership interest in a trust name, contact the general partner's office and see what documentation is needed.

h. Business Interests

A living trust can be a good way to transfer business interests to beneficiaries, since the hassles and delays of probate can be extremely damaging to a business. Transferring title to a business depends on the form of ownership.

- An unincorporated, solely-owned business is easiest to transfer. Since there is no title document for the business itself, all that needs be done is list the business on a trust schedule. Then, any ancillary title documents of property owned by the business, such as real estate, must be re-registered in the trustee's name.
- Stock in a solely-owned corporation can be transferred by preparing the appropriate corporate records, transferring ownership to the trust, and then re-registering the share certificates in the trust's name.
- An owner's interest in a shared business partnership or corporation is the most complicated to re-register in the trust's name. First, the partnership agreement or corporate by-laws must be checked to be sure they permit transfer of an owner's interest to a living trust. Then, the appropriate records authorizing the transfer must be prepared, and signed by all required to approve the transfer. Finally, the title document—corporate shares or partnership certificate (if there is one)—must be re-registered in the trust's name.

Often the complicated part of a living trust for a business is arranging for continuity and management of the business after the owner's death. (This is discussed in Chapter 28, Business Ownership and Estate Planning.)

i. Motor Vehicles

Before you decide to transfer your vehicle by trust, check out your state's special probate avoidance transfer laws to see if you can use your will to transfer your car outside of normal probate. (See Chapter 13, State Law Exemptions From Normal Probate.) This will save you from having to deal now with the Department of Motor Vehicles, and the hassles that inevitably entails. Also, is your car really worth enough to bother? Many cars are financed, and aren't that significant an asset to warrant placing in a trust. Finally, you have to check with your insurance company to be sure they'll continue your insurance if the car is technically owned by your trust. Many insurance companies are reluctant to insure cars owned by a living trust, claiming they can't be sure who are authorized drivers. If after all this, you decide you do want to transfer your motor vehicles by your living trust, and you can get insurance for this, you'll need to contact your state Department of Motor Vehicles and see what form it requires to accomplish this.

j. Other Property With Documents of Title

As stated above, all other property with documents of title which is transferred to a living trust must be re-registered in the trustee's name. For example, if you want to transfer a promissory note to your living trust, complete a "Notice of Assignment," formally placing title to the note in the name of the trustee. (And, of course, you'd also list the promissory note on a trust schedule.) Other types of property which can be assigned to a living trust include patents and copyrights.

3. After Your Trust Is Completed

After your living trust has been completed and all property with documents of title re-registered in the trustee's name, it still requires some attention. Obviously, you need to store it securely. You may also want copies of it. In addition, you obviously need to keep it up-to-date by making necessary changes as you acquire and dispose of major items of property or find that, for one reason or another, your beneficiaries have changed. Again, you can do this technical work or you can have a lawyer do it for you. But a lawyer can't know of changes in your personal life that would result in your wanting, or needing, to amend your living trust—changes such as divorce, marriage, having a child, selling a major trust asset. So you have some responsibility for keeping your trust up-to-date, even if you turn the legal work over to your lawyer. Let's now look at these issues individually.

a. Storing Your Living Trust

It's usually best to store your living trust document with your other important papers. Some people use a safe deposit box jointly owned with their successor trustee for this purpose. Others use a secure place in their home, such as a home safe, fireproof metal box or file cabinet. The important thing is that the successor trustee knows where the trust document is and has fast access to it. Whether you reveal the contents of your living trust to your successor trustee is a personal decision. As you know from reading Chapter 1, Personal Concerns and Estate Planning, we are generally in favor of openness and suggest that you at least let your successor trustee know what's in the trust. After all, he'll find out eventually.

b. Making Copies of Your Living Trust

If you prepare your own living trust, you will need to provide photocopies of your trust to organizations that keep property with ownership (title) documents in order to successfully transfer title to trust property. This includes banks, brokers, mutual funds and limited partnerships. Also, you may decide you want copies for other reasons, such as to give to your successor trustee or beneficiaries. And if you store your original trust document in a safe deposit box, you may want to keep a copy at home. It's fine to make as many copies as you need, as long as there is only one original—that is, one living trust document you have actually signed. You should never sign or notarize any copies. Doing this creates a duplicate original which can raise serious legal problems, especially if you decide to amend or revoke your trust. Photocopying the page of your original living trust with your signature and notary seal is okay, and does not create a duplicate original.

c. Registering Your Trust

The laws of the following states provide that you can or must register your living trust document with the local court: Alaska, Colorado[6], Florida,[7] Hawaii, Idaho, Maine, Michigan, Nebraska[7], North Dakota and Tennessee[8] (applies only to resignation or removal of a trustee.) However, there are no legal consequences or penalties if you don't register your trust. So, for practical purposes, if you live in one of these states it's entirely up to you whether to bother registering your trust or not.

Registration of a living trust with a court doesn't give that court any power over the trust unless there's

---

[6] Registration not required until grantor's death, and no registration required then if all trust property promptly distributed to beneficiaries.

[7] Registration optional.

[8] Registration applies only to resignation or removal of trustee.

a dispute. But if there is a dispute, a lawsuit can always be filed, even if the trust wasn't registered.

To register a living trust, the trustee must file a statement with the court where the trustee resides or keeps records. The statement normally must include:

- the name and address of the trustee
- an acknowledgment of the trusteeship
- the name(s) of the trust grantor(s)
- the name(s) of the original trustee(s)
- the date of the trust document.

4. Amending or Revoking Your Living Trust

A living trust can usually be amended or revoked while the grantor, or grantors, live. However, often a shared living trust document provides that it can only be amended by both spouses, while both are alive. This is to guard against one spouse being able to pull a fast one with trust property in the event of a dispute or divorce. When one spouse dies, his or her portion of the trust becomes binding and irrevocable and the property is distributed according to the trust's terms by the successor trustee. The surviving spouse can now amend or revoke his or her own portion of the trust, like any other single person.

a. Amending a Living Trust

You must amend your living trust by a written document. Usually simply called "Amendment to the [name] Living Trust."

Amendments are usually for simple, clear changes—such as adding a new beneficiary, deleting a beneficiary, changing a successor trustee, or deleting property from the trust. Amendments are not appropriate for making major revisions or wholesale changes in your living trust. Attempting major revisions by amendment creates risks of confusion or inconsistency. To achieve major changes, you need to revoke your trust and prepare a new trust document.

Examples:

Mr. Howard decides he will give his gold coin collection to his (new) friend Ron Kolbert, not to William Boyd. He amends his trust as follows:

1. The following language is added to the trust: Ron Kolbert shall be given the gold coin collection listed on Schedule A, or if Ron Kolbert doesn't survive the grantor, the property shall be given to Mario Martinelli.

2. The following is deleted from the trust: William Boyd shall be given the gold coin collection listed on Schedule A, or, if William Boyd fails to survive the grantor, that property shall be given to Mario Martinelli.

Mr. Howard must then sign and date the amendments before a notary.

Any trust amendment must be notarized. You can give a copy of the amendment to anyone who has a copy of your trust, but this isn't always mandatory. For example, there's usually no reason to give an amendment to a bank or brokerage company which required a copy of your trust to transfer title of an account into the trust's name.

Some people wonder why they can't make amendments to a trust simply by retyping a page on the original document. For example, suppose you want to name a new beneficiary for property listed on your property schedule and eliminate one beneficiary currently listed. Why can't you simply detach the page where the beneficiaries and gifts are listed, have the new information typed on a replacement page and reassemble the pages? The answer is that, as a practical matter, you might very well be able to do this without your trust encountering subsequent legal trouble. But this approach does risk the possibility that someone could challenge the trust on grounds it was improperly altered by making changes after it had been notarized. This is particularly true if an excluded beneficiary is resentful about losing a gift and makes an issue of how the trust was changed. In sum, making "informal" changes is not legally proper, and is unwise.

b. Adding Property to Your Trust

Often, it isn't necessary to formally amend your trust simply to add additional property to it. Many living trust forms specifically give you the right to add "after acquired" property to your trust. You can add property to your trust simply by listing it on the appropriate schedule and transferring title to it (if it has a title document) to the trust's name.

Just because property has been added to your trust does not mean you've provided for who will receive it after your death. So you often need to amend your trust to name the beneficiary for newly added property. There are, however, a couple of important exceptions to this requirement. First, if you've left all the property in the trust to one beneficiary, or to several to share, you don't need to amend your trust to state who receives newly listed property. It will go to the beneficiary(ies) you named to get everything. Likewise, if you want the newly added property to go to the residuary beneficiary, you don't need to amend the trust.

Property added to the trust can be one of two types: property you owned before the trust was created but didn't transfer to the trust, or property you acquired after the trust's creation. In both instances, you need to be sure that if the property has a title document, it appears in the trustee's name. With newly acquired property, you can simply take title in the trustee's name when you get that property; it will automatically become part of the trust. For example, real estate purchased in the name of "Denis Clifford as trustee for The Denis Clifford Trust," would go directly into the trust. Property you previously owned must have title re-registered in the name of the trustee.

c. Revoking Your Living Trust

As long as the grantor or grantors live, she, or they, can revoke a living trust at any time, for any reason. Revocation must be done in a written document, signed by the grantor or grantors. A shared trust can usually be revoked by either spouse any time. The reason either spouse can revoke the marital trust, but it takes both to amend it, is that revocation simply returns both spouses to the status quo. By contrast, in event of divorce or (other) bitter conflict, it's risky to permit one spouse to amend a trust that governs both spouse's property.

If a grantor wants to revoke a trust because a massive overhaul is required to reflect the grantor's current desires and situation, a new trust must be created. This requires a lot of work—as much as went into creating the original, now revoked, trust. The trust should be given a different name than the revoked trust. This can be something as simple as adding a "II" to the old name—for example, "The Denis Clifford Living Trust, II." Or you can change, or add, a date to the new trust—for example, "The Denis Clifford Revocable Living Trust dated Jan. 19, 1992." Then title to all trust property must be re-registered in the name of the trustee of the new trust.

Even if a living trust is revoked, it's rare that a new one isn't created afterwards. After all, the reason a living trust was established in the first place—to avoid probate—certainly hasn't gone away. If a trust is revoked, it ceases to have any legal existence, and property cannot be transferred by it. When a trust is revoked for this reason, you must be sure that you've transferred title to all former trust property back into your own name. Or you could transfer property directly from the old trust to the new trust before you revoke the old one, to save a step.

Because of the work involved, revoking a trust should be a last resort. Most changes in circumstances can be handled by a trust amendment. In our experience, it's not often that a person's situation and desires change so drastically that a new trust need be prepared. But of course, there certainly are those times when revocation is essential, as when the creators of a shared trust got divorced.

If you do revoke your living trust, it's prudent to track down and destroy all copies of your old trust, to diminish the possibility someone could claim you didn't really intend to revoke it (an unlikely possibility in any case). ■

10

Joint Tenancy and Tenancy by the Entirety

This chapter explains what joint tenancy is and how it works, and explores the advantages and drawbacks of using joint tenancy to avoid probate. The chapter also explains how tenancy by the entirety, a form of joint tenancy available in many, but not all, states for married couples only, works.

A. What Is Joint Tenancy?

Joint tenancy is one way co-owners, called "joint tenants," can own property together. Under some circumstances, it is a useful probate avoidance tool, because all property held in joint tenancy carries with it the "right of survivorship." This means that when one joint tenant dies, his or her ownership share of the joint tenancy property is "automatically" transferred to, and becomes owned by, the surviving joint tenant(s), without the need for probate.

Example: Ron and Linda own their house and a stock account in joint tenancy. At Ron's death, ownership of his one-half share of the house and stock account automatically goes to Linda, who becomes 100% owner of this property, without probate.

The automatic right of a surviving joint tenant or tenants to inherit is basic to this form of ownership. You cannot leave your interest in joint tenancy property to anyone but the other joint tenant(s).[1] Property owned in joint tenancy passes automatically to the surviving joint tenant(s) even if a deceased joint tenant provided to the contrary in a will or living trust. By contrast, other forms of shared ownership, such as tenancy in common or community property, don't create a right of survivorship, and an owner's share of such property can be transferred by will (and become subject to probate) or living trust.

Any number of people can own property together in joint tenancy, but they must all own equal shares. All joint tenant owners share equally in all income, profits and losses from their property. If an ownership document specifies different percentages or shares of ownership, it's a tenancy in common, not a joint tenancy, and there's no right of survivorship for the co-owners.

Unequal Ownership of Property

If you want to own property in unequal shares, you must do it as tenants in common. For example, two people living together may decide to own property in unequal shares because one person initially has more money to invest in the property than does the other. (Contracts and forms to create a tenancy in common and to switch to joint tenancy ownership should ownership shares become equal are contained in the *Living Together Kit* and the *Legal Guide for Lesbian and Gay Couples,* both published by Nolo Press.) Property held in tenancy in common does not avoid probate automatically. However, this can be accomplished by each owner putting his or her interest in the property in a living trust. (See Chapter 9, Revocable Living Trusts.)

It's common that real estate, or land, is owned in joint tenancy, but any type of property can be owned in this manner and avoid probate. Bank accounts, automobiles, boats and mobile homes are all routinely held in joint tenancy for just this reason.

[1] In most—but not all—states, while all the joint tenant owners are alive, any joint tenant does have the right to terminate ("sever," in legal lingo) the joint tenancy and, by doing so, create tenancy in common ownership. If this is done, each tenant in common may leave his share of the property to anyone he chooses.

STATES THAT HAVE RESTRICTED OR ABOLISHED JOINT TENANCY

The following states have, by law, limited or abolished joint tenancy, as described:

Alaska	No joint tenancy in real estate, except for husband and wife.
Pennsylvania	A presumption against joint tenancy, which can be overcome by clear statement of intent to create one.
Tennessee	No joint tenancy for any property, except for husband and wife.
Texas	No joint tenancy in any property, unless there's an agreement in writing between joint owners.

If you want to explore the possibilities of using joint tenancy in any of these states, see a lawyer.

B. Tenancy by the Entirety

"Tenancy by the entirety" is a form of property ownership that is similar to joint tenancy, but is limited to married couples. If you do not live in a state which specifically allows, by statute, for tenancy by the entirety, you cannot use it. Tenancy by the entirety is available in the following states:

Alaska*	Maryland	Oklahoma
Arkansas	Massachusetts	Oregon*
Delaware	Michigan*	Pennsylvania
District of Columbia	Mississippi	Tennessee
Florida	Missouri	Vermont
Hawaii	New Jersey*	Virginia*
Indiana*	New York*	Wyoming*
Kentucky*	North Carolina*	

*Allowed only for real estate.

Like joint tenancy, property owned in tenancy by the entirety does not go through probate when one spouse dies; it automatically goes to the surviving spouse. So if you're married and own property in tenancy by the entirety and avoiding probate is your basic estate planning concern, you don't need to transfer that property to a living trust.

Tenancy by the entirety property doesn't avoid probate, however, if both spouses die simultaneously. If spouses die at the same time, each spouse's half-interest in the property is passed to the beneficiaries named in the residuary clauses of their wills. If a spouse didn't make a will, the property passes to the closest relatives under their state's "intestate succession" law.

C. Simultaneous Death of Joint Tenants

Many joint tenants, as well as married tenants by the entirety, are concerned about what will happen to the property if the couple who owns it dies simultaneously. After all, if there's no surviving owner, the right of survivorship that's central to joint tenancy has no meaning. To deal with this highly unlikely but still potentially worrisome possibility, you have two choices:

- You can name a beneficiary, who would inherit the property in the event of simultaneous death, in your back-up will. If the property passes under your will, however, it will probably go through probate.
- You can transfer the property to your living trust, and each spouse can name an alternate beneficiary to receive his or her share of the property. It's a bit more paperwork, but you're assured that probate will be avoided even in the event of simultaneous death.

Even if you transfer joint tenancy or tenancy by the entirety property to a living trust, you should still prepare a will. Your will serves as your final back-up device to make sure that, whatever happens, you've named a beneficiary for your property, not left any of it to be distributed according to state law. (See Chapter 14, Wills.) It's wise to make a will, but you don't normally state in it who gets joint tenancy property in case of the simultaneous death of all joint tenants, since this is truly a remote possibility. Your will's residuary clause, which passes all property not specifically given to other beneficiaries to a beneficiary or beneficiaries named to take everything that's left over, takes care of the problem.

Example: Tom and Mary Jones, owners of a house in joint tenancy, die together in a plane crash. One-half of the joint tenancy property is included in Tom's estate and is transferred by his will to his residuary beneficiary, his son by a prior marriage. The other half is included in Mary's estate and is transferred by her will to her residuary beneficiary, her sister. If either Tom or Mary had no will, the property would be distributed to his and her legal heirs. If Tom and Mary had named each other as residuary beneficiaries in their wills, the property would go to their alternate residuary beneficiaries.

In contrast to a will, using a living trust does not work to dispose of property owned in joint tenancy in the case of the simultaneous death of all joint tenants. The reason has to do with a conflict between the legal structure of living trusts and joint tenancy ownership. Legal trusts only work for property technically owned by the trust, but joint tenancy only works for property owned by individuals.

D. Joint Tenancy in Community Property States

This section is of interest to people who live in or own real property in a community property state: Arizona, California, Idaho, Nevada, New Mexico, Texas, Washington or Wisconsin. If you don't live in one of these states, go on to Section E.

Most property accumulated by either spouse during a marriage is the community property of both. (See Chapter 3, State Property Ownership Laws, Section B, for a discussion of the rules.) Spouses can, and commonly do, hold their community property in joint tenancy with each other to avoid probate when the first spouse dies. Doing this can make good sense. However, for certain important income tax reasons (explained in Section E3 of this chapter), it's important to be able to show the IRS that community property held in joint tenancy for probate avoidance purposes is still community property.

One standard way to achieve this is to hold title in joint tenancy and prepare a separate simple written document, signed by both spouses, declaring that identified property "retains its character as community property, despite our holding title to this property in joint tenancy, which we do solely for convenience, to avoid probate." Another possible method is to state on the ownership document itself that the property is "community property held in joint tenancy." However, many title companies refuse to permit transfers of real estate into "community property held in joint tenancy," maintaining the two legal forms are inconsistent. Since, in the real estate world, it's often sadly true that "the law is whatever the title companies say it is," it's safer to rely on the first method suggested, holding title in joint tenancy with a separate document stating the property remains community property. Interestingly, neither title companies nor the IRS have any objection to this. It's the all-too-frequent legal story: What you cannot do directly, because of institutions, courts or misapplication of legal technicalities, you can do indirectly—if you know the proper indirect method.

Although the vast majority of spouses in community property states who hold property in joint tenancy do so with one another, one spouse might wish to place property into joint tenancy with someone other than the other spouse. If the property is the separate property of the transferring spouse, there's no ownership problem, since it's her property to do with as she wishes. (But see Section E, below, for possible tax disadvantages.) However, if the property is community property, serious ownership problems can develop between the surviving spouse and the surviving joint tenant. The reason for this is simple: Each spouse automatically owns one-half of all community property, whether or not his or her name appears on property ownership documents. Thus, the surviving spouse can successfully contend that the deceased spouse only had authority to transfer half of the community property into joint tenancy with someone else. This point may seem a little confusing. If so, this example should help.

Example: Mrs. Abruzzi, who has one daughter, owns a house as her separate property. She remarries Mr. Mykenas. For several years, they use their community property income to pay mortgage payments on the house. Mrs. Abruzzi decides to transfer the house into joint tenancy with her daughter to avoid probate at her death. When Mrs. Abruzzi dies, Mr. Mykenas could claim that part of the house was community property because community funds were used for mortgage payments. Half of the community property portion of the house is his. Mrs. Abruzzi has no legal right to transfer his portion to her daughter.

If you're married, check carefully before creating a joint tenancy with anyone but your spouse. If you're married and want to transfer property into joint tenancy with someone other than your spouse, be sure that the property is 100% your separate property, or that your spouse approves the transfer in writing. If you have any doubts, have your spouse agree (in writing) that this property is your separate property before you create the joint tenancy with someone else. Doing this can be tricky, so see a lawyer.

E. Tax Concerns Affecting Joint Tenancy

Before deciding whether you want to use joint tenancy in your estate planning, you should under stand the potential tax implications of holding property as joint tenants. The major tax concerns are estate taxes, gift taxes, income tax "basis" rules and property tax reappraisals. We know wading through this probably sounds dreary, but hang in there—it's not that difficult. And you do need to know this material before you can sensibly resolve whether or not you want to use joint tenancy.

[2]The exception is joint tenancy property purchased before 1977. In that case, all the worth of the property is included in the estate of the first joint tenant to die. See Section E3, below.

1. Federal Estate Taxes

Owning property as a joint tenant doesn't reduce your taxable estate for federal estate tax purposes. The federal government includes the value of the deceased's jointly-owned property in the taxable estate.[2] How that value is determined depends on whether the joint tenancy owners were married (including spouses owning tenancy by the entirety property) or not.

a. Marital joint tenancies

The tax rule for marital joint tenancies is simple. When a husband and wife own property as joint tenants or tenants by the entirety, one-half of the market value of the joint tenancy property, as of the date of death of the joint tenant, is included in the federal taxable estate of the first spouse to die, no matter what amount of money either spouse actually put up to buy the property.

Example: Lou and Isabelle are married and live in New York. During their marriage they purchased real estate as tenants by the entirety. Isabelle actually paid the entire down payment for the property from her savings. After purchase, mortgage payments were shared more or less equally by both spouses. Isabelle dies. The IRS rules provide that 50% of the market value of the property on the date of her death is included in her taxable estate. This is true even if she is fact put up more than 50% of the total cost of the property.

Either spouse may transfer separately-owned property into joint tenancy with the other spouse without any liability for gift taxes. No gift taxes are assessed against any gift made between a husband and wife, no matter how much it is worth. (See Chapter 15, Estate Taxes, Section A.)

b. Unmarried joint tenancies

The IRS rules defining the worth of a non-married joint tenant's share in joint tenancy property are more tricky than for married couples. Under the IRS rules, the value of a deceased joint tenant's interest is based on how much each joint tenancy contributed to the acquisition of the jointly-owned property. If the deceased put up all the money to purchase a piece of joint property, the full market value of the property (at death) is included in the taxable estate. If the deceased paid half the cost of acquiring the property, 50% of its worth is included in his taxable estate.

Crucially, with the exception of married couples covered above, the IRS *presumes* that the first joint tenant to die contributed all of the money for the purchase of jointly-owned property. The IRS also presumes that the first joint tenant to die paid for all capital improvements, if additional expenses were made for that. The surviving joint tenant(s) can overturn this presumption by proving that the survivors made cash or other contributions toward buying or maintaining the property. To the extent the surviving tenants can prove that they put up part of the purchase price, mortgage payments or other expenses, the value of the joint tenancy property interest included in the deceased's taxable estate will be reduced proportionately. Therefore, one risk for unmarried people of holding property in joint tenancy is that, unless good records are kept, the full value of the jointly-owned property will be subject to death taxes twice.

Example: Decades ago, Phil and his sister Patsy bought a house as joint tenants. They each contributed half the purchase price and paid off the mortgage equally, but any records that can prove that have long since vanished. Patsy dies in 1993. The full 1993 market value of the house is included in her taxable estate, since the IRS presumes she contributed all the purchase price and Phil has no proof to rebut this presumption. Phil, the surviving joint tenant, owns the entire house until he dies in 1994. The full 1994 market value of the house is included in his taxable estate, because he now owns all the property. Had Phil and Patsy kept records, only half the value of the house would have been included in Patsy's taxable estate.

2. Joint Tenancy as a Taxable Gift

Creating a joint tenancy (except between married couples) may involve making a taxable gift. To understand the basics of how gift taxes can affect joint tenancy, all you need to know is that the federal government assesses taxes against any gift over $10,000 made to any person, other than one's spouse, in a calendar year. (Gift taxes are explained in Chapter 16, Gifts and Gift Taxes.)

Gift taxes can affect joint tenancy because the IRS takes the position that, except for joint bank accounts (discussed below), a taxable gift is made when joint tenancy is created if the owners don't pay equally for the property. Thus, if one person puts up all the money to purchase property, but another is listed as a joint tenant, the person who puts up the money makes a legal gift of half-ownership of the property. If the value of that gift exceeds $10,000, the giver must file a gift tax return and gift taxes are assessed. Likewise, if a sole owner of property (worth more than $20,000) transfers ownership into joint tenancy with another person, a taxable gift has been made, because the half given away is worth more than $10,000.

Example: Martha transfers her house, worth $300,000 (all equity), into joint tenancy with her son Richard solely to avoid probate. The IRS position is that she has made a taxable gift of one-half the value of the house (less the $10,000 exempt amount).

There are two exceptions to the IRS rule that a taxable gift is made whenever a sole owner places property in joint tenancy. First, if a bank account is opened in joint tenancy, with one person actually making all or most of the deposit, there's no taxable gift. Second, this exception also applies to buying a savings bond in joint tenancy. Only when a person who didn't contribute half the original bank deposit or bond cost takes possession of more than his original contribution (by withdrawing money from the bank account, or selling an interest in the bond) is there a taxable gift.

PAYING GIFT TAXES ON A GIFT OF JOINT TENANCY PROPERTY

Normally, no gift taxes must actually be paid when a gift of joint tenancy is made. Any tax assessed is deducted from the giver's estate/gift tax credit. (See Chapter 15, Estate Taxes, Section A.) In other words, cash will not have to be spent, out-of-pocket, to pay any gift tax assessed, but a gift tax return must still be prepared and filed, a hassle to many people.

3. Federal Income Tax Basis Rules

In most cases, someone who inherits joint tenancy property gets a break on income taxes if she eventually sells the property. To understand this, you need to understand the tax concept called a "stepped up" basis.

Under federal law, the basis of inherited property is increased, or "stepped up," to its market value as of the date that the deceased owner dies. In other words, if B inherits property from A, B's basis in the property is its market value when A died, *not* its basis to A.

Example: Grant's basis in his house was $120,000. Grant dies and leaves the house to Serena under Grant's will. The market value of the house when Grant died was $350,000. When Serena inherits the house, her tax basis for it is stepped up to that market value of $350,000. If Serena sells the house for that amount, she has no taxable gain.

If the market value of property has risen above the original owner's basis, it's clearly desirable for an inheritor of that property to receive a "stepped up" basis to the value as of the date of the owner's death. In the above example, if Serena had only received Grant's basis in the house of $120,000 and she then sold the house for the market value of $350,000, she would have a taxable profit (or capital gain) of $230,000. Instead, because of the stepped up basis, she has no taxable profit.

While all property transferred on an owner's death receives a stepped up basis, property transferred by gift during the owner's life does not get a stepped up basis for the receiver of the gift.

Okay, now to apply this to joint tenancy. The general IRS rule for joint tenancy is that a surviving joint tenant gets a stepped-up basis only for one-half the value of the property, the half owned by the deceased owner. The half owned all along by the surviving joint tenant retains its original tax basis.

Example: Ellen and Julie buy an investment property (a rental house), in joint tenancy, for $100,000. Each contributes the same amount to the down payment and operating expenses. When Ellen dies, the property is worth $200,000. The basis of Ellen's half share of the property is "stepped up" to $100,000. The basis of Julie's half remains at $50,000, her share of the original purchase price. So Julie's new total net basis becomes $150,000.

In common law states, the stepped up basis rules, as applied to joint tenancy, do not create any special problem when expenses of buying the joint tenancy were shared equal, or it was created between spouses. But the stepped up basis rules are different for joint tenancy property when one of the owners did not contribute an equal share to the purchase price (except for spouses). As previously discussed, federal tax law includes in the estate of the first joint tenant to die the full market value of the property, less "any part that is shown to have originally belonged to such other person," and was not acquired from the deceased by the other person as a gift. (Section 2040, Internal Revenue Code.)

What does this mean? It means that if someone transfers solely-owned property into joint tenancy as a gift, the entire value of that property will be included in the giver's taxable estate. And because the entire value is included in that estate, all of the property will receive a stepped-up basis.

TAX BASIS OF PROPERTY

Put simply, the "basis" of property is the overall dollar cost to the owner of his interest in that property. To determine the profit, or loss, if an owner sells property, you deduct the owner's basis from the selling price. For example, Gus buys stock for $50,000, which is his tax basis for the stock. Two years later Gus sells the stock for $70,000. His taxable profit is sale price ($70,000) less basis ($50,000), leaving $20,000 profit.

The basis is not always simply equal to the owner's original purchase price. For example, the basis of real estate is its purchase price, plus the cost of any capital improvements, less any depreciation.

Example: Ardmore buys a house for $100,000 and puts $30,000 into capital improvements. There has been $10,000 depreciation. Thus the property's basis is $120,000. If Ardmore sells the house for $350,000, his taxable profit (sales price minus basis) is $230,000.

Example: Mary transfers her house, worth $250,000 (all equity), into joint tenancy with her son, Ed, who pays nothing for his share (it's a gift). When Mary dies, the house is worth $340,000. The full value of the house—$340,000—is included in her taxable estate, because Ed didn't contribute any cash for the property. And because the full value of the house is included in Mary's taxable estate, all of that property receives a stepped-up basis. So, Ed's basis is $340,000.

Sharp-eyed readers may have noticed a problem here. Wasn't Mary supposed to file a gift tax return when she originally transferred the house into joint tenancy with Ed? Yes, that's what the law requires. Since a gift tax was assessed, doesn't Ed become the full legal owner of half the property, so that only half of its value is included in Mary's estate, and only half of it receives a stepped-up basis? The answer is no. Despite Mary's filing the gift tax return, the IRS includes all the value of the property in her estate and all the property receives a stepped-up basis. Mary's estate does receive a credit for the gift tax previously assessed.

a. Note on Community Property Held in Joint Tenancy

Tax basis rules are different for married couples who live in the eight community property states. Both shares of community property held in joint tenancy are entitled to a stepped-up basis upon the death of a spouse, no matter what contributions were made to the initial purchase. Thus, if a husband and wife own community property real estate in joint tenancy worth $2 million at the husband's death, the basis of *both* the husband's and wife's share of that real estate is stepped-up to $1 million (no matter who paid for what, originally).

But to get the full stepped-up basis, you must prove to the IRS that the joint tenancy property is community property. Otherwise, only the half of the deceased spouse gets the stepped-up basis. So if you're married and hold any community property in joint tenancy, be sure you can prove it retained its character as community property. As mentioned in Section B, above, the best method to do this is to prepare a simple written statement signed by both spouses that they are holding community property "in joint tenancy for convenience only, to avoid probate, and that the property retains its character as community property." It's also a good idea to keep records showing that community property was used to purchase or make capital improvements to the property.

b. Joint Tenancy Property Acquired Before 1977 in Common Law States

For spouses or other co-owners in common law states who acquired joint tenancy property before 1977, the tax basis rules were, and remain, different. Prior to 1977, the tax law was that the full value of joint ownership property was included in the value of the estate of the first owner to die. So all the property received a stepped-up basis to its value as of the owner's death. While Congress changed this rule, beginning in 1977, to the present rule (if co-owners paid equally, only the deceased owner's portion is subject to estate tax at current market value, and only that portion gets the stepped-up basis), courts have held that this change was not retroactive. So the previous rule continues to apply to property acquired before 1977.

In some circumstances, this can result is significant income tax savings for the surviving joint owner, if she subsequently sells the property.

Example: Rob and Sue bought a farm for $30,000 in 1955, as tenants by the entirety in a common law state. Rob died in 1993. Under the pre-1977 tax law, the full current value of the property, $3,400,000, is included in Rob's taxable estate. However, no estate taxes must be paid because all Rob's interest in the farm goes to his wife, under the rules of tenancy by the entirety, and all property left to a surviving spouse is free of estate tax.

Because the full value of the farm was included in Rob's taxable estate, all of it receives a stepped-up basis to its value at Rob's death. So the basis of the farm, to Sue, is now $3,400,000. If she immediately sold the property for the market value, she should have no taxable gains. By contrast, if Rob and Sue had bought the farm after 1977, and the same figures applied, only Rob's half of the property would get a stepped-up basis, in this case, $1,700,000. Sue's half would retain her share of the original basis, which is one-half of $30,000, or $15,000. So Sue's total basis would be $1,715,000. If she immediately sold the property, her taxable gain would be $1,685,000.

The moral: Spouses and others who bought property in joint tenancy before 1977 have a big tax incentive to keep that form of ownership, rather than transferring the property to a different form of ownership, such as placing it in a living trust.

4. State Income Tax Basis Rules

State tax basis rules can also be quite complicated. However, in general, there's little need to worry about state basis rules. State income taxes take small enough bites that, in our opinion, they aren't worth bothering about when you're doing estate planning. Also, joint tenancy applies most often to real estate, and land obviously can't be moved from a high tax state to low or no tax one.

If you have a large estate and want to be extremely cautious and review the impact of your state's basis rules on your estate plan, see a tax lawyer or other tax expert.

5. Local Property Taxes

In some areas of the country, real property is reassessed for local property tax purposes every time it changes hands. This usually means that taxes go up, sometimes a lot if your property hasn't been reassessed recently.

In general, creating a joint tenancy interest in real property isn't a "change of ownership" if the original owner is one of the new joint tenants. In California, for example, there is no property tax reappraisal if you transfer your property into joint tenancy with yourself and others. However, as a general rule, if the original owner isn't one of the new joint tenants, then any "creation, transfer or termination" of a joint tenancy interest is a change of ownership, and the property will be reassessed. Before relying on this advice, however, contact your local property tax assessor and determine the specific rules for what types of transfers trigger the reassessment of property.

Example 1: Mrs. Jefferson owns two pieces of real estate. She transfers title to the first lot to herself and her husband, Raymond, as "joint tenants with right of survivorship." She transfers title to the second lot to herself and her daughter, Lila, as "joint tenants with right of survivorship." There has been no change of ownership in either of these transfers for reassessment purposes in most states. A few, states or local jurisdiction, though, impose transfer taxes in these situations. Also, when Mrs. Jefferson dies, there may be a reappraisal, depending on state property tax rules.

Example 2: Mrs. Jefferson transfers (by gift or sale) a third lot to her son and his wife "Raymond Jefferson and Lila Jefferson, as joint tenants with right of survivorship." There has been a "change of ownership," since the original owner, Mrs. Jefferson, isn't one of the new joint tenants. This is likely to trigger a property tax reassessment in many states.

F. Drawbacks of Joint Tenancy

We've already discussed the advantageous fact that joint tenancy property avoids probate, and the tax basis rules applicable to joint tenancy. In addition, as part of deciding whether to use joint tenancy, there are certain possible risks you should consider.

1. Any Joint Tenant Can End the Joint Tenancy

In most states, as long as all joint tenants are alive, any of them can terminate the joint tenancy, whether or not the other owners consent to it. Some states require a formal court partition (division) of the property before an owner can end the joint tenancy. In other states, any joint tenant has the power to end it, and sell his interest in the jointly-owned property, at any time. In either case, if there's a sale to a new owner, he takes his interest as a tenant in common with the remaining original owners. If the remaining (original) owner, and the new (tenant in common) owner conflict, either can ask a court to partition the property into equal halves. If that isn't feasible, the court will order a sale with the proceeds divided in equal shares.

The risk that a co-owner may sell her share of the property may not be serious for couples or close friends who purchase property together with money they each contribute. In this situation, if a divorce, separation or other reason to end the joint tenancy occurs, each joint tenant simply gets her fair share. However, if solely-owned property is transferred into joint tenancy by an older person in the form of a gift, the situation is quite different. The older person has given up ownership of half his property. And unlike putting property into a living trust, he can't change his mind later and take it back.

Example: Sid transfers his house into joint tenancy with his nephew Joe. Then the two have a bitter fight. Sid wants to regain sole ownership of the house. Joe says, "Nothing doing. I'm half owner, legally, and there's nothing you can do about it." Worse, Joe can then try to sell his half-interest in the house. If he does, Sid will share ownership with a stranger.

In short, one question to answer before you transfer property into joint tenancy is: Do you absolutely trust that your joint-tenant-to-be won't sell the property or do anything with the ownership interest that's adverse to you? If you have any doubts, joint tenancy isn't for you.

A living trust may be a better way to transfer property ownership. To eliminate the risk of giving property to someone in joint tenancy who could then sell his interest in the property, or turn into someone whom you later don't get along with, we advise people in Sid's situation to create a revocable living trust naming Joe as beneficiary. Then, if Joe and Sid have a falling out, Sid can simply amend the trust and change beneficiaries.

2. Creditors and Joint Tenancy

Creditors of any joint tenant may go after (legally "attach") that tenant's individual interest, but not the other joint tenants' interests. If there is an attachment, a court may order the whole property sold to reach the debtor's share.

Generally, upon the death of one owner, the surviving owner takes the property free of any responsibility for the deceased's debts. But, in a number of states, a creditor of the deceased owner can go after the property if:

- the deceased person had pledged his interest in the property as security for a loan
- the creditor sued, got a judgment and initiated legal steps to collect the money before the deceased died, or
- the creditor can show that the joint tenancy arrangement was a scheme set up solely to defraud creditors.

3. Incapacity

Any form of shared ownership can become difficult if one owner becomes incapacitated. The other owner(s) may need someone with legal authority to act for the incapacitated owner, particularly to sell the property or refinance it. The best way to authorize someone to act for you if you become incapacitated is by use of a durable power of attorney for finances (discussed in Chapter 26, Incapacity: Health Care and Financial Management Directives). To be secure about possible incapacity, owners of joint tenancy property should be sure each has prepared a durable power of attorney. Otherwise, there's a risk a court proceeding will be required if one owner becomes incapacitated.

G. When Joint Tenancy Makes Sense

By now, some of you may have read our negative comments about the risks of joint tenancy as a damning indictment against using it under all circumstances. Please don't. In some situations, owning property in joint tenancy certainly does make sense. For people who value simplicity (joint tenancy is easy to create), and whose situations don't involve the drawbacks and risks we've discussed, joint tenancy can work fine.

1. Married Couples

A married couple (or any couple) who is buying a house can sensibly use joint tenancy or tenancy by the entirety if each spouse wants the other to receive that spouse's interest in the house on his or her death. Indeed, buying a house in joint tenancy or tenancy by the entirety is probably the major way this form of ownership is used.

2. Transfers When Death Is Imminent

If a sole owner of property is likely to die soon, transferring that property into joint tenancy can be a useful last minute probate avoidance device if no previous estate planning has been done.

Example: Avram Berg, who is old and in rapidly-declining health, lives in a coop apartment in Manhattan. Avram wants the apartment to go to his daughter, Molly, whom he trusts totally—and he wants to avoid probate. He also loathes paperwork and wants the transfer accomplished as simply as possible. Avram can simply transfer ownership of the property into joint tenancy with his daughter. It requires less paperwork than a living trust. He doesn't worry about filing a gift tax return, since by the time it's due, there will probably be an estate tax return instead. And since Molly didn't contribute any cash for the purchase of the coop, it will all receive a stepped-up basis to the market value at Avram's death.

Transfers of solely-owned property into joint tenancy are less desirable if the original owner is likely to live an appreciable time. In this situation, a gift tax return must actually be filed (well, it's supposed to be); then there's more paperwork, and possible subsequent estate tax credit calculations when the original owner dies. For long-term planning with solely-owned property, a living trust remains a better method.

3. Purchase When Co-Owners Contribute Equal Amounts and Want the Other to Receive Their Share at Death

It's common that partners, whether personal or business, take title to newly-acquired property in joint tenancy when they want the other to inherit their share.[3]

[3] Remember, this does not apply to married couples As explained in Section E3, for tax basis reasons, you want to be sure that all shared ownership property can be demonstrated to be community property.

Example: Isadora and Randall plan to buy a house together. If either dies, they want the other to receive his or her share, outside of probate. Each fully trusts the other. If they take title in joint tenancy, they achieve their estate planning goal with a minimum of bother. Since each owns half the house, there's no basis problem; only the deceased owner's half-interest in the house will receive a "stepped-up" basis, no matter how they hold title to the house.

H. Creating a Joint Tenancy for Property With Documents of Title

There are two ways property with documents of title can be placed in joint tenancy:

- Two or more people buy or acquire property and take title in joint tenancy.
- A person who owns property can transfer title into joint tenancy with another person or people.

Joint tenancy is commonly used for many types of property with documents of title, including real estate and bank accounts or safe deposit boxes. (Joint bank accounts and safe deposit boxes are discussed in Chapter 11, Pay-on-Death Designations, Sections B & C, with "pay-on-death" bank accounts, because these kinds of accounts are similar in many ways.)

1. The Language Required

To own property in joint tenancy, the title document must contain words that clearly demonstrate the owners' intention. In most states, joint tenancy may be created by using the phrase "in joint tenancy" or "as joint tenants" in the ownership document. In some states, it's traditional or required to use the phrase "joint tenants, with right of survivorship," or "in joint tenancy with right of survivorship." This is sometimes abbreviated "JTWROS." Sometimes, the following is used: "Joint tenancy, not as tenants in common, and with right of survivorship." Simply listing the owners' names joined by "and" or "or" is not normally adequate to create a joint tenancy, although a few states allow it.

You may not remember how you took title to a piece of real estate, or your car, or your bank account. To see if shared ownership property is held in joint tenancy, look on the deed (for real estate) or the title slip (for other kinds of property, such as cars). If it doesn't say the co-owners own the property "as joint tenants" or "with right of survivorship" or similar language, the property isn't held in joint tenancy.

If you decide to transfer some of your existing property into joint tenancy, you must learn your state's law to learn the exact wording needed. If you're transferring real estate, any reliable title

INDIVIDUAL GRANT DEED

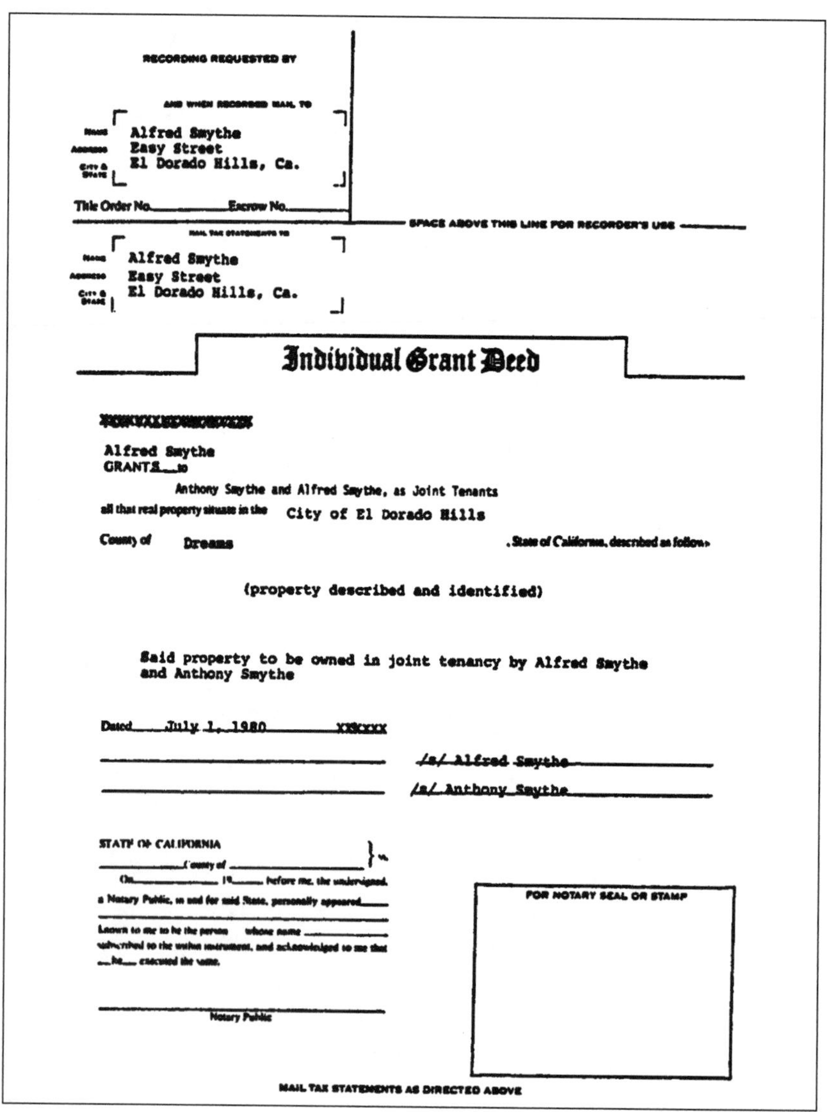

RECORDING REQUESTED BY

AND WHEN RECORDED MAIL TO

Name Alfred Smythe
Address Easy Street
City & State El Dorado Hills, Ca.

Title Order No.______ Escrow No.______

SPACE ABOVE THIS LINE FOR RECORDER'S USE

MAIL TAX STATEMENTS TO

Name Alfred Smythe
Address Easy Street
City & State El Dorado Hills, Ca.

Individual Grant Deed

Alfred Smythe
GRANTS to

Anthony Smythe and Alfred Smythe, as Joint Tenants

all that real property situate in the City of El Dorado Hills

County of Dreams, State of California, described as follows:

(property described and identified)

Said property to be owned in joint tenancy by Alfred Smythe and Anthony Smythe

Dated July 1, 1980

/s/ Alfred Smythe

/s/ Anthony Smythe

STATE OF CALIFORNIA
County of ______ } ss.

On ______ 19__ before me, the undersigned, a Notary Public, in and for said State, personally appeared ______ known to me to be the person whose name ______ subscribed to the within instrument, and acknowledged to me that __he__ executed the same.

______
Notary Public

FOR NOTARY SEAL OR STAMP

MAIL TAX STATEMENTS AS DIRECTED ABOVE

company or lawyer can tell you.[4] You'll find that a few states have special requirements governing how a joint tenancy is created. For example, in Florida, a joint tenancy can be created only in an instrument of transfer—a deed made when property is sold. In South Carolina, a joint tenancy for real estate must use the words "with right of survivorship." And in Oregon, the functional equivalent of joint tenancy is created by using the phrase "tenancy in common with right of survivorship."

2. Real Estate

To demonstrate how simple joint tenancy can be, here is a deed used to transfer solely-owned real estate into joint tenant. In this deed, Alfred Smyth has created a joint tenancy in real property between himself and his son Anthony, by giving Anthony a "joint ownership" interest in the real property.

[4] Nolo Press publishes *The Deeds Book,* by Randolph, which contains all the forms (deeds) and instructions necessary to transfer real property into joint tenancy in California.

I. Creating Joint Tenancy for Personal Property Without Documents of Title

You can create joint tenancies for personal property without documents of title, such as valuable paintings, jewelry or even for your shoes. (To remind you, "personal property" is all property except real estate.) To create a joint tenancy for personal property that doesn't have a formal document of title, all you have to do is declare in a written document that you and the co-owners own the property "in joint tenancy" or "as joint tenants." The document doesn't need to be filed with the County Recorder, unlike deeds putting real property in joint tenancy. However you should have the document notarized

Example: Guy and Danielle have been together for years. They have acquired a considerable amount of household furnishings, including appliances, furniture and glassware. Each wants the other to receive all their property when one of them dies. They want to avoid probate and the possibility that a member of either's family could claim any of their property. So, Guy and Danielle execute a joint ownership document, reciting that all the household furnishings listed in it are their joint tenancy property. ■

11

Pay-on-Death Designations:

Bank Accounts, U.S. Government Securities, Stocks and Bonds, Retirement Plans, Motor Vehicles

In a pay-on-death designation, the owner of some property formally names another person, or persons, to receive that property, or whatever is left of it, when the owner dies. Property in a pay-on-death account avoids probate. When the owner dies, the property goes directly to the named beneficiary. Pay-on-death designations have become widely used, particularly for retirement plans, government securities and bank accounts. More recently, some states have adopted laws allowing the use of pay-on-death registration for vehicles or securities (stocks, bonds or stock brokerage accounts).

Pay-on-death accounts can be desirable because they avoid probate with a minimum of paperwork. Normally, an institution, such as a bank or the U.S. Treasury Department, provides you with one simple form where you designate the beneficiary, and that's it. The beneficiary, of course, has no rights to any of the property until your death.

If you want to leave property to a minor, and there is some chance you will die before the minor reaches 18 (and who can know?), a pay-on-death designation usually isn't advisable (even if it's permitted for that type of property), since minors can't own property outright and pay-on-death accounts do not allow you to establish adult supervision for property left to them. Therefore, the minor's parent or guardian may end up having to establish a formal, court-supervised property guardianship, which is a considerable hassle. (See Chapter 6, Children, Section C.) It's better to put the property into a living trust that also contains a Uniform Transfers to Minors Act gift to the minor, or use a simple child's trust to provide built-in management for property left to minors.

Pay-on-death bank accounts have long been used in estate planning. The depositor names a beneficiary on the bank account form. The beneficiary receives any money in the account when the depositor dies.

Bank Accounts Can Be Decent Investments

If you have substantial amounts of cash, you may believe that bank accounts are not a sensible investment, whatever their estate planning benefits. After all, even extremely safe investments, such as mid- or long-term U.S. Government bonds, are often touted as producing a better return on your money. And, of course, if all goes well, more speculative investments in stocks, bonds, real estate, precious metals, or commodities can substantially outperform bank accounts. But investing aggressively in these ways means taking risks. People are badly burned in such gambles all the time. (Even U.S. Government bonds can be losers if interest rates soar.) In short, we believe that, for many readers, as part of pursing a diversified investment strategy, putting at least a significant amount of money in a federally-insured bank can make excellent sense. Remember W. C. Fields' investment strategy—"All my money's tied up in currency." Generally, bank accounts, especially certificates of deposit for six months or longer, aren't bad investments. On the average, they yield in interest at least twice as much as the most stocks pay in dividends, which means the stock price must increase significantly before people who buy it do as well as they would if they made a safe and secure bank deposit.

A. Pay-on-Death Bank Accounts

Here we look deeper into how pay-on-death bank accounts work. This type of account is called by various names by different banks in different parts of the country. Common names include "informal trust," "pay-on-death" account, "bank trust account," and a "Totten trust."[1] Whatever it's called, it works the

[1]The name "Totten" perhaps comes from some long forgotten Mr. Totten, or is perhaps derived from the German "Tod," meaning death.

same way. You open an account in your name, as depositor, and as "trustee for the benefit of [your beneficiary, whomever you name to receive whatever money is in the account when you die]." As long as you live, the beneficiary has no rights to any money in the account. You can spend it freely, and, indeed, spend it all, if you want to, or need to. After your death, the beneficiary can promptly obtain whatever money remains in the account simply by presenting the bank with proof of identity and a certified copy of the death certificate.

Example: Ray Jones wants to leave cash, probate-free, to his two daughters. He simply opens a pay-on-death trust certificate of deposit account as "Ray Jones, depositor, as trustee for Michelle and Mary Jones, equal beneficiaries." After he dies, his daughters go to the bank, present a death certificate and proof of their identities to bank officials, and then remove and divide equally all money in the account.

1. Advantages of Informal Bank Trust Accounts

There are normally no risks in creating an informal bank trust or pay-on-death bank account. As noted, unlike joint tenancy bank accounts, the beneficiary cannot withdraw any money from the account while the depositor is alive. In addition, the depositor can close the account any time, and can change the beneficiary at any time.[2] Also, the depositor can deposit or withdraw any amount desired (subject, of course, to any penalties the bank applies on early withdrawal from C.D. accounts). Because the depositor retains complete control over the account until death, establishing a pay-on-death account isn't a gift, and therefore doesn't involve gift tax concerns. (See Chapter 16, Gifts and Gift Taxes.) Only when the beneficiary gets the money at the depositor's death does legal ownership of that money change.

2. Opening an Informal Bank Trust Account

An appealing aspect of an informal bank trust account is that it's so easy to open. Most banks, including most credit unions, and savings-industrial loan companies, have standard forms for opening this kind of account; they will do the paperwork for you. A pay-on-death or informal bank trust account may either be a newly-opened account or an existing account to which you add a trust designation. Banks don't normally charge extra fees for holding your money in an informal bank trust account.

Generally, any regular bank account, including checking, savings, or certificates of deposit accounts, may be used as informal bank trust accounts. In practice, trust accounts are usually savings accounts, since it's more likely there will be substantial funds in this type account at the account on the depositor's death. Not only do checking account balances fluctuate, but most don't pay interest, so aren't suitable places to keep substantial sums.

3. Estate Taxes

The money in an informal bank trust account is included in the taxable estate of the depositor. (See Chapter 15, Estate Taxes.) So this type of trust only works as a probate avoidance device, and will not save on federal or state death tax, assuming your estate is large enough to pay them.

[2]If the beneficiary dies before the depositor, and no new beneficiary is named, the money would be transferred under the residuary clause of the depositor's will, if there is one.

4. Before You Open an Informal Bank Trust Account

If you decide to open an informal bank trust account, there are a few concerns you should be aware of and ask about at your bank:

- **Notice to beneficiaries.** In the majority of states, simply opening a trust account or adding a trust designation to an existing account is all you need to do. However, in a few states, an informal bank trust account is created only if the beneficiary is notified of the deposit. Your bank will know your state's rules for what kind of notice, if any, must be provided.
- **Early withdrawal penalties.** If the type of bank account you choose for an informal bank trust account requires holding a deposit for a set term, or paying a substantial penalty for early withdrawal—as would be the case, for example, for a six-month certificate of deposit—the penalty is usually waived if the depositor dies before that term expires and the beneficiary claims the funds.
- **Spouse's share of estate.** If you try and disinherit your spouse, the person you name as trust beneficiary may not get all the money in your informal bank account. The reason is simple. In many states, funds deposited in an informal bank trust account are included in the assets against which a surviving spouse who hasn't received from one-third to one-half of the total estate is given a legal right to take. (See Chapter 3, State Property Ownership Laws, Section C.)
- **State death tax.** If your state has a state death tax (see Chapter 15, Estate Taxes, Section C), immediate death tax liens (legal claims) may be imposed on informal trust bank accounts, and the liens must be removed before the funds can be transferred to the beneficiaries. This is normally done by demonstrating to the tax authority that the estate has ample funds to pay tax and is routine for most estates.

B. Joint Tenancy Bank Accounts

Here we look at other bank devices that can be used in estate planning to transfer property outside of probate. These are not pay-on-death accounts, but can be used to achieve the same goals as those accounts.

A joint tenancy bank account can be a useful means of avoiding probate, especially when two people are already a family unit and are sharing income and expenses. Most banks have standard joint tenancy account forms, and most types of bank accounts may be owned in joint tenancy, including checking, savings and certificates of deposit. To open such an account, all people involved sign the account papers as "joint tenants with right of survivorship." (Some banks abbreviate this "JTWROS.") When one joint tenant dies, the other can (within the limits on the account and by the procedures described below) obtain all the money in the account, with no need to go through probate.

In most joint tenancy bank accounts, either person can withdraw any or all of the money in the account at any time. If the purpose of the account is for shared expenses—as the family account of a husband and wife—this isn't normally a problem. If it is, inquire if a bank will let you require two signatures for withdrawals on a joint tenancy account. Many will.

A joint tenancy account is generally not a good idea if your purpose is to transfer your own money at death to someone else by changing the ownership document for the account to list the other person as a joint owner. A joint tenancy account exposes you to the risk that the other person can remove the money while you're alive—unless, as just mentioned, two signatures are required to withdraw money. But this means you'll have to get someone else's signature each time you want to withdraw your own money from the account. If your main goal is to avoid probate for money in your own account, an "informal bank trust account," discussed above in Section A, allows you to retain full and exclusive control over your money while you live and still have the account avoid probate.

One question that commonly arises when considering creating a joint bank account by adding someone's name to your individual account is whether doing so means you've made a legal gift, and therefore have to concern yourself with gift tax. Happily, there's no legal gift made by creating a joint bank account or depositing money in it. However, a gift is made by the depositor if the other person takes money out of the account. Under IRS rules, the other person could remove up to $10,000 per year, without there being any gift tax liability. (The legal rules for gifts and gift taxes are discussed in Chapter 16, Gifts and Gift Taxes.)

C. Joint Tenancy Safe Deposit Boxes

A joint tenancy safe deposit box can be a sensible place to keep important papers—wills, funeral instructions, burial or body donation, veteran, union death benefits or pension documents. This is true because either joint tenant can normally obtain instant access to the documents when they are needed.

If you decide to get a joint tenancy safe deposit box, be sure to specify on the bank account cards whether the co-owners share ownership of all contents of the box. This can be particularly important if you keep valuable objects, such as jewelry, in the box. In some states, joint tenancy rental of a safe deposit box gives both joint tenants access to the box, but doesn't necessarily create ownership rights to that box's contents unless it's clearly spelled out. Of course, if you don't want the other person with access to the box to own certain property in it, be sure it's clear that the joint tenancy in the safe deposit box is for access only. And of course, you would also want to leave the property in the box by your living trust or will.

Don't store estate planning documents in a safe deposit box that may be sealed after an owner's death. In some states with state death tax, safe deposit boxes are sealed by a bank as soon as it is notified of the death of an owner. The contents cannot be released until the box is inventoried by a government official. So if your state has a death tax, check with your bank's officials to see whether the safe deposit box will be sealed upon death of a joint tenant, and how one gets the box unsealed. Usually this can be done reasonably quickly and easily. If not, however, a safe deposit box isn't a good place to store documents that you want to be readily available at your death, including your living trust and will.

D. Naming a Pay-on-Death Beneficiary for Government Securities

You can hold U.S. Treasury Department Securities (T-bills) in a pay-on-death account form. The Treasury Department, or your investment advisor (if you have one), can provide you with the correct form. In that form, you register ownership of your securities in your (the purchaser's) name, followed by "payable on death to [whomever you name as beneficiary]." If a minor (or incompetent adult) is beneficiary, that status must be stated on the registration. But, as we've suggested already, it's not advisable to use a pay-on-death registration for a gift to a child. Likewise, it's similarly undesirable for making a gift to an incompetent person. In both cases you need a device, such as a trust, which allows you to impose adult supervision for the gift without any requirement of court supervision.

E. Naming a Beneficiary for Stocks and Bonds

In a number of states, you can add a pay-on-death designation to individual securities (stocks and bonds) or broker accounts under the Uniform Transfers-on-Death Security Registration Act. The Act has been adopted in the following states:

Arkansas	North Dakota
Colorado	Ohio
Kansas	Oregon
Minnesota	Virginia
Missouri	Washington
Montana	West Virginia
Nebraska	Wisconsin
New Mexico	Wyoming

The Act allows residents of those states to utilize pay-on-death registration for any securities account, or for individual stock certificates. In these states, if you register your stocks, bonds, stock bond accounts, mutual funds or other securities in a "pay-on-death" account form, the beneficiary or beneficiaries you designate will receive these securities after your death. No probate will be necessary. If you life in one of these states, your broker can provide the forms you'll need to name a beneficiary for your securities or security account.

If you don't live in one of these states, and you want to avoid probate of securities/stock accounts, you have to use some other form acceptable to the institution involved—such as a living trust or joint tenancy—to transfer the account to our beneficiary. If you actually have possession of stock certificates themselves, you must contact the transfer agent of the company you own stock in.

If you can't use a pay-on-death designation for your securities, it's usually better to use a living trust rather than joint tenancy. With a living trust:

- the beneficiary of the living trust has no right to the property while you live; and
- you can change the beneficiary or end the living trust if you wish.

With joint tenancy, you cannot decide to remove the joint tenant as co-owner, and that person can legally sell his half of the stock/securities at any time.

F. Using a Pay-on-Death Designation for a Retirement Plan

With many retirement plans, both individual or institutional, you can name a beneficiary to receive any money left in the plan, or that you remain entitled to, at your death. An individual retirement account, such as an IRA, Keogh or a 401(k) plan, is not designed to provide funds for someone after your death, but to provide money for you while you are alive. Thus the IRS mandates that you commence withdrawing funds from such accounts by, at the latest, age 70-1/2, and annual adjustments are made each year after that, according to your life expectancy, to determine how much you are required to withdraw. (These types of retirement plans are discussed further in Chapter 29, Social Security and Pensions, Section B.) Nevertheless, since people do not die according to life expectancy tables, many, if not most, die with money remaining in an IRA or Keogh, or owed them by an institutional retirement plan. Also, people who are ill and know they won't live nearly as long as the IRS life expectancy tables project, can take the minimum allowable amount from these accounts, and thus easily pass a substantial sum free of probate. So it's always a good idea to name a beneficiary, and probably an alternate beneficiary, for any of these types of retirement plans.

G. Car Registration

The state of Missouri pioneered using car registration as a probate avoidance device. California has recently adopted a similar law (although at least a year after it's been adopted, local DMV offices have not heard of it and have no forms for it). Under these laws, a car owner can designate on the vehicle title document a person or persons to receive ownership of the car when the present owner dies. The new owners obtain title to the car (and the car itself) without any court proceedings.

Other states are currently considering legislation similar to Missouri's and California's. Hopefully, this type of transfer-on-death car registration will soon become a widely-used method of probate avoidance for the cars that are part of nearly every estate. ■

12

Life Insurance

Life insurance has long been a part of much estate planning in the United States. Indeed, one fear many people have of the phrase "estate planning" is that it's a cover for hard-sell visits by life insurance agents. Although life insurance is vastly oversold and not needed as part of many people's estate plans, it can be very useful, especially for parents of young children and those who support a non-working spouse or a disadvantaged or incapacitated adult.

A. An Overview

In addition to providing money to support dependents in a situation where the provider's estate isn't large enough to do the job, life insurance can help solve several other common estate planning problems. These include:

- **Providing immediate cash at death.** Insurance proceeds are a handy source of cash to pay the deceased's debts, funeral expenses, and income or death taxes.[1] Lawyers and financial advisors call cash and assets that can quickly be converted to cash "liquid." If your estate has almost all "non-liquid" assets (real estate, collectibles, a share in a small business), there may be a substantial loss if these assets must be sold quickly to raise cash to pay bills, as opposed to what they could be sold for later if there was enough ready money from insurance or other sources to meet all pressing bills. Obviously, if your estate includes bank accounts or marketable securities—or your inheritors won't need ready cash—you won't need to purchase insurance for this purpose.
- **Probate avoidance.** Normally, the proceeds of a life insurance policy avoid probate because you name your beneficiary in the policy instead of by a will. This means that money can be transferred quickly to survivors with little red tape, cost or delay (see Section C, below). However, if you have established a living trust and other probate avoidance devices, you really don't need life insurance to accomplish this goal.
- **Death tax reduction.** When an insurance policy is not legally owned by the person who is the insured (as explained in Section E), the proceeds are excluded from the insured's taxable estate. This can significantly reduce death tax liability of the insured's estate. Obviously, though, this is only a benefit for people whose estates are large enough to face death tax liability in the first place.

  Example: Alicia Perez's estate consists of several valuable pieces of real estate and a one-half interest in a profitable antiques store, but includes very little cash and no life insurance. When she dies, she owes debts of $40,000 (aside from mortgages) and death taxes totaling $120,000. To raise this money, her inheritors must sell some of her real estate or her interest in the store. Unfortunately, the country is suffering a mild recession, and the market value of both antiques and real estate is down. To make matters worse, canny real estate people spread the word that this is a "distress sale" to raise money for estate obligations. As a result, the price the inheritors receive when they sell one of the pieces of real estate is far below what they would receive if they had the flexibility to choose when to sell the property. Had Alicia purchased an insurance policy with a pay-off at death of $160,000 or more, the need to sell other assets would have been avoided.

Having indicated some of the reasons life insurance can be desirable, let us again emphasize that simply buying some is not an adequate way to plan an estate. Indeed, many, if not most, people who have no financially-strapped dependents simply don't need life insurance. Those who decide to purchase

[1] Federal estate taxes are due nine months after death, so cash to pay them doesn't have to be raised immediately.

insurance should know exactly why they are buying it, the best type of policy for their needs, and of course, should buy no more than they need. (As a group, Americans certainly believe in life insurance, holding over two trillion dollars worth, far more, per capita, than any other country.)

Here are some questions to ask yourself to help evaluate your life insurance needs.

1. Long-Term Needs

First, determine whether it makes sense for you to purchase insurance to provide financial help for family members over the long term by taking into consideration the following:

- How many people are really dependent on your current earning capacity over the long term? If the answer is "no one," it's doubtful that you need life insurance.
- How much money would your dependents really need, and for how long, if you died suddenly? Don't accept life insurance salesperson hype on this one. Very few people need to be supported for the rest of their lives.
- When you determine how much money your dependents will need, subtract the amounts that will be available from public and any private insurance plans that already provide coverage. Social Security and dependents' benefits will almost surely be available, and you may also be covered by union or management pensions or a group life insurance plan.
- And don't forget to subtract any other likely sources of income, such as the help reasonably affluent grandparents would assuredly provide for your children in case of disaster. Also, remember that bright kids often get scholarships, and dependent spouses caring for young children can usually return to work at some point.

2. Short-Term Needs

Now you should assess whether you need life insurance for short-term needs.

- How long is it likely to be, after you die, before your property is turned over to your inheritors? If your property will avoid probate, there's usually little need for insurance for short-term expenses, unless you have no cash, securities or other "liquid" assets. By contrast, if the bulk of your property is transferred by will, and therefore will be tied up in probate for months, your family and other inheritors may need the ready cash insurance can provide. While a probate court will usually promptly provide a family allowance or allow a spouse or other inheritor access to funds, it can still be nice to have insurance proceeds available.
- What assets would be available to take care of immediate financial needs? Aside from buying insurance, there are other, cheaper, ways of providing ready cash, such as leaving some money in joint or pay-on-death bank accounts, or placing marketable stocks and other securities in joint tenancy.
- If you are sole owner of a business, how much cash would it need on your death? Do you want, and expect, that some of your inheritors will continue the business? If so, do you think there will be a sufficient cash flow so the new owners can successfully maintain the business? How much is your death likely to affect (reduce) cash flow? Do you need insurance proceeds to cover any cash flow shortage of the business?

  If you don't plan to have your inheritors continue the business, the questions are simpler. Will there be enough cash so the business can continue to stay live until it is sold? Is there really anything to sell? For many personal service businesses, the answer is no—the business goes when the person providing the service dies.

BUYING INSURANCE

If you don't own life insurance and think you want it, you need to talk to an insurance salesperson or broker. Normally, a salesperson sells for one company only, while a broker can place your policy with one of several. In theory, this would seem to be a reason to prefer a broker, but in practice, the integrity of the person you are dealing with is more important than is the legal relationship to an insurance company or companies.

If you do contact an insurance salesperson, look for a person who will function as an ally, offering additional information and proposing alternatives—not forcing you. If you get too much quick-sell pressure, contact someone else. And here's one more tip: some salespeople don't recommend that you buy term insurance, or try to talk you out of it, for no other reason than they get a much higher commission from selling you whole life or universal. (See Section B, below, for an analysis of the pros and cons of various types of life insurance.)

Before you contact anyone who sells insurance, you should have a good idea of what kind of policy you need and how much it should cost. The cost of the same insurance can vary considerably from company to company. Often, relatively small mutual companies charge lower rates than some of the giants of TV advertising, and some broker's charge lower "discount" commissions.

Resources: There are some books that explain the ins and outs of life insurance, including buying life insurance. A couple of the better life insurance books are:

- *Winning the Insurance Game,* by Ralph Nader and Wesley J. Smith (Doubleday).
- *Your Life Insurance Options,* by Alan Lavine (John Wiley and Sons, Inc.)

You can also contact a free life insurance rate-shopping service, which will provide information on the costs of different companies' policies. These resources include:

- Select Quote, 800-343-1985
- Insurance Quote, 800-972-1104

These organizations make money if you buy a "product" (life insurance) they recommend, so use any information they give you as a starting point. But it can be useful information, even if they have some self-interest in promoting the product.

B. TYPES OF LIFE INSURANCE

If you are interested in life insurance, any salesperson will be delighted to explain the bewildering array of policies available to you. But unless you educate yourself first, it's all too easy to get mesmerized by insurance policy lingo and end up paying too much for a policy that may not even meet your needs. Basically, for estate planning purposes, there are two main types of life insurance: term, which provides insurance only, with no savings feature, and some form of cash-value life insurance, which returns at least some money to a policy holder who survives the coverage period. These include whole life, universal life and variable life (discussed below). Any of these types of life insurance can be purchased with one lump sum, called a "single-premium payment," which can be a useful estate planning device if you have sufficient funds and want to lock in your life insurance now. And finally, annuity policies, which typically pay out a fixed sum each month, can be very useful in planning certain types of estates. We explain each in the sections which follow.

1. Term Insurance

Term insurance provides a pre-set amount of cash if the insured dies while the policy is in force. For example, a five-year $130,000 term policy pays off if you die within five years—and that's it. If you live beyond the end of the term, you get nothing (except, of course, the continued joys and sorrows of life itself). With term insurance, you pay only for life insurance coverage. The policy does not also have a savings feature. You don't accumulate any savings or cash surrender value from the policy.

Term insurance is the cheapest form of coverage. As a candid life insurance man once said, "It provides the most bang for the buck, no question." There are many types of term insurance, such as policies that have an automatic right to renew for an additional term, but these options don't change the basic fact that term insurance pays off if you die during the policy time period and doesn't pay anything if you live beyond that period.

Term life insurance is particularly suitable for younger people with families, who want substantial insurance coverage at low cost. Since the risks of dying in your 20's, 30's or 40's are quite low, the cost of term insurance during these years is as reasonable as life insurance prices get. Also, if you only need insurance for a short time, say to qualify for a business loan, term is your best bet. However, the older you are, the more expensive term insurance becomes when you compare how much you have to pay in premiums to the pay-off value of the policy. This, of course, is understandable, as the older you are, the greater the chance you will die during the policy term.

As mentioned above, term policies offered by different companies have all sorts of differences, some fairly significant. For example, some policies are automatically renewable at the end of the term without a medical examination, often for higher premiums, and some are not. Some have premiums

How Safe Is Your Insurance Company?

As a number of surprised and angry insurance policy owners have leaned to their dismay, insurance companies can encounter serious financial trouble, and even go broke. For instance, some insurance companies invested heavily in junk bonds and "go-go" real estate deals during the '80s, and paid the price of insolvency when glimmers of fiscal (and societal) sanity returned to these economic areas in the '90s. Other companies were, for whatever reason, mismanaged, and didn't have sufficient assets to pay off all their policies.

There is no national or federal insurance guarantee fund for life insurance companies similar to FDIC insurance for bank depositors. In 47 states, there is some sort of industry-sponsored state guarantee fund. (Colorado, Louisiana, New Jersey and Washington, DC have no such funds at all.) While these funds offer most policy holders the reasonable hope that they won't lose everything they invested if their insurer goes broke, you still certainly don't want to have to wait for state regulators to take charge of an insolvent company, investigate and finally—and it can take a while—determine how much money you get back.

To avoid this sad scenario, your best bet is to check the reliability of the insurer you plan to buy a policy from. There are several major companies that provide rating systems for the financial stability of insurance companies. It's prudent to check your insurance agency against one—and even better, two—of these rating systems, to be sure the company you're interested in got top grades.

The names of the major rating companies are:

- A.M Best (Best Insurance Reports)
- Duff & Phelps
- Moody's Investors Service
- Standard and Poor's.

You should be able to locate the reports of these companies at a large public library. If not, your insurance agent should be able to assist you with locating their business offices and phone numbers. Each company has a slightly different code for its rating—for instance, A.M. Best's top two ratings are "A+" and "Contingent A+," whereas Standard and Poor's top two ratings are "AAA" and "AA+." Each company will provide you its rating code system. So you simply need to understand precisely what that code means.

set for a period of years, whereas others only guarantee a premium rate for the first year. After that, the rate can go up. Some can also be converted from a term to whole life or "universal" policy during the term, again without needing to requalify. But as we've said, no term insurance has cash surrender value; unlike whole life or universal insurance, term doesn't build up any recoverable cash value that you can borrow against or collect when the policy ends.

2. Cash Value Life Insurance

With a cash value life insurance policy, the premium payments cover more than the actuarial cost of the risk of death. The excess money goes into some type of savings, or investment, account. Income that builds up in this account is not taxable, until the money is actually distributed to the owner, or the beneficiaries.

A trustworthy insurance agent is a must. There are a bewildering number of variations of cash value life insurance policies. Without writing an entire book on the subject, it's impossible to explain the names of every possible option to you here. We can tell you the basic forms of cash value life insurance, and offer two pieces of advice: First, many of these variations are of the "bells and whistles" type, minor differences that don't mean nearly as much as some insurance agents may claim. Second, when it comes to fine-tuning your needs, your selection of an insurance agent is crucial. Unless you are prepared to do an immense amount of research yourself, you'll have to rely somewhat on the advice of your agent. So you surely need one you trust.

a. Whole Life Insurance

Whole life (sometimes called "straight life") insurance provides a set dollar amount of coverage should you die while the policy is in force in exchange for fixed, uniform payments. What distinguishes it from term insurance is that whole life also has a savings feature. If you keep the policy in force long enough, it builds up a "cash reserve," which you can borrow against or, after the passage of a number of years, cash in.

The premiums for whole life, especially in the early years of a younger person's policy, are much greater than needed to cover the actuarial risk of death. In other words, insurance companies take in substantially more money on whole life policies during their first few years than they pay out for proceeds for insureds who die. The insurance company invests the surplus. Some of the surplus becomes the insured's cash reserve, which grows over time. Like savings held in a bank, the cash reserve earns interest, paid by the insurance company. After a set time, usually several years, the policyholder has the right to cash in the policy and obtain the cash reserves. The amount is sometimes called the "cash surrender value" of the policy. A policyholder who cashes in a policy gets a lump sum, but, of course, is no longer insured. Another way to get money back on the policy, but to keep the insurance in force, is to borrow against the policy. Funds borrowed from the cash or surrender value of an insurance policy are deducted from the proceeds paid at death, if the insured dies without having paid off the loan. When the policy ends, the insured may chose to receive the cash that's accumulated or choose from a list of other options, which might include renewal or receiving payments over time, in the form of an annuity.

Whole life is more expensive than term life insurance, especially in the early years of the policy. This makes sense, since buying insurance and savings is obviously more costly than only buying insurance. Over the length of a policy, it will typically cost a middle-aged person several times more money to obtain the same amount of coverage if she chooses whole life rather than term.

On the other hand, whole life is usually automatically renewable, unlike many term policies; with whole life, the insurance period can be extended without a new physical examination of the insured.

The problems with whole life are typically twofold:

- Insurance is mostly needed by younger people with small children who don't have adequate savings to cope should a main income-provider die. But people in this group usually can't afford relatively expensive whole life policies either. Usually it's better to buy a much more affordable term policy.
- People who do have enough money to adopt a savings and investment plan have many choices as to how to proceed. On balance, most experts (including the authors) believe that there are a number of ways to do this that are more cost-effective than purchasing life insurance.

b. Universal Life Insurance

Universal life combines some of the desirable features of both term and whole life insurance, and offers other advantages. Over time, the net cost usually is lower than whole life insurance. With universal life, you build up a surplus, or cash reserve, as with whole life. Insurance companies invest this surplus in fixed-income assets. Usually the investment is in assets that pay short-term fixed yields, such as treasury bills or short-term corporate loans. When interest rates are low, as they were in the early 1990s, the return on a universal life policy will likely be quite low, too. Nevertheless, a universal cash reserve policy typically pays a higher rate of return than traditionally paid by whole life. But the interest paid on universal life varies significantly from company to company, so you need to investigate carefully which companies consistently achieve a better performance. Also, be warned that interest payments aren't permanently fixed, and can be affected by market conditions if there's a crash.

Aside from potentially higher interest rates, the main advantage of universal life over whole life is that universal is far more open and flexible. For example, you can vary your policy payments, or amount of coverage, or both, from year to year. Again, in contrast, whole life creates set payments for a set amount of proceeds, which cannot be varied during the period of the policy. Also universal life policies normally provide you with better consumer information. For example, you are told how much of your policy payments goes for company overhead expenses, reserves and policy proceed payments, and how much is retained for your savings. With whole life, you are typically told only the interest rate paid on your cash reserve.

Universal life can also act as a kind of tax shelter. The interest the company pays on the cash (surrender) value of the policy is not taxed as it is earned and accumulates. Only if the insured withdraws any interest is it subject to tax. Certain partial interest withdrawals can even be made without paying tax if the insured has owned a universal policy at least 15 years. By contrast, the interest on bank accounts is subject to tax in the year it is paid, even if left untouched in the account.

There can be other significant advantages to universal life; an insurance agent will be glad to explain them to you.

c. Variable Life Insurance

Variable life, sometimes called "variable universal life insurance," refers to policies in which cash reserves are invested in securities, stocks and bonds. In a sense, these policies combine an insurance feature with a mutual fund. Since over the past decade, prices on the stock market have risen dramatically overall, variable life policies have usually produced the best return. But of course, there's a potential downside to this also. These policies are basically almost sure to offer bring unpleasant surprises when financial markets decline.

3. Single-Premium Life Insurance

With single-premium life, you pay, up-front, all premiums due for the full duration of the policy. Normally, any policy with a savings feature can be purchased with a single premium. Obviously, this requires the expenditure of a large amount of cash—$5,000, $10,000 or often much more, depending on your age and the dollar amount of the policy. A reason to commit so much cash to buying an insurance policy is that it enables the purchaser to give the fully-paid-for policy to new owners. As explained in Section E of this chapter, there can be truly significant estate tax savings if someone other than the insured owns the policy, since the gift tax obligation is computed on the current—not future—value of the policy. And because there are no more payments to make, a gift of a single-premium policy doesn't involve risks that the new owners will fail to make payments and cause the policy to be canceled.

4. Joint Life Insurance (Second to Die Insurance)

Joint life insurance (also called "second to die" insurance) is a relatively new type of insurance. It provides a single policy that insures two lives, usually spouses. When the first spouse dies, no proceeds are paid. Indeed, the policy remains in force, and premiums must continue to be paid, as long as a spouse lives. The policy only pays off on the death of the second spouse.

Why would any couple want such a policy? Mainly for use as part of an estate plan for wealthier couples (normally people with over $1,200,000), since that defers most estate taxes until the death of the second spouse. None of this is of interest to people with moderate-sized estates or smaller, so if you are in this category, you don't need to read this section. For those of you still reading, all you need to know about estate taxes right here is that:

- all property left to a spouse is free of estate tax
- property worth up to $600,000 can be transferred to anyone free of estate tax
- many spouses make use of "marital life estate" trusts to effectively guarantee that each spouse gets to take advantage of his or her own $600,000 estate tax exemption, with the result that the couple will have no estate tax liability for a combined estate of $1,200,000.[2]

Estate taxes are discussed in some detail in Chapter 15. Using a "QTIP" trust to postpone taxes otherwise due on one spouse's death until the second spouse dies is covered in Chapter 19, Other Estate Tax-Saving Marital Trusts, Section A. If yours is a larger estate, please read all this material before even trying to make decisions.

Now let's apply these tax rules to insurance needs. Let's say a husband and wife own $5,200,000 worth of property, all shared. Each spouse's share is worth $2,600,000. Each spouse creates an estate plan leaving $600,000 to be divided amongst their children, and $2,000,000 to go to the surviving spouse. When one spouse dies the other receives this $2,000,000 free of estate tax. But now when this (second) spouse dies, he or she will have an estate of $4,600,000. Of this $600,000 is estate tax exempt. The remaining $4,000,000 that is subject to estate

[2]This estate tax break can be used by unmarried couples, too. See Chapter 18, Estate Tax-Saving Bypass Trusts, Section D.

taxes will be hit for a hefty $2,200,000. Surely the beneficiaries—the couple's children—will be delighted if the couple also provided a source of funds to help pay these taxes, rather than have them all taken from the estate itself.

So, enter joint life insurance. When additional funds are wanted to help pay estate taxes on the death of the second spouse, the policy pays off.

This type of insurance can be particularly desirable when a major family asset is a family business, or real estate interests—assets that aren't liquid, and which the survivors may not want to sell. Or suppose two children inherit a family business, but one doesn't want to keep it going. The other could use her share of the insurance proceeds as an initial buy-out payment, so she could retain ownership of the business.

Because two lives are insured, the premium payment for joint life policies are comparatively low compared to policies on one person's life. But, of course, this is also heavily influenced by the age and the health of the insured couple. It's those old insurance companies' actuarial tables again: The odds on two people dying in X time period are less than on one.

The federal tax statute governing second-to-die life insurance is somewhat ambiguous, and tax experts have questions about how it will be interpreted by the courts. You want to be sure that no part of the policy is included in the estate of the first spouse to die. If it is, you may wind up with double taxation, with the proceeds also included in the estate of the second spouse to die.

Because this is a new and complex area, you need to check with a good estate planning lawyer with current knowledge of the tax rulings on these types of policies, and to discuss this issue with your insurance agent to ensure your joint policy will have the effect you intend.

5. "First to Die" Life Insurance

"First to die" life insurance is, as the name indicates, the reverse of joint life insurance. With a first to die policy, two (or occasionally more) people, usually business partners or co-owners, are insured under one policy. Because these policies are usually maintained as a part of a business buy-out agreement, usually the company or partnership itself buys and maintains the policy. When the first insured dies, the policy pays off, with the funds typically paid to the company or partnership. Effectively, this means payments go to the other owners of the policy, normally the deceased's business co-owners.

A first to die policy will be significantly cheaper to pay for than if both, or several, business owners or partners are each insured for the same amount by the business. Obviously, insuring against only one death exposes an insurance company to lower risks, and lesser proceed payments, than if several people are insured for the same amount.

When one business owner dies, the proceeds can be used to pay off the worth of the deceased owner's interest, under a buy-out clause. Or, if the deceased owner's beneficiaries wish to, and are allowed to, participate in the business, the funds can be used for the costs of whatever adjustments and problems the business faces because of the death of an owner.

Example: Paul, Gabe and Liz are equal partners in a video rental store. Their partnership agreement provides that if a partner dies, the two surviving partners can buy out that partner's interest according to a set valuation formula. The business does not have a great deal of ready cash. Almost all the available cash the partners had was consumed by opening the business, acquiring inventory and operational costs.

So the partnership buys a "first to die" policy covering the lives of the three partners. The partners have made a rough guess of how much the business is worth now, and paid for a policy that pays off about half this value.

In theory, they only need coverage for one-third of the value, but they hope and expect their business will increase, so want to include some allowance for increased value of a deceased partner's interest.

If a partner dies, the life insurance pays the proceeds to the partnership. The value of the deceased partner's interest is determined from the formula. The two surviving partners pay this amount to the deceased partner's inheritors. If there are any insurance proceeds left over, the partners can use them however they agree upon. And when everything is wound up, the two surviving partners now own the business 50/50.

6. Annuities

Basically, an annuity is a policy in which an insurance company contracts to pay the policy beneficiary a certain cash amount each year, or month, instead of one lump sum upon death. There are all sorts of annuity policies and combinations of annuity payment plans with cash-value life insurance policies. Some people who don't trust their own ability to hold onto money even purchase an annuity policy when times are good, naming themselves as beneficiary. They thus provide themselves with a set income for life, beginning at a specified age.

An estate planning advantage of an annuity is that you can buy one that will provide periodic payments to someone you believe is unable (too young, or too much of a wastrel) to handle one large lump sum insurance payment. In this sense, annuities work somewhat like a trust.

However, even if you want to arrange for periodic payments to a beneficiary, you should consider other alternatives, including establishing a trust (see Chapter 17, An Overview of Ongoing Trusts), before choosing an annuity policy. Why? Because, as is usually true with insurance policies, annuity policies tend to be a relatively expensive way to meet your objective. Also, they are not flexible. For example, if special needs of the beneficiary arise, such as an extended illness, the payments normally cannot be increased, as they often can be with a well-designed trust. In short, buying a more prosaic type of insurance and having the benefits put in trust should you die, to be administered by a trusted friend or family member with a reasonable amount of discretion to vary pay-outs to meet the needs of the trust beneficiary, is usually a wiser choice.

C. Life Insurance and Probate

The proceeds of a life insurance policy are not subject to probate unless the deceased's estate is named the beneficiary of the policy. If anyone else, including a trust, is the beneficiary of the policy, the proceeds are not included in the probate estate, and the proceeds are paid to the beneficiary without the cost or delay of probate. Except when your estate will have no ready cash to pay anticipated debts and taxes, there is no sound reason for naming your estate, rather than a person(s) or trust for another person, as the beneficiary if beneficiaries of an insurance policy.

Think again before naming your estate as a life insurance beneficiary. In our experience, the problem of a deceased person having substantial debts and no liquid assets is fairly rare. In most instances, estates contain enough cash, or other assets that can be sold for cash, to pay debts and taxes.

Unless life insurance proceeds are used for estate costs, they will be distributed to someone, eventually. So it seems foolhardy to reduce the amount inheritors receive from your life insurance because of probate costs—or add to the time your inheritors must wait before they get this money.

D. Choosing Life Insurance Beneficiaries

As you know, when you buy life insurance, you name the policy's beneficiaries—those who receive the proceeds when you die. As long as you are the owner of a life insurance policy, you can change beneficiaries, as long as you are mentally competent. You can't, however, change a beneficiary of an insurance policy simply by naming a new beneficiary in a will or living trust. If one person is named as a beneficiary of a life insurance policy, but another person is named as the beneficiary of the policy in the insured's will or living trust, the first person remains the legal beneficiary.

1. Community Property States

If you live in a community property state (see Chapter 3, State Property Ownership Laws, Section A, for a list) and buy a policy with community property funds, one-half of the proceeds are owned by the surviving spouse, no matter what the policy says about the beneficiary. This result can be, and often is, varied by a written agreement between the spouses, in which one spouse transfers all interest in a particular insurance policy to the other spouse.

2. Minor Children as Beneficiaries

If you want your minor children to be the beneficiaries of your life insurance policy, you should arrange some legal means for the proceeds to be managed and supervised by a competent adult. If you don't, the insurance company would likely require that a court appoint a property guardian for the children before releasing the proceeds. As discussed in Chapter 6, Children, this is not desirable, since it necessitates court proceedings and court supervision of life insurance proceeds left to benefit your children—costs and hassles the children won't benefit from. There are several ways to prevent this:

- Rethinking your plan to name minors as beneficiaries of your life insurance policy, and instead, naming a trusted adult beneficiary such as a spouse, who you are confident will use the money for the children's benefit.
- Naming your living trust as the beneficiary of the policy, if your minor children are beneficiaries of the trust. In the living trust, you define how the proceeds are to be used for your children. The proceeds are managed as part of a children's trust created in the living trust.
- Naming a person you trust as property guardian for your minor children in your will. You can do this in your will.

Grandparents or other non-parents who name minors as beneficiaries of their life insurance policies can name their living trust as beneficiary of the policy and create child's trusts for the minor beneficiaries in that living trust.

In general, naming a living trust as beneficiary for life insurance proceeds is the best strategy for effectively leaving that money to benefit minors. The advantage of using a living trust over a property guardian named in a parent's will is that a guardianship must end when the minor becomes a legal adult. Trusts can be continued until each child reaches whatever age you've decided is best for the child to receive property outright. Also, property guardianships normally require court supervision, while children's trusts do not.

E. Transferring Ownership of Life Insurance Policies to Reduce Estate Taxes

This section is important only if your estate will face federal estate taxes. As we stated earlier, an estate must be worth $600,000 (unless you have made substantial gifts during your life) before this occurs.

1. Estate Taxes and Life Insurance Proceeds

One way federal estate taxes can be reduced is by transferring ownership of a life insurance policy. Whether or not life insurance proceeds are included in the deceased's taxable estate, and so subject to federal death taxes, depends on who owns the policy when the insured dies. If the deceased owned the policy, the proceeds are included in the federal taxable estate; if someone else owned the policy, the proceeds are not included.

Example: Melissa purchases and owns an insurance policy covering her life, with a face value of $200,000, payable to her son, Jeff, as beneficiary. Melissa's business partner, Juanita, owns a second policy, covering Melissa's life for $400,000, payable to Juanita. She will use these proceeds to pay Jeff, Melissa's sole inheritor, the worth of Melissa's interest in the business. Melissa dies. All the proceeds of Melissa's policy, $200,000, are included in her federal taxable estate. However, none of the $400,000 from the policy Juanita owns is part of Melissa's federal taxable estate, because Melissa did not own the policy.

Fortunately, an owner of life insurance has the right to assign or give ownership of the policy to any other adult, including the policy beneficiary. (The only exceptions are some group policies, which many people participate in through work, and which don't allow you to transfer ownership.) We say "fortunately" because the value of the policy that is given away during the insured's life will be substantially less than the amount it pays off on death, with the result that the total tax bill will be substantially lower.

When considering whether you want to transfer ownership of your life insurance policies, you need to read and understand Chapter 15, Estate Taxes, and resolve three important questions.

1. What is the estimated net value of your estate?

2. What is the amount of your life insurance proceeds?

3. Will including the proceeds of your insurance policies in your taxable estate affect your federal estate tax liability?

If your estate is larger than $600,000 (or it is less but you made large gifts during your life), there will be estate tax savings if you transfer ownership of the policy. But there is a trade-off: Once the policy is transferred, you've lost all your power over it, forever. What this really amounts to is, you cannot cancel it or change the beneficiary. To make this point bluntly, suppose you transfer ownership of your policy to your spouse, and later get divorced. You cannot cancel the policy or recover it from your now ex-spouse. Nevertheless, in many situations, the trade-off is worth it, as for example when you transfer policy ownership to a child (or children) you have a close and loving relationship with.

The IRS has some special rules about determining who owns a life insurance policy when the insured dies. Gifts of life insurance policies made within three years of death are disallowed for federal estate tax purposes (and often for state death tax purposes, too). This means that the giver would still own the policy, since the gift was not effective as a matter of law.

Example: Louise gives her term life insurance, with proceeds of $300,000, payable on death, to her friend, Leon, in 1990. She dies two years later. For federal estate tax purposes, the gift is disallowed, and all the proceeds, $300,000, are included in Louise's taxable estate. If Louise had transferred the life insurance policy more than three years before her death, none of the proceeds would have been included in her taxable estate.

The message here is clear: If you want to give away a life insurance policy to reduce estate taxes, give the policy away as soon as feasible. (And don't die for at least three years.)

Another IRS regulation provides that a deceased person who retained any "incidents of ownership" of a life insurance policy is considered the owner. The term "incidents of ownership" is simply legalese for keeping any significant power over the transferred insurance policy. Specifically, if the deceased has the legal right to do any one of the following, the proceeds of the policy will be included in his taxable estate for tax purposes:

- change, or name, beneficiaries of the policy
- borrow against the policy, pledge any cash reserve it has or cash it in
- surrender, convert or cancel the policy
- select a payment option—decide if payments to the beneficiary can be a lump sum or in installments, or
- make payments on the policy. This doesn't mean the policy must be fully paid up, but simply that the original owners cannot retain any legal right to pay any of the premiums as they become due.

If the life insurance policy is transferred from the original insured owner to a beneficiary, the transaction is regarded as a gift by the tax authorities. So, if a long-standing policy with a present value of more than $10,000[3] is transferred to one person, gift taxes will be assessed. Even so, the amount of gift tax assessed will be far less than the tax cost of leaving the policy in your estate. This is because the proceeds payable under a policy when the insured dies are always considerably more than the worth of the policy while the insured lives.

Example: Eugene transfers ownership of his universal life insurance policy to his son, David. The cash surrender value of the policy when he transfers it is $22,000.[4] Eugene dies four years after giving his son the insurance policy, which pays $300,000. None of this $300,000 is included in Eugene's federal taxable estate. (Nor are the proceeds considered income to David, for federal income tax purposes.)

2. How to Transfer Ownership of Your Policy

You can give away ownership of your life insurance policy by signing a simple document, called an "assignment" or a "transfer." To do this, notify the insurance company, and use its assignment or transfer form. There's normally no charge to make the change. Also, the policy itself will usually have to be changed to specify that the insured is no longer the owner.

After the policy is transferred, the new owner should make all premium payments, unless of course the policy is fully paid up. If the previous owner makes payments, the IRS might contend that the previous owner was keeping an "incident of ownership," so the proceeds of the policy must be included in the deceased owner's federally taxable estate—precisely what you're trying to avoid. If the new owner doesn't have sufficient funds to make the payments, the previous owner could give her money to be used for these payments. In other words, it's okay for the previous owners to make payments indirectly by giving money to the new owner, but it's

[3]Gifts of $10,000 or less to one person in a calendar year are gift tax free. Even if the policy is larger than this and gift taxes are assessed, they don't have to be paid. The amount of the gift tax is simply subtracted from the amount of the $600,000 federal estate and gift tax credit. For more, see Chapter 16, Gifts and Gift Taxes.

[4]Gift taxes are assessed on $12,000, the value of the gift exceeding $10,000.

a no-no for the previous owner to make payments directly to the insurance company.

If you give a paid-for single-premium policy to a new owner, there's no question about who makes future payments. There aren't any. Because it's paid for in full once it's purchased, single-premium life can be a particularly convenient type of policy to give to a new owner in order to reduce the giver's estate taxes. However, there can be a drawback here, too. The value of the policy, at the time of the gift, may exceed $10,000, so gift tax will be assessed on all value over this $10,000. By contrast, if the giver gives a policy worth less than $10,000, and then every year gives the new owner no more than $10,000 to pay for annual premiums, no gift tax will be assessed.

F. Life Insurance Trusts

An irrevocable life insurance trust is a legal entity you create for the purpose of owning life insurance you previously owned. As explained in Chapter 21, Other Estate Tax-Saving Trusts, Section B, an irrevocable trust is, like a corporation, simply a legal entity, distinct from any human being.

Creating an irrevocable life insurance trust is a means of transferring ownership of life insurance from the insured to a new owner—the trust. As with transferring ownership of a life insurance policy to another person, the major reason to create an irrevocable life insurance trust is to reduce death taxes, especially federal estate taxes, by removing the proceeds of an insurance policy from your taxable estate. Since the trust owns the policy, not you, the proceeds aren't part of your estate.

Why create a life insurance trust, rather than simply transfer a life insurance policy to someone else? One reason is that there's no one you want to give your policy to. In other words, you want to get the proceeds out of your taxable estate, but you want to exert legal control over the policy and avoid the risks of having an insurance policy on your life owned by someone else—perhaps a spouse or child you don't trust to pay policy premiums. For example, the trust could specify that the policy must be kept in effect while you live, eliminating the risk that a new owner of the policy could decide to cash it in.

Example: Mrs. Brandt is the divorced mother of two children, in their 20s, who will be her beneficiaries. Neither are sensible with money. Mrs. Brandt has an estate of $500,000, plus universal life insurance which will pay $300,000 at her death. She wants to remove the proceeds of the policy from her estate. If she doesn't, $200,000 of her estate will be subject to federal estate tax. However, there's no one Mrs. Brandt trusts enough to give her policy to outright. With the controls she can impose through a trust, however, she decides it's safe to allow her sister, the person she's closest to, to be the trustee of a life insurance trust for the policy. She creates a formal trust, and transfers ownership of the life insurance policy to that trust.

There are strict requirements governing life insurance trusts. If you want to gain the estate tax savings:

- The life insurance trust must be irrevocable. If you retain the right to revoke the trust, you will be considered the owner of the policy and the proceeds will be taxed in your estate upon death.
- You cannot be the trustee. You must name either an independent adult or an institution to serve as trustee.
- You must establish the trust at least three years before your death. If the trust has not existed for at least three years when the person who set it up dies, the trust is disregarded, for estate tax purposes, and the proceeds are included in the settlor's taxable estate.

Get legal help for a life insurance trust. If you decide you want to create or explore using a life insurance trust, you'll need to see a lawyer. Tax complexities must be considered: How will future premium payments be made? If the person establishing the trust makes the payments directly, or even indirectly, how will that affect estate taxes? Personal concerns also have to be carefully evaluated. For example, what happens if the settlor has a child after the trust becomes operational? Or gets divorced? Marries or remarries? There aren't any standard answers to these questions.

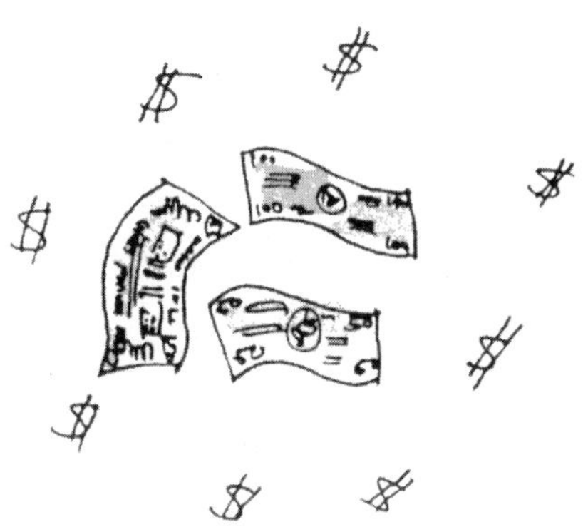

G. Taxation of Insurance Proceeds

Cash policy proceeds payable to a beneficiary after an insured's death are exempt from *all* federal income taxes. However, if the proceeds are paid in installments, any interest paid on the principal is taxable income to the recipient. Likewise, the proceeds of an insurance policy are exempt from state income tax in most states. ■

13

State Law Exemptions From Normal Probate

As a general rule, property left in a will must go through probate. However, there are exceptions; a number of states' laws allow a certain amount of property to be left by will, either free of probate or subject only to a very simplified probate process.[1]

It's important to understand that there are two basic types of state law exemptions to normal probate. Some states have adopted one type, some the other, some both, and some neither. A summary of each state's laws is provided in Section C.

The first type eliminates probate altogether for small amounts of property, usually in the $5,000 to $60,000 range. Where this type of law is in effect, a qualifying inheritor can collect property given him by completing an affidavit (a statement signed under oath), and presenting the person or institution holding the property with whatever additional proof state law requires—such as a copy of the will, a certified copy of the death certificate, or personal identification. The property is then simply turned over to the inheritor.

The second type of state law exemption to probate provides a summary court procedure far simpler—and normally faster and cheaper—than conventional probate. Where available, these laws typically apply to transfers to a surviving spouse and sometimes other close family members. How simplified the procedure is, and what types of property it applies to, varies by state. Some summary procedures are easy enough to do without a lawyer. Others still require a lawyer, so they result in at least some attorney's fees, court costs and delays.

[1]Aside from the laws discussed in this chapter, some states have very specialized methods to avoid probate in specific circumstances, such as property owned by a military veteran who dies in a state veterans' home, or permitting payment of wages up to $50. Since these statutes almost always involve small amounts of property in narrow circumstances, and aren't germane to planning an estate, they're not covered.

A. Using Your State Laws in Estate Planning

How can you use your state's probate exemption laws in your estate planning? Generally, by combining a will that qualifies for probate exemption or simplified probate under state law with other probate avoidance techniques for the rest of your property.

Few, if any, readers of this book will be able to totally avoid probate solely by using their state's probate exemptions laws. Most estates are worth far more than the $5,000-$10,000 of property that can normally be transferred completely free of probate. And even when it comes to planning to use simplified probate procedures (in the states where they are available), most people will find that only a small part of their property qualifies.

Fortunately, in California, New York and in some other states, the probate-exemption law can still be valuable, even if you have a larger estate than the exempted amount. This is because you can combine this method with other probate avoidance devices, such as living trusts and joint tenancy. For instance, in California, property worth up to $60,000 can be transferred by affidavit probate-free, with the rest of a larger estate transferred by other probate avoidance devices, such as a living trust. Similarly, in New York, property worth up to $10,000 can be left probate-free by will, and the rest of the estate transferred by other probate avoidance devices.

Unfortunately, many states probate exemption laws don't allow this method to be combined with other probate avoidance devices. In these states, it is the total amount of property in the entire estate, not just the property subject to the will, which determines if the dollar limits of the probate exemption law has been exceeded.

B. State Law Probate Exemption Rules

Each state's probate exemption law is different. Section C, below, contains a chart summarizing each state's law. This chart provides three categories of information for each state:

1. the amount of property that can be transferred by will free of probate
2. the amount of property that can be transferred by will through summary (simplified) probate
3. the citation to the state's probate exemption statute (law).

The summary chart is designed to give you sufficient information to decide whether you want to investigate the usefulness of your state law for your estate planning. The chart does not set forth the operational details of your state's laws, which would require a book in itself.

The chart does not tell you whether you can combine your state law's exemptions from normal probate (if any) with other probate avoidance methods. This is because, oddly, state laws usually ignore this issue; what is permitted is determined by accepted custom and practice in the legal community. If you learn from the chart that your state has a probate exemption law you might want to use in your estate planning by preparing a will that qualifies for the exemptions, you should take one or more of the following steps to determine your state's precise requirements and accepted legal practice:

- Read the statute yourself. In Chapter 30, Using Lawyers, Section B, you'll find a discussion of how to research legal statutes.
- Contact the clerk of the court that handles probate matters to see if they provide any consumer information or will answer your questions;
- Consult a lawyer who knows about the accepted practices. Since you're asking for limited and specific information, the fee should be reasonable.

The probate exemption rules and legal customs of the four largest states—California, New York, Texas and Florida—are examined in detail in Sections D, E, F and G. In California and New York, the accepted legal practice is that you can combine a will qualifying for probate exemption laws with other probate avoidance methods.

The chart in Section C also does not define how each state's law calculates its dollar limit for purposes of determining the value of property exempt transfer by will—that is, whether they apply to your gross estate (the market value of everything you own with no deduction for debts), net estate (market value less debts and encumbrances) or net probate estate (net value only of property left by will). Obviously this can make a big difference. A car worth $10,000 on which you owe $8,500 might be valued at $10,000 in one state and $1,500 in another. Again, the statutes are normally not clear on this. How the value of property that can be transferred free of probate is calculated in each state is usually a matter of custom in the legal community, so you will need to check further if this is relevant to your situation.

1. Reading the State Law Probate Exemption Chart

As an example of how to read the probate exemption law chart in Section C, let's look at Illinois. The chart provides:

ILLINOIS

Category 1: Affidavit Procedure Instead of Probate: $25,000, personal property; also, if all beneficiaries agree, and are Illinois residents, and no state inheritance or federal estate taxes due.

Category 2: Summary Probate: $50,000

Category 3: Statutes: Illinois Annotated Statutes, Ch. 110 1/2, Sections 25-1+ and 9-8+

> **NOTE FOR CALIFORNIA, MARYLAND AND WISCONSIN READERS**
>
> Residents of these three states are fortunate. In California, Nolo Press publishes a detailed book, *How to Probate an Estate*, by Julia Nissley, which explains step-by-step how California's probate exemption law works and provides all forms necessary to handle a probate proceeding without a lawyer.
>
> In Maryland, there's a simplified form of probate available for estates of any size.
>
> In Wisconsin, there's a state-mandated procedure for probating a deceased's solely-owned property informally without an attorney. An interested person applies to the Probate Registrar, who will assist with the informal probate.

Category 1: Affidavit Procedure Instead of Probate

This category tells you whether the state has a law allowing any property left by a will to be transferred by affidavit, free of normal probate. If there's a "no" in this category, the state doesn't have this kind of law.

Using an affidavit procedure means the inheritor(s) state, on a notarized document, that the will of the deceased left them certain specified property. To obtain this property, the inheritor simply presents the affidavit, personal I.D., and a copy of the deceased's will to whoever holds that property. No actual court proceedings (notice of hearings, hearings before a judge, formal pleadings) are required. Some states still require a relatively simple affidavit to be filed with a court or court clerk. Others don't require any judicial filing at all.

If a dollar figure is listed in this first category, it means the state has a law allowing property up to that dollar amount to be transferred by this affidavit method. Next, any restrictions on the type of property that can be transferred are listed; many states allow only personal property, not real estate, to be transferred. In any case, real estate is normally so valuable these days that it's unlikely that an interest in real estate would fall below the dollar limits, unless that ownership is a small percentage of the property. Finally, any restrictions on who the beneficiaries can be are summarized ("only to spouse and children").

The chart doesn't set forth the precise information which must be in an affidavit if one is required. To determine this, you'll need to research your state's law.

To return to our Illinois example, Category 1 states "$25,000, personal property." This means personal property worth up to $25,000 can be transferred by affidavit, free of probate, in Illinois. Then this category states "also, if all beneficiaries agree, and are Illinois residents, and no state inheritance or federal estate taxes are due." This means there is another type of affidavit transfer, free from normal probate in Illinois, if the specified requirements are met—all beneficiaries must be Illinois residents and agree to the transfer outside of probate, and no death taxes can be owed.

Category 2: Summary Probate

This category provides the same kind of information as Category 1 for those state laws that offer a simplified version of probate for certain amounts of property. Many states, such as Illinois, have both an affidavit procedure and a separate summary probate procedure. The actual operation of these laws varies widely from state to state. Most importantly, the statutes themselves usually don't specify that probate attorney fees must be reduced from those charged for normal probate.

To return again to our Illinois example, Category 2 reads: "$50,000," without any other restrictions. This means property worth up to $50,000—either personal property or real estate—can be transferred by summary probate.

Category 3: Statutes

This category gives you the legal citation to your state's probate exemption statute.

If your state has two statutes, one for an affidavit procedure and another for simplified probate, both citations are given. In such cases, the first citation given is to the affidavit procedure statute. The citations are to the first section of the relevant statute. The + symbol after the statutory cite means that other pertinent sections follow the first section that's noted.

The Illinois example states: "Illinois Annotated Statutes, Ch. 110-1/2, Sections 25-1+, 9-8+." This means the statute for the $25,000 affidavit procedure is found in Section 25-1 and those immediately following of Chapter 110-1/2 of the Illinois Statutes. The statute for the $50,000 summary probate procedure is found in Section 9-8 and those immediately following of Chapter 110-1/2.

C. Summary Chart of State Law Exceptions to Normal Probate

ALABAMA

Affidavit Procedure Instead of Probate: No

Summary Probate: $3,000, personal property only

Statute: Code of Alabama, Title 43, Ch. 2, Section 690+

ALASKA

Affidavit Procedure Instead of Probate: No

Summary Probate: No dollar limit

Statute: Alaska Statutes Title 13, Ch. 6, Sections 13.16.080

ARIZONA

Affidavit Procedure Instead of Probate: $30,000, personal property and $30,000 real property

Summary Probate: No (except for certain types of family property)

Statute: Arizona Revised Statutes, Sections 14-3971+; 14-1973+

ARKANSAS

Affidavit Procedure Instead of Probate: $50,000

Summary Probate: Limited amounts only for surviving spouse or dependents

Statute: Arkansas Statutes Annotated, Sections 28-41-101+

CALIFORNIA

Affidavit Procedure Instead of Probate: $60,000, personal property, and real property interest, $10,000 plus any vehicles owned by the deceased (cars, mobile homes, trucks), up to $5,000 of back pay, and all joint tenancy property.

Summary Probate: To surviving spouse, community property petition, no dollar limit

Statute: California Probate Code, Sections 13050, 13100+,13200+, 13500+

COLORADO

Affidavit Procedure Instead of Probate: Net estate, $27,000

Summary Probate: Limited to amount set by several other statutes

Statute: Colorado Revised Statute Sections 15-12-1201+

CONNECTICUT

Affidavit Procedure Instead of Probate: $20,000 personal property only

Summary Probate: No

Statute: Connecticut General Statutes Annotated §45a-273+

DELAWARE

Affidavit Procedure Instead of Probate: $12,500, personal property only. Beneficiaries can only be spouse, grandparents, children or other specified relations, trustee or funeral director

Summary Probate: No

Statute: Delaware Code Annotated, Title 12, Sections 2306+

DISTRICT OF COLUMBIA

Affidavit Procedure Instead of Probate: No (except if entire estate is no more than two cars, and all debts and taxes are paid)

Summary Probate: $10,000

Statute: District of Columbia Code, Title 20, Section 351+

FLORIDA

Affidavit Procedure Instead of Probate: No (except for very small estates with less than specified exceptions)

Summary Probate: $25,000, property in Florida subject to probate; $60,000 for estate left primarily to family members)

Statute: Florida Statutes Annotated, Sections 735.301+; 735.201+, 735.101+

GEORGIA

Affidavit Procedure Instead of Probate: No

Summary Probate: No

Statute: [No applicable statute]

HAWAII

Affidavit Procedure Instead of Probate: $5,000

Summary Probate: $20,000 property in Hawaii

Statute: Hawaii Revised Statutes, Sections 560:3-1201; 560: 3-1205

IDAHO

Affidavit Procedure Instead of Probate: $5,000

Summary Probate: No dollar limit (Statute provides useful do-it-yourself instructions)

Statute: Idaho Code, Sections 15-3-1201+

ILLINOIS

Affidavit Procedure Instead of Probate: $25,000, personal property

Summary Probate: $50,000 and no U.S. taxes due

Statute: Illinois Annotated Statutes, Ch. 110 1/2, Sections 25-1+, 9-8+

INDIANA

Affidavit Procedure Instead of Probate: $15,000, personal property only

Summary Probate: No dollar limit (if all heirs agree)

Statute: Indiana Statutes Annotated Sections 29-1-8-1+; 29-1-7.5 1+

IOWA

Affidavit Procedure Instead of Probate: No

Summary Probate: $50,000 total value of probate and non-probate Iowa property only to surviving spouse; $15,000 to parent or grandchild; $10,000 to relatives

Statute: Iowa Code Annotated: Section 635.1+

KANSAS

Affidavit Procedure Instead of Probate: No

Summary Probate: No dollar limit

Statute: Kansas Statutes Annotated, Sections 59-3201+; 3301+

KENTUCKY

Affidavit Procedure Instead of Probate: No

Summary Probate: By agreement of all beneficiaries; when spouse receives probate estate under $7,500 (intestate only, or where renunciation of will by spouse)

Statute: Kentucky Revised Statutes: Sections 391.030+, 395.450+

LOUISIANA

This book is not applicable in the state of Louisiana.

MAINE

Affidavit Procedure Instead of Probate: $10,000

Summary Probate: Limited to amounts set by several other statutes

Statute: Maine Revised Statutes Annotated, Title 18A, Sections 3-1201+

MARYLAND

Affidavit Procedure Instead of Probate: No (except if entire estate is no more than two cars, or a boat worth less than $5,000)

Summary Probate: No limit

Statute: Annotated Code of Maryland Estates and Trusts Law, Sections 5-601+

MASSACHUSETTS

Affidavit Procedure Instead of Probate: None

Summary Probate: $15,000, personal property; for close family only

Statute: Massachusetts General Laws Annotated, Ch. 195, Sections 16, 16A

MICHIGAN

Affidavit Procedure Instead of Probate: No

Summary Probate: $5,000; and cars worth less than $25,000 given to surviving spouse or heirs, if no other property

Statute: Michigan Compiled Laws Annotated, Sections 700.102

MINNESOTA

Affidavit Procedure Instead of Probate: $10,000

Summary Probate: $30,000

Statute: Minnesota Statutes Annotated, Sections 524.3-120

MISSISSIPPI

Affidavit Procedure Instead of Probate: No

Summary Probate: No

Statute: Not applicable

MISSOURI

Affidavit Procedure Instead of Probate: $15,000

Summary Probate: No

Statute: Annotated Missouri Statutes, Trusts & Estates, Section 473.097

MONTANA

Affidavit Procedure Instead of Probate: $7,500

Summary Probate: Limited to amounts set by several other statutes

Statute: Montana Code Annotated, Title 72-3-1103+, 72-2-801+

NEBRASKA

Affidavit Procedure Instead of Probate: $10,000

Summary Probate: Limited to amounts set by several other statutes

Statute: Revised Statutes of Nebraska, Sections 30-24, 125+

NEVADA

Affidavit Procedure Instead of Probate: $25,000 (court petition must be filed)

Summary Probate: $100,000

Statute: Nevada Revised Statutes, Section 145.010+, 146.070+

NEW HAMPSHIRE

Affidavit Procedure Instead of Probate: No (except $500 to surviving spouse or other immediate family)

Summary Probate: $5,000 personal property

Statute: New Hampshire Revised Statutes Annotated, Ch. 553: 31+

NEW JERSEY

Affidavit Procedure Instead of Probate: No (only if die intestate, then $10,000 to spouse, or $5,000 to others)

Summary Probate: No

Statute: New Jersey Statutes Annotated, 3B-10-3; 3B-10-4

NEW MEXICO

Affidavit Procedure Instead of Probate: $20,000

Summary Probate: Limited to amounts set by several other statutes

Statute: New Mexico Statutes, 45-3-1202, 45-3-1204

NEW YORK

Affidavit Procedure Instead of Probate: $10,000 personal property (plus certain types of exempt property, to specified dollar limits)

Summary Probate: No

Statute: Consolidated Laws of New York Annotated, Surrogates' Court Procedure Act, Section 1301+

NORTH CAROLINA

Affidavit Procedure Instead of Probate: $10,000, personal property only

Summary Probate: No

Statute: General Statues of North Carolina, Ch. 28A, Section 25-1.1

NORTH DAKOTA

Affidavit Procedure Instead of Probate: $15,000

Summary Probate: No dollar limit

Statute: North Dakota Code, Sections 30.1-23-01+, 30.1-23-01+

OHIO

Affidavit Procedure Instead of Probate: No

Summary Probate: $25,000

Statute: Ohio Revised Code Annotated, Section 2113.03

OKLAHOMA

Affidavit Procedure Instead of Probate: No

Summary Probate: $60,000

Statute: Oklahoma Statutes Annotated, Title 58 Sections 241+

OREGON

Affidavit Procedure Instead of Probate: $25,000 personal property; $60,000 real estate

Summary Probate: No

Statute: Oregon Revised Statutes, Section 114.505+

PENNSYLVANIA

Affidavit Procedure Instead of Probate: No

Summary Probate: $10,000 personal property

Statute: Pennsylvania Statutes Annotated, Title 20, Sections 3102+

RHODE ISLAND

Affidavit Procedure Instead of Probate: No (except person(s) who paid funeral costs, last bills, etc., up to $10,000)

Summary Probate: No

Statute: No applicable statute

SOUTH CAROLINA

Affidavit Procedure Instead of Probate: $10,000 (but affidavit must be approved and signed by a judge)

Summary Probate: $10,000

Statute: Code of Laws of South Carolina, Section 62, 3-1201; 3-1203+

SOUTH DAKOTA

Affidavit Procedure Instead of Probate: $10,000

Summary Probate: $60,000

Statute: South Dakota Codified Laws, Section 30-11A-1+

TENNESSEE

Affidavit Procedure Instead of Probate: $10,000

Summary Probate: No

Statute: Tennessee Code Annotated, Title 30, Ch. 4, Section 101+

TEXAS

Affidavit Procedure Instead of Probate: $50,000

Summary Probate: No dollar limit if will writer provides that "no other action shall be had in county court" [other than] the probating and recording of his will and the return of an inventory

Statute: Texas Probate Code, Sections 137+, 145+

UTAH

Affidavit Procedure Instead of Probate: $25,000

Summary Probate: No dollar limit

Statute: Utah Code, Title 75, Section 3-1201+

VERMONT

Affidavit Procedure Instead of Probate: No

Summary Probate: Limited to amounts set by several other statutes

Statute: Vermont Statutes Annotated, Title 14, Section 1901+

VIRGINIA

Affidavit Procedure Instead of Probate: $5,000 personal property, and $5,000 owed deceased from bank or employment

Summary Probate: No

Statute: Code of Virginia, Sections 64.1, 122.2+

WASHINGTON

Affidavit Procedure Instead of Probate: $60,000 personal property

Summary Probate: No dollar limit (if decedent was "solvent")

Statute: Revised Code of Washington Annotated, Title 11, Section 62.010+; Title 11, Section 68.010+

WEST VIRGINIA

Affidavit Procedure Instead of Probate: $100,000

Summary Probate: No

Statute: West Virginia Code, Ch. 44-3A-1+

WISCONSIN

Affidavit Procedure Instead of Probate: $10,000

Summary Probate: $30,000, plus Wisconsin has an "informal" probate procedure that doesn't require a lawyer and has no dollar limit

Statute: Wisconsin Statues Annotated: Sections 867.01+

WYOMING

Affidavit Procedure Instead of Probate: $30,000

Summary Probate: $70,000

Statute: Wyoming Statutes Annotated, Sections 2-1-201; 2-1-205+.

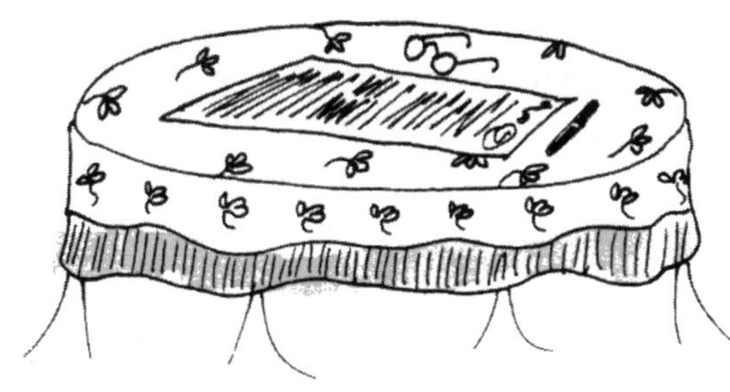

D. California Exemptions From Normal Probate

California has two simplified probate procedures:

1. The "community property petition" allowing all property left to a surviving spouse to be transferred by summary probate.

2. What is commonly called the "Affidavit of Right"[2] allowing property worth less than $60,000 (with no interest in real estate in excess of $10,000) to be transferred by affidavit entirely outside of probate.

1. The Community Property Petition

By using a community property petition, a surviving spouse can readily obtain the portion of the deceased spouse's property left to him or her. It makes no difference if it's jointly owned community property or the deceased's separately-owned property. There's also no dollar limit either on the total amount of the estate or the amount of the property that can be transferred to the surviving spouse by this method. Even if some of the deceased's share of the community property is left to others, the spouse can still obtain his or her portion of it left through a will, without the expense of probate.

The community property petition is a simple one-page, two-sided form that can be prepared by a surviving spouse who is entitled to property of a deceased spouse, either from a will (or by intestate succession if there was no will). The petition is filed with the local probate court, which sets a hearing date. Notice of the hearing must be given to certain people, including all beneficiaries named in the will. Then the hearing is held, and the property ordered transferred to the surviving spouse unless someone contests the petition, which is very rare. Most surviving spouses should be able to handle the process without a lawyer. The steps needed to file a community property petition, and to get court-approval, are explained in detail, including sample forms, in *How to Probate an Estate,* by Nissley (Nolo Press).

[2]Technically, this may also be called "Affidavit under California Probate Code Section 13100."

2. The Affidavit of Right

If a deceased left, by will or intestate, property worth less than $60,000 (net), and no interest in real estate worth more than $10,000, the inheritors can obtain that estate by filing a simple form, called an "Affidavit of Right," with the people or organizations holding the deceased's property.[3] In addition, the inheritors can also collect all of the following under the Affidavit of Right: all vehicles owned by the deceased, no matter how much they are worth, and up to $5,000 owed in back pay. Further, the value of any joint tenancy property does not count toward the $60,000 limit. The purpose of the Affidavit of Right is to enable beneficiaries of a deceased who left a small estate to obtain the cash and other assets they inherit immediately without a lot of red tape. The Affidavit can be prepared and filed by the inheritors who are entitled to the deceased's estate, either by will or, if there's no will, by the laws of intestate inheritance. If there's more than one beneficiary under a will (or the intestacy laws if there's no will), all the beneficiaries must sign the Affidavit of Right. A copy of the Affidavit is then presented to persons or organizations holding the property left by the will; they must promptly release the assets to the beneficiaries. Sample forms and instructions are contained in *How to Probate an Estate,* by Julia Nissley (Nolo Press).

An Affidavit of Right doesn't have to be filed with any state agency. No court or other probate proceeding is required. There's no procedure to verify the inheritor's declaration that the deceased's net estate in California is worth less than $60,000. In this one instance, the law appears to go by the honor system.

Example: Harry Billings dies in Los Angeles, California. Under Harry's will, his sole beneficiary is his adult daughter, Myra. Harry owned no real estate. His estate is worth $65,500: a CD worth $42,000;

[3]Except for any interest in real estate worth less than $10,000, which still must be transferred through a regular probate proceeding.

personal property (stereo, household furniture, two valuable cameras, some rare books) worth $15,000; a car (owned outright by Harry) with a market value of $6,000, and back wages owed Harry (unused vacation pay) of $2,500. Even though Harry's estate, left by his will, exceeds $60,000, all of the property may be collected by Myra by Affidavit of Right. His CD and personal possessions are worth a total of $57,000, under the $60,000 limit. Separate exemptions allow his car and back wages to be claimed by Affidavit of Right.

Myra simply completes the Affidavit of Right and attaches one copy each of the will and death certificate. She then gives one set of the documents, plus her own I.D., to Harry's bank, a second set to the holder of the personal property—in this case, Harry's landlord—a third set to the DMV, and a fourth set to the company that owes Harry the back vacation pay. The bank and the holder of Harry's personal property must release it to her promptly. The Department of Motor Vehicles will re-register the car in Myra's name, and the company will turn over Harry's unused vacation pay to her.

The affidavit must state, under oath, that the total value of the deceased's estate in California is less than $60,000. However, as we've explained, certain items, such as vehicles, no matter how much they are worth, don't count towards the $60,000 limit.

What about property transferred by a living trust or informal bank trust account? The California Affidavit of Right statute isn't clear, but as previously mentioned, standard California legal practice has long assumed that property in a living trust or informal bank trust account isn't counted toward the $60,000 limit. Thus, savvy Californians with good-sized estates can use other probate avoidance methods to pass their valuable items of property and rely on the Affidavit of Right procedure to avoid probate on the rest, which they leave by will.

Example: Teresa has an estate consisting of a house in Los Angeles, with equity of $620,000; a summer cottage at Stinson Beach, with equity $220,000; the furnishings of her two houses worth $40,000; a bank account of $60,000; life insurance with total proceeds of $300,000; and various heirlooms worth a total of $45,000. At her death, she wants her children to receive all her property, except for the heirlooms, which she intends to give to cousins and other relatives. Teresa doesn't think of herself as wealthy; she acquired her houses years ago, when "a dollar was a dollar" and prices low. But, in fact, her taxable estate now amounts to $1,285,000. Rather than have all this property subject to regular probate:

1. She transfers the houses and furnishings into a living trust, naming her children as beneficiaries;

2. She creates a pay-on-death bank account for hersavings, naming her children as beneficiaries;

3. She assigns ownership of her life insurance policies outright to their beneficiaries, and gives up all ownership of them.

Now, only the heirlooms, worth less than the $60,000 limit, remain in Teresa's probate estate. She can distribute these by her will, and her inheritors can claim them simply and speedily by using an Affidavit of Right.

E. New York Exemptions From Normal Probate

New York law provides a simple affidavit procedure for estates of personal property (no real estate) worth less than $10,000. Also, New York exempts *entirely* certain property of a deceased spouse which is set aside for the surviving spouse, or the deceased's minor children if there is no spouse. The total amount of property that can be set aside for family use is $26,150. All property set aside for family use isn't counted as part of the $10,000 that can be exempted from probate. Thus, in theory, an estate totaling $36,150 could be eligible for New York's affidavit procedure if the maximum amount of exempt property was left to a surviving spouse or minor children.

Under the affidavit procedure, the deceased's executor acts as a "voluntary administrator," preparing an affidavit listing the property and beneficiaries and filing it with the probate court (called "surrogate court") clerk. The executor then has authority to collect the deceased's personal property and distribute it to the beneficiaries according to the will or the intestacy laws.

Although the statute isn't clear about whether the affidavit procedure can be combined with other probate avoidance devices, accepted New York legal practice is that it can be. Thus, if someone transfers big-ticket items like houses and stocks by living trust, she could then transfer small personal gifts, with a total value less than $10,000, by her will free from normal probate.

F. Texas Exemptions From Normal Probate

Texas has two simplified probate procedures:

1. An affidavit allowing summary transfer of estates worth less than $50,000, and

2. A summary probate with no dollar limit.

Also, Texas probate is normally quite easy. An uncontested estate can be heard by a judge within ten days of filing a petition for probate.

1. The Affidavit

Under Texas law, certain small estates can be transformed by use of an affidavit filed with the clerk of the county court. The affidavit procedure is available only if the estate has a value, *excluding* homestead and exempt property, of less than $50,000. Exempt property is certain community property that can be "set aside" for the deceased's family—including an automobile, household furnishings, clothing, food and last wages. Homestead property is community real estate protected under Texas law.

All people receiving part of the estate must sign and swear to the affidavit. The affidavit can be filed by any beneficiaries only if 30 days have passed since the deceased has died and no one has filed for formal probate. The affidavit must list the estate's assets and liabilities, the names and addresses of all people receiving part of the estate, and whether they take that property under a will or by intestacy. If there's a will, it usually is filed with the affidavit, although this isn't required by statute.

After the affidavit is filed with the county court clerk, the clerk issues a certified copy of the affidavit to the beneficiaries. The affidavit entitles them to collect debts owed the deceased, collect and receive estate property, and to have title to automobiles, bank accounts, stocks or real estate transferred. Anyone releasing or transferring property to someone on the authority of such an affidavit is discharged from any further liability on that property. The responsibility for properly disposing of the property falls on the person collecting the property with the affidavit.

A creditor can prevent collection by affidavit by filing for formal probate within 30 days of the deceased's death. And, even if collection by affidavit occurs, those who collect the deceased's property remain liable to the estate creditors.

Since all those with rights to an estate must sign it, the affidavit is practical only if there are no disputes about who should receive what property. Although title can be transferred under the authority of the affidavit, others can dispute it later. (Where title may be disputed, the summary probate procedure described in Section 2 below may be more desirable.)

The $50,000 ceiling on the value of estates collectable by affidavit limits the use of the process. Most estates containing real property will exceed that limit. However, since the value of homestead property is excluded from the $50,000 calculation, the statute may have broader use with small estates where a spouse survives the deceased. This is because the family home, often the principal estate asset, would be excluded from the $50,000 calculation. Therefore, where there's a surviving spouse, a moderate-sized estate, including the family house, might be collected and distributed by the affidavit process. However, where there's no surviving spouse, the affidavit process will be limited to small estates.

2. Summary Probate

The Texas summary probate has no dollar limitations. Under this procedure, the executor files an application to probate the will, exactly as in traditional probate. A hearing is then held on the validity of the will. If the will is proved valid, and it's shown that the estate has no outstanding debts or other problems, the court orders summary probate, dispensing with many of the tedious steps of normal probate. (The Texas statute is silent, however, on whether summary probate means reduced attorney's fees, which means that it's up to your inheritors to negotiate.)

The court order admitting the will to probate serves the same function as the small estate's affidavit: it authorizes transfer of the deceased's property to those entitled to it under the will. Furthermore, since the will has been proved in court, title to the property transferred in this way isn't open to challenge. This avoids a problem that sometimes occurs with the small estates affidavit. However, Texas summary probate does normally require an attorney, so the major drawback of normal probate is still involved and it isn't therefore a satisfactory alternative to probate avoidance techniques.

G. Florida Exemptions From Normal Probate

Florida law provides three different types of simplified probate. However, all three are quite restrictive, and therefore of no use to most Florida readers who wish to plan their estate to avoid probate.

1. Simplified Family Probate

Family members can petition a probate court for a simplified form of probate (called "Family administration") if there's a will and:

- The primary beneficiaries are the surviving spouse and/or "lineal descendants" (children, grandchildren) and/or "lineal ascendants" (parents, grandparents, etc.) and any specific or general gift to others is a minor part of the estate; and
- The value of the gross estate, for federal estate tax purposes, is less than $60,000; and
- The entire estate consists of personal property.

Thus a family, or any member, can petition for simplified probate only if the total net value of the estate is less than $60,000, and none of it is real estate. This net value includes all property transferred by a living trust or joint tenancy, since the worth of this property is included in the federal taxable estate. Most Florida readers' estates will be well in excess of the relatively modest amount of $60,000.

2. Summary Probate

Florida law also permits summary probate (called "summary administration") if 1)there's a will and 2) the value of the entire estate subject to probate in

Florida, less the value of property exempt from creditors, is less than $25,000. Property exempt from creditors, under Florida law, includes:

- Homestead property (basically, a house) exempted under the state constitution
- A "family allowance," specified by statute, for the support of the deceased's family
- Certain property of a deceased—household furniture, furnishings and appliances (up to a net value of $10,000), cars, personal effects not disposed of by will (up to a net value of $1,000)—which can be claimed by the deceased's surviving spouse or minor children.

Again, this summary probate procedure is too restrictive for most people to use. The amount left by will can't exceed $25,000. The wording of the statute indicates that you can't combine summary Florida probate with probate avoidance devices. For example, suppose you transfer all your property by living trust, except for personal items worth $15,000 which you leave to a friend by a will. Can your friend obtain this property by "summary" probate? Probably not.

3. No Probate Required

For certain very small estates, Florida doesn't require probate. These estates can consist only of personal property, not real estate, that is:

- exempt from creditors under Florida law or the state constitution, and
- not worth more than "the amount of preferred funeral expenses and reasonable and necessary medical and hospital expenses of the last 60 days of the last illness." ■

14

WILLS

A will is what many people think of when they first consider estate planning. This makes sense. As almost everyone knows, a will is a document that specifies who gets your property when you die.

After reading this far, you're surely aware of the major problem caused by leaving property by a will—the legal requirement that most wills must go through probate. Indeed, a substantial portion of this book is devoted to explaining methods of avoiding this expensive, time-consuming process. However, despite the downside of probate, a will should still be part of every estate plan.

A thorough estate plan, which we particularly encourage older people to prepare, avoids probate. With this kind of plan, you normally need only a simple will, which we call a "back-up will." A typical back-up will enables you to:

- make some specific gifts to named beneficiaries
- name a residuary beneficiary and alternate for any property subject to your will that is not specifically given to other beneficiaries
- name personal and property guardians and alternates for your minor children, and
- name your executor.

As we will discuss below, a will can also be an excellent interim estate planning device for younger adults who sensibly decide to put off more in-depth estate planning until later.

A. Why Prepare a Back-Up Will?

If you prepare a thorough estate plan, including the use of probate avoidance tools such as joint tenancy, pay-on-death accounts and a living trust, do you still need a back-up will? Yes. It's always sensible to have a back-up will as part of your estate plan for one or probably more of the following reasons:

- **To name a personal guardian for your minor children.** You need a will to achieve the vital goal of naming a personal guardian for your minor children, if you have any. You can't use a trust to appoint a personal guardian. Also, in your will you can appoint a property guardian for your children to manage any of their property not otherwise legally supervised by an adult. (As discussed in Chapter 6, Children, Section C, it's generally preferable to leave your minor children property as part of a children's trust, or using the Uniform Transfers to Minors Act, rather than relying on a property guardian named in a will, which you name only as a back-up.) As discussed in Section B below, younger people with minor children, who don't have much property, may decide that because naming a personal guardian is the primary thing they're worried about, a simple will is all the estate planning they currently need.
- **To dispose of suddenly acquired property.** Anyone may end up acquiring valuable property at or shortly before death, such as a sudden gift or inheritance, a lottery prize or a share of joint tenancy property because of simultaneous death. Of course, it's sensible to promptly revise your estate plan to name a specific beneficiary to receive this property. But what if you don't get around to it before you become mentally incapacitated, or die? If you have a will, that property will go to your residuary beneficiary, who, by definition, takes "the rest of your property." Unfortunately, there's no easy way to leave left-over property through a living trust, since, by definition, property must be formally added to the trust for it to be subject to the trust provisions.
- **To dispose of property not transferred by a probate avoidance device.** This is really the same point as we just made above, for a slightly different type of property. If you buy property but don't get around to planning probate avoidance for

it (by placing it in your living trust, for example), a will is a valuable back-up device, ensuring that the property will go to whomever you want to have it (your residuary beneficiary), and not pass under the intestate laws. Similarly, if somehow you've failed to transfer some of your existing property to a probate avoidance device—either intentionally or because you didn't properly complete transfers of title—a will prevents that property from passing under the intestate laws.

- **To give away property someone left you that is still in probate.** If someone has left you property by will, and that property is still enmeshed in probate when you die, you can't arrange to transfer it by a probate avoidance device such as a living trust, since you don't have title to the property. But again, under your will, that property goes to your residuary beneficiary.
- **To disinherit a child or spouse.** As explained in Chapter 6, Children, Section E1, you can expressly disinherit a child in your will. You can disinherit a spouse in your will only if you live in a community property state. (See Chapter 5, Beneficiaries, Section H.)
- **To name your executor.** In your will, you name your executor, the person with legal authority to supervise distribution of property left by your will, and to represent your estate. It can be a good idea to have an executor even if you have also set up a living trust and named a successor trustee to manage it when you die, because banks and other financial institutions can be reassured to know an executor exists. The successor trustee and executor are often the same person.
- **In case probate is not required.** As explained in Chapter 13, State Law Exemptions From Normal Probate, some states don't require probate, or greatly simplify probate, for small or modest estates. If your estate qualifies for simplified treatment, there's no need to use a series of probate avoidance devices—a will is all you need. And in some states, even larger estates can make use of simplified probate. For example, California allows personal property worth up to $60,000 to be transferred by a will without any probate. Property transferred by probate avoidance methods doesn't count toward this $60,000 limit. So, in California (and in some other states), a will can be a useful method for making small gifts—that treasured antique clock to a niece, or $3,000 to a fondly-remembered employee—once you have placed the bulk of your estate in a living trust.

B. A Will as the Centerpiece of Your Estate Plan

As just discussed, back-up wills are designed to fit as one small piece of a more complex estate plan. But obviously it's also possible not to bother with a more sophisticated estate plan, and simply leave all or most of your property by will. To do this, you'll obviously need to focus much more precisely on how to make a comprehensive will.

Despite the costs and delays associated with probate, many people decide to make a will the centerpiece of their estate plan. These include:

- People, no matter what their age or health, who simply don't want the bother of more extensive estate planning. Quite a few people say, "Yes, I guess I should probably do full-scale estate planning, but I never get around to it, so I'd better at least make a will now and think about the full-scale plan later." After all, a simple will easily achieves their basic goal of distributing their property as they see fit, with as little disturbance to themselves as possible. Sure a will is likely to lead to probate, but the goal of probate avoidance, as sensible as it is, should never obscure the more important goal of seeing to it that your property will go to the people and organizations you want to receive it.
- Healthy younger people who know that, statistically, they're unlikely to die for decades. These people primarily want to be certain their basic wishes for their property are carried out in the very unlikely event they die unexpectedly. A will achieves this goal, with considerably less paperwork than does a living trust. And as you acquire property, and people close to you are born and die, it can be a lot easier to make a new will than to amend a living trust. Accordingly, many younger people rely primarily on a will and make a probate-avoiding estate plan when they're older and more settled.
- Parents of minor children. The primary estate planning goal of many young parents—single or in couples—is to ensure, to the best of their abilities, that if they die, their children are well provided for and cared for. A will allows parents to name a personal guardian (something that can't be done in a living trust), while also allowing them to establish a simple children's trust to delay the age at which the kids get their hands on the money. Years later, of course, if the parents accumulate considerable property, they may want to engage in more thorough estate planning.

C. Options If You Decide You Want a More Complex Will

If you decide to prepare a more complex will, you can either draft one yourself or hire a lawyer. Happily, many—perhaps most—people can safely prepare their own, without the cost of a lawyer, using Nolo's excellent computer software package, *WillMaker*. The *WillMaker* program allows you to draft and print out a valid will with surprising ease. If you have access to a Windows, DOS, or Macintosh computer, *WillMaker* could be exactly what you need. Or, if you prefer a book, you can use *Nolo's Simple Will Book,* a thorough manual that Denis authored to enable you to prepare a will safely covering most people's needs.

With *WillMaker* or *Nolo's Simple Will Book,* you can do any of the following:

- make gifts of cash or specific items of property
- name alternate beneficiaries for each gift
- name a residuary beneficiary to receive all property subject to the will not given to other-named beneficiaries
- name personal and property guardians for your minor children, and also name successor guardians, in case your first choices can't serve
- name different personal or property guardians for different children (*Nolo's Simple Will Book* only)
- establish a basic trust for any property you leave to your children. This allows you to specify the age at which each child gets his or her property outright. In the meantime, the trustee can spend money for the child's basic needs, such as health, housing and education
- disinherit a child
- forgive debts
- specify what assets you want used to pay death taxes or debts
- give real estate free of a mortgage (*Nolo's Simple Will Book* only)

- establish a "no contest" clause that disinherits any beneficiary who unsuccessfully challenges your will.

D. General Information About Wills

Many people have questions about wills—how they work, what you can or can't do with one, who you can disinherit, how a will can be challenged. Here we briefly discuss (and hopefully answer) some of these major questions—which apply to all wills, back-up or not.

1. What Makes a Will Legal?

Drafting a legal will isn't nearly as complicated as most people fear. The requirements are:

- You must be at least 18-years-old in all states, except Wyoming, where you must be at least 19 to make a valid will.
- You must be of "sound mind." The fact that you're reading and understanding this book is, as a practical matter, sufficient evidence that you meet this test.
- Your will must comply with the technical will-drafting requirements of your state's law. In general, these requirements are very similar in all states, and are less onerous than many people imagine. These technical requirements are:
  - The will must be typewritten or printed on a computer printer (see Section D2, below, for a discussion of handwritten wills).
  - The will must have at least one substantive provision. The most common one gives some, or all, of your property to whomever you want to have it.
  - You must appoint at least one executor.
  - You must date the will.
  - You must sign the will in front of three witnesses—people who don't inherit under the will. Some states only require two witnesses, but using three ensures that you've met the requirements of every state and, in any case, is safer. Witnesses watch you sign your will and then sign it themselves. They must be told that it's your will they are signing, but they don't have to read it or be told what the will contains.

Those are all the basic technical requirements. There's no requirement that a will be notarized,[1] recorded, or filed with any governmental agency. Years ago, when Denis was a partner in a small law firm, he learned that some clients were disappointed that their wills didn't look more impressive. So he began stapling all wills in a blue cover-binder, and attaching a red ribbon and red wax seal. Some clients appreciated these touches—although they were certainly not legally required. If you want extras like these, you can purchase what you need at most stationery stores, for far less than if you buy them from a lawyer.

2. Are Handwritten Wills Valid?

"Holographic" is legalese for handwritten. A holographic will must be written, dated and signed entirely in the handwriting of the person making the will. It does not have to be witnessed. Holographic wills are recognized by about 25 states. We definitely don't recommend them, even in the states where they're legal, and therefore don't discuss them in detail in this book.

---

[1]However, in many states, having the witnesses sign what's called a "self-proving" affidavit, which is then notarized, can eliminate any need for a witness to testify at subsequent probate proceedings. "Self-proving" wills are explained in detail in *Nolo's Simple Will Book*, Chapter 13, Section D.

Holographic wills aren't recommended because probate courts traditionally have been very strict when examining them after the death of the writer. Since a handwritten will isn't normally witnessed, judges sometimes fear that it might have been forged. Also, there's often the need to prove that the will was actually and voluntarily written by the deceased person, which sometimes isn't easy to do. In short, given the tiny bit of extra trouble it takes to prepare a typed will and have it witnessed, it's reckless not to do it.

3. What Are Statutory Wills?

A statutory will is a pre-printed, fill-in-the-blanks, check-the-boxes will form authorized by state law. California, Maine, Michigan, New Mexico and Wisconsin have statutory wills, and other states are considering them. In theory, statutory wills are an excellent idea—inexpensive, easy to complete, and reliable. Unfortunately, in practice, statutory wills are so limited in scope they aren't useful for most people. The choices provided in the statutory forms are quite narrow and cannot legally be changed—that is, you can't customize them to fit your situation or, indeed, change them at all. For example, the California Statutory Will allows you to make one, and only one, cash gift. All your other property must go to your spouse or children. If you want to leave your car to your brother, or leave money to several charities, you are out of luck. The Michigan form allows you to make only two cash gifts (aside from household property); everything else must go to your spouse or children. Thus, these statutory wills are useful to you only if you are married and want all your property to go to your spouse (or, if she predeceases you, in trust for your minor children). But even if you're married, if you want to use your will to leave some of your property, beyond one cash gift, to relatives or friends, you cannot use the statutory will.

4. What Is a Pour-Over Will?

A "pour-over" will is one that directs that the property subject to it goes to (be "poured over" into) another legal entity, usually a trust. For example, sometimes people make their living trusts the beneficiaries of their wills. When the will property is poured over to the trust, the trust beneficiary provisions control who receives that property.

a. When Not to Use a Pour-Over Will

Pour-over wills are rarely a good idea to use with a living trust for an individual or a shared basic living trust. Pour-over wills do *not* avoid probate. All property that is left through a will—any kind of will—must go through probate, unless the amount left is small enough to qualify for exemption from normal probate laws. Probate is most definitely not avoided simply because the beneficiary of a will is a living trust.

It's generally better to simply use a standard back-up will to take care of your left-over (non-living trust) property rather than a pour-over will. In the back-up will, you can name the people you want to get the property, and skip the unnecessary extra step of pouring the property through the living trust after your death.

When used as a back-up will, a pour-over will actually has a disadvantage that standard wills don't: It forces the living trust to go on for months after your death, because the property left through the pour-over will must go through probate before it can be transferred to the trust. Usually, the property left in a living trust can be distributed to the beneficiaries, and the trust ended, within a few weeks after the person's death.

b. When You May Want a Pour-Over Will

There are, however, two situations in which you might want to use a pour-over will. With a living trust with marital life estate, a pour-over will can be desirable. With this device, the spouses want the maximum amount of property to eventually wind up in the marital life estate trust. (See Chapter 18, Estate Tax-Saving Bypass Trusts, Section C.) So each spouse writes a pour-over will, leaving his or her property to that trust. After a spouse dies, the other spouse should amend her or his will or prepare a new one, since there will no longer be a functional marital life estate trust for the surviving spouse's property to go to.

Also, if you set up, as part of your living trust, a child's subtrust to provide management for property left to a young beneficiary, you may want any property that child inherits through your will to go into that subtrust. Otherwise, you would create two trusts for the beneficiary: one in the will and one in your living trust.

5. Other Types of Wills

Although almost all readers of this book will want a formal, witnessed will, either as a back-up to a living trust or as their primary estate planning device, long experience has taught us that people will also have questions about other types of wills. Here are the most common wills that are asked about:

- **Oral wills.** Oral wills (also called "nuncupative" wills) are valid in a minority of states and, even where valid, are acceptable only if made under special circumstances, such as the will maker's perception of imminent death on the battlefield or in some other highly unusual circumstance. Clearly they are not to be relied on as a serious estate planning device.
- **Video or film wills.** Video or film wills aren't valid under any state's law. But films of a person reciting who they give property to can be useful evidence if a will is challenged, to demonstrate that the will maker was competent and didn't appear crazy or under the influence of someone else.

If you truly fear a will contest based on your lack of competence or the undue influence of a beneficiary, ask a lawyer about using videos or films to help establish that you were fully competent when your will was signed.

- **Joint wills.** A joint will is one document made by two people, who are usually married. Each leaves everything to the other when the first one dies, and then the will goes on to specify what happens to the property when the second person dies. In effect, a joint will can prevent the surviving person from changing his mind regarding what should happen to the survivors. We don't recommend joint wills. They may tie up property for years, pending the second death. Also, even if circumstances change radically, it can be unclear whether the survivor can revoke any part of the will. If you want to impose controls over property you leave to your spouse, the sensible way to do it is through a property control trust. (See Chapter 23, Trusts for Second or Subsequent Marriages, Section A.)
- **Contracts to make a will.** A contract to make a will—that is, to leave certain property to the other person who signs the contract—can be valid, but is usually not wise. The usual case in which such contracts are made is where someone provides services—care, or live-in nursing—in return for an agreement that the person receiving the care will leave property to the person providing the care. Tying up your property like this so you cannot

change your will, even if circumstances change, isn't desirable for many reasons. Most lawyers prefer to establish a trust for these situations.

If you face a situation in which you want to guarantee now that someone will receive money from your estate, see a lawyer.

- **Living wills**. A living will (sometimes called a "Directive to Physicians") isn't a conventional will at all. Essentially, a living will is a document in which the writer states that she wants a natural death and doesn't want her life artificially prolonged by use of life support equipment. They are discussed in Chapter 26, Incapacity: Health Care and Financial Management Directives.

6. What Property Cannot Be Transferred by Will?

Throughout this book, we have emphasized the fact that property transferred by a binding probate avoidance device can't also be transferred by will. Another way to make this point is to emphasize that once property is placed in one of the following forms of ownership, listing it in a will has no force and affect. The following property cannot be transferred by will:

- *all* joint tenancy property—it automatically goes to the surviving joint tenants (but if all joint tenants die simultaneously, you can transfer your share by will)
- *all* property in a living trust—it goes to the beneficiaries under the trust;
- life insurance proceeds payable to a named beneficiary or beneficiaries—they go to the beneficiaries of the policy
- retirement plans, pensions, IRAs, Keoghs, etc., payable to named beneficiaries—the beneficiaries in these programs get these assets no matter what your will says
- informal bank account trusts or pay-on-death accounts —the person you designate as beneficiary on the account document inherits, and
- contracts, as in living together, partnership, closely-held corporations, etc., where the survivor gets property or rights to it.

7. Can My Will Be Successfully Challenged?

The fact that many people worry about the possibility of challenges to their wills (or other transfer documents such as a living trust), shows how fear-ridden estate planning has become. Fortunately, the reality is that will challenges, let alone successful ones, are exceedingly rare. The legal grounds for contesting a will are limited to extreme circumstances. Basically, your will can only be invalidated if you were underage when you made it, were clearly mentally incompetent, or the will was procured by fraud, duress or undue influence.

A person has to be pretty far gone before a court will rule that she lacked the capacity to make a valid will. For example, forgetfulness or even the inability to recognize friends don't by themselves establish incapacity. Also, it's important to remember that courts will presume that the will writer was of sound mind, unless someone challenges this in a court proceeding—which is rare. Similarly, a will is rarely declared invalid on grounds it was procured by fraud, duress or undue influence; this requires proof that some evildoer manipulated a person in a confused or weakened mental or emotional state to leave his property in a way the person otherwise wouldn't have.

If you think there's any possibility anyone might challenge your will or estate plan, see a lawyer. Or if there are special circumstances, such as a seriously debilitating illness, that you believe might raise questions about your competency and the validity of your will, it's also prudent to see a lawyer. In practice, of course, this can mean having the lawyer come to see and perhaps even physically help you. For example, in many states, if you're too ill to sign your own name, you can direct that a witness or an attorney sign it for you. In any unusual physical or mental circumstances, it's prudent to have a lawyer's assistance, especially if substantial amounts of property are involved. It could always be claimed that someone too ill to sign her name wasn't mentally competent. In any subsequent court challenge to the will, the lawyer's testimony that the will maker appeared to be in full possession of his or her faculties could be very important.

8. Does Divorce Automatically Revoke Gifts Made to a Former Spouse?

Not in every state. In any case, you should always revise your will and bring your estate plan up-to-date after a divorce. (See Chapter 31, After Your Estate Plan Is Completed, Section B.)

9. What Happens If I Have a Child or Marry After I Make a Will?

If you have a child or get married after you make your will, you must revise your will, and your estate plan, to reflect your new situation. If you don't, your estate may become entangled in laws designed to protect "afterborn children" and spouses married after a will and other estate planning documents were prepared.

In any case, most people who have a child or get married after they make their will and estate plan want to revise those documents to provide for the new child or spouse.

10. Whom Should I Name as Executor?

Your executor should be the person you trust the most—and who's willing to do the job. If you plan to prepare a living trust, it's generally best that your executor be the same person you've chosen to be the successor trustee of your trust.

You can name co-executors, or even several executors, if you have good reason for it. As with successor trustees of a living trust, we generally recommend having only one trustee. However, there can be compelling reasons—family harmony is one example—for selecting more than one trustee.

One caution here: Some states require that your executor must either live in your state or, if she doesn't, must post a bond. This costs your estate money solely to provide a bond your estate won't need if your executor is honest. In any case, it's a good idea to name at least one executor who does live in your state.

11. Can I Give My Property as I Choose?

Pragmatically, you can leave property to anyone and for any purpose you choose, with the following exceptions:

- In common law states, your spouse has a right to a certain percentage of your property. (See Chapter 3, State Property Ownership Laws, Section C.)
- There are legal limits on how long you can impose controls on property after you die. If you want to mandate that property remain in your family for more than two generations, you've got problems, and must see a lawyer.

- You cannot leave money for some socially-disapproved purposes, such as a gift contingent on the divorce of the beneficiary.

12. Can I Disinherit Whomever I Wish?

Aside from the rights of a spouse mentioned above, you can disinherit anyone you choose.[2] As previously discussed in Chapter 6, Children, anyone but a child (or a grandchild, if your child is deceased) can be disinherited simply by omitting to name him or her as a beneficiary of your will or living trust. However, if you decide to disinherit a child or a child of a deceased child you must specifically state so in your will—for example, "I disinherit my son, Nero, and declare he shall receive nothing from my estate." You can also leave a child a minimal amount—$1 or so—which functions as a disinheritance. If you decide to disinherit a child, evaluate the possibility that the child will challenge your will and estate plan.

[2]Except, as previously noted, a spouse in Florida must leave his or her house to the other spouse or, if that spouse is deceased, to their children.

Possible challenge to disinheritance. If you conclude that by disinheriting a child you create risk that he or she will challenge your will or living trust (and especially if you are very ill or aged), discuss the matter with an expert before finalizing your decision.

13. What Happens If I Move?

A will drafted in one state normally remains valid if you subsequently move to another state. However, it's often advisable to draft a new will after a permanent move, because it's wise to appoint an executor of your will who is nearby. Also, if you're married and move from a common law property state to a community property state or vice versa, the marital property ownership laws of your new state may affect your will.

14. Can I Leave Property to Minors in My Will?

The answer is yes. As previously explained, minor children cannot own substantial amounts of property outright. Property you leave to minors—your own children or someone else's—can be left by using various legal methods: a child's trust, a gift made under the Uniform Transfers to Minors Act or property to be managed by a property guardian. Leaving property to be supervised by a property guardian is generally the least desirable of these alternatives. (See Chapter 6, Children, Section C.)

15. Simultaneous Death: What Happens If My Spouse or Mate and I Die at the Same Time?

This is an issue that concerns many couples, though the chances of it occurring are very remote. To handle this possibility, most wills for a married person contain what's called a "simultaneous death" clause. The purpose of this clause is to provide for what happens if a husband and wife die in the same accident and it can't be determined who died first. Under these circumstances, the clause creates the presumption that the will maker survives his or her spouse. Thus the husband is presumed to survive the wife for purposes of his will property, and the wife is presumed to survive the husband for purposes of her will property. Although at first glance this clause can certainly appear to be contradictory if contained in the wills of both spouses, it is a standard, well-accepted legal device. Because each spouse's will is interpreted separately, the clause acts to distribute each spouse's property as his or her own will provides.

SIGNING AND WITNESSING YOUR WILL

To be valid, your will must be signed and dated in front of witnesses—two in most states, three in a couple. Then, these witnesses must sign the will in your presence, and also in the presence of the other witnesses.

Witnesses need only be:

- Adults (usually over 18) and of sound mind.
- People who won't inherit under the will. That means anyone who is to receive of any gift in your will cannot be a witness.
- People who should be easy to locate in the event of your death. This usually means choosing people who aren't likely to move around a lot and who are younger than you are. ■

15

ESTATE TAXES

All U.S. citizens, and anyone owning property located in the U.S., are subject to federal death taxes, called "estate taxes."

Basically, no estate taxes are required if the value of the "taxable estate" transferred at a person's death to his or her inheritors is less than $600,000. (There is discussion in Congress now to raise this figure to, perhaps, $750,000.) If the estate is over that amount, estate taxes are often assessed. If estate taxes are payable, they can take a large bite of a good-sized estate. The tax rate is determined by the size of the taxable estate, with the general rule being that the more you own, the higher the rate.

ESTATE TAX LAWS

Federal estate tax laws are found in the Internal Revenue Code. We use the conventional abbreviation "IRC." The Internal Revenue Code can be found in Volume 26 of the United States Code, the official collection of all federal statutes.

Also, a minority of states impose death taxes on property of a deceased who lived or owned real estate in that state.

Fortunately, several federal tax law deductions and credits (exemptions) allow you to leave substantial amounts of property to your beneficiaries free of estate taxes. The most important of these are:

- The "unified credit," which allows the first $600,000 of property to pass tax-free, no matter who it is left to (IRC Section 2010); and[1]
- The marital deduction, which exempts all property left to a surviving spouse—unless the spouse is not a citizen of the U.S. (IRC Section 2056(a)); and
- The charitable deduction, which exempts all property left to a tax-exempt charity (IRC Section 2055(a)).

Avoiding death taxes has nothing to do with avoiding probate. All property owned by the deceased, whatever the form of ownership, and whether it's transferred to inheritors through probate or by other means, is subject to federal estate taxes.

International estate death tax planning is a complex field. If you own property in the U.S. and also in another country, or earn income in another country, you'll definitely need to see a lawyer.

If you own assets that are clearly worth less than $600,000, you don't need to worry about federal estate taxes and therefore can skip or skim most of this chapter (though you should still check Section C to see if your estate might be liable for state death taxes). However, if you have assets worth more than $600,000, or if you are married and plan to leave your property to your spouse, who would then have a total net worth exceeding $600,000, please read on.

DEATH TAXES ON PROPERTY OUTSIDE THE U.S.

If you also own property in another country, or earn income in that country, your estate may well be subject to death taxes in that country. But also, if you earn income in another country, and are a U.S. citizen or resident, you may be subject to death taxes by the U.S. on some, or all, of the same property taxed by the other country.

[1]Assuming none of your federal "unified estate gift tax credit" has been previously used because you have made taxable gifts. Generally, gifts worth up to $10,000 to one person in a calendar year are tax exempt. Taxes due on gifts over $10,000 are deducted from your unified credit. (See Section B1 of this chapter and Chapter 16, Gifts and Gift Taxes, for more on the interrelationship of estate and gift taxes.)

If your estate is likely to be subject to federal estate tax, you'll want to resolve several important questions, including:

- How much estate tax will likely be assessed against your estate?
- How can you eliminate, or at least save on, those taxes and still achieve your other estate planning goals?
- If it's likely that there will be estate taxes due, what source of funds will be used to pay them?

NO INCOME TAXES ON INHERITED PROPERTY

Someone who inherits property is not liable for income taxes on the worth of that property. It is received income tax free. However, after a person inherits property, any income she subsequently receives from the property is considered regular income, and so subject to income tax.

The rules for capital gain tax applied to the sale of inherited property are discussed below, in Section A6.

We'll now take a closer look at federal estate taxes, the major tax imposed on larger estates.

A. FEDERAL ESTATE TAXES

To estimate your federal estate tax liability, you need to do the following:

1. Estimate your net worth (the value of everything you own minus everything you owe) to arrive at the net value of your estate.

2. Subtract all applicable estate law tax deductions, such as for charitable gifts or property left to a spouse.

3. If there's anything left over (in other words, your allowable subtractions don't reduce your estate to zero), you then need to check the estate tax table (Section A5, below) to determine the amount of estate taxes that you would owe on your "taxable estate." The result of this calculation is called, in tax-ese, the "tentative tax."

4. Subtract the "unified credit" from your tentative tax to estimate the estate tax that would be owed to the federal government.

1. The Big Picture: Gift Tax, Estate Tax and the Unified Credit

As we stated earlier, federal estate tax law allows you to take certain deductions that reduce the amount of your estate on which the estate tax is figured. So, in order to know if your estate will likely have to pay estate taxes, you need to subtract these deductions from the net value of your assets. Before we discuss these important deductions, however, let's focus on how the U.S. estate tax laws work generally.

To begin with, the basic tax law is that both taxable gifts made during one's life and one's estate transferred at death are free from all federal gift and estate taxes up to a combined value of $600,000. This tax-free treatment is accomplished, technically, by use of something called the "unified credit." The reason this credit is called "unified" is because the same tax rate applies to taxable lifetime gifts as to property left on death.

The gift tax exists in order to prevent wealthy people from giving away much or all of their property before they die and thus avoiding estate tax entirely. Once a gift exceeds $10,000 per person per year (unless the gift is to a spouse or charity), gift taxes are assessed. The amount of tax imposed on a taxable gift made during one's life is identical to the estate tax imposed on the same amount of property left on death. So there is no tax incentive for a person to make large gifts during her lifetime.

SOME THOUGHTS ON DEATH TAXES AND AVOIDING THEM

Whether or not to tax property transferred at the death of a person is a decision that every society makes for itself. In the days of "survival of the fittest" capitalism in 19th century America, for example, there were no federal estate taxes. By contrast, in some European countries today, death taxes take a very significant portion of larger estates. Modern America is somewhere in between.

Trying to reduce death taxes to a minimum through estate planning is sometimes thought of as a form of lawyer's magic, by which taxes can be avoided completely no matter how large the estate. It's true there is some gimmickry in some schemes of the very rich to avoid death taxes, although not nearly as much as was allowed 25 years ago. Certainly, there's no magic way to escape death taxes legally owned. The best estate planning can do is use lawful means to reduce, or hopefully eliminate, death taxes.

The process of planning to avoid taxation at death has been criticized by many. They suggest this is a game for the rich, and that society would be better off if people couldn't pass large sums from one generation to the next. Perhaps, although we've noticed that even most socialists seem to prefer to have whatever wealth they've acquired be given to family, friends or worthy causes rather than turned over to the government. Certainly, given present law, we believe that it makes good sense to try to preserve as much of your estate as possible for your inheritors.

Technically, here's how the unified estate/gift tax credit we just mentioned works. The unified credit is $192,800, an amount that corresponds exactly to the amount of gift or estate tax that would be owed on the transfer of $600,000 of taxable property. Practically, this unified credit has two important effects:

- First, if you make no taxable gifts during your life (which includes the vast majority of us), you will not have used any of your unified credit at the time of your death. Therefore, the first $600,000 of your estate will not be taxed by the federal government.
- Second, if you do make taxable gifts during your life, no tax will be actually owed to the government until all of your unified credit is used up. In other words, you must give $600,000 in taxable gifts before you actually start paying the government gift taxes. So even if you've made taxable gifts, if they total less than $600,000, you'll still have some of your unified credit left over to apply to your estate when you die. How much unified credit you have left over depends entirely on the amount of taxable gifts you've given.

Examples:

- Jane, who has never made a taxable gift, leaves her entire estate with a net worth of exactly $600,000 to her children. The unified credit means the entire amount is free from estate tax.
- Fred, who has never made a taxable gift, leaves his entire estate of $580,000 divided between four good friends. All of this property passes free of estate tax.
- Mike, who has never made a taxable gift, leaves his estate of $700,000 to his son. $100,000 will be taxed under federal estate tax law.
- Sally gives her nephew a gift of stock in the family business worth $710,000. Gift tax will be owed and payable on $100,000 ($710,000 gift minus $10,000 annual gift tax exemption minus

$600,000 excluded from estate tax by the unified credit).

- Cynthia gave her father a $50,000 gift when he retired in 1988 for an around-the-world cruise. She filed a federal gift tax return and reported making a taxable gift of $40,000. Cynthia died in 1994 leaving an estate with a net worth of $590,000. Estate tax will be owed on $30,000. Here's why. Because the 1988 taxable gift of $40,000, the amount that Cynthia could leave at her death free from tax was reduced from $600,000 to $560,000. When Cynthia died with an estate of $590,000, she only had enough unified credit left to shield $560,000 from estate tax; the remaining $30,000 was taxed.

Under the estate gift tax law, the very wealthy don't get full benefit of the unified credit. If your taxable estate and taxable gifts total over $10 million the unified credit begins to be phased out. This phase-out ends at $21,040,000. Still, we imagine that inheritors of such large estates will manage to get by. Also, large estates can benefit from the use of various estate tax-saving devices, from an ongoing gift program (see Chapter 16, Gifts and Gift Taxes, Section E) to a variety of estate tax-saving trusts. (See Chapter 17, An Overview of Ongoing Trusts.)

2. Estimate Your Net Worth

If you completed the property worksheets in Chapter 4, Inventorying Your Property, Section B, you should have a ballpark estimate of your current net worth (assets minus liabilities). If you didn't complete the property worksheet, you'll need to make some estimate, now, of your present net worth. Your current net worth will give you an indication if your estate is likely to exceed the $600,000 federal estate tax threshold. As a rule, most property should be valued at its current market value. However, under federal estate tax law, a few types of property can be valued on a lower dollar basis than current market value. For example, family farmland can be valued for its (continued) use as a farm, even if the land would be worth more if sold to a developer to build an apartment complex or a shopping center. (The idea here is to protect family farms.)

Of course, you can't now determine exactly what your estate will be worth when you die, so you don't need to worry about precise figures. A rough estimate of your present worth should be sufficient for estate tax planning purposes. Also, it may be hard to determine the value of some types of property, such as royalty rights or stock in a closely held corporation. You can either make your best guess here, or pay for an expert's opinion.

If your net worth exceeds $600,000, it normally makes sense to conclude that you'll have at least that much in your estate when you die, and probably more. And, as we've said, if you have significantly less than $600,000, you generally don't have to worry about federal estate taxes now. If you strike it rich, or semi-rich, later that will be the time for you to learn about estate taxes and ways to reduce them.

> **WHO APPRAISES YOUR ESTATE AFTER YOU DIE?**
>
> Having the value of an estate determined is the responsibility of the person the deceased appointed to supervise his property. This is the successor trustee if the property is left by living trust, or the executor if the property is left by will. If all property is left by joint tenancy, the surviving joint tenant has the responsibility to see if an estate tax return must be filed or taxes paid.
>
> The federal government isn't involved in appraising property in an estate. Obviously, though, the IRS can challenge and audit estate tax returns, just as it can audit income tax returns. In some states that impose death taxes, official appraisals are done as part of the death tax system. However, in the many states without official appraisals, it's the exclusive responsibility of the person supervising the estate to make a bona fide appraisal of the estate's property in order to determine if a federal estate tax return need be filed.
>
> It may often be difficult for an executor, trustee or probate attorney, to establish the market value of many items—works of art, closely held businesses, stock in small corporations, for example. Saving cost receipts, bookkeeping records and other documents containing the actual cost of items of property can be very useful and can save time and money later.[2] For large estates that have many assets (appreciated real estate, art, interests in small businesses, to name but a few), determination of the dollar amount of the estate, for federal tax purposes, can be especially tricky. Estates in this category can afford to, and usually should, hire an experienced tax accountant to handle this work.

[2]To help you keep track of these records, use *Nolo's Personal RecordKeeper*, a computer program designed specifically to record the location of all important business and personal records.

3. Subtract Estate Law Tax Deductions

As we stated earlier, federal estate tax law allows you to deduct certain amounts from your estate before estate tax is computed. In tax lingo, this is the process by which your "gross estate" is reduced to your "taxable estate." If your estate exceeds $600,000, you need to subtract these deductions to determine if your estate will actually be subject to taxes. So let's examine the two most important estate tax and gift tax deductions, property left to a surviving spouse and property left to charity.

a. Marital Deduction

All property given as a gift to a spouse or left to the spouse at death is not subject to federal gift or estate taxes, no matter how much the property is worth. This is called the "marital deduction."

Example: Pedro leaves his spouse Rebecca $5,000,000. No estate tax is owed.

b. Special Rules for Non-Citizen Spouses

No marital deduction is allowed for property one spouse leaves (or gives while living) to the other spouse if this spouse is not a citizen of the U.S. It doesn't matter that a non-citizen spouse was married to a U.S. citizen, or is a legal resident of the U.S. The surviving spouse must be a U.S. citizen to be eligible for the marital deduction.

Even without use of the marital deduction, a U.S. citizen can leave a non-citizen spouse a good deal of property free of estate tax. As we've stated, federal law provides that anyone is entitled to leave property worth up to $600,000 to individuals (and organizations) free of gift and estate tax because of the unified credit. Thus, a citizen can leave her non-citizen spouse $600,000 in property tax-free (as always, assuming no taxable gifts were made earlier).

Example: Lucy has an estate is worth $500,000. She can leave it all to her non-citizen spouse, Desi, free of federal tax. But if Lucy leaves $500,000 to Desi and $200,000 to her children, the $100,000 excess over the $600,000 tax threshold will be hit with estate tax.

Property a non-citizen spouse leaves to a citizen spouse remains eligible for the marital deduction. Congress seems to have feared that non-citizen spouses would leave the U.S. after the death of their spouses, whisking away their wealth to foreign lands, so it would never be subject to U.S. tax. Presumably, Congress thought that citizen spouses will remain here.

Congress has provided two exceptions to the rule that non-citizen spouses can't be given or left property, tax-free, under the marital deduction.

First, U.S. gift tax law provides that a citizen spouse can give the other, non-citizen spouse, up to $100,000 per year free of gift tax. (IRC Section 2525(i)(2)). Without this rule, the most a spouse could give his non-citizen spouse, free of gift tax, would be $10,000 per year, as we mentioned earlier in this chapter. Thus, a citizen spouse with an estate exceeding $600,000—say it's $900,000—could transfer it all to her non-citizen spouse, free of tax, by giving the non-citizen spouse $100,000 in each of three years, then leaving him the remaining $600,000 at death.

Second, property left by one spouse to a non-citizen spouse in what's called a "Qualified Domestic Trust" is allowed the marital deduction. (IRC Sections 2056(d)(2), 2056A.) So no estate tax is assessed on property in this trust when the citizen spouse dies, no matter how much that property is worth. With a Qualified Domestic Trust, the non-citizen spouse receives all income from the trust during her lifetime. On her death, the final trust beneficiaries must be U.S. citizens.

A Qualified Domestic Trust must meet all the following requirements:

- The surviving spouse cannot be the sole trustee. At least one of the trustees must be a U.S. citizen (or U.S. corporation), and no distribution of trust property can be made without that trustee having the right to withhold estate tax on the property.
- During his or her life the surviving spouse must be entitled to receive all income from the trust. However, if any principal is paid to the spouse, that principal is subject to federal estate tax in the year distributed.
- All additional IRS regulations governing these trusts must be complied with. (As of the printing of this edition, no IRS rules have been issued.)

Finally, if a non-citizen spouse becomes a naturalized U.S. citizen before the deceased spouse's estate tax return must be filed (nine months after death), the surviving spouse is then entitled to the full marital deduction. For a prosperous couple residing in the U.S., and who are not both U.S. citizens, obtaining the estate tax advantage of the marital deduction can be one good reason for becoming U.S. citizens.

Non-citizen spouses. These special rules mean that if you're married to a non-citizen and have an estate worth more than $600,000, you should see a lawyer for estate tax planning.

c. The Marital Deduction Is Unlimited

As we've said, if both spouses are U.S. citizens, it makes no difference how much money or property is given during life or passed at death to the surviving spouse. Whether it's $700,000 in emeralds or $10,000,000 in cash assets, it's all exempt from gift and estate taxes because of the marital deduction.

Thus, none of this property is included in the taxable estate of the deceased spouse. Likewise, it makes no difference what legal form the property left to the surviving spouse is in—whether it's community property, joint tenancy property, "quasi-community" property or separate property.

d. The Marital Deduction Is Over and Above Other Deductions

Finally, and happily, the marital deduction is in addition to all other allowable estate tax deduction and credits.

Example: Sue (who has never given taxable gifts) has an estate valued at $6,600,000. She leaves $600,000 to her children and $6,000,000 to her husband. All Sue's property is exempt from federal estate taxes—the $6,000,000 because of the marital deduction and the $600,000 because of the unified credit (her personal estate tax exemption).

The marital deduction can be a tax trap. The marital deduction, great as it is, does have a downside in some situations. Put bluntly, it can be a tax trap for couples with larger estates totaling over $600,000 for both spouses. The fact that no federal estate tax is assessed when property is left to the surviving spouse can mislead people into thinking that leaving everything to a spouse must be the best thing to do. It often is not, since increasing the size of the surviving spouse's estate can eventually result in estate tax being assessed, when there otherwise would be none, or in higher estate taxes.

Example 1: Barbara and Paul are married; each has an estate of $400,000. If Paul leaves all his property to anyone but Barbara (or a charity), his estate tax exemption shields his property from taxation because his estate is worth less than $600,000. But if Paul gives it all to Barbara, and she dies with an estate of $800,000 (her $400,000 plus her inheritance of $400,000), she will owe estate tax on $200,000, the amount over $600,000. The tax is $54,800. That money would be paid in estate taxes because of the marital deduction tax trap.

Example 2: Gustav and Marlena own community property worth $1,400,000. Each spouse's share is $700,000. If Marlena dies and leaves all her property to anyone but Gustav (or a charity), $100,000 of her estate will be subject to tax. The tax will be $23,800. But if she leaves all her estate to Gustav and he then dies with an estate of $1,400,000, he will owe estate taxes on $800,000. The tax will be $320,000. Had he not inherited her estate, the tax on his $700,000 estate would have also been $23,800. Thus the marital deduction trap cost the combined estates $272,400.

This tax trap is particularly dangerous when both spouses are elderly and the survivor isn't likely to live long enough to really benefit from legally owning the deceased spouse's property. The alternatives are having the first spouse to die leave property directly to children or other beneficiaries, or establishing some type of marital estate tax-saving trust, such as a "marital life estate trust." (See Chapter 18, Estate Tax-Saving Bypass Trusts, Section C) or a "QTIP" trust (see Chapter 19, Other Estate Tax-Saving Marital Trusts, Section A.)

Unmarried couples. There are no exemptions similar to the marital deduction for lovers or "significant others." Quite simply, the estate tax laws are written to encourage and reward traditional relationships.[3] So much so that a number of unmarried heterosexual couples eventually decide to marry to take advantage of the marital deduction.

e. Gifts to Charities

All gifts you make while you live or you leave on your death to tax-exempt charitable organizations are exempt from federal estate gift taxes. If you plan to make large charitable gifts, be sure you've checked out whether the organizations you're giving money to are in fact tax-exempt. The most common way an organization establishes that it's a tax-exempt charity is by a ruling from the IRS, under Internal Revenue Code Section 501(c)(3). (These organizations are referred to, in tax lingo, as "501(c)(3) corporations.") Organizations that are active politically are often not tax-exempt. Many charitable institutions, particularly colleges and universities, provide extensive information about tax-exempt giftgiving and offer a variety of gift plans.

Making substantial gifts to charities through trusts is discussed in Chapter 20, Charitable Trusts.

f. Other Estate Tax Exemptions

There are also federal estate tax deductions for:

- funeral expenses
- estate expenses, such as probate fees
- any claims against the estate, and
- credits for state death tax, and death tax imposed by foreign countries on property the deceased owned there.

[3]Perhaps there is a certain fairness in this, as unmarried couples normally receive significant income tax benefits if both have income. For a thorough discussion of the legal rights and responsibilities of unmarried couples, see *The Living Together Kit,* Warner and Ihara (Nolo Press), and *A Legal Guide for Lesbian and Gay Couples,* Curry, Clifford and Leonard (Nolo Press).

4. When a Federal Estate Tax Return Must Be Filed

An estate tax return (on Form 706) must be filed for an estate with a gross value over $600,000. That's gross, not net. This means that, for purposes of deciding whether a return must be filed, you don't subtract the amount a deceased owed from what he owned. Thus, there can be instances where an estate tax return must be filed even though no taxes are due.

Example: Doug's estate consists of cash (money market funds) of $100,000 and two houses. One has a market value of $400,000, with $300,000 owing on a mortgage; the other has a market value of $200,000, with $100,000 owing on a mortgage. Here's the gross and net estate figures:

Gross Estate	Net Estate
$100,000 cash	$100,000 cash
$400,000 house	$100,000 equity in house
$200,000 house	$100,000 equity in house
$700,000 total	$300,000 total

Because Doug's gross estate is more than $600,000, an estate tax return must be filed. But because his net estate is well under the $600,000 exemption, no tax will be due.

If an estate tax return must be filed, it's due within nine months of the death of the deceased, but extensions can be granted.

The executor of the deceased's will is the person legally responsible for filing an estate tax return, if due. If the deceased left no will, but transferred all property by other methods, including a living trust, the successor trustee named in the living trust is responsible for filing any estate tax return due. In perhaps the most common situation, a person creates both a will and living trust as part of her estate plan. Often the executor and successor trustee are the same person. If they are not, both must cooperate so the executor has sufficient financial information to determine if an estate tax return need be filed, and what the right figures are if one is required.

Under federal law, a deceased's property can be valued as of the date of death, or six months afterwards (referred to in tax lingo as the "alternate valuation date"). Which valuation date is desirable for your estate is a matter your successor trustee, and executor of your will, must decide with a lawyer, and perhaps a tax adviser as well.

Example: Ellen died on April 30, 1987 with a stock portfolio worth $1,000,000 on that date. As a result of "Black Monday," the stock market crash of October 1987, her stock was worth $750,000 on October 30, 1987. Her estate executor took advantage of the alternate valuation date to value her portfolio at the lower amount, and saved about $100,000 in estate taxes.

If a federal estate tax return does need to be filed, a tax expert must be hired to complete the Form 706. It is not an easy form to complete, and there are no self-help materials available to assist individuals to prepare estate tax returns.

5. How to Calculate Federal Estate Taxes

After you've estimated the net worth of your estate and subtracted the estate tax deductions (the marital deduction, charitable deduction, etc.) the next step in estimating your estate taxes is to compute the "tentative tax" from the estate tax table below. Remember, subtracting the $192,800 unified credit is the last step in calculating estate tax, so wait until you've done this last step before being concerned about the possibility that your estate will owe tax.

Here's the estate/gift tax rate schedule. To repeat, the chart shows rates before the $192,800 tax credit is deducted. As you can see, if your estate is subject to federal estate tax at all, the minimum tax rate starts at hefty 37%, increasing to a maximum of 55% for estates over $3,000,000. Clearly this is a tax worth avoiding or minimizing to the extent you can do so legally.

Remember, for very large estates—over $10 million—the unified credit is gradually phased out, and entirely eliminated for estates over $21,040,000.

The following example illustrates how to read the schedule:

Example: Bernie has not made any taxable gifts during his lifetime. His anticipated net estate, after subtracting liabilities from assets, totals about $4 million. He plans to leave $3 million to his wife and $1 million to his children. All the property he leaves to his wife is exempt from federal estate tax because of the marital deduction. His net estate subject to tax is thus $1 million. Column C on the Estate Tax Chart reveals that the tentative tax on a $1 million estate is $345,800. From $345,800 Bernie then deducts the $192,800 unified tax credit (again, the tax assessed against a $600,000 estate). Thus, Bernie determines that his estate will have to pay federal taxes of $153,000.[4]

[4]Incidentally, Bernie is an excellent candidate to give money to his kids while he is still alive. By doing this, he can reduce the size of his estate and therefore the tax. See Chapter 16, Gifts and Gift Taxes, Section E for a further discussion of how gifts can be used to reduce estate taxes.

Now follow the precise steps below to determine the tax due on a net estate (after all estate tax deductions) of $700,000.

1. Locate the amounts in Columns A and B between which the anticipated taxable estate falls	Column A = $500,000 Column B = $750,000
2. Estate tax on $500,000 (listed in Column C)	$155,800
3. Subtract the amount in Column A from the anticipated value of your estate	$700,000 - 500,000 $200,000
4. Multiply this remainder by the percentage in Column D	$200,000 x .37 $74,000
5. Add the result to the tax on the amount in Column A ($500,000), which is listed in Column C	$74,000 + 155,800 $229,800
6. Subtract the unified credit ($192,800); the difference is the estate tax liability	$229,800 - 192,800
	Tax Due = $37,000

MORE INFORMATION ON FEDERAL ESTATE TAXES

More detailed information about federal estate and gift taxes can be found in the publication "Federal and Estate Gift Taxes," IRS publication no. 448. It's available free at many IRS offices. You can also read the relevant federal tax statutes, if you dare to plunge into this morass of legalese. It is dense, even for tax professionals.

UNIFIED FEDERAL ESTATE AND GIFT TAX RATES

Column A net taxable estate over	**Column B** net taxable estate not over	**Column C** tax on amount in column A	**Column D** rate of tax on excess over amount in column A
$ 0	$10,000	$ 0	18%
10,000	20,000	1,800	20
20,000	40,000	3,800	22
40,000	60,000	8,200	24
60,000	80,000	13,000	26
80,000	100,000	18,200	28
100,000	150,000	23,800	30
150,000	250,000	38,800	32
250,000	500,000	70,800	34
500,000	750,000	155,800	37
750,000	1,000,000	248,300	39
1,000,000	1,250,000	345,800	41
1,250,000	1,500,000	448,300	43
1,500,000	2,000,000	555,800	45
2,000,000	2,500,000	780,800	49
2,500,000	3,000,000	1,025,800	53
3,000,000	infinity	1,290,800	55

6. Federal Income Tax Basis of Inherited Property

The concept of a property's basis is a tricky one, not made any easier by the fact that "basis" is not defined in the tax laws. When property is purchased, its basis is generally its cost. In fact, basis is often referred to as "cost basis." If you buy a painting for $5,000, for example, it has a basis equal to its cost—$5,000. Suppose you sell the painting two months later for $8,000 (lucky you), your taxable profit is $3,000 ($8,000 sale price minus $5,000 basis equals $3,000 gain). So a good definition of basis for our purposes is the value assigned to property from which gain or loss on sale is determined.

If you make what's called a "capital improvement" to property, such as putting in a new foundation for a house, the cost of the improvement is added to the basis of the property. Capital improvements, very roughly, last more than a year.

Basis is also often referred to in tax lingo as "adjusted basis," since the original cost basis can be adjusted up, for reasons such as capital improvements, or down, for reasons like depreciation.

Example: Green Is Good, Inc. bought an old barn to design and make bicycles. The barn cost the company $280,000; so the company has a cost basis in it of $280,000. Over the next year, Green Is Good spent $220,000 for capital improvements to the barn—installing a new fire control system and a new roof. Adding these capital improvements to the original cost basis gave the company an "adjusted basis" in the barn of $500,000.

Based on this adjusted basis, the company took depreciation deductions on its income taxes of $20,000 over two years. The property's adjusted basis now becomes $480,000 (since the deduction for depreciation lowers the adjusted basis of the property). If the barn is sold to T. Donald Boesky (who plans to use the barn for a weekend getaway) for $600,000, Green Is Good, Inc. has a taxable profit of $120,000 on the sale ($600,000 sale price minus $480,000 basis). T. Donald Boesky has a cost basis of $600,000 in the barn.

Now to move to the tax basis of inherited property. Under federal tax law, the basis of inherited property is "stepped up" to its fair market value at the date of the decedent's death.

Example: During the next 12 years, until T. Donald's death, he occasionally visited the barn but made no capital improvements to it. At the time of his death, when the barn was inherited by T. Donald Jr., it had appreciated in value to $800,000. T. Donald Jr.'s basis in the barn would thus be stepped up from the $600,000 basis that T. Donald had in it to $800,000, the fair market value of the barn at the death of T. Donald. Now, if T. Donald Jr. turns around and immediately sells the barn for $800,000, he has no profit, and thus owes no capital gain tax ($800,000 sale price minus $800,000 basis equals zero).

The fact that the basis of property is stepped up at the owner's death to its fair market value means that it's almost always desirable to hold on to highly appreciated property until it can pass at death. That way, your inheritors obtain the advantage of the stepped-up basis rule. Thus, if T. Donald sold the barn a year before he died, when it was worth $780,000, he would have had to pay federal taxes (and possibly state income taxes) on $180,000 ($780,000 sale price minus his $600,000 basis). And if T. Donald gave the barn to T. Donald Jr. during his lifetime, T. Donald Jr. would have had the same basis in the barn "as it had in the hands" of T. Donald, or $600,000. In other words, gifts are not entitled to a stepped-up basis. Only transfers at death qualify for this desirable tax treatment.

B. How to Reduce Federal Estate Taxes

What can you do to reduce federal estate taxes if you think your estate will be liable for them? Not as much as you might think. Aside from making use of the estate tax deductions discussed above, including leaving property to your spouse or to charity, the following are the major ways you can lower estate taxes.

1. Give Away Property

While you're alive, you can give away property in amounts of $10,000 or less per person per year tax-free. A couple can give $20,000 a year tax-free to one person and $40,000 to another couple. Tax-exempt gift giving works well for people who can afford it, and can be particularly advantageous for those who have several children, grandchildren or other objects of their affection. For example, a couple can give each of their three children $20,000 per year tax-free, a total of $60,000 per year. If these children are married and the couple wishes to include spouses in their gift-giving program, these amounts can be doubled. (All of this is covered in detail in Chapter 16, Gifts and Gift Taxes, Section E.)

2. Create an Estate Tax-Saving Trust

There are a number of different types of trusts that can possibly be used to save on overall estate taxes, depending on your circumstances and desires. We discuss these trusts in detail in Chapters 18 through 21. If you individually, or you and your spouse together, have an estate exceeding $600,000, be sure to check out those chapters carefully to determine if you might be able to use one or more of these trusts. Your final decision should be made only after consultation with an experienced estate planning lawyer. We do not summarize each trust here, because snappy summaries won't tell you enough to allow you to make any sensible decisions about how these trusts would work in your particular circumstances.

3. Payment of Estate Tax

Sometimes payment of estate tax can become a real problem and even destroy an estate plan. Suppose you leave your house to your son and your stock and cash to your daughter. Any remaining assets pass to your husband. You want your son to receive the house free and clear of estate taxes, so you provide that estate taxes are to be paid out of your daughter's inheritance. To make sure your daughter isn't short-changed, you leave her what you think will be enough extra to pay the estate taxes on the house.

Over the years, the house more than doubles in value, but you've spent quite a bit of your cash and sold some of your stock. Come estate tax time, much of your daughter's inheritance goes to pay the estate taxes on the house. The result is your son gets your house, which is worth twice what you figured on, and your daughter gets significantly less than you planned on giving her. So, to point out the obvious, keep your estate planning in tune with your current financial situation, especially if you're using the payment of estate taxes to balance inheritances.

Decide who pays taxes. Unless a will or living trust directs otherwise, IRS rules prorate estate taxes between all persons and non-charitable organizations inheriting the estate. This means that those receiving a larger proportion of the estate pay a larger proportion of the taxes. If you want to vary this by having certain assets used to pay your estate taxes, you'll need to state that specifically in your will or living trust.

C. State Death Taxes

Twenty-seven states and the District of Columbia have, effectively, abolished state death taxes. The rest impose death taxes on:

- all real estate owned in the state, no matter where the deceased lived; and
- the personal property (everything but real estate) of residents of the state.

1. Where Do You Live for State Death Tax Purposes?

Technically, states that impose death taxes on residents do so on all persons "domiciled in the state." "Domicile" is a legal term of art. It means the state where you have your permanent residence, where you "intend" to make your home. Generally, it's clear where a person's domicile is. It's the state where they live most of the time, work, own a home and vote. However, in some instances, where a person has two (or more) homes in different states, there may be no clear evidence which state is a person's domicile. For example, several states claimed that Howard Hughes was domiciled there. A less dramatic and more common example can be a person who owns two homes. In some circumstances, it's quite possible that more than one state would assert the person was domiciled there.

Example: Mrs. Koppel retired and moved from Michigan to North Carolina. However, she returns often to Michigan to visit her children, keeps several bank and brokerage accounts in Michigan, and never bothers to register to vote in North Carolina. Michigan might claim, on her death, that Mrs. Koppel remained domiciled there and never transferred her domicile to North Carolina.

If you do divide your residence between two or more states, make sure you make it clear which state you are domiciled in. Normally, this means being sure that you maintain all your major personal business contacts and vote in the state you claim as your domicile. Obviously, if one state doesn't have death taxes and the other is a high death tax state, you might want to establish your domicile in the no-tax state.

2. Estate Planning for State Death Taxes

If you live or own real estate in a state that has death taxes, it's sensible to consider what the impact of those taxes on your gifts will be. In many instances, the bite taken from estates by state death taxes is annoying, but relatively minor. However, in some states, larger bites can be taken, especially for property given to non-relatives. For example, Nebraska imposes a 15% death tax rate if $25,000 is given to a friend, but only 1% if it's given to your child. Also, in many states with inheritance taxes, there is no tax on property left to a surviving spouse. (See Appendix I, Chart I.) It's probably rare that someone would change the amount of property left to a beneficiary because of state death taxes, but you should at least evaluate the issue if it applies.

If your state has death taxes, it may have other laws that affect your estate planning. For example, some states with death taxes require a deceased's bank accounts or safe-deposit boxes to be "sealed" until a release is obtained from tax officials. It's normally fairly quick and easy to do this, as long as the officials are convinced the estate has enough assets to pay the taxes.

As mentioned, if you have connections with more than one state, it can be sensible to have the state of your domicile be the one with lower, or no, death taxes. For example, a couple divides their time roughly equally between Florida and Pennsylvania. Florida effectively has no death taxes. Pennsylvania imposes comparatively stiff inheritance taxes. Other things being equal, it makes sense to the couple to be domiciled in Florida.

3. Summary of State Death Tax Rules

Following is a summary of each state's tax rules, which will enable you to learn if the state where you live imposes death taxes. If it does, you can learn the specifics of those death tax rules from the charts in Appendix I.

a. States That Have No Death Taxes

Nevada is the only state that has no death taxes at all.

b. States That Effectively Impose No Death Taxes

In many states, there's no reason to concern yourself with state death taxes when you plan your estate. These states do, technically, impose death taxes on estates subject to federal estate tax—those over $600,000. And in those instances, a state death tax return must be filed. However, the maximum amount of state death tax is exactly equal to the maximum credit for state death taxes allowed under the federal estate tax law. So your estate pays, overall, no more in taxes than it would if the state imposed no death taxes. In other words, part of the tax that would otherwise be included with the federal estate tax return is paid to state tax authorities instead. This is commonly called a "pick-up" death tax. To repeat, the important point is that in these states, state death taxes are matters for accountants and estate tax preparers, and have no real impact on the amount of your estate that's left for your beneficiaries.

c. States That Impose Inheritance Taxes

Inheritance taxes are imposed on the receiver of inherited property, not the estate. Typically, state inheritance tax statutes divide receivers into different classes, such as "Class A, Husband or Wife," "Class B, immediate family— children, parents, etc.," "Class C, brothers, sisters, cousins, etc." "Class D, all others." Each class receives different death tax exemptions and is taxed at a different rate. The general rule is that the highest exemption and lowest rate applies to spouses, or "Class A."

Each of these state's inheritance tax rules are set out in Appendix I, Chart I.

d. States That Impose Estate Taxes

Some states impose a tax, like the federal government's, on the taxable estate itself, without regard to who the beneficiaries are. For state estate tax purposes, the taxable estate is all real estate in the state, and all personal property of a person who was domiciled in the state, except personal property having a specific, real location in another state. These state's estate tax rules are set out in Appendix I, Chart 2.

State	**Inheritance Taxes?**	**Estate Taxes?**
Alabama	effectively, no	effectively, no
Alaska	effectively, no	effectively, no
Arizona	effectively, no	effectively, no
Arkansas	effectively, no	effectively, no
California	effectively, no	effectively, no
Colorado	effectively, no	effectively, no
Connecticut	yes	no
Delaware	yes	no
District of Columbia	effectively, no	effectively, no
Florida	effectively, no	effectively, no
Georgia	effectively, no	effectively, no
Hawaii	effectively, no	effectively, no
Idaho	effectively, no	effectively, no
Illinois	effectively, no	effectively, no
Indiana	yes	no
Iowa	yes	no
Kansas	yes	no
Kentucky	yes	no
Louisiana	yes	no
Maine	effectively, no	effectively, no
Maryland	yes	no
Massachusetts	no	yes
Michigan	yes	no
Minnesota	effectively, no	effectively, no
Mississippi	no	yes
Missouri	effectively, no	effectively, no
Montana	yes	no
Nebraska	yes	no
Nevada	no	no
New Hampshire	yes	no
New Jersey	yes	no
New Mexico	effectively, no	effectively, no
New York	no	yes
North Carolina	yes	no
North Dakota	effectively, no	effectively, no
Ohio	no	yes
Oklahoma	yes	no
Pennsylvania	yes	no
Oregon	effectively, no	effectively, no
Rhode Island	effectively, no	effectively, no
South Carolina	effectively, no	effectively, no
South Dakota	yes	no
Tennessee	yes	no
Texas	effectively, no	effectively, no
Utah	effectively, no	effectively, no
Vermont	effectively, no	effectively, no
Virginia	effectively, no	effectively, no
West Virginia	effectively, no	effectively, no
Washington	effectively, no	effectively, no
Wisconsin	effectively, no	effectively, no
Wyoming	effectively, no	effectively, no ■

16

Gifts and Gift Taxes

We're used to thinking of gifts as a personal matter, not as an aspect of financial or estate planning. Up to a point, this is accurate; birthday, Christmas or anniversary presents don't normally have tax consequences. However, if a gift is worth more than $10,000, the rules change. Gifts in excess of $10,000 per year made to any person or non-charitable institution are subject to federal gift tax.

The federal gift tax rate is the same as the estate tax rate. Indeed, the technical name for the tax is the "Unified Estate and Gift Tax." The idea is to tax property the same way, whether you give it away during your life or leave it at your death. Another way of saying this is that taxable gifts reduce the $600,000 amount that can pass free of estate tax on death. (See Chapter 15, Estate Taxes, Section A.) For example, if you make taxable gifts totaling $400,000 while you are alive, only $200,000 worth of your property can be transferred tax-free when you die.

Taxes aren't actually paid until your $600,000 exempt amount is used up, either by making gifts during your life or leaving property at death or a combination of the two. This means that people with estates worth under $600,000 don't have to worry about actually paying gift tax. However, a federal gift tax return must be filed for any gift over $10,000 to a person per year (IRS Forms 709 or 709-A).

Giving to charity. Making large gifts to tax-exempt charities is another way to give away property and get tax breaks in return. (See Chapter 20, Charitable Trusts.)

Other Reasons to Make Gifts

This chapter focuses on the gift/estate tax consequences of making substantial gifts, which for tax purposes means any gift over $10,000 in one year to one person or non-charitable institution. But we're aware that many people, including those with estates over $600,000, are reluctant or unwilling to make big gifts simply to reduce their taxable estate. For them, the tax savings alone aren't worth the loss of the property given away.

In our experience, people are more often willing to make substantial gifts if, in addition to possible estate/gift tax savings, they believe the recipient really needs the money. For example, an adult child may need money for home repairs or a much needed vacation. Or a grandparent may want to pay for a grandchild's braces or ski trip. We also know that if parents (or one parent) give a child a down payment for a house, that may not be the end of their gift-giving concern. If they have other children, they may feel they must, or want to, give them the same amount, either now or at death.

Even if your primary motive in making the gift isn't to save on taxes, there is certainly no reason not to take full advantage of the gift tax rules.

A. The Federal Gift Tax: An Overview

Gift tax is assessed against the giver of a gift. (Technically, the tax is assessed against the transfer itself, but the IRS looks to the giver to pay any gift tax.) The recipient of a gift is not liable for federal gift tax, unless the giver failed to pay any tax actually due. Only in that case will the IRS go after the recipient for any gift tax liability.

Federal law exempts from gift tax the first $10,000 per year you give to any one person or institution. Lawyers often call this "the $10,000 annual exclusion." (Internal Revenue Code Section 2503(b).) So, for example, if you give someone $25,000, the first $10,000 of that gift is exempt from gift tax, while the remaining $15,000 is not.

> **REMINDER: THE INTERNAL REVENUE CODE**
>
> You'll see a number of references in this chapter to the "IRC," which is the conventional abbreviation for a set of tax laws known as the Internal Revenue Code. The Internal Revenue Code can be found in Volume 26 of the United States Code, the collection of all federal statutes.

In addition, some types of gifts are completely exempt from federal gift tax:

- All property one spouse gives the other, no matter how much it's worth. (IRC Section 2523(a).) However, there's a different rule if the spouse receiving the gift is not a U.S. citizen. A U.S. citizen can only give his or her non-citizen spouse up to $100,000 worth of property per year free of gift tax.
- All property given to a tax-exempt charity. (IRC Section 2522.)
- Gifts spent directly for someone's medical bills or school tuition. (IRC Section 2503(e).)

This final exemption has a couple of twists. First, the money must be paid directly to the provider of the medical service or the school. If you give the money to an ill person or student, who then pays the bill, the gift is not tax-exempt. Nor can you reimburse someone who has already paid a medical or tuition bill and have this be a tax-exempt gift. Finally, you cannot pay for a student's other educational expenses, such as room and board, and have this treated as a tax-exempt gift.

Example: Victor gives $6,000 outright to his son, $50,000 to his wife, $20,000 to CARE (a tax-exempt organization), pays $12,000 for his grandson's tuition at college and also pays $21,000 for a daughter's medical bills. All these gifts are completely exempt from federal gift tax.

Since many gifts are not to a spouse, charity or to pay education or medical costs, the fact that you can give any recipient $10,000 per year exempt from gift tax is extremely important. You can use this exemption repeatedly over a number of years to reduce the size of your estate and hence your ultimate estate tax bill.

Here are some examples of how the $10,000 exemption from gift tax works:

- You give $8,000 to a cousin in one year: There are no federal gift tax consequences.
- You give $16,000 to the cousin in one year: $6,000 is subject to gift tax.
- You give $8,000 each to two cousins: None of the $16,000 is subject to gift tax.
- You give $7,000 each to two cousins, three years in a row; none of this $42,000 is subject to gift tax.

Married couples can combine their annual exclusions, which means that they can give away $20,000 of property tax-free, per year, per recipient.

Gift taxes that are assessed against you, the giver of a gift, are not payable until and unless your taxable gifts exceed the $600,000 amount that can pass tax-free. Instead, any tax imposed on the gifts you make eats up your unified estate/gift tax credit and thus reduces the amount that can later pass tax-free. (See Section C, below, for an explanation of how the estate/gift tax credit works technically for gifts.)

Example: In the last ten years of her life, Sheila gives her two children a total of $300,000 over and above the $10,000 annual exemptions. These taxable gifts use up a portion of her unified estate/gift tax credit, reducing the $600,000 that would otherwise pass free of estate tax at her death to $300,000. Sheila dies with an estate valued at $500,000. Because some of her unified credit was used for gift tax on the $300,000 of taxable gifts, she has only enough credit left to shield another $300,000 of her estate from estate tax. Thus, Sheila's estate will owe estate tax on the remaining $200,000 of her estate.

B. What Is a Gift?

Before exploring more about gifts and estate planning, let's be sure we know what a gift is.

1. The Giver's Intent

In common understanding, a gift is the voluntary transfer of property made without receiving anything of value in exchange. (In legalese, anything of value is called "consideration.") In other words, a gift is a permanent transfer of property that isn't commercial in spirit.

From the point of view of the IRS, the crucial element in determining whether or not a gift is made is the giver's intent, which can be distinctly murky. For example, say you obtain a valuable painting from Frank. Did Frank intend to give you that painting, or loan it to you? Or was he hoping to sell it to you and wanted you to have it for a while before he mentioned the price?

If someone's intent may not be obvious (now or in the future), it is an excellent idea to accompany a gift with a written statement explaining that it's a gift, so that the status of the transaction is clear. If there is no clear written evidence, the IRS doesn't know when you transfer something for less than its market value whether you intend to make a gift or you're just a poor businessperson. So, it does the only thing it can do—it looks at the "objective evidence" and demands gift tax if the transaction doesn't appear reasonable from a commercial (economic) point of view.

Example: Linda paid $15,000 to her niece for an office lamp and deducted the $15,000 as an expense of her small business. If the IRS questions this transaction and contends it was really a gift, Linda must convince the IRS that this was a bona fide commercial transaction (for example, that the lamp was a valuable antique), not a gift disguised as a sale.

LOOKING DEEPER INTO GIFTS

For a fascinating discussion of the meaning of giving, see *The Gift: Imagination and the Erotic Life of Property*, by Lewis Hyde (Random House). The book brilliantly explores the spirit involved in giving and receiving a gift, from a Christmas present to creating a work of art, and how the giving spirit interacts with commercial culture.

2. The Recipient's Control Over the Gift

For a transaction to be a legal gift, the property must be delivered to and accepted by the recipient.

Example: Matt puts $10,000 into a drawer for Nina. There's no legal gift until Nina removes the money.

The giver must release all control over the property. If the giver retains any interest in the gift property, there is no legal gift.

Example: Sonya gives a rental house she owns to her daughter, Misha, transferring the deed into Misha's name. But Sonya continues to receive all of the rental income from the house. Legally, Sonya has not made a valid gift.

Giving real estate is often complicated. People sometimes make gifts of real estate to their children, grandchildren or other family members. A number of these gifts are later disallowed by the IRS, often because the giver held onto some important right over the property—for example, the right to receive rents from a small apartment building. To avoid this problem, you must comply with all applicable IRS rules, and understand the consequences of transferring the property. Real estate gifts are discussed in more detail in Section E2, below.

Some transactions simply can't, by law, count as taxable gifts. For instance, you can perform services—from dispensing medical treatment to repairing a trombone—freely, without being held by the IRS to have made a taxable gift of the market value of your services. Similarly, you can loan property to someone, even for an extended period of time, and there's no legal gift.

Example: Grandpa Elijah has an old Rolls Royce that he lets his grandson Jacob drive. Indeed, Elijah has basically turned the car over to Jacob, although Elijah still pays for the car insurance. There is no gift—and would not be even if Jacob paid for the insurance, since Elijah remains the car's legal owner.

If you give a tangible item (cash, an heirloom, pictures), the relinquishment of control necessary to establish a gift is usually easy to prove—the recipient gains unrestricted possession over the property. In other situations, the question of control may be more difficult to ascertain. For example, if a gift made by will or living trust is contingent on a future event, that event must be determinable by some objective standard. "To Desiree, when she becomes 21," or "when she travels to Paris" is objective; "when she's happily married" is not.

Property you place in your revocable living trust isn't a gift because you retain full control over the property and can revoke the trust if you wish. The beneficiaries have no current right to the trust property. Likewise, if you establish a trust and retain the power to change who will benefit from it, even if you, yourself, are specifically excluded as a possible beneficiary, there's no gift.

Example: Roger, a wealthy older man, puts money in a trust for his grandniece Olivia, to be used for any needs she has now, and for eventual college and graduate school costs. He appoints a trustee and gives her authority to alter the purposes for which the trust money can be spent. Roger also retains the right to substitute a new trustee. Because Roger still has so much control over the trust property, legally there has been no gift.

3. Common Kinds of Gifts

Here are some types of transactions that are legal gifts:

- Handing someone cash, a check or any tangible item, with the intention of making a gift
- Transferring title to real estate, stocks or a motor vehicle into another's name, without receiving

anything of value in exchange. Remember that if you reserve the right to receive any income from the property, such as rent or dividends, no valid gift of the entire property is made.

- Making an interest-free loan. Really? Yes. Federal law provides that an interest-free or artificially low-interest loan is a gift by the lender of the interest not charged. An "artificially low" interest rate is any rate below market interest rates when the loan was made. So, if you loan a friend $30,000 interest-free, you are making a taxable gift of the interest you didn't charge. But because of the $10,000 annual gift tax exemption discussed above, gifts of interest on most loans don't have gift tax consequences. For example, at a 10% simple interest rate, a single person can make an interest-free loan of $100,000 to a person without gift tax liability. A married couple could loan a person up to $200,000 interest-free before the annual interest would exceed $20,000, the couple's combined annual gift tax exemption.
- Transferring property to an irrevocable trust you create to benefit another person. An irrevocable trust means you can't change your mind and alter or terminate the trust once it is created. (By contrast, as we've mentioned, since a living trust is almost always revocable, naming someone as a beneficiary doesn't guarantee they will receive the property, so no gift is made.)
- Withdrawing funds someone else deposited in a joint (not community property) bank account.
- Irrevocably assigning a life insurance policy to another.
- Forgiving a debt.
- Assigning a mortgage or court judgment to someone without receiving fair compensation in return.
- Making a non-commercial transfer of your property into joint tenancy with another person. (Except for joint bank accounts; in that case, the rule is that a gift is made only when one depositor withdraws money deposited by the other.)

Partial gifts. Federal law authorizes "partial gifts." (IRC Section 2512(g).) These are gifts where you receive something of value back, but the gift is worth far more than what you received. Making a partial gift is a complex tax matter and you'll need to see a lawyer.

C. How Federal Gift Tax Works

Before you can sensibly evaluate whether you want to use gifts as part of your estate plan, you need to thoroughly understand how the federal gift tax actually works. We touched on this above; now we present a more thorough treatment of this important subject.

Gift tax applies to all gifts made by U.S. citizens and residents, and also to gifts of property by non-resident aliens if the gift property is physically located in (in legalese, has a *situs* in) the U.S. The most obvious example is real estate in the U.S.

Here are the basics.

1. The Estate/Gift Tax Credit

As we've discussed, the first $600,000 of a person's taxable gifts and estate can be transferred free of gift and estate tax because of the unified credit. And, as you now know, each person has an annual exemption from gift tax for $10,000 given per person, per year.

If you give a gift worth more than $10,000, you must file a gift tax return, and the IRS will assess a gift tax against you. However, instead of paying the tax now, the IRS requires that the amount of the gift tax be used to reduce your unified estate/gift tax credit. You cannot choose to pay gift tax now and "save" your unified credit for later use.

The unified estate/gift tax credit is $192,800. This amount is exactly the amount of tax that would be owed on $600,000 of taxable gifts or estate assets. Once a person gives enough taxable gifts to use up all of her unified credit, from that point on, gift tax is payable on any taxable gift. Also, the entire value of the person's taxable estate will be subject to estate tax after her death.

Example: Charlene, a widow, gives her niece Lucy $20,000 in 1994. Charlene has never given a gift worth more than $10,000 before. $10,000 of Charlene's gift is excluded from gift tax under the annual gift tax exemption.[1] The remaining $10,000 of the gift is subject to gift tax of $1,800. Charlene must file a gift tax return, but she does not pay the gift tax now. Instead, the $1,800 is subtracted from her unified credit of $192,800, leaving her with a credit of $191,000. When Charlene later dies, her remaining unified credit will (assuming she has made no other taxable gifts) allow her estate to transfer $590,000 free from federal estate tax.

The estate/gift tax rates are graduated, so the higher the taxable value of the gift, the higher the gift tax rate that applies to it. (See Chapter 15, Estate Taxes, Section A.) Also, the tax rate is cumulative. This means that in determining the gift tax rate applied to a current gift, the value of all taxable gifts given since January 1, 1977 must be added. Otherwise, large estates could be transferred at lower tax rates by piecemeal giving.

Example: Carol gives her niece $20,000 two years in a row. Each year, $10,000 of the gift is exempt from tax. Here is the gift tax assessed and subtracted from her unified credit.

	Year 1	Year 2
Amount given	$20,000	$20,000
Amount taxed	$10,000	$10,000
Tax rate based on	$10,000	$20,000
Tax rate	18%	20%
Tax assessed	$1,800	$2,000
Unified credit remaining	$191,000	$189,000

2. Gifts Made Near Death

Most gifts can be made up to the moment you die and qualify as legal gifts under the IRS rules. However, a few types of gifts must be made at least three years before the giver's death, or the gifts are disallowed for estate tax purposes. With disallowed gifts, the IRS acts as if the gift were never made, and includes the current value of the gift property in the giver's gross taxable estate.[2] This is for estate tax purposes only; it doesn't affect ownership of the property, which remains with the recipient of the gift.

A gift of a life insurance policy is the most significant type of gift in this category. A gift of life insurance is disallowed, for estate tax purposes, if ownership is transferred within three years of the giver's death. This can result in a substantial increase in the size of the giver's taxable estate, because the value of the life insurance proceeds the insurance company pays on the death of the insured are always worth much more than the value of the same policy given away before the insured dies. (Term insurance, which has no cash surrender value, is basically worth little or nothing before the insured dies.) For example, a whole life policy that pays $300,000 on an

[1]Had Charlene given Lucy $10,000 and then waited until January 1 of the next year and given her a second $10,000, no gift tax would be assessed at all.

[2]If gift tax has already been paid, that amount will be credited towards any estate tax due. IRC Section 2012(a).)

insured's death might be worth $50,000 two years or two days before the owner dies. Thus, if the policy owner gives away the policy and then dies within three years, the IRS will disallow the gift, and the property subject to estate tax will increase by $250,000. (Gifts of life insurance are discussed in more detail in Section E4, below.)

Another gift that is disallowed if made within three years of death is a gift from a living trust. As trustee of your living trust, you have the right to make gifts from the trust. However, if a gift is made from the trust within three years of your death, the IRS contends that the gift is not valid. (*Jalkut,* 96 Tax Code Reports (TC) 675 (1991); IRS Letter Ruling 9010005 (1990).) Thus, the gift is retroactively invalidated for the giver's estate tax. Fortunately, it's easy to get around this IRS rule. If you want to make a gift of property that has been transferred to your living trust, always withdraw it from the trust and then give it personally. Do this routinely for gifts of trust property, since you can never guarantee that you'll live for three more years.

3. The "Present Interest" Rule

Gifts are eligible for the $10,000 annual gift tax exemption only if they are what is called a gift of a "present interest." This means that the person or institution who receives the gift has the right to use it immediately. For the great majority of gifts, this is no problem. The receiver obtains full control when the gift is made. By contrast, gifts that someone can use only in the future, not when the gift was made, do not qualify for the $10,000 annual exemption. These are called gifts of a "future interest."

Example: Kim gives $10,000 outright to her friend Gayle and places another $10,000 in an irrevocable trust to benefit her friend Madeleine. Madeleine, age 32, can use principal from the trust only when she turns 35. The gift to Gayle is a gift of a present interest, because Gayle gets the money now. The gift to the trust for Madeleine is a gift of a future interest, because she has no right to the money when Kim gives it. So gift tax is assessed against the $10,000 Kim gives to the trust.

4. Gifts to Minors

Gifts to minors can qualify for the $10,000 annual exemption, even though the minor isn't given (indeed, by law, cannot be given) full present access to or control of the gift property. Federal law (IRC Section 2503(c)) provides that in order to make a gift to a minor that qualifies for the $10,000 annual exemption, three conditions must be met:

1. The gift, and any income it produces, must be used or retained in trust for the minor's benefit until he or she reaches age 21.
2. The remainder of the gift must go outright to the child when she reaches age 21.
3. If the child dies before reaching age 21, the remainder of the gift must be paid to his estate.

5. The Federal Gift Tax Return

You must file an IRS gift tax return when your regular income tax return is filed (normally, April 15) if you:

- have made non-exempt gifts over $10,000 to any person or tax-paying organization during the previous taxable year, or
- have made gifts to a tax-exempt organization over $10,000 during the previous taxable year. Although no tax is assessed for this type of gift, the IRS still requires a return to be filed. Who knows why?

The IRS does not require a gift tax return to be filed for gifts between spouses (unless the recipient is not a U.S. citizen and the gift exceeds $100,000; see

Chapter 15, Estate Taxes, Section A), or for gifts for educational or medical expenses, no matter how large the gift.

D. State Gift Tax Rules

Most states have no gift tax. Generally, when they exist, state gift tax rules and rates are the same as that state's death tax rules and rates.

Delaware	South Carolina
Louisiana	Tennessee
New York	Wisconsin
North Carolina	

For most people, state gift tax is a minor matter, and doesn't enter into their estate planning. An exception can be people with large estates who live in states that levy relatively high gift and death taxes. In this situation, some people consider whether it's worthwhile to move their home from a state that imposes gift and death taxes to one that doesn't. This can be especially sensible for those who already own homes in two states, one of which doesn't levy these taxes. (See Chapter 15, Estate Taxes, Section C, for more on this issue.)

Get more information about state gift tax. If you live in or own real estate in a state that imposes gift tax, you may want to learn exactly what the tax is and how it might affect you. Start by calling a state tax office and asking for information on the subject.

E. Using Gifts to Reduce Estate Taxes

For people with larger estates, making tax-exempt gifts while living, either to individuals or charities, can be a significant part of their estate plan. Many people make such gifts primarily for personal reasons, but with the awareness that they're obtaining estate tax benefits, too. Using gifts to reduce the size of your estate when you die can be desirable if:

- Your estimated estate will exceed $600,000; and
- The property you want to give has not greatly appreciated in value since you acquired it (if it has, it's better to transfer it at death to take advantage of more advantageous tax basis rules—see Section F); and
- You don't need all of your assets and income to live on.

This last concern, of course, requires a determination of how much money and property you need (or want) now and in the future, as well as what your resources are, including income from retirement, pensions, Social Security, savings and investments. Some people, who may not want to use up any of their principal for gifts, may decide to use some of their income for gifts.

Example: Mr. and Mrs. Tureba, in their 70s, have four children. The Turebas have an estate totaling $1,140,000: a house worth $275,000 (all equity), stocks currently valued at $120,000, savings of $340,000, and business investments of $405,000. At first, the Turebas don't feel comfortable with the thought of giving away any of this property. However, their incomes are substantially more than they need to live on. The figures are:

Retirement pensions	$ 32,000
Social Security	12,000
Mrs. Tureba's part-time job	8,000
Stocks, savings and investments	56,000
Total Annual Income	$108,000

> **THE TIMING OF GIFTS**
>
> For those who engage in extensive tax-saving gift giving, the timing of making gifts can be important. To briefly summarize what can fast become complicated, it's advantageous to make non-charitable gifts (above the $10,000 annual exemption) near the beginning of the taxable year if cumulative taxable gifts totaling over $600,000 have already been made. The reason is that although gift tax is the same, no matter when the gift is made during the year, if you make a taxable gift in January, you do not have to pay the gift tax until April of the following year. In the meantime, the income from the gift goes to the recipient rather than increasing your taxable estate.
>
> By contrast, charitable gifts are often given at the end of the tax year, so the giver can receive the income from the asset most of the year, while obtaining the charitable tax deduction for that same year.

After completing a detailed budget, the Turebas figure they spend about $35,000 a year, and taxes claim another $30,000. In short, in addition to all the money and property they have already put aside, they're saving over $40,000 per year. Facing up to the fact that this is surely more than they will ever need, the Turebas decide to give away $10,000 a year to each of their four children, rather than increase their savings. Over ten years this will result in their giving $400,000 to their children, all gift tax free.

1. Using the $10,000 Annual Exemption Repeatedly

Although the $10,000 annual gift tax exemption may not seem like a great sum, it can often be used over time to achieve substantial estate tax savings. The key is using this $10,000 exemption as fully as possible. It's a simple matter of multiplication. If you use the $10,000 annual exemption for gifts to one person for five years, you've given away five times as much ($50,000) tax-free as you would if you gave the same $50,000 to the same person in one year and qualified for only one $10,000 exemption. If you make $10,000 gifts to five recipients in one year, you've also given away $50,000 tax-free. And obviously, it follows that if you make five $10,000 gifts to five people for five years, you've given $250,000 away tax-free. (And since spouses can each make $10,000 gifts, giving as a couple multiplies your gift tax exemption by two.)

Example: Patti owns a successful small business, with an estimated net worth of $810,000. Her other assets are worth roughly $175,000. Patti intends to leave her business to her four children. To reduce the value of her eventual estate, she incorporates her business and starts giving her children stock. She can give each of her children stock worth $10,000 per year gift tax-free—a yearly total of $40,000. She wants to retain a minimum of 51% of the stock, so that she does not risk losing control of her business. So, for ten years she gives each child $10,000 worth of stock, transferring a total of $400,000 worth. She has retained $410,000 worth of stock—slightly more than half the value of the business. More importantly, she has retained voting control. (Also, she could give them "non-voting" stock and not have to worry about this.) By giving away the stock, Patti has reduced the net value of her estate to less than $600,000, eliminating estate taxes.

This example assumes the worth of the company remained the same for ten years, unlikely in the real world. In practice, Patti would have to review the worth of her company yearly with her accountant to determine how much stock she could give without endangering her voting control.

SOME THOUGHTS ON GIFT-GIVING AND TAXES

Estate planners have developed a number of ways to use gifts to reduce, or even eliminate, estate tax for many people whose estates are in excess of $600,000. Before plunging into this subject (game might be a better word), take stock of what you really feel about gifts. Will giving property to your children or grandchildren enhance their lives? Or are they not yet ready to handle or appreciate your generosity? For example, helping a hard working 21-year-old get an education or the head of a new family buy a house may be a truly great gift. By contrast, you may not want your money spent by a young person on an expensive car or two weeks in Las Vegas.

Making a gift, under both common understanding and the law, means you give away ownership of some property; you no longer control it. This loss of ownership is precisely why many people don't make substantial gifts. Sometimes this makes good sense; they need, or may need, the money. Often, however, with larger estates, the refusal to make gifts makes little economic sense. Some people, it seems, want to hang on to every nickel they've got while they're alive, whether they will ever need it or not. The pleasure of keeping all their property outweighs any possible tax benefits.

Certainly, we wouldn't encourage anyone to give away money if it meant risking sacrifices in lifestyle or the possibility of money fears or anxieties. However, those with more than adequate wealth for their foreseeable needs should seriously consider making tax-exempt gifts while alive. Aside from any tax savings, the giver can feel pleasure and satisfaction in making a gift while living and seeing the help it brings.

Gifts of privately-held stock. Determining the value of privately-held stock is tricky, and a good accountant should be consulted.

2. Making Gifts of Real Estate

Some parents want to give a house, or money to buy a house, to a child or children. Can it be done free of gift tax, even though the house is worth far more than $10,000? Often, it can.

One method is to lend the children the money, take a promissory note in return and then forgive a portion of the loan each year. But unless you want to do a fair amount of research and planning yourself, you'll need the help of an experienced lawyer or financial planner to pull this off. This type of transaction skirts the edge of what the IRS allows, and must be handled carefully.

Another way to make the gift tax-free is for the parents to buy a house and then officially sell it to their children for a fair market price. The sale is secured by a mortgage, including reasonable interest, payable annually by the child. The payments are structured so that each year's payment will be less than $10,000. Then, each year, the parents forgive the payment—that is, they don't accept it—which is a form of a gift. It's essential to do this in writing. Over time, the entire house is transferred to the child, without any gift tax being paid.

This may sound appealing, but it, too, must be very carefully arranged. The transaction must have the appearance of creating enforceable rights by the "sellers" (the parents) and real legal obligations to pay on behalf of the intended owner(s) (the children) of the home. If the IRS can establish that, from the beginning, the parents intended to forgive each year's payments, it will treat the transaction as being made all in one year and assess gift tax accordingly.

Get good information before acting. Just to have the IRS claim you've made a taxable gift of real estate (even if you eventually prevail) is a hassle you, or your inheritors, surely don't need. See a lawyer who knows how to work with the IRS rules governing this type of transaction.

Despite the risks, a properly arranged transaction can result in considerable tax savings.

Example: Jean-Paul and Monique Zelly, a married couple, buy a home for $160,000, which they pay for in cash equally. They want their son, Richard, to live in the house now and own it as soon as possible. The Zellys' estate is well over $1.2 million, so naturally they want to reduce their eventual estate tax bite as much as is legally possible. They consider giving the house outright to their son, but this seems like a bad idea, because $140,000 of the gift would be subject to gift tax (the $160,000 value less the $20,000 annual exclusion available to a couple), and the amount that each of the Zellys could pass tax-free at death would be reduced from $600,000 to $530,000.

After working with an experienced lawyer, the Zellys transfer the house to their son in exchange for a loan of $160,000 and reasonable interest totaling $48,000. All the paperwork is dutifully prepared, signed and notarized. The Zellys record a mortgage for $208,000 in their names, with the son to make payments of $16,000 a year for 13 years. ($16,000 a year isn't the total amount the Zellys could forgive—that would be $20,000 a year—but a $20,000 a year payment might raise a red flag to the IRS, who could say, "Ah, you just happened to set the payment at the maximum amount you could forgive, huh?")

As each year's payment comes due, the couple forgives it—that is, makes a gift of that amount to their son. Each year's gift is within the amount exempt from gift tax. In 13 years, the house has been fully transferred to their son, and its worth will be excluded from each of the Zelly's taxable estate. If their son were married, the Zellys could shorten the time for the transfer in half, by making the gift jointly to their son and his spouse.

Obviously, to engage in this kind of real estate gift-giving, you must have confidence and trust in the person (or people) you're transferring the property to. And you have to live long enough to complete the transfer. Otherwise, the obligation is owed to your estate, and won't be annually forgiven. If the Zellys didn't completely trust their son, this wouldn't be a wise estate planning move, since if he sold the house without their consent, it could mean trouble for them.

3. Gifts of Property That Is Likely to Appreciate

If you're prosperous and your estate will be subject to estate tax, it can make particularly good sense to give away property that you believe will appreciate substantially in the future, especially if it hasn't gone up in value much already. At first, this may seem a little complicated, but if you read what follows carefully, you'll see it really isn't.

Here is the basic idea. If property you own seems reasonably likely to go up in value substantially in the future, giving it away now not only excludes its present worth from your estate but also eliminates the value of its likely future appreciation from your estate.

Example: Brook, in her 60s, recently purchased some vacant land for $160,000 cash. The property is located in an area she believes will be ripe for development in a few years. She intends to leave this land to her niece, Laura, when she dies. If she waits to transfer the property until her death, then the market value of the property when she dies will be included in her taxable estate. But if Brook gives the land to Laura now, then all of its appreciation in value, as well as its current worth, won't be included in Brook's taxable estate.

The gift will be subject to gift tax ($10,000 of the gift will be excluded from gift tax, but $150,000 won't be). Still, if Brook is right about the land increasing in value, the gift tax assessed will be far less than estate tax imposed on the appreciated property would be at Brook's death, for the obvious reason that the appreciated property will be worth more, and therefore taxed at a higher rate.

By contrast, it usually doesn't make sense to give away property that has already gone up in value, especially if you may not live long. The reason, as more fully explained in Section F, is that the recipient of a gift has the same tax "basis" in the property as the giver did (which is, very roughly, usually what the giver paid for the property). On the other hand, an inheritor obtains a basis that is "stepped-up" to the fair market value of the property at the time of death (or sometime thereafter at the option of the estate). The concepts of "basis" and "stepped-up basis" can seem harder than they really are, so hang in there. It's important. (These concepts are discussed below in Section F, and also in Chapter 15, Estate Taxes, Section A.)

Example: Bill bought 1,000 shares of stock at $5 a share. It's now worth $30 a share and is still going up. If he gives it now to his daughter Betsy, her cost basis will be $5 per share. If he leaves it to Betsy upon his death, her stepped-up basis in the stock will probably be $30 a share or higher, depending on its market price when he dies.

This difference will be vitally important when Betsy sells the stock. If its cost basis is $5 a share and it sells for $30 a share, she will have to pay capital gain tax on the $25 per share profit. By contrast, if the basis is stepped up to $30 because the transfer is made at death, and she sells the stock at $30 a share, she won't owe any capital gain tax.

4. Gifts of Life Insurance

In some situations, making a gift of life insurance can substantially reduce or eliminate federal estate tax. In fact, from a gift tax standpoint, giving life insurance can often be the most advantageous way to transfer a large sum out of your estate, since the gift normally has a low value for gift tax purposes. But because gifts of insurance policies can be such a good tax deal for the giver, special rules apply. The most important one is that the gift must be made more than three years before you die to be effective for estate tax purposes.

Gifts of life insurance are discussed in Chapter 12, Life Insurance, Section C. Here is a summary of the advantages of giving away a life insurance policy you own on your life.

If you own the policy when you die, the proceeds paid by the policy at your death are part of your taxable estate. However, if someone else owned the policy, the proceeds aren't part of your taxable estate. It's crucial to understand that simply naming a beneficiary of a life insurance policy isn't a gift. The policy itself must be given for a gift to occur.

Of course, a gift tax obligation can be incurred when you transfer the policy to its new owner. However, the policy itself is always worth less—often lots less—than the proceeds paid at death.

Ownership of a life insurance policy must be given to someone by a document transferring ownership. Many insurance companies provide forms for this purpose, so check with your insurance agent.

Example: Kate, in her early 60s, gave a life insurance policy with a face value of $200,000 to her daughter, Ava, in 1989. The value of the policy in

1989 was only $4,000. There was no gift tax assessed when the gift was made to Ava, because the policy was worth less than $10,000. When Kate dies suddenly in 1994, the policy pays $200,000. Aside from life insurance, Kate's estate totals $560,000. The $200,000 proceeds are not included in Kate's taxable estate because she lived more than three years after the gift was made. The result is that Kate's estate, at her death, is worth $560,000, which is under the $600,000 estate tax threshold.

If you give away an insurance policy more than three years before your death, you can also make yearly tax-exempt gifts up to $10,000 per year to the new owner, who can then use that money to pay the premiums on the policy. These gifts won't cause the life insurance policy to run afoul of the federal three-year rule. So, even though you effectively, if indirectly, continue to pay for the policy, the proceeds won't be included in your taxable estate.

You can also give life insurance to an irrevocable life insurance trust. Again, to avoid having the proceeds included in your taxable estate, the policy must be transferred to the trust at least three years before your death. If this has been done, the proceeds are not included in your (the insured's) taxable estate. (See Chapter 21, Other Estate Tax Saving Trusts, Section B.)

HOW MUCH IS A LIFE INSURANCE POLICY WORTH FOR GIFT TAX PURPOSES?

If you're considering giving away an insurance policy, you'll want to know the present worth of that policy. If it's over $10,000, gift tax will be assessed on the transaction. Under IRS rules, the value of a gift of a new life insurance policy for gift tax purposes is its cost (what it would cost to buy a similar policy), not the cash surrender value. For fully paid-up policies, this value is easy to determine, but where further payments will be made, the value of the gift is harder to figure out. Under IRS rules, "all relevant facts and elements of value shall be considered." (IRS Reg. 25.2512-1.) The IRS regulations use phrases like, "the interpolated terminated reserve as of the date of the gift, plus any prepaid premiums," as a method for determining value.[3]

Fortunately, most insurance companies will provide, on request, an informal approximation of the gift tax value of a policy before you make the actual gift. They will also provide the appropriate forms (usually Treasury Department Form 938) for submission with the gift tax return, if need be.

As we've discussed above, however, the value of the gift of an insurance policy is always much lower than the proceeds paid in the event of the insured's death.

5. Gifts to Minors While You Live

You can make a gift to a minor during your life, as well as leave a minor property when you die. As we've discussed, a minor cannot legally control any

[3]Yes, these words are bizarre. All you need do with them, however, is repeat them slowly to your insurance company. They will then give you the dollar value, for gift tax purposes, of your policy.

substantial amount of property in his or her own name. An adult must have that responsibility. If, while you are alive, you make a gift directly to a child, rather than to his or her parents or guardians, you have two choices, as discussed below.

Your options are to:

1. *Give the money in a trust.* If you, while living, make a gift to a minor using a child's trust, you obtain the $10,000 annual gift tax exemption in the year the gift is made, provided that the child's trust ends when the child is 21. If, however, the trust property will not be turned over to the child until she is older than 21, you are not entitled to the annual gift tax exemption. (IRS Reg. 25.2503-4(c).) (See Section C4, above.)

2. *Appoint a "custodian" for the gift, under your state's Uniform Transfers to Minors Act (UTMA) or Uniform Gifts to Minors Act (UGMA).* Not every state has adopted the Uniform Transfers to Minors Act, but all those that haven't have adopted the Uniform Gifts to Minors Act. The UGMA only allows you to make gifts to minors while you live, not to use that Act for leaving property to minors when you die.

Using either Act, you, while you are still living, make a gift to a minor by creating a document naming the minor beneficiary. You also identify the money or property you are giving and name an adult to serve as custodian (property manager) for the gift. (The custodian's duties are discussed in Chapter 6, Children, Section C.)

In most states, the custodianship must end when the child turns 21. That obviously satisfies the IRS requirement that to qualify for the $10,00 annual gift tax exemption, a gift to a minor must be turned over to the recipient when he or she turns 21. In Alaska and Nevada, be sure to specify that the recipient receives the gift at age 21. These states' laws are unclear and could be interpreted as extending the custodianship past age 21, if you don't provide otherwise.

We want to note that gifts to minors made while one is alive are often given primarily for personal reasons, not for gift tax savings. A giver's personal motives may override maximizing gift tax savings, or those motives may work harmoniously with all applicable gift tax rules.

Example 1: Oksana, who is quite prosperous, wants to be certain her grandson Viktor and granddaughter Marya will have enough money to attend college. Viktor is 12 and Marya is 10. Oksana wants to make the gift now, so she can take pleasure in seeing that her grandchildren know their educational future is secure. She creates an educational child's trust for each, to last until the child is 26, naming their father as trustee. Oksana realizes that by doing this, she will not obtain the $10,000 annual gift tax exemption for any money she gives the trust, because, as we explained, federal tax law requires the child to receive the money outright by age 21 for the annual $10,000 exemption to apply. But Oksana wants adult supervision of the trust until the children are 26, because she doubts if any child age 21 is likely to be able to handle this sum of money responsibly. Her concern over this issue overrides any consideration of tax savings.

Example 2: Biff decides to give an expensive thoroughbred horse (which would sell for $50,000) to his niece Brenda, age 16, who has loved horses since she was small. Biff makes the gift under his state's UTMA, which requires the horse to be legally turned over to Brenda when she becomes 21—which is fine with Biff. Biff names Brenda's mother, Josette, as custodian for the gift. They all know this is only technical, since Brenda will be, and wants to be, responsible for the horse.

Biff is not assessed gift tax on $10,000 of his gift. He is assessed gift tax on the remaining value of $40,000.

F. Tax Basis Rules for Gifts

Much of this chapter has discussed why it is often advantageous, from an estate/gift tax point of view, to give away property before you die. But this isn't always the case. It's usually unwise to give away an asset (as opposed to leaving it at death) that has substantially appreciated in value since you purchased it, especially if you are older and likely to die before decades pass.

In order to understand why it is often better for the recipient to inherit appreciated property than to receive it during the giver's life as a gift, you need to understand the tax concept of "basis." While we've discussed this elsewhere (particularly in Chapter 15, Estate Taxes, Section A), it's so important, that we discuss the rules again for you here, focusing on how they apply to gifts.

The tax basis of property is the value (dollar figure) from which gain or loss on sale is determined. When property is purchased, its basis is generally its cost. In fact, basis is often referred to as cost basis. If you make major (capital) improvements to property—for example, adding a deck to your house—the cost of the improvement is added to the basis of the property.[4]

The recipient of a gift takes the same basis in the property as the giver had. This is called the "carry-over" basis, in tax jargon.

Example: Lewella's basis in her house is $100,000 (net purchase price plus capital improvements). The house now has a market value of $320,000. Lewella gives her house to Megan. Megan's (carry-over) basis in the house is $100,000. If Megan then sells the house for $320,000, her taxable profit is $220,000 ($320,000 minus her basis of $100,000).

[4]To simplify what can become very complicated tax issues, capital improvements are additions and improvement to property that increases its value, that cannot be removed, that have a useful life of more than one year and that are not normal maintenance (for example, painting a house or fixing a roof).

The basis rules for inherited property differ from those applicable to gifts. The tax basis for property a person inherits is the fair market value at the date of the original owner's death. This means the tax basis is increased (in taxese, "stepped up") from the deceased's basis to the value of the property at death.

Example: If Lewella dies and leaves her house to Megan, Megan's basis in the house is increased to its market value at Sara's death, which is $320,000.

This stepped-up basis rule means there are major (capital gain) tax savings for the recipient if an asset that has appreciated in value is transferred at death instead of given to that recipient while the giver is still alive.

Example: Edward owns a Redon pastel painting, which he bought an astute art student for $20,000. Sixty years later, an appraiser informs him it's worth $1.5 million. If Edward were to sell the painting, his taxable gain would be $1.5 million less his basis of $20,000. If he gives the painting away and the recipient sells it, the tax situation is the same—only now it's the recipient who owes capital gain tax on the profit.

By contrast, if Edward dies and leaves the painting to the same recipient in his living trust, his beneficiary's "stepped-up" basis in the painting is $1.5 million. If the beneficiary promptly sells the painting, there's no taxable gain.

1. Special Rules for Community Property

If you're married and own community property (see Chapter 3, State Property Ownership Laws, Section B, for a discussion of community property and a list of the nine community property states), an additional federal tax basis rule can be significant for your estate planning. On the death of one spouse, the basis of the community property interests of both spouses is stepped up (increased) to the property's fair market value at the time of the spouse's death.

Example: Felicia and Max are residents of the state of Washington, a community property state. They own a house they bought for $50,000. The basis of each spouse's interest is $25,000, one-half the purchase price. When Felicia dies, the market value of the house is $400,000. Because of the stepped-up basis rule for community property, the federal tax basis of each spouse's half-interest in the house steps up to $200,000. If Max sells the house for $400,000 shortly after Felicia's death, he will not owe any capital gain tax. The sale price equals the stepped-up basis of the house. In contrast, if the house had been sold before Felicia died, the total federal taxable gain to Felicia and Max would have been $350,000. (If Felicia and Max were over 55, they would have had the right to a one-time tax deduction of $125,000, so their taxable gain then would have been $225,000.)

Again, what all this means is that there's a considerable federal tax advantage for inheritors if an elderly couple retains, until one of them dies, community property that has substantially increased in value since they purchased it.

Example: Tristan and Isolde, residents of California (a community property state), have been married for 45 years. During that time, they've acquired valuable community property:

- a home, purchased for $30,000 in 1955, now worth $300,000;
- a summer home, purchased for $50,000 in 1964, now worth $300,000;
- two oil paintings, purchased for $3,000 each in 1960, now worth $100,000 each.

Tristan dies and leaves his half of the community property to their children. This means they receive $150,000 worth of the home, $150,000 worth of the summer home and a painting worth $100,000. These figures are also the children's stepped-up "bases" (plural of basis) for these assets.

Isolde, of course, still owns her one-half of the community property. Her basis in her half of the property also goes up to its market value at Tristan's death. In other words, if Isolde decided to sell her share of the oil paintings a week after her husband's death for $200,000, she would have no taxable profit. If she gave the paintings away, the recipient's basis in the paintings would be $200,000. Similarly, if Isolde and the children sold the summer home for $300,000, no tax would be owed by anyone.

2. State Basis Rules

In general, the impact of state tax basis rules on gifts or inherited property is minor, because the tax rates involved are relatively low in those states that impose gift and death taxes. Estate planning decisions are rarely affected by state basis rules. If you want to explore your state's rules, you can either research that issue yourself (see Chapter 30, Using Attorneys, Section B) or consult an accountant or tax attorney.

Stepped-Up Basis for Community Property Held in Joint Tenancy

Sometimes, title to community property is held in joint tenancy for probate avoidance purposes. Normally, only the property interest of a deceased joint tenant is entitled to a stepped-up tax basis, not the property interest of the remaining joint tenant. However, as long as community property is involved, both halves of that property are entitled to a stepped-up basis upon the death of the first spouse, whether it's held in joint tenancy or not.

Unfortunately, the IRS presumes that joint tenancy property isn't community property, unless the taxpayer can prove that it is. In addition, IRS rules are far from clear concerning what proof suffices to establish the community property status.

As a result, some estate planners advise married couples not to hold community property, especially appreciated property, in joint tenancy to be absolutely sure they obtain a stepped-up basis for both halves of their property. Using a living trust (instead of joint tenancy) allows couples to both avoid probate and eliminate worry that both halves of their community property will not qualify for a stepped-up tax basis.

Other ways to avoid this problem are:

- to hold title as "community property held in joint tenancy," if your title company permits this (see Chapter 10, Section B)
- to sign a statement that the property remains community property and is held in joint tenancy only for probate avoidance purposes.

G. Using Gifts to Reduce Income Taxes

If you are prosperous and are willing to give income-producing property to someone in a lower tax bracket while you are still alive, you can achieve some overall income tax savings in addition to the possible federal estate and gift tax savings discussed earlier in this chapter. With the current maximum income tax rate close to 40%, a gift to a person in a lower tax bracket, especially someone in the 15% bracket, will obviously result in less income tax being paid on income received from the property. Of course, you will not see the tax savings yourself, because you no longer own the property.

Beware of giving property to people under 14. This possible income tax benefit may well not apply to children under age 14. The reason is that all income over $1,000 received by minors under 14 years, from any gift (whether from their parents or otherwise), is taxed, for federal income tax purposes, at the highest tax rate of their parents. So if the parents are not in a lower bracket, this benefit is eliminated.■

17

An Overview of Ongoing Trusts

An "ongoing" trust is a trust that is intended to operate for a significant time after the death of the grantor (the person who establishes the trust). Often, but not in all cases, an ongoing trust begins to operate as a separate legal entity only at the death of the grantor. Once operational, these ongoing trusts are irrevocable and often function for many years or even decades.

The two basic functions of ongoing trusts are to:

1. Save on estate taxes

2. Impose long-term controls on the management of trust property.

Some ongoing trusts serve both purposes, some only one.

Many people need only a simple probate-avoidance living trust, not a complex ongoing trust. By the end of this chapter, you should have a pretty clear idea of whether a simple probate-avoidance trust is enough for you or if you need some type of ongoing trust as well.

This chapter explores basic features common to all ongoing trusts. The other chapters discuss the specifics of the different major types of ongoing trusts used in estate planning. We don't bother with summary explanations of these trusts here, because summaries of these devices will be of no, or very little, use. To understand these trusts, you have to dig in a bit. These trusts include:

- Estate tax-saving "bypass" trusts, including the commonly used "marital life estate" or AB trust (Chapter 18).
- Other estate tax-saving marital trusts, including a "QTIP" trust to postpone payment of estate taxes (Chapter 19).
- Charitable trusts (Chapter 20).
- Other estate tax saving trusts, including generation-skipping trusts, irrevocable life insurance trusts and grantor-retained interest trusts (Chapter 21).
- Using disclaimers where a beneficiary declines a gift (Chapter 22).
- Trusts useful to people in second or subsequent marriages (Chapter 23).
- A basic child's trust, to control property inherited by a minor or young adult (Chapter 6).
- A trust to impose controls over property (Chapter 24).

TRUST PROPERTY AND MEDICAL BILLS

Some, perhaps many, people would like to include a "catastrophic illness" clause or provision in whatever type of ongoing trust they create so they can prevent their trust assets from being used to pay medical bills if a trust beneficiary suffers a catastrophic illness. Preservation of trust assets from claims by medical providers or government agencies is often desired particularly by couples with some type of shared trust property. At the very least, the couple doesn't want both members' trust assets used to pay for one's catastrophic illness.

Unfortunately, there is no simple clause applicable in all states that will effectively achieve the desired result. Provisions designed to protect trust assets from being consumed by huge medical bills can provide some protection, if properly geared to current federal laws and regulations and your specific state's laws. But such provisions rarely, if ever, consist of a single clause or paragraph; indeed, they often go on for pages. Obviously, such a provision must be prepared by an expert. It's absolutely essential to be up-to-date on the law here.

A. Estate Tax Saving Trusts

One goal of many ongoing trusts is to save on estate taxes. There's good reason to want to cut your estate tax bill: Federal estate taxes, which kick in when a person dies owning property worth more than $600,000, are substantial. Rates start at 37% and go to 55% for estates over $3 million. (See Chapter 15, Estate Taxes, Section A.)

Any individual or couple with an estate over $600,000 should explore tax-saving trusts. A couple with a combined estate worth more than $600,000 can use an ongoing trust that becomes operational after one member dies to achieve significant savings in the couple's combined estate taxes. (See Chapter 18, Estate Tax-Saving Bypass Trusts, Section C.)

If you are under the impression that estate tax-saving trusts are an aid only to a handful of millionaires, or that they are somehow fraudulent (or at least sleazy), think again. Many prosperous folks (to repeat, those with estates over $600,000) can take advantage of what these trusts offer, and they are perfectly legal.

If you are afraid you might be overwhelmed by reading about tax-saving trusts, don't give up. You don't need to master the complexities of actually preparing most of these types of trusts. Indeed, this book contains no forms for preparing your own estate tax-saving trusts. Nolo does offer *Make Your Own Living Trust*, which contains forms you can use to prepare your own marital life estate, or AB trust (discussed in depth in Chapter 18, Estate Tax-Saving Bypass Trusts, Section C). Otherwise, these trusts are quite complex and technical, and must be prepared by a lawyer.

Beware of tax-saving trusts that seem too good to be true. Expert estate planning lawyers can sometimes come up with truly ingenious plans to fit a family's particular needs and also save on estate taxes. But some lawyers and financial planners (at the very least) push the line of what's legally safe. For example, some tout the virtues of trusts designed to save big money on income or estate taxes, while at the same time giving the grantor great powers over trust assets. The IRS looks askance at this. It's up to you to decide how safe or aggressive you want to be. But before betting a big estate on the novel theories of any estate planner—lawyer or not—it's wise to get a second, perhaps more conservative, opinion.

We want to offer you sufficient information about major types of estate tax-saving trusts so you can decide whether it's worth your time and money to hire a lawyer to create one or more for you. Also, by reading the next four chapters, you should be able to discern if a lawyer is providing helpful, accurate information and advice about estate tax-saving trusts or is primarily concerned with running up your bill.

If you still have any doubts about the value of investigating estate tax-saving trusts, consider the following analogy: When you sit down each year to fill out your income tax forms, would it ever occur to you to just skip personal exemptions and deductions you are entitled to and cheerfully send that money to the government? Well, that's exactly that you're doing if you prepare an estate plan that ignores exemptions and deductions available through the use of estate tax-saving trusts.

To make this point even more bluntly, let's look at what really happens to a hard-earned dollar (at least, we presume it was hard-earned) when it is subject to estate tax. You could call this the case of the disappearing dollar. Your original dollar earned has already been taxed by income tax—probably at roughly 30%, as a minimum (and quite possibly higher, particularly if you have to pay state income or Social Security taxes). So now you've got, at most, 70 cents left. If the 70 cents is subject to estate tax at the minimum rate of 37%, there's only 44 cents left. And for very large estates, the estate tax goes up to 55%, which leaves less than 35 cents. (And you can take another nickel away if the estate went through probate.)

B. Ongoing Trusts Used to Control Property

In addition to saving on estate taxes, ongoing trusts can also be used to provide for the management and control of property you don't want to leave outright to a beneficiary or beneficiaries. This is particularly common in second or subsequent marriages if there are children from a prior marriage. Often, each spouse wants to leave the other spouse well-provided for. At the same time, each spouse doesn't want to leave everything outright to the other spouse, because each wants the bulk of his or her property to eventually go to his or her children. An ongoing trust can be used to achieve both these goals. (See Chapter 23, Trusts for Second or Subsequent Marriages.)

An ongoing trust to control property is also desirable or essential in other circumstances, including if:

- You leave property to minors (or persons who have been declared legally incompetent) who are not legally permitted to own substantial amounts of property outright.
- You believes the beneficiary can't handle money responsibly
- The beneficiary needs what's called a "special needs trust" to provide long-term support while letting the beneficiary stay eligible for federal or state assistance.
- You decide you no longer want the burdens of administering your own property and want to turn that task over to someone else. For instance, a grantor who is old and ill may know that it's sensible to arrange for others to handle her finances. There are various methods to arrange for this, including purchasing an annuity or preparing a durable power of attorney for finances. Sometimes people prefer a trust, however, because it is a more traditional legal form, and the trust property will avoid probate on the grantor's death.

This book does not attempt to show you how to prepare one of these trusts yourself—they are complicated and definitely require a lawyer. But we hope to provide you with sufficient understanding of how these trusts work, so that you can sensibly decide whether or not to explore creating one.

The grantor's selection of the successor trustee and alternate successor trustee is especially important with a trust used to control property. The successor trustee for a trust used to control property will have an ongoing relationship with the beneficiaries. Usually, the trustee will have important decisions to make, such as how to invest trust money and whether to spend some of the trust principal for a certain beneficiary's needs. Also, there may be other sensitive personal issues involved in choosing the successor trustee—most importantly, the relationship between her and the trust beneficiaries.

BASIC ONGOING TRUST TERMS

A person who sets up a trust (that's you, or you and your spouse) is called a **grantor(s)**.

All the property you own at death, whether in a trust or owned in some other legal form, is your **estate**.

The market value of your property at your death (or six months later, if your executor or successor trustee chooses), less all debts and liabilities on that property, is your net or **taxable estate**.

The property you transfer to a trust is called, collectively, the **trust property**, **trust principal** or **trust estate**. (And of course, there's a Latin version: the trust "corpus.")

The person who has power over the trust property is called the **trustee**.

The person you name to take over as trustee after your death (or, with a trust made jointly by a couple, after the death of both spouses) is called the **successor trustee**.

The people or organizations who inherit trust property are called the **beneficiaries** of the trust. Different types of beneficiaries include:

- **primary beneficiaries**, people or institutions who will receive a specific gift you leave them
- **alternate beneficiaries**, people or institutions who will receive property if the primary beneficiary for that property dies before you do
- **life beneficiaries**, people who will receive benefits from trust property, such as income or use of the property, during their lifetime. Life beneficiaries have only limited rights (if any) to use up or sell trust principal, and no right to leave that principal to anyone
- **final beneficiaries**, people or institutions designated to receive life estate trust property outright upon the death of a life beneficiary
- **residual beneficiaries**, people or institutions you designate to receive any property owned by the ongoing trust that you haven't left to any other specifically-named beneficiaries.

C. ONGOING TRUSTS AND AVOIDING PROBATE

Ongoing trusts don't automatically avoid probate. Indeed, some ongoing trusts become operational while the grantor is alive; for these trusts, probate is not an issue. However, most ongoing trusts become operational only when the grantor dies. To avoid probate of property left in these trusts, ongoing trusts are usually a part (a big part) of a living trust. There's rarely a sensible reason to have ongoing trust property go through probate. For this reason, after a person's death, it's better to transfer her property to an ongoing trust through a living trust, rather than leave the property by will. By using a living trust, the property first avoids probate after the person's death; then the property goes to the ongoing trust.

Example: Malcha wants to establish an ongoing trust to manage the property she intends to leave to her kid brother, Carl, who is 20 years her junior. She wants to create an ongoing trust because Carl, age 28, has always squandered whatever money he's acquired and shows no signs of change. Malcha creates a trust in which the trustee controls how and when money is given to Carl from the trust. This trust will be an ongoing one and will become operational only after Malcha dies. Malcha wants to avoid probate of the property in the ongoing trust, so that trust is grafted onto a revocable living trust. That way, Malcha's property will first avoid probate and then be in the ongoing trust.

As long as Malcha lives, the living trust, and the ongoing trust contained in the living trust, are revocable. When Malcha dies, the ongoing trust becomes irrevocable and cannot be changed by anyone, including Carl.

All of the ongoing trusts discussed in the next chapters can be made part of a living trust, except those ongoing trusts that become operational before the grantor dies. To say this metaphorically, just because an ongoing trust and a probate-avoidance living trust are technically different legal animals doesn't mean they can't drink at the same pond. We stress this here because it's important to understand you don't need to risk probate by creating an ongoing trust. Please make a mental note of this, since we don't repeat it for each ongoing trust we discuss. These discussions are already complex enough.

D. How Ongoing Trusts Work

Once an ongoing trust becomes operational, it is a legal entity separate from any person or organization. It also, as we've stressed, becomes irrevocable—that is, the terms of the trust cannot be changed.

1. When an Ongoing Trust Takes Effect

A trust becomes "operational" when it actually becomes effective in the real world as a legally distinct entity. As we've mentioned, most often, this happens at the death of the person who created the trust. Once an ongoing trust becomes operational, the trustee must obtain a taxpayer I.D. number for the trust, keep accurate trust financial records, and file an annual federal trust income tax return and any state trust tax returns required. Most people don't want an ongoing trust to become irrevocable while they are alive. Understandably, they don't want to be locked into giving away some of their property during their life.

Example: Alma, age 73, creates a living trust to avoid probate. As one component of this living trust, she creates an ongoing trust for her disabled daughter. Only when Alma dies does the ongoing trust for her daughter become operational and irrevocable.

Occasionally, however, people want this ongoing trust to become operational and irrevocable during their lifetime. For example, charitable trusts are often set up this way. In these trusts, the grantor creates an irrevocable trust that is operational as soon as the trust document is signed and notarized. Trust property is promptly given to the named charity, and the grantor retains certain rights to receive income from the trust property. (See Chapter 20, Charitable Trusts.)

There can be other reasons to make an ongoing trust operational during your lifetime, rather than at your death. One example is an irrevocable life insurance trust, which must be operational at least three years before the grantor's death to obtain estate tax savings. (See Chapter 21, Other Estate Tax-Saving Trusts, Section B.)

If an ongoing trust is designed so that it takes effect while you are alive, the property placed in the trust is a gift, subject to gift tax, unless the beneficiary is a tax-exempt charity. (See Chapter 16, Gifts and Gift Taxes, Section A.) If the ongoing trust is created in a will or living trust and takes effect when you die, the property in the trust is subject to federal estate tax, if your total estate exceeds $600,000. In some states, it is also subject to state death tax. (See Chapter 15, Estate Taxes, Sections A.)

> **Avoid 'Daydream Trust' Scams**
>
> Those who believe trusts are truly lawyers' magic may seek or fall victim to what we call the "daydream" trust. In a daydream trust, the grantor wants to use an ongoing trust to:
>
> - Avoid all income taxes.
> - Shield the property from all creditors, and
> - Retain complete control over trust property or, at the very least, have full access to it in times of need.
>
> It should come as no surprise that the daydream trust is just that—a fantasy. Tax rules prevent a grantor from accomplishing the goals listed above. Obviously, it's not socially desirable to allow people to escape financial liabilities and obligations simply by use of a trust. As a result, you can't use a trust to escape responsibility for legal debts and obligations, including child support, alimony, court-ordered judgments or any other legal debt. Likewise, if you retain any control over the trust or benefits from it, the IRS will not allow the trust to be used to lower your income taxes.

2. How Long an Ongoing Trust Lasts

How long an ongoing trust lasts is determined by the trust document. Some trusts last for a set number of years, but usually termination of the trust is triggered by a certain event. The trust may, for example, last until a surviving spouse dies; when that happens, trust property is distributed to the couple's children and the trust ends. A trust for grandchildren may last until the youngest reaches age 30 or 35, or whatever age the grantor chooses, at which point the grandchildren receive all remaining trust property.

A legal rule called "the rule against perpetuities" requires a trust to have a set ending time, or set ending event. This rule prevents someone from tying up property for generations without that property ever being owned outright by anyone. For example, you can't leave property "first to my daughter, then equally to her children, then equally to their grandchildren," and so on. Society has decided that there should be a finite period during which the instructions of a deceased person can control the disposition of property. At some time, some person has to own the property outright and be free to sell it or give it away.

The intricacies of the rule against perpetuities have baffled law students for generations. For practical purposes, the rule means you can legally tie up property for only one generation—people who are alive when you die. That means you can leave trust property for your grown children to use during their lives and specify that, at their deaths, the property goes outright to their children. But if you try to impose controls on your grandchildren's freedom to use or dispose of the property, you risk running afoul of the rule against perpetuities.

If you want to impose controls on property for more than one generation, you'll definitely need a good estate planning lawyer's advice to determine if what you want is legally possible.

E. The Trustee

The trustee of an ongoing trust has serious responsibilities, and choosing a reliable trustee is an important part of creating an ongoing trust.

1. The Trustee's Duties

No matter what type of ongoing trust it is, the trustee must supervise and manage the trust property prudently and comply with any specific instructions in the trust document regarding trust property management.

> **TERMINOLOGY NOTE**
>
> Because an ongoing trust is usually created as a component of a living trust, you are the original trustee. When you die, a person you've named as trustee for the ongoing trust manages it. Often, but not always, this person is the same as the successor trustee of your living trust. So the trustee of the ongoing trust could technically be your "successor trustee." However, we refer to the person who manages an ongoing trust that become operational at your death simply as the "trustee."

The powers the trustee will have are usually set out in detail (sometimes pages of detail) in the trust document. For example, the trustee may be given the specific power to sell trust real estate, or to buy or lease new real estate.

In addition to all the terms of the trust document, general legal rules also govern the trustee. Legally, the trustee is a "fiduciary," which means she is held to the standard of highest good faith and scrupulous honesty when handling trust business (unless the trust document itself declares a lesser legal standard). Thus, unless specifically authorized in the trust document, the trustee may not personally profit from any financial transaction involving the trust.

The trustee of an ongoing trust will most likely engage in various business or financial transactions on behalf of the trust. For instance, the trustee will probably deal with banks or other financial institutions. The trustee may well be involved in other trust financial matters, from say leasing trust property to dealing with the IRS. The trustee may also have to make investment decisions, or buy or sell trust property.

Sometimes, the trustee's actual financial responsibilities can be rather simple. For example, if the trust primarily consists of a valuable house, the trustee has to be sure the house is properly maintained, and perhaps decide to sell it. But often the trustee's work is more difficult. If much of the trust money is invested, the trustee must decide if the investments are reasonable ones—neither absurdly cautious nor too risky. If the trust property includes a business or a complex investment portfolio, managing the property can be quite a task. For this reason, it's normally permissible for a trustee to hire financial or investment advisors and pay for their advice from trust assets.

The trustee of an ongoing trust must also distribute trust income (or principal) to the beneficiaries as the trust document directs or permits. Sometimes this, too, is far from simple. If the trust document allows the trustee some discretion in whether or not to distribute some trust income, or invade trust principal, on behalf of a certain beneficiary, it may not be easy for the trustee to decide what to do.

The trustee of an ongoing trust that becomes operational at the grantor's death is responsible for handling all trust paperwork—for example, getting the taxpayer ID number from the IRS and keeping accurate trust financial records. Professional help can be used here if, in the trustee's judgment, trust financial affairs necessitate it. The trustee is also responsible for having the annual trust income tax return (IRS Form 1041) filed if the trust's gross annual income is $600 or more. If any federal tax is due, the trustee must pay it from trust funds. Finally, the trustee must handle any required state income tax return.

Eventually, when the trust ends, the trustee must distribute any remaining trust property to whomever was named as the final trust beneficiary.

Because of these responsibilities, most trustees of ongoing trusts are paid. The trust document often allows the trustees to pay themselves "reasonable compensation" or a set amount per hour from trust property. Of course, you can expressly prohibit pay for your trustee, but it's not wise. Are you sure you can rely on a person who will do the work required of a trustee without compensation? And even if someone would do it, do you really think it's fair? After all, the trustee is spending time on work you created by establishing your ongoing trust.

2. Choosing the Trustee

It is evident that if you create an ongoing trust, you must give serious thought to who will serve as the trustee. The two most important criteria your trustee should meet are that you completely trust her and that she wants to do the job.

It's also desirable that the trustee have some financial common sense. You may decide, though, that you want your trustee to have considerable financial expertise. For instance, you may want a trustee who understands the difference between a balanced, fairly conservative investment portfolio (a mix of income-oriented stock and bond funds, for example) and much riskier investment in someone's great idea for a new business or speculation in real estate.

If you can find all this in one person, fine, but remember—your trustee can always hire investment advisors. Someone you trust, and who is willing to do the job of trustee, can't be purchased.

You may also face sensitive personal issues in deciding whom to choose as trustee. For one thing, your trustee will have an ongoing relationship with the trust beneficiaries.

Example: Malik has three children from his former marriage. He wants to leave the income from his estate to his wife, Libby, during her life, and on her death, have his estate divided equally among his children. Who should Malik name as trustee of the ongoing trust he creates to achieve these goals?

There's no one set answer. Malik must carefully evaluate a number of factors:

- What is the relationship between Libby and his children?
- If Libby is the sole successor trustee, will she truly guard the trust principal for his children?
- If one of his children is the successor trustee, will he be fair to Libby—or will he try to retain all the money he can so it will eventually go to himself and his siblings?
- If Libby and one of Malik's children are co-successor trustees, can they get along?
- What will happen if they can't?

Different types of ongoing trusts may raise different concerns about your choice of trustee. These issues are discussed in the subsequent chapters, which cover various types of ongoing trusts.

3. Naming More Than One Trustee

Legally, you can name two, or even several, persons to serve as co-trustees. But before you do, make sure you have some compelling reason. Having two or more people serve as trustees, for a trust that lasts a long time, can lead to serious conflict or confusion.

If you feel there are pressing family or other important reasons why you want to name co-successor trustees, definitely discuss the situation with an estate planning attorney.

If you do decide to appoint co-successor trustees, you must decide how they share authority—whether each can act separately for the trust or all must agree in writing to act for the trust. But even more important, you must have complete confidence that all your trustees will get along. Do be cautious here. Power and property can lead to unexpected results. If the co-trustees are prone to conflict, you may well create serious problems, and will be doing none of them a favor by having them share power.

If co-trustees can't agree, say, on how to manage trust property, the situation can get very messy. Your trustees could wind up in court. Not only would this probably waste trust money, but the end result might be much worse, and generate more animosity than if you had just picked one person to be trustee in the first place and let the chips fall as they may.

4. Trust Companies and Banks as Trustees

Does the financial responsibility involved in managing an ongoing trust mean that the grantor, and the beneficiaries, might be better served if a professional trustee (from a bank or private trust company) is named as a trustee? Generally, we believe not. Our strong preference is for a person you know and trust to serve as trustee, if there's someone who can do the job. A trustee should have good money sense and be reasonably knowledgeable about the financial world, but does not normally need to be an expert.

Banks can be very impersonal, perhaps paying little attention to trusts worth less than (many) millions, or treating a beneficiary as a nuisance. In addition, they charge overall management fees (and often additional fees for each tiny act), which can cost a bundle.

But if there is no person you trust who is willing to serve as trustee, and you want to create an ongoing trust, you'll have to select a financial institution as your trustee. Also, certain types of property, such as oil and gas interests, are complicated and beneficiaries can benefit from professional management of such assets. Your best bet is probably to use a private trust company, a business that specializes in trust management. They tend to be smaller and less impersonal than banks, and more focused on trust management. If you're extremely cautious, you might want to name another institution as an alternate trustee, just in case your first choice goes out of business or decides not to handle smaller trusts. But doing this means you have to make arrangements with two private trust companies—which means extra work.

A possible compromise: co-trustees. One possible alternative is to name both an individual you trust and a financial institution as co-trustees. That way, you hope to get a measure of investment savvy but still have a real person in the mix. The reality may be less inviting. Most institutions won't accept a co-trustee arrangement in the first place. And anytime you appoint co-trustees, potential problems abound. (See Section 3 above.) Unless there's a financial institution you really feel comfortable with, a better bet is just to name an individual trustee, who can hire good financial advisors if needed.

5. Choosing an Alternate Trustee

Since your ongoing trust will likely last awhile, you need to give some thought to arranging for an alternate trustee, in case, somewhere down the line, your first choice becomes unable to perform the job. Aside from naming, in your trust document, one or more alternate trustees (to serve in the order named), you can also authorize an acting trustee to name, in writing, additional alternate trustees, to serve if—and only if—all the trustee and any alternative trustees you named are unable to serve. This should ensure that the position of trustee never becomes vacant. (If it did, there would have to be a court proceeding to name a new trustee.) Also, this ensures that any trustee will at least have been chosen by someone you trust.

Example: Shannon's living trust creates an ongoing trust for her two young grandchildren, to last until they reach age 35. She names the children's mother, Carrolyn (her daughter), as the trustee and Carolyn's husband, Will, as the alternative trustee. She also includes in the trust document a provision allowing any trustee to name, in writing, additional successor trustees.

Carolyn dies a few years after the trust becomes operational, and Will becomes trustee. He writes a document naming his brother Al, then Al's wife, Jane, to serve as trustees if he can't. Before either child is 35, Will is killed in a car crash. Al then becomes the trustee.

F. Taxation of Ongoing Trusts

It is rarely desirable, at least from an income tax standpoint, to have an ongoing trust retain income generated by trust property for over a year. Trust income tax rates are now higher than individual income tax rates. An ongoing trust is taxed on all income over $100 that it retains at the close of the tax year. If the trust distributes income earned in that year to a beneficiary, that income is taxed at the beneficiary's rate, not the trust's.

Since a beneficiary's income tax rate will be lower than the trust's rate, the rule is simple: trusts that retain income (over a year) pay more in income tax, and thus ultimately have less to distribute to the beneficiaries. You must feel that, for some non-income tax reason, it's vitally important that the trust can, or can be allowed to, accumulate income if you create a trust that requires, or even authorizes, this.

Current trust tax rates begin at 15% for retained trust income up to between $600 and $1,500 and reach a top rate of 39.6% for retained trust income over $7,500. The specific income tax rates are:

Amount of Retained Trust Income	*Income Tax Rate*
$100-$1,500	15%
$1,500-$3,500	$225 plus 28% of the excess over $1,500
$3,500-$5,500	$785 plus 31% of the excess over $3,500
$5,500-$7,500	$1,405 plus 36% of the excess over $5,500
Over $7,500	$2,125 plus 39.6% of the excess over $7,500 ■

18

Estate Tax-Saving Bypass Trusts

A "bypass" trust is an ongoing trust designed to lessen overall estate taxes. The most popular form of this trust is used by couples with a combined estate exceeding $600,000. We call this type a "marital life estate" trust. It also goes by other names, such as an "AB" trust.

Bypass trusts (most importantly, marital life estate trusts), can also be used to impose restrictions over a beneficiary's rights to trust property. This type of control trust is discussed in Chapter 23, Trusts for Second or Subsequent Marriages.

Important features of ongoing trusts, including bypass trusts, are discussed in Chapter 17, An Overview of Ongoing Trusts. To gain a better understanding of the trusts covered here, make sure you know the basics covered in Chapter 17.

A. Overview of Bypass Trusts

Here's the basics of how a bypass trust works. You create an ongoing trust that will take effect at your death, and provide that one beneficiary, usually your spouse, has the right to use that trust property during his or her life.

There is no estate tax savings at your death; the property in the trust is part of your taxable estate. The benefit comes when the surviving spouse dies. The key is that your spouse never legally owned the trust property, although she did have certain rights to receive income generated by trust property, or to use trust property (a house, for example). Because the surviving spouse never legally owned the property, it isn't counted as part of her estate, for estate tax purposes, when she dies.

When your spouse dies, the trust property goes to the final beneficiaries you've chosen, usually your children. Obviously, since no estate tax is taken out of the trust property when the second spouse dies, more of your property is left for your children to inherit. By contrast, if you had left your property to your spouse outright, it would have been included as part of his taxable estate when he died.

The person you name to receive rights in the trust property during his or her life is called, fittingly, the "life beneficiary." The life beneficiary has only those rights to the trust property specified in the trust document. These rights can include receiving all trust income, using trust property (for example, living in the family home) or certain limited rights to spend trust principal for specific needs (for example, medical care).

Technically, it is the trustee who decides whether or not to spend trust principal for authorized needs of the life beneficiary. But in most tax-saving bypass trusts, the trustee and the life beneficiary are the same person. Still, the life beneficiary is never the legal owner of the trust property. She has no power to decide who receives it after her death. When the life beneficiary dies, the trust property goes to whomever you originally named in the trust document as your final beneficiaries.

Both couples (married or not) and individuals can create a bypass trust.

Example 1: Cecilia has been married to Lou for over 40 years. They have one grown child, Marietta, who is 37. Cecilia creates the type bypass trust we call a "marital life estate trust" and transfers all her major items of property, both separately-owned and her half of shared marital property, to this trust. She names Lou as life beneficiary, with the right to receive (after Cecilia dies) all income from trust property until he dies, and to use trust principal for basic needs like medical care. When he dies, the trust property will pass outright to the final beneficiary, Marietta.

Example 2: Jefferson creates a bypass trust, naming his best friend, Isaac, as the life beneficiary. Isaac has the right to receive trust income, and also live in the house the trust owns. Jefferson's trust document specifies that, when Isaac dies, the property be divided equally between Jefferson's children, the final beneficiaries.

To understand how bypass trusts actually save on estate taxes, you obviously need to know how those taxes work. (They are discussed in detail in Chapter 15, Estate Taxes.) Here we repeat three basic federal estate tax rules:

- Every person can leave a total of $600,000 at death, tax-free, whether left to one beneficiary or divided among many, unless that person made taxable gifts during life. (See Chapter 16, Gifts and Gift Taxes.) This is sometimes called the "personal exemption" from estate tax.
- Married people can leave any amount tax-free to a spouse who is a U.S. citizen. (See Chapter 15, Section A.) In tax lingo, this is called the "marital deduction."
- If you leave more than $600,000 of property outright to a beneficiary (say your brother), and a few years later he dies owning property worth over $600,000, estate tax will be levied twice on your property—once when you die and once when your brother dies.

Enter the bypass trust, where property is left for the use of a life beneficiary and then goes to a final beneficiary. Under U.S. tax law and IRS rules, the life beneficiary never becomes the legal owner of the trust property. Therefore, property in the trust is subject to estate tax when the grantor dies, but cannot be taxed again when the life beneficiary dies—hence the name "bypass" trust.

Example: Continuing with Cecilia and Lou, from the above example, let's say Cecilia had property worth $540,000 when she died. Lou, who has no separate property, has an estate worth $440,000 when Cecilia dies. If Cecilia had left her property outright to Lou, his total estate would be $980,000, with $380,000 subject to estate tax. But because Cecilia used a bypass trust, no estate tax will be due on either's death. Cecilia's $540,000 is less than the $600,000 tax threshold. And since Lou is never the legal owner of Cecilia's trust property, his estate remains at $440,000 and so (unless it grows to over $600,000 at his death) will not be subject to estate tax when he dies.

B. IRS Restrictions on Bypass Trusts

All bypass trusts must comply with applicable IRS regulations, or the estate tax savings you're after will be lost.

1. Right to Spend Trust Principal

The trustee cannot be given complete freedom to spend trust principal for the life beneficiary. If the successor trustee has such unlimited rights, the IRS will regard the life beneficiary as the legal owner of the trust property, and impose estate tax on it when the life beneficiary dies.

The IRS does, however, allow the trustee to invade (spend) the trust principal for the life beneficiary's "health care, education, support and maintenance ... in accord with his or her accustomed standard of living." (IRS Regulation 320.2041-1(c)(2).) Spending trust money for these purposes is allowed because, according to the IRS, the need for these expenditures can be judged against an "ascertainable standard." By contrast, if the trust document says that trust assets can be spent for, say, the "comfort" or "well-being" of the life beneficiary, the IRS considers this an "unascertainable" standard. In that case, the trust assets will be regarded as legally owned by the life beneficiary and taxed at his death.

This right to keep trust principal available for basic needs of the life beneficiary is crucially important to many couples. They want to conserve as much of their estate as possible for their children or other final beneficiaries, but they don't want the surviving spouse to risk running out of money for vital needs, such as health care or normal living expenses. With a bypass trust document that is properly drafted—using the language acceptable to the IRS—the surviving spouse will have the right to use any amount of principal necessary for basic expenses, including medical care; so this risk is eliminated.

Example: Walter and Marjorie, a working couple in their late fifties, own shared property worth $1.2 million. They each draft a bypass trust for their half of the property, specifying that the income goes to the other spouse for life, with the assets then going to their children. Each includes in their trust language ("powers," in legal lingo) that gives the survivor (as trustee) the right to spend trust principal for his or her health care, support and maintenance.

Each spouse has taken advantage of their personal exemption of $600,000 instead of leaving all property to the survivor and wasting the $600,000 exemption of the first spouse to die. They will avoid any federal estate tax when the second spouse dies. If their financial situation remains stable (or their wealth increases), the survivor may never need to spend trust principal. However, they have provided a security back-up for each other that allows the survivor to use all of the assets they both own if necessary for basic needs.

Restricting a spouse's right to spend principal. In some situations, particularly second or subsequent marriages, one or both spouses may not want to give the surviving spouse the right to invade trust principal, and may even want to further restrict use of trust property. Normally, this is because a spouse wants to be sure trust property remains intact for her own children or other final beneficiaries. (See Chapter 23, Second or Subsequent Marriages.)

2. The "5 and 5" Power

Another IRS rule allows the trust document to give the trustee of a bypass trust what is called a "5 and 5" power. This authorizes the trustee to invade the trust principal annually for a beneficiary, for any reason whatsoever, up to a maximum of 5% of the trust principal or $5,000, whichever is greater. The trustee can be given authority to exercise this right for the life beneficiary, the final beneficiaries, or both. The trust document must specifically state which beneficiaries are eligible to receive trust property under the 5 and 5 power.

It is certainly not mandatory to include the 5 and 5 power in a bypass trust. In fact, this power is not in favor with many sophisticated estate planning lawyers these days. They reason that it's better to include a provision allowing the trustee to invade principal for the life beneficiary's "health care, education, support and maintenance," which protects the life beneficiary in case of real need. (See Section 1, above.) The risk of the 5 and 5 power is that it can allow the life beneficiary to use up, over the years, much or even all of the trust principal for any reason whatsoever.

One advantage of a 5 and 5 power is that a final beneficiary, not just the life beneficiary, can benefit from it. If you think that one or more of the final beneficiaries may need money from the trust while the life beneficiary is alive, you can specify that the trustee can use the 5 and 5 power to benefit some, or all, of the final beneficiaries. (This is one form of a "sprinkling trust." See Chapter 24, Trusts and Other Devices Imposing Controls Over Property, Section E.) For instance, if the trust document authorized it, a trustee might use the 5 and 5 power to spend some trust principal for the educational costs of a needy final beneficiary, particularly if the life beneficiary would remain financially comfortable even after that money was spent.

The trustee does not have to exercise the 5 and 5 power for an eligible beneficiary. Each year it is up to the trustee to decide whether or not an eligible beneficiary should be given trust principal under this power. Normally there are no adverse tax consequences if the 5 and 5 power isn't exercised.

The tax rules are more complex for sprinkling trusts that include the 5 and 5 power. If you decide to consider a sprinkling trust, talk with your tax advisor or a good lawyer about the rather complicated ramifications of including a 5 and 5 power in such a trust.

C. Marital Life Estate Trusts: Bypass Trusts for Couples

For many married couples with combined estates worth over $600,000, the ideal result can be simply stated: You want the surviving spouse to have access to the deceased spouse's money, if he or she needs it, but you don't want the surviving spouse to become the legal owner of the deceased spouse's property, because then hefty estate tax will be due when the second spouse dies. You can achieve these goals with a marital life estate trust. (As we've said, this is simply a bypass trust for married couples.)

To summarize what we outlined in Section A, above, here's how it works. Each spouse creates a marital life estate trust (usually, it's added onto a basic probate-avoidance living trust). Instead of leaving his or her share of property outright to the survivor, each spouse leaves all, or at least the bulk, of his or her property to the marital life estate trust. The key point: When one spouse dies, the survivor gets only a "life estate" interest in all property of the deceased spouse that goes into the marital life estate trust. After a spouse dies, the surviving spouse continues to have his or her separate revocable living trust.

Each spouse names his or her final beneficiaries, who receive the marital life estate trust property when the surviving spouse dies. Most commonly, the final beneficiaries for both spouses are their children.

Marital life estate trusts involve complexities and drawbacks, but they do work very well for many couples and families. Indeed, they are a standard component of most estate plans prepared by lawyers for couples with a combined estate exceeding $600,000. For many older couples, the drawbacks amount to no more than relatively minor accounting and recordkeeping hassles, which they feel are well worth it to conserve up to hundreds of thousands of dollars worth of their property for their children or other beneficiaries.

DO YOU NEED A LAWYER?

You may wonder whether or not it's wise to prepare a marital life estate trust yourself, without the aid of an attorney. If you and your spouse have a combined estate worth between $600,000 and $1.2 million (and neither of you owns property in excess of $600,000), quite possibly you can go it alone. Forms and complete instructions for preparing a marital life estate trust for couples in this situation can be found in *Make Your Own Living Trust*, by Denis Clifford (Nolo Press). The marital life estate trust in that book is designed for couples who want to allow the surviving spouse the maximum legal rights over the trust property, while still gaining the estate tax-saving advantages of this type of trust.

The trust in that book is not for couples in the following situations:

- Those with a combined estate exceeding $1.2 million. Couples with larger estates should consult a good estate planning lawyer to explore more sophisticated options to reduce estate tax.
- Those who want to impose limits on the rights of the surviving spouse to use trust property. This includes many couples in second or subsequent marriages, who want to be sure the bulk of their property is preserved for children from prior marriages.
- Those who simply need a different type of ongoing trust, such as a special needs trust for a disadvantaged child or a spendthrift trust for a child who can't properly manage his money.

1. How a Marital Life Estate Trust Reduces Estate Tax

You may wonder why a married couple needs a marital life estate trust. After all, because of the marital deduction, one spouse can leave the other an unlimited amount of money free of federal estate tax. That's true. But what happens when the second spouse dies? For couples with a combined estate exceeding $600,000, the result is often an estate tax trap. For example, if spouses with a combined shared estate of $1 million (that is, each owns $500,000) leave their portion to each other, the surviving spouse will wind up with $1 million. When the surviving spouse dies, $400,000 of this $1 million will be subject to federal estate tax (the $1 million less the $600,000 personal exemption). The estate tax is $153,000. This means, obviously, that that amount will not go to whomever inherits the couple's property after both die.

Using a marital life estate trust provides estate tax savings because the property in the trust is subject to estate tax only when the first spouse dies. If there is less than $600,000 in that spouse's estate, no federal estate tax is due. The trust property isn't subject to estate tax when the second spouse dies, because, as we've stressed, the second spouse never legally owned it.

Example: Arnold and Maggie share ownership of $1.1 million worth of property. Maggie dies first, and Arnold a year later. If each leaves his or her property to the other, and the survivor leaves all their property to their two children, here are the tax consequences:

On Maggie's Death:

Gross estate (1/2 shared property)	$550,000
Final bills, burial costs, etc.	($10,000)
Net taxable estate	$540,000
Estate tax due (Because of the marital deduction.)	$0

On Arnold's Death:[1]

Gross estate (his $550,000 and $540,000 inherited from wife)	$1,090,000
Final bills, burial costs, etc.	($10,000)
Net taxable estate	$1,080,000
Tax assessed	$ 78,600
Personal $600,000 estate tax exemption	($192,800)
Estate tax due	$185,800

Now let's look at what happens if Maggie and Arnold each create a marital life estate trust, leaving their assets for the benefit of the surviving spouse for his or her life. When the second spouse dies, the trust property will be distributed to their children.

On Maggie's Death:

Gross estate (1/2 shared property)	$550,000
Final bills, burial costs, etc.	($10,000)
Net taxable estate	$540,000
Estate tax due (because of Maggie's $600,000 exemption)	$0

On Arnold's Death:

Gross estate	$550,000
Final bills, burial costs, etc.	($10,000)
Net taxable estate	$540,000
Estate tax due (because of Arnold's $600,000 exemption)	$0

[1]To make the writers' lives easier and the example clearer, none of Maggie's or Arnold's net estate has been spent, nor has any of it appreciated since Maggie died.

Neat, isn't it? By using a marital life estate trust, no estate tax at all is paid. By contrast, without the trust, $185,800 must be handed over to the government in estate tax, instead of going to the children. What's more, this also saddles the husband's executor (probably one of the children) with the hassle of having to file a federal estate tax return. And other costs may be involved if estate tax must be paid, such as appraisal fees. (However, if a marital life estate trust is used, similar costs may also have to be paid at the first spouse's death in order to divide up the property between the now irrevocable marital life estate trust and the surviving spouse's continuing, revocable, living trust.) Finally, because estate tax must be paid when Arnold dies, his assets may be tied up for nine months before what's left can be transferred to the children.

You can place whatever property you want in your marital life estate trust. You can place all your separate property and all your half of shared or community property, or any portion of either, in your trust.

If the marital life estate trust's assets appreciate substantially by the time the life beneficiary dies, this appreciation is not subject to any estate tax. The trust assets are subject to tax once, and only once—when the grantor dies.

Example: Isabel and Simon own shared assets totaling $900,000. They each draft marital life estate trusts for their $450,000 shares, with their children as the final beneficiaries. Isabel dies first, and Simon lives for another 20 years. His business is successful, and he never needs to invade Isabel's trust principal. At Simon's death, Isabel's marital life estate trust property is worth $1.5 million. Her trust assets were subject to estate tax only at Isabel's death, and no tax was due then because the value then was under $600,000. The full $1.5 million is now distributed to the children with no estate tax ever paid on these assets.

2. Is a Marital Life Estate Trust Best for You?

If you're considering a marital life estate trust, the first thing to do is to take a realistic look at your personal situation.

For some married couples, using a marital life estate trust is not the best option. Here are some guidelines:

- If a couple has a combined estate worth less than $600,000, there's no reason to bother with an estate tax-saving trust Even if one spouse leaves all his or her property outright to the other, the surviving spouse's estate will still be under the federal estate tax threshold. Of course, if during their lives their combined estate grows to over $600,000, they can then revise their plan and create marital life estate trusts.
- Younger couples may well not want to tie up one spouse's assets in a marital life estate trust. There's no set rule for what is a "younger couple." But certainly couples under 40 rarely create marital life estate trusts. With a younger couple, if one spouse dies suddenly and prematurely, the surviving spouse may well live for decades, and would be far better off inheriting the deceased spouse's property outright. Commonly, younger couples create a basic living trust, leaving each other all or most of their property outright. Then, once they're older—say in their 50s or 60s—they revoke their old trust and create marital life estate trusts. If one spouse unexpectedly dies before the couple gets around to making a tax-avoiding trust, the survivor will inherit everything estate tax free, no matter what the amount, because of the marital deduction. That surviving spouse will probably have years to use the money—and years to arrange for other methods of reducing the eventual estate tax.
- Couples where one spouse is considerably younger than the other and presumably will live much longer. Again, generally there's no need to burden the younger spouse with a trust designed to save estate tax when he or she is likely to live for many years.
- Couples who don't want to leave the bulk of their property for use of the surviving spouse, but want instead to leave substantial amounts of property directly to other beneficiaries.

These are only guidelines, not rules. We've seen couples in their late 30s prepare marital life estate trusts, because they want to be sure that they've done all they can to reduce estate tax, even with the possibility that one spouse's property may be tied up in trust for decades of the surviving spouse's life.

No matter what age you are, a marital life estate trust works best when all involved—both spouses and all final beneficiaries—understand and agree on the purposes of the trust. Again, these goals are to save on overall estate tax and at the same time give the surviving spouse maximum rights to use trust income and principal if it becomes necessary. Without this agreement, serious conflicts between the surviving spouse and the final beneficiaries may develop. This can be particularly true when there are children from a prior marriage.

A marital life estate trust is less likely to create any strife down the road if:

- Family members trust each other, are reasonably close and are able to work out any conflicts that might arise.
- The final beneficiaries understand that a couple taking the trouble to create a marital life estate trust, do a generous act; after all, the trust benefits the children, not themselves. The final beneficiaries receive much more of the couple's combined estate than they would have if the spouses had left property outright to the other.

- If the trust allows the surviving spouse, as trustee, to spend trust principal for his "support, health, education and maintenance," the final beneficiaries can be trusted to support the surviving spouse if he decides to spend trust principal for any authorized reason.

If there is any potential for conflict between the surviving spouse and the final beneficiaries of the trust, a marital life estate trust may well provoke or aggravate that conflict. After all, in theory at least, there is an inherent conflict of interest between the life estate beneficiary and the final beneficiaries. The final beneficiaries may want all the trust principal conserved, no matter what the surviving spouse needs. On the other hand, the surviving spouse may want or need to use up most or even all of the trust principal for her health care, education or maintenance.

Another conflict can arise if the surviving spouse becomes ill and can no longer serve as trustee. If a child who stands to eventually receive trust assets takes over as successor trustee, it's possible the child might be more concerned with preserving principal than with a parent's medical or other needs. We've heard of such situations, where it seemed to other family members and friends that a child disregarded his parent's basic needs and instead protected the trust principal for himself.

Conflicts can also occur if the final beneficiaries believe the surviving spouse, as trustee, is not managing the trust property sensibly—for example, by investing in very speculative stocks or risky real estate deals. If this situation arises, there can be real trouble, possibly even a lawsuit.

Final Beneficiaries in Second Marriages

Spouses in a second or subsequent marriage often want to name different final beneficiaries for each spouse's property. Each often wants children from a prior marriage as final beneficiaries. Fortunately, each spouse creates his or her own separate marital life estate trust, so each has the right to choose the final beneficiaries for his or her own trust property. (This issue is discussed further in Chapter 23, Second or Subsequent Marriages.)

3. How Marital Life Estate Trusts Are Created

Normally, a marital life estate trust is combined with a living trust. (See Chapter 17, An Overview of Ongoing Trusts.) That way, when one spouse dies, the trust property first avoids probate; then the irrevocable marital life estate trust becomes operational.

Each spouse owns his or her distinct portion of the living trust property, which includes half of any community or co-owned property, and all that spouse's separate property. When one spouse dies, that spouse's marital life estate trust becomes irrevocable. The surviving spouse, normally also the trustee, takes over management of the trust's property and must comply with all terms of the trust.

Meanwhile, the surviving spouse's living trust (that is, her portion of the couple's original living trust) continues to be revocable, as long as she lives. The surviving spouse can revoke the marital life estate trust component of her living trust and create whatever new provisions and beneficiary clauses seem appropriate now. Or, she can leave her marital life estate trust as it is. When she dies, her trust property will go directly to whomever she named as the final beneficiaries in the life estate portion of her living trust. Her marital life estate trust will never become operational, since she leaves no surviving spouse.

4. Choosing the Trustee

We discussed how to select the trustee of a bypass trust in Chapter 17, An Overview of Ongoing Trusts, Section E. There are, however, some special considerations when you're choosing the trustee for a marital life estate trust.

Most couples want the surviving spouse to serve as initial trustee of the marital life estate trust, which becomes operational when the first spouse dies. To do that, the trust document simply makes both spouses initial trustees of the marital life estate trust. Because the life estate trust doesn't become operational until one spouse dies, only the surviving spouse will actually serve as trustee.

Example: Mark and Vera have three grown children and a combined estate worth approximately $800,000. In their shared living trust document, each creates a marital life estate trust. Each specifies that all his or her property is to go into his or her life estate trust at his or her death. The document names both spouses as co-trustees of the trusts.

Mark dies first. His property goes into his marital life estate trust, which is now operational. Vera is the sole trustee and will manage the property in the trust.

The living trust document normally also names a successor trustee for the marital life estate trust to take over management of trust property if the surviving spouse becomes incapacitated. You may also want to name an alternate successor trustee.

If you don't want your surviving spouse to be trustee of your marital life estate trust, you can name someone else to be the trustee. For example, your spouse may be infirm, not sensible about financial affairs or simply uninterested.

If you wish, you can name more than one person to serve as co-successor trustees. For example, you might want to name your two adult children, or your spouse and one adult child, as co-trustees. (The potential pitfalls of naming co-trustees are discussed in Chapter 17, Section E.)

When selecting the successor and alternate successor trustees for a marital life estate trust, ask several questions about your choices:

- Does the person or persons want to serve?
- Is the person capable of handling the trustee's duties?
- Would the trust management create an undue burden on that person?
- Will the trustee be paid?
- Do you completely trust the person to manage the property as you would wish?

5. The Rights of the Life Beneficiary

When you make a marital life estate trust, you can place whatever restrictions you want on the rights of the life beneficiary (your spouse) to use trust property. You cannot, as we hope is clear by now, give the trustee broader authority to spend trust principal for the surviving spouse than is allowed by the IRS regulations discussed in Section B. To remind you, the trustee can be given all of the following rights to use trust property for the surviving spouse:

- the right to distribute all trust income to the surviving spouse
- the right to control the trust property (use it, as with a house, or buy or sell, as long as principal is conserved)
- the right to invade trust principal in any amount needed for the surviving spouse's "health, education, support or maintenance, in his or her accustomed manner of living," and

- the 5 and 5 power (Section B, above).

In some situations—particularly in second or subsequent marriages—you may want to limit the surviving spouse's rights. You can impose any restriction over his or her rights to trust property that you want to.

Example: Sam is in his sixties and is married to Diane. He has two adult daughters by his former marriage. Diane does not have children of her own. Sam's estate is worth $500,000, consisting mainly of a residence and a stock portfolio. He also has a life insurance policy that will pay $200,000 to Diane at his death. Diane has much less in assets, the total amounting to around $50,000. Sam wants to support Diane, preserve as much as possible for his daughters, use his $600,000 estate tax exemption, and take advantage of the benefit of a marital life estate trust.

Sam prepares a marital life estate trust for all his assets. The income from trust property will go to Diane for life, and the principal will go to his daughters after Diane's death. Sam worries, though, that if he dies, Diane may remarry someone who'll push her to get at the trust principal. On the other hand, he doesn't want Diane to go without medical care she might need but can't pay for herself. So he names a daughter he trusts, not Diane, to be the successor trustee. He also includes a provision in his trust that allows the successor trustee to invade the principal for Diane's health care only if all of her other assets are exhausted and the income from the trust is not sufficient. He feels that this is the best he can do for everybody, and hopes that his wife and children will agree.

Other still more restrictive provisions can be imposed if you wish. For example, the surviving spouse can be denied the right to invade principal for any reason. Or use of trust property can be strictly controlled—for instance, the surviving spouse can be given only the right to live in a house owned by the trust, not to sell it or rent it. Also, it's legal to provide that a spouse's life estate ends if he remarries. If he remarries, the trust property is promptly turned over to the final trust beneficiaries. All these types of restrictions are discussed in depth in Chapter 23, Second or Subsequent Marriages.

6. How Much Property to Place in a Marital Life Estate Trust

Presently each spouse can leave up to $600,000 in a marital life estate trust without any estate tax liability. (If Congress increases the estate tax exemption to, say, $750,000, each spouse can leave up to that amount in the trust.) If a couple has more than $1,200,000, they'll usually still want to take advantage of both of their $600,000 estate tax exemptions by creating marital life estate trusts and leaving $600,000 worth of property in them. Doing this won't, however, eliminate all estate tax on the death of the first spouse. For example, if a couple has shared property worth $1.9 million, each's share is worth $950,000. If a spouse's entire $950,000 is placed in a marital life estate trust, $350,000 will be subject to estate tax. So to reduce estate taxes further, each spouse may want to limit the amount in their marital life estate trust to $600,000, and place the remainder in another trust. (A common one is a QTIP trust. See Chapter 19, Other Marital Estate Tax-Saving Trusts, Section A.)

a. Placing More Than $600,000 in the Marital Life Estate Trust

Sometimes, a couple will decide it's sensible for each spouse to place assets worth more than $600,000 in a marital life estate trust. The reason is those old graduated estate tax rates, which start at 37% for estates over $600,000 and go to 55% for estates over $3 million. The larger the estate, the higher the percentage that will be lost to estate tax. That means that for couples with large estates, overall estate tax can be lowered if some property of the first spouse to die is taxed when that spouse dies.

If only $600,000 is put in the marital life estate trust, it passes free of estate tax. If, however, for couples with combined estates worth over $1.2 million, some property of the first spouse to die is taxed at his death, the total tax paid should be well below the amount that would be due at the death of the surviving spouse if everything over $600,000 had been left to her.

Example: Carl and Sophia have a combined estate of shared property worth $4 million. They each draft a marital life estate trust, specifying that $600,000 of property should be put in the trust when the first spouse dies. They leave all other property outright to the other. Carl dies first. If Carl's marital life estate trust contains only $600,000, and his final bills are $25,000, $1,375,000 is left to Sophia. No estate tax is due when Carl dies.

Carl's gross estate	$2,000,000
Final bills, costs, etc.	($25,000)
Net taxable estate	$1,975,000
Property in marital life estate trust	$600,000
Property left to spouse	$1,375,000
Estate tax due (because of the marital deduction and the personal estate tax exemption)	-0-

Sophia's estate is now worth $3,375,000. If her estate remains the same and she dies several years later, here's the tax picture:

Sophia's gross estate	$3,375,000
Final bills, costs, etc.	($25,000)
Net taxable estate	$3,350,000
Estate tax at 55%	$1,842,500
Estate tax credit (the $600,000 personal exemption)	($192,800)
Estate tax due	$1,649,700

Now let's suppose that Carl's marital life estate trust contains all of his assets, not just $600,000. Income to Sophia from that amount during her life would probably be sufficient for her needs, since she also owns $2 million outright. All of Carl's property is subject to estate tax when he dies; none is left outright to Sophia, so none qualifies for the marital deduction.

Here's the estate tax picture when Carl dies:

Carl's gross estate	$2,000,000
Costs, etc.	($25,000)
Net taxable estate	$1,975,000
Estate tax at 45%	$888,750
Estate tax credit (the $600,000 personal exemption)	($192,800)
Estate tax due	$695,950

And at Sophia's death:

Sophia's gross estate	$2,000,000
Costs, etc.	($25,000)
Net estate	$1,975,000
Estate tax at 45%	$888,750
(Estate tax credit) The $600,000 personal exemption	($192,800)
Estate tax due	$695,950

By increasing the size of the marital life estate trust when the first spouse dies, Carl's and Sophia's estates have paid a total of $1,391,900 in estate tax. Compared to the $1,649,700 in tax if only $600,000 had been put in the trust, they have saved $257,800 for their inheritors.

If Carl had used no marital life estate trust at all and had just left everything to Sophia, her taxable estate would have been $3,950,000. After her personal $600,000 tax exemption, her estate would pay $2,009,700 in tax.

Although it may save in overall estate tax, there's a disadvantage to placing more than $600,000 in a marital life estate trust. As you know, any amount over $600,000 is subject to estate tax when the first spouse dies. Many married couples want to keep all their wealth intact until the second spouse dies. They can accomplish this by each leaving no more than $600,000 in the marital life estate trust, and all the rest to the surviving spouse. This property can be left to the surviving spouse outright or in a QTIP trust. What's important about QTIPs for now is that property left in a QTIP trust, like property left outright to a spouse, qualifies for the marital deduction. No estate tax is due on QTIP property when the first spouse dies.

Many couples simply do not want to pay any estate tax until they must—after the second spouse's death. Moreover, placing no more than $600,000 in a marital life estate trust, no matter how much money the couple has, can be desirable, particularly when it's likely that one spouse will long outlive the other. Because of the marital deduction, the deceased spouse leaves all his property over $600,000 to his surviving spouse free of estate tax. The surviving spouse will, hopefully, have many years, even decades, to use that money. The income and potential growth in value of the assets she receives can far exceed any additional estate tax that eventually has to be paid when she dies. Also, she can take other actions to lower her eventual estate tax, such as making regular tax-free gifts. (See Chapter 16, Gifts and Gift Taxes, Section E.)

Finally, there can be other reasons to postpone estate taxes that may outweigh any higher overall tax costs. For instance, if an estate consists of property that is not liquid, such as a family-owned business or a valuable residence, it may be worth waiting and paying extra tax dollars at the second death to prevent having to sell assets to get cash for tax at the first death.

b. Spouses Who Own Different Amounts of Property

Spouses who don't own equal amounts of property need to take that difference into account when setting up a marital life estate trust. Even if the total value of the couple's property is worth less than $1.2 million, if the value of one spouse's separate property plus her interest in shared property totals more than $600,000, that spouse has estate tax decisions to make. Does she want to place all her property in a marital life estate trust, and have some estate tax paid her estate? Or does she want to leave anything over $600,000 to her husband, free of tax under the marital deduction?

To save money on estate tax, wealthy couples with different-sized estates can create marital life estate trusts designed to equalize the worth of the two estates. This way, the wealthier spouse's estate tax rate is lowered, because the estate tax rate goes up as the value of the estate increases. The other spouse's estate tax rate may become higher. But overall, the estate tax paid will still be less than if the wealthier spouse were subject to the higher tax rate on his full estate.

Example: Joe has a $2 million estate; his wife, Nelda, has $800,000 in assets. Joe's estate plan places $1.4 million in his marital life estate trust and leaves the remaining $600,000 outright to Nelda. No estate tax is due on this $600,000 gift because of the marital deduction. If Joe dies first, his taxable estate, is $1.4 million. The marital estate tax rate on this amount is 43%. Nelda receives the $600,000, making her estate worth $1.4 million. The taxable estates of the two spouses have been equalized, and overall estate tax has been lowered.

c. Using a Formula Clause

Many estate planners advise you not to specify a dollar amount of property to be put in your marital life estate trust. Instead, they recommend putting what's called a "formula" clause in the trust document. Essentially, the usual formula provides (in heavy legalese) that the assets in the marital life estate trust are to consist of exactly that amount that will reduce your federal estate tax to zero. Planners prefer such a clause because they are concerned that Congress may someday raise or lower the current tax-exempt amount of $600,000.

With a formula clause, if Congress does change the $600,000 exemption figure, you don't have to worry about changing your living trust or will, because the formula ensures that the amount put into the trust will be whatever amount is exempt from estate tax under current law. Of course, if there were a drastic change in the exemption amount—say it were lowered to $200,000—you would probably want to revise your estate plans anyway, so using a formula clause isn't a sure-fire solution to any changes in the tax-exempt amount.

If you want to place more than the exempt amount in the marital life estate trust, a formula clause is obviously not desirable. It's useful only if you decide that the best course is to place only the exempt amount (again, currently $600,000) in your marital life estate trust.

Example: Monica and Tony have a combined estate of $1.6 million. They each create a marital life estate trust for the other, using a formula clause that provides that the bypass trust will contain that amount that results in no estate tax when the first spouse dies—presently, $600,000. The remaining $200,000 (or whatever it may be when Monica or Tony dies) goes outright to the surviving spouse. Monica and Tony don't have to worry about relatively minor changes in the estate tax law, and the survivor doesn't have to worry about paying any estate tax when the first spouse dies.

7. Drawbacks of Marital Life Estate Trusts

Before deciding to use marital life estate trusts, you and your spouse should understand what you're getting into. Once one spouse dies, that spouse's marital life estate trust becomes irrevocable; it imposes limits and burdens on the survivor's use of the deceased spouse's property that cannot be changed.

a. Restrictions on the Surviving Spouse's Use of the Property

At the death of a spouse, the couple's shared property must be divided into two legally separate entities. One share is owned by the surviving spouse's revocable living trust and is under the surviving spouse's complete control. The other share is placed in the deceased's marital life estate trust. The surviving spouse and trustee are subject to all restrictions set out in the trust document. These restrictions cannot be changed.

b. Legal or Accounting Help Will Probably Be Necessary to Divide the Property

When the first spouse dies, an estate lawyer or accountant will be needed to determine how to best divide the couple's assets between the now-irrevocable marital life estate trust and the continuing revocable living trust of the surviving spouse. Each item of the couple's shared property does not have to be divided 50/50 between the two trusts, but the total value of shared property in each trust must be equal. This means there is considerable flexibility in allocating assets between the two trusts. Often it takes an expert to decide on the best division.

For example, what should be done with the family home? If full ownership of the house is placed in the marital life estate trust, the house would be valued, for estate tax purposes, at its value on the death of the first spouse. By contrast, if the house were allocated to the surviving spouse, and she survives for many more years, the house would presumably be worth more (given inflation) by the date of her death. Its increased value might result in the survivor's estate being more than $600,000, or, if her estate was already well over that, in extra tax being paid because of the increased worth of the house.

But there can also be drawbacks to including the full value of a house in the marital life estate trust. If the trust owns a house, certain tax advantages are lost. For example, a person over 55 has the one-time right to sell a house and retain up to $125,000 profit (capital gain) without tax. An irrevocable trust has no such right. So if the house may be sold in the future, it can be costly, income tax-wise, to place it in the marital life estate trust.

This just scratches the surface of the complexity of dividing a couple's property between the two trusts on the death of a spouse. Of course, not every case is complex, but the surviving spouse should at least check the matter out with an expert before actually dividing up the couple's shared property.

c. The Surviving Spouse Must File Trust Tax Returns

The trustee of the marital life estate trust must obtain a taxpayer ID number for the trust. Also, the trustee must file an annual trust income tax return for that trust. This usually isn't a big deal, but like any tax return, it requires some work.

d. Recordkeeping Can Be Complicated

The surviving spouse must keep two sets of books and records, one for the property in the surviving spouse's revocable living trust and one for the marital life estate trust property, which is legally separate from property owned by the surviving spouse.

D. Bypass Trusts for Unmarried Persons

Life estate bypass trusts can legally be used by any person, whether single or a member of an unmarried couple. In either case, the trust document names a life beneficiary to receive specified rights to the trust property, and final beneficiaries to receive the trust property when the life beneficiary dies.

You may want to consider a bypass trust if you have:

1. A desire to leave property to someone only for his or her life, then outright to others.

2. Someone you trust to serve as the successor trustee of the trust, to manage the trust property after you die, while the life beneficiary lives.

1. Bypass Trusts for Unmarried Couples

Any couple, married or not, can use an estate tax-saving bypass trust if their combined estate exceeds $600,000. Of course, the terminology is different; the trust isn't called a "marital life estate" trust, the term applied to a married person's trust. For a member of an unmarried couple, the trust is sometimes simply called a bypass trust, or sometimes a "life estate trust."

An unmarried couple can achieve the same overall estate tax savings with a bypass trust as a married couple. Of course, the marital deduction is not available for unmarried couples, so any amount one of them owns in excess of $600,000 will be subject to tax when he dies, unless another estate tax-saving trust, such as a charitable remainder trust, is used. (See Chapter 20, Charitable Trusts.) Still, the estate tax savings an unmarried couple can achieve by using bypass trusts can be substantial.

Example 1: Ira and Selma, an unmarried couple, have no children. They've been together for over 30 years, and all of their combined estate of $800,000 is held in shared ownership. Ira has a much younger brother to whom he's very close. Selma is equally close to two nieces. Ira and Selma decide to create a bypass trust. Each leaves the other his or her property in a life estate trust, rather than outright, and names his or her own relatives as final beneficiaries. As a result, they save on overall estate tax, and each ensures that his or her property will go to the desired final beneficiaries.

Example 2: Antonio and Gina are an unmarried couple with two children. Their combined estates total $1.1 million. They wish to provide support for each other for life and then leave their assets to their children. If the first to die leaves a $550,000 share outright to the other on the survivor's death, estate tax of $194,000 will be due on the entire $1.1 million. However, if each of them creates a life estate trust with the other as the life beneficiary, the children will eventually inherit all the property tax-free. This is because by establishing a life estate trust, both Gina's and Antonio's $600,000 estate tax exemption are used.

Example 3: Shizue and Takanori each own property worth $1 million. After one of them dies, they want the other to have the use of and the income from the deceased partner's property. But each also wants to preserve the bulk of their estate for other beneficiaries. Each one creates a life estate trust consisting of all his or her property, with income from the trust going to the other for his or her life. Also, each authorizes the other to use any amount of trust principal for health care or basic maintenance. At the second death, remaining assets in the trust will go to their respective relatives.

Shizue dies first and Takanori ten years later. Assuming the property values remain the same, let's look at the tax picture.

On Shizue's death:

Gross estate	$1,000,000
Federal estate tax	$345,800
(Estate tax credit)	
$600,000 personal exemption	($192,800)
Estate tax due	$153,000

On Takanori's death:

Gross estate	$1,000,000
Federal estate tax	$345,800
(Estate tax credit)	
$600,000 personal exemption	($192,800)
Estate tax due	$153,000

Takanori never owned the $1 million left by Shizue in her life estate trust, so it bypassed his estate for tax purposes. At his death, those assets pass tax-free to the relatives Shizue named in her trust document.

Now, let's look at the situation without a trust, if each had just left everything to the other. On Shizue's death, her estate taxes are the same—$153,000—after using her personal estate tax exemption.

On Takanori's death, however, you can see how not using a bypass trust costs their inheritors several hundred thousand dollars:

Gross estate	$1,847,000
Federal estate tax	$711,950
(Estate tax credit)	
$600,000 personal exemption	($192,800)
Estate tax due	$519,150

Without the trust, total estate tax would be $672,950. Using the bypass trust, total estate taxes for Shizue and Takanori were $306,000. This difference of $366,950 will go, eventually, to their final beneficiaries.

The savings would be even greater if the value of the property went up before Takanori's death. For example, if Takanori lived 15 more years, the value of the bypass trust property might rise to $1.5 million or more. That appreciation would pass to the final beneficiaries without further tax, because the property was already taxed when Shizue died.

2. Bypass Trusts for a Single Person

A single person, not a member of a couple, usually isn't concerned with providing for another person for her or his life, then having property go to other final beneficiaries. And there usually isn't any reason to look for tax savings, since there is no one other person the single person might combine his estate with, as there often is with a couple. Still, if you want to do this, a life estate bypass trust can prove every bit as desirable as it can for a couple.

Example: Gustav, a bachelor, leaves all of his property, worth $800,000, in a bypass trust with his friend Ludwig as the life beneficiary. At Ludwig's death, the assets are to go to Gustav's favorite two nephews.

Because Gustav's property is worth more than $600,000 at his death, federal estate tax is due.

Gustav's gross estate	$800,000
Federal estate tax	$253,800
(Estate tax credit)	
$600,000 personal exemption	($192,800)
Estate tax due	$61,000
Net estate to trust	$739,000

When Ludwig dies, the trust property (no matter how much it is worth at the time) passes tax-free to Gustav's nephews. This is true even if Gustav's estate property has increased greatly in value, because the trust assets have bypassed Ludwig's estate.

Now let's look at what would have happened without the bypass trust, if Gustav just left his property outright to Ludwig.

Nothing changes at Gustav's death; federal estate tax of $61,000 is still due. But when Ludwig dies, Gustav's remaining property ($739,000 after estate tax was paid) will be added to all other property Ludwig owned, for estate tax purposes. If Ludwig's estate, when he dies, was worth 1.4 million (including the amount he received from Gustav). Here are the tax figures.

Ludwig's gross estate	$1,400,000
Federal estate tax	$512,800
(Estate tax credit)	
$600,000 personal exemption	($192,800)
Estate tax due	$320,000

In sum, single people who want to support another person for life, then have their property benefit other younger beneficiaries, can sensibly use a bypass trust. ■

19

Other Estate Tax-Saving Marital Trusts

(QTIPS, QDOTS and more)

This chapter covers trusts, other than the marital life estate trusts discussed in Chapter 18, that married couples can use to achieve estate tax goals.

Single people look elsewhere. Because estate tax laws treat the married and unmarried differently, we do too. This chapter covers tax-saving trusts only available for the legally married. Unmarried people—whether couples or single—should skip this chapter and instead move to the next chapter that concerns them.

- **QTIP Trusts.** The most commonly used is labeled a Qualified Terminable Interest Property trust in federal tax law. Usually, this obtuse jargon is shortened to "QTIP." A QTIP trust allows a married person to name the surviving spouse as the life beneficiary of the trust property. When the second spouse dies, the property passes to final beneficiaries named by the first spouse. So far, it sounds just like a marital life estate trust, right? However, unlike a marital life estate trust, with a QTIP, when the first spouse dies all the property in the trust is exempt from estate tax, no matter how much it's worth. This is because under IRS rules, property in the QTIP trust qualifies for the unlimited marital deduction.

  However, property remaining in the QTIP trust when the second spouse dies is subject to estate tax. So taxes are postponed, not eliminated. The principal reason to use a QTIP is to avoid paying any estate tax when the first spouse dies, which makes more money available to the survivor.

  QTIPs are useful only if you and your spouse have a combined estate exceeding $600,000. And generally, QTIPs aren't used unless a couples' combined estate exceeds $1.2 million. Couples with estates worth between $600,000 and $1.2 million generally use only a marital life estate trust.

IRS Requirements for a Valid QTIP Trust

In order to qualify as a valid QTIP trust under federal law (IRC Sec. 2056(b)(7)), the trust document must specify all of the following:

1. All income from the trust must be distributed to the surviving spouse at least annually.
2. The spouse can demand that the trust property be converted to income-producing property.
3. No one, not even the surviving spouse, may spend the principal of the trust for the benefit of anybody but the spouse.
4. The executor of the deceased spouse's estate must elect, on the deceased's federal estate tax return, to have the trust be treated as a QTIP.

The following estate tax-conserving trusts that might be of interest to married couples are covered:

- **QDOT Trusts.** If you're married to a non-citizen and you have an estate worth over $600,000 that you want to leave to your spouse, consider a QDOT trust. (Section B.)
- **Widow's Election Trusts.** Very occasionally, a married couple will consider using a "Widow's Election" trust, which enables the first spouse to die to name final beneficiaries for both spouse's estates. (Section C.)
- **Marital Deduction Trusts.** This type of trust has been largely replaced by QTIP trusts. On rare occasions, a couple will use a marital deduction trust, which provides the estate tax postponement of a QTIP, but unlike a QTIP, permits the surviving spouse to name the final beneficiaries of this trust. (Section D.)

A. QTIP Trusts

The four basic purposes of a QTIP trust are to:

1. Postpone estate tax on the estate of the first spouse to die until the second spouse dies.

2. Leave money and property for the use (but not ownership) of your surviving spouse when you die.

3. Name final beneficiaries (often, children or grandchildren) to receive the trust property at the death of your spouse.

4. Allow for some after-death (lawyers call it "post-mortem") flexibility. As we discuss below, your executor (the person in charge of carrying out the terms of your will) can evaluate the estate tax situation and choose whether or not a QTIP you've created should actually become operational.

Find a knowledgeable lawyer. To prepare a QTIP trust, you need an expert estate planning lawyer. A good one. Many complex issues can arise when actually preparing the trust, and a mistake can be fatal, estate tax-wise. The IRS regularly refuses to grant trusts QTIP status because they didn't conform to all applicable federal regulations. In that case, of course, estate tax isn't postponed, and the major benefit of a QTIP is wasted. (For tips on finding a good lawyer, see Chapter 30, Using Lawyers, Section A.)

1. How QTIP Trusts Work

A QTIP trust is similar in many aspects to a marital life estate trust. In each case, a spouse is the grantor (the person who creates the trust). Each spouse in a couple can create a separate QTIP trust for his or her property, whether it's separate property, their half of shared property, or both. In both QTIPs and marital life estate trusts, the surviving spouse is the life beneficiary. The original grantor gets to name the final trust beneficiaries (normally, his or her children) to receive the trust property when the surviving spouse dies.

The big difference between these two types of trusts is that with a QTIP, no federal estate tax is assessed against trust property when the first spouse dies—no matter how much that property is worth. With a regular marital life estate trust, property above $600,000 is subject to estate tax when the grantor dies.

You can use a marital life estate trust and a QTIP trust together. Indeed, using these two trusts for each spouse is the foundation of many estate plans for wealthier people. Property worth up to $600,000 is placed in the marital life estate trust and is exempt from estate tax when the grantor dies. All that spouse's remaining property goes to the QTIP, again exempt from tax when the spouse dies. (Combining these two types of trusts in an estate plan is discussed further in Chapter 25, Combining Ongoing Trusts, Section A.)

Example 1: Li-shan leaves $600,000 in a marital life estate trust and $900,000 in a QTIP trust, with her husband as life beneficiary of both trusts. No federal estate tax is due on the QTIP trust property when Li-shan dies, because that property qualifies for the unlimited marital deduction. The $600,000 in the marital life estate trust is exempt because of Li-shan's personal estate tax exemption. By contrast, if Li-shan had left $900,000 in the marital life estate trust and $600,000 in the QTIP trust, with her husband as life beneficiary, $300,000 of the marital estate trust would be subject to estate tax when Li-shan dies. The tax would be $115,000.

Example 2: Bernice, who is married to George, has an estate worth 2.6 million. She creates both a marital life estate trust for property worth $600,000, and a QTIP trust for the remaining 2 million. The advantage of using both trusts is that she is able to use her personal $600,000 estate tax exemption. If she left the entire $2.6 million in a QTIP trust, no estate tax would be due when she died, but the whole amount would be taxed at her husband's death. She would never use her $600,000 exemption, and the $192,800 estate tax savings the exemption offers would be lost.

QTIPs at a Glance

- A QTIP trust creates a life estate for the surviving spouse, who is entitled to:
  - use trust assets, such as a residence, for her lifetime;
  - receive trust income regularly
  - invade trust principal to the extent allowed by the trust document.
- In the trust document, the grantor names final beneficiaries, who will inherit the QTIP trust assets when the surviving spouse dies.
- No estate tax is assessed on the death of the grantor.
- When the surviving spouse dies, the full net value of the property in the QTIP (as of that date) is included in his taxable estate.
- The QTIP assets do not go through probate after the death of the surviving spouse.

2. Long-Term Tax Consequences of QTIP Trusts

It's vital to understand that estate tax on QTIP trust property is not eliminated. When the second surviving spouse dies, tax must be paid on all property in his estate. Under tax law, this includes the full net worth of all property in the QTIP, as of the date of the surviving spouse's death.

Example: Bernice leaves property worth $2 million in a QTIP, with George, her husband, as life beneficiary. George has an estate of $1 million of his own. He dies a few months after Bernice. George's total estate, including property in the QTIP, is $3 million. Of that amount, $600,000 is exempt from federal estate tax, so $2.4 million will be subject to estate tax.

Because all of the value of QTIP property is included in the taxable estate of the second spouse to die, the tax rate will almost always be higher than if the first spouse had left that property by other methods, including making use of the $600,000.

Example: Gregor creates a QTIP trust for his wife, Natalie, with Gregor's children as final beneficiaries. Gregor's estate is worth $875,000. Natalie's estate is worth $225,000. If Gregor dies first, Natalie's total estate will be $875,000 + $225,000 = 1.1 million. The tax rate on this sum will be higher than the rate that would have been applied to Gregor's $875,000 at his death. And if Gregor had given Natalie $275,000 during his lifetime and the couple had each established a marital life estate trust to take advantage of each spouse's $600,000 personal exemptions, no estate tax would ever be due.

If the property in the QTIP trust increases in value during the surviving spouse's life, that increase is subject to estate tax when that spouse dies. Again, this is not true for property in a marital life estate trust. With a marital life estate trust, the value of the trust property for tax purposes is determined only once, at the date of death of the grantor spouse.

Example: Ivan creates a QTIP trust with property that is worth 1.1 million when he dies. By the time his wife, Olga, dies 12 years later, the value of the trust property has risen to 1.6 million. This total 1.6 million is included in Olga's taxable estate.

3. Who Can Benefit From a QTIP Trust

QTIPs are very popular with estate planners. But why, given the possible tax drawbacks just discussed? Most importantly, because many wealthier couples decide that postponing tax payment until the second spouse dies is worth the eventual tax cost. Many spouses strongly do not want to have any of their estate eaten up by tax when the first spouse dies, even if more taxes are paid in the long run. Moreover, it's far from clear, usually, that it must cost more in the long run. With a QTIP, a surviving spouse who outlives the other by a significant period of time—say a few years or more—will receive income from all the deceased spouse's property, without having had any taken out to pay estate tax. This money the surviving spouse receives from the trust property may exceed any additional tax paid on that spouse's death.

But why use a QTIP instead of leaving property outright to the surviving spouse? Of course, in some cases, this is done. But many couples prefer the control a QTIP provides—the power of the original grantor to name the final beneficiaries for the trust. Many spouses want to be sure their children, not other final beneficiaries, will receive the bulk of their estate, no matter what happens with the surviving spouse. A unique advantage of a QTIP trust is that it allows you to use the marital deduction for estate tax purposes (that is, have the trust property treated, tax-wise, as if the surviving spouse inherited it outright) and simultaneously allows you to impose controls over this property and specify who eventually inherits it.

Finally, because each member of a couple can create separate marital life estate trusts and QTIPs, neither spouse must sacrifice his or her personal $600,000 estate tax exemption. Rather, the usual plan, as we've said, is for each spouse to create a marital life estate trust to use his or her personal $600,000 estate tax exception, and a QTIP trust to postpone payment of estate tax on any additional property.

QTIPs are commonly used when one spouse in a second marriage is older and more affluent than the other. Typically, the wealthy spouse wants to provide adequate financial resources during the other spouse's life, but also wants the trust property go to his kids by an earlier marriage after the surviving spouse's death. A marital life estate trust alone won't work well here because it depends on each spouse owning a significant part of the couple's property (as is usually the case in long-term marriages). But a QTIP does the job nicely. A full 100% of the wealthier spouse's property is available for the surviving spouse's use, as life beneficiary, because no estate tax is levied when the first spouse dies.

Example: Sam's assets are worth $800,000 when he marries Angela, his second wife, who has very little property of her own. If Sam dies before Angela does, he wants to be sure she is provided for, but he also wants to ensure that his children from his previous marriage are the final beneficiaries of his property.

Sam feels that Angela may need all the income his $800,000 could provide. For this reason, he does not want to create a normal marital life estate trust, under which $200,000 would be taxed on his death. Also, Sam does not want to give Angela $200,000 (which he could do, tax-free, because of the marital deduction) and thus reduce his estate to $600,000. He wants to preserve his principal, to the extent possible, for his children.

So Sam creates a QTIP trust, containing all of his assets, which will become effective at his death.

Angela is the life beneficiary. Sam designates his children as the trust's final beneficiaries, to receive all that's left when Angela dies. No tax will be due at Sam's death (if Angela is still alive) because all property in a QTIP trust takes advantage of the unlimited marital deduction. Income will go to Angela for her life. Also, if he chooses, Sam can specify that trust principal can be used for Angela's "support, education, health or maintenance" in any amount. Or, at the other extreme, he can prohibit any invasion of the principal, to be sure it's all conserved for his children. (See Section 4, below.)

If you are in a second or subsequent marriage, you must try to balance the interests and needs of your current spouse and your children from a former marriage. (See Chapter 23, Trusts For Second or Subsequent Marriages.) Exactly how these needs are balanced depends on each situation—there is no formula for how to use a QTIP trust in estate plans.

Example: Sol is married to Rosalie and has two children from a previous marriage. His estate is worth $1.7 million. He creates a QTIP trust of $1.1 million to take effect at his death. All of the income from the trust will be paid to Rosalie for her lifetime, and at her death the assets of the trust will go to his children.

Sol also leaves $300,000 outright to each child. No estate tax will be due on this $600,000, because of Sol's personal estate tax exemption.

Thanks to the marital deduction, no tax is due on the $1.1 million in the QTIP trust at Sol's death. At Rosalie's death, estate tax will be due on the remaining trust assets, which will be counted as part of Rosalie's taxable estate.

4. The Surviving Spouse's Rights

The surviving spouse must be given the sole right to all income from property in the QTIP trust. Also, the surviving spouse must have the right to require that the trustee sell non-income-producing property and invest the sale proceeds in income-producing property. If either of these criteria is not met, the IRS will rule that the QTIP property doesn't qualify for the marital deduction.

a. All Trust Income Must Go to the Surviving Spouse

The surviving spouse must receive all of the income from a QTIP trust if the trust becomes operational at the first spouse's death (that is, the QTIP election is made; see Section A6, below). There are no exceptions to this rule. The trustee must distribute all income periodically (at least annually) to the spouse, and cannot accumulate income in the trust. If the surviving spouse becomes incapacitated, the trustee must spend the income for the spouse's benefit.

PROTECTING TRUST ASSETS FROM HUGE MEDICAL BILLS

Many couples worry that medical bills will eat up property left to a surviving spouse. And it's true that because trust income must be paid to the surviving spouse, it's not possible to "protect" that income if the surviving spouse incurs major medical bills. The trust income belongs to the spouse and, as such, is liable for medical bills she owes.

If, however, a QTIP trust allows a trustee to spend trust principal for medical needs, it is possible to draft provisions that protect the trust principal from being used to pay huge medical bills that would otherwise be covered by government aid programs. But drafting these provisions is quite a complex matter. They require an attorney who is also an expert in government health care and asset-protection rules. (See Chapter 30, Using Lawyers, Section A.) Some estate planning attorneys are experts in both government protection rules and QTIP trusts; many aren't. Be sure your attorney is qualified to prepare these types of clauses. It will probably cost you more in legal fees, but the security of knowing it will be done right should be well worth the extra cost

b. Trust Assets Are Available Only to a Spouse During Life

As long as the surviving spouse lives, the trustee of a QTIP trust cannot spend any of the assets of the trust for the benefit of anyone else. In general, this rule protects both the surviving spouse, who receives a continuing income, and the final beneficiaries, who are to later receive the trust principal.

But occasionally it can be troublesome. For example, suppose the surviving spouse remarries, no longer really needs the trust income and would just as soon end the trust and have its assets distributed to the final beneficiaries. Can't be done. A QTIP trust cannot end until the second spouse dies.

Or suppose that one of the final beneficiaries really needs some money from the trust, and the surviving spouse wants to give it. Officially, the trust's income, as well as the assets, cannot be spent directly on anyone else during the surviving spouse's lifetime. If the surviving spouse wants to help out, she must do so indirectly. All trust income is hers to do with as she wishes, so once she receives some income, she can give it to the needy final beneficiary. And if, atypically, the trust document allows the surviving spouse to spend trust principal for any reason, she can take as much principal as she wants and give it away. But if, as is common, her rights to spend trust principal are restricted or nonexistent, she won't be able to get any of this principal to the needy final beneficiary.

Example: Mark directs that a QTIP trust be created at his death, with the income going to his wife, Alice. Alice has no rights to spend trust principal. At Alice's death, the assets of the trust will pass to his five children from two previous marriages.

Several years after Mark dies, Alice remarries a wealthy man. But the income from the trust continues to go to Alice.

Meanwhile, Mark's oldest son, Edward, has business trouble and desperately needs money to keep afloat. Because the trustee cannot touch the income or the assets of the QTIP trust for the son's benefit, the business fails. This is hardly what Mark would have wanted. (Of course, the surviving spouse could give money to Edward. But she can give only her own money, which includes income from the trust, not trust principal.)

c. The Spouse Can Demand That Trust Property Produce Income

You can put any kind of property into a QTIP—a house, furniture, money, stock, even a business—but the surviving spouse has the right to demand that any non-income-producing property be converted into a form of property that does produce income. Thus if the trust includes a safe deposit box full of krugerands or a collection of valuable antique chairs that are not income-producing, the surviving spouse can demand this property be sold and the profits invested in income-producing property.

Example: Gretchen creates a QTIP trust and names her husband, Lloyd, as the life beneficiary. The trust assets consist of stocks, bonds, a residence and a vacation home. After Gretchen's death, Lloyd decides that the income is not enough for him to live on in the manner he's used to. Using his authority as trustee, he sells the vacation home and invests the proceeds in property that yields income for him, such as bonds.

5. Powers That May Be Given to the Surviving Spouse

Now we move on to powers a grantor is allowed by the IRS to include in a QTIP, but are not mandatory.

a. The Power to Spend Trust Principal

As we've stated, a surviving spouse must receive all the income from property in a QTIP trust. There is no flexibility here. But when it comes to permitting principal to be spent (invaded), it's a different story—you have great flexibility.

Because the surviving spouse is considered, for estate tax purposes, the owner of all property in the QTIP, she can be given the right to invade trust principal for any reason she wants, for any amount she wants. However, it's unusual to grant such broad power to spend trust principal. After all, this, in effect, leaves the property outright to the surviving spouse. If that's what you want, just do it directly, and no estate tax will be imposed (because of the marital deduction). Most QTIP trust grantors want to impose some restrictions on the surviving spouse, to protect the principal for the final beneficiaries.

Sometimes, the surviving spouse has no right to spend trust principal, period. In other situations, the right to invade principal is defined very specifically and narrowly, such as for emergency health care only. The trust document can limit the right to spend trust principal to the IRS objective need standard, allowing invasion only when necessary for the surviving spouse's "education, health care, support or maintenance." (IRS Reg. 20.2041-1(c)(2).)

If the surviving spouse has the right to spend trust principal, there's an inherent risk of conflict between the spouse and the final beneficiaries, so the trust document creating the trust should be very specific about the spouse's rights. The last thing you want is a fight over what assets can and cannot be used, or what standard the spouse must meet to justify spending principal.

The surviving spouse frequently serves as trustee of a QTIP trust. If, however, broad invasion powers are granted, you may want to name a disinterested party as trustee or co-trustee, to avoid or at least reduce the chances of hostility and conflict between the beneficiaries.

b. The "5 and 5" Power

The "5 and 5" power is a distinct right, allowing the trustee to spend trust principal for the life beneficiary. It's discussed in Chapter 18, Estate Tax-Saving Bypass Trusts, Section B. This right can be incorporated into a QTIP trust. It gives the spouse the right to get $5,000 or 5% of the trust principal, whichever is greater, each year. There are no restrictions on how the surviving spouse can spend this money.

The surviving spouse does not have to use this 5 and 5 right in any one year. But if it is not used in one year, that year's right is lost. In other words, the right is not cumulative, year to year.

Example: Isabelle is the trustee and life beneficiary of a QTIP trust established by her late husband. The trust document includes a 5 and 5 power. If she doesn't exercise this right this year, she cannot take an extra 5% or $5,000 out of the trust principal next year.

The 5 and 5 power is not currently used much by sophisticated estate planners, because more controlled methods of allowing the surviving spouse access to the trust principal are usually preferable.

c. The Power to Distribute Trust Property Among Beneficiaries

One of the most important features of a QTIP trust is the power of the original grantor to control who gets the trust assets when the surviving spouse dies. Often, a grantor specifies that the assets go to his or her children. But a trusted spouse who survives many years after the other spouse's death may be in a far better position to know just which of a group of final beneficiaries designated by the grantor need more than others, or which ones don't really need an inheritance at all. With a QTIP trust, the grantor can choose the group of possible final beneficiaries, but let the surviving spouse decide how much each one actually inherits. The surviving spouse formally makes this decision in her living trust or will. In legal terms, this is called giving the spouse "a limited power of appointment" over the assets in the trust.

Example: Sara is remarried to Emmanuel, nine years younger than herself. Sara fully trusts Emmanuel and is confident he loves her family. Sara has two children, Alison and Lori, from her prior marriage. When Sara prepares her QTIP, Alison has two young children (and wants more) and Lori is single. Sara wants to provide for her own children but also make direct gifts to her grandchildren.

In her QTIP, she specifies that her children and grandchildren will be the final beneficiaries of the trust. She states that each daughter will receive 30% of the trust property, and that the remaining 40% shall be divided among all her grandchildren alive when final distribution of the trust assets is made. She doesn't want to specify the precise divisions now because there may be (she hopes) additional grandchildren. And if Emmanuel survives her by a considerable time, she believes he will be in a far better position to decide how much money shall be given to each grandchild. So she gives Emmanuel authority to make the decision regarding actual distribution to the grandchildren.

Allowing the spouse to make such a decision can produce a fair and just distribution—one that may not have been foreseeable when the trust was created. One child may have completely dedicated himself to the family business, another may have special needs, and one child may have amassed such a large estate that he needs less than the others.

Granting this power to the spouse is not very common in QTIPs. Most grantors want absolute control over who the final beneficiaries are. But if you have complete confidence in your spouse's judgment, granting this power can be sensible, especially when some desired beneficiaries are very young (or even not yet alive) when the trust is prepared.

6. The "QTIP Election"

A unique aspect of QTIPs is that the executor (also called personal representative) named in your will must elect, on your federal estate tax return, to place property you left in a QTIP in that trust. (An estate tax return must be filed for any estate with a gross value exceeding $600,000, even if no tax need be paid. See Chapter 15, Estate Taxes, Section A.) Your executor has the final say here. You cannot require that he elect QTIP tax treatment for your property. If the QTIP election isn't properly made by the executor, no valid QTIP trust exists, period.

The QTIP election itself amounts to marking the correct box on the estate tax return and then listing the property that is to go into the trust. Seems simple, but it has surely been done wrong. In one case, an executor hurriedly filed an estate tax return, forgot to mark the box and then sought IRS permission to file an amended return electing a QTIP. Nope, said the IRS, which sometimes seems to take special delight in denying proposed QTIP trusts from "qualifying" and thus being eligible for the marital deduction.

a. Making the Election

Deciding how and whether to make the QTIP election can be difficult. The executor has several choices:

- not to elect the QTIP
- elect that all property the deceased left in the (possible) QTIP trust actually be treated as QTIP property, or
- elect to have only a portion of the trust property treated as a QTIP. For example, the executor can elect to have 60% of the trust property treated as a QTIP and 40% not. That 40% would be subject to estate tax now.

These options make possible a great deal of strategic after-death tax planning. This is desirable, because it allows key tax decisions to be made in light of current circumstances rather than being frozen years before. But in some family situations, it can require the wisdom of Solomon (not to mention high quality tax advice) to decide which election option to take.

In larger estates, this QTIP election is sometimes used to equalize the value of each spouse's estate. For example, sometimes it makes estate tax sense to choose not to elect a QTIP and allow the deceased spouse's possible QTIP trust property to be included in his taxable estate. If electing the QTIP would result in the surviving spouse's estate being much larger than that of the first spouse to die, higher overall estate tax would be paid. So in such a case, after the first spouse's death, the executor might elect to go ahead and pay any estate tax assessed against that deceased spouse's property, because the tax rate is lower on this amount of property than it would be if this property were combined, for estate tax purposes, with the surviving spouse's.

This means the surviving spouse must accept higher tax payments now in exchange for overall tax savings later. If he doesn't, there can be a real power struggle between him and the executor. Of course, often he is the executor, so this problem is eliminated.

Another option is for the executor to elect to have only a percentage of the deceased spouse's property receive QTIP treatment. This is called a partial QTIP election. This, too, can be used to lower overall estate tax. Any percentage of the trust property not elected to receive QTIP treatment still must, under IRS rules, be used for the surviving spouse's benefit. This portion can technically be left in the QTIP trust, but does not receive QTIP estate tax treatment. Two separate financial records must be kept—one for the trust property receiving QTIP treatment and one for the trust property that does not receive QTIP treatment. Less commonly, the percentage of the property that does not receive QTIP treatment could go to into a separate trust, particularly a marital life estate trust.

Example: Ben has an estate worth $2 million. He is married to Gloria and has children from a first marriage. Gloria has her own property worth $2 million. Ben puts his $2 million in a QTIP for Gloria, with the income to go to her and the assets to go later to the children from his first marriage.

At Ben's death, if the executor elects the full QTIP, these are the tax consequences:

Ben's gross estate	$2,000,000
Marital deduction for QTIP property	($2,000,000)
Estate tax due	$0

At Gloria's death:

Gloria's gross estate	$4, 000,000
Estate tax at 55%	$1,840,800
Personal $600,000 tax exemption	($192,800)
Estate tax due	$1,648,000

Now suppose that the executor elects to have only 50% of Ben's property qualify for QTIP trust treatment. The other half must, under IRS rules, be used solely for the surviving spouse's benefit.

At Ben's death:

Ben's gross estate	$2,000,000
Property given marital deduction for half of QTIP treatment	($1,000,000)
Taxable estate	$1,000,000
Estate tax	$345,800
Personal $600,000 tax exemption	($192,800)
Estate tax due	$153,000

At Gloria's death:

Gloria's gross estate	$3,000,000
Estate tax	$1,275,800
Personal $600,000 tax exemption	($192,800)
Estate tax due	$1,083,000

By electing to have only half of the trust property qualify for the QTIP, $602,000 in eventual estate tax is saved for the final beneficiaries. The savings is possible because of the graduated estate tax. Electing a full QTIP would cause the second estate to be taxed at 55%. But with half of it taxed now, Ben's estate fell in a lower bracket, only 41%. (Chapter 15, Estate Tax, Section A, contains an estate tax rate chart.)

A number of issues can contribute to the decision your executor makes regarding the QTIP election. One factor is simply that circumstances may have changed (indeed, they always do, according to Buddha) since you prepared the QTIP trust. Your original estate plan may not be the most financially desirable one after your death.

Example 1: Steve has an estate worth about $1.05 million. He drafts a QTIP trust for $950,000 of his assets and a marital life estate trust for the remaining $100,000. His wife, Esther, has property of her own worth about $200,000. She will get the income from both trusts, and the principal from both will go to Steve's son, Zack, upon Esther's death.

Several years later, Esther inherits property worth $450,000, making her own estate now worth $650,000. Steve neglects to revise his estate plan. When Steve dies, if the QTIP goes into effect, Esther's estate will now be worth over $1.5 million for tax purposes—well over the $600,000 threshold at which estate tax is due.

Instead, when Steve dies, his executor looks at the whole picture and decides to make only a partial QTIP election for 16%, or $150,000, of Steve's estate. That means $900,000 remains and will go into the marital life estate trust. It will be subject to estate tax immediately, though Steve's estate will receive a credit (his personal credit) for the tax due on the first $600,000.

Esther will still get the income from both trusts, and Zack will still inherit the principal when she dies.

Example 2: Daniel, a retired teacher, creates a QTIP trust for Martha, his second wife, with the principal to go later to his children. His assets consist of savings of $50,000, life insurance of $100,000, his residence and personal belongings. The QTIP trust will defer tax and allow Martha to use the house and furnishings for as long as she lives.

Daniel does not consider himself wealthy. He paid $30,000 for his house 40 years ago. But at his death, his real estate is appraised at $750,000, and his total net estate is $900,000. His executor elects to have QTIP treatment for only one-third of the property. The rest, $600,000, will pass tax-free because of Steve's personal exemption. This $600,000 will remain in the trust, for Martha's benefit and use, even though it doesn't receive QTIP tax treatment. Any estate tax on the QTIP portion is deferred until Martha's death.

b. Complexities of Making a Partial QTIP Election

An executor can make a partial QTIP election only in terms of a percentage or fraction of the total property originally left for the QTIP. For example, a trustee can elect to have 40% or 63% or one-third of the total property originally left for the QTIP actually qualify for QTIP tax treatment. What the executor cannot do is specify that certain specific assets be included in or excluded from the QTIP. The IRS simply doesn't allow that kind of property maneuvering with a QTIP.

The real world consequences of a partial QTIP election can be difficult. For example, there can be much paperwork if two-thirds of your house is owned by a QTIP trust and one-third owned by another trust. Also, it can complicate matters like real estate tax or refinancing. Because of the complexities involved, partial QTIP election is not often recommended by many sophisticated estate planners.

7. The Reverse QTIP Election

A "reverse QTIP election" is a special legal procedure designed to avoid losing the million dollar exemption allowed for assets that skip generations. (See Chapter 21, Other Estate Tax-Saving Trusts, Section A.) Without a reverse QTIP election, all assets that are left by a grandparent to a grandchild (skipping the middle generation) or in other generation-skipping plans are subject to an extra tax, called the Generation-Skipping Transfer Tax or GSTT.

Sometimes a QTIP trust leaves the trust principal, at the death of the surviving spouse, to the grantor's grandchildren or other beneficiaries more than one generation away. When this happens, the law allows the surviving spouse (the life beneficiary) to be considered the one transferring the property for GSTT purposes. This means up to $1 million can go to the grandchildren GSTT-free, because there is a $1 million standard exemption from the GSTT. However, when a reverse QTIP election is made at the first spouse's death, the first spouse who died is legally the person who makes the eventual transfer to the grandchildren. This preserves that first spouse's $1 million GSTT exemption and allows the second spouse to transfer another million to grandchildren free of the Generation Skipping Transfer Tax.

This reverse QTIP election is concerned only with generation-skipping trusts and the Generation-Skipping Transfer Tax. It is an entirely separate matter from the basic QTIP election, where the executor decides whether or not to use a QTIP, and if so, how much property to actually place in the QTIP trust.

8. Planning for a QTIP

A QTIP must be planned for and created in the trust document before you die. No one has any authority to create one, and obtain its estate-tax postponing advantages, after you die.

a. Choosing Your Trustee

A vital issue you must decide is who will be the trustee, or trustees, of your QTIP trust. The trustee can be (and usually is) your surviving spouse, but a child or someone else entirely can serve. Above all, choose the person you trust the most—and, of course, one who is willing to serve.

Do you believe that your spouse can be fully trusted to protect the trust principal, the final beneficiaries' inheritance? Do the final beneficiaries believe that your spouse can be trusted to protect their interests? If the answer is "no," or even "I'm not positive," perhaps a child should serve as co-trustee. Or, if you believe one of your children (and not your spouse) has the wisdom to best balance the needs of the surviving spouse against the final beneficiaries' rights to their eventual inheritance, you may want to name the child as sole trustee.

Obviously, there's no one-size-fits-all answer when it comes to choosing the trustee. A good lawyer may be able to help, by focusing your attention on your personal situation, but the final decision is definitely yours. (Choosing a trustee is discussed further in Chapter 17, An Overview of Ongoing Trusts, Section E.)

Remember also that the executor of your will has the authority to decide if property in the trust should actually receive QTIP treatment. So it's common to have your QTIP trustee be the same person as your executor.

Since by law you cannot deny the executor the power to decide whether or not to elect QTIP tax treatment for property you include in your QTIP trust, it's obviously vital that you have an executor you trust completely to make the best judgment in light of the interests of all trust beneficiaries—life beneficiary and final beneficiary.

B. Trusts for Non-Citizen Spouses: QDOTs

If you and your spouse are U.S. citizens, you can skip this section.

If you are married to someone who is not a citizen of the United States, property you leave to that spouse will not be entitled to the unlimited marital deduction. In plain English, you cannot leave your non-citizen spouse an unlimited amount of money free of federal estate tax. Congress eliminated the marital deduction for property a U.S. citizen leaves to his or her non-citizen spouse because it wanted to prevent non-citizen spouses from inheriting large amounts of money and then leaving the country, with the result that no U.S. estate tax would ever be paid on this money. The rule applies even if the non-citizen is married to a U.S. citizen or is a legal resident of the U.S.

What's the best way to deal with this issue? Certainly, it may make excellent sense to have the non-citizen spouse become a U.S. citizen. Usually, this is possible, given some time. If, for whatever reason, a spouse doesn't obtain U.S. citizenship, there remains one very important estate tax exemption that can be used by a citizen spouse for property left to a non-citizen spouse. It's the $600,000 personal estate tax exemption, which is available to each spouse, no matter whom he or she leaves property to. (See Chapter 15, Estate Tax, Section A, for more on the personal exemption.) So a citizen can leave her non-citizen spouse up to $600,000 worth of property free of federal estate tax. But any amount over $600,000 left outright by a U.S. spouse to a non-citizen spouse is subject to estate tax at the regular rates, which begin at 37% and rise to 55% for amounts over $3 million.

For estates over $600,000, there is one exception to the rule denying the marital deduction to property left to a non-citizen spouse. All property, no matter what its value, left by one spouse to a non-citizen spouse in what's called a "Qualified Domestic Trust" (QDOT) is allowed the marital deduction. (IRC Section 2056(A).) This means that when the citizen spouse dies, the federal estate tax that would otherwise be assessed on property in a QDOT is deferred until the second spouse dies. Especially when the non-citizen spouse is younger and is likely to need as much income as possible, this is a big advantage, because money that otherwise would be paid to the government for tax goes into the trust. QDOTs are used only by spouses with an estate exceeding $600,000, because only these estates must pay federal estate tax.

There are strict federal laws governing QDOT trusts. For example, if any trust principal is distributed to the non-citizen spouse during her life, estate tax is assessed on the amount distributed. Thus, if the trust pays for $150,000 from principal for a spouse's medical bills, that amount is immediately subject to estate tax. The tax rate depends on how much of her $600,000 personal estate tax exemption the citizen spouse had used up. If all of her property went into the QDOT trust, none of it was subject to estate tax when she died. So the estate tax rate would be the rate applied to $150,000, or 32%. By contrast, if the husband had left $600,000 in trust for his children, and all the remainder of his property in the QDOT, his $600,000 exemption would have been used up when he died. So the tax rate on the $150,000 would be 37%. If another $100,000 of principal is subsequently spent for the spouse's needs, the tax rate would increase accordingly.

Income the non-citizen spouse receives from the QDOT trust is taxable to him as regular income. But this is true for any person, whether a U.S. citizen or not, for income received from any ongoing trust.

When the surviving non-citizen spouse dies, the QDOT trust assets are subject to estate tax. The tax is based on the value of the assets in the trust when the non-citizen spouse dies. In this regard, QDOTs are similar to QTIPs. Any increase in value in the trust property during the life of the surviving spouse is subject to estate tax on her death, unlike property in a marital life estate trust.

Gifts to Non-Citizen Spouses

Under a special gift tax regulation, a citizen spouse can give up to $100,000 per year, free of gift tax, to a non-citizen spouse while both are living. (IRS Reg. 2523(i)(2).) By contrast, if both spouses were citizens of the U.S., they could give any amount to each other, free of gift tax. (See Chapter 16, Gift and Gift Taxes, Section A.) While the annual $100,000 exemption allowed for gifts to non-citizen spouses is more limited than for gifts to citizen spouses, it is still a substantial amount. A U.S. citizen with an estate over $600,000 should consider whether making gifts to her non-citizen spouse of up to $100,000 a year would be a sensible estate planning strategy.

A valid Qualified Domestic Trust must meet all of the requirements of a regular marital life estate trust and also the following special requirements:

- At least one of the trustees of the trust must be either a U.S. citizen or a U.S. corporation. Thus, the surviving spouse cannot be the sole trustee.
- The surviving spouse must be entitled to receive all income from the trust.

- When the trust is created, it must comply with any additional IRS regulations that have been issued. Although this requirement is expressly stated in the federal QDOT statute, when this book was printed, there were no IRS regulations governing QDOTs, even though the law is a few years old. Presumably, the IRS will eventually issue some regulations regarding QDOTs, but they are clearly not in a rush.
- The QDOT trust must be elected by the executor of the grantor's estate on the estate tax return (just like a QTIP trust).

Here's an example of how a QDOT can work:

Example: Juan, a U.S. citizen, has an estate worth $2 million. He is married to Maria, who is a legal resident of the United States but not a citizen. Juan's estate plan includes an outright bequest of $600,000 to Maria. This amount is exempt from federal estate tax because of Juan's personal exemption. The remaining $1.4 million will go into a QDOT trust for Maria's benefit during her life, and will be distributed, at her death, to their children. Juan appoints his brother Ricardo, who is a U.S. citizen, to serve as co-trustee with Maria of the QDOT trust. (Legally, Juan could also use a U.S. bank or other institution as a co-trustee.)

At Juan's death, his executor makes the election for the QDOT trust on Juan's federal estate tax return. No estate tax is due at this time because of the personal tax exemption and the marital deduction QDOT trust. Maria will receive all of the income from the trust for her life and may receive necessary principal for her support. At Maria's death, the assets remaining in the trust will be subject to estate tax.

The QDOT rules have one opening that is an incentive to a non-citizen spouse to become a U.S. citizen. If the spouse becomes a citizen before the deceased spouse's estate tax return is filed (generally, nine months after the death) or before any distribution of principal is made to the non-citizen spouse, property in the trust will receive the full marital deduction, and assets may be invaded during the spouse's lifetime without paying estate tax. The trust is no longer a QDOT and the remaining assets will only be subject to tax when the surviving spouse dies.

A QDOT trust doesn't necessarily have to be created before the grantor's death. If someone who is married to a non-citizen prepared a trust before the federal QDOT law applied, or simply didn't know of that law, the surviving non-citizen spouse can request of the IRS that the trust document be "reformed" to meet the guidelines of a QDOT trust. For example, if a citizen simply left all property outright to a non-citizen spouse, the spouse can request the creation of a QDOT trust and obtain an estate tax deferment for the property.

As we've said, the rules governing QDOTs, estate tax and non-citizen spouses are special and complicated and new IRS regulations are expected. If you're married to a non-citizen and have an estate worth more than $600,000, see a lawyer for estate planning.

C. Widow's Election Trusts

This rather peculiar trust with the unfortunate name can be used only by married couples. It is not confined to the benefit of just a wife. Either spouse can create a widow's election trust for the other.

This type of trust is a hybrid designed to use the $600,000 estate tax exemption and take advantage of the unlimited marital deduction. In a sense, it does some of the same things you can accomplish by establishing a QTIP trust and backing it up with a marital life estate trust. (See Section A, above.)

Widow's election trusts are not very common, and with good reason. Only if one spouse wants to control the disposition of both spouse's property, and the other spouse agrees to this, are they useful. Such control by one spouse is rarely desired these days. Widow's election trusts are basically a relic from the time when men presumed it was best for them to control the disposition of family money, including property owned by their wives—and their wives accepted this view.

Among other problems, the tax rules governing widow's election trusts are so complicated that just reading about them can bring about a case of fatigue. However, bear with us, and we will outline the main tenets involved, so you will have at least a basic understanding of how these trusts work. Then, if you wish to pursue one as part of your estate plan, get out your checkbook and proceed to the most experienced trust attorney you can find.

Good advice is essential. These trusts are so rare and complicated that relatively few estate planning lawyers really understand how they actually work. If you want to consider one, locate an expert lawyer who is knowledgeable about widow's election trusts.

With a widow's election trust, one spouse, traditionally the husband, leaves property to the other in trust, on the condition that the surviving spouse will "elect" to place her own property in the trust. The husband names the final beneficiary for this trust. Usually, the surviving spouse (presumed to be the wife) receives only the income, for her life, from the now-combined assets of both spouses. When the surviving spouse dies, all trust assets go to the final beneficiaries. By using this trust plan, the grantor can control both spouses' property, designate the final beneficiaries and avoid probate at the death of the surviving spouse. But the surviving spouse loses the right to name the beneficiaries for her own estate.

Example: Leon and Petra have a combined estate worth $3 million. Leon drafts a widow's election trust for his $1.5 million share. He names his children from a prior marriage as final beneficiaries. He leaves these assets to Petra only if she elects at his death to transfer her $1.5 share into the same trust. She will then receive the income from all of the assets for life, and on her death, the trustee will distribute the assets to Leon's children. Petra has no children of her own, so she does not object to this plan.

Why would anyone use a widow's election trust? Most of all, simply for the desire for control—the need of some people to keep all of both spouses' property together for management (or ego) purposes.

One very difficult aspect of these trusts is figuring out the estate tax rate applied to the trust property of the first spouse to die. This involves using actuarial tables and formulas, looking at the age of the surviving spouse and how much income the spouse can expect to be paid. Determining the tax rate is exceedingly tricky, and too complex to explain in detail here. Again, you'll need top-notch professional advice.

D. Marital Deduction Trusts

A marital deduction trust (authorized in IRC Section 2056(b)(5)) is similar to a QTIP trust in many ways, but differs in a couple of aspects. These days, marital deduction trusts are used in rare situations, when one of their special features is desired.

You may want to create a marital deduction trust if:

- You want the trustee to be able to give away trust principal while your spouse is still alive.
- You want your spouse to choose who will inherit trust property after her death

Marital deduction trusts are quite technical and must comply with applicable tax law and IRS rules. Any marital deduction trust must be drafted by an expert experienced with this type of trust.

Like a QTIP, one spouse creates a marital deduction trust, naming the other spouse as the life beneficiary. Trust property qualifies for the marital deduction, so no estate tax on property in the marital deduction trust is paid when the first spouse dies. The trust property that remains when the second spouse dies is included in the taxable estate of the surviving spouse.

Historically, a major purpose of a marital deduction trust was to have property managed for a surviving wife who had not "earned" it, in the sense that she had not actually worked in the husband's business and was presumed—the innocent lamb—to be unable to manage financial matters. So property left in a marital deduction trust was managed by an independent (or, at least, male) trustee. An independent trustee is not legally required for these trusts, but it definitely was the practice.

It's certainly far less common now for a husband to believe this about his wife, so a major reason for using marital deduction trusts has been largely eliminated by cultural change. And even if a husband or wife wants an independent trustee to manage property left in trust for the other, a QTIP trust can serve that purpose.

1. Determining the Final Beneficiaries

With a marital deduction trust, the surviving spouse must be given the right to determine who will receive the trust property at her death. This is called a "Power of Appointment." (See Chapter 24, Trusts and Other Devices for Imposing Controls Over Property, Section G.) This is in direct contrast to a QTIP trust, where the grantor can, and normally does, name the final beneficiaries.

2. Making Gifts of Trust Principal

The trustee of a marital deduction trust can, if authorized by the trust document, make gifts of trust principal to other trust beneficiaries during the life of the surviving spouse. This is not permitted under QTIP trust rules.

This flexibility may be desirable because it may not be at all clear when you prepare a trust whether your surviving spouse will need access to the trust principal during his lifetime. Perhaps one or more of the final beneficiaries will genuinely need some of the trust principal while the surviving spouse is alive. One way to handle these uncertainties is to create a marital deduction trust and give the trustee power to make gifts from the principal.

Example: Peter drafts a marital deduction trust for his wife, Lisa. Lisa will receive all income from the trust and can choose who will inherit the assets at her death. During her life, the trustee (who can be Lisa, if that's what Peter chooses) is authorized to give, during her life, trust principal to each of their two children.

Peter dies. Lisa is quite well off from her own property, but one of their children loses his job, and he and his family are threatened with eviction from their recently-purchased home. Lisa, as trustee, decides to allocate $30,000 of trust principal to her child, bailing him out of this crisis.

This gift is a taxable event for estate tax purposes. Since the trust property will be part of Lisa's taxable estate, she will use $20,000 of her $600,000 estate/gift tax exemption by making this distribution. (It's $20,000 because the first $10,000 is exempt under the annual gift tax exclusion.See Chapter 16, Gifts and Gift Taxes, Section A, for an explanation of the unified gift and estate tax system.)

3. Trusts Where Assets Must Go to the Estate of the Surviving Spouse

An "estate" trust is a special type of marital deduction trust where, when the surviving spouse dies, all remaining trust principal must go into his or her estate. (IRC Section 2056 (b)(1); IRS Reg. 20.2056(3)—2(b)(iii).) One desirable feature of this type of trust is that the trust property can be, and remain, non-income-producing.

Example: Suzanne's property holdings include several acres of woodland, and a very small house (almost a shed) by the side of a river. Suzanne grew up spending much happy time on this land (and in the river) and she wants to be sure the land is preserved for her children, if possible. As it is now, the land is not income-producing, the shed has no electricity and only rudimentary plumbing. Suzanne doesn't want the shed rented out, even if it could be, so she leave the land in a marital deduction estate trust, with specific directions in the trust document that the land may not be sold while the trust lasts.

Another feature of this type trust is that income does not have to be paid out to the spouse, but may, at the trustee's option, be accumulated, increasing the amount of the trust principal. If this occurs, income is taxed at the trust's higher tax rate. In rare instances, this disadvantage may be thought to be offset by the fact that the trust principal does increase, allowing more money to be used for business growth or other investment purposes. ■

20

Charitable Trusts

Let's start with the most basic point: Establishing a charitable trust involves making a gift, often a substantial one, to a charity. If you want to do that, it makes sense to explore how using a trust may allow you to do it in a way that is advantageous from a tax point of view. As you'll see, there are several charitable trusts to choose from that can offer significant financial benefits, depending on your situation.

By contrast, if your basic estate planning goals are to pass on your property to family or friends, make a few minor charitable gifts and pay less estate tax, then a charitable trust is probably not for you. The income tax and estate tax breaks charitable trusts can offer probably won't make up for the amount of property that is given to a charity instead of your family.

A. An Overview of Charitable Trusts

There are two basic types of charitable trusts, each identified by its own obtuse name. They are:

- charitable remainder trusts, including popular pooled charitable trusts (IRC Section 664), and
- charitable lead trusts (IRC Sections 664, 671).

These trusts have certain features in common:

- **They become operational while you are alive.** A basic purpose of charitable trusts is not simply to make a gift to a charity, but also to provide some income (or other benefits) to you or to some beneficiary or beneficiaries. You can name several beneficiaries to share the payments made from the trust. Or you can name one beneficiary (your child) to receive payments after another beneficiary (your spouse) dies. But the longer the payment period to your beneficiaries, the lower the income tax deduction for the gift to charity. (See Section B1, below.)
- **They are irrevocable.** Once you create a charitable trust and it becomes operational, it is irrevocable. You cannot change your mind and regain legal control of the property you have given to the trust.
- **Only tax-exempt charities are eligible.** In order to obtain the tax benefits, you must make the gift to a charity that is approved by the IRS. Normally, this means a charity that has gained tax-exempt status under Section 501(c)(3) of the Internal Revenue Code.[1] The IRS does distinguish between valid charities and "public charities." A valid charitable gift may be made to either. However, the IRS maintains a long list of acceptable public charities, which include educational institutions, research organizations and well-known institutions like United Way or CARE. Usually, the easiest way to determine if the charity you want to make a gift to is an approved charity is to contact the IRS and see if it appears on their public charities list.
- **You get an income tax break.** The value of the charitable gift is deductible from your income tax. (See Section B, below.)

1. The Basics of Charitable Remainder Trusts

With a charitable remainder trust, you name an income beneficiary or beneficiaries, and a final beneficiary, which is always the charity.

The income beneficiary can be (and often is) yourself, but it can be your wife, mate, child or anyone else. And, as we've said, there can be more than one income beneficiary. This person (or persons) receives a set payment from the trust or a set percentage of the worth of trust property for the term defined

[1]Other types of organizations, such as social welfare groups, are tax-exempt under other subsections of 501(c).

in the trust. For example, the income beneficiary might receive 7% of the value of the trust per year, or a fixed sum of $X per year. However, you cannot give the income beneficiary the right to receive all trust income, except for spouses in certain situations.

You state, in the trust document, how long the income beneficiary will receive income from the trust property. This payment period can be a set number of years, or until the income beneficiary dies. The income beneficiaries have only the specified right to trust income during their lives. They never legally own the trust property, and it can never be included in their taxable estate.

The charity itself is usually the trustee of the trust property. As trustee, the charity is responsible for making proper payments to an income beneficiary. The trustee normally converts any non-income producing property, from raw land to artworks, into income-producing property.

Gift tax may be assessed on the money received by the income beneficiary. If an income beneficiary is anyone other than you or your spouse, the payments from the trust are considered a taxable gift from you to that person. If more than $10,000 in income is received per year, you will be assessed gift tax on the excess over $10,000 and will have to file a federal gift tax return.

Trust property isn't included in your taxable estate, either, which means that your heirs get an estate tax break. The net value of the trust assets, as of the date they become solely owned by the charity (that is, when the income beneficiary's interest ends), is excluded from your taxable estate.

2. The Basics of Charitable Lead Trusts

With a charitable lead trust, income from the trust property is given to the charity for a set period of time. Once that period is over, the trust property goes back to you or someone else you named to receive it. In other words, charitable lead trusts function in the reverse of charitable remainder trusts with regard to beneficiaries.

Charitable lead trusts are not as widely used as charitable remainder trusts. They are discussed further in Section D, below.

3. Selecting a Trustee for a Charitable Trust

You can serve as trustee of your own charitable trust, or you can choose whomever you prefer to be trustee.[2] However, most people choose the charity itself to serve as trustee.

Most large public charities won't allow you to serve as trustee. These charities want their own investment staff managing all gifts made to them, including yours. Large charities have experienced investment staffs, and many people prefer to turn money management and investment decisions regarding their trust property over to them, rather than burdening themselves with this responsibility. Also, a larger charity can offer you other services. They may assist you in preparing the trust document. They may also administer the trust free of any charge for the trustee's services. Finally, while you probably can't impose investment decisions over the charity serving as trustee, you can direct where you want the trust property to go after the income beneficiary's interest ends. For instance, if the trust will benefit a school, you could usually require that the property be used only for scholarship purposes in a certain field.

Matters can be different if you're making a gift to a smaller, less-established charity. Its cause may be noble, and its staff dedicated, but that's far from a guarantee of experience and sophistication regarding

[2]Special rules apply if you use a pooled income trust; in that case, the charity is always the trustee. (See Section C3, below.)

investments. So with a small, new charity you may decide that it's wisest to name yourself as trustee, to better manage your property. But check to be sure the charity will allow this; even some small charities insist on being named as trustee of a charitable trust.

With a charitable remainder trust, there may be other good reasons to choose someone other than the charity to be trustee, if you can. The interests of the income beneficiary and the final beneficiary (the charity) can conflict. The income beneficiary may want the trust assets managed to maximize current income, whereas the charity will likely be concerned with long-term growth. Fortunately, such a conflict is not invariably the case, and indeed seems rare.

KNOW YOUR CHARITY

Many people make charitable gifts to charities they know well, whether from publicity or personal experience. If you don't know the charity so well, you may well want to investigate the charity thoroughly, including its history, current management and its plans. Several books evaluate charities and list what percentage of their funds actually go for charitable services. You can also ask for annual financial reports from charities you are interested in.

Before you choose a trustee, do two things:

1. Work with a lawyer knowledgeable in charitable trusts. An experienced lawyer should be able to help you clarify what your needs are and how much risk you might take on if the charity is trustee. The lawyer should also be able to suggest other possible trustees, aside from yourself—perhaps a corporate trustee, like a private trust company.

2. Investigate how the charity would work as trustee. If the charity is the trustee, you can't control what the trust assets are invested in, so it's vital that you trust the charity's investment personnel. Who in the charity will actually be doing the trustee work? Does that person seem open, and easy to talk to? Do you feel confidence in her judgment and human sympathies? How sophisticated is the potential trustee, and her staff, in money and investment management?

Don't choose the charity to be the trustee unless you are confident that the organization, and the people in it who will actually manage your trust and its property, will protect the income beneficiary's interests. If a charity you feel is dubious regarding financial management insists it be trustee, don't create a charitable trust benefiting that institution. Any trustee, including a charitable organization, has what's called a "fiduciary duty" to do what's best for all the trust beneficiaries. But you want to rely on real people you actually trust, not abstract legal duties.

NAMING A BACK-UP CHARITY

To protect your income tax savings from a charitable trust, consider naming another tax-exempt charity as a back-up final beneficiary, or provide in the trust document that the trustee can choose another charity if this need arises. In the unlikely event that the chosen charity becomes defunct or loses its IRS tax-exempt standing, this ensures that there can be no (retroactive) loss of any income tax deduction. It also ensures that the charitable gift can never be subject to estate tax, because there will always be some valid, IRS tax-exempt charity entitled to receive the trust property when the income beneficiary's term ends.

B. The Income Tax Deduction

You may get substantial income tax advantages by creating a charitable trust. With a charitable trust, you can, over time, deduct the full value of the gift to the charity from your income tax. The fact that a charitable remainder trust makes payments to you or some other beneficiary for many years doesn't change this basic rule.

Where things get tricky, though, is determining what is the actual value of the gift to the charity for income tax deduction purposes. With a charitable remainder trust, the value of your gift to charity is not simply the value of the property when you give it to the trust. The IRS deducts from this value the estimated value of the income beneficiary's right to receive payments from the trust property.

With a charitable lead trust, things are reversed. The income tax deduction is the estimated value of the income the charity will receive during the set period it receives it.

Once the IRS determines the worth of a gift to a charitable trust, you are entitled to a 100% income tax deduction of this amount. But this deduction cannot be taken in a single year. Rather, you can deduct a certain percentage of the tax worth of the gift in the year it is made, and deduct the rest over the next four years.

The amount of the first year's deduction depends on how the IRS classifies the charity. IRS regulations allow you to deduct the value of a gift to some charities up to 50% of your adjusted gross income for the first year. Donations to other charities qualify for only a 30% deduction. For a gift to a charity to be eligible for the 50% deduction, that charity must be classified by the IRS as a "public" charity. Most widely-known charities meet this requirement, such as schools, churches, the Salvation Army, the American Cancer Society and many environmental organizations. Many private foundations, however, do not meet this public charity requirement. If your gift is made to one of these charities, you will receive an income tax deduction of only up to 30% of your adjusted gross income the first year. To determine whether your charity makes you eligible for the 50% or 30% deduction, contact the IRS.

Example: Christopher creates a charitable remainder trust, with the charity CARE as the final beneficiary. He names himself as the income beneficiary. The IRS will determine the worth of his gift, for income tax purposes, by subtracting the value of his retained interest in the income from the trust principal. He may take 50% of the value of his gift, as the IRS has determined it, as an income tax deduction for that year.

If, instead, Christopher had given the money to a tax-exempt foundation not in the IRS 50% category, he would have been able to deduct only 30% of the value of the gift on that year's income tax return. Over each of the next four years, he would deduct 17.5% per year.

1. Determining the Value of a Gift to a Charitable Remainder Trust

If you make an outright gift to charity, the income tax deduction permitted by the IRS is the gift's value (more precisely, the net value to you) at the time you make it. For example, if you write a $100,000 check to the Audubon Society, you're entitled to a $100,000 income tax deduction.

By contrast, if you make a gift to a charitable remainder trust while you are alive, determining the amount of your tax deduction is, as we've just said, more complicated. The IRS determines the value of the charitable gift in the trust from tables that estimate your life expectancy (or that of whomever is the income beneficiary), interest rates and what the charity is expected to receive (that is, how much principal will be left) when the income beneficiary's interest ends. The more the charity is expected to get, the bigger the tax deduction; the larger the expected return to income beneficiary, the lower the deduction.

Example: Zola, who is 80 years old, creates a charitable remainder trust. She gives $600,000 to her favorite charity, Save the Children, and retains the right to receive income equal to 6% of the trust principal annually for her life. After her death, the charity will receive all remaining trust property outright.

Curt, who is 40 years old, creates the same kind of trust, with the same amount of property and the same retained income rights. Under IRS rules, the value of Zola's gift to the charity is worth more than Curt's, which means she can take a larger tax deduction. The reason is that Curt, who is just 40, will probably live much longer than 80-year-old Zola, so the trust will pay out more money to Curt than Zola.

The fact that the IRS calculations are influenced by prevailing interest rates means that the precise valuation of the tax worth of a gift to a charitable remainder trust depends on when the gift is made. So to determine the actual value of your gift through a charitable trust for IRS purposes, you need to see an expert who has the most current IRS tables. You could dig up the tables yourself, but figuring out how to use them, interweaving estimated interest rates, your life expectancy, and the value of the charity's interest, is definitely not easy; indeed, for the uninitiated, it's close to impossible.

2. Giving Appreciated Property to a Charitable Trust

One of the most desirable aspects of a charitable trust is that it provides a method to turn highly appreciated assets into cash without paying any capital gain tax. If you donate a non-income-producing asset in a charitable trust, the charity can convert it into an income-producing one. Though a charity isn't legally required to do so, it surely will if the asset—say an appreciated house or painting—isn't producing any, or much, current income. And, whatever the profit from such a sale, no capital gain tax is assessed; charities are simply not liable for capital gain tax.

Here's how it works. You donate an appreciated asset to the charity using a charitable remainder trust. The charity sells it for its current market value, without any subtraction for capital gain tax. As the grantor, you benefit in two ways. You get a tax deduction based on the sales price (the current value) of the asset; also, the income you receive from the trust property will be based on the amount the charity received when it sold that property—which will obviously be higher than if capital gain tax had to be paid out of the sale's profits.

Example: Toni owns stock currently worth $300,000, which she paid $20,000 for 20 years ago. She creates a charitable remainder trust, naming the N.A.A.C.P. as the charity-beneficiary. She funds her charitable trust with her stock. The N.A.A.C.P. sells the stock for $300,000 and invests the money in a safe mutual fund. Toni, as the income beneficiary, will receive income from this $300,000 for her life.

Technically, there is a capital gain (profit) of $280,000 on the stock sale—that is, the sale price less Toni's original $20,000 purchase price. But no capital gain tax is assessed against the charity (or Toni), because charities are simply not liable for capital gain tax. Had Toni sold the stock herself, however, she would have had to pay the capital gain tax. In effect, by making this charitable gift, she has converted an asset with a tax basis of $20,000 to one really worth $300,000.

Toni's trust document specifies that her annual income from the charitable trust will be 7% of the value of the trust property (currently worth $300,000). The IRS calculation of Toni's income tax deduction will also start from a gift worth $300,000.

C. A Closer Look at Charitable Remainder Trusts

There are different types of charitable remainder trusts. Each one offers different advantages and drawbacks. Briefly, the three main types are:

- **Annuity trusts** which pay the income beneficiary a fixed amount each year
- **Unitrusts** which pay the income beneficiary an amount equal to a percentage of the trust assets each year
- **Pooled income trusts** which let you contribute to an existing charitable trust and receive income for a set time.

1. Charitable Remainder Annuity Trusts

This type of trust provides a fixed dollar amount of income (an annuity) to the trust's income beneficiary, regardless of the value of the trust assets. When creating the trust document, you name the income beneficiary—often yourself—and the term of the annuity period—often your lifetime. You also state the precise dollar amount of annual income that must remain the same throughout the period the life beneficiary receives trust payments.

Once you have established the set yearly payment figure, and the trust is operational, you can't later change that figure. For instance, if you create a trust worth $250,000 and specify that the charity pay you $10,000 a year for the rest of your life, you can't subsequently say, "Oops. I forgot about inflation. How about $15,000 a year?" No deal.

You can, theoretically, make the payments as high as you wish. There is no IRS limit on maximum payments allowed. However, practically, there are limits. First, the higher the set payment rate, the lower your income tax deduction. Second, if the payment is set quite high, it might require yearly spending of principal, possibly using up all the gift before the payment term is over. Obviously, this defeats your desire to make a gift to the charity. Third, a charity is unlikely to accept a gift, particularly if it must serve as trustee, where it is likely, or even possible, that all the trust property will be consumed (spent) before the charity is entitled to receive this property outright.

The advantage of this type of trust is that if the trust somehow has lower-than-expected income—for example, during a period when interest rates are extremely low—the income beneficiary still receives the same annual income. The trustee must invade the trust principal, if necessary, to obtain the amount of the annuity. This can't be done with other types of charitable remainder trusts.

If you create a charitable remainder annuity trust, you don't obtain a hedge against inflation. Payments from an annuity trust remain the same, even if there's significant inflation or the trust assets significantly increase in value.

You cannot give additional assets to a charitable remainder annuity trust after it's operational. (IRS Reg. 1.664-2(b).) Once the trust is created and funded, that's it. Of course, you could create a new, second trust, but this is a fair amount of bother, especially with subsequent recordkeeping. So you should carefully decide, before creating a charitable remainder annuity trust, how much money you want to put in it and how large an annuity you want.

There are income tax advantages to using an annuity trust. The same property contributed to an annuity trust has a higher value for income tax deduction purposes than if placed in a charitable remainder unitrust. If you are not concerned about inflation and wish to reduce your estate tax and income tax, an annuity trust is often a better choice than a unitrust.

Example: Jack sets up his charitable remainder annuity trust with $600,000. He specifies he is to receive a guaranteed annuity each year of $25,000. To determine his income tax deduction, the IRS looks at his anticipated life span, subtracts what he is supposed to receive each year and then values the gift to the charity. The value of the gift for income tax purposes will be higher than if Jack had given the same $600,000 in a charitable remainder unitrust.

CHARITABLE REMAINDER ANNUITY TRUSTS AT A GLANCE

1. Grantor funds trust with appreciated (if possible) trust assets.
2. Grantor takes income tax deduction.
3. Trustee converts all assets into income-producing assets. No capital gain tax is due on profits of sale.
4. Trustee pays set amount of income to income beneficiary for the annuity period.
5. At end of annuity period, trust assets go outright to charity. The value of these assets is not subject to federal estate tax.

2. Charitable Remainder Unitrusts

With this popular form of a charitable remainder trust, the trustee pays income each year from the trust to an income beneficiary—again, usually the grantor. But instead of a fixed amount, the income beneficiary gets a percentage of the current value of the trust property. For example, the trust document could specify that the income beneficiary receives 7% of the value of the trust assets yearly. Each year, the trust assets must be reappraised to obtain a current worth figure. If the value of the trust assets increase because of wise investment decisions by the trustee, the payments received by the income beneficiary increase. Similarly, because the income beneficiary receives a fixed percentage, not a flat dollar amount, if inflation pushes up the dollar value of the assets, the payments to the income beneficiary go up accordingly. Thus a charitable remainder unitrust can serve as a hedge against inflation, in contrast to an annuity trust, where payments remain fixed no matter how rampant inflation becomes.

The trust income beneficiary must, under IRS rules, receive a payment of at least 5% of the value of the trust assets each year. There is no upper limit. But here again, practical considerations, such as the grantor's desire to make a gift to charity, and the charity's willingness to accept and manage the trust property, mandate that the percentage be reasonable. If it is excessive, it may consume all the trust property during the income beneficiary's period of payment.

In certain situations, the trust document can direct that the income beneficiary be given all the income from the trust:

- if the spouse of the grantor is the income beneficiary, or
- if the trust property consists of the grantor's residence or family farm.

The creator of a charitable remainder unitrust can, later on, transfer more property to the trust, but the power to make additional gifts must be expressly provided for in the original trust document. (IRS Reg. 1664-3(b).)

Here's an example of how a charitable remainder unitrust can provide income tax relief, reduce estate tax and provide other benefits:

Example: Felix, age 60, earns a very comfortable salary and owns assets worth $3 million. Much of his property consists of his home and stock that he bought years ago. The stock has appreciated enormously in value; it cost $400,000 and is now worth $1.6 million. It currently pays very little in dividends.

If Felix, himself, sells the stock and buys income-producing assets, he'll be obligated to pay capital gain tax of $336,000. Setting up a charitable remainder unitrust offers one way to avoid this tax and guarantee income later, when Felix retires. Felix establishes a charitable remainder trust with himself as the income beneficiary for life and his alma mater, his state's university, as the final beneficiary. Felix funds the trust with the stock.

For income tax purposes, his donation to the charity is the full market value of the stock, less the IRS deduction based on his retained interest, age and current interest rates.

The trustee of the charitable trust sells the stock and receives $1.6 million, which means a profit of $1.2 million. This profit is not taxed. The trustee reinvests this entire amount into a well-paying investment. The trust document requires income to be paid to Felix at 6% of the trust value annually for life. This figure will be $96,000 the first year; it will change each year as the value of trust assets changes.

So far, Felix has avoided paying capital gain tax while turning an asset that paid little income into one that pays him much more. But there is even more good news. Felix has also reduced his estate to a level where much less estate tax will be due at his death. Felix has given money to the school for its eventual use instead of giving it to Uncle Sam. And he has a guaranteed income for life.

If Felix lives for 20 years while receiving income from this trust, the trust should pay him at least $96,000 x 20, or $1.92 million. If the trustee invests the original $1.6 million wisely, that principal amount should also increase significantly in 20 years. If the principal increases, Felix will obviously receive more than $96,000 a year.

CHARITABLE REMAINDER UNITRUSTS AT A GLANCE

1. Grantor funds trust (with appreciated assets, if possible).
2. Grantor takes income tax deduction
3. Trustee converts all assets into income-producing assets. No capital gain tax due on profits of any sale.
4. The value of the trust property is redetermined annually.
5. Trustee pays percentage of revalued trust assets to income beneficiary annually as income.
6. At income beneficiary's death, trust assets go outright to charity. Value of these assets is not subject to estate tax.

3. Pooled Income Trusts

A popular type of charitable remainder trust is a pooled income trust, which allows people of more modest means to take advantage of charitable income tax deductions, donate to their favorite charity and receive an income for a set period. You don't set up your own pooled income trust, the charity does it. You simply donate money to the charity, and it pools your donation with other money it's been given, and manages all the money in one big trust. By law, the minimum amount you can give is $1,000.

Not every charity offers pooled income trusts, but most large ones do. If a pooled fund is available, the charity will surely be delighted to discuss it with you, and help set up the paperwork.

Pooled income trusts operate very much like mutual funds. The donor contributes money, bonds or stocks to the charity. (Highly appreciated stock is desirable, because, as we've discussed, the charity can sell it for its present market value and pay no capital gain tax.) The charity pools a number of individuals' donations, invests the money and pays interest to the donors according to its earnings. You can specify that your earnings be retained until you reach a certain age, such as retirement age of 65 or 70, with payments to start then. The charity receives what remains of your gift after your death. If invested wisely, chances are the charity's share may have appreciated in value significantly by them.

Gifts of tangible property to a pooled trust, from real estate to jewelry, are not permitted under federal law. This is not true for other types of charitable trusts.

In a pooled charitable trust, the charity is always the trustee—you have no option here. If you don't think that a charity will manage your gift well, that pooled income charitable trust is simply not for you.

Pooled income trusts can be attractive for many reasons. The charity does all of the work of setting up the trust and managing the assets. Also, unlike other charitable remainder trusts, you can easily add amounts to the trust after the initial contribution. So if you don't have a large portfolio or cash to donate at one time, you can still build a nice retirement income and at the same time benefit a good cause, by donating smaller amounts over years.

A deduction from your income tax is allowed every time you make a donation. The amount of the deduction is figured by using the IRS tables to value the charity's remainder interest. (See Section B1, above.)

Example: Yuki is a businesswoman in her 40s with a salary of $80,000 a year. She is not married and has no children. She wants to support her favorite museum and also plan for her retirement. Yuki contributes $10,000 to a charitable pooled fund managed by the museum and takes her income tax deduction, the exact amount of which is determined by the IRS tables. A year later she does the same thing.

She keeps this up for 20 years, adding more in high income years and less in years when she has unexpected expenses. By age 65, when she needs the income, her pooled shares, having been well-managed by the fund, are worth around $400,000. She will receive whatever income this amount generates.

Yuki has accomplished both of her goals—giving a substantial amount to charity and providing a retirement fund for herself.

CHARITABLE POOLED INCOME TRUSTS AT A GLANCE

1. Donor contributes assets to charity.
2. Donor takes income tax deduction.
3. Charity combines assets with other contributions in a fund.
4. Fund pays income to donor according to fund's income on all pooled gifts.
5. Donor can make additional gifts. If so, donor takes further income tax deductions.
6. Fund keeps paying donor for life on the donor's total contributions.
7. At donor's death, contributed assets go outright to the charity.

Checking out a pooled charitable trust. The pool must meet strict federal requirements in order for your contributions to be tax deductible. (IRC Sections 170(f)(2)(A), and 642(c)(5).) These include who can serve as trustees and how contributions are combined and invested. If you are dealing with a "brand name" charitable pool, you should be safe. If not, and your own investigations have not reassured you that the charitable pooled trust you're considering fully complies with federal law (and this may not be easy to determine), it is sensible to take all the information you can gather about the trust to a good tax advisor.

D. A Closer Look at Charitable Lead Trusts

A charitable lead trust works in reverse fashion from any form of charitable remainder trust. In a charitable lead trust, the charity initially receives a set amount of income from the trust for a set period, usually a number of years. If the charity's income from the trust property drops below the set level, the charity can invade the trust principal to pay itself the set amount. At the end of the set period, the trust principal goes to the final beneficiaries named by the grantor, usually a spouse or children.

Charitable lead trusts, which become operational during the grantor's life, are not currently popular with most estate planning experts. But when the final beneficiaries don't need their inheritance right away, a charitable lead trust created upon death of the grantor can occasionally be a satisfactory device for saving on estate tax, giving to charity and still (eventually) benefiting one's family or other beneficiaries.

Charitable lead trusts do not offer all the same tax advantages as charitable remainder trusts. But they do offer some of the same income tax advantages. For instance, if you donate appreciated property to a charitable lead trust, and the charity then sells it, no capital gain tax is assessed. Also, tax law allows you an income tax deduction of the amount that the charity is expected to receive, based on the IRS tables.

Charitable lead trusts that become operational while the grantor lives are used rarely, because they involve a significant income tax drawback: Income from the trust paid to the charity (during the set payment period) is taxed to the grantor, because the assets will revert back to him or his inheritors later. So the grantor must pay income tax on income the charity, not he, receives. Not a highly desirable state of affairs. Still, these types of trusts are occasionally used, mainly by the very wealthy. They can make sense if you have highly appreciated assets that you want to ultimately remain in the family, not be given to charity.

Example: Clark, a wealthy industrialist in his early 50s, wants to take advantage of every tax break he can find. He and his wife have many assets that will let them continue to live very well when they retire.

With the help of his lawyer, Clark creates a charitable lead trust, funded with real estate that he long ago paid $100,000 for and which is now worth $2 million. He chooses as the income beneficiary a research institute for the cure of Parkinson's disease and sets the income payments to the institute at 8% of the trust assets a year. At Clark's death, the trust assets are to go to his children.

The trustee sells the real estate and invests the proceeds in mutual stock funds. Clark avoids a large capital gain tax that would have been assessed if he personally sold the property, because the charity isn't taxed on the sale. Clark takes an immediate income tax deduction of the charity's projected income from these assets, based on the IRS tables that consider his life expectancy and interest rates. He knows he will have to pay tax on the income the charity obtains from these assets, but he hopes the gain he's achieved from avoiding capital gain tax will cancel out this drawback.

Even more important to him, Clark is able to leave the trust property to his children. Also, he feels satisfaction that he has contributed to the possible cure of a horrible disease.

It's impossible to say exactly how much income tax Clark will pay on what the trust earns during his life, because it depends on how long he lives and on income tax rates. Let's say Clark lives for 25 more years. If the trust earns 8% a year, that's $80,000. Income tax the first year would be $24,800. If the value of the trust keeps going up, the tax savings will be eaten away.

If a charitable lead trust becomes operational on the grantor's death, any negative income tax consequence to the donor is avoided. He won't be earning any more income. (Death solves that concern.) The purpose of the trust becomes the reduction of estate tax.

Naming a Child's Trust as the Final Beneficiary of a Charitable Lead Trust

When children or young adults are the final beneficiaries of a charitable lead trust, it can be a good idea to create a children's trust to receive the trust principal, in case the children are not old enough or responsible enough to handle the money when the charitable term ends. (Children's trusts are discussed in Chapter 6, Children, Section C.) If children are the final beneficiaries, one child may need more money than the others, so a "family pot" children's trust may be advisable. Professional help here is a must.

There are two basic types of charitable lead trusts:

- Unitrusts, where a set percentage of the trust's net worth is paid to the charity for a period of years. The actual amount paid can vary over the years, as the trust assets are reappraised each year.
- Annuity trusts, where the grantor provides that a set dollar amount is to be paid to the charity each year.

Charitable Lead Trusts at a Glance

1. Grantor funds trust, with appreciated assets if possible.
2. Grantor takes income tax deduction.
3. Trustee converts all trust assets into income-producing assets.
4. Income goes to charity for set period.
5. Grantor pays income tax on trust income paid to charity.
6. At grantor's death, all trust property, including appreciation, goes to beneficiaries.

Example: Rachel directs in her living trust that, upon her death, a charitable lead trust of $1 million be established for a period of 15 years. During those years, income payments of $80,000 annually will go to her favorite charity. At the end of the period, the remainder will go to her niece. The charity's interest in the trust is calculated by the IRS tables. In this case, it will probably be around $800,000. This $800,000 is deducted from the taxable value of Rachel's estate. If Rachel's property is worth over $3 million at her death, so that her estate is in the 55% estate tax bracket, her estate saves $440,000 in estate tax.

E. TYPES OF CHARITABLE TRUSTS: A COMPARISON

TYPES OF CHARITABLE TRUSTS				
	Charitable Remainder Unitrust	**Charitable Remainder Annuity Trust**	**Pooled Income Trust**	**Charitable Lead Trust**
Primary goals	Income tax and estate tax savings; hedge against inflation	Income tax and estate tax savings; fixed income for life	Income tax and estate tax savings; income (possibly for retirement)	Income tax and estate tax savings (though they can cause significant tax disadvantages); preservation of trust assets for final beneficiaries
Property you can transfer to trust	Money or tangible property	Money or tangible property	Money only	Money or tangible property
Transfer additional property later?	Yes	No	Yes	Yes, if permitted in original trust document
Income tax deduction available to you	Smaller than with annuity trust, because IRS values the charity's share as less	Larger than with unitrust, because IRS values the charity's share higher	Yes	The value of charity's income interest for set period
Trustee	Anyone you choose, including yourself or the charity	Anyone you choose, including yourself or the charity	The charity only	Anyone you choose, including yourself or the charity as trustee
Income beneficiary	You or anyone else you name	You or anyone else you name	You or anyone else you name	The charity
Final beneficiary	The charity	The charity	The charity	You or beneficiaries you name
Income paid to income beneficiary	Fixed percentage of trust assets each year	Fixed dollar amount each year, even if trust principal must be used	Interest earned from donor's contribution to the pool	Fixed dollar amount or percentage of trust assets, whichever you specify in trust document ■

21

Other Estate Tax-Saving Trusts

People with larger estates can use a number of different types of trusts to save on overall estate taxes. "Larger" here means individuals with estates over $600,000 or couples with a combined estate of $1.2 million. (This assumes that the couple used marital life estate trusts to preserve each spouse's $600,000 estate tax exemption. (See Chapter 18, Estate Tax-Saving Bypass Trusts, Section C.) The tax-saving trusts described in this chapter can be used by anyone, whether married, in an unmarried couple or single.

The trusts discussed in this chapter are complicated. You'll need a lawyer to prepare the trust documents.

A. Generation-Skipping Trusts ("GST")

A generation-skipping trust provides income to one generation of beneficiaries (called the middle or second generation) and then leaves the trust property outright to the next generation. The benefit of a generation-skipping trust is that up to $1 million will avoid estate tax when the second generation (usually your children) dies. In the right situation, these trusts can save a family a bundle on overall estate taxes.

Example: Alex, a grandparent, establishes a generation-skipping trust of $1 million. His children, the middle generation receive the income generated by the trust property while they are alive. They're called the income beneficiaries. When Alex's children die, no estate tax is assessed against the trust principal. The entire amount is turned over to his grandchildren, who are termed the final beneficiaries.

There are no estate tax savings when the grandparent dies. But this type of trust works to transfer up to $1 million tax-free because the middle generation (Alex's children) is never the legal owner of the trust property. That means that the property in the generation-skipping trust isn't subject to tax when the middle generation dies and the trust property is turned over to the grandchildren.

Use of a generation-skipping trust is not limited to your direct descendants. It can be used anytime you have beneficiaries in two subsequent generations and, of course, a sizable amount of money you're willing to tie up for a generation.

Example: Monroe, who has a lot of money, decides to leave $1 million to his niece and her three grandchildren in a generation-skipping trust. His niece, the "middle generation," receives trust income for her life. When she dies, the trust ends and the property is distributed equally among her three children.

This loophole has a limit, however: any money in this type of trust exceeding $1 million is subject to tax, called the "generation-skipping transfer tax" (GSTT), when the middle generation dies. Members of a couple can each transfer $1 million free of GSTT.

This section discusses some important aspects of generation-skipping trusts. But be warned—using these trusts is complicated, and we provide only an overview of the subject. If you decide a generation-skipping trust makes sense in your family, you absolutely need an expert who is knowledgeable in the field of generation-skipping transfers to prepare your trust.

Congress created the GSTT because it wanted to put an end to one of the favorite estate-tax loopholes used by the very rich. (See "One Way the Rich Stayed Rich," below.) Every dollar over $1 million left in a generation-skipping trust is subject to the highest existing estate tax rate at the time the GSTT tax is applied, when the middle generation dies.[1] Currently this rate is 55%. This 55% GSTT tax is in addition to whatever estate tax was paid on the trust property at the death of the original grantor (the older generation).

Trusts for "non-lineal" descendants. Fussy actuarial rules apply if you create a trust to benefit your "non-lineal" descendants (that is, anyone except children, grandchildren and so on), to determine which generation they are in. Basically, the rules provide that a "generation" occurs every 25 years, except the "child" generation starts when a beneficiary is over $12^1/2$ years younger than the grantor.

ONE WAY THE RICH STAYED RICH

Before the adoption of the generation-skipping transfer tax, when Congress put a $1 million limit on the right to pass money to one's grandchildren free of estate tax, people with many, many millions (even billions) of dollars would leave the bulk, or even all, of their property in generation-skipping trusts. Estate taxes were, of course, due when the trust grantor died, but no taxes at all would be assessed when the middle generation died. These types of trusts enabled the very wealthy to escape all estate tax in every other generation. And the income from a trust of many millions normally proved quite sufficient for the middle generation to live an affluent lifestyle. Since Congress created the GSTT in the 1980s, there is no tax advantage in creating a generation-skipping trust worth more than $1 million.

[1]The tax is defined in IRC Section 2611, which refers to several other IRC sections.

1. Is a Generation-Skipping Trust for You?

You must have a substantial estate—usually at least a couple of million (individually)—before using a generation-skipping trust makes sense. Property in a generation-skipping trust cannot be spent for a surviving spouse, and the middle generation cannot have unrestricted use of it. So you want to be sure that your spouse and children will be well provided for at your death before you create a generation-skipping trust that will benefit the second generation down, usually your grandchildren.

Example: Abigail is a widow with two children and four grandchildren. Each of her children is established in a successful career and is quite prosperous. Abigail has an estate of $2.5 million. She decides to leave $750,000 outright to each of her children and create a generation-skipping trust for the remaining $1 million. This trust will become operational on Abigail's death. The trust will pay all income to Abigail's children, equally, during their lifetimes. When one child dies, all trust income will go to the surviving child. When the surviving child dies, the trust assets will be divided equally among Abigail's grandchildren, with no additional estate tax due.

a. Will Your Spouse Need Your Property?

No money from a generation-skipping trust, either income or principal, can be paid to a surviving spouse. So these trusts are only sensible if your spouse is already fully provided for—from his own property, other property you leave for his benefit, or both. Even if your spouse were to suffer some economic disaster and lose all his money after your death, he would have no right to receive any income, let alone principal, of the generation-skipping trust. If the income or limited rights to principal from the marital life estate trust weren't sufficient for her needs, he would be in trouble.

Example: Roberta and Byron own shared property worth $3.2 million. Neither has any separately-owned property. Thus, each one's estate is worth $1.6 million, half the total. Each spouse creates the same estate plan: $600,000 is left in a marital life estate trust, with the surviving spouse having maximum powers to spend trust principal for health care or other needs. Each spouse feels that with their own $1.6 million, and the income generated by it, as well as possible use of principal in the marital life estate trust, they are sufficiently protected economically. So each spouse leaves $1 million in a generation-skipping trust for their children and grandchildren. Each directs that any estate tax due on their death be paid from the amount directed to the generation-skipping trust. Since each's estate totals $1.6 million, federal estate tax of $345,800 will be due when that spouse dies. So the amount actually going into the generation-skipping trust will be $654,200—well under the $1 million GSTT exempt amount.

b. Will Your Children Need Your Property?

If you establish a generation-skipping trust, your children (the second generation) will not have outright ownership of any of the trust property (principal) except under limited circumstances. They can receive only trust income or, if expressly allowed by the trust document, amounts from trust principal deemed necessary by the trustee for their "health, education or maintenance." (This is the IRS "objective" standard for invasion of trust principal by life beneficiaries. See Chapter 18, Bypass Trusts, Section B.)

What this amounts to is that, for most people, a generation-skipping trust makes sense only if you're sure your children (the middle generation) will be financially comfortable without the assets in the trust. If this isn't the case, you'll probably want to simply leave them the property outright. Particularly if members of the middle generation are reasonably young and may survive you by decades, you may not feel secure tying up a lot of money in such a way that they can reach it only in limited circumstances.

2. Creating Two Generation-Skipping Trusts

Each member of a couple (married or not) can transfer $1 million in a generation-skipping trust free of GSTT. Thus, a wealthy couple can create two generation-skipping trusts for their children and grandchildren, placing a total of $2 million in the trusts. Each spouse creates a separate trust.

In second or subsequent marriages, each spouse may want to create a generation-skipping trust for her or his own children from a prior marriage, and for their children's children.

3. How the GSTT Works

Any gift to a beneficiary two generations down, no matter how it is made, is subject to the GSTT. As we've said, the GSTT tax rate is the highest rate on the federal estate tax scale, currently 55%.

If the amount in the original trust or gift exceeds $1 million, the GSTT applies when any property or money is actually distributed to the third generation beneficiary.

a. Transfers Subject to the GSTT

This chapter focuses on generation-skipping trusts, where the final beneficiaries receive their property only after the middle generation dies, and the GSTT, if applicable, is assessed then. But there are also two other types of transfers subject to the GSTT. If you consult an expert about leaving substantial amounts of property to your grandchildren, you can explore whether either of these other types of transfers could be desirable in your situation.

The two other types of generation-skipping transfers are:

- A "direct skip" is an outright gift to someone two (or more) generations down. For instance, if you leave $2 million outright to a grandchild, $1 million of that gift is exempt from the GSTT. The other $1 million is taxed at 55%. Also, the entire $2 million is included in your taxable estate, and so is subject to estate tax at your death. So the property is taxed twice.
- A "taxable distribution" is a payment from the trust to someone two generations down, while the middle generation is still alive. If a generation-skipping trust directs or permits payment to a beneficiary two generations removed from the grantor, any such payments will be taxed under the GSTT, if the amount in the trust originally exceeded $1 million.

b. How and When the GSTT Is Assessed

If you use a generation-skipping trust, the generation-skipping transfer tax will be due when the income (middle generation) beneficiary dies and the trust property goes to the final beneficiaries. In tax lingo, this event is called a "taxable termination."

However, whether or not a generation-skipping trust is subject to the GSTT is determined when the grantor dies—that is, when the trust becomes operational—not when the middle generation dies. If the amount in the trust at the time the grantor dies is less than $1 million, no GSTT will apply when the trust assets are eventually distributed to the grandchildren, even if the worth of the those trust assets has increased significantly by that time.

Example: Frank is a widower with two children and four grandchildren. His total estate is worth $1.9 million. He sets up a generation-skipping trust of $1 million to take effect at his death. This $1 million is included in Frank's taxable estate when he dies. Frank has directed that all estate tax due on his death be paid from his other assets, not from property in the generation-skipping trust. So the full $1 million goes into the trust. The trust will pay the income to his children for their lifetimes. When they die, the principal goes to the grandchildren. When the children die, the property in the trust is worth $3.5 million. No GSTT is assessed, because the amount in the trust when Frank died did not exceed $1 million.

The amount of money in the trust, for GSTT purposes, is determined after any estate tax assessed on, and payable from, the amount left in trust has actually been paid.

Example: Abigail funds her generation-skipping trust with her entire estate of $1.5 million. The income will go to her children for their lives, and when they die the assets will go to her grandchildren. Federal estate tax of $363,000 (on her $1.5 million) will be due at Abigail's death. So the amount of her property left to go into the generation-skipping trust will be $1,137,000. The amount over the GSTT $1 million exemption, $137,000, will be subject to the GSTT when all Abigail's children have died.

Abigail's children are never the legal owners of the trust property, so none of it is included in their taxable estates when they die. By the time they die, the value of the property in the trust has risen to $2.2 million. No GSTT is assessed on this amount. Rather, when the grandchildren receive the trust property, the GSTT is assessed on $137,000, the amount by which the original trust exceeded $1 million. The tax rate is 55%, so the tax paid is $75,350.

Determining in advance the exact tax rate that will be applied to property placed in a generation-skipping trust is not easy, especially when some of this property will be used to pay some portion of the grantor's estate tax. To really understand how this works means deciphering tax concepts like "inclusion ratios" and "applicable fractions." (The intrepid may wish to study IRC. Sections 2601, 2602.) A certified public accountant (CPA) or lawyer with estate tax experience is a big help here.

4. Options With Generation-Skipping Trusts

You have some flexibility when you set up a generation-skipping trust. For example, under some trusts, trust income can be made available to the grandchildren—for example, for their education—while their parents (the middle, income generation) are still alive.

In addition, other estate planing devices can be useful in combination with a generation-skipping trust. Most common is use of a bypass trust, usually a marital life estate trust, with a generation-skipping trust. (See Chapter 18, Bypass Trusts, Section C.) Another of these is a disclaimer. (See Chapter 22, Disclaimers.) Combining generation-skipping trusts with other trusts is discussed in Chapter 25, Combining Ongoing Trusts, Section C.

B. Irrevocable Life Insurance Trusts

After your death, all the insurance proceeds paid from a policy you owned are included in your taxable estate. (See Chapter 12, Life Insurance.) If the payout is large, it may easily push the value of your estate past the $600,000 federal estate tax threshold. So finding a way to remove life insurance proceeds from your taxable estate can save your heirs a bundle in estate tax if you have a taxable estate exceeding $600,000—or you will when the life insurance payoff is included.

One way to remove life insurance proceeds from your estate is to use an irrevocable life insurance trust. This trust is a legal entity you create while you are alive. It becomes the owner of life insurance you previously owned as an individual. Because the policy is owned by this legally independent trust, the insurance proceeds from this policy are not included in your taxable estate. Normally, the beneficiaries of the policy remain the same as they were before you set up the trust, which is simply a legal vehicle to remove ownership of the policy from your estate.

Irrevocable life insurance trusts aren't for everyone, or even most people. Indeed, simply transferring the policy by a gift is normally a better approach, if there's someone you trust to give the policy to. (See Chapter 12, Section C, for a discussion of the advantages and drawbacks of giving away your life insurance policy.) Life insurance trusts are for those who don't want the risks involved in giving their policy outright to another person. For instance, when the beneficiary of the life insurance isn't yet mature enough to be trusted with ownership, an irrevocable life insurance trust can be very desirable.

If you want to create or explore using a life insurance trust, see an experienced lawyer before you trundle off to your insurance company. In addition to the complexities of any irrevocable trust, there are also problems unique to a life insurance trust.

1. IRS Requirements

There are strict IRS requirements governing irrevocable life insurance trusts. To gain the estate tax savings this type of trust can offer, you must conform to these rules.

a. The Trust Must Be Irrevocable

The life insurance trust must be absolutely irrevocable. If you retain any right to revoke or amend the trust, or affect the insurance policy in any way (such as naming a new beneficiary), the IRS will consider you to be the legal owner of the policy. That means the proceeds will be included in your taxable estate.

b. The Trustee Must Be Independent

There must be an "independent" trustee for the trust. You cannot be the trustee, nor can any members of your immediate family. "Immediate family" means directly in your family line—your spouse, children, grandchildren or parents. Neither can a beneficiary of the trust serve as trustee. You must name an independent adult who doesn't stand to benefit from the insurance policy, or an institution, to serve as trustee. However, there are no rules against your being very close to the trustee, or choosing one you are sure will act in your best interests.

Because you create the trust document that establishes the trustee's powers, you have more control over an independent trustee than you would over someone to whom you gave an insurance policy outright.

Example: Pilar is the divorced mother of two children, in their 20s, whom she has named as beneficiaries of her universal life insurance policy. It will pay $300,000 at her death. In addition to the insurance policy, Pilar has an estate of $500,000. She wants to remove the proceeds of the policy from her estate. If she doesn't, her estate will be subject to federal estate tax, which, of course, begins for estates over $600,000.

But Pilar has a problem. Although she loves her kids dearly, neither child is sensible with money, and she doesn't trust them enough to give her policy to them outright. She fears they might fail to make the premium payments, or possibly even cash in the policy in a time of financial desperation. She wants to be sure the policy is kept in force until her death, so that all the proceeds—far more than the cash-in value of the policy—will be distributed to her children on her death. And even if she felt comfortable giving away the policy to her children, she might have to make subsequent premium payments herself. If she did this, the IRS would regard her as the legal owner of the policy, and so include all the proceeds in her taxable estate. (See Chapter 12, Life Insurance, Section C.)

Pilar decides to name her sister, Julianna, the person she's closest to, to be the trustee of an irrevocable life insurance trust for the policy. As an independent trustee, Julianna has full power over the life insurance policy.

If Julianna cashed the policy in, she would receive no benefit. A trustee cannot legally profit from managing trust property (that's called a "conflict of interest" or "self-dealing"—prohibited acts for a trustee). Also, even if she managed illegally to cash in the policy, she wouldn't receive the cash surrender value herself; it's the trust, not herself personally, that owns the property. The cash-in money would remain in the trust.

c. The Trust Must Exist for at Least Three Years Before Your Death

You must establish the trust at least three years before your death. If the trust has not existed for at least three years when you die, the trust is disregarded for estate tax purposes, and the insurance proceeds are included in your taxable estate.

This three-year rule is obviously crucial. It means that if you want to establish an irrevocable life insurance trust, you should do so promptly. It would clearly be unfortunate for you to create an irrevocable life insurance trust and die before the end of the three-year period, negating all estate tax savings the trust offered.

The reason for this three-year rule is that the estate tax savings offered by an irrevocable life insurance trust (or any transfer of life insurance ownership) can be so substantial that the IRS wants to prohibit last-minute transfers of life insurance, in anticipation of death. (Three years seems like a pretty long "last minute.") But sensible or not, the rule exists. If you want to create an irrevocable life insurance trust, do it now. There are no benefits from waiting.

2. Paying Insurance Policy Premiums

One major concern when creating an irrevocable life insurance trust is how future premium payments to the insurance company will be made. If you set up the trust, you cannot directly make the payments, or the IRS will consider you to have retained some control or interest in the policy. This means, as we've warned before, that all the proceeds payable on your death will be included in your taxable estate.

At least two payment options are available to you. First, you can give money to the beneficiaries each year so that they can make the payments themselves. Of course, you'll have to trust the beneficiaries to spend that cash on policy premiums. Second, you can include what are called "Crummey" trust provisions (so named because someone named Crummey was the first to have this type of trust validated) in your irrevocable life insurance trust.

Here's how Crummey trust provisions work. The trust document provides that each year, each trust beneficiary has the right to receive up to $10,000 from the trust property ($10,000 is the maximum that can be given to a beneficiary free of gift tax). Usually, the beneficiaries have a deadline, say January 15, to obtain their money for the year.

Each year, you give up to $10,000 per person to the trust. Now things get tricky. Each year the beneficiaries decline to accept this amount of money. By doing this, the gift is converted from a "future interest" (not eligible for the annual $10,000 gift tax exemption) into a gift of a "present interest"—which means it qualifies for the $10,000 annual gift tax exclusion. (This distinction is discussed in Chapter 16, Gifts and Gift Taxes, Section C.) The trustee uses this declined money to pay that year's insurance premium. Any balance left over after the year's premiums have been paid is saved in the trust for future premium payments.

If neither of these methods provides enough cash to pay the yearly insurance premium, what can you, the grantor, do? Perhaps you could purchase a single-premium policy, so there's no worry about future payments. Another approach is simply to give money to the trust and be assessed gift tax on the gift.

3. When Circumstances Change

Sometimes tricky personal concerns arise preparing or living with an irrevocable life insurance trust. For example:

- What happens if you get married, divorced or you have a child after setting up an irrevocable trust? Legally, it's up to the trustee to decide who the beneficiaries of the policy should be. Of course, a trustee who cares for you will probably revise the insurance beneficiaries as you want. For example, the trustee could add your new child as a beneficiary of the life insurance policy.
- Suppose you get divorced, and your ex-spouse is one of the beneficiaries of the life insurance policy and also of Crummey trust provisions you created to pay the premiums? Here's where matters can get very touchy. If the trustee simply removes the ex-spouse as a beneficiary of the policy, the ex-spouse could claim the trustee is not really "independent." With personal complexities like these, you must see a lawyer.

C. Grantor-Retained Interest Trusts: GRATs, GRUTs and GRITs

Names to the contrary, this section is not about lifting weights or southern cooking. Here we discuss three types of irrevocable estate tax-saving trusts. Their common feature is that you retain either income from trust property, or use of that property, for a period of years. Then the trust ends, and the property goes to the final beneficiaries you've named. These types of trusts are called:

- Grantor-Retained Annuity Trusts (GRATs)
- Grantor-Retained Unitrusts (GRUTs), and
- Grantor-Retained Income Trusts (GRITs).

The primary purpose of these irrevocable trusts is to save on gift and estate taxes. Anyone considering one of these trusts must have enough wealth to feel comfortable giving away a substantial hunk of property. If you believe you'll want or need full control over all your property until you die, these trusts are not for you. To achieve the tax savings, you must follow several steps:

- First, you place property in one of these trusts, but you also retain some interest in that property for a set period. The retained interest can be income generated from the trust property, or the right to use that property—such as living in a trust-owned house. You name final beneficiaries to receive the trust property at the end of the set period.
- By creating this trust, you've made a gift of the property that will eventually be given to the final beneficiaries. But because you have retained an interest in the trust property, the value of the gift, for gift tax purposes, is reduced, and is less than the property's market value.
- If you survive the set period, the property is transferred outright to the final beneficiaries. No new taxes are assessed then. The only taxes ever assessed on this transaction were the gift taxes when the property was first placed in the trust. And because you no longer own the property, the entire amount cannot be included in your taxable estate on your death.

As you'll see, the trick here is for you to outlive the set time, so that the trust property is turned over to the final beneficiaries during your lifetime. If you don't, all the property will be included in your estate, for estate tax purposes—and your planning will be wasted. Any gift tax previously assessed against you will be credited to any estate tax due on your death.

Anyone, whether married or single, can use a grantor-retained interest trust. Because estate tax breaks for single people are few and far between, a grantor-retained interest trust can be an attractive tax-avoidance technique for a wealthy single person.

Here's a rough example to show you how these trusts work. We'll get into the legal details soon enough.

Example: Phyllis, age 65, creates a GRAT (that's a grantor-retained annuity trust). She funds it with her house, worth $100,000, and retains the right to live in the house for 15 years. She names her daughter as the final beneficiary. The value of the gift (her house) to the trust is determined when she creates the trust. Phyllis outlives the 15-year period she set. When she becomes 80, the house, now worth $225,000, is legally turned over to her daughter. Because gift tax was assessed on the $100,000 value of the house at the time the trust was created, Phyllis has avoided paying gift tax on $125,000. Moreover, she has removed the house from her taxable estate, for the obvious reason that she's no longer the owner of it.

As you've probably already suspected, this trust has potential risks. When she turns 80, Phyllis will no longer own her house. Legally, she must pay her daughter reasonable rent. Of course, her daughter could forgive the rent as it becomes due, making a gift of the rent to her mother. If the rent totals more than $10,000 in a year, the daughter will have to file a gift tax return. (See Chapter 16, Gifts and Gift Taxes, Sections C and E.) Worse, her daughter could decide to sell the house and Phyllis would have no recourse. And, as we discuss below, if Phyllis does not survive the time period she set in the trust document, the whole game collapses, and nothing is achieved, taxwise.

1. Overview of GRATs, GRUTs and GRITs

GRATs, GRUTs and GRITs vary in some important aspects—such as how payment to the grantor is determined—but all have much in common. These trusts can enable you to make a gift to people you love, save on gift taxes and save again on estate taxes. A good deal.

To create this type of trust, you make a gift to the trust, naming yourself as the beneficiary of a specific retained interest in the trust property for a set period. You also name final beneficiaries to receive the trust property when this period ends. You can be, and usually are, the initial trustee of your trust.

Once established, the trust is irrevocable—you can't change your mind and take back any property from the trust. No matter how much you may need that property, it can never again be yours outright.

At the end of the set period of your retained interest in the trust property, or at your death—whichever is first—that property goes to the final beneficiaries of the trust.

Creating a grantor-retained interest trust involves risk. For estate tax purposes, you in effect make a bet that you will outlive the set period. If you survive this set period (set by you in the trust document), the remaining value of the trust property will not be counted in your taxable estate. If you don't, the trust assets, complete with all appreciation in value, are included in your taxable estate—you gain nothing, estate tax-wise, and the money and time spent drafting the trust and administering it will have been wasted. Your estate will, however, get credit for any gift tax paid when the trust was created.

For gift tax purposes, the value of the gift you make to the trust is determined when the trust is established. This value never changes. You hope that while you have a retained interest in the trust property, the value of that property will increase significantly. If you outlive the time period, and the property is turned over to the final beneficiaries before your death, this increase in value will never be subject to gift tax or estate tax.

For gift tax purposes, the value of your gift to the final beneficiaries is lower than the actual market value (less any encumbrances) of the property at the time the trust was created. This is because you retained an interest in the gift, such as receiving income from the trust, for the set period. To determine the gift tax value of your gift, the value of your retained interest is subtracted from the total net value of the property at the time the trust is created. So gift tax is assessed on the value of the gift to the final beneficiaries, according to complex IRS tables. The annual $10,000 exclusion from gift tax is not available because the gift is not one for present use by any beneficiary but rather for use in the future. However, when you make your gift to the irrevocable trust, no gift tax must actually be paid, unless you have already used up your personal $600,000 estate tax exemption by previous gifts. (See Chapter 16, Gifts and Gift Taxes, Section A.)

2. Grantor-Retained Annuity Trusts (GRATs)

To establish a GRAT, you transfer some valuable asset, from cash to real estate to stocks to any property with significant value, to the trust. Under the terms of the trust document, the trustee (usually yourself) pays you, from the trust, an annual fixed sum (an annuity) for a set term of years. At the end of this term, the remaining trust assets go to the final beneficiary, perhaps your child, as the trust document directs. (IRC Section 2702.)

The benefit of a GRAT results from the fact that the IRS values the gift to the final beneficiaries only when the trust is established, not when the remaining trust property is later distributed, as long as you outlive the set term period. Your retained interest greatly reduces the value of the gift for gift tax purposes, even though the final beneficiary will normally receive (at a minimum) the full amount given.

Example: Hattie, a widow 60 years old, has assets worth $2 million. She sets up a GRAT with $1 million. The trust will last for 15 years and will pay Hattie $40,000 a year during the term. At the end of the term, or when Hattie dies, whichever happens first, the remaining trust assets will go equally to her three children. The value of the gift to the trust for gift tax purposes is set by an IRS formula that considers Hattie's life expectancy, the amount in the trust ($1 million) and subtracts Hattie's annuity interest ($40,000 times 15 years, or $600,000).

After subtracting the $600,000 value of Hattie's retained interest, the gift is worth $400,000 when given. But now the IRS tables take into account Hattie's age and life expectancy and the interest rates when the trust is created. As a result, the value of the gift for gift tax purposes will be less than $400,000.

The IRS tables used to determine the gift tax value of a gift to a GRAT are nearly impenetrable to all but real experts. Rather than bore, and quite possibly confuse, you with a detailed explanation of how they work, we'll simply say they are one big reason you must see an expert if you want to set up one of these trusts.

GRATs AT A GLANCE

1. You create and fund the trust, establishing the dollar amount of the annuity you will receive each year for the set period.
2. The value of gift for gift tax purposes is determined when you fund the trust.
3. The trustee pays you an annuity annually.
4. When the annuity term ends, trust assets go to the final beneficiary.

Now let's continue the above example, to see in more depth how a GRAT works.

Example: The value of the gift to Hattie's children, for gift tax purposes, is determined at the time the trust is created. If Hattie has not used any of her gift and estate tax exemption by making other taxable gifts, no tax payment will actually be due at that time, because the gift is valued under $600,000. Instead, the value of the gift is deducted from Hattie's $600,000 exemption.

Over time, the assets in the trust may well appreciate in value. This increase in value is not subject to tax. So, the real gift to her children may well actually be more than the taxable value of the gift.

Suppose Hattie's $1 million trust yields an actual annual return of 7%. That means income of $70,000 for the trust during the first year. After Hattie receives her $40,000 annuity, the extra $30,000 of income increases the amount of money in the trust. If this goes on year after year, with the trust assets increasing in worth, the same return of 7% obviously yields more than $70,000 annually. For instance, the second year the return will be 7% of $1,030,000. And so it goes. The $1 million not only stays intact for the children, but gradually increases.

The more benefit you retain from the trust property, the less the property is worth for gift tax purposes. It follows then that the younger you are, and the longer the term during which you will benefit from the gift, the lower the taxable value of the gift. Likewise, the higher the annuity payments to you, the lower the taxable value of the gift.

Example: Hattie, our grantor above, funds her GRAT with $1 million, retaining an annuity of $40,000 annually. But this GRAT is only for a period of ten years, rather than 15.

Now her total benefit is $40,000 x 10, or $400,000, rather than $600,000 for the 15-year period. The gift tax value of the gift to the final beneficiary increases to closer to $600,000. (As we've said, the exact figure will be different, because of the IRS calculation tables.) That means a higher gift tax assessment.

If the value of the gift to the final beneficiaries exceeds $600,000, you will have to pay gift tax when the trust is funded.

Example: Max places $1 million in a GRAT and reserves a $20,000 annuity for himself for ten years. This results in a total benefit to him of $200,000 and a gift (to the final beneficiary) worth roughly $800,000. (Again, the IRS tables must be used to determine the precise taxable value of the gift.) Because the value of the gift exceeds Max's $600,000 estate tax exemption, Max will have to pay gift tax on the roughly $200,000 over the exempt amount when the trust is funded.

a. Increasing the Tax Savings From a GRAT

A GRAT is an irrevocable trust, which normally means it functions as a separate taxable entity. It can be constructed, however, in such a way that all income and capital gain from the trust are taxed to the grantor. This is called making the GRAT a "grantor trust." This way, more money is given to the future final beneficiaries.

A GRAT set up as a grantor trust can yield another potentially valuable tax saving, if assets contributed to the trust go up substantially in value. Normally, if trust assets appreciate, the final beneficiaries of the GRAT would have to pay capital gain tax on the appreciation. To grasp what this means, a little review of cost basis rules is in order. (Basic rules are covered in more detail in Chapter 15, Estate Taxes, Section A5.)

When you make a gift of property (land, stocks, jewelry or whatever) to someone other than a spouse during your life, the recipient receives and owns the property with your original cost basis. For example, if you give your child a house that you paid $40,000 for and is now worth $200,000, the child's tax basis will be $40,000. If the child then sells the home for $200,000, he will owe capital gain tax on $160,000. In contrast, if the child inherited your house at your death, his cost basis would automatically increase to the actual market value as of the date of your death. If he sold it for that amount, no capital gain tax would be owed. This is why many people, especially elderly people, sensibly postpone making outright gifts of appreciated property until their death.

Fortunately, if you use a GRAT, the final beneficiaries don't have to receive the gift at your original basis. Instead, you can legally change the basis of low-basis property in a GRAT, so that when the final beneficiaries receive the property, their cost basis is equal to the current market value of that property. The beneficiaries can sell the property when they receive it, without any capital gain tax being assessed. You can accomplish this bit of tax code magic by purchasing low-basis assets from the trust just before the set term ends, and replacing them with recently purchased assets.

Example: Joanne funds her GRAT with a combination of cash and stocks and makes it a grantor trust. This means she personally, not the trust, pays the tax on any income the trust makes, and also pays any capital gain tax if the trust sells any stock for a profit. Just before her set (annuity) term ends, she purchases all stock in the trust that has appreciated in value since it was placed in the trust. She replaces the stock with stocks of similar market value, recently purchased. When her annuity term ends, the children receive stock which has a basis at, or close to, its current market value, not stock with a low cost basis. If they'd received low-cost basis stocks, this would result in a big capital gain tax when they eventually sold the stock.

3. Grantor-Retained Unitrusts (GRUTs)

Don't you just love the jargon? Fortunately, you can comprehend it, contrary to what some high-priced tax lawyers would like you to believe. A grantor-retained unitrust, or GRUT, is very similar to a GRAT, except for one important difference: The income payment to you (the grantor) is not a fixed amount annually. Instead, the amount is equal to a percentage of the value of the trust assets for that particular year. In that case, the annual payments you receive would also get larger.

Each year, the trust must be revalued so it pays you the percentage of the new current value of its assets. Assuming a decent economy, in a well-managed trust the income, as well as the worth of the assets themselves, should gradually increase over the years.

If the set percentage is larger than the trust's earnings—for example, you're entitled to 8% of the trust's net worth, but the trust property earned only 5% this year—the rest comes out of the principal. The reverse is also true. Any trust income above the percentage set for you is added to the trust assets.

Just as with a GRAT, the gift tax value of the gift to the final beneficiary is established when the trust is created.

Because your annual payment is based on the value of the trust property, a GRUT can give you some hedge against inflation. For example, say you have $1 million in a GRUT and get 7% of the value of the trust assets per year. If suddenly there's 20% annual inflation, the dollar value of the trust assets will, presumably, also increase by roughly 20%, to $1.2 million. Obviously, 7% of $1.2 million is a higher number than 7% of $1 million. But all you are really doing is keeping up with inflation. In real dollar terms, you receive the same amount, although you receive more (inflated) dollars. (If the trust assets drop to a worth of $800,000, you receive less money.) No such hedge against inflation is available to grantors of a GRAT. They receive a set dollar amount every year, period.

Example: Ravi, aged 60, has an estate worth $900,000. He creates a GRUT of $300,000 that will last for ten years. Then the trust assets go to his friend Monica. The trust specifies that during the ten-year period, Ravi will receive, annually, 8% of the trust's net worth.

The first year, the trust pays out $24,000 to Ravi—8% of $300,000. If Ravi outlives the ten-year period, Monica will likely receive more than $300,000, and surely far more than the value the IRS assigned the gift Monica received when the trust was created. In addition, Ravi will have removed the $300,000 from his taxable estate.

Like a GRAT, the taxable value of the gift to the final beneficiary, for gift tax purposes, depends on an IRS formula. The formula considers how much you can expect to receive, your age and how long the trust is supposed to last. The older you are, the more valuable the gift; the longer the term of the trust, the lower the gift value.

GRUTs at a Glance

1. You create and fund the trust, establishing the percentage return you will get each year for however many years you want the trust to last.
2. The value of the gift, for gift tax purposes, is determined when you fund the trust.
3. Trustee pays you the established percentage of assets.
4. Trust assets are appraised annually.
5. Trustee pays you a percentage of the trust assets' worth annually.
6. When the term ends, the trust is terminated and trust assets go to the final beneficiary.

4. Drawbacks of GRATs and GRUTs

The potential benefits of a GRUT or GRAT are rarely worth the risks involved unless you are very wealthy. If you have $10 million, putting $2 million in a GRUT or GRAT makes more sense than putting $500,000 in one if you have $2 million. Also, an expert must set up the trust, which is complicated and expensive.

There can be other drawbacks to use of a GRAT or GRUT. Whether they are likely to affect you depends on your family and tax situation. You should be aware of these drawbacks and evaluate how they could affect you and your beneficiaries before you create one of these trusts.

a. You Lose Control Over Trust Assets

As we've already stressed, once a GRAT or GRUT is established and operational, you lose legal ownership of the trust property. You can't later on turn around and decide that the income you receive from the trust isn't enough, and insist on higher payments. Nor can you get the trust assets turned back to you personally. Further, you cannot add to, or subtract from, the trust principal. Under the IRS rules, the amount put in the trust must stay there, period. Practically speaking, this means that if you or someone in your family suffers a financial disaster, the trust property isn't available to help out.

Further, if you do outlive the set term, you lose all benefit from the trust assets because they go to the final beneficiary at the end of the set term. Suppose you live for another ten years after the trust ends. You may well have become accustomed to the payments from the trust—or worse, may need them for expenses, such as medical costs. But anything you receive from the trust property (after the trust ends) will have to be a gift to you from the final beneficiaries—if they choose to make it. Also, a beneficiary who gives you more than $10,000 will have federal gift tax assessed on the amount over $10,000.

b. Estate Tax Savings Are Not Guaranteed

Usually the biggest concern involved in deciding whether to use a GRAT or GRUT is the possibility that you won't outlive the period you've set to receive income from the trust. If you die before the set period has ended, all the trust property is legally part of your estate. All your possible estate tax savings are lost.

If you are married, you can plan to defer taxes in such circumstances by having the trust assets go to you spouse. All property left to your spouse can pass estate tax-free under the marital deduction. If the surviving spouse is young and healthy, that spouse can make or revise her own estate plan to try to soften the estate tax blow when she dies.

But if the surviving spouse is elderly or in poor health and may not live long (thus triggering a larger estate tax), or if you are single, your untimely death and the resulting addition of the trust property to your estate could mean higher estate taxes. In hindsight, another form of estate plan, such as a program of direct gift-giving, would have been preferable.

c. The Final Beneficiary May Have to Pay Capital Gain Tax

Stocks and bonds, as well as other property, are often used to fund GRATs and GRUTs. Over time, these assets are likely to go up in value. If they do, and unless you buy them back from the trust (usually near the end of the set term; see Section B2a, above), the cost basis of this property when the final beneficiaries receive it will be lower than its market value. The difference may be substantial. If it is, the final beneficiaries will have to pay a hefty capital gain tax if they sell the property.

Example: Mona funds a 15-year GRAT with stock currently worth $200,000 that she bought for $100,000. At the end of the term, the stock will go to her friend Kim. During the 15-year period, the value of the stock climbs to over $400,000. Mona cannot afford to repurchase the stock before the term ends because she doesn't have a spare $400,000. At the end of the 15-year period, Kim receives the stock, now worth $420,000. Her cost basis in the property is $100,000, Mona's original basis. If she promptly sells the stock, she will owe capital gain tax on $320,000. (Of course, Mona's heirs get an estate tax break, because she has removed from her estate an asset that would be valued at $420,000 on her death.)

If the final beneficiary must pay capital gain tax, this of course reduces the real value of the gift. This loss must be balanced against any estate tax savings your inheritors gain because the property is removed from your taxable estate. By contrast, if you choose to retain ownership of the property until death and not create a GRAT or GRUT, the property's basis will be stepped up to its market value as of your death. In that case, if your inheritors promptly sell the property, no capital gain tax will be assessed.

Example: Mona simply leaves her stock to Kim, using a living trust. When she dies, the stock is worth $420,000. Kim's cost basis for the stock will be the full $420,000. If she promptly sells the stock for $420,000, she has obtained no taxable profit on the sale, so she will not owe any capital gain tax.

5. Grantor-Retained Income Trusts (GRITs)

If you set up this type of trust, you receive *all* income from the trust assets for a set period. The assets go to the final beneficiary when you die or the term ends. GRITs were enormously popular before 1990, when Congress took away any tax savings if the trust assets eventually benefit your family. "Family" includes your spouse, lineal descendants, ancestors, siblings and spouses of any members named above.

The law left one exception. The one remaining form of GRIT that can save on taxes and be used for family members is called a "residence GRIT."

a. Qualified Residence GRITs

You may still sensibly use a GRIT that will ultimately benefit family members, if it is funded only with your personal residence and nothing else. (IRC Section 2702.) This personal residence may be either your primary residence or a vacation home. (If you have both, and want to place both in GRITs, you will need two separate trusts, one for each house.) If the vacation home is sometimes rented by others, to qualify for a GRIT, you must actually use it each year for the greater of 14 days, or 10% of the time it is rented—that is, if it is rented for 180 days a year, you must personally use it for at least 18 days, 10% of 180 days.

Here's how the residence GRIT works. You put your residence into a trust for a set period, usually about ten years. Your retained "income interest" during the term is the right to occupy the residence. At the end of the set period, the property goes to the final beneficiary you named in the original trust document.

A couple who own a home in shared ownership must create two residence GRITs, one for each person's share. There is no language in the relevant federal statutes authorizing a couple to set up a single residence GRIT for both of their interest in a shared home. A GRIT is an individual trust and gift. The value of the grantor's retained interest is determined, in part, by his or her individual life expectancy.

If you set up a residence GRIT, you are usually the trustee. The trust document gives you full control over management of the house—it's almost like retaining actual home ownership. Among other things, this means that you can still take an income tax deduction for mortgage interest and real estate taxes on the house.

When carefully drafted, the trust document creating your GRIT can allow you to make additional payments to the trust for mortgage payments, taxes, insurance and improvements. The document should also give you freedom to sell the property and reinvest the proceeds in another home.

Possibly more important, you can also retain rights, under IRS rules, to reinvest sale proceeds and avoid capital gain tax by use of:

1. The one-time $125,000 exclusion from capital gain tax if you're over 55, and

2. Buying a new home within the time allowed by the IRS, currently 24 months.

The taxable value of the gift to the trust—the residence—is based on an IRS formula that considers the term of years of the trust, your age and current interest rates.

Example: Lucille, 60 years old, funds her GRIT with her primary residence, worth $1 million. The term of the trust is for 15 years, after which the residence will go to her son. The gift tax value of the gift to her son is figured by IRS formulas. In this case, Lucille's retained interest is worth about $750,000. So for gift tax purposes, the gift to the son is worth about $250,000.

If Lucille survives the 15-year term, her son will receive the house. Since the house will not be part of Lucille's taxable estate, the only tax assessed was on the $250,000 gift, when the trust was funded. (No tax would actually be paid, as long as Lucille hadn't already used up her personal $600,00 estate/gift tax exemption.) If Lucille doesn't survive the term, her son still gets the house on her death, but the full current value of the house is included in Lucille's taxable estate. Lucille's estate will get credit for gift tax previously paid.

b. "Reversionary Interests" in a GRIT

You can structure a GRIT so that you have the right to purchase back the property from the trust before the term ends. This is called a "reversionary interest." Because the IRS views you as the property's owner until the set period ends, you have no taxable gain or loss on this purchase. Why bother to do this? Because your five beneficiaries will be in a better tax position than if you didn't buy back the house.

Here's the basics of how this technique works: You, the donor, buy the house back from the trust for the current market price. The basis of the house then becomes what you just paid for it, not your own original basis. (Unless you repurchase the house, its basis does remain your original basis.)

The house is transferred back into your name. The IRS does not tax this transaction.

The trust now has the cash of your purchase price. When the trust term period ends (assuming you outlive the set term), the money is turned over to your final beneficiaries. No taxes are assessed.

You retain the house until your death. At your death the house receives a stepped-up basis to its current market value.

This technique only makes sense if you have large amounts of money, since you must put up cash to buy the house back from the trust. Also, this technique is very new, and under scrutiny by the IRS. You must see an expert lawyer if you want to explore using this technique in your estate plan.

Here's an example of how this technique can be beneficial.

Example: Harry places his $1 million residence in a 15-year GRIT and retains a reversionary interest. His cost basis in the house is $300,000.

If Harry survives the 15-year term, the house is turned over to his final beneficiaries. They take it at his cost basis. If they later sell it, they'll pay a substantial capital gain tax, since the house's market price should be at least the $1 million it was when Harry placed it in the trust.

Now, look at what happens if Harry has enough money to buy the house back from the trust, just before the 15-year period expires. The house's market value is now $1.3 million. Harry pays $1.3 million to the trust of the house. Harry now owns the house; the trust has $1.3 million in cash. No taxes are assessed on this transaction when the trust period ends. The entire $1.3 million is turned over to Harry's final beneficiaries, free from tax.

Harry receives the house back at his original $300,000 basis. But when he dies, the house receives a stepped-up basis. So the house's inheritors have as their basis in the property its value as of Harry's death.

Many estate planners suggest that married couples include a specific type of reversionary interest clause in a residence GRIT. This clause directs that if one spouse dies before the end of the term, the house is to be returned to the spouse's estate and given to the surviving spouse, so the unlimited estate tax marital deduction can be used.

Example: Celeste puts her summer cottage in a GRIT that will last 15 years; at the end of that period, the cottage will go to her daughter, Anna. But Celeste keeps a reversionary interest in the cottage so that if she dies during the term of the trust, the cottage reverts to her estate instead of going to her daughter. This would result in the property actually passing to Celeste's husband, so no estate tax will have to be paid if Celeste dies during the term.

RESIDENCE GRITs AT A GLANCE

1. You create trust and fund it with your house. You retain the right to live in the house, or sell it and buy a new one.
2. The value of gift for gift tax purposes is determined when you transfer the house to the trust.
3. Near the end of the trust term, you can repurchase the home from the trust if you wish.
4. When the term ends, the trust is terminated and the final beneficiary receives the house.

c. Drawbacks of Residence GRITs

As with all grantor-retained interest trusts, the flip side of the potentially big tax advantages of a residence GRIT are potentially big disadvantages. Most of the drawbacks of a GRIT are the same as for a GRAT or GRUT, covered above in Section B3. One drawback unique to a residence GRIT is that at the end of the set term, unless you have the resources to repurchase the house, you live in a home belonging to someone else. If you want to stay, and don't pay fair rent to the final beneficiaries, the IRS considers that a legal gift by the final beneficiaries to you. For the wealthy, paying rent is often just another good way to pass on money to their children without gift tax and also to reduce their estate, and consequently its tax. But for people with less means, it could surely be a burden.

Some risks are reduced or eliminated if you are very wealthy. For example, if you have a bundle of cash, you can buy back the property near the end of the term if it goes up in value.

> **Remember King Lear**
>
> In a perfect world, a parent might create a residence GRIT for the benefit of a child or grandchild, who will lovingly allow the parent to continue to reside in the house until death. The child or grandchild would then, at the death of the parent, move in or sell the house.
>
> Sadly, this is not always what happens. (Surprise—there's need and even greed in some families.) When several children are the final beneficiaries, they may decide to sell the property as soon as they become its legal owners. If they need the money and don't care what happens to the parent (the grantor), that parent could find herself out on the street.
>
> Even if the parent is wealthy and could afford another house, a GRIT might make it easier for a well-meaning child to pack a parent off to a nursing home. After all, the child could rationalize, it's not even the parent's house any more.
>
> Making another trust the final beneficiary of a residence GRIT can sometimes alleviate these potential problems, if you select a trustee who'll treat you honorably. Still, the trustee has a legal obligation to the final beneficiaries to produce the most income possible from the trust, which might necessitate selling the house. And if you can't trust your own kids, how can you be confident a separate trustee will be more reliable?

d. "Regular" GRITs

Congress eliminated the advantages of regular GRITs for the benefit of direct family members, but it did not exclude the tax benefits of GRITs for other beneficiaries. In fact, nieces, nephews and cousins, as well as friends, can still be final beneficiaries for GRITs funded with property other than a personal residence. This is one strategy unmarried couples can use—and indeed, come out ahead on—since they are not legally "family."

If you set up a regular GRIT, you receive all of the income for a set term from the trust property. The gift tax value of the gift consists of what the final beneficiary is expected to receive at the end of the set term. As with all of the other grantor-retained interest trusts, the IRS values the gift property for tax purposes when the trust is established, and does not want to revalue it again when the property is distributed to the final beneficiaries. Your income interest is subtracted from the total worth of the property to value the gift. The IRS tables used for this calculation take into account current interest rates, your age and the length of the term. The actual gift is usually substantially discounted for gift tax purposes.

Example: Joseph creates a ten-year GRIT for the benefit of his long-time companion, Al. He funds it with a stock portfolio worth $1 million. Because he will receive all of the income for ten years, the gift to Al in the GRIT is valued at less than half the value of the stock, no more than $500,000. It retains the gift tax value no matter what the property is worth ten years later when Al receives it (assuming Joseph is still alive). If Joseph doesn't survive the term, the full value of the trust assets is included in his taxable estate, just as if he had done nothing.

Like the other trusts discussed above, the shorter the term, the larger the taxable gift to the final beneficiary. But if you are in good health, and especially if you are single, regular GRITS still offer an attractive method of giving gifts, reducing the size of an estate and saving on taxes at the same time.

> **"REGULAR" GRITs AT A GLANCE**
>
> 1. You create and fund the trust, specifying how long it is to last.
> 2. The value of gift for gift tax purposes is determined when you fund the trust.
> 3. The trustee pays you all income annually.
> 4. When the term ends, the trust is terminated and trust assets go to the final beneficiary.

6. Questions to Ask About a Grantor-Retained Interest Trust

If a GRAT, GRUT or GRIT sounds appealing for your situation, you need to sit down with an estate planning expert and carefully assess your situation. An expert should compare using any of these trusts with other possible estate planning alternatives. Make sure you get the answers to these questions:

- How do the tax savings from this type of trust compare with simply giving the gift directly (with any gift tax assessed), or making the gift over a period of years, using the $10,000 annual gift tax exemption repeatedly and allowing the beneficiary to invest the money you give?
- What are the likely savings overall, taking into consideration possible capital gain tax paid by the final beneficiary if he sells the trust property?
- What are the chances you will buy back appreciated property near the end of the set term if you retain a reversionary interest in trust property?
- Given your age, health and economic situations, and feelings about money and security, can you risk parting with these assets irrevocably?
- Is your family situation stable enough that you can confidently rely on your present feelings about who you name your final beneficiaries to remain valid for years?
- Is it better to create a grantor-retained interest trust and pay gift tax now (if necessary) on the gift property? Or is it wiser to hang on to the property and let your estate pay any estate tax on this property after your death?
- Is a grantor-retained interest trust really desirable, considering your overall financial picture and the possible alternatives, including:
  - the $600,000 estate tax exemption
  - a program of tax-exempt $10,000 gifts over a number of years
  - using a marital bypass trust so both spouses' estate tax $600,000 exemption is used
  - QTIP trusts
  - charitable trusts
  - life insurance policies owned by others on your life.

Answering these questions, and other personal ones that will surely come up, is time-consuming and requires a high level of expertise in estate planning. If your expert can't answer them or thinks that they are not important, quickly find another expert, a genuine one. ■

22

Disclaimers: After-Death Estate Tax Planning

It may sound strange, but the term "estate planning" is expansive enough to include the possibility that, after you die, one or more of your beneficiaries will decide to decline to accept part or all of the property you left them. Refusing to take a gift is called "disclaiming" it. A beneficiary has the legal right under federal law (IRC Section 2518) to disclaim or refuse all, or any part, of a gift. If a beneficiary disclaims any property, it goes to whomever you specified in your trust or will to receive it if the primary beneficiary cannot or does not take it. (If you foresee that a beneficiary might want to disclaim property inherited from you, you can also specify, in your will or trust document, who will receive it if it is disclaimed. See Section D, below.)

You may wonder why anyone in our materially-oriented society would be so unworldly as to refuse property left to him or her. It's not because the people who disclaim are noble or saintly. (They may be, but that's not what disclaimers are about.) The main reason people disclaim gifts is to lighten their individual or their family's overall estate tax burden.

A. Advantages of Disclaimers

Disclaimers can be an efficient way for a beneficiary who already has plenty of property to pass a bequest along to another person (usually a family member) who has less, and by doing so, save on estate taxes. The person who winds up with the gift is usually the alternate beneficiary for that gift, or, if you didn't name an alternate beneficiary, your residuary beneficiary.

1. Estate Tax Savings

Here's how using a disclaimer can save on estate taxes. Under federal tax law, any property disclaimed by a beneficiary is never legally owned by that person, which means it cannot be included in that beneficiary's taxable estate at death. In addition, no gift tax is assessed against the person who disclaims a gift (in effect, giving it to someone else), again, because the person never owned it.

Disclaimers can be particularly useful when the primary beneficiary already has a large estate and receiving the gift would add significantly to his eventual estate tax, but the alternate beneficiary has much less wealth.

Example: Roger, an elderly widower, has an estate worth $540,000. He leaves it equally to his two children, George and Carlotta, with the provision that if one of them cannot or does not take his or her half, it will go to the other. When Roger dies, his middle-aged children are in very different financial shape. Carlotta is a prosperous graphic designer, with an estate of roughly $800,000. Her husband has a similar-sized estate. George hasn't fared so well financially. His real estate business (his latest enterprise) was marginal from the start five years ago, and has been in a serious slump over the past year. George has very little savings and a child with special educational needs.

Carlotta and George are close. Carlotta decides to disclaim her half of her father's estate ($270,000), so the entire $540,000 goes to George.

Carlotta disclaimed the gift—that is, gave the money to George—not primarily to save on estate tax, but because she felt he needed it and she didn't. But a pleasant side benefit is that there will be a significant estate tax savings. If Carlotta had accepted her half, her total estate would have grown to $1,070,000, increasing her eventual estate tax liability. George's estate is about $540,000, after his inheritance. So his estate will not be subject to estate tax (unless, of course, it increases in value to over $600,000 before his death).

Disclaimers can also be desirable if the primary beneficiary is older and may not live long, and the alternate beneficiary is younger.

Example: Barton leaves his estate of $500,000 to his sister Elizabeth, who is in her late 70s and has, herself, an estate of $800,000. Because Barton's estate is less than $600,000, no federal estate tax is due when he dies, no matter who inherits it. The alternate beneficiaries for Barton's estate are Elizabeth's two children, both in their 30s, with very little property. If Elizabeth accepted the gift, her estate would total $1.3 million, and substantial estate tax ($277,000) would be assessed on her death. If Elizabeth instead disclaimed the gift, it would be divided between her two children. And at Elizabeth's death (assuming she still has $800,000), only $200,000 is subject to estate tax.

Clearly, disclaiming property can result in substantial estate tax advantages. But unlike a bypass trust (see Chapter 18, Estate Tax-Saving Bypass Trusts, Section A), which is established in advance to save on estate taxes, it's solely up to the beneficiary to make the decision to disclaim a gift or not. A beneficiary who is insecure, needy or even a tad greedy may choose not to disclaim property, even though doing this might be the wisest choice in light of "objective" personal needs and overall estate tax consequences. But after all, the gift was left to that beneficiary. Disclaiming may make sense from an estate tax point of view, but it's hard to see it as a moral obligation.

2. Fine-Tuning Gifts

Disclaimers can allow beneficiaries to make adjustments regarding who gets what. This can be done to equalize beneficiaries' financial positions. Also, beneficiaries can, effectively, trade property between them, so that each gets—or at least, comes closer to getting—what he or she wants. The power to disclaim can also help beneficiaries avoid problems of owning something together, having to come up with the money to buy out co-owners, or having to sell property that one of them loves.

Example 1: Tony, a bachelor, leaves his entire estate to his two nephews, Phil and Angelo, in equal shares. Each is the alternate beneficiary for the other's gift.

Among the assets at Tony's death is an ocean beachfront vacation home. Phil, with a sizable estate of his own, dislikes ocean beaches and spends his summers in the mountains, by freshwater lakes and rivers. Angelo, on the other hand, is not as well-off financially and has vacationed every summer of his life at the beach cottage. Phil disclaims his one-half interest in the beach property, keeping it out of his already large estate (and paying no gift tax whatever) when it then goes to Angelo.

Example 2: Now assume Phil and Angelo are on an equal financial footing, but Phil still dislikes the beachfront home. Now it might be appropriate for Angelo to disclaim something of value equal to the vacation home in exchange for Phil's disclaimer. Phil has avoided inheriting the beachfront property and then making a gift of his share of the home to Angelo, which would result in substantial gift tax.

Disclaimers can also be used when a person decides she wants the property to go to the next in line for the gift.

Example: Babette leaves her house to her three children, in equal shares. Her living trust provides that the alternate beneficiaries for each child's share are his or her children. When Babette dies, all three of her children are quite well off. Two intend to accept their share of the house. One child, Fritz, disclaims his share, because he decides it's wiser to let it pass to his children, who are in their early 20s and starting their careers (or, at least, starting to earn money). Fritz knows his children will find much security in the financial nest egg his disclaimer provides for each.

If Babette had specified that the alternate beneficiaries for the house were her other children, Fritz would not have disclaimed his share. He would not have wanted that share divided between his brother and sister, bringing no benefit to his children.

3. Adjusting for Unforeseen Circumstances

Disclaimers can also be a lifesaver under pressing circumstances. For instance, a person may be over-generous or over-optimistic regarding his finances in his estate plan, and his financial situation at his time of death may turn out to be worse than he anticipated. Beneficiaries can use disclaimers to achieve fair results—results the person would surely have wanted if he'd known how his finances would turn out.

Example: Sven, who's doing well in business, prepares a living trust that leaves $200,000 each to his three children and the rest of his estate to his spouse. Later, after some business setbacks and an extended illness, his wealth has dwindled. When Sven dies, there will be almost nothing left for his widow after the $600,000 is given to his children. The children generously disclaim their inheritance so the money will go to their mother for her support.

This sounds good—indeed, ideal—but there is, of course, an obvious risk if a disclaimer is needed for this purpose. A child may be unwilling to give up an inheritance, no matter what hardship that creates for the surviving parent. In the situation described above, it would have been wiser for Sven to rewrite his living trust after his business reversals, simply leaving all his property to his spouse.

B. Couples and Disclaimers

Couples, whether married or not, can sometimes cut their tax bills significantly by using disclaimers. It's common for each member of a couple to leave everything to the other, with the children named as alternate beneficiaries. That surviving mate, they hope, will pass the deceased person's property on to their children. Especially when spouses or mates are relatively young and don't have a big estate, this makes sense. Why tie up property in a trust when a surviving spouse may need that property for decades?

But a couple who had modest property holdings at the time they prepared their estate plan may turn out to be quite prosperous when one spouse dies decades later. In situations like this, the surviving spouse's ability to disclaim part of the deceased spouse's estate, and have it go directly to their children, can achieve substantial overall estate tax savings. (A surviving spouse can also disclaim property and have it go into a trust that benefits that spouse. See Section C4, below.)

Example: While in their mid-50s, Boris and his wife Natasha created their estate plan, leaving all of their property to each other. Each named their three children as alternate beneficiaries. By their late 70s, they have an estate worth $800,000.

Boris dies first, leaving his $400,000 share to Natasha. Natasha is not in good health. If Natasha disclaims $200,000 of her inheritance, it will go directly to their children. Also, there's a possibility that Natasha may end up in a nursing home or need major health care. If so, her entire estate could be gobbled up with distressing speed. But if Natasha had previously disclaimed $200,000 inherited from Boris, that property cannot be subject to claims from any of her medical or heath care providers.

Why would Natasha disclaim $200,000, rather than more or less than this amount? Because as the chart below shows, this would allow her to receive the maximum amount possible form Boris and still not have her estate subject to estate tax when she dies (assuming the value of her estate remains the same).

	Without Disclaimer	*With $200,000 Disclaimer by Natasha*
Value of Boris's estate	$400,000	$400,000
Estate tax due	-0- (because of the marital deduction)	-0- (because of marital deduction and Boris's personal $600,000 exemption)
Value of Natasha's estate	$800,000	$600,000
Amount actually taxable	$200,000 (her $800,000, less her $600,000 personal estate tax exemption)	-0-
Estate tax	$75,000	-0-

Now suppose Boris and Natasha had the same size estate, but Boris died suddenly in his late 50s. Natasha might well sensibly decide not to disclaim any of Boris's estate. It could be ten, 20 or many more years before her death, and she may well want or need all the $800,000 during her lifetime.

When a surviving spouse wants to disclaim an interest in property the spouses own together, that spouse can disclaim only that portion that was left to her by the deceased spouse. The other half of the property is and remains owned by the surviving spouse; obviously, no disclaimer of that portion is possible.

Example: Yaphet and Malika together own property worth $850,000. Yaphet also has well over $1 million in separate property. They each leave their half of the shared property to each other, with their three children as alternate beneficiaries. After Malika dies, Yaphet wants to disclaim all he can, so it will go to his children. He can disclaim only Malika's one-half share of their shared property, a total of $425,000. He cannot disclaim his own one-half share of that property (or, of course, his separate property), because that wasn't left to him by Malika—he owned it all along.

C. IRS Rules for Disclaimers

A Federal law requires that a beneficiary's disclaimer must be "qualified." This means that it must meet certain rules set out in IRC Section 2518. If these rules aren't complied with, the person disclaiming will not avoid legal ownership of that property for estate tax purposes, and the major purpose of the disclaimer is lost. The IRS requirements are:

- The disclaimer must be in writing.
- A disclaimer by an adult must be completed within nine months of the death of the person leaving the property.
- A minor who has been left property must disclaim within nine months of reaching age 18.
- The person who disclaims property may not accept any benefit from the property before disclaiming it. (An exception exists for a surviving spouse—see Section 4, below).

- The person refusing the property may not direct where the property then goes. The original will or trust document determines who receives the disclaimed property.

1. The Disclaimer Must Be in Writing

A beneficiary who wants to disclaim inherited property—for whatever reason and whatever the type of property—is responsible for putting the disclaimer in writing. The beneficiary must deliver the written disclaimer to whomever is in control of the property at that time. This is usually the successor trustee of a living trust or the executor (personal representative) of a will.

Example: In her living trust, Carla leaves a money market account to her son, Francisco, and another of roughly equal value to her daughter, Eva. The trust provides that if either child dies before Carla does, the money goes to the other. She names Francisco as successor trustee of her trust.

At Carla's death, Eva is financially comfortable, but Francisco is struggling. Eva is also aware of the fact that her mother spent much more on her college and graduate education, while Francisco chose not to go to college. She wishes to disclaim so he can receive the money directly from Eva's estate without it being a taxable gift from her.

As successor trustee, Francisco is bound by law to follow the directions in his mother's trust. If Eva calls him up and tells him to take her money, he can't legally do it. He needs the written disclaimer so he can follow the trust instructions and satisfy IRS regulations. Only when armed with the signed disclaimer from Eva will he have the power to change his mother's primary instructions and take the money himself. (See Section D, below, covering complexities that can arise when a trustee of a living trust disclaims trust property or receives it by disclaimer.)

2. The Disclaimer Must Be Made Within a Certain Time

IRS rules require that a disclaimer must be made by adults within nine months of the death of the original giver—that is, the trust grantor or will writer.

DISCLAIMERS BY MINORS

A minor can disclaim a gift within nine months of becoming age 18. This raises some odd questions, such as who manages the property until the minor turns 18? What can be done with it? Who may benefit from the property during this time? Is the life of the estate prolonged? The answers depend on state law.

Generally, state laws are unclear regarding allowing a child to disclaim an income interest that has been left him in a trust without losing his eventual inheritance of the trust assets. It's a very complicated estate tax issue.

Legal advice for possible disclaimer by a child beneficiary. If you are the parent or guardian of a minor who has been left property and think it's possible the minor would want to disclaim that property at age 18, seek some good professional advice.

The nine-month period allows enough time, hopefully, for the adult survivors to begin getting back on their feet emotionally and to get the information they need to make wise financial decisions.

Example: Makoto dies suddenly, leaving a wife, Hanako, in her 60s and two adult children. His will leaves everything to Hanako or, if she doesn't survive him, to the children. Makoto's elder son, Keiji, who is executor of the will, sees immediately the estate is worth about $1 million, more than Hanako, who has substantial assets of her own, needs. When Keiji hires a lawyer to probate the will, the lawyer advises changing things around for tax purposes. But no one in the family wants to think about these issues shortly after Makoto's death.

The nine-month period gives the attorney time to draft a tax-savings plan and explain it to the family. Also, the family has a chance to look at the situation and assess who needs what, and when.

In the end, Hanako decides to disclaim $600,000. This allows Makoto's estate to use its entire personal estate tax exemption (for the $600,000, which now goes to the children as alternates). Now Hanako inherits only $400,000, so her own estate is smaller, and the estate tax that will be due on it at her death is lower. But it's not only tax savings that motivate Hanako. She believes her children need this money now, when they are working hard and trying to raise their own children. With the disclaimer, they get it, with no taxable gift having been made by Hanako.

The nine-month deadline may seem straightforward, but it can get a little complicated when someone wants to disclaim property that was co-owned with the deceased. This situation most commonly arises when a married person dies and leaves his or her share of co-owned property—a house, perhaps—to the surviving spouse.

Figuring out the deadline for making a disclaimer depends on how the property was owned: as community property or joint tenancy property, for example. If the property was owned as community property or as tenancy-in-common property, the nine-month period begins when the person who left a share of the property dies. If the property was held in joint tenancy or tenancy by the entirety, however, you need to follow other rules, which vary from state to state. (For a discussion of joint tenancy, see Chapter 10, Joint Tenancy and Tenancy by the Entirety, Section A.)

a. Disclaiming Joint Tenancy Property

Most states allow one co-owner to divide joint tenancy property while both owners are alive. In other words, one owner is free to do what she likes with her interest in the property—such as separate the owners' interests and sell her share—while the other owner lives. In these states, the nine-month disclaimer period begins to run at the first owner's death.

A number of states, however, still do not allow one co-owner of joint tenancy property to transfer his or her share while the other owners are alive. Technically, the disclaimer period in these states starts to run when the joint tenancy is created. Thus a disclaimer after death would be too late in almost all cases, unless one owner happened to die within nine months of purchase of the property.

b. Disclaiming Tenancy by the Entirety Property

A number of states permit marital property to be held in "tenancy by the entirety," a special kind of joint tenancy for married couples only. (See list in Chapter 10, Joint Tenancy and Tenancy by the Entirety, Section B.)

In most of these states, the time limit for disclaimers of tenancy by the entirety property is nine months after the couple acquired the property. Normally, property held in this way cannot be unilaterally severed or divided by one spouse. Both spouses' consent is needed. In effect, this means there is no right for a surviving spouse to disclaim deceased spouse's interest of tenancy by the entirety property. Only if the spouse died within nine months of when the couple acquired the property would a disclaimer be possible.

To find out your state's specific rules regarding disclaimers of joint tenancy or tenancy by the entirety property, you'll need sound professional advice.

3. The Person Disclaiming Property May Not Benefit From Disclaimed Property

With one important exception, discussed below in Section 4, a beneficiary who wants to disclaim property cannot use or accept any benefit from the property, however brief the use or slight the benefit. One danger here is when a beneficiary takes a small benefit from a large gift. For example, if a beneficiary receives rent from gift real estate for a short time and then decides he wants to disclaim the entire gift, it's too late. The disclaimer will not be valid for estate tax purposes.

Also, a beneficiary who will still receive any benefit from the property after the disclaimer cannot disclaim the property. For example, a beneficiary cannot disclaim property that then goes into a trust that will, or even could, pay the beneficiary any income from the trust. For example, if a beneficiary disclaims a gift that goes into a family pot trust with 15 potential beneficiaries, including the person who disclaimed, the disclaimer is not valid. The property still goes to the next beneficiary in line, but the transaction is considered, legally, a simple gift, and the giver may be assessed gift tax if the property is valuable enough.

4. The Exception for Surviving Spouses

There's one exception to the general rule that a beneficiary can't receive any benefit from disclaimed property. A surviving spouse who disclaims a gift can still receive some benefits from it. This makes possible some flexible estate planning.

One strategy is to arrange things so that a surviving spouse can disclaim money inherited from the other. If the property is disclaimed, it goes into a marital life estate trust, with the surviving spouse as life beneficiary. Income from the trust goes to the spouse, if needed. When the second spouse dies, the trust assets go to the couple's children (or other beneficiary they chose). The IRS never considers the second spouse to die the legal owner of the disclaimed property, even though he benefited from that property.

Example: Benjamin and Esther, in their 40s, own shared property worth $800,000. Each has an estate worth $400,000. In their estate plan, each leaves their property outright to the other.

However, they worry about what will happen if they acquire considerably more valuable property but don't get around to revising their plan. Then there would be substantial federal estate taxes when the surviving spouse died, and a marital life estate trust might be desirable. (See Chapter 18, Estate Tax-Saving Bypass Trusts, Section C.) On the other hand, the surviving spouse may need or want the entire estate, not just the right to get income from the property, as a marital life estate trust would provide. How can Benjamin and Esther decide now what's wisest? The answer is, they don't have to.

Suppose their total estate is worth $2 million when Esther dies. Esther leaves her $1 million to Benjamin, subject to his right to disclaim. Benjamin could disclaim $600,000 of the gift and accept $400,000 of it. In other words, Benjamin could decide that his own estate of $1 million plus $400,000 from Esther is enough for him to own outright. The $600,000 now goes into a marital life estate trust. By using the disclaimer, Esther's estate and Benjamin's estate each take advantage of the $600,000 personal estate tax exemption, saving an enormous amount in estate taxes and giving more, eventually, to the children.

When the estates of the spouses are unequal, disclaimers can be used similarly, placing property where it's wisest for estate tax purposes. The goal is to equalize the value of both spouses' estates, or at least make them closer in size. The reason for this is that old graduated estate tax and the personal $600,000 estate tax exemption. If one spouse has an estate of $4 million, and the other has nothing, they will pay more estate tax than if each spouse owned property worth $2 million.

Disclaimers used to equalize, or balance, spouses' estates are often used in combination with other estate tax saving devices, such as marital life estate trusts or QTIP trusts. (See Chapter 18, Estate Tax-Saving Bypass Trusts, Section C, and Chapter 19, Other Estate Tax-Saving Marital Trusts, Section A.)

Example: Guido, 60 years old, is married for the second time, to Sophia. Guido's assets total $3 million, and Sophia's financial worth is negligible. Guido wants to ensure that Sophia is taken care of in the case of his death, but he wants his estate to eventually pass to the children of his first marriage.

He creates a plan that will pay income to Sophia for her support from two trusts, one a marital life estate trust of $600,000 and the other a QTIP trust consisting of his other assets. (Property in a QTIP trust is subject to estate tax when the second spouse dies.) Guido directs that the income and then the principal of the QTIP trust be used up, if necessary, before paying Sophia income from the marital life estate trust. At Sophia's death, the assets remaining in both trusts will go to Guido's children

If Sophia disclaims any amount of the QTIP trust property, it will go into the marital life estate trust. She remains entitled to receive the income from that trust if she needs it. However, the amount in the marital life estate trust is subject to tax at Guido's death, instead of at Sophia's death, when the property in the QTIP trust will be subject to estate tax.

Here's a chart of estate tax consequences if Sophia accepts all Guido's property or disclaims $1 million of it.

	Without Disclaimer	*With $1,000,000 Disclaimer by Sophia*
Value of Guido's estate	$3 million	$3 million
Estate tax due	-0- (on the $600,000 amount in the marital life estate trust (because of Guido's personal estate tax exemption)	$408,000 (because disclaimed $1 million goes into marital life estate trust, which then has a total value of $1.6 million, where it is subject to estate tax on Guido's death)
Value of Sophia's estate when she dies	$2.4 million	$1.4 million
Estate tax due	$784,000	$320,000
Total estate tax paid	$784,000	728,000

The estate tax saving is not the only benefit of this kind of strategy; much greater savings are lurking in the wings. A wise and creative trustee can fund the marital life estate trust with high-growth assets (he hopes). If these assets do grow significantly in value during the surviving spouse's life, they will not be taxed at her death. This increase in value passes to the children free of estate tax.

At the same time, the property in the marital QTIP trust can be converted to high-yield assets, providing comfortable support for the surviving spouse. If she lives for 15 years, this trust may be spent down for her support, so the estate tax due at her death may actually be even lower than in the example above.

D. Disclaimers and Living Trusts

Someone who both serves as the successor trustee of a living trust and inherits trust property may run into complications if he or she wants to disclaim property. The basic rule is that if such a person has any authority to direct where any of the disclaimed property will go, she can't disclaim it unless she resigns as trustee or declines the authority to direct distribution of trust property (assuming this is permitted under state law).

Example: Tsultrim and Yeshe each create a living trust, providing that on a spouse's death, $600,000 of that spouse's property goes directly into a trust for their children. Any remaining property goes outright to the surviving spouse. The surviving spouse will serve as trustee of the children's trust and have broad trustee powers, including the authority to distribute trust principal and income to the children if they need it.

Yeshe dies first. The couple's estate turns out to be large, so it would be desirable, from the overall estate tax viewpoint, for Tsultrim to disclaim the property Yeshe's left to him and let it go into the children's trust. Estate taxes would be lower in the long run if some tax were paid on part of Yeshe's property at her death.

But as long as he serves as trustee of the trust for the children, Tsultrim can't disclaim any of the property Yeshe left him. That's because, as trustee, he has the authority to direct the distribution of property to the trust beneficiaries. To have a valid disclaimer, he will have to also disclaim this authority or resign as trustee altogether.

Many living trusts do not allow the trustee to determine who receives any trust income or property. The beneficiaries and their shares are all specified in the trust document. But if a beneficiary is considering disclaiming property that will then go into a trust, and the beneficiary has any powers at all over the trust assets, expert advice is really needed. A legal power to direct who gets the disclaimed assets may not be readily apparent, but may be discovered upon a closer review. Even a power by the trustee to allocate income and principal might cause a disclaimer to fail.

If you're preparing a living trust, be sure to discuss disclaimer possibilities with your attorney, and be sure the trust document is drafted so that this potential problem is eliminated, to the extent possible.

Even though disclaimers are expressly authorized by federal law, incorporating a specific disclaimer provision in your living trust or will can be a real favor for your beneficiaries. A clause permitting beneficiaries to disclaim gifts you leave them tells beneficiaries that you know about disclaimers and personally authorize them. A beneficiary who wants to make a disclaimer doesn't have to worry about going against your desires. Also, not all beneficiaries (or successor trustees or executors) know about disclaimers, so specifically authorizing them can be a good means of alerting your beneficiaries that they exist.

You might want to work out potential problems in advance, when you prepare your estate plan, rather than leaving them unresolved until your death. For example, if your successor trustee would have to resign to make her disclaimer valid, obviously it's important who the alternate successor trustee will be.

You can also direct who is to receive property that one of your beneficiaries disclaims. This would only be desirable if you decide that if a beneficiary disclaims, you don't want the gift to go the alternate beneficiary. This might be the case if the alternate beneficiary is likely to be in the same financial position as the primary beneficiary, as can be the case with husband and wife.

Example: Chang, a widower, leaves all of his $300,000 estate to his son Tai, with Tai's wife as the alternate beneficiary. But Chang also provides in his living trust document that should Tai disclaim any property, it then goes to Chang's favorite nephew. When Chang dies, Tai's and his wife's assets are quite large; neither Tai nor his wife needs the inheritance. By contrast, the nephew, who is just starting out in business, really needs the money. Tai disclaims the gift, and the $300,000 goes directly to the nephew.

Because Tai never owns the property, his own estate is not increased for estate tax purposes. Nor has he made a taxable gift by disclaiming the gift and letting it go to Chang's nephew.

If Tai had accepted the gift, he could remove it from his estate by subsequently giving it to the nephew. But this would mean Tai would be assessed gift tax on $290,000, the taxable portion of the gift.

If you anticipate that a disclaimer may make sense, you can include a brief letter or note in the envelope with your will or living trust alerting the executor or successor trustee so beneficiaries can be told. You can suggest that it may be wise to make no distributions whatsoever until all concerned have consulted a tax advisor. ■

23

Trusts for Second or Subsequent Marriages

In many second or subsequent marriages, one or both spouses may feel truly conflicted about estate planning. On the one hand, a surviving spouse may really need additional income from, or the use of, the other spouse's property to live comfortably. On the other hand, children from a former marriage may believe they are entitled to inherit the property once their parent dies. Even if the children aren't insistent, they may have financial needs and resent their inheritance being tied up while the other spouse lives. This situation—which can be dicey at the best of times—becomes even more complicated when one's current spouse and children from a former marriage are estranged from each other.

This chapter discusses how you can use a trust to try to balance the interests and needs of all concerned. Essentially, this type of trust imposes controls over your property after your death, so that the surviving spouse has some use of it, or income from it, but does not have unlimited rights to use it. By this control, you seek to ensure that most or all of the trust principal will remain intact for your children.

Trusts imposing controls over property can be used in many situations, not just those involving second or subsequent marriages. (Trusts for those needs are discussed in Chapter 24, Trusts and Other Devices for Imposing Controls Over Property.) This chapter focuses exclusively on concerns of spouses in second or subsequent marriages, because for many people this is a central concern of their estate planning.

UNMARRIED COUPLES

This chapter talks in terms of subsequent marriages and surviving spouses, because most people who do this type of estate planning are married. But the principles apply equally to unmarried couples with children from previous relationships, previous marriages or both.

A. How a Property Control Trust Works

A common way to avert conflict between your children and present spouse over property you leave them is to create a trust, similar to the marital life estate trust discussed in Chapter 18, Estate Tax-Saving Bypass Trusts, Section C, but with some important differences. There is no one, broadly accepted term for the type of trust we discuss here. We call it a "marital property control trust."

This type of trust imposes restrictions and controls over the rights of the surviving spouse to the property placed in the trust. The surviving spouse is the life beneficiary of the trust, which means she receives benefits from the trust as long as she lives. However, her rights to use trust property, to receive trust income, or spend trust principal, are as limited as the grantor (the deceased spouse) determined they should be. These restrictions are expressly stated in the trust document.

A marital property control trust is in marked contrast to a marital life estate trust intended to save on estate tax, where the surviving spouse is usually granted the maximum rights to use and invade trust property allowed under IRS rules. The purpose of restricting the surviving spouse's rights in a marital property control trust is to protect the trust principal, so that it remains intact (or at least close to intact) until the surviving spouse dies. Then, the trust property goes outright to the grantor's children from a prior marriage, or other final beneficiaries the grantor named.

Example: Lisi and Greg get married in their late 30s. Lisi has a child from a prior marriage; Greg has two children from his prior marriages. Lisi and Greg have a child together, Dory. Neither spouse has an immense estate: Lisi owns property worth $400,000, and Greg owns property worth $310,000. Together they own a house that cost $320,000. Each contributed half the down payment for the house, and they share mortgage payments equally.

Each spouse creates a marital property control trust. The other spouse, as life beneficiary, has these rights:

1. To remain in the house for life.

2. To receive the income from any property placed in the trust.

3. To spend trust principal only for medical costs that can't be paid for from other resources.

Each spouse names the final beneficiaries for his or her trust. Lisi decides that her final beneficiaries are Dory and her daughter from her prior marriage, who will divide her trust's principal 50/50. Greg, who is not close to his children from his prior marriage, names them and Dory as his final beneficiaries. Dory will receive 60% of his trust property and the other two children will equally divide the remaining 40%.

Whether or not your estate is under the $600,000 estate tax threshold, you may want a marital property control trust. Since the purpose of this trust is to preserve assets for your final beneficiaries, it is immaterial whether those assets will be subject to estate taxes on your death. This is in contrast to a marital life estate trust used to save on estate taxes, for couples with a combined estate over $600,000. (You can, however, use a marital property control trust both to restrict the surviving spouse's right and save on estate tax. See Section D, below.)

Example: Benny and Belle, each in their late 50s, marry. Benny has two children, ages 26 and 24, one each from two prior marriages. Belle has one child, age 19, from her prior marriage. Benny has an estate worth roughly $375,000; Belle's is worth $230,000. Neither spouse has enough saved to be truly financially independent should the other die first. Each creates a marital property control trust, allowing the other spouse income for life from the trust but absolutely no right to invade trust principal. This way, they've each ensured that their estate will remain intact, to be received by their child or children after the surviving spouse dies.

Marital property control trusts are no guarantee that family conflicts and tensions will be eliminated, or even reduced. But they can achieve at least some control over your assets, and give you the comfort that you've done your best to provide for your spouse and your children.

HOW TO SET UP A PROPERTY CONTROL TRUST

A marital property control trust usually is combined with a living trust to avoid probate. In that case, the marital property control trust remains revocable, as a component of the living trust, as long as you live and are mentally competent. After your death, the trust property is transferred to the ongoing martial property control trust, without probate proceedings. At that point, the marital property control trust becomes irrevocable. (See Chapter 17, An Overview of Ongoing Trusts.)

B. Restricting the Surviving Spouse's Rights Over Trust Property

You may impose a wide variety of restrictions on your surviving spouse's rights over the property in a marital property control trust. For instance, the surviving spouse may be given the right to receive income from the trust, but no right whatsoever to spend (invade) trust principal. Or you can name someone else, not the surviving spouse, to be the trustee of the trust. This, obviously keeps one source of real world power from the surviving spouse. If someone else is the trustee, presumably there's less chance that the trustee will abuse his authority and give the surviving spouse more than the trust document allows.

Example: Leticia, in her 70s, marries Ben, also in his 70s. Leticia has been married twice before, and has one grown child from each marriage. Her estate consists of her house, worth $275,000 (all equity), and savings of $580,000. Ben owns much less, about $40,000 in savings and stocks. He also receives a modest pension plus Social Security.

Leticia wants her property to eventually go to her two children, equally—but if she predeceases Ben, she doesn't want him thrown out on the street. She creates a marital life estate trust for control of her property, appointing the older of her two children as trustee. She arranges for her house and savings to go into the trust.

The trust document gives Ben the right to remain in the house, with all its current furnishings, for his life. If he leaves it for more than four consecutive months, whether to move to some tropical paradise or a nursing home, the house and furnishings can be sold or rented if the trustee decides that's desirable. Leticia is leaving it up to her oldest child, as trustee, to decide what should happen to the house if Ben vacates it for more than four months. Leticia doesn't want to require that the house be turned over to her children in these circumstances. She just wants to protect her children, and not have the house empty, or rented out by Ben, for a long time. Leticia fully trusts her oldest daughter to make a wise decision if this matter comes up. In legalese, this is called giving the trustee "compete discretion" to decide the matter.

Ben also is to receive $5,000 per year from the income generated by the money in the trust. If the trust's annual income is lower than $5,000, Ben receives that lesser amount. If the income exceeds $5,000, Ben can be given any portion of the additional income if the trustee determines he needs it for basic needs, such as health care or basic maintenance.

Each marital property control trust involves the unique circumstances of the couple and final beneficiaries involved. There are no set rules dictating what's right. You must try to foresee the future needs of the surviving spouse and balance those needs with your desire to protect most, if not all, of the principal for your final beneficiaries.

Finally, if your spouse and children don't get along, you may need to face the possibility that you will not be able to create a trust that will make all of them happy. In this case, you simply have to arrive at a resolution that seems the most wise and fair to you.

Here is a non-exclusive list of controls that can be placed over the surviving spouse's right to trust property:

- The survivor can live in a house owned (or partially owned) by the trust, but has no right to sell it.
- The survivor can live in the house and can sell it, but only for the purpose of buying another residence, and then only with the approval of all trust beneficiaries.
- The survivor can live in the house but cannot sell it or rent it. And if the survivor moves into a nursing facility and remains there for more than 90 consecutive days, the house must be turned over to the trust's final beneficiaries.
- The survivor (who is not the trustee) will be paid trust income only as the trustee determines it is necessary for medical care or basic needs.
- The survivor is named co-trustee with one of the final beneficiaries. Any decision regarding trust income or property, including distribution of income to the surviving spouse, requires approval of both trustees. (Clearly, if you include this kind of provision, be certain there's good will between the co-trustees.)
- The survivor may drive a valuable car owned by the trust, but can sell it only with consent of at least one final beneficiary.
- The survivor must follow specific directions set out in the trust document, down to how he can

use many items of trust property and care for valuable antiques.

- All rights of the surviving spouse to the trust property end if he or she remarries.

Example: Dottie and Sam have been living together for six years. Dottie is in her 50s and is the sole owner of a prospering women's clothing company. She owns, free and clear, a house worth $360,000, which she bought over 25 years ago. Her business is worth perhaps $200,000. (It's usually fairly hard to determine the market value of a small business, because often there is no actual market for it.) Her other assets total $230,000, so her total estate is worth $790,000. Sam owns property worth $400,000.

Dottie has no children. She wants to leave her estate, eventually, to her niece, Betsy, who works with her in her business. Sam wants his property divided between his two children.

Dottie decides that Sam could need income beyond what his $400,000 may generate, to continue to live in the comfortable style they've enjoyed together. Also, she wants to keep her business intact—most of all, so that Betsy can eventually inherit it, but also so it can produce income for Sam. So Dottie creates a restricted marital life estate trust, with Sam as the life beneficiary. She names Betsy as trustee, because Betsy will manage the business, owned by the trust. Sam is entitled to:

1. Live in their house for the duration of his life.

2. Sell it and buy another place, if Betsy consents.

3. Receive 25% of any profits from the clothing company (leaving the rest so the business can expand or maintain itself), or any income from other assets in the trust.When Sam dies, all the trust property goes to Betsy. Since Dottie's estate totals $790,000 now, there will likely be estate tax due on it when she dies unless she suffers drastic business reverses or other financial losses that bring the value of her estate below $600,000. Dottie specifies that any estate tax be paid from the other assets in her trust, not from the business or the house, so she can preserve these two assets for Sam, and then Betsy.

Sam also creates a trust that allows Dottie the income from his assets for her life but prohibits her from having the right to spend principal. When Dottie dies, his property will be divided between his children.

Sam's children do not get along well with Dottie, so he's reluctant to appoint one of his children as trustee of his trust. He feels confident that Dottie would not abuse the position of trustee. So he names her to be trustee, with the provision that she must give both children copies of the trust's annual income tax return, so they can see that the principal is not being spent.

C. The Role of the Trustee

Obviously, choosing the right trustee for a marital property control trust is vital. The trustee will have authority to manage the trust property and to make any payments the surviving spouse is entitled to. Also, the trustee may have some enforcement—or at least checking-up—responsibilities, to be sure that the surviving spouse's use of trust property complies with trust requirements. So the trustee normally has all the duties and powers of a trustee of any ongoing trust, plus possibly some delicate personal responsibilities that can require diplomacy or making tough decisions.

Choosing the trustee can be a difficult task, requiring some serious thought. If your current spouse and your children are on good terms or, better yet, really trust each other, you may not face much of a problem. Still, even when the nicest of people are involved, you should understand that there's an inherent potential for conflict between the surviving spouse and the final beneficiaries. The surviving spouse may want or need to spend trust property, including the principal. The final beneficiaries clearly have an interest in preserving as much of the trust principal as possible. And even nice people can at times act in self-interested, and even mean-spirited, ways.

Whatever rules and restrictions you place over the surviving spouse's rights to trust property, it will be the successor trustee who must actually enforce these rules. So it's best if both you and all the beneficiaries have complete trust in this trustee. If such a person exists in your family—and it might be the surviving spouse or one of the children—you're lucky. But certainly, it's not unheard of that your children from a prior marriage don't really trust your current spouse sufficiently to want him to be sole successor trustee. Similarly, the spouse may not want his rights—including, perhaps, such basic rights as where he can live—to be supervised by a child with whom he has a hostile relationship.

If you find yourself facing this situation, it should be no surprise that there's no magic solution that will please everyone. The best you can do is think long and hard about who is most likely to be fair to all involved, and to be seen by all as fair. If your spouse and children trust another family member—a sister, perhaps—choosing her to serve as trustee, assuming she's willing, may be the best solution. If the potential for conflict and mistrust between the surviving spouse and the final beneficiaries is severe, you may need to look for a more unconventional solution.

Example: Alberto is married to Miranda and has one child, age 12. Alberto also has a son, Francesco, age 23, from a prior marriage. To put it bluntly, Francesco and Miranda can't stand each other. What's worse, Alberto thinks neither of them is a particularly good money manager. After discussing this successor trustee problem with Miranda, they agree that a trusted friend, Benito, should serve as successor trustee. Francesco has known Benito for many years, likes him and is relieved when Alberto tells him that Benito, not Miranda, will be the successor trustee. Since Benito is Alberto's age and may predecease Miranda, Alberto puts a provision in his trust that allows Benito to appoint, in writing, alternate successor trustees to serve, in the order nominated, in case Benito, himself, can't do the job. Benito names his wife, Carla, to be the first alternate successor trustee.

Another possibility is simply to name whomever you feel will be fairest, even if that person is your spouse or a child mistrusted by others involved, and let the chips (and sparks) fall as they may.

1. Naming a Financial Institution as Trustee

If you can't find any family member or friend you think would be a suitable trustee, you have a serious problem. Your last resort is to name a financial institution, such as a private trust company, to serve as trustee. As we've discussed before, there can be real drawbacks to this. (See Chapter 17, An Overview of Ongoing Trusts, Section E.)

Many financial institutions will not handle trusts with property worth less than $250,000 or even $500,000. This eliminates many marital property control trusts altogether. Also, financial institutions usually charge hefty fees for serving as trustees. Finally, these institutions can be quite bureaucratic and impersonal, especially when handling trusts that seem like small potatoes to them. So if you must name one as trustee, try to establish a personal relationship with someone you can trust in the institution first.

2. Naming Co-Trustees

It's rarely a good idea to name co-trustees for a marital property control trust. You may hope to reduce potential conflict by naming your spouse and one of your children to serve as co-trustees, but if they don't get along, it could well make matters worse. The result could be a case of trustee gridlock, where each person's vote cancels out the other. Even a simple matter like payment of trust income could wind up in a court battle, if the trustees don't agree what "income" is. And if your spouse and your child or children get along, why bother with co-trustees?

If you want, you can impose reporting requirements on the trustee, such as requiring that the trustee provide annual trust income tax returns to all trust beneficiaries, or even copies of all monthly trust bank account statements. This allows non-trustee beneficiaries to check up on the trust without risking co-trustee power struggles.

D. Savings on Estate Taxes

For couples in second marriages with combined estates exceeding $600,000, a marital property control trust can be used for dual purposes: both to impose controls over the surviving spouse's rights to trust property and to save on overall estate taxes.

Example: Khosro and Maheen, a couple in their late 70s, have an estate worth $1 million, with each owning half. Their home and personal belongings are valued at $400,000, and savings and stocks total $600,000. Khosro has a child from his previous marriage and Maheen has two from hers. They have no children from their marriage.

Each spouse creates a marital property control trust for all of his or her property. The trust documents provide that trust income will go to the surviving spouse, who also will have use of the home. The principal will be maintained for their respective children. The surviving spouse is not given the right to spend trust principal, even for health needs. On the death of the first spouse, no federal estate tax will be due, because the trust property is less than $600,000. (See Chapter 14, Estate Taxes, Section A.

The surviving spouse will receive income from the deceased spouse's share of their stocks and savings, which is $300,000. If interest rates average 6%, this property will generate income of approximately $18,000 a year for the surviving spouse. Khosro and Maheen both feel that when combined with Social Security and retirement benefits, this amount of income is sufficient. In case of an emergency, the surviving spouse naturally can use that spouse's own assets, but not the assets in the marital property control trust, thus preserving the trust assets for that grantor's child or children.

Khosro and Maheen are also pleased that no estate tax will be due on either of their deaths, because each will use their personal estate tax exemptions. Their entire $1 million estate (plus all appreciation in the trust assets) will pass tax-free and intact to their children.

There is nothing tricky about using a marital property control trust to achieve estate savings. Basically, you (with a lawyer's help) prepare the trust document, imposing whatever controls you want to over the surviving spouse's rights to trust property. The trust property is subject to estate tax when you die. If your estate is under $600,000, all the trust property is exempt from estate tax at your death. And because it's never legally owned by your surviving spouse, it will not be subject to tax when the surviving spouse dies.

So it's not a question of drafting a different trust to achieve estate tax savings. That would be necessary only if you wanted to allow the surviving spouse the maximum power over trust assets the IRS allows, which is that trust principal can be spent for the surviving spouse's "education, health care, support or maintenance." It is rare that a grantor in a second or subsequent marriage wants to allow a surviving spouse this broad a right to invade trust principal, because this could result in the devouring of much or even all of that principal.

OTHER SOLUTIONS

What do you do if you are considering using a marital property control trust both for control and tax savings, and anticipate conflict between beneficiaries? First, you should realize that there are no iron-clad rules here. You really do have to come up with your own individual solutions. For instance, you could buy an annuity or insurance policy with the proceeds going to the survivor and leave all other property to the children. Or, particularly if you have a substantial estate, you could leave your children a hefty chunk outright and leave the rest in trust with your spouse as the life beneficiary and grant him, as trustee, fairly generous powers to spend trust principal. The principal may never be touched, but even if it is gobbled up, at least the children have already gotten something.

E. WORKING WITH A LAWYER

If you decide you want a marital property control trust, you'll need to have the trust document prepared by a good estate planning lawyer. There are too many options and possibilities for you to safely prepare one yourself. A good estate planning lawyer will have had experience with other people in second or subsequent marriages, and may be able to offer helpful suggestions for resolving your particular problems. She can also draft trust language that clearly and unambiguously expresses what you want. With this type of trust, it's especially important to avoid any possibly unclear or ambiguous phrases in the trust document. You don't want to leave any opening for beneficiaries to fight over what you really intended.

Although you will need a lawyer, you can still do much of essential work yourself. (See Chapter 30, Using Lawyers, Section A.) After all, it's best not to wander into a lawyer's office and start discussing your situation at $200 or more per hour. Try to work out a tentative plan of what you want before your first visit. The principal issues with a restricted marital life estate trust used to control property are practical, human ones: working out what's fair (as best you can) and deciding who will be best able to carry out your decisions as successor trustee for your trust. These concerns may be easy to state but, in real life, they can be quite difficult to resolve. The best advice we can give is to be candid with yourself. Focus on your specific situation, and try to face family and domestic realities, even if they're not all rosy and romantic. Once you've carefully thought about your situation, needs and desires, write down your specific concerns and what, if any, special problems you anticipate. This should mean less time spent with a lawyer, thus reducing your fee—which likely will still be enough to make you blink. ■

24

Trusts and Other Devices for Imposing Controls Over Property

In a number of situations, sensible estate planning includes the use of an ongoing trust to impose controls over beneficiaries' rights to trust property. One such situation—married people who want to ensure that their property eventually goes to their children from prior marriages—is discussed in Chapter 23, Second and Subsequent Marriages.

We call the types of trusts discussed here "property control trusts." Here are some of the circumstances in which you might want to consider using one:

- One of your beneficiaries is a minor and cannot legally manage more than a small amount of property. (Children's trusts are discussed in Chapter 6, Children, Section C.)
- A beneficiary is a young adult who is not yet mature enough to sensibly manage significant sums of money or property. (Also discussed in Chapter 6.)
- A beneficiary is disabled and will always need help managing property. ("Special needs trusts" are discussed in Section C of this chapter.)
- You believe a beneficiary is improvident with money, and his rights to trust property must be restricted. ("Spendthrift trusts" are discussed in Section D of this chapter.)
- You want the trustee to have the authority to decide how to distribute trust income or principal among several beneficiaries. ("Sprinkling trusts" are discussed in Section E of this chapter. For minor children, this type of trust is called a "family pot trust," discussed in Chapter 6, Children, Section C.)

A property control trust is usually quite a complex legal animal. In most of them, you are trying to impose sensible limits on what can happen with trust property in the future. But since the future cannot be foreseen, you're struggling with what is, at best, very difficult: How to create a trust document that will last for a long time and achieve what you want, in spite of future uncertainties. Some property control trusts, particularly sprinkling trusts, allow the trustee broad powers to decide how to use the trust property for a named group of beneficiaries. This flexibility is desired because the grantor knows he cannot foresee future events and necessities well enough to decide, now, on distribution of trust property.

We don't mean to suggest you shouldn't create a property control trust, if that's what you believe is best. But be aware that without being able to see into the future, you cannot be absolutely certain that you'll achieve what you want. Still, in spite of the inherent uncertainties, the property control trusts discussed here have proved effective over the years for many, many people. Generally, using one of these trusts is far more desirable than not trying to arrange for the handling of a difficult beneficiary situation at all.

Most of the property control trusts discussed here become operational only after your death. There are a couple of exceptions, discussed below, where a trust can become operational either when initially created or on the grantor's death.

See an attorney to prepare a property control trust. All the types of property control trusts discussed in this chapter must be prepared by a knowledgeable estate planning attorney. These trusts inherently involve dealing with uncertainties, and can tie up property for decades. Drafting a trust with such complex matters is not easy. There are no self-help materials that reliably show you how you can prepare one yourself.

A. Exemption Trusts

An exemption trust is simply a trust in which you leave $600,000 or less for any beneficiary or beneficiaries. It's called an exemption trust because the amount in the trust—under $600,000—is exempt from federal estate tax. An exemption trust becomes operational after your death.

The basic purpose of exemption trusts is to control trust property. Usually, property is left for the use of one or more beneficiaries for a number of years or, more likely, for life. They are called the "income" beneficiaries, although the trustee can also be given rights to spend trust principal for them. Eventually, that property goes to the final beneficiaries.

The property placed in an exemption trust is not subject to estate tax, unless your total estate, including property in the exemption trust and all property outside it, exceeds $600,000. If your total estate was less than $600,000 when you died, the property in the trust will never be taxed by the federal government, no matter how much the property is worth when it's distributed to the final beneficiaries.

Example: Delilah wants her sister Ruth to be able to live in her house, with equity worth $350,000, for her lifetime. She wants the house to go to Ruth's son after Ruth dies. She creates an exemption trust for the house. Ruth is named as the life beneficiary, and will have the use of the house during her life. Upon her death, the house will go to Ruth's son. The house stays out of Ruth's estate for tax (and probate) purposes because she never legally owns it. Even if Ruth lives for 20 years and the house value climbs to $1 million, no tax is due at her death.

You can use an exemption trust also, even if you have an estate exceeding $600,000. A common situation is where you want to leave some property in trust for your children and grandchildren, and other property to your spouse.

Example: Roger, a prosperous businessman, is 66 years old. He creates an exemption trust of $600,000, with the rest of his assets to go outright to his wife, Monique. In the exemption trust, he specifies that each of his two daughters (who serve as co-successor trustees) will share the income from the trust for life, unless either has a child who begins college. If this occurs, income from the child's parent's portion of the trust will be used for college expenses. Any remaining income goes to the child's parent. If there are, eventually, several children in college, the trustee can spend trust principal to pay for costs that aren't covered by trust income. When a child graduates from college or graduate school, trust income reverts to that child's parent. When one parent dies, her remaining trust principal is to be divided equally between her grandchildren.

Roger chose $600,000 to place in this trust because that amount will be free of federal estate tax. Since all the rest of his property is left outright to his spouse, it is not liable for estate tax because of the marital deduction. (See Chapter 15, Estate Taxes, Section A, for a review of basic federal estate tax rules.)

An exemption trust offers you these basic advantages:

- The assets in the trust can be used to benefit more than one income beneficiary for whatever period you name, and then go to the final beneficiaries. By contrast, in a marital life estate trust or a marital deduction trust, there can only be one life beneficiary, the surviving spouse.
- If your estate is under $600,000, you can pass on all the trust assets to the final beneficiaries free of estate tax.
- You can include in the trust property that produces little or no income, such as unimproved land or valuable art works. By contrast, in a QTIP trust, if the property isn't income-producing, the surviving spouse, as life beneficiary, can demand

that the property be sold and the proceeds invested in income-producing property. (QTIP trusts are discussed in Chapter 19, Other Estate Tax-Saving Marital Trusts, Section A.)

- Some or all of the trust principal can be made available to either the income or final beneficiaries when needed. Usually the trustee decides if a beneficiary needs to spend (invade) trust principal under general standards set out in the trust document.

B. Educational Trusts

A relatively common type of property control trust is one created to help beneficiaries pay for college or other schooling. These trusts are rarely set up by parents of children—they just pay educational costs directly, out of their own pockets. They are more commonly created by a grandparent or other older relatives who want to help young relations.

Creating an educational property control trust often involves resolving many rather difficult issues:

When should the trust become operational? If the beneficiaries are very young, and you are unlikely to live until a child begins college, this is not a serious problem. You can arrange for the trust to become operational at your death. But what happens if the children are older, near or at college age? You may well want the trust to become operational now, while you live.

If you create the trust now, there can be significant tax consequences. The property you give to the trust will be a taxable gift. The gift tax exemption for educational costs won't apply, because that works only for money paid directly to an educational institution. (See Chapter 15, Gifts and Gift Taxes, Section C.)

If the trust becomes operational while you're alive, do you want to be the initial trustee or appoint someone else who would continue to serve after your death?

How does a grandchild qualify for benefits? Does a grandchild have to attend college or school full-time to receive trust benefits? What constitutes "full-time"? What qualifies as a college or school? And if a grandchild discovers another way to learn—for example, becomes an apprentice to a metal sculptor—does the successor trustee have authority to approve the payment of trust benefits? What about graduate school? Would those expenses be covered from the trust?

Can unequal payments be made to different beneficiaries? If one grandchild attends Columbia Medical School, while the other grandchild goes to a non-tuition community college, their expenses will vary greatly. Lawyers call a trust where a trustee can pay different amounts of principal or income to different beneficiaries based on their needs a "pot" trust—all the dough is in one pot. By contrast, if you want each child to have the same amount of money, you should set up separate trusts for each grandchild.

What happens if more grandchildren are born? How can the trust include them as possible beneficiaries? Accomplishing this is largely a matter of proper legal drafting of the trust document, by an expert lawyer.

What happens if no grandchildren attend college? Can the trust income be used for grandchildren's "emergencies?" What kinds? What do you want to happen with the trust principal?

When does the trust end? What happens to any money left in the trust when it does end? Is distribution left up to the trustee.

If you think you want to create an educational trust, first try to tentatively resolve the types of questions posed above and any other questions you think of. Write out your basic thoughts and resolutions of the issues. Then you'll need to see an experienced estate planning attorney.

If need be, she should be able to help you clarify your desires regarding the trust. Then you must rely on her skillful drafting of the trust document to turn your desires into an educational trust that works as you intend. If you have worked out what you want as best you can before you see an attorney, you'll have a framework to work from that should focus what you and the attorney do, and thus lower your fees.

C. Trusts for Persons With Special Needs

Parents or others who care about someone who is disabled by serious physical or mental problems can face difficult estate planning questions. Understandably, they may want to provide for the disabled person, to the extent possible, for as long as that person lives. If the disabled person cannot be expected to sensibly manage property, the property must be left in a property control trust. And the trust document must be carefully drafted, so that the trustee has enough flexibility to deal with the beneficiary's medical or other special needs.

There is no standard special needs trust that can be used in all circumstances. A trust created to provide for a disabled beneficiary must be geared to his or her particular needs and problems, as well as how much money you can afford to place in the trust. If you're uncertain whether or not a given amount will cover all the beneficiary's expenses, you may want to prioritize what you anticipate the most important needs of the beneficiary will be and set them out in the trust document, to provide guidance for the trustee on spending trust money. At the other end of the spectrum, you can leave it up to the trustee to decide how much, and when, to spend trust income or principal for the beneficiary's needs.

1. Choosing the Trustee

A primary concern with a special needs trust is making sure you select a trustee and successor trustee(s) who are willing and able to do the job. The trustee's responsibilities include being attentive to the disabled person's situation, discerning what is needed, and providing for those needs to the extent possible. The trustee will need to be in close contact with the disabled person—the trust beneficiary—so it is essential that the two get along. And finally, the trustee should have the savvy to deal with various institutions, from banks to money market funds to medical providers, and quite possibly, government agencies.

2. Eligibility for Government Assistance

Usually a major concern with a special needs trust is how to prevent the trust from rendering the beneficiary ineligible for government assistance, such as Supplemental Security Income (SSI) or medical or educational aid. This fear is very real, since a disabled person who is the legal owner of any substantial amount of property usually must use up most of it before government assistance is available. In some circumstances, if a disabled person acquires property, the government may even demand reimbursement for past benefits.

Obviously, this rule can have nasty consequences. Even if the property left to the disabled person is substantial, it may be used up fairly quickly. The disabled person will then become eligible once more for governmental assistance, but none of the trust property will remain for emergencies or the many needs governmental assistance doesn't provide for.

Technically, the beneficiary is not the legal owner of the trust property—the trustee is. But this fact alone doesn't mean that a government agency won't try to consider the trust principal (as well as, of course, any trust income the beneficiary actually receives) as part of the beneficiary's property, when it comes to determining eligibility for government aid.

If you can provide enough trust money to take care of all the beneficiary's needs, you may not need to worry about the disabled beneficiary's eligibility for government benefits. Of course, how much money must be in the trust before you reach this point is a personal, subjective decision. But few people can leave millions, or anything approaching it, in a special needs trust. Most people who create one of these trusts have far less money.

What can you do? You can, of course, elect not to give any property to the disabled beneficiary in the first place and let the person rely exclusively on government benefits. But if, like most people, you are rightly skeptical of relying on public programs to provide total care for someone with special needs, this is not a solution you'll be eager to accept.

Fortunately, there is a better choice. You can establish a property control trust that allows the trust property to be used for the benefit of the disabled person without affecting eligibility for public assistance.

Under U.S. Social Security Administration (SSA) guidelines, the property in a special needs trust doesn't affect eligibility for Social Security assistance if the beneficiary cannot:

- control the amount or frequency of trust payments, or
- revoke the trust and use the property.

In other words, the beneficiary can have no rights to demand and receive money from the trust, either income or principal. Nor can the beneficiary simply revoke the trust and obtain the trust principal. All power over the trust principal, including payment of income or principal to the beneficiary, must be given to the trustee.

Local SSA offices have wide latitude in interpreting these SSA guidelines. For example, some local SSA offices require that the trust document show the trust creator didn't "intend" the trust property to be used as the primary source of aid or income for the disadvantaged person.

Statutes and SSA regulations pertaining to eligibility for government programs change frequently. Further, each state has its own regulations about eligibility for government programs (many aid programs, primarily funded by the federal government, are administered through state agencies). These regulations also can change quickly.

Thus, the key to drafting a trust for a disabled person is up-to-date knowledge of:

- relevant federal law
- SSA rules and court interpretations of them
- local SSA practices, and
- state rules and regulations.

Because the government rules here are complex and can change suddenly, a distinct legal subspecialty has developed: lawyers who prepare special needs trusts. The truth is that you really need not only an estate planning expert here, but someone who is knowledgeable in drafting special needs trusts. (See Chapter 30, Using Lawyers, Section A, for a discussion of how to find the right lawyer for you.) You most definitely should not attempt to do it yourself. There are no detailed self-help or other information about how to prepare these trusts. Nor can you safely rely on a general practice lawyer, most of whom are not knowledgeable enough to properly prepare a special needs trust.

D. Spendthrift Trusts

Put bluntly, a spendthrift trust is designed to minimize an unreliable beneficiary's ability to squander trust principal. The "spendthrift" beneficiary may be someone who simply has no head for money (like some of our dearest friends and relatives), and could easily waste trust principal if controls weren't placed on his right to get at it. This type of trust is also used when a beneficiary has an addictive personality and might spend trust principal on drugs, alcohol, gambling or some other compulsive indulgence. Creating a spendthrift trust is an attempt to balance concern for the beneficiary with a realistic appraisal of his more wasteful or destructive behaviors.

The term "spendthrift" may sound like a harsh epithet to apply to a loved one, but sitting down to work out a sensible estate plan demands facing realities, even painful ones. If you want to help someone who is financially irresponsible, a spendthrift trust that provides rigid control of the property may be warranted.

With a spendthrift trust, the beneficiary is never the trustee. The trustee can spend trust money for the beneficiary's needs, or make income payments directly to the beneficiary, as the trust document directs or permits. The beneficiary has no right to spend trust principal. Nor does he have the legal right to pledge trust principal, or future income expected from the trust, as security for a loan.

Example: Pierre wants to leave money to his son, Maurice, a charming fellow who's always spent money as if he were a millionaire. So Pierre creates an ongoing spendthrift trust for the benefit of Maurice, to take effect after Pierre dies. The trust will be managed by Pierre's prudent bourgeois brother Jean-Paul, who will dole out trust income to Maurice on the first of each month. If Jean-Paul predeceases Maurice, first Jean-Paul's wife, Anne-Marie (also quite prudent) and next their son Thierry (a chip off the old block) will serve as trustee.

Under the terms of the trust, Maurice cannot obtain the trust principal or pledge his expected trust income to obtain credit. The trust will end when Maurice becomes 50, by which point Pierre hopes he'll have learned financial prudence. If not, Pierre simply accepts the risk that he'll waste the trust principal at that age.

At the extreme, a spendthrift clause can give the trustee power to cut off benefits, temporarily or even permanently, to a beneficiary who becomes uncontrollably self-destructive. Income withheld could be accumulated in the trust or paid to another beneficiary named in the trust document.

Giving the trustee this power, however, is rarely if ever wise. It imposes a troubling burden on the trustee, who must decide what behavior by the unreliable beneficiary is so bad that income may be withheld. Even if certain offending behaviors are spelled out in the trust document, it's the trustee who must actually make the factual determination of whether the beneficiary's behavior justifies withholding income payments. How is the trustee to make this determination? Must he play detective, or hire a professional to spy on the beneficiary?

Perhaps the most that you can sensibly do here to describe, in the trust document, specific, objective acts which, if undertaken by the beneficiary, would allow the trustee to withhold income payments. For example, the trust document could provide that if the

ADDING SPENDTHRIFT PROVISIONS TO ANY ONGOING TRUST

Even when a beneficiary is presumed to be financially responsible, some estate planning lawyers include spendthrift clauses in any ongoing trust. These clauses usually prohibit the beneficiaries from assigning money they expect to receive from the trust to someone else, or from using the trust principal as collateral to obtain a loan. The purpose of such clauses is simply to protect the trust assets from creditors as much as possible.

Including a spendthrift clause in an ongoing trust doesn't have to be seen as an insult to your beneficiaries. Ongoing trusts can last for a very long time, and you have no way of seeing into the future. An unforeseen nightmare may occur—for example, a beneficiary could become involved in a nasty divorce with a spouse who attempts to grab hold of every asset she or he can. (We know of a man who, before leaving his wife, inventoried the food in their refrigerator, and later claimed his estimate of its worth as part of their community property.) Or a beneficiary could be sued, with all assets, including trust principal, considered up for grabs. Even a medical provider occasionally attempts to obtain funds from trust assets that you would not want used for that purpose.

As long as a spendthrift clause is not designed to defraud creditors, it is legally acceptable and may be a good idea to protect the trust property.

beneficiary were convicted of certain types of drug offenses, payments could be withheld. But even here, is this really the wisest course? Even if the beneficiary were in prison (where access to drugs should be greatly reduced), wouldn't receiving income payments from the trust be a help? Having some personal cash could ease a prisoner's life in many ways, from purchasing canteen food to affording good legal representation.

A less draconian method is for you to direct the trustee to continue to make payments for the benefit of a beneficiary who's become obviously self-destructive (such as paying his rent, food bills or other basic needs) but withhold direct payments to that beneficiary. This still imposes on the trustee the burden of evaluating the beneficiary's behavior, with all the difficulties that involves. But sometimes imposing such a burden is necessary, particularly when the beneficiary's behavior could become (or already is) truly dangerous.

In other situations, you may decide that the trustee must make regular (monthly or quarterly) payments to the beneficiary, regardless of the beneficiary's behavior. These payments can be defined in the trust document as all of the trust income, a set amount, or a percentage of trust income. But however the payments are defined, if you choose this option, you must accept the risk that the beneficiary won't spend the money wisely. Once the beneficiary actually receives the trust income, he can spend it however he wants. No trust can prevent a beneficiary from squandering money once it's in his pocket.

The rigidity of spendthrift trusts can be a problem down the road. What happens if the beneficiary needs more money than the monthly payment allowed? Does the trustee have the power to spend trust principal if the beneficiary becomes ill and lacks funds to pay medical bills? Or suppose the beneficiary sees the error of his wasteful ways and decides to settle down and go to dental school. Can the trustee use the principal to pay the beneficiary's tuition? You may decide to allow the trustee to spend trust principal for the beneficiary, either for specific needs or as the trustee determines is desirable.

E. Sprinkling Trusts

Perhaps the most flexible property control trust of all is termed a "sprinkling" or a "discretionary" trust. Under either lingo, this type of trust gives the trustee authority to "sprinkle" both the income and principal of the trust between named beneficiaries. (Sometimes this is called allowing "sprinkling" powers.)

A sprinkling trust differs from other trusts, including all other trusts designed to control property, in that you don't specify what property each beneficiary gets, or when. Rather, you leave money in the trust and name the group of possible beneficiaries. The trustee determines which of these beneficiaries will receive payments from trust income or principal, and how much.

You can, however, give the trustee rules to follow in the trust document. For instance, the trustee could be allowed to spend trust principal only for a beneficiary's educational or medical needs. Or a trustee might have the power to sprinkle only trust income, not principal. Or he could have the power to give no more than 20% of the trust principal to any one beneficiary in any one year.

If the trustee decides it's best, income may be accumulated in the trust instead of being handed out to any beneficiaries. However, the income tax rate applied to retained trust income will probably be higher than the rate applied to trust income received by beneficiaries. (See Chapter 17, An Overview of Ongoing Trusts, Section F.) Therefore, it's unlikely that a trustee would decide to retain trust income, effectively costing the beneficiaries money in higher taxes.

By law, you must name an independent ("disinterested") trustee—that is, a trustee who has no financial interest in how the trust money is distributed, but is dispassionate enough to hand out money as it's genuinely needed. Thus, a surviving spouse normally should not serve as trustee of a sprinkling trust. (See Section 3, below.)

1. Sprinkling Marital Life Estate Trusts

A sprinkling marital life estate trust can be appropriate for a couple with a large estate, when the surviving spouse has plenty of assets and may not need or want regular income payments. To make sure trust assets are available to the surviving spouse in an emergency, you can include provisions allowing invasion of principal for the surviving spouse's health care or other basic needs. Creating "sprinkling powers" in a marital life estate trust can accomplish several goals:

- **Helping other beneficiaries:** You can take care of possible needs of other beneficiaries, such as your children, during the surviving spouse's life. At an extreme, for example, if a wealthy surviving spouse marries someone even wealthier, the trustee can choose not to pay anything at all to that spouse, but to spend (or save) all the trust income and assets for the children or other named beneficiaries.

  More commonly, one child beneficiary may need more money for education or support than another. When the beneficiaries are young, a sprinkling trust allows great flexibility over the years and makes the assets available when necessary.

- **Income tax savings.** If your surviving spouse will be well off, you can achieve income tax savings by channeling some trust income to beneficiaries in lower tax brackets, such as adult children or children over 14 with low incomes. (Income paid out to children 13 or younger is taxed at their parents' rates; see Chapter 6, Children, Section C.)

Example: Akira and Mariko have a shared estate totaling $3 million. They have two young children, and Akira also has a teenaged son by a former marriage.

Akira drafts a sprinkling marital life estate trust placing $600,000 of his property in the trust. His remaining property will go into a QTIP trust, with his wife as life beneficiary and Akira's three children as the final beneficiaries. (See Chapter 19, Other Estate Tax-Saving Marital Trusts, Section A, for a discussion of QTIP trusts, which are used to defer payment of estate tax.) If he dies first, the trustee of the marital life estate trust will have the power to sprinkle both income and principal to Mariko and to any of the children for their support for the rest of Mariko's life. Upon Mariko's death, the remaining assets will be distributed to Akira's children. The trust document specifies that this division shall take into consideration how much from the trust has been previously paid to each.

Akira accomplishes several purposes with this trust plan. He takes advantage of his $600,000 personal federal estate tax exemption and defers all estate tax on his remaining $900,000 until Mariko's death.

Akira also makes funds available early on for his teenaged son, who will be facing college and perhaps graduate school expenses. And if Mariko doesn't want some or all of the income, she can always disclaim it (see Chapter 22, Disclaimers, Section A), building a larger trust principal for the children to inherit later.

2. Other Uses of Sprinkling Trust Provisions

Sprinkling trust provisions can be used in a wide variety of property control trusts. For example, if you want to leave property for minor children or young adults, you may create a "family pot" trust. This is a kind of sprinkling trust, where you choose to let the trustee decide, according to the actual needs and circumstances of the children, how much money to pay to each child. If you have full confidence in the trustee, this approach may be wiser than trying to foresee now which children will need what in the future, or simply dividing the trust principal equally between the children and ignoring the possibility that one may legitimately need far more than another.

Similarly, a grandparent may create a sprinkling trust for grandchildren or, for that matter, for adult children. Sprinkling trust provisions can work well in any situation if you totally trust the trustee, and there are a number of beneficiaries who may need payments from the trust for a long period of time.

3. Choosing an "Independent" Trustee

No matter the type of sprinkling trust, a key to making one work well is to appoint a disinterested, independent trustee, whom you trust completely. Because a sprinkling trust is intended to operate over a lengthy period, you also need to select at least one successor trustee, and often an alternate successor trustee, with similar care.

An "independent" trustee means a trustee who cannot benefit from the trust—that is, is not a beneficiary of any kind. Even someone who is named as an alternate beneficiary (or fourth alternate, for that matter) cannot serve. If the trustee is financially "interested" in the trust, the IRS may consider her to be the legal owner of all the trust property and include it in her taxable estate when she dies, which is definitely not what you want.

This is the reason the surviving spouse should not be the trustee of a sprinkling marital life estate trust. As the life beneficiary, the surviving spouse obviously has an interest in trust payments. Indeed, normally, as you know, he receives all trust income during his life. But creating a sprinkling trust clause means there are other possibilities. Allowing the surviving spouse to be the trustee in this situation, when there are sprinkling provisions in the trust, means the IRS will regard him as the legal owner of all trust property. That property will be included in his taxable estate when he dies, and thus the grantor's personal $600,00 estate tax exemption will have been wasted.

You need a trustee who, although he or she has no financial interest in how the trust money is distributed, is personally interested in the welfare of the beneficiaries and will remain alert to their financial needs. A sprinkling trust, by its very nature, can create conflict among the beneficiaries. After all, they may all think they need money—and a lot of it—from the trust, so the trustee may have some serious personal as well as financial issues to handle. If you can't find a legally independent but emotionally involved person who'll do the job, and who you fully trust, a sprinkling trust isn't for you.

F. Trusts to Manage Your Own Property

If you tire of coping with your property and financial affairs, you can arrange for someone else to manage your property. One method is for you to put your property in a trust, to be managed by a trustee for your benefit. The trustee would have the authority to spend any amount of trust income or principal for you. You can define as carefully as you like in the trust document what standard of living you expect. (Of course, there must be sufficient assets in the trust to pay for that standard of living.)

Unlike the other trusts discussed in this chapter, there's no need to have this type of trust be irrevocable. Indeed, there are real drawbacks to making the trust irrevocable. The consequences of that are that the trustee must obtain a trust taxpayer ID, maintain trust financial records, and file an annual trust income tax return. None of this would benefit you.

There is one possible pitfall here. Under IRS regulations, if you are not one of the trustees of a revocable trust for your benefit, then the tax requirements applied to irrevocable trusts apply to this revocable trust as well. One simple way to avoid this problem is for you to name yourself and some other person as co-trustees and provide in the trust document that either trustee may act for the trust. The other person, as co-trustee, in reality becomes the sole manager of the trust property. But as long as you remain one of the official trustees, no tax reporting obligations are imposed on the trust.

There are other devices that you can use to allow another person to manage your property for you. One method is to give another person authority, using a document called a durable power of attorney for finances, to manage the property. (As we discuss in Chapter 26, Incapacity: Health Care and Financial Management Directives, Section B), it's always a good idea to create a durable power of attorney for finances as part of your estate plan.) A durable power of attorney for finances, however, does not give authority over property in a living trust.

If you have transferred property to a living trust, there is no need to create a new trust to handle that trust property in case you become incapacitated. A standard clause in a well-drafted living trust authorizes your successor trustee to take over management of your trust property, if necessary, for your benefit as long as you live. (See Chapter 9, Revocable Living Trusts, Section B.) If this happens, the living trust remains revocable, if you regain the ability to manage your affairs.

Malcolm hopes Jamal will see the light and cease using drugs, so he surely doesn't want to cut Jamal out irrevocably. So in his living trust he creates a power of appointment in his best friend, Ted. Ted will decide, after Malcolm's death, if Jamal can be given property outright because he has been clear from drugs for a specified period of time. (Of course, determining this may not be easy.) If Ted decides Jamal still suffers from drug addiction, then the property left for Jamal will go into a trust for him, managed by Ted.

G. Powers of Appointment

A "power of appointment" is simply the power to determine how someone's assets are distributed after his or her death.

Example: In her living trust, Anita authorizes her husband, Frederico, to distribute all her property among her children as he wishes, if he outlives her. If he doesn't outlive her, Anita grants the same authority to her brother, Marcello.

There can be a number of sensible reasons to use a power of appointment. Generally the most common reason is that you are unsure, when you prepare your estate plan, exactly who you want your beneficiaries to be. In this case, you don't want to create a sprinkling trust, because there the trustee normally has the power to distribute trust money only among beneficiaries named in the trust document. If you trust someone—a spouse, brother or friend—completely, it may make sense to postpone the choice of beneficiaries, or what property named beneficiaries will receive, until later.

Example: Malcolm, a widower, has two children: Veronica, age 24, and Jamal, age 22, who has a serious drug problem. Malcolm certainly doesn't want to leave any property outright to Jamal if he's still using drugs when Malcolm dies. On the other hand,

1. Kinds of Powers of Appointment

There are two kinds of powers of appointment: "general" and "special" (also called "limited"). A general power of appointment often has adverse estate tax consequences, while a limited power of appointment does not.

General power of appointment. You name a person to distribute your property to whomever she chooses—including herself. Authorizing a general power of appointment is rarely a good idea. Under IRS rules, the person who has a general power of appointment will have the full value of the property subject to that power included in her taxable estate at her death. This is true even if she never gives any property to herself, had no intention of doing so, and in fact gave it all to someone else. The practical effect is that this property is subject to estate tax twice—once when you die and once when the person to whom you gave the power of appointment dies.

Example: In his living trust, Martin gives his wife Helen a general power of appointment over property worth $500,000. Martin's total estate is worth $900,000, so it is subject to federal estate tax. Ellen's estate is worth $700,000, aside from the property subject to the general power of appointment. Shortly after Martin's death, Ellen gives the entire $500,000 to their three children. Nevertheless, when Ellen dies, the entire $500,000 is included in her taxable estate, because she had the power to give all this money to herself if she had chosen to. So the $500,000 has been included in two taxable estates, which is clearly undesirable.

Special or limited power of appointment. This kind of power to appoint is limited as you see fit. Most importantly, the person who has the power cannot give the property to himself, use it to pay his creditors or leave it in his estate. This eliminates the double estate tax problem of a general power of appointment.

Typically, if you give someone a limited power of appointment, you specify which people (beneficiaries) the holder of the power can give property to. For instance, the person appointed can be given only the right to divide property among your four children. Or the person can be directed to give at least 15% of your property to each of the children, with the remaining 40% to be distributed among them as the person with the special power of appointment determines.

Example: Woody sets up a marital life estate trust, leaving the income from the trust to his wife, Janet, and the principal to their three children upon Janet's death. He includes a limited power of appointment authorizing Janet to direct how the trust assets will pass to the children, if she so chooses. Janet lives for 20 years after Woody's death and receives the income from the trust. During that time, Sarah, one of the children, gives birth to a severely disabled child. The other children are all well-off financially and don't, in Janet's opinion, need money from the trust.

Janet considers what Woody would want if he were alive and could make the decision. Then, in her will, she exercises her limited power of appointment, by leaving 75% of the trust property outright to Sarah, with the understanding that Sarah will use the money primarily for her disabled child's needs. The other 25% of the trust property is divided between the other two children.

Just because a limited power of appointment is included in a trust document does not mean that this power must be exercised. If circumstances have not changed, or if the original directions of distribution appear equitable, the person holding the limited power of appointment can just leave the situation alone. If there were no original directions, just a list of possible beneficiaries, then the holder of the limited power of appointment must decide who receives what property. Otherwise, the property will probably be divided equally between the named beneficiaries. But state law could compel other results here, so it's not a risk to take; make sure the person to whom you give a power of appointment understands this.

Limited powers of appointment and disclaimers: With a limited power of appointment, problems can arise if the person given the power also wants to use a disclaimer at the grantor's death. If one disclaims (refuses) property that then goes into a trust, the one disclaiming cannot then direct where the disclaimed property eventually goes. So disclaiming is inconsistent with having any power of appointment, even a limited one. (See Chapter 22, Disclaimers, Section C.) See a good estate planning lawyer if you think this problem might come up.

2. Limited Power of Appointment in QTIP Trusts

Limited powers of appointment are also occasionally used in QTIP trusts. A QTIP trust is basically a device to defer estate tax until the death of a surviving spouse, while allowing the first spouse to die to name the final beneficiaries for his estate. (See Chapter 19, Other Estate Tax-Saving Marital Trusts, Section A.)

When a surviving spouse is given a limited power of appointment over QTIP trust property, the surviving spouse simply has some control over the final distribution of the assets in the QTIP trust, within the limits the grantor imposed. The grantor can choose the final group of beneficiaries, such as his children, and allow a spouse to determine the amounts received by each one. The grantor, then, still controls who the final beneficiaries are—just not how much each receives.

Example: Gert leaves $1 million in a QTIP trust with the income going to her much younger husband, Raphael, for his life. She gives him a limited power of appointment to choose at his death how much each of her four children by a previous marriage will receive of what is left. Raphael may benefit for many years from the trust, and he may adjust the final outcome according to the children's needs. But if he remarries (and Gert suspects that he might well), the trust terms prevent him from shifting these assets to his new bride or to anyone else. ■

25

Combining Ongoing Trusts

This chapter is only for individuals who have estates exceeding $600,000 in value. Those with smaller estates can skip this chapter.

Many individuals and couples find it desirable to use more than one trust in their estate plans. There are no fixed rules or customs regarding how to combine trusts. The trust combinations presented in this chapter can give you a sense of the possibilities offered by combining different types of trusts. What combination, if any, is right for you is a matter for you to decide after reading this chapter, perhaps doing more research, and certainly consulting an estate planning expert.

It should come as no surprise that if you use two or more different types of ongoing trusts in your estate plan, it will be complex and tricky to work out the precise details of that plan. You will definitely need an expert estate planning lawyer, and your legal bill will probably be substantial. But since you must have considerable wealth before it's worth combining different trusts, and since doing so can save you and your inheritors a bundle, the lawyer's cost is probably well worth it.

A. Combining Two Estate Tax-Saving Trusts

A QTIP trust is a marital trust where the surviving spouse receives a life interest in trust property. (See Chapter 19, Other Estate Tax-Saving Marital Trusts, Section A.) Usually, the spouse who creates the trust names the final beneficiaries, who receive the property when the second spouse dies. No estate tax is due when the first spouse dies, no matter how much the property in the QTIP trust is worth. A common estate plan for wealthier couples, whose combined estate exceeds $1.2 million, is for each spouse to create two trusts: a marital life estate trust for up to $600,000 and a QTIP trust for all the rest. (See Chapter 18, Estate Tax-Saving Bypass Trusts, Section C, for more on marital life estate trusts.) With the combination of these two trusts, each spouse achieves several desirable goals:

- Each spouse uses his or her own $600,000 federal estate tax exemption.
- All property over and above each spouse's $600,000 exemption is placed in the QTIP trust and qualifies for the unlimited marital deduction; this means that no federal estate tax at all must be paid on the death of the first spouse. (If all a spouse's property were in the marital life estate trust, all amounts over $600,000 would be taxable. Property in a marital life estate trust does not qualify for the marital deduction.)
- The first spouse to die determines who will ultimately receive all his property after the surviving spouse dies. If all the property instead went to the surviving spouse with no strings attached, it would not necessarily pass, at the surviving spouse's death, to the people the first spouse would have wanted to inherit it.

Example: Miles and Simian, in their early 50s, have been married over 25 years. They have two children and a substantial estate (almost all co-owned) worth over $4 million. Their estate plan consists of each preparing a marital life estate trust, funded with $600,000, with the surviving spouse as life beneficiary. Because this allows each spouse to take advantage of his or her personal exemption, no federal estate tax will be paid on this money. Each spouse's remaining property (roughly $1.4 million) will be placed in a QTIP trust, with the surviving spouse again as life beneficiary. The surviving spouse is entitled to all income from the trust during his or her life, and can spend trust principal for "education, health care, maintenance and support." (This is the

IRS "objective" standard for invasion of principal. See Chapter 18, Estate Tax-Saving Bypass Trusts, Section B.)

The couple's children are final beneficiaries of both trusts. Neither spouse thinks it's likely that the other would run wild if one died suddenly, but who can tell what might happen if one spouse survives the other by 20 or 30 years—a remarriage? A second family of stepchildren? A sudden urge to seek thrills and bet millions at the race track? A QTIP trust protects the children from any of these remote possibilities.

Combining a QTIP and a marital life estate trust can also be useful if you're in a second marriage and want to provide for both your spouse and your children from a prior relationship.

Example 1: Malcolm, age 60, has been married to Sadie, age 47, for four years. He has three children from a former marriage. Sadie has a small estate of her own, consisting of savings and stock worth $50,000. Malcolm, on the other hand, owns his house and a varied portfolio; his assets are worth a total of $800,000. He also has a life insurance policy that will pay $100,000 to Sadie at his death.

Although his children seem to like Sadie, Malcolm senses uneasiness among them about whether they'll actually receive the inheritance they've been expecting from him. Wanting to take care of everybody, if possible, and also to create no hard feelings, Malcolm musters the following plan.

Upon his death, his assets are to be divided into two trusts. One is a marital life estate trust, which will consist of property worth $600,000, the amount than can pass free of federal estate tax. The second is a QTIP trust for all his property exceeding $600,000. Malcolm decides to name Sadie and his daughter Hilda, the most level-headed of his children and the one who gets along with Sadie the best, to be co-trustees of both trusts.

Malcolm provides in the QTIP trust document that the income goes to Sadie during her life, and also that the trust principal may be used, if the co-trustees agree it is needed, for Sadie's health care or basic maintenance. When Sadie dies, the QTIP trust principal is to be divided among his three children.

The amount that would go to the QTIP if Malcolm died suddenly is about $200,000. But since Malcolm is 60 and still working, this amount could increase.

No tax is due on the QTIP trust property at Malcolm's death because of the marital deduction. At Sadie's death, what remains in this trust will be subject to estate tax as part of her estate. But if, as seems likely, her entire estate is not over $600,000, including the value of the QTIP property, no federal estate tax will be assessed.

Malcolm provides that the marital life estate trust will contain his house, and Sadie will have the right to live in it for her life. The trust will also pay income to Sadie for her life, but she will have no right to invade the principal. Malcolm has decided that the principal in the QTIP should be sufficient to protect Sadie in case of serious financial need. This way, he's preserved at least $600,000 for his children, while he's treated Sadie fairly. He's also protected at least $600,000 of his estate from estate tax, and possibly more, up to all the amount in the QTIP.

Example 2: Carla has assets worth $950,000; her husband Peter's property totals $200,000. They are both in their late 60s, and Carla has three children by a previous marriage. She wants to avoid estate tax and also make sure Peter can live comfortably for the rest of his life if she should die first, but she wants all she owns to go eventually to her children.

To help her children in the years when they are establishing families of their own, Carla makes specific gifts in her living trust of $50,000 to each of her three children. She also creates a marital life estate trust for $450,000, which uses up the rest of her personal tax exemption of $600,000. Peter will receive the income from this trust, and upon his death the principal will go equally to her children. Peter is not given any right to invade the principal of this trust. And he is not named as trustee. Rather, Carla names her most reliable child as trustee.

Carla creates a QTIP trust for her remaining assets. Income from this trust goes to Peter during his life, and the principal can be invaded if needed for his support. At Peter's death, all assets remaining in the QTIP trust also go to Carla's children. Carla names her child as trustee of the QTIP trust, too.

This is the tax picture:

At Carla's Death:

Taxable estate	$950,000
QTIP trust (tax postponed because of the marital deduction)	$350,000
Gifts left to children	$150,000
Marital life estate trust	$450,000
Credit for personal $600,000 exemption	$192,800
Federal estate tax	$0

At Peter's Death:

Taxable estate (his own property plus the QTIP principal)	$550,000
Credit for personal $600,000 exemption	$192,800
Federal estate tax	$0

B. Combining a Charitable Trust With Other Estate Tax Saving Trusts

If you want to leave some of your property to causes you care deeply about, you are eligible for some tax breaks. For example, gifts made to charities through a charitable trust are exempt from estate tax. (See Chapter 20, Charitable Trusts.) The other potential benefits from using a charitable trust are that you take an income tax deduction on the worth of the property to charity, and also avoid paying capital gain tax, if the charity sells appreciated assets you gave it.

Unless you are extremely wealthy or don't want to leave property to any individuals, however, you may understandably be reluctant to give or leave significant assets to a charity. Fortunately, if you set up a charitable trust, you can have your cake and eat it too—that is, make the charitable gift, but do it in such a way that the value of the property donated is replaced in your estate, so that your other beneficiaries receive as much as they would have without the charitable trust.

A major method of achieving this is to create both a charitable trust and an irrevocable life insurance trust. The proceeds of the life insurance policy will be roughly equal to the amount your individual beneficiaries would have inherited from you if you hadn't made the charitable gift.

Irrevocable life insurance trusts are discussed in Chapter 21, Other Estate Tax-Saving Trusts, Section B. Basically, such a trust owns your life insurance policy—which means that the policy proceeds are not included in your estate, for tax purposes, when you die.

Here's a summary of how you could use a life insurance trust to replace money "lost" to individual beneficiaries because of a charitable gift:

1. First, you make a gift to charity through a charitable trust.

2. You create the life insurance trust. You fund it, for the purpose of making premium payments, with the income tax-savings you obtained by making the charitable gift. This means there is no significant actual cost to you to create and fund the trust. You choose a life insurance policy that will pay out, at

your death, more or less the same amount that you gave the charity.

3. You include "Crummey provisions" in your life insurance trust document. These clauses allow gifts you make to the trust to qualify for the $10,000 annual gift tax exclusion. (See Chapter 21, Section B.) Otherwise, if you gave money directly to the trust, it wouldn't qualify. The Crummey provisions further provide that for each gift you make to the trust up to $10,000 per trust beneficiary, that beneficiary has the right to take that money from the trust. Because the beneficiaries have this right, each gift of up to $10,000, allegedly for a different beneficiary, qualifies for the annual gift tax exclusion. So if there are three beneficiaries, you can give up to $30,000 a year to the trust free of gift tax.

4. Next comes the fancy part. The beneficiaries, who are wise to the scheme, always decline to take their $10,000. The money remains in the trust and the trustee spends it on insurance premiums. (This is allowed by another provision in the trust document.) The net effect is that you have indirectly paid the insurance proceeds (you can't pay them directly and have the life insurance trust be regarded as a separate taxable entity), without any gift tax being assessed.

Example: Aldo has four children and an estate worth $2 million. He funds a charitable trust with land currently worth $400,000. He bought the land for $170,000. The charity sells the land and buys stock that will provide payments to him for life. The charity will take what remains of the trust assets at his death.

When he creates the trust, Aldo obtains a significant income tax deduction. Also, by giving the land to charity, he avoids capital gain tax on the increase in value of $230,000 when the land is sold and converted to income-producing assets. And by removing $400,000 from his estate, he saves on estate tax, lowering his taxable estate to $1.6 million.

The property Aldo has given to charity would have gone to his children. But if he had kept the property, it would have been subject to estate tax, in the 50% bracket, when he died. So $200,000 of the $400,000 would have been gobbled up by tax: Thus his children have actually lost only $200,000 because of his charitable gift.

Aldo creates an irrevocable life insurance trust. He buys and transfers to the trust a life insurance policy for $200,000. He includes "Crummey" provisions in the life insurance trust, so he can give, free of gift tax, up to $40,000 a year to the trust—$10,000 for each of the life insurance trust's beneficiaries, his children. As we've just discussed, after the proper dance is performed by the beneficiaries, the trustee can use these funds to pay the premiums of the life insurance policy.

If you are in reasonably good health (and especially if you're young), replacing the donated assets by life insurance is usually the preferred choice. If you are elderly, in poor health, or uninsurable for any reason, other replacement methods can be attempted.

Example: After Aldo establishes his charitable trust, he discovers that he is ill and that insurance on his life would be too costly, if available at all. He still sets up an irrevocable trust for his children and donates income to it. He will be subject to gift tax on the money he donates to the trust, but the trustee purchases assets he and Aldo hope will greatly appreciate in value. (Easier hoped for than accomplished, of course. It's not hard in a rising market, but otherwise, as many real estate investors have learned in the 90s, it can be quite difficult indeed.) Depending on the expertise of the trustee and some luck, the $50,000 each child would have received but for the charitable gift may eventually be recouped.

C. Combining Three Different Estate Tax-Saving Trusts

In larger estates, it may be desirable to combine several different estate tax-saving trusts. For instance, you could use a marital life estate trust for property worth up to $600,000, to be sure you take advantage of your personal estate tax exemption. You might also use a QTIP trust for much of the rest of your property. But for reasons discussed above, you might also want to use a charitable trust.

Wealthy couples may want to benefit their family and other inheritors and charities, and also minimize overall estate tax. With the right planning, a couple can achieve all of these goals and pay no estate tax whatsoever when the first spouse dies.

Example: Guillermo and Maria, a couple in their late 70s, have an estate of $4 million owned equally. They have no children. Although they would like to leave several young friends an inheritance, they want the bulk of their estate to go to charity and not to the government in taxes.

They create a living trust document that will create two separate trusts when the first spouse dies—a marital life estate trust and a QTIP trust for that spouse's property. Guillermo and Maria also each create a charitable trust with a total value of $500,000 per person, benefiting their alma mater. Under the terms of each spouse's charitable trust, income of 6% of the value of the trust assets will go to that spouse yearly, and will continue until the second spouse dies. When this occurs, the trust assets will be used to establish a scholarship fund for needy students at the university. The establishment of that irrevocable charitable trust reduces each one's taxable estate by $500,000. They also obtain an immediate income tax deduction.

Upon the death of the first spouse, the marital life estate trust of $600,000 will become effective. Income generated by trust property will go for the support of the other spouse. At the death of the second spouse, assets in this trust will pass tax-free to Marta, the daughter of a close friend.

Also on the death of the first spouse, a QTIP trust will become operational. Placed in this trust will be any other assets owned by the first spouse to die, except for the $600,000 in the marital life estate trust. (Each spouse's charitable trust was funded on creation and is not added to when a spouse dies.) At the death of the surviving spouse, half of the assets in the QTIP trust will be divided equally among five friends. The other half will be given to cancer research. However, the QTIP trust gives the surviving spouse a "limited power of appointment," allowing him or her to name other final beneficiaries. Because this power of appointment is limited, he or she cannot name herself, his or her estate or creditors as final beneficiaries.

Guillermo dies first. At Guillermo's death, no federal estate tax is due on the property in the marital life estate trust, because the amount in the trust is not over $600,000. And no tax is due on assets in the QTIP trust because of the marital deduction.

After Guillermo's death, Maria continues to receive the 6% income from the charitable trusts and income from the QTIP. She also has the right to spend the QTIP trust and marital life estate trust principal for health care or basic needs and to receive the income from, and use of, the property in the marital life estate trust. Of course, she also has her share of their original property.

After Guillermo's death, Maria no longer needs her existing estate plan, which includes a marital life estate trust and QTIP trust. She revokes those trusts and creates a new living trust, leaving $600,000 of her own property to three nieces and the rest to various charities. Thus no estate tax will be due on Maria's own property when she dies.

At Maria's death, the assets of Guillermo's marital life estate trust go to Marta. Also, the assets of the charitable trust, which are also not part of her estate, establish the scholarship fund.

The assets in the QTIP trust are part of Maria's taxable estate. If half of this property is left to friends, as originally provided by Guillermo, that portion is subject to estate tax. Marta doesn't exercise her power of appointment, so the remaining assets in this trust go to a tax-exempt cancer research foundation, as Guillermo specified, and no tax is due on that amount.

The result of all this is that Guillermo and Maria have provided for the survivor to continue to live very well, while transferring at least $1.2 million to their young friends and the bulk of their estate to charity—and at most, paying a relatively small percentage of their overall estates in estate tax.

D. Using Ongoing Trusts and Gift-Giving to Reduce Estate Tax

Ongoing trusts can be combined in a number of ways to reduce estate tax for the wealthy. If you are wealthy, you can leave gifts to your spouse, children, grandchildren and charity, all by using different trusts. The goal here is, as usual, to make all these gifts while paying a minimum of estate tax. Here's an example of combining a generation-skipping trust, a charitable remainder unitrust, an irrevocable life insurance trust, a marital life estate trust and a QTIP trust, all in one estate plan.

Example: Doris is 65 and married to Ted, her second husband. She has two children from her first marriage, both of whom are financially comfortable, and six grandchildren. Doris's estate is worth $5 million; Ted has a much smaller estate of $70,000.

If she dies first, Doris wants Ted to be properly supported, but she also wants most of her assets to go eventually to her children and grandchildren. She also wishes to contribute a sizable portion of her estate to charity. First she sets up a charitable remainder unitrust of $1 million. (See Chapter 20, Charitable Trusts, Section C.) Ted and Doris will receive income from the trust annually. Next, she takes an income tax deduction based on the value of her gift to the charitable trust. Using the money saved on income tax, she purchases life insurance by funding an irrevocable life insurance trust. The beneficiaries of the life insurance are her children; they will receive an amount roughly equal to the amount she gave to charity. Proceeds from the life insurance trust will not be included in her estate for estate tax purposes. She also establishes a marital life estate trust for $600,000 of her assets. At her death, $600,000 will go into a marital life estate trust, with the income to be paid to Ted for his life. When Ted dies, this trust's assets are divided between her children.

Next, she establishes a generation-skipping trust of $1 million, with income paid to her children during their lives. This trust will be subject to federal estate tax when Doris dies, but not when the middle generation dies. When they die, this trust's assets will be distributed to the grandchildren. Because these trust assets skip a generation and were worth less than $1 million when the trust was created, no estate tax will be paid on these assets when the children die. (See Chapter 21, Other Estate Tax-Saving Trusts, Section A.)

The remaining $2.4 million will go into a QTIP trust, with all income to Ted for life, and the assets to her children at his death. The trustee, one of Doris's children, can use the principal of this trust for Ted's medical care or basic support if the trustee decides it is needed. No estate tax will be due at Doris's death on these assets because of the marital deduction; they will be subject to estate tax when Ted dies.

Finally, during Doris's life, she also adopts a plan of giving gifts from her present income to keep her estate from increasing and eventually resulting in more estate tax. She gives $10,000 annually, gift tax-free, to each of her two children, their spouses and the six grandchildren. This is a total of ten people, so $100,000 a year is given away tax-free. (See Chapter 16, Gifts and Gift Taxes, Section E, for more on gift-giving programs.)

With this plan, Ted will receive income from the QTIP trust, the marital life estate trust, and the charitable remainder trust for his lifetime. So Doris has assured the support of her husband, given a large amount to charity and reserved the bulk of her assets for her children and grandchildren. She has avoided probate fees at both deaths for the entire amount and saved an enormous amount in estate tax.

E. Combining Estate Tax-Saving Trusts With Property Control Trusts

Sometimes an estate tax-saving trust and a trust for property control are combined as a central part of an estate plan. Indeed, more than one of either basic type of trust may be used. For example, you could use two trusts for estate tax-saving purposes, and two others for property control purposes.

Example: Parnell, in his 60s, has an estate worth $1.8 million. He recently married Moira, who has little property of her own. He has two children from his prior marriage—a daughter, Maeve, who he worries cannot handle money, and a son, Padraic, who is severely disabled. Parnell wants to leave some property for Padraic's needs, and ensure, as best he can, that Padraic will remain eligible for the government medical and rehabilitation services he now receives. Parnell also wants to provide for Moira if she outlives him, and leave some property on her death to Padraic and Maeve.

After working with an expert lawyer, Parnell decides to create three trusts:

1. A special needs trust for Padraic, to be funded with $600,000 at Parnell's death. (See Chapter 24, Trusts and Other Devices for Imposing Controls Over Property, Section C.)

2. A QTIP trust for the remainder of his property, to provide income for Moira and postpone estate tax on the $1.2 million left in his estate. (See Chapter 19, Other Estate Tax-Saving Marital Trusts, Section A.) Maeve and Padraic are the final beneficiaries of this trust and will divide the trust property equally when Moira dies. Parnell specifies that Padraic's share of this property will be added to his special needs trust.

3. A spendthrift trust Parnell creates for the property Maeve will eventually receive from the QTIP trust when Moira dies. (See Chapter 24, Section D.) The spendthrift trust will become operational only after Moira dies.

Parnell still has many matters he must resolve. For example, who should be trustee of the QTIP trust? Can Moira invade the trust principal? Who is the trustee of the spendthrift trust? How long will it last? Can the trustee decide that Maeve has become financially responsible and turn the trust principal over to her? With Padraic, Parnell faces the problems involved in creating any special needs trust.

Parnell also has to decide what he'll tell his family members about his estate plan. Moira surely needs to know about the QTIP, but how much does he want to tell his children? If he's not on good terms with Maeve, maybe he doesn't want to tell her about the spendthrift trust. But letting her discover this only after he dies could be very hurtful. Parnell decides he will write Maeve a letter, explaining his estate plan, and why he's decided it's best to leave her property in a spendthrift trust. Parnell knows Maeve has a fierce temper. He hopes that by writing her, he'll lessen the chance of a screaming fight between the two of them, Parnell being no saint himself. But if Maeve has some time to reflect on Parnell's plan, maybe they can simply talk about it later, without rancor. Parnell also informs Padraic that he's created a special needs trust to try to protect him over the years. ■

26

Incapacity: Health Care and Financial Management Directives

We tend to think of estate planning as something we do now to take care of what happens when we die. While this definition has the advantage of being neat and tidy, it's a bit too simple. As we grow older, many of us face the stern reality that before we die we may not be mentally or physically competent for some period of time, sometimes an extended period. We believe that a thorough estate plan must consider this possibility.[1] This chapter discusses how a person can ensure that his or her rights, dignity and wishes are protected if he or she were to become incapable of making or communicating decisions regarding the difficult choices about medical interventions. It also discusses how a person's finances can be managed if he or she were to become incapable of handling them.

If your health deteriorates and you become incompetent to make financial or medical decisions, there must be another adult with legal authority to make financial and medical decisions for you.

There are two ways to deal with this possibility:

1. Do nothing, and, if you ever become incapacitated, let a judge appoint someone, called a conservator or guardian (depending on the state) to make decisions for you. Court proceedings for incapacitated persons are almost always undesirable, unless you have no choice. These proceedings are costly, time-consuming and expose to public concern what most people prefer to keep private.

Sometimes, people simply ignore the requirement of court proceedings: a niece signs her ill aunt's name to the aunt's retirement check, for example. Unfortunately, there's an unpleasant legal term for this act—forgery. So ignoring the law isn't wise, and often not practical either. Over an extended period of time, it's hard to adequately manage another's affairs by continually signing his name to financial documents, especially if he owns different types of property.

2. Complete documents called "durable powers of attorney" to make your own binding choice of who will have authority to act for you regarding your finances and health care in the event of your incapacity. You can also create what is commonly called a "directive to physicians" or a "living will" to specify to doctors what medical treatment you want provided or withheld.

Because planning for possible incapacity is so inextricably related to estate planning, we briefly review the issues involved here.

A. Health Care Decisions

The increasing use of life-sustaining medical technology over the last decades has raised fears in many that our lives may be artificially prolonged against our wishes. The right to die with dignity, and without the tremendous agony and expense for both patient and family caused by prolonging lives artificially, has been addressed and confirmed by the U.S. Supreme Court, the federal government and the legislatures in every state.

This individual right also protects against the situation where doctors might wish to provide a patient with less extensive care than he or she would like. For example, a doctor may be unwilling to try experimental treatments or maintain long-term treatments on a patient who he or she feels has slim chances of recovering.

In 1990, the United States Supreme Court held that every individual has the constitutional right to control his or her own medical treatment. The Court also expounded that "clear and convincing evidence" of a person's wishes must be followed by medical personnel—even if those wishes are directly opposed by the patient's family. (*Cruzan v. Director, Missouri Dept. of Health*, 497 U.S. 261.)

[1] A related concern is financial planning for long-term medical care. These matters are discussed in *Beat the Nursing Home Trap: A Consumer's Guide to Choosing & Financing Long-Term Care*, by Joseph Matthews (Nolo Press).

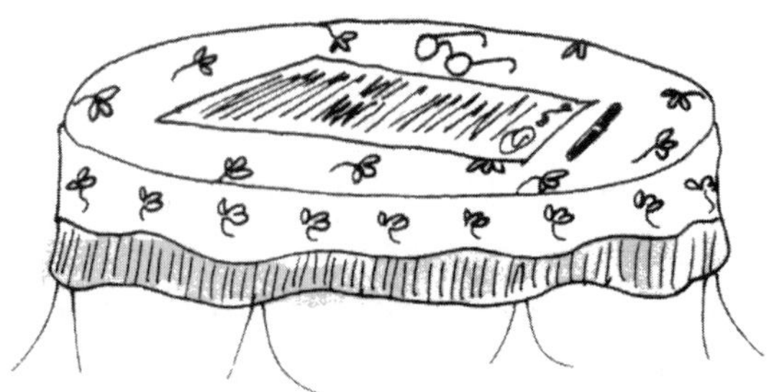

1. Documents Protecting Choices of Medical Care

In response to the legal right to control one's own medical treatment, every state now has laws authorizing individuals to create a simple document that provides the "clear and convincing evidence" of that person's wishes concerning life-prolonging medical care. Depending upon the state, the document may be called by one of several different names: Living Will, Medical Directive, Directive to Physicians, Declaration Regarding Health Care, Durable Power of Attorney for Health Care.

The directions expressed in the document are to be followed if an individual is no longer capable of communicating to medical personnel his or her choices regarding life-prolonging and other medical care.

It is important to note that many of these documents take effect only when a patient is diagnosed to have a terminal condition or to be in a permanent coma. These documents are not used when a person is able to communicate those wishes to doctors in any way or is only temporarily unconscious. However, a durable power of attorney for health care can become effective whenever the person who creates it (the "principal") decides.

Your written medical care instructions can help alleviate your fears, whether your fear involves unwanted medical treatment being administered to you or desired medical treatment being withheld. It can also help relieve family members from having to make agonizing decisions about a loved one's medical treatment. This can be particularly important when family members have different ideas about what care you should receive. Also, doctors and hospitals have their own rules and beliefs about what is proper medical treatment, and even if your family knows your wishes and tries to have them followed, medical personnel would not necessarily be bound to follow them without a valid document you have signed.

2. Differences Among Types of Medical Care Documents

The two basic types of document to direct medical care are a Living Will (also called Directive to Physicians or Declaration) and a Durable Power of Attorney for Health Care or Health Care Proxy. A Living Will—in some states referred to as a Directive to Physicians or a Declaration—is not a will at all, but a document stating a person's decision to receive or not to receive certain medical treatment.

The basic difference between the two types of document is simple. The Living Will or Declaration is a statement made by you directly to medical personnel which spells out the medical care you do or do not wish to receive if you become terminally ill and incapacitated. It acts as a contract with the treating doctor, who must either honor the wishes for medical care that you have expressed—or transfer you to another doctor or facility that will honor them.

In a Durable Power of Attorney or Health Care Proxy, you appoint someone else (your "attorney-in-fact") to oversee your doctors and health care providers to make sure they provide you with the kind of medical care you wish to receive. You can specify in the document what type of care you want, or don't want. You can specify in the document what type of care you want or don't want. In some states, you can also give the person you appoint the broader authority to make decisions about your medical care on your behalf.

> **WHEN YOUR STATE FORM IS NOT ENOUGH**
>
> As mentioned, when it comes to medical directives, there are many state differences in the forms and formats used. Some state laws mention that a specific form must be followed for a directive to be valid. However, since the Supreme Court ruled in the *Cruzan* case that every individual has a constitutional right to direct his or her own medical care, the most important thing for you to keep in mind is that your directions should be clear and in writing to doctors and other medical personnel. If you feel strongly about a particular kind of care—even if your state law or the form you get does not address it—it is a good idea to include your specific thoughts in your written document. If you are using a specific state form that does not adequately address your concerns, write them in on the form with the additional request that your wishes be respected and followed.

3. What to Include in a Medical Directive

The trend in the laws controlling health care directives is to provide that individuals may direct their own medical care both if they are diagnosed to be in a permanent coma and if they have a terminal condition. Another trend is to allow individuals the right to direct what "comfort care"—care which doctors feel may alleviate pain and which may or may not prolong life—should be provided or withheld.

The problem many people have in filling out their state forms on directing health care is that they are not sure how to fill in the blanks—and are not sure what much of the terminology means. Although medical technology and treatments are evolving over time, filling out the forms is not as difficult as it may seem at first. In most health care documents, you can direct:

- that all life-prolonging procedures be provided
- that all life-prolonging procedures be withheld, or
- that some be provided, while others are withheld.

The following medical procedures and treatments are usually considered to be in the category of "life-prolonging."

- **Artificial breathing apparatus, such as a respirator or ventilator.** Some people specify that they wish artificial breathing while they are conscious, but not if they lapse into unconsciousness.
- **Artificial administration of food and water, also called nutrition and hydration.** As with artificial breathing, some people want artificial food and water administered as long as they are conscious, but not if they become unconscious. Others want artificially-administered food and water if they are diagnosed to be in a permanent coma, but not if they become terminally ill. A few states, however, do not permit a doctor or hospital to withhold artificial food and water even if you request that it be withheld. Again, if you feel strongly that you would like artificial food and water withheld, but you are living in a state that restricts your right to direct that, write your request on the health care directive you fill out—and ask that your wishes be respected and followed, as is your constitutional right.
- **Comfort care—including relief from pain and discomfort, usually through medication.** Many people specify that they do want pain medication, but do not want any other life-prolonging measures.

To make an informed decision about which procedures you do and do not want, as well as about others which might pertain to your particular medical condition, it may be a good idea to discuss your medical directive with your physician. He or she can explain the medical procedures more fully and can discuss the options with you. You will also find out whether your doctor has any medical or moral objections to following your wishes. If he or she does object and will not agree to follow your wishes regardless of those objections, you may want to consider changing doctors.

Even when you have specified your wishes in a medical directive regarding life-prolonging and comfort care medical treatment, certain decisions may still be difficult to resolve:

- when, exactly, to administer or withhold certain medical treatments
- whether or not to provide, withhold or continue antibiotic or pain medication, and
- whether to pursue complex, painful and expensive surgeries which may serve to prolong life but cannot reverse the medical condition.

To deal with these situations, in most states, the document called a Durable Power of Attorney for Health Care or Living Health Care Proxy allows you to appoint someone who understands your wishes and whose judgment you trust to make these decisions in accordance with your wishes and in your best interest. To help the appointed person make and carry out these decisions, the power of attorney or proxy form may include specific authorizations:

- to give, withhold or withdraw consent to medical or surgical procedures
- to consent to appropriate care for the end of life, including pain relief
- to hire and fire medical personnel
- to visit you in the hospital or other facility even when other visiting is restricted
- to have access to medical records and other personal information, and
- to get any court authorization required to obtain or withhold medical treatment if, for any reason, a hospital or doctor does not honor the document.

4. Using Durable Power of Attorney for Health Care

A durable power of attorney for health care can go into effect when signed, or only if the writer subsequently becomes mentally incapacitated and is unable to handle his or her own health care decisions. This later type is called a "springing" durable power of attorney. It is sensibly created as a kind of insurance protection against the possibility that you later need it.

A durable power of attorney for health care that becomes operational and effective on signing by the principal can be advisable for someone with a life-threatening illness, or who is facing major surgery, or who knows he's declining into advanced stages of Alzheimer's disease.

Example: Sara is seriously ill, faces major surgery, and knows that for some time she will be unable to make all her own medical and health care decisions. She prepares a durable power of attorney for health care, delegating to her sister, Kennel, the authority to make health care decisions for her. To make sure that her own wishes are complied with, she inserts several restrictions regarding Kennel's power. Specifically, Sara wants to be operated on by Dr. June Lee at Mattan Hospital. So, in defining the attorney-in-fact's authority, she includes the following clause:

"My attorney-in-fact shall comply with my stated desire that all surgery performed on me be done at Mattan Hospital, 134 Ridge Road, Linda Vista, California, by Dr. June Lee, unless Dr. Lee is unable to perform such surgery."

5. Choosing an Attorney-in-Fact or Proxy

There are a number of things to consider in choosing a health care attorney-in-fact or proxy. Some are obvious: you should choose someone who understands your wishes and whom you trust to follow those wishes.

But there are a few other things you should also consider, such as appointing someone who:

- is likely to be present when decisions need to be made—most often, this means someone who lives nearby or who is willing to travel and spend time to be at your side during your hospitalization
- would not easily be bullied or intimidated by doctors or family members who disagree with your wishes, and
- is capable of understanding your medical condition and the proposed life-prolonging measures.

It is also a good idea to appoint a second person as a backup or replacement attorney-in-fact or proxy to act if your first choice is unable or unwilling to serve. Make it clear, however, that the second person is only a back-up. It is not a wise choice to appoint co-proxies: two people who must make decisions would only complicate the process.

Do not appoint your doctor as attorney-in-fact: Although your doctor is an important person for your attorney-in-fact or proxy to consult concerning all health care decisions, you should not appoint your doctor to act as attorney-in-fact or proxy. The laws in most states specifically forbid treating physicians from acting in this role—to avoid the appearance that they may have their own interests at heart and so may not be able to act purely according to your wishes.

6. Changing Your Mind—and Documents

Any type of medical directive can be changed by the person who made it as long as he or she remains legally competent to do so. Therefore, neither your decisions about health care nor about the proxy you have named are final decisions. Anytime you wish to change the terms or proxy, however, you must prepare a new document and date, sign and have it witnessed and possibly notarized again—depending on the formalities that must be followed in your state. You should also make sure that all copies of the document you made earlier are destroyed.

7. Legal Rules and Conditions

As mentioned, each state makes its own rules concerning medical directives. Here are some of the rules and conditions of which you should be aware.

Required form. In some states, you must use a form specifically required by special provisions in state law. (See Section 8, below).

No proxy. Many states recognize living wills but do not have any legal provision for the appointment of a proxy in their health care directive. In these states, if you want to appoint someone to supervise your care and make sure that your wishes are followed, you must prepare a durable power of attorney for health care in addition to a living will. Make sure that your description of the medical treatment you do or do not want is exactly the same in both documents.

8. Obtaining the Right Medical Directive Form

Be advised that the laws on medical directives and forms approved for use frequently change, so a particular form which was the right one in your state several years ago may by now have been replaced by a different, more complete form.

In most instances, you do not need to consult a lawyer to prepare a Living Will, Directive to Physicians, Power of Attorney for Health Care or other medical directive form. The forms are usually quite simple and can be obtained, free or for a nominal fee, from a number of sources, such as:

- **Senior referral and information.** The white pages in most telephone directories have a listing for Senior Referral & Information. This number refers people to various agencies, groups and other sources of assistance for seniors. Call your local Senior Referral & Information number and ask where you can obtain your state's official medical directive form.
- **Local senior center.** Often, your local senior center will have copies of your state's form for medical directive. If it does not have a copy, it may be able to obtain one for you.
- **Consumer organization.** The national non-profit organization Choice in Dying (formerly the Society for the Right to Die) is one of the nation's oldest patients' advocacy groups. It welcomes donations, but will provide free information on your state's current laws on medical directives and can provide current forms. Send a stamped, self-addressed envelope, along with your request for information on your state's medical directive law, to:

  Choice in Dying
200 Varick Street
New York, NY 10014-4810
- **Computer program.** Nolo Press has developed an easy-to-use software program, included as part of *WillMaker*, that helps you prepare and update a medical directive for any state—as well as a regular legal will and final arrangements such as body donation, cremation or burial and funeral wishes. It comes with a manual providing necessary background information and leads you step-by-step through the process.

QUALIFICATIONS FOR WITNESSES

Many states require that two witnesses see you sign your health care documents and that they verify in writing that you appeared to be of sound mind and signed the documents without anyone else influencing your decision.

Each state's qualifications for these witnesses are slightly different. In many states, for example, a spouse, other close relative or any person who would inherit property from you, is not allowed to act as a witness for the document directing health care. And many states prohibit your attending physician from being a witness.

The purpose of the laws restricting who can witness your documents is to avoid any appearance or possibility that another person was acting against your wishes in encouraging specific medical care. States that prevent close relatives or potential inheritors from being witnesses, for example, justify their restrictions by noting that these people may be specially influenced by another person's health care.

9. What to Do With Your Completed Documents

Once you have completed the documents directing your medical care, there are several steps you should take with them.

Signing, witnessing, notarizing. Every state law requires that you sign your documents—or direct another person to sign them for you—as a way of verifying that you understand them and that they contain your true wishes.

Most state laws also require that you sign your documents in the presence of witnesses. The purpose of this additional formality is so that there is at least one other person who can attest that you were of sound mind and of legal age when you made the documents.

In addition to the requirement that witnesses sign your medical directives, some states also require that you and the witnesses appear before a notary public and swear that the circumstances of your signing, as described on the documents, are true. In some states, you have the option of having a notary sign your document instead of having it witnessed.

Making and distributing copies. Ideally, you should make an effort to make your wishes for your future health care widely known. Keep a copy of your health care directives, and give other copies to:

- any physician with whom you now consult regularly
- any attorney-in-fact or health care proxy you have named
- the office of the hospital or other care facility in which you are likely to receive treatment
- the patient representative of your HMO or insurance plan
- close relatives, particularly immediate family members—a spouse, children, siblings
- trusted friends, and
- clergy or lawyer, particularly if you are in regular contact with the clergy or lawyer but you do not have a family member who lives nearby.

Keeping your documents up-to-date. Review your health care documents occasionally—at least once a year—to make sure they still accurately reflect your wishes for your medical care. Advances in technology and changes in health care are two changes in course that prompt many people to change their minds about the kind of medical care they want.

In addition, you should consider making new documents if:

- you move to another state
- you made and finalized a health care directive, but did so many years ago, before there likely were substantial changes to your state's law controlling them, and
- the proxy or representative you named to supervise your wishes becomes unable to do so.

> **KEEPING TRACK OF COPIES**
>
> Keep a signed copy of your medical directive in an easily accessible place at home—someplace you could easily describe to someone else if they had to retrieve it for you.
>
> Also, keep a list of all the people and places that have copies of your medical directive. Then, if you change the terms of the directive, you will be able to retrieve each of the copies or have them destroyed.

B. Financial Management Decisions

To arrange for someone to manage your property if or while you become incapacitated, you can use a durable power of attorney for finances. This document can provide you with some peace of mind that your money and property will be managed by a trusted person, in accordance with your wishes, without need for a court-appointed guardian or conservator.

A durable power of attorney for finances can be effective immediately on signing, or only if the principal becomes incapacitated and unable to manage his or her financial affairs. The document (called a "springing" durable power of attorney for finances) can be tailored to a person's specific financial situation, authorizing an attorney-in-fact to take care of financial matters ranging from buying holiday gifts and keeping a garden tended, to paying bills, making bank deposits, handling insurance, Social Security and other paperwork—even selling a home or other property. And the durable power of attorney for finances can also ensure that there is someone to pay for needed pain relief, comfort care or other medical treatment which may not be fully covered by Medicare and health insurance.

The success of any power of attorney arrangement depends upon the trust and understanding between you and the person you appoint to handle your affairs as your attorney-in-fact. This understanding and trust can be helped along to the extent you put specific instructions in the document regarding particular financial actions you do and do not wish the attorney-in-fact to take with your money or property. Some people also appoint a second attorney-in-fact in the same power of attorney document, with a provision that both must agree to any transaction over a certain amount.

As with durable power of attorney for health care, you can change the attorney-in-fact or other terms of the document at any time, as long as you are legally competent.

1. Powers of Attorney and Medicaid

There are several ways to protect your assets from the reach of a nursing facility while still qualifying for Medicaid. Some of these methods, however, might turn out to require a transfer of assets after you no longer have the capacity to do this personally. If you create a durable power of attorney for finances, you may want to include the power to transfer title of property and other assets to your spouse, children or other specifically-named people—the same people to whom you would want the property to pass after your death.

2. Durable Powers of Attorney for Finances and Living Trusts

Many living trusts provide that the successor trustee is to manage the trust property if the grantor becomes incapacitated. Even if you use a durable power of attorney to appoint someone (your attorney-in-fact) to handle your property if you become incapacitated, property in your living trust still remains subject to your successor trustee, not the attorney-in-fact. This division is typically only one of terminology, not substance, as most people appoint the same person to handle both jobs.

Some people who plan to transfer all of their property under a living trust ask why they need bother with a durable power of attorney for finances at all. The reason is that you're likely to receive income, even if you become incapacitated, from pensions, Social Security and other sources, and you will need an attorney-in-fact of a financial durable power of attorney to deal with this money, and maintain your personal bank account, pay bills, etc.

C. Guardianships and Conservatorships

Most of the advice in this chapter may not apply to you if you are concerned about a person who is already incapacitated and unable to make decisions. At that point, the person can no longer enter into legal documents and arrangements or delegate responsibility for decisions to others. Yet there is a danger that without prior legal arrangements such as a durable power of attorney or living trust, financial institutions, government agencies, health care providers and bureaucrats of every variety will either refuse to take action regarding the person's affairs—or will take actions without regard for your wishes or for what you know are the person's wishes.

In this situation, you may have to go to court to ask a judge to appoint you or another friend or relative to act on the person's behalf. There are procedures in every state to do this. Some states have only one legal category, usually called guardianship, while others have a second category, usually called conservatorship and often limited to financial matters.

In general guardianship proceedings, the legal question is whether or not a person has become "incompetent" to handle any of his or her own affairs. In about half the states, this requires that medical evidence of incompetence be presented to the court. In more limited proceedings to establish a financial conservatorship or guardianship only (see below), the court can act if it finds that the person is unable to handle financial affairs even though not completely legally incompetent.

In conservatorship or guardianship proceedings, a person has a right to appear in court with an attorney and to consent or object to all proposed authority. In many states, if the person does not have an attorney, the court may appoint one. Similarly, any change in the conservator or guardian's authority requires an additional court order to which the person can consent or object. The conservator or guardian is held responsible for mismanagement of the person's property.

In some states, it is possible to handle conservatorship proceedings without the assistance of a lawyer if no one challenges the need for the conservatorship and its scope. More complicated guardianship procedures, however, do require the assistance of a lawyer, particularly if the person alleged to be incompetent, or anyone else, does not agree that the guardianship is needed or that the person seeking to be guardian is not the right person for the job.

1. Financial Conservatorship or Guardianship

A conservator or guardian can be appointed by a court solely to protect a person's property—savings, real estate, investments. He or she can also conduct daily financial affairs, such as paying bills, or arrange for services when the person is unable to do so. This type of limited management assistance is appropriate when the person is still capable of caring for himself or herself, but because of disorientation or disability is unable to carry out personal business affairs efficiently. In this situation, the conservator or guardian does *not* have power over the person's personal conduct, but has authority over financial or other affairs as the court orders.

An advantage of a limited conservatorship or guardianship is that it leaves the person free to make many important decisions independently: where to live, with whom to associate, what medical care to receive, how to handle property. Nonetheless, it is still a court process in which a judge makes a ruling, occasionally against the person's will, that gives another person authority over some parts of his or her life. It is therefore a procedure to be used only if voluntary procedures such as a durable power of attorney are no longer possible.

2. Full Guardianship

Full guardianship is an extreme measure that severely restricts the legal rights of a person based on a court's finding of legal incompetence. It reduces that person's legal status to that of a minor, with no control over her or his own money or property, decisions about medical care or institutionalization. A person under full guardianship even loses the right to vote.

If a person retains some degree of orientation and capability, a legal finding by a court that he or she is incompetent can be emotionally devastating and, in fact, self-fulfilling. The person deemed legally incompetent may well give up the will to care for himself or herself and become much less competent than before. Obviously, full guardianship is a very serious step, to be taken when a person's mental condition leaves no other choice such as a durable power of attorney. ■

27

Body Organ Donation, Funerals and Burials

People facing the grief and reality that someone they love has died face other immediate problems—disposing of the body and arranging the ceremonies desired to mark the death. It's hard to even talk directly about a body once life has left it; the word "corpse" sounds unfeeling and "cadaver" is worse. Statutes often refer to a dead body as "the remains," a word technically accurate and almost as disturbing. Perhaps it's because we don't like to think about death that the language we have invented for it's so awkward. But, however it is described, the reality is the same: a dead body must, somehow, be removed from the place of death and disposed of, rapidly. And then, if desired, commemorative ceremonies need to be scheduled.

Most people die in hospitals or nursing homes. These institutions want a dead body removed quickly. So it's near-inevitable, if no planning has been done, for family or friends to turn to "professionals"—funeral homes. Often this is done without reflection, or even much knowledge, of what the traditional funeral establishment offers or what it charges for its services. This passive approach often means family and friends pay far too much for a funeral they don't even like—and worst of all, for funeral goods and services that don't suit the person who has died.

Grief, guilt, sorrow, religious conviction, doubt, or whatever else survivors are feeling often leave them distraught and confused. In these circumstances, the expense of practical problems can seem trivial. However, we believe it's no slight to the deceased, or to the feelings of those who survive, to suggest that nothing is gained by needless expense. Funerals can be expensive. Indeed, the traditional funeral, which can easily cost thousands of dollars, is one of the most expensive items normally purchased by an American family. To many, including these authors, this is a huge and unnecessary cost to comply with the biblical injunction: "Remember, man, thou art dust and to dust thou shall return."

A. Making Your Own Choices

More and more people are reflecting on what they want to happen to their bodies when they die, and making choices that have emotional meaning for them, as well as saving their families needless expense.

Broadly viewed, there are four choices available:[1]

1. Donating the entire body to a medical school. This must be arranged beforehand. If this is done, the body is usually cremated—and the cremains buried or scattered. However, family members or friends can request that the body be returned when the study is complete—usually within a year or so.

2. Donating specific body organs can also be donated to an organ bank. If organs are donated, the rest of the body is normally returned to those responsible for cremation or burial, which means that you still must arrange for its disposal.

3. A traditional funeral service conducted by a commercial funeral home, with cremation or body burial.

4. A simple funeral service, without embalming of the body, provided either through membership in a cooperative funeral society or by independent arrangements,[2] with either cremation or burial.

Planning for the immediate, practical aspects of your death is essential to make sure your wishes are carried out. To take one example, if you wish to donate body parts or organs, it's almost essential to authorize it, in writing, before your death. Similarly, if you want a non-traditional funeral, such as cremation with your ashes scattered over the sea, it may not

[1]We don't cover some of the more esoteric options—cryonics (body freezing), for example.

[2]How to handle funeral/burial problems yourself, with organizational help, is discussed in Nolo's *WillMaker* computer program, which has a whole module (with help) on burials and funerals, and also in *Caring For Your Own Dead,* by Carlson (Upper Access Books).

happen unless you arrange the details yourself. (Each state has rules governing how and where ashes may be scattered.) Even for a traditional commercial funeral, planning is desirable. Costs for similar death goods and services vary widely—for example, caskets are commonly marked up from five to ten times their retail costs. So comparison shopping can often result in big savings.

In our view, there's really no sensible reason to plan how to save money on probate fees or estate taxes and then toss a chunk of it away on an overpriced funeral. Equally important, there's no reason to dread thinking about what kind of death notice and ceremonial service will be fitting, if you want them. Once you've decided what is appropriate, you need to convey your intention to others, preferably in a written declaration.

B. Leaving Written Instructions

Whatever decisions a person makes regarding the disposition of his body should be put in writing. Under most states' laws, written burial instructions of a deceased person are binding, assuming, of course, the instructions don't violate state laws on body disposition. Even where laws do not specifically require that a deceased person's instructions be followed, they almost always are. You can also assure that your wishes are followed by joining a local funeral or memorial society. (See Section F2, below.)

Commonly, written instructions are included in a will. This is not the best choice, because it may take time to locate and read a will—and dead bodies are most often disposed of quickly. A better approach is to prepare your instructions in a separate document, and to also include them in your will. However they're drawn up, written instructions should be kept in a safe and readily accessible place, known to whoever will have the responsibility for implementing them. Or, simpler yet, give a copy to the person you've chosen to be responsible for carrying out your desires. Make sure the funeral society you have joined or the mortuary you've chosen also has a copy of your wishes.

If no legally binding written instructions are left by the person who has died, the next of kin (the closest family relation) has legal control over the disposition of the body. This can pose insoluble problems for a friend or lover of the deceased, who knows the deceased wanted a specific type of disposition that the next of kin opposes. Without legally binding written instructions, the friend or lover is powerless to prevent the next of kin from controlling the disposition.

About Death Certificates

Whenever a person dies, a physician must complete a death certificate shortly after the death and file it with the appropriate governmental agency, often a local registrar of health. Certified copies of the death certificate will be needed to transfer certain types of property to those legally entitled to them. For example, to collect money from a pay-on-death bank account or to end a joint tenancy of real estate, the inheritors need a certified copy of the death certificate. To wind up a probate avoidance living trust, the successor trustee will often need several copies of the death certificate.

C. Donating Your Body or Organs

If you want to leave your body, or parts of it, for medical research or instruction, you have two choices:

1. You can leave your entire body to medical science, usually a medical school, or

2. You can donate certain of your body organs or tissues to transplant facilities.

You cannot do both, because medical schools generally won't accept a body from which any part has been removed (except sometimes for eye transplants).

The procedure for donating a body to a medical school is simple: contact the school, see if it needs bodies, and, if so, what legalities and forms it requires. Most medical facilities don't pay to obtain bodies, but most will absorb the cost of transporting a body—unless you die very far from the institution. Many, but not all, medical schools won't accept bodies that are too old or too diseased, or where death occurred during surgery. So it's important to have a back-up plan if you're thinking about body donation. You can call the National Anatomical Service at 718-948-2401 to find out more specifics about body donation in your locale.

Some medical schools are currently not accepting whole body donations. By contrast, the need for many types of organ donations is great. Heart transplants get the most publicity, but many more organs, tissues and bones can and are being transplanted, including middle ear, eyes, liver, lungs, pancreas, kidneys, skin tissue, bone and cartilage, pituitary glands, and even hip or knee joints. A gift of a vital organ is one of the most precious and loving acts one can make. We know this well, as we have a friend who was saved from blindness by a cornea transplant.

Every state has adopted the Uniform Anatomical Gift Act. Under this act, any mentally competent adult can promise to make after-death organ donations. Obviously, to authorize this you have to sign the proper forms. In some states you can do this as part of renewing your driver's license, or simply obtain the form from your local Department of Motor Vehicles. Your doctor and local hospital should be aware of what is required in your state. Also, under the Act, a person's family can agree to organ donations if the person is brain dead, but body organs have been kept alive by a life support system.

Time is truly of the essence for the successful removal of donated body parts, so anyone desiring to have organs removed on death should make arrangements beforehand, and discuss those intentions with family and friends. Most people put off making these arrangements, no matter how intensely they may want to donate their organs. With donation of body parts, the limits of this logic of procrastination are starkly seen, since we never know when death may come.

D. Services and Ceremonies Following a Death

Many people wish to have input about the ceremonies held after their deaths. You may have a favorite church or synagogue where you would like the service held, or a particular priest, pastor or rabbi to conduct it. You may know how you want the service to be conducted. Of course, in many religious and spiritual communities, the broad outlines of rituals that accompany a death are well-established. Usually, however, when it comes to the particular prayers to be read and songs to be sung, there's room for personal choice. If the service won't be held by a religious institution, individual input becomes more urgent. It's sad to attend, as both of us have, funerals of good friends held in a commercial funeral homes where not one personal word was said.

If you have specific ideas about ceremonies you want held after your death, the best way to make your wishes known in writing. Simply include a brief statement as part of your burial instructions. (See Section B, above.)

E. Death Notices

When someone dies, one of the first things that most families do is notify others. For close friends and relatives, phone calls normally work. But what about notifying the many other people whose lives have been touched by the deceased, such as former neighbors, golf partners, sailing or bowling friends, retired business associates and other friends? Doing this promptly is important, as many of these people will wish to attend one or more of the events which usually occur very soon after death, such as a wake, lying-in, funeral or memorial ceremony. And other people will wish to communicate with the family and extend their sympathy.

In many communities, notification is handled by a local newspaper, with either a death notice or an obituary.

Death notices generally must be paid for, and consist of small print listings of the date of death, names of survivors, and location of any services.

An obituary is a news item, usually prepared by the staff of the newspaper. It runs in standard type, contains a small headline (for example, "Former Local School Principal Dies") and is free. In small towns, many local newspapers prepare obituaries for a large percentage of people who die, giving more space to those who were locally prominent. In large metropolitan papers, however, very few people's deaths are sufficiently newsworthy to qualify for obituaries, and even fairly prominent people have their deaths recorded in the paid death notices, if at all.

Death notice information must be submitted to newspapers promptly. This can raise a real problem for survivors. Just when they are beset by difficult emotions and serious practical problems, someone has to call in to the newspaper office with details of the dead person's life and survivors. While newspapers are commonly very understanding and provide a lot of help, it still can be difficult. Common problems involve remembering or locating dates, parents' full names, details of key events, correct spellings for clubs and other affiliations, to mention just a few.

One solution to this problem is to prepare your own death notice. This might sound a bit macabre, but it will probably only take you a little while, and those who are later spared the task will surely be appreciative. Just look at the appropriate newspaper, follow the general form it uses and write one out.

What about an obituary? At least for many local newspapers, you can help write the news story about your death in advance. The paper will have a form on which you can list all relevant biographical information, including your education and employment history, civic responsibilities, names of children, and so on. If this form is filled out in advance, it can be given to the paper immediately after death, and will be used to write the news story. In addition to completing this form, however, you may want to actually try your hand at writing your own obituary, leaving blank your date of death. Does this sound weird? Well, yes, a little, perhaps, but remember, if you don't do it, someone you love may have to deal with a reporter precisely when there will be far more pressing practical and emotional concerns occasioned by your death. To get an idea of what an obituary should look like, read a few in your local paper. In our experience, if a family submits a well-written, factual obituary immediately after a person's death, a local newspaper is likely to use a good part of it, or at least echo its major themes.

F. Funerals

For funerals, you have two basic options—use a commercial funeral home or make arrangements in advance through a non-profit funeral or memorial society.

1. Commercial Funerals

The traditional American funeral, as provided by a commercial funeral home or mortuary, normally includes the following:

- The funeral director takes care of the paperwork required for death and burial certificates, and removes the body from the place of death and embalms it.
- The deceased's embalmed body is shown at an open— or closed—casket ceremony. Many funeral parlors have their own chapels and encourage all services to be held there, rather than in churches.

Funerals are always products of culture. Our own culture, which has long studiously avoided death, is also made nervous by trying to decide what type of funeral is appropriate. In some ages, expensive funerals and burials were scorned as ostentatious, wasteful, and the norm was a simple, dignified and inexpensive service. In other times, as in 17th century England, expensive funerals and grand tombs were in vogue for those with status and wealth.

There is no one American cultural tradition concerning funerals and burials. Many Americans do hold ceremonies when a person dies, of course, and many ethnic and religious traditions are deeply ingrained, such as the Jewish custom of burial within 24 hours or the Irish wake. But, generally speaking, for those not close to their ethnic roots, there's still a significant cultural vacuum. As should come as no surprise, that vacuum was filled by creating the funeral business.

Before the Civil War, burials in America were most often simple affairs—a religious ceremony, a plain pine box, and quick burial. Undertakers did not exist until roughly the 1860s; originally they practiced some other trade, often carpentry. During the Civil War, bodies of dead soldiers were embalmed so they could be shipped home for burial. Then, undertakers emerged as a distinct trade; they later evolved into funeral directors and began to proclaim themselves professionals. With this, the plain pine box was transformed into a luxurious coffin. Funerals became theater, and their cost rose accordingly. Embalming the dead body and showing the embalmed remains became standard funeral parlor practice—a practice which obviously adds substantially to the cost of burial, and one not used (and indeed regarded as barbaric) in most other countries. The funeral industry also developed a rationalization for embalming. It claimed that viewing the embalmed body is useful for the living, because seeing a lifelike body enables the viewers to cope with their grief. The term they invented for this is "grief therapy." Recently, some funeral homes are offering "after care" help to a widow or widower, sometimes including support groups and professional therapists.

As many people sense, there's something odd, as well as expensive, about traditional American funerals. This shift in attitude was originally sparked by Jessica Mitford's book *The American Way of Death* (Simon & Schuster), a pioneering examination of commercial American culture in one of its more rapacious and grotesque areas. Written with wit and grace, Mitford's book (now over three decades years old, but still influential) raised many questions about American funeral customs.[3] As a result of her book and the efforts of many others, many beneficial legal changes have occurred, allowing alternatives to conventional funeral parlor practices.

Legal reform has also aided the growth of funeral societies, which, in turn, have introduced real price competition into the commercial funeral business. Now some commercial funeral homes have begun to advertise less expensive funerals. So, if you do want

[3]Another fine book is Ruth Harmer's *The High Cost of Dying* (Crowell-Collier Press).

to patronize a traditional funeral parlor, shop around for the best prices on costs and services. Mortuaries are legally required to give those who ask a detailed price list of their goods and services.

a. Embalming

The greatest expense of a traditional funeral is embalming the body. Generally, state law doesn't require embalming unless the body will be transported by common carrier, such as a commercial plane, or county health officials order embalming as a protection against the spread of contagious disease (a *very* rare event). There are those who claim that embalming is a necessary health measure, but there's little evidence to support this. If a body must be preserved for a short time, refrigeration is at least as reliable, and far cheaper.

In embalming, preservative and disinfectant fluid is injected into the arterial system and body cavities, replacing blood. Embalmed bodies aren't preserved for eternity, though medical science can do this for exceptional reasons (keeping Lenin's body on display, for example). Generally, an embalmed body begins to decompose rapidly within a few weeks.

By embalming the body, a funeral parlor can preserve it sufficiently to allow open-casket viewing of the body at a funeral service, a popular practice with some Americans. How one feels about this is, of course, a private matter. The important point is to realize that open-casket viewing—and embalming—are far from inevitable practices. The choice is up to survivors or anyone who makes plans for his own burial.

BEWARE OF PREPAYMENT PLANS

Shopping around for the most suitable and affordable funeral goods and services is a wise consumer idea. However, be extremely cautious about paying in advance—or prepaying—for them.

While there are a number of legal controls on how the funeral industry can handle and invest funds earmarked for future services, there are many reported abuses of mismanaged and stolen funds. A great many other abuses go unreported by family members too embarrassed or too grief-stricken to complain.

There are additional pitfalls. When mortuaries go out of business, the consumer who has prepaid is often left without funds and without recourse. Also, many individuals who move to a new locale during their lifetimes are dismayed to find that their prepayment funds are nonrefundable—or that there is a substantial financial penalty for withdrawing or transferring them. In addition, money paid now may not cover inflated costs of the future—meaning that survivors will be left to cover the substantially inflated costs.

If you are interested in setting aside a fund of money to pay for your final arrangements, a more prudent approach for most people is to set up a Totten Trust—a trust or savings plan earmarked to pay for your final arrangements—with a bank or savings institution. Most will do so for a very slight charge, the trust funds are easily transferred or withdrawn if need be and you have complete control over the money during your life.

b. Costs

A major factor in the total cost of a funeral—and the item most grossly marked up—is the price of the casket. Not surprisingly, funeral directors generally urge as expensive a casket as possible. Anyone who's ever been casket shopping can tell you it's a bit like visiting a car dealership. There's always a larger, fancier model available, with more expensive options. The question all too often becomes not how much a casket costs, but how much are you willing to pay. In most facilities, rental caskets are available for a slight charge, for those who wish to be cremated or who choose not to purchase a casket.

The cost of a traditional funeral can easily add up to many thousands of dollars. In addition to the casket, there's normally a charge for each extra, and there are a lot of possible extras, including flowers, special burial clothing, additional limousines, clergyman's honorarium, music and cards. Also, watch out for fraudulently tacked-on fees—"handling" charges, AIDS body handling costs, etc.

Flowers have become traditional at American funerals. A significant percentage of all flowers sold by commercial florists in America are sold for funerals. Not surprisingly, the florist industry resists any attempt to reduce the sending of flowers to funerals. Some people prefer that money which would have been spent on flowers be given to a particular charity. Sometimes funeral notices or announcements state "Please Omit Flowers." Whether flowers are a beautiful and moving statement or an unnecessary expense is a choice each person can make; again, the point is to realize that there's a choice.

Finally, transporting a body from a distant place of death, or to a distant burial place, is particularly expensive. If you must arrange for the return of a body from a distant place of death, consult a customer service representative of the airlines to make sure you get the most affordable rates.

2. Funeral Societies

Funeral societies are private, nonprofit organizations, open to any who wishes to join. They are devoted to the concept of simple, dignified burial services for a reasonable cost. There's usually a small membership fee for joining. Members are entitled to the burial programs offered through the society. Funeral societies don't generally employ their own morticians, or own their own cemeteries; rather, they have contracts of varying types with cooperating local mortuaries and crematoriums. The societies make a price list of goods and services available—and members choose the mortuary and service they would like. After a death, the society ensures that only the services selected are performed and billed for.

Specific policies, funeral costs and options vary somewhat from organization to organization, but the basics are common to all. Dignified, simple funerals can be arranged for hundreds of dollars, not thousands. Members are concerned not only with reducing the excessive costs, but at least equally with what they believe are the excesses and lack of spiritual values inherent in many commercial funerals. As the literature of the funeral societies notes, in the traditional funeral the emphasis is on the dead body—lying in an open casket, the body embalmed, often painted, rouged, or otherwise altered cosmetically in the belief that the embalmer's skills will make a more lifelike body, and that viewing a lifelike dead body is a sign of respect or affection.

Funeral societies want new members and readily provide information on their programs, services and membership rules, as well as the names of all cooperating mortuaries. If you move, there's a good chance you can transfer your membership to another society; there are funeral societies in most urban areas of the United States.

There are about 150 funeral societies in the U.S. To locate one near you, check the phone book or contact:

The Continental Association of Funeral
and Memorial Societies
6900 Lost Lake Road
Egg Harbor, Wisconsin 54209
800-765-0107

G. CREMATION

Cremation means the burning of the body. Cremation is common in many parts of the world. For example, over half of those dying in England are cremated. It's opposed by certain religions, such as Muslims, and Greek and Jewish Orthodox creeds. Catholics are supposed to receive the permission of their local bishop to be cremated, but the Catholic Church no longer bans cremation outright.

Be careful if you make a direct arrangement with a profit-making cremation organization. Some have been known to rip off customers, charging for "handling," "transportation" or "disposal" fees. Regular fees commonly are $900 or more for a "basic" cremation, plus possible additional charges of $350 to $700 for scattering the ashes, and $1,500 to $20,000 for urn placement.

Despite the risk of excessive costs, many people have been able to arrange for sensibly-priced cremations. Indeed, cremations are now quite common, used for roughly half the deaths in the U.S.

By law in many states, a crematory cannot require that a casket (rather than a bag) be used in cremation. This makes sense, as it seems particularly needless to pay for an expensive wood casket that is almost immediately burned. Cheaper wood caskets are often used, by custom, if no contrary directions are given. And most facilities also make rental caskets available for a slight charge.

Whether and how ashes can be scattered depends on state law. Scatterings were rare a few generations ago, but there has been a marked increase in their number as the number of cremations has grown. Cremated remains can be removed from the place of cremation or inurnment and disposed of by scattering by the person with the legal right to control the remains. A permit is usually required for scattering, whether at sea or over private land. The crematory or mortuary involved should handle the paperwork. Once again, giving specific instructions regarding disposition can save considerable trouble.

H. BURIALS

A body must be disposed of in a lawful way. Unless it's cremated and the ashes scattered or kept in an urn or in a licensed columbarium, it must be buried somewhere. Often this means the remains must be buried in a cemetery (graveyard, if you prefer the more descriptive word).

In this country, there's a wide variety of cemetery types, including profit-making ones, large mutually-owned ones, church burial grounds, small co-ops, municipal ones, and national cemeteries, in which most veterans and their spouses, are entitled to free burial.

Although there is a wide variety of types of cemeteries, most American cemeteries are private businesses. To be buried in a privately-owned one you have to buy your way in. Private cemeteries are normally separate businesses from funeral homes, although they often have working relationships with one another. Sometimes, though, they compete, and some cemeteries sell caskets. Usually, the fact that private cemeteries are separate means only that there's one more transaction to arrange—buying a funeral plot. This purchase can often be arranged through a funeral society or a funeral home. If there's a specific cemetery you desire, you should be sure the funeral home or society can arrange for that particular purchase. Also, you might save money if you select your own cemetery as prices can vary significantly.

Probably the best known private graveyard in the world is Forest Lawn Cemetery in Los Angeles. Evelyn Waugh's justly famous satire of Forest Lawn, *The Loved One,* hasn't diminished the success of this cemetery. Many people still choose (or their relatives choose) to be buried in its "splendor." Depending on how much splendor is desired, this can be quite expensive indeed.

Cemetery costs, like everything else, are going up. The minimum cost includes:

1. the plot

2. the coffin enclosure, which normally consists of a vault or grave liner of concrete and steel. Cemetery owners sometimes say vaults are required to prevent the land bordering the grave from eventually collapsing. Although this danger is often nonexistent or exaggerated, yearly vault sales have recently been estimated to amount to nearly one-half billion dollars. Many vaults are bought through a funeral director, although they are usually cheaper if bought from a cemetery;

3. opening and closing the grave

4. upkeep.

Many cemeteries sell "perpetual care," which they claim means that the grave will be attended "for eternity." This sounds pretty grandiose until you realize that as graves don't require much care—what this really means is that the grass will be cut. And even this task doesn't amount to much in many modern urban cemeteries, which have eliminated the use of headstones, substituting plaques that are planted flush to the ground, so as not to interfere with the power mower.

If you haven't got enough to worry about, you could worry about what will happen when we run out of cemetery land. It'll take a while, surely, although one expert suggests that in only 500 years, at the present rate of graveyard growth, all the land in the United States would be graveyards.

Finally, if there's to be a headstone or plaque, why not create your own epitaph? It's your last opportunity for self-expression.

Among our favorite epitaphs are:

Cast a cold eye, on life, on death. Horseman, pass by!

—Yeats

and the classic:

On the whole, I'd rather be in Philadelphia.

—W.C. Fields ■

28

Business Ownership and Estate Planning

If you own an interest in a small business, whether you're a sole proprietor, a partner in a partnership or a shareholder in a closely-held corporation, estate planning can get complicated fast. Indeed, if a substantial part of your estate is a profit-making business of significant value, there's seldom a "simple" estate plan. By definition, you need to plan carefully both at the business and personal level. Here we provide an introduction to what is involved. In addition, you will want to get help from an experienced estate planner with strong business and tax experience.

The special estate planning problems for small business owners usually break down into three broad areas:

- operation of the business
- probate avoidance, and
- estate tax concerns.

A. Operation of the Business

In this section we look at issues you will have to resolve if you want your business to continue after you die and show you how to plan to achieve your goal.

The basic questions you must ask yourself if you do want your business to continue include:

- Do you want the business to continue to be run by your beneficiaries after your death?
- Is there some other way you want the business to continue?
- Is it really possible to continue the business if you're not there?
- Do you want the business sold and the money received divided between your beneficiaries?

Whether or not you are a sole owner of your business will, in large measure, determine your response to these questions.

A business can be held in two ways:

- **Sole proprietorship.** If the business is a sole proprietorship, by definition you are its only owner and, subject to the rights of your spouse, your estate planning problems are comparatively simple. But after you decide who you'll leave the business to, you'll need to ask two questions:

  1. Will your beneficiaries want to continue the business?
  2. If so, are they up to it?

  If the answer to both questions is yes, you'll want to plan so there will be a smooth transfer of ownership and management. This includes making sure that the beneficiaries know how the business works, and also that the business has sufficient cash to carry them over whatever rough spots they encounter in their first few months of ownership. On the other hand, if the answer to either of the above questions is no, you will need to arrange to have the business either sold or managed by a professional manager.

- **Partnership/small corporation.** If you are a partner in a partnership (including the general partner of a limited partnership) or own stock in a closely-held (non-public) corporation, you have a more difficult task. Before you even worry about your beneficiaries, you must first take into account the rights of surviving co-owners regarding your share of the business. It is very common for the surviving principals of a business to have the contractual right to purchase the share of a principal who dies from her estate. If co-owners do have this right, two important questions should be addressed: How will your share be valued, and how will the money be found to actually buy it? Often, to resolve these issues, a buy-out method has been pre-established, in corporate bylaws, a shareholders' agreement or in a partnership agreement. But if not, and you are starting from scratch, obviously, the buy-out agreement should be planned so as to not destroy the business or force it to be sold to outsiders.

B. Death Tax and Probate Concerns

Once you have dealt with any concerns about the operation of the business, you will have to choose an estate planning device to actually transfer your share of the business, or the money from a buy-out, to your beneficiaries. With a buy-out, money often comes in over a period of years, so you'll also need to adopt a legal device to actually funnel the money to your beneficiaries. Often, you can arrange to have the payment made to your living trust, and have the trustee distribute this payment to beneficiaries, as defined by you in the trust.

Of course, in addition to seeing that your business, or money you receive from its sale, gets to your beneficiaries, you'll want to reduce death taxes on your business assets to the extent possible. You also want to consider ways to have your business interests avoid probate, not only to save on probate fees, but also to assure prompt transfer of ownership.

C. Practical Business Problems

The death of the sole or part owner of a small business is likely to seriously disrupt that business. If no planning has been done, the disruption can be catastrophic, sometimes even resulting in the failure of a sound business. Let's now look more thoroughly at how your business will be affected by your death, and the steps you can take to see that the value you have built up over years of hard work really does benefit the people you care about.

1. Individual Ownership

It's rarely desirable to simply close down or sell a solely-owned business immediately on the death of its owner, unless it's a one-person service business. Even if your beneficiaries do not want to run the business over the long term, you'll want them to have some flexibility in the timing of the sale—which means the business must be capable of continuing in a profitable fashion for a while. One way to achieve at least short-term continuity is for key employees, the owner and beneficiaries to agree in writing that these employees will stay around and continue to run the business for a period of time after, perhaps in exchange for a small portion of the eventual sale proceeds. Another way to accomplish this is to incorporate the business and make the key employees officers of the corporation and minority stockholders. (Obviously, the officers can still quit at any time, but they are less likely to do so if they have an equity interest in the business.)

If there's more than one beneficiary, questions commonly arise about what happens after the death of the original owner. Suppose one of the new owners wants to sell out and the others don't. Or suppose they all want to sell, but don't see eye to eye about how best to do it. Or suppose the new owners want to operate the business but disagree on how to proceed? If a business has any real value that is likely to survive the death of its sole proprietor, questions such as these should be anticipated and resolved as part of the estate planning process.

In some situations, a sole proprietor wants the business to continue but doesn't trust his ultimate beneficiary to run it. If there is a trusted employee who can manage the business, she may be the logical person to take over. This sort of situation can necessitate a fairly complex legal structure, and is a good illustration of why professional estate planning help is typically needed.

Example: Hank Jackson is the sole proprietor of a thriving print shop. He wants to leave the management of the company in the hands of his friend, trusted employee and longtime co-worker Ed Brown, for Brown's life. When Ed dies, the business will be given to Hank's grandchildren, who, Hank knows, will almost surely decide to sell the business promptly. Jackson incorporates the business. As part of his living trust, he establishes an ongoing life estate trust and provides that, when he dies, his shares will be placed in this trust. Ed Brown is named as trustee of this ongoing trust, with power to control the shares and thus manage the corporation. The trust also provides that Brown is to receive 50% of the business's profits during his life, with the other 50% divided between Hank's grandchildren. After Brown dies, the trust will be dissolved and the business transferred to Jackson's grandchildren.

In this situation, Brown's rights as trustee are vital. Because Brown is given broad power, he can hire himself to run the corporation at a good salary, in addition to receiving his 50% share of the profits. Or, he can take a more back-seat role, paying someone else to run the business on a day-to-day basis and receiving only his share of the profits left over.

Jackson will probably not want to try and dictate how Brown is to run the company, but may want to institute some controls, such as requiring that at least some profits be reinvested back into the business. He might do this to protect against any possibility that Brown would be tempted to overemphasize policies that will prefer short-term profit (in which he shares) over the long-term value of the business (which goes to the grandchildren).

Jackson should also provide (in the trust document) for what happens if the grandchildren disagree about what to do with the business. Do some have the right to buy out others? If so, how is the sale price to be determined, and how is the money to be raised?

2. Businesses With More Than One Owner

When business ownership is shared between two or more people, whether the form of that business is a partnership or a corporation, each co-owner must carefully consider the other owner's rights when engaging in estate planning.

a. Controlling the Disposition of a Shared Ownership Business

It's common that a partnership agreement, corporate bylaws or a shareholders' agreement controls the disposition of a deceased co-owner's interest in the business. If this is the case, each partner or shareholder must create a personal estate plan that is in harmony with this document.

In the absence of an owners' agreement, the rights of the surviving owners are determined by the laws of the state where the business is located. Put bluntly, it is not wise to rely on these laws, since they are highly unlikely to fit your or your family's needs. For instance, state laws generally require that a partnership must be dissolved on the death of a partner unless the partnership agreement provides differently. State laws often also define how partnership property is to be valued, in the absence of agreement between the partners, with the result that it's often valued too low. So, to repeat, it's obviously unwise to leave such crucial issues up to state law. It is essential that co-owners of a business resolve, in writing, exactly what's to happen when one owner dies.

b. Determining the V alue of a Deceased Owner's Interest

It's important to establish, in advance, a method to value a deceased owner's interest in a shared ownership business for several reasons. Someone who inherits an interest in a business may well want to sell that interest. In some cases, sale is prohibited by previous agreement between the original owners. But in most situations, the beneficiaries do have a right to sell, although the other owners often have the first option to buy out the beneficiaries. To get all parties to agree on a fair method to determine the sale price, after an owner's death, can be problematic, to say the least—sometimes even resulting in a lawsuit. To forestall this nasty possibility, it's better for co-owners of a business to agree in advance of an owner's death how interests in the business are to be valued. Even if the beneficiaries don't have the right to sell, they will still need to know the worth of their inheritance for death tax or other purposes. Although the IRS is not bound by private valuations of a business, it is likely to accept a valuation (or valuation formula) that appears reasonable, especially for a business with no readily ascertainable market value.

Any of the conventional methods for determining the value of a small business can be adopted in a partnership agreement or corporate bylaws (or shareholders' agreement) to value a deceased owner's share.

The owners can agree to:

- Establish a fixed dollar amount for the deceased owner's share.
- Have the business interest appraised. This often means agreeing on a particular person to do the appraisal in advance and then abiding by the value of her post-death appraisal.
- Determine the book value of the business interest. This is the total value of all tangible assets of the business, less the business liabilities, and is normally calculated each year as part of preparing a financial statement.
- Use the "capitalization" of net earnings formula. This method is useful in some types of businesses where there are generally net earnings, and the numerical multiplier used to calculate the value of the business has been generally defined and accepted in the trade. This method basically involves a method of multiplying annual net earnings (or net earnings averaged over however many years you pick) by a "multiplier," to determine the value of the business. To come up with a reasonable multiplier, you need to investigate carefully what's the norm for your type of business. You'll also usually need to consult with an experienced business attorney.
- Give the surviving owner the right to match any outside bona fide purchase price, sometimes called "the right of first refusal." For this method to work, there must be an outside offer. Since this can rarely be assured beforehand, it's sensible to have a backup method for determining the worth of a deceased owner's interest also included in the partnership agreement, corporate bylaws or shareholders' agreement.

> **FAMILY BUSINESS ESTATE FREEZES**
>
> Until 1987, a common estate planning device for a family-owned corporation was what's called a "freeze" of the majority owner's interest in the business. Usually, the majority owner, or co-owners, were single people or couples in the older generation. Essentially, a freeze involved a gift of common stock (at a low value) to the owner's children, with the owner retaining preferred voting stock. All appreciation in the worth of the business was later attributed to the common stock. Because this stock was legally owned by the children, none of the appreciation (nor the original worth of the common stock) was included in the taxable estate of the owner.
>
> Unfortunately for family businesses, Congress has basically eliminated an owner's ability to "freeze" the current value of her business. Congress has adopted an exceedingly restrictive, and even more complex (indeed, confusing), set of laws controlling attempted estate freezes and family stock transfers. However, in the right circumstances, a few loopholes remain. Certainly, some lawyers still try sophisticated, on -the-edge (or slightly over it) stock manipulations of family corporations in an effort to lower the eventual worth of an owner's family business stock. If a lawyer proposes such a scheme to you, do your best to figure out what he or she is suggesting. And be sure to ask your lawyer why she thinks this is legal, in light of Congress's basic elimination of estate freezes. In other words, why would the IRS accept the lawyer's scheme?
>
> Congress's elimination of estate tax freezes has not done away with tax-free gifts of stock completely. Under the general gift tax exemption, an owner of stock can give, free of gift tax, stock worth up to $10,000 ($20,000 in the case of a married couple) per person, per year. A tricky issue here is how you fairly value the stock in a closed or small corporation, which usually has no ascertainable market price. So there's some room here for creative accounting, if it's done right—that is, by an expert.

c. Payment for a Deceased Owner's Interest

Assuming a valuation method is chosen in advance, some means of actually paying the deceased's beneficiaries for their interest should also be agreed on by the business owners. Purchasing life insurance is one way to do this. Each owner can purchase life insurance on the other owner's life; the purchaser is the beneficiary of that policy. Or the business itself can purchase insurance for all owners, with proceeds paid to the surviving owners. Or the surviving owners can be allowed to pay the deceased's beneficiaries over time, and use the income from their business to make the payments. Again, the key point is for the owners to agree, in writing, on their plan for buy-out payments.

If the business is a corporation, buy-out agreements can become quite complicated. For instance, if the business buys the deceased's stock from the estate, is that purchase price taxed to the deceased's estate as a dividend, which means more taxes will be owed? It can be, under some circumstances. This is one more reason to check your estate planning carefully with an expert if you're a co-owner of a corporate business.

3. Partnerships

If your business is a partnership, you should state in your partnership agreement what will happen when a partner dies. Below are two examples of how partnership agreements can be structured to handle the eventuality. For more information on how to write a partnership agreement to deal with these issues, see *The Partnership Book,* by Clifford and Warner (Nolo Press). This book provides a number of ready-to-use clauses designed to fit different needs. You can also use *Nolo's Partnership Maker,* a DOS computer program that allows you to prepare a legally enforceable partnership agreement in any state. You can select and assemble clauses for your agreement as you desire. These materials include on-line legal help screens, a glossary, a tutorial and a manual that take you through the process step-by-step.

Example 1: Ned, a partner in N.J.D, has agreed with his other two partners (J. and D.) that the survivors will continue the business after one of them dies. Ned wants the value of his ownership interest to go to his children. The other partners have similar wishes. To achieve the dual goals of keeping the business going and providing for beneficiaries, Ned and his partners decide that management of the partnership business will be kept legally separate from the ownership interest of the partner's beneficiaries. To do this, they agree in the partnership agreement that the partnership share of a deceased partner will be placed in a trust for the benefit of his beneficiaries. The surviving partners will serve as trustees, with power to manage the business as they see fit. A deceased partner's beneficiaries will have the right to one-third of the partnership profits. The surviving partners also can, at their option, buy out the beneficiaries' share of the partnership. A formula to value this share is established in the partnership agreement, along with a payment schedule. If the buy-out isn't completed in the defined period of time, the trust ends and the beneficiaries can sell their partnership share to outsiders.

Example 2: Jason and Pat are equal partners in the J-P Co. When Jason dies, he wants his partnership interest to go to his son. Pat wants her interest to be divided between her three children. Both Jason and Pat want to avoid probate. Equally important, both want the surviving partner to have the opportunity to continue the business. Neither wants the child or children of the first partner to die to be able to liquidate the partnership.

Jason and Pat agree on the following estate plan: Both create living trusts in which they place their interests in the partnership business. They check their partnership agreement and recall that each partner must approve the other's transfer of his or her partnership interest, so each signs a document formally giving approval to the other's transfer to the living trust.

Finally, they amend the partnership agreement to put in the solution they've worked out allowing the surviving partner to continue the business: The amended partnership agreement provides that a partner with 51% ownership of the business has exclusive control over it. The other partner or his or her beneficiaries have rights to income from the partnership if it makes a profit, but no rights to manage it or dissolve it. When a partner dies, the value of his 50% or her interest in the partnership will be determined by a carefully-defined appraisal method. Then the surviving partner has the right to buy 1% of that deceased partnership interest, for 1/50 (or 2%) of the appraised worth of that interest. Thus, the surviving partner will obtain 51% of the business and have exclusive control over it.

In this situation, it's important for all to be aware that a deceased partner's beneficiaries have no rights to manage or liquidate the business, and that their income from it depends entirely on the decisions of the surviving partner. So, for this sort of plan to work well for all concerned, each partner must totally trust the other (which is what partnerships should be about).

4. Corporations

Although the legal form of a corporation is different from a partnership, the same types of estate planning problems must be resolved by the owners of closely-held (non-public) corporations: how to value the interest of a deceased owner, how to provide continuity, and how to protect the interests of both the surviving owners and beneficiaries. The shareholders should resolve these issues in a written agreement which is incorporated in corporate documents, typically either the bylaws or a separate shareholders' agreement.

Example: Frederick Smith and Rachel Twardzick are a married couple with three adult children. They are also the co-owners of a thriving plant store and commercial plant rental business. The couple entered the business with a kiss and high hopes, and even though many of their hopes have been fulfilled, they have never gotten around to incorporating the business or creating a written partnership agreement. Even without a written partnership agreement, they are partners, because of their actions.

After many years, and more than a few gray hairs, they decide it's time to discuss their respective estate planning needs. Each wants to leave a majority of ownership of the store to the surviving spouse, with some of it divided between their three adult children.

They decide to incorporate the business as "Plants, Inc." and divide the stock equally between themselves. Each shareholder then creates a probate-avoiding living trust and transfers all of his or her stock in Plant's, Inc. to it. The trust document provides that when each parent dies, the trust is to distribute two-thirds of the stock to the surviving spouse and the remaining third equally between the three children. A detailed provision is also included in the bylaws, defining how each child's interest can be valued and purchased by the other children if they all desire that. But if they don't, it can't be sold to an outsider.

The corporate bylaws are also custom-designed to prevent the children from selling their stock as long as one parent lives. In addition, the bylaws give managerial control to the majority shareholder, the surviving spouse. Frederick and Rachel privately agree that the survivor will leave all of his or her stock to the children, but they don't make a formal contract to require this, because they believe that binding the survivor to dispose of property to the kids they both love dearly is just plain unnecessary.

D. Avoiding Probate and Reducing Estate Taxes

Once planning is done at the business level, each business owner obviously needs to do personal estate planning, to find the best method to transfer his business interest while avoiding probate and minimizing estate taxes. Let's briefly look at what's involved in each.

1. Probate Avoidance

It's often disastrous for a small business to become enmeshed in probate. Probate is, of course, costly. But worse, it ties up the business under court control for a year, or often longer. It can be burdensome, even destructive, to have to seek a probate court's approval for business decisions. If you doubt this, ask yourself if you want a judge supervising your business for months, or years. You can plan to avoid probate of your business interest by using either a joint tenancy or a living trust. For a number of tax and ownership reasons discussed in detail in Chapter 9, Revocable Living Trusts, and Chapter 10, Joint Tenancy and Tenancy by the Entirety, a living trust is usually the best choice. Let's look at how this might work for a sole proprietorship and for shared ownership businesses.

a. Individual Ownership

Placing your business in a living trust is commonly the best means to avoid probate of a solely-owned business. The living trust allows the business to be transferred to its beneficiaries promptly, without any risk of loss of control while you live.

If your business has many debts and creditors' claims, probate may be desirable, because it provides a convenient forum for having those claims resolved. Also, if the business might possibly have any toxic claims made against it, probate is desirable to provide a cut-off period for such claims. (See Chapter 7, Probate and Why You Want to Avoid It, Section D, for more on these issues.) These problems are unusual. Most business owners, even those with a defined list of known creditors, should plan to avoid probate. And few face claims for toxic damage. For most solely-owned businesses, a living trust works fine.

Example 1: Sam is the sole owner of a New York restaurant. The business is not incorporated. Sam conducts the business under his name "dba [doing business as] The Manhattan Bar and Grill," and has filed the appropriate business and tax forms with city licensing agencies. Sam will leave the business to his son, Theodore. Sam creates a living trust and names Theodore as the beneficiary to inherit the restaurant. Sam lists the restaurant on Schedule A of the trust: "The restaurant dba The Manhattan Bar and Grill...[street address]... and all assets, supplies, accounts receivable, good will or other property of the business." Sam then checks with the city licensing agencies, which inform him that they do not require any paperwork for the living trust to be effective. Of course, when Theodore inherits the business, he'll need to complete a new "dba" form.

Example 2: Natalie is sole owner of the Stay-Potted plant store. She wants to leave her interest in the store as follows:

30% to her close friend Donna;

25% to her niece Cindy;

15% to each of her three brothers (totaling 45%).

After investigating her options, she decides to incorporate and then transfer the stock of the corporation into a living trust. The trust provides that each of its beneficiaries receives the percentage of shares of stock she's specified. Natalie also prepares the appropriate corporate records, according to the corporation's bylaws, to approve her actions. She decides she won't worry about management and continuity of the business after she dies. It's up to her beneficiaries. If they agree to run the business and can run it—fine. If that doesn't work out, they can sell the business.

b. Shared Ownership Businesses

For shared ownership businesses—whether partnerships or corporations—living trusts are normally the best probate avoidance devices. The partnership agreement, corporate bylaws or shareholders' agreement should specifically permit each owner to transfer her interest to a living trust. If the document does not provide for this, it should be amended or revised so that it does. Then, each owner creates her own living trust, consistent with any requirements of the partnership agreement, bylaws or shareholders' agreement (such as the right of surviving principals to buy out the deceased's share), and transfers her interest in the business to that trust. The trust then works like any other probate avoidance living trust, as explained in Chapter 9. The business property transferred to the trust is listed on Schedule A, for example as:

The grantor's shares in the ZT Corporation.

The grantor's partnership interest in the AB partnership.

Then, any business asset transferred to the living trust with a document of title must be re-registered in the trust's name.

Example: Vikki and Sloane each own one-half of the stock in Go-Get-'Em, Inc. which owns two apartment houses. Both Vikki and Sloane create living trusts for their business interests. Each must do the following to transfer his or her share of the business into the living trust:

- Prepare the appropriate corporate records and resolution authorizing and approving the transfer.
- Prepare new corporate shares, listing the living trust as owner.

2. Reducing Estate Taxes

There are special federal estate tax rules for small businesses (called "closely held" businesses in tax lingo) which can be used to lighten or reduce death taxes. To learn if these detailed rules apply to your business and whether it's sensible for you to plan to use them, you'll need to see a tax expert. Here's a summary of how these rules work:

- Estate taxes assessed against the value of a small business can be deferred five years and then paid in ten annual installments. In other words, the final payment isn't due until 15 years after the owner's death. The principal Internal Revenue Code restriction here is that the value of the small business must exceed 35% of the total estate or 50% of the taxable estate.

  Example: Andrew owns the Ace Pharmacy, which has a net worth of $500,000. Andrew dies. His total estate, including the pharmacy, is worth $1,000,000. The federal estate taxes assessed against the estate are $153,000. However, half the value of Andrews' estate is his small business, so half of his estate taxes can be postponed, and paid over 15 years.

- Real estate used in a family trade or business or as a family farm can be valued for estate tax purposes at its value for the present use, rather than at its "highest and best" use. For example, a family farm doesn't have to be valued for its (possibly much higher) worth as a potential location for a shopping center or subdivision, but can be valued on the basis of its worth as a farm. This valuation rule can provide a real break for family businesses, as the value of the real estate can be reduced up to a maximum of $750,000, the difference between "present use" and "best use." However, there are several requirements that must be met for the rule to apply:
  - The value of the family business or farm must be at least 50% of the overall estate.
  - The value of the real estate of that business must be at least 25% of the overall estate.
  - The family business must be passed at the death of deceased to a member of his family.
  - The deceased or a member of his family must have used the real estate for the business in five of the eight years preceding the decedent's death.
  - There are restrictions on the sale and use of the real estate for ten years (and in some cases 15 years) after the estate tax break. During this time, the family must agree to notify the IRS if the property is sold or no longer used for the business and may be required to repay some or all of the estate taxes if the ownership or use of the real estate changes.
- Significant income tax savings are permitted for corporate stock redeemed to pay estate taxes assessed against family businesses or farms. ■

29

Social Security and Pensions

Upon retirement, most people are entitled to payments from one or more retirement programs, such as Social Security payments, military benefits, private and public employee pensions, union pension plans, or an individual IRA or Keogh Account Planning for a financially comfortable retirement can be a complicated field, and we don't pretend to cover it here. For more information on these subjects, see *Social Security, Medicare and Pensions*, by Joseph Matthews, and *Beat the Nursing Home Trap*, by Joseph Matthews, both published by Nolo Press.

Although we don't focus on retirement issues here, we do note the obvious; estate planning and retirement planning are related. For example, in drafting their estate plan, a married couple should consider each spouse's rights under pension plans. If a surviving spouse can expect to get generous monthly pension checks that will cover living expenses, with a little left over, the other spouse may sensibly decide to leave at least some money and property directly to children or friends. On the other hand, if a surviving spouse won't receive adequate pension income, the other spouse would more likely leave all property to him. Similarly, buying a life insurance policy on the life of a breadwinner makes great sense if there will be little continuing income should he or she die, and much less if a generous pension will be in the offing.

Another important estate planning question is, what happens if a family breadwinner dies before becoming eligible for retirement benefits? Do the benefits he would have received had he lived go to the surviving spouse or children? If so, how much, under what circumstances, and for how long? Obviously, it's important to be able to answer these questions before you plan your estate.

Which gets us to the central point of this chapter. It's important to clearly understand how much you will receive in retirement benefits and, if you are married, what, if any, rights, a surviving spouse will have to a deceased spouse's retirement plan. For example, Social Security and other public programs normally protect a deceased covered worker's surviving children and spouse. But there's no legal requirement that a private or union pension plan pay benefits to a surviving spouse or anyone else. Some are generous, some are miserly, and some don't even bother to say "tough luck, friend."

In the rest of this chapter we will briefly discuss how the principle retirement benefit plans work. It will be up to you to find out more about the ones that affect you.

RETIREMENT BENEFITS:
ESTATE TAX AND PROBATE STATUS

Retirement plan payments earned by a deceased spouse and paid to a surviving spouse or other beneficiary are normally exempt from probate. All lump-sum retirement or pension payments—such as the remaining balance in an IRA, profit sharing account or 401(k) plan—are subject to estate tax. If the deceased's estate, including a lump-sum retirement payment, exceeds $600,000, taxes will be assessed. Of course, if a spouse names the surviving spouse as the beneficiary for a lump-sum payment, this money is not taxable, because of the unlimited marital deduction. Payments made to a survivor over time are taxed as income to the survivor, not as part of the deceased's estate.

A. Social Security

The most extensive retirement program is the federal Social Security system. Despite periodic anxieties that the program will run out of money, it manages to make regular payments to millions and will surely continue to do so. Payments usually begin at age 65 (although it's possible to elect to receive smaller payments at age 55, or even younger if you become blind or disabled).

More pertinent to estate planning, Social Security also provides payments to many categories of family survivors of covered wage earners, even if these people are not entitled to payments based on their own earnings record:

- A widower or widow who is 65 or older receives, for life, 100% of the deceased spouse's Social Security benefits if the deceased spouse was over 65 at death. If the surviving spouse is between ages 60 and 65, there is a reduction in benefits according to a set formula. (Remarriage after age 60 doesn't terminate benefits.) A surviving spouse cannot receive double benefits, both on the basis of the deceased spouse and because of his own Social Security contribution. However, the surviving spouse can choose to receive whichever payment is larger.
- Unmarried children up to 18 (or 19, if attending high school full time) receive benefits.
- Children disabled before age 22 can get benefits for as long as they're disabled. This program is of particular interest to parents with a mentally or physically disadvantaged child who will need continuing lifetime care. It means they can create an ongoing "special needs" trust (see Chapter 24, Trusts and Other Devices for Imposing Controls Over Property, Section C) to supplement Social Security income; they don't have to start from scratch.
- Divorced widows or widowers, if the marriage lasted at least ten years, receive payment for life. It's possible for both a surviving spouse and an ex-spouse to collect Social Security based on the same deceased wage earner. A divorced widow or widower can receive full benefits at age 65, and reduced benefits from age 60.
- Under certain circumstances, grandchildren, great grandchildren, and dependent parents age 62 or older may be eligible for payments.

In addition, Social Security pays one lump-sum death payment of $255 to the surviving spouse or child eligible for benefits.

People under 70 who receive Social Security payments as the survivor of a deceased worker may have the payments reduced if they work and their earnings exceed "exempt amounts" set by law. An unlimited amount can be earned by a person over 70 without a reduction in payment.

Under federal law the decedent's own last monthly Social Security check must be returned to the Social Security Administration. The amount is not prorated. The full last monthly check must be given back. It's important to note here that Social Security payments are paid by the government a month late. In other words, the check for January is received during early February. So, if a recipient died on February 1, the check that arrives in March must be returned.

B. Profit Sharing, IRA and 401(k) Retirement Programs

As you doubtless know, Individual Profit Sharing plans (formerly known as Keogh plans), IRA (Individual Retirement Account) and 401(k) plans are retirement plans you fund yourself from your own earnings, without paying income taxes on the money contributed. A Keogh plan is for the self-employed. By contrast, any income earner can create an IRA. A 401(k) plan is for an employee of a company who has established this type of retirement program. The employee defers receiving some wages, having them paid instead into the 401(k) plan. Income taxes in all these plans are due when money is withdrawn after retirement; if there is an early withdrawal, tax is owed and a penalty imposed.

Profit Sharing, IRA and 401(k) plans were not intended as estate planning devices. In theory at least, you create one of these plans to provide for yourself after retirement, not to make gifts after your death. However, in practice, IRAs, Profit Sharing and 401(k) plans often contain money when the account owner dies, and so become part (sometimes a significant part) of an estate. As mentioned earlier, any lump-sum payment from a Profit Sharing, IRA or 401(k) plan is included in the deceased's taxable estate, unless the payment is left to a surviving spouse. In that case, the payment is exempt from estate taxes because all property, no matter what the source, left to a surviving spouse is free of estate tax. By contrast, periodic payments made to a beneficiary after a retirement plan owner's death are not included in the deceased's estate, but are treated as ordinary income, taxable to the beneficiary.

Because the federal government doesn't officially recognize IRAs, Profit Sharing plans and 401(k) accounts as estate planning devices, it requires that you must begin to take money from your account when you reach age 70½. Then the percentage of the total that you must withdraw each year is determined by your age and statistical life expectancy, or your age/life expectancy and someone else's, such as a spouse.

An advantage of having money in an IRA, Profit Sharing or 401(k) account that many people don't consider is that any money left in the account at death goes to a named beneficiary free of probate. You simply specify the beneficiary or beneficiaries on the account documents. The money can be paid in a lump sum, or in installments, in the form of an annuity.

After the death of the person who funded an IRA, Profit Sharing or 401(k) plan, or who is the beneficiary of a organization retirement program, a named beneficiary can have some options regarding how he receives the money over time. In fact, fairly complicated rules can apply to the beneficiary's choice of what time period payments will be made to him. If the deceased person (who established an account) hasn't required a lump-sum distribution at her death, the beneficiary can elect to take the money remaining in the account over a five-year period. As another option, the beneficiary can elect to have the money paid out over the same period of time she would have had if she were the creator of the plan. Making this choice is a complex matter, and it's usually wise to consult a pension expert before you make your final choice.

1. Do Not Name Your Living Trust as Your Beneficiary

Some people wonder about naming their living trust as the beneficiary of their IRA, Profit Sharing or 401(k) plan. Generally, this is not desirable. Following are the drawbacks of naming your living trust as the beneficiary:

- Since there is no probate needed for IRA and Keogh plans in the first place, there is no need to name your living trust as beneficiary in an effort to avoid probate.
- Distribution cannot be based on estimates of how long you and the beneficiary, such as your spouse or living-together partner, will live. They can only be based on your own life estimate. The result is, usually, a higher amount of money must be withdrawn each year, and therefore there may be little or no money left in the account for your spouse if he or she survives you.
- At your death, all money remaining in the account must be distributed within five years. Longer distribution periods are available if you name an individual to be beneficiary.

2. Rollover IRAs

There's one peculiar type of IRA called a "rollover IRA." It is created by employees of a company that has a retirement plan if the following occurs: After a set time, depending on the plan, employees obtain what's called a "vested interest" in the plan. In other words, they have the right to obtain the money set aside for them in the plan if the company goes broke, or just decides to discontinue the retirement plan, for whatever reason. The employees with a vested interest in the terminated plan are legally entitled to obtain the money set aside for them in the now-discontinued company retirement plan. When an employee receives his money, he has 60 days to put it into ("roll it over") a new (or existing) IRA plan in his name. If this is done, there are no adverse tax consequences to the employee. If the money is not rolled over into an IRA within 60 days, the money is then treated as having been distributed to the employee. He will then owe income tax on the money, plus a 10% penalty charge for a premature distribution of retirement funds.

RESOURCES FOR RESEARCH ON PENSIONS AND RETIREMENT PLANS

The IRS publishes a series of booklets explaining various rules applicable to different pension or retirement plans. IRA publication #590 covers individual retirement arrangements, such as IRAs. IRS publication #560 covers retirement plans for the self-employed, such as Keoghs. And publication #575 covers pension and annuity income.

These publications are not easy reading. They're complex and technical. And, unfortunately, there are no books we know of that provide an adequate explanation of the intricacies and choices available with pensions or retirement plans.

If you want help understanding the details of your pension or retirement plan and can't get what you want from the IRS publications, you'll need to see a pension-plan expert, or a lawyer knowledgeable in this specialized field.

C. Pensions

There is no law that requires an employer to offer a pension plan. However, if a company chooses to do so, ERISA, the general federal law covering pensions and distributions from them, requires that every pension plan must spell out who is eligible for coverage. Pension plans do not have to include all workers, but they cannot legally be structured to benefit only the top executives or otherwise discriminate—for example, by excluding older workers. The plan administrator for your company's pension program (assuming it has one) can tell you whether or not you are eligible to participate.

If you are eligible to participate in your employer's pension program, the administrator must provide you with several documents needed to understand the plan.

- **A summary plan description.** Explains the basics of how your plan operates. ERISA requires that you be given the summary plan within 90 days after you begin participating in a pension plan, and that you must be given any updates to it.

  This document will also tell you the formula for vesting in the plan—if it is a plan that includes vesting—the formula for determining your defined benefits or the defined contributions that your employer will make to the plan, and whether or not your pension is insured.

- **A summary annual report.** A yearly accounting of your pension plan's financial condition and operations.

- **Survivor coverage data.** A statement of how much your plan would pay to any surviving spouse should you die first.

Your plan administrator is also required to provide you with a detailed, individual statement of the pension benefits you have earned, but only if you request it in writing or are going to stop participating in the plan because, for example, you change employers. Note, however, that ERISA gives you the right to only one such statement from your plan per year.

Where to Get More Information

If you want more detail on your rights to receive benefits from a private pension plan, there are a number of free brochures available from:

American Association of Retired Persons (AARP)
601 E Street, NW
Washington, DC 20049
202/434-2277

Another organization that offers a number of publications relating to pensions is:

The Pension Rights Center
918 16th Street, NW; Suite 704
Washington, DC 20006
202/296-3778

D. Other Retirement Programs

There are many other types of retirement benefits: military benefits, railroad benefits, state and federal employment retirement, union pension plans, and so on. The benefits these programs may provide survivors depend on the specific provisions of each program. To find out, you'll need to check the rules of each program that applies to you. Once you do, it shouldn't be difficult to integrate this information into your estate plan. ■

30

USING LAWYERS

Some readers will decide that, with the aid of this book and other Nolo resources, they can do all the estate planning they need themselves, without a lawyer. Other readers will conclude that they need the help of a lawyer[1] to safely plan their estate. Here we discuss how to use a lawyer, if you need one—how to find a good lawyer, how to evaluate a lawyer and what type of lawyer you'll need (including the level of expertise necessary).

Also, we discuss in some depth the option of doing your own legal research. Even if your situation is one for which we've stated you'll definitely need a lawyer, that doesn't prohibit doing some legal research yourself, going deeper into one or more topics than we can here. After all, the more you know about the broad legal issues involved in estate planning and the particular legal tools you are considering incorporating in your plan, the more likely you are to make good choices and the lower your eventual legal bill should be. Otherwise you could end up in a situation in which the lawyer not only sells you information you could have mastered for yourself, but, because of her superior knowledge, may tend to dictate, or at least heavily influence, your decision-making.

Of course, there's no requirement that you do any legal research at all. It takes effort. Many readers who decide to hire a lawyer will conclude they've gone as deep into advanced estate planning as they can to by reading and understanding this book. That surely is a reasonable response. After all, unless you really are ready to invest a fair number of hours climbing the estate planning learning curve, you won't acquire enough expertise to creatively challenge and debate the lawyers recommended solutions.

[1]Ambrose Bierce defined a lawyer as "one skilled in circumvention of the law."

A. HIRING A LAWYER

If you do determine that you want an expert's assistance, obviously you don't want to hire a lawyer at random and say "tell me what to do." As an intelligent consumer, you not only want to gain at least as much knowledge about your problem as you conveniently can, but you also want to invest sufficient time to be sure the person you hire is honest, knowledgeable and provides good service for your dollar.

Be true to yourself. Your estate plan should express your intentions. No one else can know those intentions. Sometimes, when people think, or fear, that they need a lawyer, what they are really doing is longing for an authority figure (or believing one is required) to tell them what to do. Keep in mind only you can decide who should get your property, and how and when they should get it. An estate planning expert is only your paid employee (advisor), not your mentor.

1. What Kind of Legal Expert Do You Need?

The first question to decide is whether you need a lawyer, or if you will be better served by a financial expert such as an accountant or financial planner. Don't just assume a lawyer is your best choice. For example, questions about federal estate taxes or how to calculate tax basis rules on the sale of appreciated property can often be better answered by an experienced CPA than a lawyer. Similarly, for some financial decisions, such as what type of insurance to buy to fund a small business buy-out, you may be better off talking to a financial planner. But for most estate planning concerns, you do need to see a lawyer. There are, basically, three categories of estate planning lawyers:

- general practice lawyers
- estate planning specialists, and
- very specialized lawyers working in one very difficult aspect of estate planning.

The type of lawyer right for you will depend on what your estate planning concerns and need are. Let's look at each type of lawyer in more detail.

a. General Practice Lawyers

General practice lawyers handle all sorts of cases, and don't specialize in estate planning. If your needs are basic, such as a garden variety living trust or will, or to check some provision of your state's laws, a competent attorney in general practice should be able to do a good job at a lower cost than more specialized attorneys.

Similarly, if your small business needs to customize its partnership agreement or corporate bylaws to allow for a surviving principal to buy out the shares of a deceased principal from his or her inheritors, a general practice lawyer should do fine.

b. Estate Planning Specialists

Specialists in estate planning often confine their practice to estate work only. As we've stated in this book, for any type of sophisticated estate planning work, you need to see a specialist. Estate planning, as this book may have convinced you, is often a complex matter. To do a good job, a lawyer often needs to be absolutely up-to-date on estate tax law and regulations, the rules governing ongoing trusts and numerous other details. Whether your concern is to establish an ongoing trust for estate tax savings, handle issues raised by a second marriage, set up an ongoing gift-giving program while you live, or any one of many other possible complex matters—you need an expert.

An expert may charge relatively high fees, but if she's good, she's worth it. Most general practice lawyers are simply not sufficiently educated in estate planning to handle complex matters.

c. Very Specialized Lawyers

These lawyers specialize in a particularly difficult aspect of estate law. For example, to prepare a "special needs" trust for a disabled person, a lawyer must be current on federal and state regulations regarding trust property and eligibility for government benefits. Even most estate planning experts don't have sufficient expertise for this. Other instances where a specialized estate planning lawyer is generally needed include arranging to protect your assets if you or your spouse must go to a nursing home, or you own property in two or more countries and need an attorney who's expert at multinational estate planning.

Unfortunately, finding the person with the specialized skills you need isn't always easy. In some states, such as California, state bar associations certify lawyers as expert estate planners, but this is no guarantee they are competent in one of the very specialized areas of estate planning. You simply have to ask until you find a lawyer with the experience you need.

It's important that you feel a personal rapport with your lawyer. You want one who treats you as an equal. (Interestingly, the Latin root of the word "client" translates as "to hear, to obey.") When talking with a lawyer on the phone or at a first conference, ask specific questions that concern you. If the lawyer answers them clearly and concisely—explaining, but not talking down to you—fine. If he acts wise, but says little except to ask that the problem be placed in his hands (with the appropriate fee, of course), watch out. You are either talking with someone who doesn't know the answer and won't admit it (common), or someone who finds it impossible to let go of the "me expert, you peasant" way of looking at the world (even more common).

As you already know, lawyers are expensive, and expert lawyers are more expensive. Lawyers charge fees usually ranging from $150 to $400 or more per hour, with experts at the higher end of the scale. While fancy office trappings, muted gray suits and solemn faces are no guarantee (or even a good indication) that a particular lawyer will provide top notch service in a style you will feel comfortable with, this conventional style will almost always ensure that you will be charged at the upper end of the fee range. At Nolo, our experience tells us that high fees and quality service don't necessarily go hand in hand. Indeed, many of the attorneys we think most highly of tend to charge moderate fees (for lawyers, that is), and seem to get along very nicely without most stuffy law office trappings.

Be sure you've settled your fee arrangement—in writing—at the start of your relationship. Depending on the area of the county where you live, generally, we feel that fees for a general practice lawyer in the range of $150 to $225 per hour are reasonable in urban areas, given the average lawyer's overhead. Expert estate planning lawyers usually cost more, sometimes a lot more. In rural counties and small cities, excellent general help may be available for a little less. Again, estate planning experts will cost more. In addition to the amount charged per hour, you also want a clear commitment from the lawyer concerning how many hours he expects to put in on your problem.

2. Getting Referrals to a Lawyer

All this sounds acceptable, you may think, but how do you find a lawyer? Ours is such a lawyer-ridden society that it's unusual if one hasn't already found you. There is a growing surplus of lawyers; one out of every 280 Americans will be one by 1996. (If we just look at white males, the figure is less than one out of 100.) The difficulty, of course, is not just finding a lawyer, but retaining one who is trustworthy, competent, and charges fairly. In addition, as noted above, many readers will need to find an estate planning expert, not just a general practitioner who says "no problem" when you ask if she does living trusts. A few words of advice on how you can find a good lawyer may be helpful.

When looking for a good lawyer, especially an estate planning expert, personal routes are the traditional, and probably best, method. If a relative or good friend who has excellent business and financial sense found an estate planning lawyer he recommends, chances are you'll like him too. Failing this, check with people you know in any political or social organization you're involved with, especially those with a large number of members over age 40. Assuming they, themselves, are savvy, they may well be able to point you to a competent lawyer who handles estate planning matters and whose attitudes are similar to yours.

Another good approach is to ask for help from a lawyer you are personally acquainted with and think well of, even if she doesn't work in the estate planning area. Very likely she can refer you to someone trustworthy who is an estate planning expert.

Also, check with people you respect who own their own small businesses. Almost anyone running a small business has a relationship with a lawyer, and chances are they've found one they like. Again, this lawyer will probably not be an estate planning expert, but he'll likely know one, or several.

If you are a member of a legal insurance plan, you may be offered sophisticated estate planning assistance from a referral panel member at a reduced fee. Some of these referrals may be to excellent lawyers. In our experience, however, too often lawyers who sign up to do cut-rate work are not the best alternative. Excellent lawyers, particularly good estate planning experts, tend to have lots of work, and don't need to cut fees to gain clients.

Also, be cautious when dealing with bar association referral panels. Never assume a listing on a referral panel is a seal of approval. While lawyers are supposed to be screened as to their specialty to get on these panels, screening is usually perfunctory. Often the main qualification is that the lawyer needs business.

3. Checking the Lawyer Out

It's desirable to personally evaluate any lawyer you've been referred to before you agree to have her handle your estate plan. Don't hesitate to question the lawyer, no matter how expert she is considered to be. But to ask sensible questions, you need to have done some preparation; you should have at least a rough general idea of what you want to do. Also, you need enough information (gleaned from this book or other sources) to intelligently pose the questions you need to ask and evaluate the lawyer's answers.

If, in your first discussion with a lawyer, he or she appears uncomfortable because you've done some thinking and general planning yourself, back off. You need an lawyer who's open and sympathetic to people who want to actively participate in handling their own legal affairs.

Keep in mind that in any field, certainly including estate planning, there are good high-priced experts and bad ones. It's all too easy to get a

HIRING A LAWYER TO REVIEW YOUR ESTATE PLANNING DOCUMENTS

Hiring a lawyer solely to review a will or living trust you've prepared from a Nolo resource sounds like a good idea. It shouldn't cost much, and seems to offer a comforting security. Sadly though, it can be difficult to find a lawyer who will accept the job. The reason is, many lawyers feel that by reviewing a document for a relatively small fee they become just as legally responsible for a client's entire estate plan situation as if they did all the work from scratch. Or, put more directly, many lawyers see every client as the author of a future malpractice claim, or at least, the source of later hassles and simply don't want to get involved for a modest fee.

To counter this mentality and help provide self-helpers with the coaching and advice they often need, Nolo Press has advocated unbundling legal services. The idea is that a customer should be able to contract with a lawyer for only the services wanted and the lawyer should have no broader liability beyond providing those services competently. With new phone law services, and lawyers who are setting up businesses to provide advice only, this approach is sure to be more common soon. But in the meantime, if you have trouble finding a lawyer who will help you help yourself, all you can do here is to keep trying to find a sympathetic lawyer. It will help if you are prepared to pay a decent fee so that the lawyer can take the time necessary to carefully review your work.

mumbo-jumbo speaking lawyer who confuses you at first, and enrages you later, when you receive his exorbitant bill for what may even turn out to be needless work. Don't be afraid to keep looking until you find a lawyer you like. Many people who have had unhappy experiences with lawyers (and we all know some) only wish they had done so.

How Many Lawyers Does a Couple Need?

Sounds like a joke question, right? Unfortunately, it isn't. Most couples can safely use one lawyer for both spouses' estate planning. However, if there's a potential conflict between different spouse's desires, then perhaps each needs a separate lawyer. This is most likely to be the case in a second or subsequent marriage, particularly if children from one or both spouse's prior marriage(s) don't get along with the other spouse.

Despite this possibility, relatively few couples will decide their interests are, or could be, so in conflict that each one must hire his or her own lawyer. But in an atypical situation—say where the estate lawyer is a good friend of one spouse and the other spouse's children are suspicious that somehow they'll get cheated of their inheritance or where one spouse can be extremely domineering and opinionated—one or both spouses may sensibly decide they want independent advice regarding their estate planning. In this case, choosing two lawyers can be a sensible form of insurance against possible later claims of undue influence or unfair representation by a single attorney.

4. Typing Services

If you determine that you can accomplish your estate planning goals without consulting a lawyer or other estate planning experts, you may still want to consult someone who is familiar with Nolo resources and knows how they can be used. A typing service may be able to assist you in the following ways:

- supply a fast-track questionnaire to help you prepare a will, living trust and other estate planning documents
- guide you through relevant portions of appropriate Nolo resources
- review your drafts and suggest additional reading where necessary
- type or print your estate planning documents on high-quality paper.

For routine estate planning form preparation for knowledgeable self-helpers with estates smaller than $600,000, typing services can be a good choice. They normally charge from $25 to $450, depending on the documents.

When using a typing service, it is important to understand that they are very different from lawyers. They can't give legal advice or represent you in court—only lawyers are allowed to do those things. When you use a typing service, you remain responsible for the decision-making in your situation. For instance, you, and you alone, must decide what property to put into a living trust and who to leave that property to. You cannot, legally, pass this responsibility on to a trust typing service.

People at a typing service should be up-front with you about not being attorneys and not providing legal advice. The following statement, posted in a well-known typing service near San Francisco, summarizes its services well:

WE ARE NOT ATTORNEYS

We are pro per assistants. Attorneys represent people. We assist people to represent themselves. If you want someone to represent you, you'll need to hire an attorney. If you want to "do it yourself," we can help. We believe that representing yourself is the only way to gain, and keep, control over your own life and your own legal problems. You don't need legal training to use the courts or manage your own legal affairs.

A recommendation from someone who has used a particular typing service is the best way to find a reputable one in your area. The services often advertise in classified sections of local newspapers under Referral Services, usually immediately following *attorneys*. Also many offices have display ads in local throwaway papers like the Classified Flea Market or Giant Nickel.

B. Doing Your Own Research

Learning how to do your own research into estate planning law can provide real benefits. Not only are you likely to save money on professional fees, you'll gain a sense of mastery over an area of law, generating more confidence that your estate plan really meets your needs and giving you a head start should you ever want to research other legal questions.

Some aspects of estate planning law are fairly easy to research. For example, to answer questions concerning technical aspects of the state laws affecting wills or probate avoidance, you often need only to check the relevant statutes of your state to find the particular provision that concerns you.

In addition, if you want to try drafting a particular legal form, you may well find that it's easier than you think (aside from the option of using a Nolo resource to prepare the form). Lawyers commonly draft forms largely by copying out fairly standard language (they call it "boilerplate") from legal form books. Indeed, once you take a look at these form books, you may be surprised to see how lawyers (or, typically, their paralegal assistants) can recycle "canned" language and charge hefty amounts for this limited service. For example, many wills and living trusts are copied by lawyers directly out of standard legal form books. Even in more complicated situations of will or trust drafting, all lawyers do, in many instances, is to check several standard legal form books. Obviously, you can do at least some of this for yourself, if you can locate the right books.

1. Research Aids

If you decide you want to do your own research, how do you go about it? First, you need an introduction to how law libraries work. If you can't hire your own law librarian, the best book explaining how to do your own legal work for non-lawyers is *Legal Research: How to Find and Understand the Law,* by Steve Elias and Susan Levinkind (Nolo Press). It shows you, step-by-step, how to find answers in the law library and is, as far as we know, the only legal research book written specifically for non-professionals. Nolo also publishes an excellent two-and-one-half hour video, *Legal Research Made Easy*, in which law librarian and legal research professor Bob Berring shows you how to conduct first-class legal research step-by-step.

Next, locate a law library (or a public library with a good law collection). There's often one in your principal county courthouse, although its quality depends a lot on your state. County law libraries are normally supported by tax dollars or by the fees paid to file court papers. In our experience, their librarians are sensitive and generally most helpful and courteous to non-lawyers who want to learn to do their own legal research. If the county library is not adequate, your best bet is a law school library. Those in state colleges and universities supported by tax dollars are almost always open to the public.

Even with the assistance of a sympathetic law librarian and a research aid, digging into the law can be intimidating at first. We urge you to stay with it. After a while—perhaps sooner than you anticipate—you'll understand the materials and how you can use them.

2. How to Approach Research Problems

In this section, we suggest a general strategy you can use when you want the answer to an estate planning legal question and must start from scratch. The basic nature of this strategy is easy to articulate: You start from the general—for instance, a concern to minimize estate taxes, if possible—and proceed to the specific—the possible ways this might be done in your situation. Of course, in theory there can be questions that have no answer (federal estate taxes, for example, can usually be eliminated), simply because they've never been decided by a court or legislature. But in reality, for most questions which are likely to affect your estate plan, there will be an answer, and it won't be too hard to find.

Look for target resources. As with any broad approach to problem-solving, doing systematic legal research—starting with the general and moving in an ordered way to the specific—isn't always necessary. Obviously, if someone else has already done this and published material that focuses on how to solve your particular problem, you can save time if you locate it. You can start here by checking the catalogue of Nolo resources at the back of this book. Next, if you need to, you can check the subject in your local law library or in the legal section of a nearby bookstore.

Step 1: Focus Your Issue

Focus on the basic subject you want to research. This will help you locate the right initial research resource. Does your question concern wills, trusts, or federal estate taxes? Take a little time to articulate your question to yourself. The sharper the focus of your inquiry, the easier it will be to obtain the answer. It may help you to discuss your problem with a law librarian. They are experts at pigeonholing questions into the right categories for further research.

Step 2: Focus on Relevant Legal Language

The next step is to come up with some terms that will enable you to locate a basic resource book about your subject. Think of several key words or phrases that come up in your question or issue, using synonyms and related words where possible. If you have read this book carefully and use the Glossary, this shouldn't be difficult. For example, if you want to know more about leaving property in trust to a disadvantaged child, you could check "trusts," "irrevocable trusts," "children," "government benefits," and "disadvantaged" or "handicapped."

Step 3: Locate a Basic Resource

In a law library, use the card catalogue (or better yet, ask the law librarian) to locate a book that will provide basic information about your subject. This basic background reading will help you understand the law that applies to your issue, possibly provide some initial answers to your question, and give you reference to more specific sources.

As you look for books, keep in mind that any over a few years old are likely to contain information that is no longer current. The most useful materials are those that are updated regularly by new editions or "pocket part" inserts inside the back cover. Once you locate a basic resource, use its index to look up the terms you came up with in Step 2.

In the estate planning field, there are several categories of background books:

- **Overall estate planning.** There are many books covering estate planning in general. One of the best is Kess and Westlin, *The CCH Estate Planning Guide* (Commerce Clearing House). In reading these resources, please remember that they are written by estate planning attorneys, for attorneys, and often have predictable prejudices against a do-it-yourself approach. So, you may need to ignore an author's attitude as you get to the solid legal information.
- **How-to-do-it estate planning books for lawyers.** Many states have estate planning books prepared for practicing lawyers. These books contain specific clauses and forms for wills or trusts, and many other "hands on" materials. For example, in California, the Continuing Education of the Bar (CEB) publishes several useful estate planning books, including *Drafting California Irrevocable Inter Vivos Trusts; Drafting California Revocable Inter Vivos Trusts; California Will Drafting;* and *Estate Planning for the General Practitioner.* Comparable books in New York are published by the Practicing Law Institute (PLI) and include:
    - *Estate Planning,* Manning
    - *Use of Trusts in Estate Planning,* Moore
    - *Stocker on Drawing Wills,* Stocker
    - *Income Taxation of Estates and Trusts,* Michaelson & Blattmaehr.

  In other states, the best way to locate this type of book for your state is to ask the law librarian or look in the subject matter card catalog.
- **Comprehensive research books on one area of estate planning law.** There are legal treatises covering certain major aspects of estate planning. For example, for federal estate taxes there's *The CCH Federal Estate and Gift Tax Code* (and IRS Regulations); and for trusts, Cohan and Hemmerling, *Inter Vivos Trusts* (Shepard's Citations); and Peschel and Spurgeon, *Federal Taxation of Trusts; Grantors and Beneficiaries* (Warner, Gorham and Lamont). And there are also a number of popular self-help tax guides.
- **Legal encyclopedias.** These provide an overview of virtually every legal topic. They are so broad that they rarely provide help in resolving a particular estate planning problem. The encyclopedias are indexed by subject and can be used much the

same way as a regular encyclopedia. There are two national legal encyclopedias: *American Jurisprudence* (Am.Jur.), generally the more up-to-date and better written, and *Corpus Jurum Secundum* (CJS) which contains numerous references to court decisions on any legal point.

There are also encyclopedias published for specific states (mostly the larger states). Unless you are dealing with a clearly federal topic (like federal estate and gift taxes), it is a good idea to first use a state encyclopedia. The material there is likely to be more specific than is an article in a national encyclopedia. Ask your law librarian whether there is an encyclopedia for your state.

- **Law review articles.** These are collections of articles published by law schools and various law-based organizations. The articles tend to focus on trends in the law or on important new statutes or court decisions. Thus, if your research topic involves issues that are current—for example, major changes in federal estate tax law—or you want to know something about your state's new probate procedures, you stand a good chance of finding something relevant in a law review article. Don't expect practical advice from a law review article, though; they are written from an academic point of view and are usually fairly theoretical. *Legal Research: How to Find and Understand the Law,* mentioned above, gives thorough instructions on how to find and use law review articles.

Step 4: Read Statute(s) or Case(s) Referred to by Background Resource

Once you have read a basic background resource, you may have as much information as you need. However, if you want to be assured that the law is as it is represented to be in the book, you will need to check the source material. In other words, once you grasp the background of the law, you may need or want to read the law itself.

Fortunately, almost all basic background resources are heavily footnoted. This means the resource will refer you to statutes and court opinions. Your next step, therefore, will be to read these law sources. Be warned, however, that many statutes are difficult to understand without considerable effort. The major research sources here are:

- **Federal statutes.** These are found in the volumes of the United States Code. The best research source here is called the U.S. Code Annotated (U.S.C.A.) which, after setting forth statutes, contains references to court decisions (cases) and other pertinent materials.

  Note on Federal Tax Statutes: Located in the United States Code, Title 26, the tax statutes are so abstruse and dense it is often impossible to determine their meaning, at least not without hours and hours of grueling effort. If you try to read the tax code, use it in conjunction with some of the more user-friendly tax treatises or guides listed above.

- **State laws (statutes).** State statutes contain detailed rules that affect estate planning, including probate, special probate exemptions, and trusts. State laws are called "codes," "laws," or "statutes," depending on the state. Usually, you want to locate the "annotated" version, which most states have. Annotated codes usefully contain both the statutes and summaries of relevant court decisions and cross-references to articles and commentaries, which you may want to read, too. In short, they let you get your hands both on the relevant law and how it's been interpreted.

  Once you have located the volumes that contain your state's laws, find and read the specific statute that concerns you, if you already have the numbered reference (citation) enabling you to find it. If you don't have a citation, check the index for the statutes covering the general subject that concerns you. In some states, the statutes are further divided into subject areas, often called "codes." If this is done, there will typically be a civil code, penal code, vehicle code, and so on. You will normally find the laws you want for estate planning in the volume of statutes dealing with your state's basic civil or probate laws.

Statutes are numbered sequentially. If they are divided into codes, numbers normally start over for each. In any case, once you locate the correct number (and if necessary, code) in the index, it's easy to find the statute you need. If you have trouble, the law librarian will usually be happy to help. And don't forget to check the supplement inside the back of the book, which contains recent law changes (if any) and court decisions about the statute.

- **Court opinions.** Court interpretations of statutes, and court decisions on matters that aren't covered by statute, are as much a part of our law as the statutes themselves. Court decisions are collected in bound volumes, and indexed in books called "digests," which a law librarian can help you find.

  How do you know whether the courts have addressed the issue you are interested in? First, as mentioned, if you check out background resources, you will almost always find reference to significant court decisions in the area, complete with a case citation which tells you the volume and page number of the bound volume where the court case can be found.

- Annotated codes (statutes) are another source of relevant case citations. The one sentence summaries of court decisions that directly follow the statutes in these codes include citations to the cases. By skimming these summaries, you have an excellent chance of picking up on any case that may bear on your issue.
- The subject matter index to state and national case digests (discussed in *Legal Research: How to Find and Understand the Law)* is another source of case citations.

Reading cases can be tricky. Basically, all cases set forth the facts that the court relied on to make its decision, the issue the court was asked to decide, the court's decision, and the reason for the decision. For a case to be applicable to your issue, its facts and the legal issue decided must be roughly the same as your situation.

Step 5: Make Sure Your Answers Are Up-to-Date

Law is always changing—a cliché, but true nevertheless. But for you the question is more focused; when you find a case or statute that seems pertinent, your next question should be, "Is this still good law?" There are several techniques for bringing the fruits of your research up-to-date. For statutes, the main technique is to check the pocket part, as explained in Step 4. If you want to be fanatical, you can also check to see whether your legislature has passed any new statutes on your subject since the pocket part was published.

The main technique for updating cases is a tool called *Shepard's Citations*. *Shepard's* tells you all the instances the case you are interested in has been referred to in other cases. This will tell your whether your case has been overruled by subsequent cases. *Legal Research: How to Find and Understand the Law* covers how to use *Shepard's*.■

31

After Your Estate Plan Is Completed

If you are serious about planning your estate, you'll eventually get the job done. What next? A celebration isn't out of place. Why not gather those you love, break out your favorite beverage and toast—"To Life!"

But although your big job is complete, you've still got more to do—storing your documents safely, deciding how much of your plan to communicate to your family and others, and making any necessary future revisions to your plan. So this chapter discusses what you may need to do once your planning documents have been completed.

A. Storing Your Estate Planning Documents

Completion of an estate plan means that you have created some important documents: a will, probably a living trust, quite possibly an ongoing trust, or even several, as well as other forms, such as a durable power of attorney for health care, and one for finances, and perhaps a joint tenancy deed, business ownership documents or written instructions for your funeral or donations of body parts. Obviously, you want to keep all these documents in a safe place, where you can readily find them. There is no big secret to accomplishing this. Any secure place can be used for storage: a safe in your house or office, or even a locked drawer in your home file cabinet. Some people have used a bank safe deposit box. If you do this, you must make sure that your executor or successor trustee has ready legal access to that box. Check with your bank to see what it requires to allow your executor/trustee to get documents from the safe deposit box. Also check with them to make sure the safety deposit isn't sealed, under state law, when one owner dies. (Some states that have death taxes require this. See Chapter 15, Estate Taxes, Section C.)

While you may want to keep at least some of your estate planning documents private while you live, you also surely want them to be promptly accessible to whoever will handle your affairs at your death. This is especially true for documents that deal with your wishes as to organ transplants and funeral or burial instructions, which must be immediately available. So once you have settled on a sensible storage place, let the person who will wind up your affairs know what you've decided, and how to obtain the documents.

What about making copies of your estate planning documents? You may have to produce copies of your living trust to financial institutions, such as a brokerage company, where you have an account you want placed in trust. Whether or not to make copies for personal reasons is up to you. Often people do want copies—to give to their executor or successor trustee, family members or friends. If you do need or want copies, you can have a lawyer (if you have one) make them for you, and pay accordingly, or make the copies yourself. In either case, follow the same approach:

- Photocopy the documents you want people to see or have. These copies are not legal originals, since they are not signed.
- Never sign a copy. If you do, it could legally qualify as a "duplicate original." If you later decide to change, amend or revoke the document, you have to change each duplicate original as well.

- To be extra safe, mark "copy" in ink on each page. This isn't legally required, but it insures that no one can claim a copy is an original.

B. Revisions

Estate plans shouldn't be changed frequently. If impromptu changes ("I'll show her, I'll cut her out of my estate!") occur often, you have an underlying family or personal problem to examine. Major life events, however, obviously can call for estate planning changes. For example, if any of the following events occur, you should review your plan:

- You sell or otherwise dispose of any property you've specifically mentioned in your will or living trust.
- Marriage. This one is particularly important, as your new spouse will have a right to inherit a share of your estate determined by law if you don't update your will.
- Divorce. In some states, the fact of a divorce ends a former spouse's right to inherit under a will. In other states, it doesn't. Often even more important, other property left to a divorced spouse using other estate planning devices may not be affected by a divorce.
- Birth of a child. The rule here is similar to that for marriage.
- Death of a beneficiary.
- Your financial situation changes significantly.
- You move to a new state. This is particularly necessary if you are married and move from a common law property state to a community property state or vice versa. (See Chapter 3, State Property Ownership Laws, Section D, for a detailed discussion of the issues that should concern you.)
- You acquire or sell substantial property.
- You want to change the successor trustee of your living trust, or the executor (personal representative) of your will.
- You want to change the personal guardian you have named for your minor children or, if you have established a children's trust, the person or institution you have named as trustee.

If you do decide to change your estate plan, you must decide whether you need, or want, to create entirely new documents or simply modify your existing ones. This can depend both on how complex your changes are and the estate planning document involved.

1. Property You No Longer Own at Your Death

Estate planning transfer devices, such as wills or living trusts, don't become binding until your death. Before then, you can sell, transfer or give away any property you own. So what happens when you dispose of property but don't change your will or trust? For example, what happens if your will leaves your son your 1988 Chevy, but by the time you die, you've already sold it and purchased a 1995 Buick?

To summarize what can be a complicated area of law: if you've given someone a specific piece of property (say the Chevy) but you no longer own it when you die, that beneficiary is out of luck. The fact that you own a Buick doesn't help the beneficiary. Lawyers call this "ademption"; people who don't inherit the property in question are often heard to use an earthier term. Obviously, the way to avoid creating this type of problem is to keep your estate plan up to date. If you've sold or transferred any item that is also specifically given away in your will or living trust, revise those documents.

2. Living Trusts

Living trusts can be revised by the following methods:

- Most living trusts have a clause permitting additions of property to the trust after it has been created (called an "after-acquired property" clause). If your trust has such a clause, you can add property by listing it on the trust schedule and taking title to that property in the trustee's name.

  This method does not automatically require you to name a new beneficiary for this new trust property. If you don't, it will go to the residuary beneficiary of your living trust unless you've provided that "all property" on the trust schedule goes to some other beneficiary. If you only add property to a trust schedule, you do not have to have the trust notarized again.
- Amend the trust. As discussed in Chapter 9, Revocable Living Trusts, you can make a formal amendment to your trust, to add or delete beneficiaries, change gifts, or name new successor trustees. The amendment must be properly signed by the grantor, or grantors, and notarized.
- Revoke the old trust and prepare a new one, reflecting your current intentions. This is the least desirable method. You'll have to get the new trust document notarized. Worse, you'll have to re-register property in the trustee's name, as trustee of the new trust. That's a lot of work, and hardly, if ever, necessary.

3. Wills

There are only two ways to change a formal witnessed will:

- Prepare a formal witnessed codicil to the will.
- Destroy the old will and make a new one.

Let's briefly examine each procedure.

a. Make a Codicil

A codicil is a formal legal method for making changes to a will after the will has been drafted, signed and witnessed. A codicil is a sort of legal "P.S." to the will. It must be typed or printed, with a formal heading like "Codicil to Will of Beth Thoreau." The text of the codicil then identifies the date of the original will and defines the change made.

I give $3,000 to my friend Al Smith

I give my silver tea set to Bertha Weinstock, and revoke my gift of that tea set to Mary Warbler, now deceased.

The codicil then must be prepared, signed and witnessed with all the formalities of a will. Because of this requirement, it can make more sense to prepare a new will entirely, if you are using a computer will program, such as Nolo's *WillMaker*. It won't take you any longer to prepare a new will than a codicil, and the signing and witnessing requirements for both are the same. A codicil must be signed and dated by the will maker in the presence of at least two—or even better, three—witnesses, who are told that it's a codicil to the maker's will and then sign their names. The witnesses don't have to be the same as those for the original will, though it's a good idea to use the original witnesses if they're available. Sample codicil forms can be found in Nolo's *WillMaker* computer program or in *Nolo's Simple Will Book*.

b. Make a New Will

If a major revision of the will is desired, it's better to draft a new will and revoke the old one than to use a codicil. A will that has been substantially re-written by a codicil is an awkward document and can be confusing. It may not always be clear what the relationship of the codicil to the original will provisions means. One advantage of using a computer will program (such as Nolo's *WillMaker*) is that it's quite easy to make changes and print out a whole new will.

If you make a new will, your old will should be revoked (canceled). This can be done as long as you are alive and mentally competent. You can do this by either:

- destroying the will itself (and all copies, if you can get your hands on them)—rip 'em up and throw 'em out; *and*
- stating in the new document you prepare that you revoke all previous or earlier wills you have made.

We strongly recommend that you do both.

4. Joint Tenancy

If you've established a joint tenancy, are you stuck with it? No—one joint tenant can normally transform the joint tenancy into a tenancy in common, which eliminates the right of the other co-owners to automatically inherit. (See Chapter 10, Joint Tenancy and Tenancy by the Entirety, Section F.) However, it takes agreement of all the joint tenants to allow any one to become the sole owner of the property. If all joint tenants agree to end a joint tenancy, they can sign a document (a deed, for real estate) transferring the property into whatever new form of ownership is desired.

If you want to transfer your share of joint tenancy property into tenancy in common, and the other owner(s) don't consent, you'll need to see a lawyer to learn the procedures required in your state, unless you live in California. In the Golden State, *The Deeds Book* by Randolph (Nolo Press) shows you how to do this.

5. Informal Bank Account Trusts

You can amend or revoke an informal bank account trust (pay-on-death account) at any time. You can change a beneficiary simply by deleting the old one and entering a new one on the bank registration form; sometimes the bank will require that a new, separate form be completed. You can also end the trust simply by closing it or by spending all the money the account contains. If the account is empty when you die, obviously the beneficiary gets nothing.

6. Insurance

If you are the owner of an insurance policy, you can cancel the policy or change the beneficiary of that policy. If you are not the legal owner of the policy, you have no right to cancel the policy or change the beneficiary, even if the policy insures your own life.

7. Ongoing Trusts

Most ongoing trusts do not become irrevocable until the grantor's death. Some, however, such as charitable trusts, become irrevocable upon creation. Once an ongoing trust has become irrevocable, it, by definition, can't be changed or revoked. Until an ongoing trust is irrevocable, it can be freely changed or revoked by the grantor. ■

32

After a Death Occurs

When someone who has created an estate plan dies, another someone (or several someones) must take actions to carry out the deceased person's plan. This is not a book that covers after-death work in depth. That is a subject for another big book. But here in this chapter we can offer you general summaries of basic estate transfer tasks that someone may need to do after a person dies. We also refer you to other Nolo resources that describe, in more detail, how to carry out tasks connected with a specific legal document, such a will or living trust.

A. Wills

When the will writer dies, the person named as executor is responsible for carrying out the terms of the will. This includes handling probate—normally by hiring a probate lawyer—and then, once probate is completed, distributing property governed by the will to the beneficiaries named in that document.

If a child's trust is created in the will, the executor is also often named as trustee of that trust, and so can have ongoing duties of managing the trust property. If property is left to a minor under the Uniform Gifts to Minors Act, the executor must turn that property over to the custodian for that gift.

Further, some executors have additional responsibilities. If a federal or state estate tax return must be filed, it's the executor's legal responsibility to see this is done. For federal taxes, the filing threshold is normally $600,000. (See Section D, below.) Also, in wealthier estates, where a QTIP trust is part of a deceased spouse's estate plan, the executor must decide whether to "elect" to have estate tax on the trust property postponed until the surviving spouse dies. (See Chapter 19, Other Estate Tax-Saving Marital Trusts, Section A.)

B. Probate Avoidance Living Trusts

With a living trust designed solely to avoid probate, the successor trustee is responsible, after a grantor dies, for carrying out the terms of the trust. This basically means transferring the trust property to the beneficiaries named in the trust. Nolo's living trust resources—*Make Your Own Living Trust* and *Living Trust Maker* (computer program) contain detailed instructions of how each major item of property can be formally transferred from the trust into legal ownership by the designated beneficiary. Below we briefly discuss the major issues.

1. Who Serves as Trustee

With a basic shared trust, the surviving spouse serves as trustee after one spouse's death. With an individual trust, or when the surviving spouse dies, the successor trustee is in charge.

2. More Than One Successor Trustee

If more than one person is named in the trust document as successor trustee, they all serve as co-trustees. This does not, however, mean all trustees must agree on all decisions. Whether each trustee must formally agree on any action taken with regard to the living trust property, or whether one trustee can act independently, depends on the terms of the trust document.

If more than one successor trustee is named, but cannot serve, the other(s) remain as trustee(s). The person named as alternate successor trustee does not take over unless all the people named as successor trustees cannot serve.

3. If a Trustee Resigns

A trustee can resign at any time by preparing and signing a written resignation statement. The ex-trustee should deliver the notice to the person who is next in line to serve as trustee. With a well-drafted living trust, any trustee, including the last acting trustee, can appoint someone else to take over if no one named in the trust document can serve.

Normally, it would be the last, or alternate, successor trustee who named someone else to act as trustee if the need arises. The appointment must be in writing, signed and notarized.

4. Management and Distribution of Trust Property of a Single Person's Living Trust

Normally, the job of the successor trustee of a single person's living trust is simply to transfer, outright, to the designated beneficiaries, the property the now-deceased grantor left them in the living trust. Only if the successor trustee is also trustee of a child's trust created in the living trust are ongoing duties required of him.

It is not the trustee's responsibility to sell or manage living trust property.

Example: Jamie is Elliot's successor trustee. Elliot's living trust leaves his house to his children, Clarence and Grace. Elliot dies. Jamie, as trustee, deeds the house from the trust to Clarence and Grace, who can do with it what they wish—live in it, rent it or sell it. Jamie cannot sell the house and divide the proceeds between the beneficiaries—that's not his decision to make.

Normally, after the grantor dies, her living trust continues to exist only as long as it takes the successor trustee to distribute trust property to the beneficiaries. In many cases, a living trust can be wound up within a few weeks after a grantor's death. But if an ongoing business is involved, this may be more trouble.

No formal termination document is required to end a living trust. Once the trust property has been distributed, the trust ends.

5. Management and Distribution of Trust Property With a Shared Living Trust

Coping with what happens next when one grantor dies is more complex for a successor trustee under the terms of a shared living trust. Eventually, the successor trustee (usually a surviving spouse or living together partner) must divide the living trust property into two portions. Each portion goes into a new trust entity, as provided for by the original trust document.

- One living trust entity contains the deceased spouse's share of trust property not left to the surviving spouse. The terms of this trust cannot be changed, and it cannot be revoked. Property is promptly distributed to its beneficiaries by the successor trustee unless the grantor provided for its ongoing management, as would be the case for property left to a minor.
- A separate living trust entity, which, as a practical matter, can be—and usually is—a continuation of the original trust, contains the surviving spouse's trust property (usually including any of the deceased spouse's share of the trust property that is left to the surviving spouse). The surviving spouse remains free to amend the terms of this trust, or even revoke it.

Though this may sound complicated, it often isn't. If, as is common, much of the trust property is left to the surviving spouse, that spouse may have little to do beyond distributing a few items to the deceased's other beneficiaries. Usually, the original trust was drafted so that the trust property he or she inherits is already in the original living trust, and remains there.

When all the property in the deceased spouse's trust has been distributed to the beneficiaries, that trust ceases to exist. No formal termination document is required.

The other living trust contains only the surviving spouse's property and remains revocable. The surviving spouse is free to change it as he or she wishes.

Example: Edith and Jacques create a basic shared living trust. They transfer their house, which they own together, into the trust, and name each other as beneficiaries. Edith names her son as alternate beneficiary.

When Jacques dies, Edith inherits his half-interest in the house. Because of the way the trust document is worded, she doesn't have to change the trust document to name a beneficiary for the half-interest in the house that she inherited from her husband. Both halves will go to her son at her death. She may, however, want to amend the trust to make her son the primary beneficiary and name someone else to be alternate beneficiary.

When the second spouse dies, the successor trustee named in the trust document takes over as trustee. The process of winding up this living trust is the same as that for an individual trust.

6. Property Left to Children

Living trust property given for a child's benefit is normally left in a child's trust, or through the Uniform Transfers to Minor's Act. In either case, the successor trustee must turn the child's property over to the adult manager of the child's property—the trustee of a child's trust or the custodian of an UTMA gift. If the successor trustee serves in one of these capacities as well, she must manage the property until it is turned over to the child.

C. Ongoing Trusts

As we've discussed, an ongoing trust is one that is irrevocable, usually becoming so on the grantor's death, and generally continuing to exist for an extended period of time. An ongoing trust is usually combined with a probate-avoidance living trust. First, probate is avoided. Then the ongoing trust becomes operational and may well last for years, or decades. As we discussed in the chapters covering ongoing trusts, the trustee's job will be much more complex here than with a simple probate-avoidance trust.

As an example, let's consider a living trust with marital life estate and see what happens when one spouse dies. As we hope you remember from Chapter 18, Estate Tax-Saving Bypass Trusts, Section C, the purpose of this type trust is to save on overall estate taxes. With a living trust with marital life estate, both spouses are the original trustees. When a spouse dies, the surviving spouse becomes sole trustee, and the living trust splits into two trusts: the irrevocable marital life estate trust (of the deceased spouse) and the revocable surviving spouse's trust.

The surviving spouse, as trustee, must first distribute any trust property the deceased spouse left to specifically named beneficiaries. Each spouse can make gifts of trust property to beneficiaries other than the other spouse. Then the trustee must establish and maintain the marital life estate trust.

A major task in establishing a marital life estate trust is to figure out how best to divide the couple's property between the ongoing marital life estate trust and the surviving spouse's trust. Property must be clearly labeled as being owned either by the marital life estate trust or by the surviving spouse's living trust. Any allocation of equally-owned shared trust property is valid, as long as each trust gets 50% of the overall total worth. But each specific item of property does not have to be split, with half going to each trust. For example, a house, worth (net) $300,000 can be placed in the marital life estate trust, as long as other property with a total worth of $300,000 is placed in the surviving spouse's trust.

Dividing the marital life estate trust property wisely usually requires the services of a lawyer or tax accountant. This subject is discussed in depth in *Make Your Own Living Trust.*

Establishing the ongoing, irrevocable marital life estate trust may require some re-registering of title of some of the deceased spouse's living trust property. For example, if the surviving spouse decides that it is wisest to put all of a shared ownership house in the living trust into a marital life estate trust, a new deed should be prepared to reflect this, listing the trustee of the ongoing trust as the new owner.

Example: Moira and Joseph O'Sullivan have created the Moira and Joseph O'Sullivan Living Trust. In each, each one creates a marital life estate trust. Joseph dies. Moira, with the help of an accountant, divides the living trust property between her now separate living trust and the newly-operational marital life estate trust. Property with documents of title transferred into the marital life estate trust must be reregistered into the name of the trustee of this new trust. Thus the property would be registered as held by "Moira O'Sullivan, as trustee of the Joseph O'Sullivan Marital Life Estate Trust."

The marital life estate trust also needs a federal taxpayer ID number. The surviving spouse must keep appropriate trust financial records and file a federal trust tax return every year. The IRS will want it clear which trust owns what. Annual state trust tax returns may also be required, in states with income taxes.

The spouse manages the property in the marital life estate trust and receives any income it generates. Management can include making sensible investment decisions, which may necessitate the hiring of a professional investment advisor.

The surviving spouse's trust goes on as before. It remains revocable and can be changed at any time. No tax return needs to be filed for this trust.

After the death of the surviving spouse, the successor trustee winds up both trusts by distributing all property (except for any specific gifts made by the surviving spouse) of both trusts to each trust's final beneficiaries. The successor trustee must file a final tax return for the marital life estate trust. The successor trustee also manages any property left in a child's subtrust and files a closing tax return for the second spouse.

D. Preparing and Filing Tax Returns

If a state death tax or federal estate tax return must be filed for the grantor of a living trust, getting this done is the responsibility of the executor (personal representative) named in the deceased person's will, and any successor trustee of the deceased's living trust. Usually, these positions are held by the same person. Also, a final federal income tax return (and state tax return, if one is required) must be filed for a marital life estate trust after both spouses die.

A federal estate tax return must be filed if the decedent's gross estate was worth more than $600,000. It is due nine months after the decedent's death. Tax matters can get quite tricky. The trustee may need professional help, and is entitled to pay for it out of the trust assets. For instance, for federal estate tax purposes, property can be valued as of the date of death or as of six months after death. This is just one of many complexities that can be involved in completing a federal estate tax return.

In addition to estate tax returns, a final income federal tax return (and state return, if there's a state income tax) must be filed for the deceased. Legally, this is the responsibility of the executor of the deceased's will, who is normally the same person as the survivor trustee.

The successor trustee can get a helpful 20-page set of instructions, "Instructions for Form 706," from the Internal Revenue Service. Another useful IRS publication is called "Federal Estate and Gift Taxes" (Publication 448).

E. Trustee's Reports to Beneficiaries

Generally, a trustee is legally not required to make any report of trust income, transactions or any other aspect of trust management to any beneficiary. There are two exceptions:

- The trustee of any operational trust may be required by the terms of the trust to give reports, such as copies of the trust's annual federal trust tax return, to all the trust beneficiaries.
- A few state's laws require the trustee to distribute an annual report to the beneficiaries. For example, Washington law requires distributing "a written itemization of all current receipts and disbursements made by the trustee." (Revised Code of Washington, Section 11.106.020.) In most family situations, these laws have little or no impact, since beneficiaries trust the trustee, and don't insist on these legal rights.

F. Collecting the Proceeds of a Life Insurance Policy

How to collect insurance proceeds after the insured person dies is not strictly speaking part of estate planning, but nevertheless people want to be sure their beneficiaries know how to collect these proceeds. Normally, this isn't a problem—they can be collected soon after the insured person's death by submitting an insurance company claim form and a certified copy of the insured person's death certificate to the company. The beneficiary may also have to file a copy of the policy, and proof of identify as the named beneficiary, if the insurance company requires it.

Although this is normally routine, there can be several flies in the ointment. In some states with state death taxes, insurance proceeds above a certain amount cannot be released until the tax officials approve. Since the insured person owned the insurance policy, the insurance proceeds will be part of her taxable estate, and the state tax officials must first be satisfied that the estate has other sufficient assets to pay state death taxes before they authorize release of the proceeds to the beneficiaries. Also, in other instances, some companies have been known to delay payments for months, so that they can collect interest on the money for a longer time. If this happens to you, a letter to the insurance commissioner of both your state and of the one where the company is headquartered (with copies to the offending company) will normally pry the money loose pronto.

G. Obtaining Title to Joint Tenancy Property After One Owner Dies

The major benefit of joint tenancy is the "automatic right of survivorship." But obviously, the words on a deed to real property or certificate of title to a car don't magically change the day one joint tenant takes that last breath. Until someone acts, the legal title will not be changed to the survivor(s) name. What "automatic right of survivorship" really means in this context is that compared to most legal tasks it's possible to transfer title to the surviving owner fairly easily, quickly and cheaply, without probate. This is true for all joint tenancies, whether of real estate or personal property.

To get the deceased owner's name off the ownership document, so that the surviving joint tenants can fully function as legal owners, they must:

- establish with the appropriate government official or recorder of title that the joint tenant has died by filing a copy of the death certificate; and
- file a document establishing that the surviving owners are sole owners to the property.

A lawyer can be hired to do this, but is normally unnecessary, as the procedures are routine. If a lawyer is hired, however, be sure the fee charged is a reasonable hourly one. An unfortunate practice in many states is for a lawyer to propose charging one-third of what the probate fee would be to transfer joint property to the survivors. Usually, this is far too high a fee; the work is neither complicated nor time-consuming.

For example, to terminate a joint tenancy in real estate, you need to file a certified copy of the deceased's death certificate and a form called "Affidavit of Death of Joint Tenant," or something similar, with the county office of property records where the property is located (called the "County Recorder" in many states). The affidavit is a standard legal form, available in many office supply stores. On this form, the surviving joint tenant states that a joint tenant has died. In some states, such as California,[1] a new deed doesn't need to be completed. After the affidavit and death certificate have been recorded, title to the property can be transferred or sold by the survivor by signing a deed "as surviving joint tenant."

Tax liens. In some states that have state death taxes, tax liens (legal claims) may be imposed on all of a deceased person's property, and title cannot be transferred until the lien is removed. Removing the lien may involve posting a bond, filing a final inheritance tax return, or otherwise satisfying the tax authorities that taxes will be paid. In those states, a major hassle for the surviving joint tenant can be obtaining a release of the tax lien. You'll need to locate the governmental agency that imposes and releases these tax liens, and see what is required to release them.

Federal estate taxes. Joint tenancy property can also be liable for a proportionate share of a deceased's federal estate taxes, if the estate is large enough to be subject to them. Federal taxes are assessed if the net estate is over $600,000. The taxes due will depend on the size of the overall taxable estate, which probably won't be determined for some time. But if the surviving owner must wait until the full amount of estate taxes are known (or even worse, paid) before obtaining clear title to the joint tenancy property, the practical advantages of the right of survivorship are severely diminished. After all, one purpose of a right of survivorship is to obtain clear title fast. Fortunately, the IRS will usually allow clear transfer of joint tenancy property if there's an estimate of the value of the property in the estate and clear indication that there are enough other assets to pay off all estate taxes. The proof required that all taxes due can be paid from the remaining taxable estate will vary depending on the size, complexity and liquidity of the estate. ■

[1]Detailed how-to information as to all the steps required to transfer any kind of joint tenancy property in California is contained in *How to Probate an Estate,* by Julia Nissley (Nolo Press).

33

Some Estate Plans

This chapter presents eight different estate plans. Each discusses the needs of a person or couple and the estate plan they decide upon. As we stated at the beginning of this book, we don't believe that relying on pre-set formula plans is a sensible way for anyone to form a personal plan. Rather, the purpose of providing these plans is to illustrate how the estate planning methods discussed in this book can be assembled into a coherent plan.

A. A Couple in Their 50s

Abel and Rachel Rublestam are in their 50s. They live in a non-community property state. They have two children, Isaiah and Rebecca. Isaiah is married and has two young children, one of whom is severely physically disabled. Rebecca is attending college.

Their property. The Rublestams share ownership of all their property. Their estate consists of a co-op apartment worth $350,000 ($100,000 equity), stocks and savings worth $80,000, life insurance on each spouse which pays $200,000 on death, and their one-third ownership of the R-S corporation, a family business. It's hard to determine the exact value for their business interest. As a rough guess, they decide it's worth $500,000.

Their estate planning goals. The Rublestams want to plan now to avoid probate. They also realize that their net combined estate is worth more than $600,000, and that the estate of the second spouse to die would face a federal estate tax. Nevertheless, each wants to leave all their property outright to the other. At their ages, neither wants the restrictions a marital life estate trust imposes. After all, if one unexpectedly dies soon, the survivor, who will have a life expectancy of 25 to 30 years, may well need all the property they have both accumulated, not just the income. They decide to postpone estate tax planning until later in their lives, accept the risk that if one dies prematurely, it may increase the eventual estate taxes on the property they leave to their children.

Their plan. To avoid probate, the Rublestams prepare a marital living trust. They use their trust to leave each other their apartment, stocks and corporation shares. Each names both children as alternate beneficiaries, in case both spouses die together. They carefully transfer title to these assets to the trust's name, having already checked that the bylaws of their co-op apartment association and the R-S corporation permit this.

Each spouse names the other spouse as beneficiary of their life insurance policy.

The Rublestams each prepare a basic will. Each also prepares a durable power of attorney for heath care authorizing the other spouse to make health care decisions if one becomes incapacitated. Each durable power of attorney specifically authorizes a spouse to terminate life support equipment if the other has a terminal illness. Each also prepares a durable power of attorney for finances, naming the other as his or her attorney-in-fact.

When they're older, the Rublestams intend to investigate how to reduce estate taxes, and how they can create a trust to benefit their disadvantaged grandchild. They also plan to eventually make tax-free gifts of $10,000 per year each to their children, but decide that they are not ready to do this yet.

B. A Prosperous Couple in Their 70s

Robert and Teresa Casswell are a prosperous married couple in their early-70s. Both are retired and live comfortably on their savings, assets and retirement payments. They live in a non-community property state and share ownership of all their property equally. The Casswells have four children.

Their property. A house worth $450,000 (all equity; they paid off the mortgage years ago), a summer home worth $125,000 ($75,000 equity), stocks and mutual funds worth $65,000, cash savings of $160,000, art works valued at $125,000, jewelry valued at $50,000 and miscellaneous personal property worth a total of $45,000. Their current total net worth is $1,505,000, all of which is in both their names. Of course, they hope the value of their estate will increase by the time a spouse dies.

Their estate planning goals. Robert and Teresa each want to leave most of their property to the surviving spouse and then to their four children in equal shares. They also want to make small gifts to friends, relatives and charities. Because their combined estate is relatively large, they also want to plan to avoid probate and reduce estate taxes to the extent feasible.

Their plan. Robert and Teresa decide to establish a shared living trust to avoid probate. As part of that trust, each spouse creates a marital life estate trust of $600,000, to reduce eventual estate taxes, and a QTIP trust for all property the first spouse to die owns above $600,000. Each spouse names their four children as the final beneficiaries of his or her marital life estate trust and QTIP trust.

When the first spouse dies, all the property in his or her estate will be exempt from estate taxes. Estate taxes will be assessed on all property above $600,000 in the surviving spouse's estate when he or she dies. As of now, the total amount in the surviving spouse's estate will be $905,000. Each spouse has an estate of $752,500. So the first to die will leave $600,000 in the marital life estate trust, and $152,500 in the QTIP, making the surviving spouse's total estate $905,000.

In their living trust, each spouse also specifies several personal gifts to friends and charities. The successor trustee for the trust, after both spouses die, will be the Casswells' eldest daughter, a stable, savvy woman who lives near them and is respected by the other children. They have discussed this with her and mentioned it to the other children; happily, none of the others objected.

The Casswells work out the basic ideas of how they want their living trust, marital life estate trust and QTIP trust to work. Then they see a lawyer to draft and prepare the actual trust.

The Casswells also prepare basic back-up wills and durable powers of attorney for health care and for finances.

Because their estates are substantial, the Casswells might consider making gifts to their children. Each can give $10,000 per year to each child gift tax-free, for a combined total of $80,000 annually. They could decide to wait until one spouse dies. If the surviving spouse thus feels secure enough to give away money, he or she can give $40,000 per year to the children.

C. A Wealthy Couple in Their 70s

Rabia and Alfonso have been married for over 35 years. Rabia is 70, Alfonso is 79. They have two grown children in their early 40s. Rabia has one child, in his late 40s, from a former marriage.

Their property. Rabia and Alfonso's shared estate has a total net worth of $8,300,000. In addition, Rabia has separate property—a rental house worth $180,000, owned free and clear—she inherited from her mother.

Their estate planning goals. Because Rabia and Alfonso have a wealthy estate, they want to save on estate taxes, leave much of their property for the eventual use of their two children, and also make a gift to charity. Also, Rabia wants to leave a gift to her son from her prior marriage.

Their plan. Each spouse's share of their common property is $4,150,000. Rabia, of course, has an additional $180,000 of her separate property.

First, they create a shared living trust to avoid probate of their property.

Next, each spouse decides to leave $600,000 in a marital life estate trust, with their two children as the final beneficiaries. This way, each spouse makes use of his or her own $600,000 estate tax exemption.

Then, each spouse decides that they have enough money to create a generation-skipping trust of $1,000,000 (less any portion of estate taxes due paid from this sum). For Alfonso, this trust is relatively simple. His two children will be the middle generation, and their children (his grandchildren) the final generation. But Rabia wonders if she should also include her son from her first marriage, and his children, as beneficiaries of her generation-skipping trust.

After some reflection and soul-searching, she decides not to. Her son doesn't get along very well with one of her other children, so having both be beneficiaries of the same trust could come problematic. Also, the logistics of have a generation-skipping trust for these different children seems unwieldy. Rabia decides, instead, that she will leave her son a substantial mount of money outright, when she dies. So, as a part of her living trust, Rabia makes an outright gift of her separate property home (worth $180,000) and $320,000 from her shared property to her son, a total gift of $600,000. She directs that no estate taxes be paid from this gift.

Finally, each spouse creates a QTIP trust for the balance of their estate left over after their other trusts have been funded, or gifts made . As you know, using a QTIP trust postpones estate taxes on the property until the second spouse dies. Alfonso names his two children to divide equally all money in his QTIP trust. Rabia distributes the property held by her QTIP trust to her final beneficiaries differently: 40% to each of her children with Alfonso, and 20% to her son from the earlier marriage.

Alfonso and Rabia complete their estate plan by each preparing:

1. a simple will
2. a durable power of attorney for health care, and
3. a durable power of attorney for finances.

D. A Widow in Her 80s

Ida Grant, a widow, lives in California. She wants to leave the bulk of her estate to her one child, Carla. She also has a four-year-old Irish terrier, which she loves and wants to provide care for after she dies. Finally, she wants to make a number of small gifts to friends and charities.

Her property. Mrs. Grant's estate consists of a house that she and her husband bought in 1937 for $5,000. It now has a market value of $460,000. Mrs. Grant has household furnishings worth $20,000, a car worth $5,000, and savings of $200,000. She lives primarily on interest from her savings and Social Security.

Her estate planning goals. Mrs. Grant values simplicity. She wants to transfer her gifts by the simplest means possible, but she also wants to avoid probate.

Her plan. Mrs. Grant considers transferring her house into joint tenancy with her daughter Carla, whom she trusts absolutely, because this seems to provide the simplest probate-avoidance transfer method. However, Mrs. Grant learns there will be serious disadvantages if she uses joint tenancy. The IRS will require that a gift tax return be filed because Mrs. Grant is giving a half-interest in the house to her daughter. No tax will actually be paid because the house is worth less than $600,000, but still, it's a hassle to prepare and file the tax return.

Mrs. Grant decides to use a living trust for her house. This allows the house to avoid probate. When she prepares her living trust, Mrs. Grant names Carla as the trust's beneficiary and successor trustee. She then signs and records a deed transferring the house from herself to the trustee of the trust. When listing the house as part of the trust property on the trust schedule, Mrs. Grant includes "all household furnishings" as part of the trust property, so her daughter will receive this property outside of probate as well.

Mrs. Grant considered establishing an ongoing trust to provide care for her dog. However, when she checked this possibility out,[1] she learned that trusts for animals are not legal. A better approach, she learned, is to handle the problem informally. Mrs. Grant discussed her concern with Carla, who was not a dog lover. Carla suggested that the dog, and a sum of money necessary to care for it, be left to Betty Planquee, a good friend who had indicated she would accept the responsibility.

Mrs. Grant learns that, under California law she can transfer property worth less than $60,000 by her will free of probate. She has her savings in two money market accounts. She divides the money in those accounts so that one contains less than $60,000. She changes title to the other, larger account into an informal bank trust account, naming her daughter as beneficiary, and so avoids probate of that account. Then, using the simple back-up will, she makes several cash gifts to close friends:

> *I give the sum of $20,000 to my good friend and long-time veterinarian, Arthur Pedronnzi.*
>
> *I give the sum of $5,000 to my good friend and faithful gardener, William Service.*
>
> *I give the sum of $5,000 and my dog Cherry Blossom to my friend Betty Planquee.*
>
> *I give the sum of $2,500 to my friend Mary Bale.*
>
> *"I give the sum of $2,500 to my friend Roberta Anthony.*

She includes in her will a residuary clause stating: "I give all my remaining property subject to this will to my daughter, Carla." Under this clause, any of her property not specifically transferred under the terms of her living trust or will would go to Carla. This includes any property she might get after the will was prepared.

Notice that Mrs. Grant didn't name any alternate beneficiaries. She wanted to keep her will simple, and decided that if any of her friends died before her, she wanted that money to go to her daughter under the terms of the residuary clause. And she doesn't even want to consider the possibility that her daughter could die before her.

Mrs. Grant also prepares two durable powers of attorney, one for health care and one for finances, naming her daughter Carla in both as her attorney-in-fact, to act for her if she becomes incapacitated and can't make medical or financial decisions herself.

E. A Couple in Their 30s

Mark Ryan and Alicia Lopez are married, in their 30s, with two young children. Mark is employed as a carpenter; Alicia works part-time as a proofreader for a publisher. They live in Texas, a community property state.

Their property. They own their house (heavily mortgaged) in joint tenancy. It's the only major asset of their estate. They also own two cars, an old Ford and an older VW station wagon, the well-used furnishings of their home, personal possessions such as clothing, books and electronic equipment, and two savings accounts—one shared with $2,000, and

[1] *Dog Law*, by Randolph (Nolo Press) has a detailed discussion of how best to provide for a dog that may survive its owner.

another with $6,000 in Mark's name, an account he had before they were married.

Their estate planning goals. Mark and Alicia's main concern is providing for their children's care, both financial and personal, if both parents die. They don't need to worry about federal estate taxes, because their estate is well below the $600,000 minimum subject to federal tax. And because their house is owned in joint tenancy, their major asset will avoid probate, unless they die simultaneously.

Their plan. Mark and Alicia decide they don't want to create probate-avoiding living trusts now, as they don't have a lot of property and, statistically, are unlikely to die for many years. They prepare a will leaving all their non-joint tenancy property, except Mark's savings account, to each other. In their wills, they name their children as alternate beneficiaries, to receive all property covered by the wills and the house, in case both parents die simultaneously.

Mark and Alicia learn, to their mutual surprise, that they disagree on what should be done with Mark's $6,000 savings account. Alicia believes it should be handled like all their other property; indeed, she points out that Mark can officially convert the account to community property by simply depositing it in their joint account. Mark states that he wants to keep exclusive control over the account, as his own separate property. Further, he wants to use his will to give it to his brother, Herb, a struggling artist whom he is very close to. Alicia, who has long felt Herb was a no-goodnik, becomes upset that Mark wants to hold out on his own family. After all, if Mark died, she and the kids would need every cent they could get their hands on. As Mark starts to get angry, Alicia realizes they need to slow down and talk it out.

It takes a couple of days, but finally they arrive at a compromise. Mark will transfer $3,000 of his account into their shared account. He can give the other $3,000 to Herb in his will.

Only after they resolve their problem do Mark and Alicia approach the issue they both agree is most important—providing for their two children as best they can if the unlikely occurs and they die simultaneously. They agree on who should be the children's personal guardian (named in their wills)—Alicia's sister Joan, who has stated that she's willing to do the job. They also name Joan as the children's property guardian. They decide that some life insurance is necessary, at least until their savings increase and the children are older. They decide to purchase $150,000 term life policies on each of their lives, realizing that because both work and the family needs two incomes to get by, it's not enough just to insure Mark's life. In case they both die simultaneously, they establish a children's trust in both their wills. If both parents die, the insurance proceeds will be paid to the trust and managed for the children's benefit until they become 35.

Finally, Mark and Alicia each prepare a durable powers of attorney for health care and a separate one for finances, each naming the other to make health care or financial decisions in case he or she becomes incapacitated.

F. A Single Man in His 60s

Dick Daughterty, a lifelong bachelor, wants to leave some of his property to his sister, some to her three children, and much to many friends.

His property. Dick has personal possessions worth $75,000, two extremely valuable antique cars worth a total of $120,000, jewelry worth $25,000, a limited partnership business interest in a real estate venture worth $60,000, stocks now worth $47,000 and savings of $45,000. He doesn't own any real estate.

His estate planning goals. Dick is most concerned with who gets his property, not how they get it. He spends considerable time evaluating exactly who gets what, making several lists and numerous revisions before he decides how it's best to distribute his property.

Since Dick's estate is worth less than $600,000, he doesn't have to worry about federal estate taxes. However, he definitely doesn't want his estate to have to pay probate fees.

His plan. Dick creates a probate-avoiding living trust. In his trust, he specifies the many beneficiaries he's chosen, identifying each item of property that goes to each. Then he transfers all his property, except his savings account, to the living trust. Specifically, he goes to the Department of Motor Vehicles and re-registers his cars in the trust's name. Likewise, he writes the Office of the General Partner for the limited partnership and instructs it to re-register ownership of his shares under the trust's name.

Dick changes his savings account into an informal bank trust account and names his three best friends as equal beneficiaries of the account.

Next, he prepares a basic will, although, at present, none of his property will be transferred by will. His will covers the possibility he may subsequently acquire property which he isn't able to transfer to his trust before he dies.

Then he prepares two durable powers of attorney—one for health care and the other for finances. He names his best friend, Al, to be his attorney-in-fact for both, and another friend, Jacqueline, to be alternate attorney-in-fact for both if Al can't serve. Dick is particularly concerned about health care decisions. If he's incapacitated, he wants to be treated by his personal doctors. If he needs to be hospitalized, he wants to be taken to a specific local hospital. And he does not want life support technology used to artificially extend his life if he has a fatal, irreversible disease. So he drafts a durable power of attorney that incorporates all his specific desires, making them legal and mandatory.

Finally, Dick prepares his funeral plan and instructions and gives them to Al, to insure they're carried out.

G. A Couple in Their 60s, in a Second Marriage

Miriam and Ira Bloom are a married couple in their 60s. It's the second marriage for each. Miriam has one child, now 32, from her first marriage; Ira has two, who are 33 and 36, from his first marriage. The Blooms live in New York, a common law state.

Their property. Miriam and Ira share ownership of a $200,000 house ($160,000 equity), savings of $80,000, stocks worth $55,000, and miscellaneous furnishings worth approximately $15,000. Each separately owns a car. Ira owns, as his separate property, real estate worth $340,000 ($250,000 equity), limited partnership interests worth $80,000, and savings of $40,000. Miriam owns a coin collection worth $5,000 and mutual funds worth $185,000.

Their estate planning goals. Both Miriam and Ira want to provide for each other, but each also wants to ensure that their children from their prior marriages are well provided for as well. Ira's total estate is now worth $525,000. Miriam's is worth $345,000. Neither's estate is large enough to be subject to federal estate taxes, but they do want to avoid probate fees.

Their plan. Miriam and Ira agree that each will leave their shared ownership property outright to the other. Any New York state death taxes assessed against either's estate will be paid from this shared property. Each's separate property will be left in a marital life estate trust for the other spouse, with the property in the trust to ultimately go to the deceased spouse's children. Then they see a lawyer to draw up the trust document. The surviving spouse will be the trustee of the life estate trust. Each spouse fully trusts the other to manage the trust property, and is confident he or she will conserve the trust principal for their children. But both spouses know that their children are somewhat mistrustful of this arrangement. So, the spouses agree that the surviving spouse will send the deceased spouse's children yearly reports of the trust's financial status (a copy of the trust's annual tax return will suffice) to reassure them that the property isn't being squandered.

Because one of Ira's children still needs financial support for education, he places $20,000 of his separate savings in an informal bank account trust (pay-on-death account) for her, so she will immediately get money, without delay, should he die before she graduates. If the daughter completes her education with Ira's help before he dies, he can, if he wants to, revoke the informal bank account trust and place the account in his living trust.

The Blooms also each execute durable powers of attorney for health care and finances, naming the other spouse as the attorney-in-fact.

Finally, the Blooms prepare simple basic wills.

H. An Unmarried Couple in Their 40s

Pat and Mercedes have lived together for 13 years. They have no children. They have a written living together contract, stating that they share ownership of their house and its furnishings, and that all other property of each is his or her separate property. They've also recorded a deed to the house, listing their shared ownership of it.

Their estate planning goals. Each wants to leave his or her interest in the house and furnishings to the other. Each wants to leave separate property to family and friends. Each wants to avoid probate of all their property. Neither's estate will be subject to federal estate taxes. And each wants to ensure that the other can make medical and financial decisions if one becomes incapacitated.

Their plan. They decide to create three living trusts: one for their shared property and one for each one's separate property. This, they conclude, will be clearer than lumping all their property into one trust. In each trust, they refer to their written property agreement and state that it remains binding when one—or both—die. In their shared trust, each gives his or her interest in the house and furnishings to the other. In their individual living trusts, they make the gifts of their own property to the beneficiaries they've chosen. Both of them leave some of their separately-owned property to each other, but also make a number of other gifts to friends and relations. When their trusts are complete, they both complete all paperwork necessary to transfer all assets with title (ownership) documents to the trust.

Each also prepares a basic will and leaves all property subject to those wills (none now) to the other.

Finally, Pat and Mercedes each prepare a durable power of attorney for health care and one for finances, naming the other as their attorney-in-fact, with authority to make decisions if one becomes incapacitated.

Other Nolo Resources

Some of the plans discussed in this chapter recommend a form contained in another publication of Nolo Press. It is necessary for us to refer you to other Nolo resources, since this book, *Plan Your Estate,* is Nolo's overview book on estate planning. As you can see, it is undoubtedly big enough. Of necessity then, a number of detailed forms and instructions are only set out in the Nolo books that focus more deeply on an individual component of the estate planning process. These resources are listed in this book's Introduction, in Section D, and in the Nolo catalog at the end of this book, under "Estate Planning and Probate." ■

Glossary

Part of the hold that the legal profession has over us has to do with its use of specialized language. It is easy to be intimidated and uncomfortable when we don't know what lawyers and judges are talking about. It is only beginning to dawn on many of us that legal language is sometimes consciously, and occasionally even cynically, used to keep us intimidated, and that the concepts behind the obtuse language are often easily understandable. We'd rather use only plain English throughout this book and eliminate legalistic jargon altogether, but unfortunately we are stuck with a legal system that often creaks into motion best when "magic" (sometimes four-syllabic) words are used. (Lawyers call such words "terms of art.")

If you don't find a confusing term defined here, try a standard dictionary, but be sure to read the entire definition, as specialized legal meanings are often listed last. Or, for family matters, check *Nolo's Pocket Guide to Family Law.* As a last resort, try *Black's Law Dictionary,* available in all law libraries.

Note Definitions in quotes and with the symbol (B.) following are taken from Ambrose Bierce's *The Devil's Dictionary.*

A/B trust A lawyer's phrase for a "marital life estate trust."

Abatement Cutting back certain gifts under a will when it is necessary to create a fund to meet expenses, pay taxes, satisfy debts or take care of other bequests which are given a priority under law or under the will.

Abstract of Trust A condensed version of a living trust, which leaves out the key parts of what property is in the trust and who are the beneficiaries. An Abstract of Trust is used to establish, to a financial organization or other institution, that a valid living trust has been established, without revealing specifics of property or beneficiaries the person who created the trust wants to keep private and confidential.

Accumulation Trust A trust where trust income is retained, and not paid out to beneficiaries until certain conditions occur.

Acknowledgment A statement in front of a person who is qualified to administer oaths (e.g., a Notary Public) that a document bearing your signature was actually signed by you.

Ademption The failure of a specific bequest of property to take effect because the property is no longer owned by the person who made the will at the time of his death.

Administration (of an estate) The court-supervised distribution of the probate estate of a deceased person. The person who manages the distribution is called the executor if there is a will. If there is no will, this person is called the administrator. In some states, the person is called "personal representative" in either instance.

Adopted Children Any person, whether an adult or a minor, who is legally adopted as the child of another in a court proceeding.

Adult Any person over the age of 18. All states allow all competent adults to make wills, except that in Georgia, you must be 19 to leave real estate.

Affidavit A written statement made under oath.

Annuity Payment of a fixed sum of money to a specified person at regular intervals.

Augmented Estate A method used in a number of states following the common law ownership of property system to measure a person's estate for the purpose of determining whether a surviving spouse has been adequately provided for. Generally, the augmented estate consists of property left by the will plus certain property transferred outside of the will by gifts, joint tenancies and living trusts. In the states using this concept, a surviving spouse is generally considered to be adequately provided for if he or she receives at least one-third of the augmented estate.

Autopsy Examination of the body of a deceased person to determine the cause of death.

Basis This is a tax term which has to do with the valuation of property for determining profit or loss on sale. If you buy a house (or a poodle) for $20,000, your tax basis is $20,000. If you later sell it for $35,000, your taxable profit is $15,000. A **stepped-up basis** means that you have been able to raise this basic amount from which taxes are computed.

Beneficiary A person or organization who is legally entitled to receive gifts made under a legal document such as a will or trust. Except when very small estates are involved, beneficiaries of wills only receive their benefits after the will is examined and approved by the probate court. Beneficiaries of living trusts receive their benefits outside of probate, as provided in the document establishing the trust. A primary beneficiary is a person who directly and certainly will benefit from a will or trust. A contingent beneficiary is a person who might or might not become a beneficiary, depending on the terms of the will or trust and what happens to the primary beneficiaries. For example, a contingent beneficiary might get nothing until and unless the primary beneficiary dies, with a portion of the trust corpus still remaining.

Bequest An old legal term for a will provision leaving personal property to a specified person or organization. In this book it is called a "gift."

Bond A document guaranteeing that a certain amount of money will be paid to those injured if a person occupying a position of trust does not carry out his or her legal and ethical responsibilities. Thus, if an executor, trustee or guardian who is bonded (covered by a bond) wrongfully deprives a beneficiary of his or her property (say by blowing it during a trip in Las Vegas), the bonding company will replace it, up to the limits of the bond. Bonding companies, which are normally divisions of insurance companies, issue a bond in exchange for a premium, usually about 10% of the face amount of the bond.

Bypass trust Any trust that creates a life estate for a life beneficiary, with the trust principal going to the final beneficiary when the life beneficiary dies.

Charitable trust Any trust designed to make a substantial gift to a charity, and also achieve income and estate tax savings for the grantor.

Children For the purposes of *Plan Your Estate,* one's children are: (1) the biological offspring of a will maker, (2) persons who were legally adopted by a will maker, (3) children born out of wedlock if the will maker is the mother, (4) children born out of wedlock if the will maker is the father and has acknowledged the child as being his as required by the law of the particular state, or (5) children born to the will maker after the will is made, but before his or her death.

Child's trust A trust created for a minor child, or young adult.

Codicil A separate legal document which, after it has been signed and properly witnessed, changes an existing will.

Common law marriage In a minority of states, couples may be considered married if they live together for a certain period of time and intend to be husband and wife.

Community and separate property Eight states follow a system of marital property ownership called "community property," and Wisconsin has a very similar "marital property" law. Very generally, all property acquired after marriage and before permanent separation is considered to belong equally to both spouses, except for gifts to and inheritances by one spouse, and, in some community property states, income from property owned by one spouse prior to marriage.

In most marriages, the main property accumulated is a family home, a retirement pension belonging to one or both spouses, motor vehicles, a joint bank account, a savings account, and perhaps some stocks or bonds. So long as these were purchased during the marriage with the income earned by either spouse during the marriage, they are usually considered to be community property, unless the spouses have entered into an agreement to the contrary. If the property was purchased with the separate property of a spouse, it is separate property, unless it has been given to the community (the couple) by gift or agreement.

If separate property and community property are mixed together (commingled) in a bank account and expenditures made from this bank account, the goods purchased are usually treated as community property unless they can be specifically linked with the separate property (this is called "tracing").

Under the law of community property states, a surviving spouse automatically receives one-half of all community property. The other spouse has no legal power to affect this portion by will or otherwise. Thus, the property which someone may leave by will or other method consists of his or her separate property and one-half of the community property.

Conditional gift A gift which passes only under certain specified conditions or upon the occurrence of a specific event. For example, if you leave property to Aunt Millie provided she is living in Cincinnati when you die, and otherwise to Uncle Fred, you have made a "conditional gift."

Conservator Someone appointed by a court to manage the affairs of a mentally incompetent person.

Contract An agreement between two or more people to do something. A contract is normally written, but can be oral if its terms can be carried out within one year and it doesn't involve real estate. A contract is distinguished from a gift in that each of the contracting parties pledges to do something in exchange for the promises of the other.

Creditor As used in this book, this means a person or institution to whom money is owed. A creditor may be the person who actually lent the money, or he may be a lawyer or bill collector who is trying to collect the money for the original creditor.

Curtesy See **Dower and curtesy**.

Custodian A person named to care for property left to a minor under the Uniform Gifts (or Transfers) to Minors Act.

Death taxes Taxes levied on the property of a person who died. Federal death taxes are called "Estate Taxes." State death taxes (if any) go by various names, including "inheritance tax."

Debtor A person who owes money.

Decedent A person who has died.

Deed The legal document by which one person (or persons) transfers title (recorded ownership) to real estate to another person or persons. If the transfer is by a grant deed, the person transferring title makes certain guarantees or warranties as regards the title. If the transfer is by quitclaim deed, the person transferring does not make any guarantees, but simply transfers to the other persons all the interest he has in the real property.

Descendant A person who is an offspring, however remote, of a certain person or family.

Devise An old English term for real estate given by a will. In this book, it is called a "gift."

Disclaimer The right to refuse to accept property left to you by trust or will.

Domicile The state, or country, where one has his or her primary home.

Donor One who gives a gift. A **donee** is one who receives a gift.

Dower and curtesy The right of a surviving spouse to receive or enjoy the use of a set portion of a deceased spouse's property (usually one-third to one-half) in the event the surviving spouse is not left at least that share and chooses to take against the will. Dower refers to the title which a surviving wife gets, while curtesy refers to what a man receives. Until recently, these amounts differed in a number of states. However, since discrimination on the basis of sex is now illegal in most cases, states generally provide the same benefits regardless of sex.

Durable power of attorney A power of attorney which remains effective even if the person who created it (called the "principal") becomes incapacitated. The person authorized to act (called the "attorney-in-fact") can make health care decisions and handle financial affairs of the principal.

Encumbrances If property is used as collateral for payment of a debt or loan, the property is "encumbered." The debt must be paid off before title to the property can pass to a new owner. Generally, the value of a person's ownership in such property (called the "equity") is measured by the market value of the property less the sum of all encumbrances.

Escheat We put this in here because it's one of our favorite legal words; it means property that goes to a state government because there are no legal inheritors to claim it.

Estate Generally, all the property you own when you die. There are different ways to measure your estate, depending on whether you are concerned with tax reduction (the taxable estate), probate avoidance (the probate estate) or net worth (the net estate).

Estate planning What this book is about—the art of continuing to prosper when you're alive, then dying with the smallest taxable estate and probate estate possible, and passing your property to your loved ones with a minimum of fuss and expense.

Estate taxes Taxes imposed on your property as it passes from the dead to the living. The federal government exempts $600,000 of property and all property left to a surviving spouse. Taxes are only imposed on property actually owned by you at the time of your death. Thus, estate planning techniques designed to reduce taxes usually concentrate on the legal transfer of ownership of your property while you are living, to minimize the amount of such property you own at your death.

Equity The difference between the current fair market value of your real and personal property and the amount you owe on it, if any.

Executor The person named in your will to manage your estate, deal with the probate court, collect your assets and distribute them as you have specified. In some states this person is called the "personal representative." If you die without a will, the probate court will appoint such a person, who is called the "administrator" of the estate.

Exemption trust A bypass trust funded with $600,000 or less.

Final beneficiaries People or institutions designated to receive life estate trust property outright upon the death of a life beneficiary.

Financial guardian See **Guardian of the Minor's Property.**

Funding a Trust Transferring ownership of property to a trust, in the name of the trustee.

Funeral "A pageant whereby we attest to our respect to the dead by enriching the undertaker, and strengthen our grief by an expenditure that deepens our groans and doubles our tears." (B.)

Future interest A right to property which cannot be enforced in the present, but at some future time.

Generation-skipping trust An estate tax-saving trust, where the principal is left in trust for one' s grandchildren, with one's children receiving only the trust income.

Gifts As used in *Plan Your Estate,* any property you give to another person or organization, either during your lifetime, or by will or living trust after your death.

Gift taxes Taxes levied by governments on gifts made during a person's lifetime.

Grantor The person who establishes a trust; also sometimes called a "settlor" or "trustor."

Grantor retained income trusts Various types of trusts where the grantor retains some interest in the trust property during his life.

Guardian of the minor's property Termed "property guardian" in this book, this is the person you name in your will to care for property of your minor child not supervised by some other legal method, such as a minor's trust. Also sometimes called "the guardian of the minor's estate," or "financial guardian."

Guardian of the person An adult appointed or selected to care for a minor child in the event no biological or adoptive parent (legal parent) of the child is able to do so. If one legal parent is alive when the other dies, the child will automatically go to that parent, unless the best interests of the child require something different, or (in some states) the court finds the child would suffer detriment.

Hearse "Death's baby carriage." (B.)

Heirs Persons who are entitled by law to inherit your estate if you don't leave a will or other device to pass property at your death.

Holographic will A will that is completely handwritten by the person making it. While legal in many states, it is never advised except as a last resort.

Incidents of ownership All (or any) control over a life insurance policy.

Inherit To receive property from one who dies.

Inheritance taxes Taxes some states impose on property received by inheritors from a deceased's estate.

Inheritors Persons or organizations who inherit property.

Instrument Legalese for document; often used to refer to the document which creates a trust.

Insurance "An ingenious modern game of chance in which the player is permitted to enjoy the comfortable conviction that he is beating the man who keeps the table." (B.)

Inter vivos trusts See **Living Trusts.**

Intestate To die without a will or other valid estate transfer device.

Intestate succession The method by which property is distributed when a person fails to distribute it in a will. In such cases, the law of each state provides that the property be distributed in certain shares to the closest surviving relatives. In most states, these are a surviving spouse, children, parents, siblings, nieces and nephews, and next of kin, in that order. The intestate succession laws are also used in the event an heir is found to be pretermitted (not mentioned or otherwise provided for in the will).

Irrevocable trust Means what it says. Once you set it up, that's it. Unlike a revocable, probate-avoidance trust, you can't later revoke it, amend it, or change it in any way.

Issue Legalese for one's direct descendants—children, grandchildren, etc.

Joint tenancy A way to take title to jointly owned real or personal property. When two or more people own property as joint tenants, and one of the owners dies, the other owners automatically become owners of the deceased owner's share. Thus, if a parent and child own a house as joint tenants, and the parent dies, the child automatically becomes full owner. Because of this "right of survivorship," a joint tenancy interest in property does not go through probate, or, put another way, is not part of the probate estate. Instead it goes directly to the surviving joint tenant(s) once some tax and transfer forms are completed.

Placing property in joint tenancy is a common tool used in estate planning designed to avoid probate. However, when property is placed in joint tenancy, a gift is made to any persons who become owners as a result. Thus, if Tom owns a house and places it in joint tenancy with Karen, Tom will have made a gift to Karen equal to one-half the house's value. This may have gift tax consequences.

Lawful "Compatible with the will of a judge having jurisdiction." (B.)

Lawyer "One skilled in circumvention of the law." (B.)

Legacy "A gift from one who is legging it out of this vale of tears." (B.)

Letters testamentary The term for the document issued by a probate court authorizing the executor to discharge her responsibilities.

Life beneficiary A person who can receive use of trust property, and benefit of trust income for his or her life, but who doesn't own the trust property itself (the "principal") and has no power to dispose of the trust property upon his or her own death.

Life estate The right to use trust property, and receive income from it, during one's lifetime.

Life insurance trust An irrevocable trust designed to own life insurance and reduce the size of the original owner's taxable estate.

Liquid assets Cash or assets that can readily be turned into cash.

Living trusts A trust set up while a person is alive and which remain under the control of that person until death. Also referred to as an "inter vivos trust," a living trust is an excellent way to minimize the value of property passing through probate. This is because it enables people (called "grantors") to specify that money or other property will pass directly to their beneficiaries at the time of their death, free of probate, and yet also allows the grantors to continue to control the property during their lifetime and even end the trust or change the beneficiaries if they wish.

Living will A document where you provide that you do not want to have your life artificially prolonged by technical means, but choose a natural death.

Marital deduction A deduction allowed by the federal estate tax law for all property passed to a surviving spouse. This deduction (which really acts like an exemption) allows anyone, even a billionaire, to pass his or her entire estate to a surviving spouse without any tax at all. This might be a good idea if the surviving spouse is relatively young and in good health.

If the surviving spouse is likely to die in the near future, however, tax problems are usually made worse by relying on the marital exemption. This is because the second spouse to die will normally benefit from no marital deduction, which means the combined estate, less the standard estate tax exemption, will be taxed at a fairly high rate. For this reason, many older couples with adequate resources do not leave large amounts of property to each other, but rather, leave it directly to their children so that each can qualify for a separate tax exemption.

Marital life estate trust As used in *Plan Your Estate,* a trust giving a surviving spouse (or mate) a life estate interest in property of a deceased spouse or mate. This type of trust is designed to save on eventual estate taxes by giving a surviving spouse (or member of an unmarried couple) the income from the property of the first spouse to die (not the property itself). It can also be called an "A/B trust," or "spousal bypass trust," or an "exemption trust."

Marriage A specific status conferred on a couple by the state. In most states, it is necessary to file papers with a county clerk and have a marriage ceremony conducted by an authorized individual in order to be married. However, in a minority of states called "common law marriage" states, you may be considered married if you have lived together for a certain period of time and intended to be husband and wife. These states are: Alabama, Colorado, District of Columbia, Georgia, Idaho, Iowa, Kansas, Montana, Oklahoma, Pennsylvania, Rhode Island, South Carolina and Texas.

Unless you are considered legally married in the state where you claim your marriage occurred, you are not married for purposes of *Plan Your Estate.*

Mausoleum "The final and funniest folly of the rich." (B.)

Minor Persons under 18 years of age. A minor is not permitted to make certain types of decisions (for example, enter into most contracts). All minors are required to be under the care of a competent adult (parent or guardian) unless they qualify as emancipated minors (in the military, married or living independently with court permission). This also means that property left to a minor must be handled by a guardian or trustee until the minor becomes an adult under the laws of the state.

Mopery Not genuine legalese, but a humorous facsimile, such as "indicted on two counts of mopery."

Mortgage A document that makes a piece of real estate the security (collateral) for the payment of a debt. Most house buyers sign a mortgage when they buy; the bank lends money to buy the house, and the house serves as security for the debt. If the owners don't pay back the loan on time, the bank can seize the house and have it sold to pay off the loan.

Net taxable estate The value of all your property at death less all encumbrances and your other liabilities.

Next of kin The closest living relation.

Ongoing trust Any trust that is designed to be irrevocable and be operational for an extended period of time.

Pay-on-death designation A method of providing, on a property account form, who will inherit what remains of that property when you die. Most commonly used for bank accounts.

Personal property All property other than land and buildings attached to land. Cars, bank accounts, wages, securities, a small business, furniture, insurance policies, jewelry, pets, and season baseball tickets are all personal property.

Pour-over will A will that "pours over" property into a trust. Property left through the will must go through probate before it goes into the trust.

Power of appointment Having the legal authority to decide who shall receive someone else's property, usually property held in a trust.

Power of attorney A legal document where you authorize someone else to act for you. *See also* **Durable Power of Attorney.**

Pretermitted heir A child (or the child of a deceased child) who is either not named or (in some states) not provided for in a will. Most states presume that persons want their children to inherit. Accordingly, children, or the children of a child who has died who are not mentioned or provided for in the will (even by as little as $1) are entitled to a share of the estate.

Probate The court proceeding in which: (1) the authenticity of your will (if any) is established, (2) your executor or administrator is appointed, (3) your debts and taxes are paid, (4) your heirs are identified, and (5) your property in your probate estate is distributed according to your will (if there is a will).

Probate estate All of your property that will pass through probate. Generally, this means all property owned by you at your death less any property that has been placed in joint tenancy, a living trust, a bank account trust, or in life insurance.

Probate fees Because probate is so laden with legal formalities, it is usually necessary to hire an attorney to handle it. The attorney will take a substantial fee from the estate before it is distributed to the heirs.

Property control trust Any trust that imposes limits or controls over the rights of beneficiaries, for one of a number of reasons. These trusts include:

Special needs trusts designed to assist disadvantaged persons with special physical or other needs;

Spendthrift trusts designed to prevent a beneficiary from being able to waste trust principal;

Sprinkling trusts which authorize the trustee to decide how to distribute trust income or principal among different beneficiaries.

Proving a will Getting a probate court to accept the fact after your death that your will really is your will. In many states this can be done simply by introducing a properly signed and witnessed will. In others, it is necessary to produce one or more witnesses (or their affidavits) in court, or offer some proof of the will maker's handwriting. Having the will maker and witnesses sign an affidavit before a notary public stating that all will-making formalities were complied with usually allows the will to "prove" itself without the need for the witnesses to testify, or other evidence.

QDOT trust A trust used to postpone estate taxes, when more than $600,000 is left to a non-U.S. citizen spouse by the other spouse.

QTIP trust A marital trust with property left for use of the surviving spouse as life beneficiary. No estate taxes are assessed on the trust property until the death of the life beneficiary spouse.

Quasi-community property A rule that applies to married couples who have moved to Idaho or California. Laws in those states require all property acquired by people during their marriage in other states to be treated as community property at their death.

Real estate A term used by *Plan Your Estate* as a synonym for the legalese "real property."

Real property All land and items attached to the land, such as buildings, houses, stationary mobile homes, fences and trees are real property or "real estate." All property which is not real property is personal property.

Recording The process of filing a copy of a deed with the county land records office. Recording creates a public record of all changes in ownership of property in the state.

Residual beneficiary Can have various meanings, including: a person who receives any property left by will or trust not otherwise given away by the document; a person receiving the property of a trust after the life beneficiary dies.

Residue, residuary estate All property given by your will or trust to your residuary beneficiary after all specific gifts of property have been made—that is, what's left.

Right of survivorship The right of a surviving joint tenant to take ownership of a deceased joint tenant's share of the property.

Rule against perpetuities A rule of law which limits the durations of trusts (except charitable ones). The workings of the rule are very complicated, and have baffled law students for generations. Very roughly, a trust cannot last longer than the lifetime of someone alive when the trust is created, plus 21 years.

Separate property In states which have community property, all property which is not community property. See also **Community and separate property**.

Spouse In *Plan Your Estate,* your spouse is the person to whom you are legally married. If you later remarry, you will need to make a new estate plan, with new documents, if you wish to leave property to your new spouse.

Successor trustee The person (or institution) who takes over as trustee of a trust when the original trustee(s) have died or become incapacitated.

Surviving spouse's trust Where a couple has created a living trust with marital life estate, the revocable living trust of the surviving spouse, after the other spouse has died.

Taking against the will The ability of a surviving spouse to choose a statutorily allotted share of the deceased spouse's estate instead of the share specified in his or her will. In most common law property states, the law provides that a surviving spouse is entitled to receive a minimum percentage of the other spouse's estate (commonly one-third to one-half). If the deceased spouse leaves the surviving spouse less than this in, or outside of, the will, the surviving spouse may elect the statutory share instead of the will provision ("take against the will"). If the spouse chooses to accept the share specified in the will, it is called "taking under the will." See **Dower and Curtesy**.

Taxable estate The portion of your estate that is subject to federal or state estate taxes.

Tenancy by the entirety In some states, joint tenancy between spouses.

Tenancy in common A way for co-owners to hold title to property that allows them maximum freedom to dispose of their interests by sale, gift or will. At a co-owner's death, his or her share goes to beneficiaries named in a will or trust or to the legal heirs, not to the other co-owners. Compare **Joint tenancy**.

Testamentary trust A trust created by a will.

Testate Someone who dies leaving a valid will, or other valid property transfer devices, dies "testate."

Testator A person making a will.

Title Document proving ownership of property.

Totten trust A simple savings bank trust, revocable at any time before the death of the depositor (also called "pay-on-death" account).

Trust A legal arrangement under which one person or institution (called a "trustee") controls property given by another person (called a "settlor" or "trustor") for the benefit of a third person (called a "beneficiary"). The property itself can be termed the "corpus" of the trust.

Trust corpus or res The property transferred to a trust. For example, if a trust is established (funded) with $250,000, that money is the corpus or res.

Trust merger Occurs when the sole trustee and sole beneficiary are the same person. Then, there's no longer the separation between the trustee's legal ownership of trust property from the beneficiary's interest, which is the essence of a trust. So, the trust "merges" and ceases to exist.

Trustee The people or institutions who manage a trust and trust property under the terms of the trust.

Trustee powers The provisions in a trust document defining what the trustee may and may not do.

Uniform Gifts/Transfers to Minors Act A series of state statutes that provide a method for transferring property to minors.

Usufruct Included because it's another of our favorite legal words, meaning the right to use property, or income from it, owned by another.

Will A legal document in which a person states various binding intentions about what he or she wants done with his or her property after death. ■

Appendix

State Death Tax Rules

CHART 1. INHERITANCE TAXES

Following are the rules for each state which imposes inheritance taxes:

CONNECTICUT

Class AA: Surviving spouse

Class A: Parent, grandparent, adoptive parent or natural or adopted descendant

Class B: Son or daughter-in-law of child (natural or adopted) who has not remarried. Stepchild, brother or sister (full or half or adopted), brother or sister's children (descendants, natural or adopted)

Class C: All other persons

	Taxable Amount			Tax Rate
Class AA				No Tax
Class A	50,000	to	150,000	3%
	150,000	to	250,000	4%
	250,000	to	400,000	5%
	400,000	to	600,000	6%
	600,000	to	1,000,000	7%
	1,000,000		And Over	8%
Class B	6,000	to	25,000	4%
	25,000	to	150,000	5%
	150,000	to	250,000	6%
	250,000	to	400,000	7%
	400,000	to	600,000	8%
	600,000	to	1,000,000	9%
	1,000,000		And Over	10%
Class C	1,000	to	25,000	8%
	25,000	to	150,000	9%
	150,000	to	250,000	10%
	250,000	to	400,000	11%
	400,000	to	600,000	12%
	600,000	to	1,000,000	13%
	1,000,000		And Over	14%

DELAWARE

Class A: Spouse

Class B: Parent, grandparent, child (by birth or adoption), son- or daughter-in-law, lineal descendant, or stepchild

Class C: Brother, sister, their descendants; aunt, uncle, their descendants

Class D: All others

	Taxable Amount			Tax Rate
Class A	70,000	to	100,000	2%
	100,000	to	200,000	3%
	200,000		And Over	4%
Class B	25,000	to	50,000	2%
	50,000	to	75,000	3%
	75,000	to	100,000	4%
	100,000	to	200,000	5%
	200,000		And Over	6%
Class C	5,000	to	25,000	5%
	25,000	to	50,000	6%
	50,000	to	100,000	7%
	100,000	to	150,000	8%
	150,000	to	200,000	9%
	200,000		And Over	10%
Class D	1,000	to	25,000	10%
	25,000	to	50,000	12%
	50,000	to	100,000	14%
	100,000		And Over	16%

INDIANA

Class A: Spouse, parents, children, grandchildren

Class B: Sibling, nieces and nephews, son- or daughter-in-law

Class C: All others

Taxable Amount			Base Tax		Plus %	of Amt Over
Class A						
0	to	25,000	0	+	1%	0
25,000	to	50,000	250	+	2%	25,000
50,000	to	200,000	750	+	3%	50,000
200,000	to	300,000	5,250	+	4%	200,000
300,000	to	500,000	9,250	+	5%	300,000
500,000	to	700,000	19,250	+	6%	500,000
700,000	to	1,000,000	31,250	+	7%	700,000
1,000,000	to	1,500,000	52,250	+	8%	1,000,000
1,500,000		And Over	92,250	+	10%	1,500,000
Class B						
0	to	100,000	0	+	7%	0
100,000	to	500,000	7,000	+	10%	100,000
500,000	to	1,000,000	47,000	+	12%	500,000
1,000,000		And Over	107,000	+	15%	1,000,000
Class C						
0	to	100,000	0	+	10%	0
100,000	to	1,000,000	10,000	+	15%	100,000
1,000,000		And Over	45,000	+	20%	1,000,000

Tax Rate columns: Base Tax, Plus %, of Amt Over.

Exemptions

1. Spouse: All tax
2. Child under 21 at death: $10,000
3. Child over 21 at death: $5,000
4. Parents: $5,000
5. Other Class A: $2,000
6. Class B: $500
7. Class C: $100

IOWA

Class 1: Spouse

Class 2: Parent, child, lineal descendant

Class 3: Sibling, son- or daughter-in-law, stepchild

Class 4: All others

Class	Taxable Amount			Tax Rate
Class 1				No Tax
Class 2	0	to	5,000	1%
	5,000	to	12,000	2%
	12,000	to	25,000	3%
	25,000	to	50,000	4%
	50,000	to	75,000	5%
	75,000	to	100,000	6%
	100,000	to	150,000	7%
	150,000		And Over	8%
Class 3	0	to	12,500	5%
	12,500	to	25,000	6%
	25,000	to	75,000	7%
	75,000	to	100,000	8%
	100,000	to	150,000	9%
	150,000		And Over	10%
Class 4	0	to	50,000	10%
	50,000	to	100,000	12%
	100,000		And Over	15%

Exemptions

1. Each son and daughter: $50,000
2. Father or mother: $15,000
3. Any other lineal descendant: $15,000
4. Any estate not exceeding $10,000

KANSAS

Class A: Lineal ancestors and descendants; stepparents, stepchildren, adopted children, lineal descendants of adopted child or stepchild, spouse or surviving spouse of son or daughter, spouse or surviving spouse of an adopted child or stepchild

Class B: Siblings

Class C: All others

	Taxable Amount			Tax Rate
Class A	0	to	25,000	1%
	25000	to	50,000	2%
	50,000	to	100,000	3%
	100,000	to	500,000	4%
	500,000		And Over	5%
Class B	0	to	25,000	3.0%
	25,000	to	50,000	5.0%
	50,000	to	100,000	7.5%
	100,000	to	500,000	10.0%
	500,000		And Over	12.5%
Class C	0	to	100,000	10%
	100,000	to	200,000	12%
	200,00		And Over	15%

Exemptions

(Taxable amount begins after taking applicable exemption)

1. Spouse: All tax
2. Class A: $30,000
3. Class B: $5,000
4. Qualified real estate: to $750,000, if left to family member and used for family farm or business

KENTUCKY

Class A: Parent, spouse, child, stepchild, adopted child, or grandchild

Class B: Sibling, nephew or niece, daughter- or son-in-law, aunt or uncle

Class C: All others

	Taxable Amount			Tax Rate
Class A	0	to	20,000	2%
	20,000	to	30,000	3%
	30,000	to	45,000	4%
	45,000	to	60,000	5%
	60,000	to	100,000	6%
	100,000	to	200,000	7%
	200,000	to	500,000	8%
	500,000		And Over	10%
Class B	0	to	10,000	4%
	10,000	to	20,000	5%
	20,000	to	30,000	6%
	30,000	to	45,000	8%
	45,000	to	60,000	10%
	60,000	to	100,000	12%
	100,000	to	200,000	14%
	200,000		And Over	16%
Class C	0	to	10,000	6%
	10,000	to	20,000	8%
	20,000	to	30,000	10%
	30,000	to	45,000	12%
	45,000	to	60,000	14%
	60,000		And Over	16%

Exemptions

1. Spouse: All tax
2. Infant/child: $20,000
3. Mentally disabled child: $20,000
4. Parent: $5,000
5. Child or step-child: $5,000
6. Grandchild: $5,000
7. Class B: $1,000
8. Class C: $500

LOUISIANA

Class 1: Spouse, descendants, lineal ancestors

Class 2: Collateral relatives (siblings, their children)

Class 3: All others

	Taxable Amount			Tax Rate
Class 1	0	to	20,000	2%
	20,000		And Over	3%
Class 2	0	to	1,000	No Tax
	1,000	to	21,000	5%
	21,000		And Over	7%
Class 3	0	to	500	No Tax
	500	to	5,500	5%
	5,500		And Over	10%

Exemptions

1. Spouse: All tax if death in 1992 or after
2. Class 1: $25,000 if death is in 1987 or after

MARYLAND

Class 1: Spouse, parent, children, grandparent, descendants, stepchild, stepparent

Class 2: All others

	Taxable Amount	Tax Rate
Class 1	All Amounts	1%
Class 2	All Amounts	10%

Exemptions

1. Spouse: First $100,000 of personal property; all real property
2. Property administered under small estates law

Special tax rates

Spouse of descendant: 1% for first $2,000 of jointly-owned savings; thereafter at 10%

MICHIGAN

Class 1: Spouse, parent, grandparent, sibling, son- or daughter-in-law, children and adopted children

Class 2: All others

	Taxable Amount			Tax Rate
Class 1	0	to	50,000	2%
	50,000	to	250,000	4%
	250,000	to	500,000	7%
	500,000	to	750,000	8%
	750,000		And Over	10%
Class 2	0	to	50,000	12%
	50,000	to	500,000	14%
	500,000		And Over	17%

Exemptions

1. Spouse: $65,000
2. All other Class 1: $10,000
3. Family-owned business—no tax if transferred to qualified heir

MONTANA

Class 1: Spouse, lineal descendant or child, and lineal ancestor

Class 2: Siblings, their offspring, son- or daughter-in-law

Class 3: Uncle, aunt, or first cousins

Class 4: All others

	Taxable Amount			Tax Rate
Class 1	0	to	25,000	2%
	25,000	to	50,000	4%
	50,000	to	100,000	6%
	100,000		And Over	8%
Class 2	0	to	25,000	4%
	25,000	to	50,000	8%
	50,000	to	100,000	12%
	100,000		And Over	16%
Class 3	0	to	25,000	6%
	25,000	to	50,000	12%
	50,000	to	100,000	18%
	100,000		And Over	24%
Class 4	0	to	25,000	8%
	25,000	to	50,000	16%
	50,000	to	100,000	24%
	100,000		And Over	32%

Exemptions

1. Spouse or child or lineal descendant: All tax
2. Lineal ancestors: $7,000
3. Class 2: $1,000
4. Charitable, educational, religious gifts: All tax

NEBRASKA

Class 1: Spouse, parent, child, son- or daughter-in-law

Class 2: Uncle, aunt, niece, nephew or their descendants or spouses

Class 3: All others

	Taxable Amount			Tax Rate
Class 1	0	to	10,000	No Tax
	10,000		And Over	1%
Class 2	0	to	2,000	No Tax
	2,000	to	60,000	6%
	60,000		And Over	9%
Class 3	0	to	5,000	6%
	5,000	to	10,000	9%
	10,000	to	20,000	12%
	20,000	to	50,000	15%
	50,000		And Over	18%

Exemptions

1. Spouse: All tax
2. Class 1: $10,000
3. Class 2: $2,000
4. Class 3: $500

NEW HAMPSHIRE

Class 1: Spouse, lineal ancestors, and descendants, their spouses and all adopted children in descendant's line of succession

Class 2: All others

	Taxable Amount	Tax Rate
Class 1	Any Amount	No Tax
Class 2	Any Amount	18%

Exemptions

1. Property left to care for cemetery lots
2. Contributions to charities
3. Members of household of deceased (must have lived with deceased from age 5-15): All taxes
4. Step-children, step-parents, descendants and their spouses: All taxes

NEW JERSEY

Class A: Spouse, parent, grandparent, children, step-children, direct descendants

Class B: Sibling, daughter- or son-in-law

Class C: All others

	Taxable Amount			Tax Rate
Class A				No Tax
Class B	0	to	1,100,000	11%
	1,100,000	to	1,400,000	13%
	1,400,000	to	1,700,000	14%
	1,700,000		And Over	16%
Class C	0	to	700,000	15%
	700,000		And Over	16%

Exemptions

1. Class B: First $25,000
2. Life insurance proceeds: All tax
3. Pension to surviving spouse: All tax

NORTH CAROLINA

Class A: Spouse, lineal descendants, ancestor, stepchild, adopted child, or son- or daughter-in-law whose spouse is not entitled to any beneficiary interest in property of deceased

Class B: Sibling, their issue, aunt or uncle

Class C: All others

	Taxable Amount			Tax Rate
Class A	0	to	10,000	1%
	10,000	to	25,000	2%
	25,000	to	50,000	3%
	50,000	to	100,000	4%
	100,000	to	200,000	5%
	200,000	to	500,000	6%
	500,000	to	1,000,000	7%
	1,000,000	to	1,500,000	8%
	1,500,000	to	2,000,000	9%
	2,000,000	to	2,500,000	10%
	2,500,000	to	3,000,000	11%
	3,000,000		And Over	12%
Class B	0	to	5,000	4%
	5,000	to	10,000	5%
	10,000	to	25,000	6%
	25,000	to	50,000	7%
	50,000	to	100,000	8%
	100,000	to	250,000	10%
	250,000	to	500,000	11%
	500,000	to	1,000,000	12%
	1,000,000	to	1,500,000	13%
	1,500,000	to	2,000,000	14%
	2,000,000	to	3,000,000	15%
	3,000,000		And Over	16%
Class C	0	to	10,000	8%
	10,000	to	25,000	9%
	25,000	to	50,000	10%
	50,000	to	100,000	11%
	100,000	to	250,000	12%
	250,000	to	500,000	13%
	500,000	to	1,000,000	14%
	1,000,000	to	1,500,000	15%
	1,500,000	to	2,500,000	16%
	2,500,000		And Over	17%

Exemptions

All Class A beneficiaries and gross estate less than $250,000

OKLAHOMA

Class 1: Parent, child, child of spouse, descendant

Class 2: All others

	Taxable Amount			Tax Rate
Class 1	0	to	10,000	No Tax
	10,000	to	20,000	1.0
	20,000	to	40,000	1.5
	40,000	to	60,000	2.0
	60,000	to	100,000	2.5
	100,000	to	250,000	3.0
	250,000	to	500,000	6.5
	500,000	to	750,000	7.0
	750,000	to	1,000,000	7.5
	1,000,000	to	3,000,000	8.0
	3,000,000	to	5,000,000	8.5
	5,000,000	to	10,000,000	9.0
	10,000,000		And Over	10.0
Class 2	0	to	10,000	1.0
	10,000	to	20,000	2.0
	20,000	to	40,000	3.0
	40,000	to	60,000	4.0
	60,000	to	100,000	5.0
	100,000	to	250,000	6.0
	250,000	to	500,000	13.0
	500,000	to	1,000,000	14.0
	1,000,000		And Over	15.0

Exemptions

(Taxable amount begins after taking applicable exemption)

1. Spouses: All tax
2. Other Class 1: $175,000

PENNSYLVANIA

Class A: Grandparents, parents, spouse, lineal descendants, widower or widow of child, spouse of child

Class B: All others

	Taxable Amount	Tax Rate
Class A	All Amounts	6%
Class B	All Amounts	15%

Exemptions

1. Spouse: All property held jointly
2. Family: $2,000
3. Life insurance proceeds
4. Social security death payments
5. Employments benefits
6. Family exemption

SOUTH DAKOTA

Class 1: Issue, adopted child, child

Class 2: Ancestor of decendant

Class 3: Sibling or their issue or son- or daughter-in-law

Class 4: Aunt or uncle

Class 5: All others

Class 6: Any person if in business with decendant for 10 or 15 years before death of decendant

	Taxable Amount			Tax Rate
Class 1	0	to	30,000	No Tax
	30,000	to	50,000	3.75%
	50,000	to	100,000	6.00%
	100,000		And Over	7.50%
Class 2	0	to	3,000	No Tax
	3,000	to	15,000	3.00%
	15,000	to	50,000	7.50%
	50,000	to	100,000	12.00%
	100,000		And Over	15.00%
Class 3	0	to	500	No Tax
	500	to	15,000	4.00%
	15,000	to	50,000	10.00%
	50,000	to	100,000	16.00%
	100,000		And Over	20.00%
Class 4	0	to	200	No Tax
	200	to	15,000	5.00%
	15,000	to	50,000	12.50%
	50,000	to	100,000	20.00%
	100,000		And Over	25.00%
Class 5	0	to	100	No Tax
	100	to	15,000	6.00%
	15,000	to	50,000	15.00%
	50,000	to	100,000	24.00%
	100,000		And Over	30.00%
Class 6	0	to	15,000	3.00%
	15,000	to	50,000	7.50%
	50,000	to	100,000	12.00%
	100,000		And Over	15.00%

Exemptions

1. Spouse: All tax

TENNESSEE

Class A: Spouse, child, lineal ancestor or descendant, sibling, stepchild, son- or daughter-in-law, adopted child

Class B: All other

Taxable Amount	Tax Rate		
	Base Tax	*Plus %*	*of Amt Over*
$440,000	$30,200	9.5%	$440,000

Exemptions

(Taxable amount begins after taking applicable exemption)

Classes A and B: $600,000

CHART 2. ESTATE TAXES

Following are the rules for each state which imposes estate taxes.

MASSACHUSETTS

Taxable Amount			Tax Rate			
			Base Tax		Plus %	of Amt Over
All Classes						
0	to	50,000	5% of the taxable estate			
50,000	to	100,000	2,500	+	7%	50,000
100,000	to	200,000	6,000	+	9%	100,000
200,000	to	400,000	15,000	+	10%	200,000
400,000	to	600,000	35,000	+	11%	400,000
600,000	to	800,000	57,000	+	12%	600,000
800,000	to	1,000,000	81,000	+	13%	800,000
1,000,000	to	2,000,000	107,000	+	14%	1,000,000
2,000,000	to	4,000.000	247,000	+	15%	2,000,000
4,000,000			547,000	+	16%	4,000,000

Exemptions

Estates under $600,000

MISSISSIPPI

Taxable Amount			Tax Rate			
			Base Tax		Plus %	of Amt Over
0	to	60,000	0		1%	0
60,000	to	100,000	600	+	1.6%	60,000
100,000	to	200,000	1,240	+	2.4%	100,000
200,000	to	400,000	3,640	+	3.2%	200,000
400,000	to	600,000	10,040	+	4.0%	400,000
600,000	to	800,000	18,040	+	4.8%	600,000
800,000	to	1,000,000	27,640	+	5.6%	800,000
1,000,000	to	1,500,000	38,840	+	6.4%	1,000,000
1,500,000	to	2,000,000	70,840	+	7.2%	1,500,000
2,000,000	to	2,500,000	106,840	+	8.0%	2,000,000
2,500,000	to	3,000,000	146,840	+	8.8%	2,500,000
3,000,000	to	3,500,000	190,840	+	9.6%	3,000,000
3,500,000	to	4,000,000	238,840	+	10.4%	3,500,000
4,000,000	to	5,000,000	290,840	+	11.2%	4,000,000
5,000,000	to	6,000,000	402,840	+	12.0%	5,000,000
6,000,000	to	7,000,000	522,840	+	12.8%	6,000,000
7.000,000	to	8,000,000	650,840	+	13.6%	7,000,000
8,000,000	to	9,000,000	786,840	+	14.4%	8,000,000
9,000,000	to	10,000,000	930,840	+	15.2%	9,000,000
10,000,000	and Over		1,082,840	+	16.0%	10,000,000

Exemption

$600,000, taxable amount begins after taking exemption

NEW YORK

Taxable Amount			Tax Rate		
			Base Tax	*Plus %*	*of Amt Over*
0	to	50,000	0 +	2%	0
50,000	to	150,000	1,000 +	3%	50,000
150,000	to	300,000	4,000 +	4%	150,000
300,000	to	500,000	10,000 +	5%	300,000
500,000	to	700,000	20,000 +	6%	500,000
700,000	to	900,000	32,000 +	7%	700,000
900,000	to	1,100,000	46,000 +	8%	900,000
1,100,000	to	1,600,000	62,000 +	9%	1,100,000
1,600,000	to	2,100,000	107,000 +	10%	1,600,000
2,100,000	to	2,600,000	157,000 +	11%	2,100,000
2,600,000	to	3,100,000	212,000 +	12%	2,600,000
3,100,000	to	3,600,0002	72,000 +	13%	3,100,000
3,600,000	to	4,100,000	337,000 +	14%	3,600,000
4,100,000	to	5,100,000	407,000 +	15%	4,100,000
5,100,000	to	6,100,000	557,000 +	16%	5,100,000
6,100,000	to	7,100,000	717,000 +	17%	6,100,000
7,100,000	to	8,100,000	887,000 +	18%	7,100,000
8,100,000	to	9,100,000	1,067,000 +	19%	8,100,000
9,100,000	to	10,100,000	1,257,000 +	20%	9,100,000
10,100,000		And Over	1,457,000 +	21%	10,100,000

Tax credits

Tax	*Credit*
$0 to $2,750	Full credit (No tax)
$2,750 to $5,000	Difference between tax and $5,500
$5,000 or more	$500

OHIO

Taxable Amount			Tax Rate			
			Base Tax		*Plus %*	*of Amt Over*
0	to	40,000	0	+	2%	0
40,000	to	100,000	800	+	3%	40,000
100,000	to	200,000	2,600	+	4%	100,000
200,000	to	300,000	6,600	+	5%	200,000
300,000	to	500,000	11,600	+	6%	300,000
500,000		And Over	23,6000	+	7%	500,000

Exemption

Marital deduction for the lesser of the federal marital deduction or one-half of adjusted gross estates greater than $500,000

Tax credit

Lesser of $5,000 or amount of tax

Index

D

E

F

G

M

N

O

P

Q

R

U

	Edition	Price	Code

BUSINESS

Title	Edition	Price	Code
Business Plans to Game Plans	1st	$29.95	GAME
Getting Started as an Independent Paralegal—Audio	2nd	$44.95	GSIP
How to Finance a Growing Business	1st	$29.95	GROW
How to Form a California Nonprofit Corporation—w/Corp. Records Binder & Disk (PC & Mac)	1st	$49.95	CNP
How to Form a Nonprofit Corporation, Book w/Disk (PC)—National Edition	2nd	$39.95	NNP
How to Form Your Own California Corporation	8th	$29.95	CCOR
How to Form Your Own California Corporation—w/Corporate Records Binder & Disk—PC	1st	$39.95	CACI
How to Form Your Own Florida Corporation, (Book w/Disk—PC)	3rd	$39.95	FLCO
How to Form Your Own New York Corporation, (Book w/Disk—PC)	3rd	$39.95	NYCO
How to Form Your Own Texas Corporation, (Book w/Disk—PC)	4th	$39.95	TCI
How to Start Your Own Business: Small Business Law—Audio	1st	$14.95	TBUS
How to Write a Business Plan	4th	$21.95	SBS
Marketing Without Advertising	1st	$14.00	MWAD
Taking Care of Your Corporation, Vol. 1, Book w/Disk—PC	1st	$26.95	CORK
The California Nonprofit Corporation Handbook	6th	$29.95	NON
The California Professional Corporation Handbook	5th	$34.95	PROF
The Employers Legal Handbook	1st	$29.95	EMPL
The Independent Paralegal's Handbook	3rd	$29.95	PARA
The Legal Guide for Starting & Running a Small Bus. on Disk—Windows	1st	$24.95	RUNSW1
The Legal Guide for Starting & Running a Small Business	1st	$22.95	RUNS
The Partnership Book: How to Write a Partnership Agreement	4th	$24.95	PART
Trademark: How to Name Your Business & Product	1st	$29.95	TRD

	Edition	Price	Code
CONSUMER			
Fed Up With the Legal System: What's Wrong & How to Fix It	2nd	$9.95	LEG
Glossary of Insurance Terms	5th	$14.95	GLINT
How to Win Your Personal Injury Claim	1st	$24.95	PICL
Nolo's Law Form Kit: Hiring Child Care & Household Help	1st	$14.95	KCHLD
Nolo's Pocket Guide to California Law	3rd	$10.95	CLAW
Nolo's Pocket Guide to California Law on Disk—Macintosh	1.0	$24.95	CLM
Nolo's Pocket Guide to California Law on Disk—Windows	1.0	$24.95	CLWIN
Nolo's Pocket Guide to Consumer Rights (California Edition)	2nd	$12.95	CAG
The Over 50 Insurance Survival Guide	1st	$16.95	OVER50
What Do You Mean It's Not Covered	1st	$19.95	COVER
ESTATE PLANNING & PROBATE			
5 Ways to Avoid Probate—Audio	1st	$14.95	TPRO
How to Probate an Estate (California Edition)	8th	$34.95	PAE
Make Your Own Living Trust	1st	$19.95	LITR
Nolo's Law Form Kit: Wills	1st	$14.95	KWL
Nolo's Simple Will Book	2nd	$17.95	SWIL
Plan Your Estate	3rd	$24.95	NEST
Write Your Will—Audio	1st	$14.95	TWYW
FAMILY MATTERS			
A Legal Guide for Lesbian and Gay Couples	8th	$24.95	LG
Divorce & Money: How to Make the Best Financial Decisions During Divorce	2nd	$21.95	DIMO
How to Adopt Your Stepchild in California	4th	$22.95	ADOP
How to Do Your Own Divorce in California	20th	$21.95	CDIV
How to Do Your Own Divorce in Texas	5th	$17.95	TDIV
How to Raise or Lower Child Support in California	3rd	$18.95	CHLD
Nolo's Pocket Guide to Family Law	3rd	$14.95	FLD
Practical Divorce Solutions	1st	$14.95	PDS
The Guardianship Book (California Edition)	2nd	$24.95	GB
The Living Together Kit	7th	$24.95	LTK
GOING TO COURT			
Collect Your Court Judgment: 19 Ways to Get Paid When You Win A Lawsuit (CA Edition)	2nd	$19.95	JUDG

	Edition	Price	Code
Everybody's Guide to Municipal Court (California Edition)	1st	$29.95	MUNI
Everybody's Guide to Small Claims Court (California Edition)	11th	$18.95	CSCC
Everybody's Guide to Small Claims Court (National Edition)	5th	$18.95	NSCC
Fight Your Ticket (California Edition)	6th	$19.95	FYT
How to Change Your Name (California Edition)	6th	$24.95	NAME
Represent Yourself in Court: How to Prepare & Try a Winning Case	1st	$29.95	RYC
The Criminal Records Book (California Edition)	4th	$21.95	CRIM
Winning in Small Claims Court—Audio	1st	$14.95	TWIN

HOMEOWNERS, LANDLORDS & TENANTS

	Edition	Price	Code
Dog Law	2nd	$12.95	DOG
For Sale by Owner (California Edition)	2nd	$24.95	FSBO
Homestead Your House (California Edition)	8th	$9.95	HOME
How to Buy a House in California	3rd	$24.95	BHCA
Neighbor Law: Fences, Trees, Boundaries & Noise	2nd	$16.95	NEI
Nolo's Law Form Kit: Leases & Rental Agreements	1st	$14.95	KLEAS
Safe Homes, Safe Neighborhoods: Stopping Crime Where You Live	1st	$14.95	SAFE
Tenants' Rights (California Edition)	12th	$18.95	CTEN
The Deeds Book (California Edition)	3rd	$16.95	DEED
The Landlord's Law Book, Vol. 1: Rights & Responsibilities (California Edition)	4th	$32.95	LBRT
The Landlord's Law Book, Vol. 2: Evictions (California Edition)	5th	$34.95	LBEV

HUMOR

	Edition	Price	Code
29 Reasons Not to Go to Law School	4th	$9.95	29R
Devil's Advocates: The Unnatural History of Lawyers	1st	$12.95	DA
Nolo's Favorite Lawyer Jokes On Disk—DOS	1.0	$9.95	JODI
Nolo's Favorite Lawyer Jokes On Disk—Macintosh	1.0	$9.95	JODM
Nolo's Favorite Lawyer Jokes On Disk—Windows	1st	$9.95	JODWI
Poetic Justice: The Funniest, Meanest Things Ever Said About Lawyers	1st	$9.95	PJ

IMMIGRATION

	Edition	Price	Code
Como Obtener La Tarjeta Verde: Maneras Legitimas de Permanecer en los EE.UU.	1st	$24.95	VERDE
How to Become a United States Citizen	4th	$12.95	CIT
How to Get a Green Card: Legal Ways to Stay in the U.S.A.	1st	$22.95	GRN

	Edition	Price	Code

MONEY MATTERS

Title	Edition	Price	Code
Chapter 13 Bankruptcy: Repay Your Debts	1st	$29.95	CH13
How to File for Bankruptcy	5th	$25.95	HFB
Money Troubles: Legal Strategies to Cope With Your Debts	3rd	$18.95	MT
Nolo's Law Form Kit: Buy & Sell Contracts	1st	$9.95	KCONT
Nolo's Law Form Kit: Loan Agreements	1st	$14.95	KLOAN
Nolo's Law Form Kit: Personal Bankruptcy	1st	$14.95	KBNK
Nolo's Law Form Kit: Power of Attorney	1st	$14.95	KPA
Nolo's Law Form Kit: Rebuild Your Credit	1st	$14.95	KCRD
Simple Contracts for Personal Use	2nd	$16.95	CONT
Smart Ways to Save Money During and After Divorce	1st	$14.95	SAVMO
Stand Up to the IRS	2nd	$21.95	SIRS

PATENTS AND COPYRIGHTS

Title	Edition	Price	Code
Copyright Your Software	1st	$39.95	CYS
Patent It Yourself	3rd	$39.95	PAT
Software Development: A Legal Guide (Book with disk—PC)	1st	$44.95	SFT
The Copyright Handbook: How to Protect and Use Written Works	2nd	$24.95	COHA
The Inventor's Notebook	1st	$19.95	INOT

RESEARCH & REFERENCE

Title	Edition	Price	Code
Legal Research: How to Find & Understand the Law	3rd	$19.95	LRES
Legal Research Made Easy: A Roadmap through the Law Library Maze—Video	1st	$89.95	LRME

SENIORS

Title	Edition	Price	Code
Beat the Nursing Home Trap: A Consumer's Guide	2nd	$18.95	ELD
Social Security, Medicare & Pensions: The Sourcebook for Older Americans	5th	$18.95	SOA
The Conservatorship Book (California Edition)	2nd	$29.95	CNSV

SOFTWARE

Title	Edition	Price	Code
California Incorporator 1.0—DOS	1.0	$90.30	INCI
Living Trust Maker 2.0—Macintosh	2.0	$55.96	LTM2
Living Trust Maker 2.0—Windows	2.0	$55.96	LTWI2
Nolo's Partnership Maker 1.0—DOS	1.0	$90.96	PAGI1
Nolo's Personal RecordKeeper 3.0—Macintosh	3.0	$34.96	FRM3

	Edition	Price	Code
Patent It Yourself 1.0—Windows	1.0	$160.96	PYW1
WillMaker 5.0—DOS	5.0	$48.96	WI5
WillMaker 5.0—Macintosh	5.0	$48.96	WM5
WillMaker 5.0—Windows	5.0	$48.96	WIW5

WORKPLACE

	Edition	Price	Code
How to Handle Your Workers' Compensation Claim: (California Edition)	1st	$29.95	WORK
Rightful Termination	1st	$29.95	RITE
Sexual Harassment on the Job	2nd	$18.95	HARS
Workers' Comp for Employers	2nd	$29.95	CNTRL
Your Rights in the Workplace	2nd	$15.95	YRW

ORDER FORM

Code	Quantity	Title	Unit price	Total

Subtotal

California residents add Sales Tax

Shipping & Handling ($4 for 1st item; $1 each additional)

2nd day UPS (additional $5; $8 in Alaska and Hawaii)

TOTAL

Name

Address

(UPS to street address, Priority Mail to P.O. boxes)

FOR FASTER SERVICE, USE YOUR CREDIT CARD AND OUR TOLL-FREE NUMBERS

Monday-Friday, 7 a.m. to 6 p.m. Pacific Time

Order Line	1 (800) 992-6656 (in the 510 area code, call 549-1976)
General Information	1 (510) 549-1976
Fax your order	1 (800) 645-0895 (in the 510 area code, call 548-5902)

METHOD OF PAYMENT

☐ Check enclosed

☐ VISA ☐ MasterCard ☐ Discover Card ☐ American Express

Account # Expiration Date

Authorizing Signature

Daytime Phone

Allow 2-3 weeks for delivery. Prices subject to change.

NEST 3.2

NOLO PRESS, 950 PARKER ST., BERKELEY, CA 94710

Take 2 minutes & Get a 2-year NOLO *News* subscription free!*

CALL
1-800-992-6656

FAX
1-800-645-0895

E-MAIL
NOLOSUB@NOLOPRESS.com

OR MAIL US THIS POSTAGE-PAID REGISTRATION CARD

*U.S. ADDRESSES ONLY.
TWO YEAR INTERNATIONAL SUBSCRIPTIONS:
CANADA & MEXICO $10.00;
ALL OTHER FOREIGN ADDRESSES $20.00.

With our quarterly magazine, the **NOLO** *News*, you'll

- **Learn** about important legal changes that affect you
- **Find out first** about new Nolo products
- **Keep current** with practical articles on everyday law
- **Get answers** to your legal questions in *Ask Auntie Nolo's* advice column
- **Save money** with special Subscriber Only discounts
- **Tickle your funny bone** with our famous *Lawyer Joke* column.

It only takes 2 minutes to reserve your free 2-year subscription or to extend your **NOLO** *News* subscription.

REGISTRATION CARD

NAME ______________________ DATE ______________

ADDRESS ______________________

______________________ PHONE NUMBER ______________

CITY ______________________ STATE ________ ZIP ________

WHERE DID YOU HEAR ABOUT THIS BOOK? ______________________

WHERE DID YOU PURCHASE THIS PRODUCT? ______________________

DID YOU CONSULT A LAWYER? (PLEASE CIRCLE ONE) YES NO NOT APPLICABLE

DID YOU FIND THIS BOOK HELPFUL? (VERY) 5 4 3 2 1 (NOT AT ALL)

SUGGESTIONS FOR IMPROVING THIS PRODUCT ______________________

____

WAS IT EASY TO USE? (VERY EASY) 5 4 3 2 1 (VERY DIFFICULT)

DO YOU OWN A COMPUTER? IF SO, WHICH FORMAT? (PLEASE CIRCLE ONE) WINDOWS DOS MAC

YOUR PRIVACY IS IMPORTANT TO US. WE PROMISE NOT TO SELL, RENT OR LEND YOUR NAME AND ADDRESS TO ANY OTHER BUSINESS OR ORGANIZATION.

NEST 3.2

NOLO IN THE NEWS

"Nolo helps lay people perform legal tasks without the aid—or fees—of lawyers."

—USA TODAY

[Nolo books are ..."written in plain language, free of legal mumbo jumbo, and spiced with witty personal observations."

—ASSOCIATED PRESS

"...Nolo publications...guide people simply through the how, when, where and why of law."

—WASHINGTON POST

"Increasingly, people who are not lawyers are performing tasks usually regarded as legal work... And consumers, using books like Nolo's, do routine legal work themselves."

—NEW YORK TIMES

"...All of [Nolo's] books are easy-to-understand, are updated regularly, provide pull-out forms...and are often quite moving in their sense of compassion for the struggles of the lay reader."

—SAN FRANCISCO CHRONICLE